East Central European Migrations During the Cold War

East Central European Migrations During the Cold War

—

A Handbook

Edited by
Anna Mazurkiewicz

DE GRUYTER
OLDENBOURG

ISBN 978-3-11-073683-0
e-ISBN (PDF) 978-3-11-061063-5
e-ISBN (EPUB) 978-3-11-060790-1

Library of Congress Control Number: 2018956630

Bibliografic information published by the Deutsche Nationalbibliothek
The Deutsche Nationalbibliothek lists this publication in the Deutsche Nationalbibliografie;
detailed bibliografic data are available on the Internet at http://dnb.dnb.de.

© 2020 Walter de Gruyter GmbH, Berlin/Boston
This volume is text- and page-identical with the hardback published in 2019.
Cover image: © Anna Mazurkiewicz
Printing and binding: CPI books GmbH, Leck

www.degruyter.com

Contents

Tables & Charts —— XI

Introduction (Anna Mazurkiewicz) —— 1

1	**Albania (Agata Domachowska) —— 9**	
1.1	Albanian migration in historical perspective —— 9	
1.2	The aftermath of World War II —— 15	
1.2.1	The political situation in Albania after World War II —— 17	
1.3	Major migration streams from Albania during the Cold War —— 20	
1.3.1	Albania's internal migration —— 23	
1.3.2	The political activities of Albanian émigrés —— 25	
1.3.3	Covert operations in Albania during the Cold War —— 37	
1.4	Albanian migration since 1989 —— 39	
1.5	Archives and Literature —— 43	

2 Baltic States: Estonia, Latvia and Lithuania (Pauli Heikkilä) —— 45
2.1 Regional migrations in historical perspective —— 45
2.2 The aftermath of World War II —— 46
2.2.1 Balts as Displaced Persons —— 48
2.3 Major migration streams during the Cold War —— 52
2.4 Political activities in exile —— 53
2.4.1 The USSR and Baltic émigrés —— 58
2.4.2 Political cooperation among Baltic exiles —— 61
2.5 Migration since 1989 —— 64
2.6 Archives and Literature —— 64

3 Bulgaria (Detelina Dineva) —— 68
3.1 Bulgarian migration in historical perspective —— 68
3.2 The aftermath of World War II —— 74
3.3 Major migration streams during the Cold War —— 78
3.3.1 Migration policy —— 78
3.3.2 Immigration —— 80
3.3.3 Emigration —— 82
3.3.4 Political emigration —— 83
3.3.5 The scope of Bulgarian migration and dominant settlement areas —— 84
3.4 Political activities in exile —— 88
3.4.1 The Bulgarian National Committee and the Bulgarian National Front —— 90

3.4.2	Unfulfilled hopes and disappointment — 93	
3.4.3	Bulgarian State Security and émigré organizations — 95	
3.5	Migration since 1989 — 96	
3.6	Archives and Literature — 97	

4	**Czechoslovakia (Michael Cude and Ellen Paul)** — 101	
4.1	Migrations in historical perspective — 101	
4.2	The aftermath of World War II — 104	
4.3	Major migration streams during the Cold War — 105	
4.3.1	Czech/Czechoslovak organizations — 107	
4.3.2	Slovak organizations — 113	
4.3.3	Sudeten Germans, Rusyns, Hungarians, and other ethnic minorities — 116	
4.4	Czech and Slovak political activities in exile — 120	
4.4.1	Early Cold War — 120	
4.4.2	Era of *détente* — 127	
4.5	Migration since 1989 — 132	
4.6	Archives and Literature — 133	

5	**Germany (Bethany Hicks)** — 136	
5.1	German migration in historical perspective — 136	
5.2	The aftermath of World War II — 138	
5.2.1	Migration and mobility in occupied Germany, 1945–1949 — 138	
5.3	Major migration streams during the Cold War — 142	
5.3.1	German migration before the Berlin Wall, 1949–1961 — 142	
5.3.2	German migration after the Berlin Wall, 1961–1989 — 148	
5.3.3	Migration and the Peaceful Revolution of 1989 — 151	
5.4	Political activities in exile — 160	
5.5	Migration since 1989 – during and after unification — 160	
5.6	Archives and Literature — 165	

6	**Hungary (Katalin Kádár Lynn)** — 168	
6.1	Hungarian migration in historical perspective — 168	
6.1.1	The aftermath of World War II – the refugee crisis — 169	
6.1.2	Post-World War II Hungarian policy related to migration — 171	
6.2	Major migration streams — 173	
6.2.1	1944–1945: the "45-ers" — 173	
6.2.2	The 1947 exodus: the "47-ers" — 175	
6.2.3	The 56-ers: emigration after the Hungarian Revolution of 23 October – 10 November 1956 — 177	
6.3	Repatriation — 177	
6.3.1	Repatriating the Hungarian postwar exodus: 1945–1951 — 177	
6.3.2	Repatriation after the 1956 Hungarian Revolution — 180	

6.4	Hungary's minorities: Motivations for emigration —— 181	
6.4.1	Hungarian Jews —— 181	
6.4.2	The ethnic German minority —— 182	
6.4.3	Hungary's Roma —— 183	
6.4.4	Resettlement and Supporting Organizations —— 184	
6.5	Political activities in exile —— 184	
6.5.1	The 45-ers' organizations —— 184	
6.5.2	The 47-ers' organizations —— 186	
6.5.3	The 56-ers' organizations —— 187	
6.5.4	Hungarian cooperation with other émigré political, cultural, artistic, and scientific groups —— 188	
6.5.5	Infiltration: communist actions against émigré groups and leaders —— 188	
6.6	Hungarian migration until 1989 —— 190	
6.7	Archives and Literature —— 191	
7	**Poland (Sławomir Łukasiewicz) —— 193**	
7.1	World War II and Polish migration —— 195	
7.1.1	Evacuations and escapes —— 197	
7.1.2	Population transfers by the Nazis —— 198	
7.1.3	Population transfers by the Soviets —— 200	
7.1.4	German expellees —— 201	
7.1.5	Post-war returns and arrivals to Poland (Sławomir Łukasiewicz) —— 202	
7.2	Major emigration streams, 1945–1989 —— 204	
7.2.1	Post-war standstill —— 204	
7.2.2	Emigration of Jews from Polish People's Republic —— 205	
7.2.3	The emigration of Germans from People's Poland —— 206	
7.2.4	Repatriation campaigns and migrations after 1956 —— 207	
7.2.5	The 'Solidarity' period —— 209	
7.2.6	Spatial distribution —— 212	
7.3	Political activities in exile —— 218	
7.3.1	The main political power structures —— 218	
7.3.2	Social and political life in exile —— 222	
7.3.3	The government-in-exile's international position —— 226	
7.3.4	Political thought in exile —— 228	
7.3.5	The People's Republic and the Polish diaspora —— 231	
7.3.6	Interactions with the home country —— 234	
7.4	Migration since 1989 —— 237	
7.5	Archives and Literature —— 238	
8	**Romania (Beatrice Scutaru) —— 243**	
8.1	Romanian migration in historical perspective —— 243	

8.2	The aftermath of World War II —— **245**	
8.3	Major migration streams across "the nylon curtain" —— **246**	
8.3.1	Choosing freedom over security —— **247**	
8.3.2	Restricted freedom of movement —— **248**	
8.3.3	Migration streams: an overview —— **252**	
8.3.4	Who, how and where? —— **257**	
8.3.5	A new form of migration: international adoptions —— **265**	
8.4	Political activities in exile —— **268**	
8.4.1	Building a new life on the other side of the Iron Curtain —— **268**	
8.4.2	Political mobilization: between democratic tradition and anti-Communist fight —— **270**	
8.4.3	The mission to inform —— **274**	
8.4.4	Culture as resistance —— **277**	
8.5	Migration since 1989 —— **279**	
8.6	Archives and Literature —— **282**	

9   Ukraine (Anna Fiń) —— 286

9.1	Conditions and course of Ukrainian migration —— **289**
9.2	The aftermath of World War II —— **291**
9.3	Major migration streams during the Cold War. The third wave of Ukrainian emigration —— **293**
9.4	Political activities in exile —— **301**
9.4.1	Anti-Communist diaspora activity —— **307**
9.4.2	Interethnic cooperation —— **316**
9.5	Migration since 1989/1991 —— **319**
9.6	Archives and Literature —— **322**

10   USSR (Alexey Antoshin) —— 326

10.1	Russian migrations in historical perspective —— **326**
10.2	The aftermath of World War II —— **331**
10.3	Major migration streams from the USSR during the Cold War —— **333**
10.3.1	Repatriation and the 'Second Wave' of Soviet emigration —— **333**
10.3.2	Emigration of Soviet Jews in the 1960s–1980s. —— **341**
10.3.3	Emigration of Soviet Germans —— **346**
10.3.4	The "Free World" and the Émigré —— **348**
10.4	Political activities in exile —— **356**
10.5	Migration since 1991 —— **362**
10.6	Archives and Literature —— **362**

11   Yugoslavia (Brigitte Le Normand) —— 368

11.1	Migrations in historical perspective —— **368**
11.2	The aftermath of World War II —— **368**

11.3	Major migration streams during the Cold War —— **370**
11.3.1	1945–1954: Deciding who was in and who was out —— **370**
11.3.2	1954–1990: Opening the borders —— **378**
11.4	Political activities in exile —— **385**
11.5	Migration since 1989 —— **388**
11.6	Archives and Literature —— **391**

Selected Bibliography —— 396

Authors' Biographical Notes —— 426

Index —— 431

Tables & Charts

Table 1.1 Albanian Population at Each Census, 1945–2001 —— 24
Table 8.1 Main Romanian ethnic groups' migration from 1990 to 1992 —— 281
Chart 8.1 Evolution of Romanian legal migration between 1957 and 1989 —— 254
Chart 8.2 Romanian citizens travelling abroad —— 258
Chart 8.3 Illegal migration of Romanians from 1941 to 1982 (percentage) —— 262
Chart 8.4 Evolution of Romanian migration according to the citizens' ethnic origin (1975–1989) —— 264
Chart 8.5 Evolution of Romanian migration in the main destination countries (1990–1992) —— 280
Table 9.1 Main countries of destination and number of Ukrainian immigrants during the first and second wave of migration —— 290
Table 9.2 Ukrainian ethnic structure with changes between 1939 and 1989 —— 291
Table 9.3 Class structure of Ukrainian society, 1939–1970 —— 293
Table 9.4 Main countries of destination and number of Ukrainian immigrants during the third wave of migration —— 294
Chart 9.1 Countries of Destination and the Number of Ukrainian immigrants during the Third Wave of Migration, 1944–1955 —— 295
Table 9.5 The number of Ukrainians in the DP camps in Germany and Austria in the three occupation zone 1946–1950 —— 298
Table 9.6 The number of Ukrainian refugees from Germany and Austria, 1947–1957 —— 298
Table 9.7 Emigration of Ukrainians and other nationalities from DP camps, 1947–1951 —— 299
Table 9.8 Organization of Ukrainian life in DP camps in three occupation zones —— 300
Table 9.9 The chronological development of Ukrainian institutions of higher learning and research centers during the DP period —— 303
Table 9.10 The estimated number of Ukrainian diaspora in 1989 —— 321
Table 10.1 Numbers and centers of the Russian diaspora in the inter-war period —— 328
Table 10.2 Number of Soviet citizens repatriated with the assistance of Western Allies by March 1946 —— 335
Table 10.3 Distribution of Soviet émigrés around the world —— 339

Introduction
Anna Mazurkiewicz

This handbook offers a unique look at migrations from East and Central Europe during the Cold War. Each of the authors of eleven chapters included herein is familiar with regional and foreign archives, with state of art in the field, fluent in the language of the country described and willing to share their knowledge and expertise in this exceptional academic guide. For general readers interested in the history of East and Central Europe, this volume can serve as a survey of major migration streams in the context of political history of the Cold War. For scholars, especially historians and sociologists, it points to new research areas, as Cold War migrations merit a thorough, in-depth study. This volume addresses problems of Cold War migrations on a transnational level. Since it contains a survey of the current state of art in the field in thirteen countries, with additional focus on further research, it is intended as a starting point for anyone interested in pursuing the study of regional migrations after World War II.

The handbook's regional scope directs scholarly attention to international processes related to migration, rather than the internal and domestic population shifts resulting, for example, from population transfers, urbanization, and industrialization. Consequently, emphasis in this volume was placed on emigration from the home country and further on – outside of the Communist bloc. Due to the Kremlin's control of political, social, and economic matters in the subjugated areas, common traits in the history of migration in the region are to be indicated in each chapter. Individual national perspectives show the patterns of realizing goals set forth by Moscow. At the same time, they also illustrate distinctive characteristics of migration patterns that have resulted from the local regimes' policies and were conditioned on regional socioeconomic, political, or ethnic peculiarities.

This volume is the result of international cooperation of authors from eight countries – historians, sociologists, and political scientists.[1] We have received encouragement and support from a number of organizations since 2012, including: The Institute of National Remembrance in Poland (within the framework of its "Polish Political Emigration 1939–1990" Central Research Program), the University of Gdańsk (a hub for our project), as well as the European Social Science History Conference that accepted our multiple sessions over the years. This allowed us to strengthen our team by meeting new scholars and developing this particular project.

---

[1] For more on the origins of the project and detailed state of research see Anna Mazurkiewicz, "Emigracja polityczna z krajów Europy Środkowo-Wschodniej w relacjach międzynarodowych czasu zimnej wojny – stan badań i projekt syntezy" in *Polska Emigracja polityczna 1939–1990. Stan badań*, ed. Sławomir Łukasiewicz (Lublin: IPN, 2015), 336–394. For the abbreviated version in English see: Mazurkiewicz, "Political Emigration from East Central Europe during the Cold War," *Polish American Studies* 72, no. 2 (Autumn 2015): 65–82.

The first problem that a researcher must resolve before attempting to write about the countries between the Adriatic, Baltic, and Black Seas is to define this area and decide which countries to include. The historical, geographic, linguistic, and religious differences of this region are immense, and the debate on what really constitutes East and Central Europe has persisted for decades. During the Cold War, the Soviet Union's domination over the countries of East and Central Europe meant single rule over this multicultural region. Therefore, does "Eastern Europe," consisting of Soviet satellites, suffice to describe it?

Throughout the twentieth century, definitions of East and/or Central Europe changed along with the dramatic events that characterized this region's history and its geopolitical shifts. Today, East Central Europe is the most common term used to describe the area encompassing regions which used to be called "Central Europe," "East," "Eastern," or "middle" (Mitteleuropa) – with a variety of combinations as to the countries which were included. The changes in name and the composition of the East/Center were and remain politically conditioned, of course, and mirrored the geopolitical context of the times.

During the Cold War, the region was often described simply as Eastern Europe. In the last two decades, there has been a noticeable attempt to change the "eastern character" and hence pre-war concepts were revived. The change in the description from East to Central Europe in the 1990s epitomized the changing place in Europe of countries like Poland, Hungary, the Czech Republic, and Slovakia. When Robert Magocsi published a historical atlas of this region in 1993, it was entitled *Historical Atlas of East Central Europe*, which the author explained as "central third of the European continent." Consequently, the twenty-first century edition saw the change in title to "Central Europe."[2] Nevertheless, it included information on Poland, the Czech Republic, Slovakia, Hungary, Romania, Slovenia, Croatia, Bosnia-Herzegovina, Yugoslavia, Macedonia, Albania, Bulgaria, as well as Greece, eastern parts of Germany, Lithuania, Belarus, Ukraine, Moldova, and western Turkey.

As of now, academics often use "Central and Eastern Europe" thus nuancing between the "central" or Visegrad countries (Poland, Czech Republic, Slovakia, Hungary), and their neighbors to the East. The countries to the South are referred to as Southeastern Europe (Romania, Bulgaria, Albania, and former Yugoslavia); the Baltic countries are described as part of Northeastern Europe. Using geographical descriptors may in fact be useful as the divisions in this region usually follow latitudinal rather than longitudinal patterns. However, should we continue to stick to geographical descriptions, our readership should be informed why Austria, Greece or Finland are not listed among the East Central European countries. Politics does

---

[2] Paul Robert Magocsi, *Historical Atlas of East Central Europe* (Seattle/London: University of Washington Press, 1993); Idem, *Historical Atlas of Central Europe* (Seattle: University of Washington Press, 2002), xi, xiii, 186, 203, 222.

change the way we describe a given region at a given time. So how should a historian describe this area during the Cold War?

In the bipolar world of the Cold War, the best description could be "Eastern Europe" – a term that has almost become archaic since the fall of Communism. Undoubtedly, this term is a by-product of the East-West divide, an ahistorical look at the area of diverse cultural heritage. The Soviet domination, however, did create an area in which peoples, economies, and cultures were amalgamated under pressure (coercion). This fact also conditioned migration processes, as well as relations among the anti-Communist exiles and various diasporas in the West.

"Eastern Europe" represents the artificial character of the "bloc" created in Europe by Moscow. Also, moving from one side of the Iron Curtain to the other quite clearly and evidently indicated a movement from one bloc to the other (notably from East to West). The émigrés from the Soviet dominated countries crossed heavily militarized borders to the "Free World" and hence it is indeed quite difficult to point to the "central" or "median" area. Finally, "Eastern Europe" was the term commonly used at the time by Western diplomats, politicians and journalists.[3] Anne Applebaum claims that eight countries were representative of how Western Europeans and Americans understood "Eastern Europe": Albania, Bulgaria, Czechoslovakia, Yugoslavia, the German Democratic Republic, Poland, Romania and Hungary. However, at least in the context of the American foreign policy there were at least four varied policy models applied to the countries of this region: German policy, post 1948 policy towards Yugoslavia, the three Baltic States, and the six "captive" countries: Poland, Czechoslovakia, Hungary, Romania, Bulgaria and Albania. Eleven countries and at least four regional policy types made up "Eastern Europe." All of these policy slants were of course conditioned on the strategic goals and American policy towards the USSR in general.

Formally, American policy towards the countries between the Baltic, Adriatic, and Black Seas was outlined in the agreements reached during the Big Three conferences in Teheran, Yalta, and Potsdam. Of all the countries of the region, only the American policy towards the three Baltic States was not covered by the agreements reached at Yalta. The Baltic States were occupied by the USSR in 1940, and then by Nazi Germany (July 1941), followed by another Soviet aggression in the summer of 1944. The US government did not recognize the annexation of the Baltic States and continued to recognize and support diplomatic representatives of these nations. Moreover, while non-Communist Poles largely considered Yalta a synonym for appeasement and a betrayal by the western Allies, other countries of the region often interpreted it as a promise of free elections and continued American and British interest in the faith of the region's political and economic future. These hopes were futile, as the Big Three agreements carried no practical provisions to ensure their re-

---

3 Anne Applebaum, *Iron Curtain: The Crushing of Eastern Europe 1944–1956* (New York/London: Doubleday, 2012), xxiv–xxv.

alization. By the end of 1945 Soviet troops and/or security and intelligence operatives were present in nearly every country of the region.

The peculiar character of the Cold War was shaped by the fact that it was not just a confrontation among hostile governments, diplomats, and generals. One of the major elements of this global struggle, a collision of political, social, and economic systems, was an unprecedented battle for the hearts and minds of peoples in both camps. This included both people "voting with their feet" as well as psychological warfare between adversary propaganda and intelligence agencies. The role played by the émigrés, especially those who lived in the "Free World" as well as migration policies implemented in the East, were an important part of this confrontation. With regard to how they identified their regional interest, it is important to emphasize that the exiles consequently called the region of their origin: Central Europe, East Central Europe, and most commonly, Central Eastern Europe as well as "captive nations/countries". This was their way of confronting the Cold War discourse. They took a clear stand against "Eastern Europe" which in their minds implied permanent character of the Soviet domination. Therefore, we should consider it a political choice and a refusal to acknowledge the *status quo* of Soviet domination in Europe.

The arrival of political exiles from Communist-dominated countries to the West prompted the creation of special American psychological warfare programs to support democratically oriented dissenters. In the bipolar world of the late 1940s, the United States literally stood out as the sole power where anti-Communist political exiles, considering themselves surrogate opposition, or representatives of the "silenced peoples," could address their hopes for both political and financial support. In need of American assistance, the East Central European exiles agreed to work within the framework established by the US government with the help of the private organizations and individuals. The creation of the National Committee for a Free Europe/Free Europe Committee (FEC) – the single most important organization established to deal with political exiles from Soviet-dominated countries of East Central Europe – mirrored American policy. Exiles from the six "Yalta" countries were considered for support, as were the three Baltic States that Kremlin turned into Soviet republics. Exiles from other European Soviet republics were not considered for the FEC-administered programs but qualified for programs designed for the Soviet Union (AMCOMLIB and Radio Liberty). The American understanding was that the countries that were independent in 1939 were to be included in the "East European" exile support programs. The large and older Ukrainian or Russian anti-Communist political diaspora were considered for programs designed for the USSR.

A separate problem was that of Yugoslavia. Following Tito's expulsion from Cominform, for two years, the Americans working with the political exiles from this country were clearly confused as to the nature of their relations. When FEC was created in 1949, Croat, Serbian, and Slovene peasant party leaders were supported, the king in exile was consulted and the process of creating the Yugoslav freedom committee and radio broadcasts was publicly announced. By 1951, the FEC internal memoranda confirmed that the creation of a Yugoslav committee was "prevented" due to a peculiar position of Yugoslavia on the international stage and the nationalistic agendas of various political groups in exile. This does not mean that the financial support for carefully selected, individual Yugoslav exiles was terminated. Even King Peter II Karađorđević received "heavy subsidies."[4]

East Germans figured among the non-represented "captives" and were not included in the concept of East Central Europe formulated by both the exile political organizations and the FEC. While it would be incorrect to ignore the German Democratic Republic when describing captive East Central Europe, as previously mentioned, American policy in Germany constituted a separate policy field for the US government. In the opinions expressed by the political exiles united in the Assembly of Captive European Nations (1954–1972), Germany's unification constituted one of the key European problems that had to be resolved in conjunction with a general European settlement that provided for the elimination of Soviet domination of their homelands.

Undeniably, "Eastern Europe" was an artificial and temporary creation, the existence of which was continuously questioned by exiles from the said region ever since it was coined in the late 1940s. Even in the context of the Cold War, calling this area "Eastern Europe" blurs and obscures the complex political nuances involved. Furthermore, it belittles the efforts of the exiles and denies them agency in the Cold War confrontation. Throughout their political activities in exile, their European self-identification included the word: Central. Therefore, in order to avoid any doubt, the volume's title (and scope) encompasses both Central and Eastern Europe.

Interconnected with the geographic scope of Cold War migrations from the region is another issue, though. What chronological boundaries should be applied to such survey? Military conflict, occupation policies, and border changes that resulted from World War II forced millions of Europeans out of their homes. Therefore, when deliberating Cold War migrations, one must consider the post-1939 movements of large groups of escapees, refugees, émigrés, displaced persons, both state orchestrated and spontaneous deportations, evacuations, transfers and population exchanges, expulsions, as well as returns or the influx of people expelled or resettled from other territories. Because of the complex nature of the migrations caused by World War II and their particular regional determinants, this volume offers a geopolitical and demographic panorama of nations reshaped by the war and the decisions made in Teheran, Yalta, and Potsdam. Furthermore, while mapping the dispersed East Central Europeans in the postwar world, factors influencing their decisions to return home or remain abroad and their reasons for staying home or choosing to escape are indicated.

---

4 Anna Mazurkiewicz, *Uchodźcy polityczni z Europy Środkowo-Wschodniej w amerykańskiej polityce zimnowojennej, 1948–1954* (Warsaw: Instytut Pamięci Narodowej; Gdańsk: Uniwersytet Gdański, 2016), 267–357.

This volume is organized by country. All authors have maintained a coherent chapter structure to make navigating through this material for comparative purposes easier. Consequently, each chapter contains the following sections: a survey of pre-1939 traditional migration patterns, a summary of major population transfers resulting from World War II, a periodization of migrations during the Cold War, and a characterization of major migration streams from the country of the author's respective focus. This handbook covers the period between the final months of War (1944/1945) and final months of Communist rule (1989/1991).

The section on political activities in exile resulted from the academic exchanges that this team of scholars held during international conferences in Vienna, Valencia, Gdańsk, and Warsaw between 2014 and 2016. Émigré political activities emerged as a common scholarly interest of our group. Situating the émigrés in the Cold War context requires giving them agency, indicating their transnational ties, and examining their (intended or unintended) impact on international relations. Thus, these sections combined may serve as an example of transnational research with easily discernible regional patterns for several of the analyzed countries (e.g. the nine "captive nations"), and clearly visible divergences for others (e.g. the GDR).

There are, of course, many other common traits of the history of migration from East Central Europe. These can be approached from two perspectives representative of the Cold War divide. From the Western perspective, common traits of the history of migrations from East Central Europe include: immigration laws, repatriation campaigns, assistance to the escapees, the role of migrants in the domestic policies of the host countries (potential gains and threats to domestic security), the use of émigrés by propaganda and intelligence agencies, and the study of conflict and cooperation among ethnic groups, their problems of adaptation and integration. Adopting the Eastern perspective results in studies on border traffic control and passport policies (including repatriation campaigns, amnesties), control over ethnic minorities (resettlement, expulsion), state punitive policies (expulsions, deportations), as well as contacts with the émigrés, including intelligence activities and two-way propaganda flows, and the attempts of regimes to block their impact on society.

However, the question remains as to how to compare East Central European migrations if the purpose of this handbook is to enhance our understanding of certain migration patterns. We can identify several common traits of the history of migration in East Central Europe between 1945 and 1989, such as limitations imposed on the freedom of movement of citizens, refugee waves stemming from social upheavals and rebellions, state organized resettlement actions or campaigns to prompt Jewish, German, or other minorities to leave. Furthermore, the common traits of the history of migrations in East Central Europe during the Cold War can be grouped into at least five areas that encompass their international and transnational aspects.

The first area deals with émigré activities on behalf of their respective homelands and includes the analysis of the political activities of various nationals in exile. These range from political and information activities oriented toward the homeland (e.g., via broadcasts) to direct contacts with the underground (sending cash, goods, printed materials, or sharing information). Such political activities also include official ties (e. g. cultural, economic, religious) of diaspora members with representatives of their respective regimes and the dynamics within exile groups that seemed to share the common feature of the "politics of schism."

The two other research areas where common regional traits can be indicated have already been mentioned above, namely, the policies of Communist regimes and the response of the "Free World" to the migrants from behind the Iron Curtain. In order to characterize the regional patterns and supranational themes, one needs to collect data from the exit countries as well as the countries of settlement. When looking for evidence of Kremlin's directives, it will be useful to look at the timing of repatriation campaigns and amnesties, to compare the aims and methods of the satellite regimes' monitoring returnees, as well as their efforts to either discredit the émigrés or encourage their collaboration with the regime. The examination of Western assistance and resettlement policies as well as the use of émigrés for psychological warfare and intelligence and paramilitary operations plays an important role in exemplifying regional schemes, including the sponsorship of uniting regional organizations in exile.

We need to be able to compare and evaluate political, cultural, humanitarian, economic, and scientific activities of the émigrés and their contacts with their homeland in a new light—as a weapon of intelligence and psychological warfare. It is important to emphasize that agency did not rest only with the two superpowers but that both the exiles and the opposition leaders behind the Iron Curtain had their own agenda and means of maintaining contacts. The examination of their actions should not be limited to their use by the antagonistic regimes. Given the émigrés' prolonged stay abroad, it is also useful to signal the problems related to the integration of East Central European émigrés into Western societies.

The fourth topic deserving a comparative analysis is the place East Central European émigrés occupied on the international stage. All of the upheavals in Soviet-dominated regions that resulted in people fleeing their homelands led to international crises. Were the responses of the international community dissimilar, and why? Diplomatic negotiations across the Iron Curtain over "releasing" certain groups or individuals also offer an intriguing ground for comparisons. Finally, the role and impact of émigré political activities in forums like the United Nations or the Council of Europe, as well as their operations in the "non-aligned nations" prompt scholars to follow the transnational and international traits in cooperation among the émigrés from various countries of the region. These actions become especially intriguing when carried out by Western-supported émigré organizations formed abroad, such as party internationals, federalist organizations, or result from efforts to form regional lobbies in exile.

The study of Cold War political emigration from East Central Europe is not complete without an epilogue on the scale of migrations in the first years following the collapse of Communism between 1989 and 1993. Five million Europeans left East Central Europe during this period. This scale of migration can only be related to the post-War years of 1945–1946. Obviously, it is almost impossible to compare the situation of disintegrating Yugoslavia with that of Czechoslovakia or Albania's opening of its borders. In the 1990s East Central Europe saw the movement of both war refugees and economic migrants. However, adding such a section provides readers with a valid insight as to how lifting limitations on travel prompted a new stream of migration from East to West. The scale of return migration is also mentioned for this particular period.

Finally, but not less important, all chapters in this volume contain descriptions of major archival collections recommended by the authors for conducting research in this field. In addition, each chapter ends with brief annotated bibliography. For readers' convenience, scholarly publications (monographs, edited volumes, journal articles, doctoral dissertations, edited primary sources) used by all authors were gathered in a single, comprehensive bibliography at the end of the volume. Rather than serving as the ultimate encyclopedia, this volume encourages further research and can be considered as a useful handbook and guide to European migration patterns.

The authors would like to express their appreciation for suggestions, comments and encouragement, editorial remarks, assistance with translation and proofreading from a number of esteemed scholars. Our special thanks go to: Anna Bischof, Wim Coudenys, Eduards Bruno Deksnis, Alla Karanukh, Magdalena Nowak, Marius Petraru, Francis D. Raška, Francesca Rolandi, Prokop Tomek, Benjamin Tromly, Jim Todd, István Vida, Ieva Zaķe, and Inga Zakšauskienė.

1 Albania

Agata Domachowska

There are currently approximately 6 million Albanians in Europe. They live in ethnically compact settlements in large areas in the southwestern part of the Balkan peninsula, primarily (around half of them) in the Republic of Albania, in the Republic of Kosovo, the western part of Macedonia, the northern part of Montenegro, the southern part of the Republic of Serbia (the Preševo Valley), and in the northern part of Greece – Chameria (Çamëria, gr. Τσαμουριά). There are also Albanian minorities in other countries, namely, Turkey, Italy, Germany, Switzerland, and Great Britain. This chapter focuses on Albanian migration during the Cold War only from Albania and not, for example, from Yugoslavia (especially from Kosovo).

This chapter characterizes Albanian migration during the forty-five years of the Communist regime. Through a careful review of the existing literature on Albanian migration, this paper explores migration from a historical perspective and establishes the basis for a better understanding of current Albanian migration. It also adds new findings to the body of knowledge, especially with regard to internal migration. Communism influenced internal and international migration patterns in various ways and shaped migration in the immediate post-Communist years (1990–1993).

1.1 Albanian migration in historical perspective

For Albania, the Second World War began in April 1939 when Italian troops, led by general Guazzoni, sailed into its harbors. On 25 March 1939 the King of Albania, Zog I (Ahmet Zogu), was given an Italian proposal for an agreement under which Albania would voluntarily become an Italian protectorate. On 5 April 1939 Italy delivered its ultimatum, which expired at noon the following day. Count Ciano, the Italian foreign minister, made four requests, none of which were accepted by the Albanians.[1] Italian troops marched into Albania on 7 April 1939 (Good Friday). Just before the invasion, the Albanian Legation in Paris issued the official communiqué: "In the name of the Government and entire people we emphatically protest against Italy's barbarous action. As the Albanian Parliament, having yesterday evening unanimously rejected an

---

[1] "The first was the complete control of the infrastructure including ports, airfields and roads to be used in a situation when the Albanian sovereignty was in danger. [...] The second request was to have a secretary general in every ministry of the administration. [...] The third was the request to give full civic and political rights to Italians in Albania. [...] The fourth and final request was to promote the Italian legation to an embassy, which was only a change in protocol," Peter Tase, "Italy and Albania: The political and economic alliance and the Italian invasion of 1939," Academicus International Scientific Journal 6 (2012), http://www.academicus.edu.al/nr6/Academicus-MMXII-6-062-070.pdf, (accessed 7 March 2015).

ultimatum containing conditions unacceptable to a free people, large naval and air forces began a violent bombardment of open towns, massacring women and children."[2]

With the exception of the coastal towns and Shkodra, Italians met with little resistance. Moreover, Albania had no support from its neighbors. Intimidated by the Italian military, neither Yugoslavia nor Greece wanted to face an open conflict with that country. Benito Mussolini decided to install a puppet government in Albania. The Italian Foreign Minister went to Tirana in order to set up a provisional government. Albania was incorporated into the Italian state and Victor Emmanuel III became King of Albania. For the next five years, Albanian territory was initially under Italian and from 1943 under German control.[3]

Despite Albania's initial ties to Yugoslavia, it was Zog I's foreign policy that placed the country into total subservience to Italy. Albania in 1939 became an Italian protectorate. King Zog I quickly forgot about previous Yugoslavian support in restoring power and choosing to boost relations with Italy.[4] The Tirana Treaty (of the Tirana Pact) strengthening Italian political and economic influence in Albania was signed in 1926.[5] Furthermore, King Zog I received a gift from Mussolini of several million lire and a promise of Italian assistance to develop Albanian economy despite that every agreement signed by both parties favored Italian interests.

The royal family and the government were among the first Albanians who left the country after Italian troops invaded the country. King Zog I and his wife, queen Geraldine, and their two-day old son Leka, left for Greece (Salonika) on 7 April 1939. From Greece, they went to Egypt from which they then travelled to France. The royal family moved to London after the Nazi invasion of France in 1940.[6] When World War II came to an end they decided to leave Great Britain for Egypt, where they lived until 1952, as guests of King Farouk, himself of Albanian origin.[7]

---

[2] "Albania occupied. Resistance collapses. King Zog leaves country. Italian Minister at helm," *West Australian*, 10 April 1939, 7; Ramadan Marmullaku, *Albania and the Albanians* (London: Hurst, 1975), 39.
[3] According to Antonina Zhelyazkova, "Today Albanians do not hold a bad memory of the Italian occupation, since for about four years more than 350 Italian enterprises were opened in this economically underdeveloped country, roads were built and administrative buildings were erected. That was also the short period of time when the debacle of Yugoslavia and Greece led to a redrawing of the Balkan frontiers, and the Albanians came closer to the ideal of national union and the dreams of Great Albania – Western Macedonia and the larger part of Kosovo were annexed to Albania," Antonia Zhelyazkova, "Albanian identities," in *Albania and the Albanian identities*, ed. Antonia Zhelyazkova (Sofia: International Center for Minority Studies and Intercultural Relations, 2000), 55.
[4] Towards the end of 1924 Ahmet Zogu returned to power. A republic with Ahmet Zogu as president was established in January 1925. In 1928 Zogu consolidated his power and proclaimed Albania a 'parliamentary and hereditary monarchy' with himself as 'King of the Albanians,' bearing the title of Zog I, Ramadan Marmullaku, *Albania and the Albanians* (London: Hurst, 1975), 36.
[5] Marmullaku, 34.
[6] Robert Elsie, *Historical Dictionary of Albania* (Plymouth: Scarecrow Press, 2010), 499–500.
[7] As the great great grandson of Muḥammad Ali, an Ottoman army commander of Albanian origins who seized control of Egypt in 1805, Farouk was part of a long monarchical tradition that had evolved

There is no doubt that during World War II there were outflows of emigrants, but the main one occurred in 1944 when Communists took power in Albania. Yugoslavian influence played a significant role in establishing the Communist Party of Albania (*Partia Komuniste e Shqipërisë*, PKSH).[8] Josip Broz Tito, at that time the President of the League of Communists of Yugoslavia, decided to send his delegates Miladin Popović and Dušan Mugoša, both of whom were present at the Tirana Founding conference (8–15 November 1941), to Albania.

The creation of a Communist party was possible after the success of temporally reconciling the ideological differences among three of the most important Communist organizations: the Korça Group, the Shkodër Group, and the Youth Group. Enver Hoxha, a member of the Korça group, believed to have been more influenced by Communism than other groups, was elected secretary of the Provisional Center Committee, that comprised Qemal Stafa, Koci Xoxe, Tuk Jakova, Kristo Themelko, Ramadan Citaku, and Gjin Marku.[9] All of these individuals agreed to fight for the national independence of Albania.

However, not all Albanians were supporters of the Communists. In the next two years (1942–1943), the following three main groups would emerge as opponents of the Communists:

The National Front (Balli Kombëtar) – the Albanian national organization founded in November 1942. Midhat Frashëri (Mid'hat bey Frashëri), a prominent political figure, was one of its leaders. The main objectives of Balli Kombëtar were formulated in "The Decalogue" – a ten-point political program.[10] Its primary goal was the crea-

---

from Muhammad Ali's ambitious military despotism to a modern, albeit weak constitutional monarchy. *Leka I Zogu*, http://www.telegraph.co.uk/news/obituaries/royalty-obituaries/8926722/Leka-I-Zogu.html (accessed 8 March 2015).

8 As emphasized by Tadeusz Czekalski, "A model for the Albanian Communists was the creation of the headquarters of Yugoslav Partisans in June 1941. This organization, which was controlled by Communists, was given the pleasant-sounding name of the national independence movement and attracted representatives of various groups who were against the Italian occupation. Tito and Hoxha agreed about the necessity of creating a unified leadership. That's why Hoxha took control of the National Independence Movement and became the leader of the growing partisan army," Tadeusz Czekalski, *The Shining Beacon of Socialism in Europe: The Albanian State and Society in the Period of Communist Dictatorship 1944–1992* (Kraków: Wydawnictwo Uniwersytetu Jagiellońskiego, 2013), 19. Although the Communist Party of Albania was only formed in 1941, the workers' movement in Albania was of much earlier origin. Tadeusz Czekalski, "Between Longstanding Hostilities and Unwanted Alliances – the Crucial Aspects of Balkan Policy of Albanian State in Twentieth Century," *Suleyman Demirel University. Journal of Social Sciences: Special issue on Balkans* 2, (December 2012): 92.

9 Arshi Pipa, *Albanian Stalinism: Ideo-Political Aspects* (New York: Columbia University Press, 1990), 56.

10 Mithat Frashëri, the son of the famous Abdyl bey Frashëri (and the nephew of Sami and Nami Frashëri – prominent Albanian nationalists), was born on 25 March 1879 in Joanine. At the beginning of the 20th century, he worked for the Ottoman administration in Salonika. At that time, he also became politically active. Frashëri was one of the signers of the Albanian Declaration of Independence (1912). In 1920, he was appointed chair of the Albanian delegation to the Paris Peace Conference.

tion of 'Ethnic Albania', which included Albania, Kosovo, part of southern Serbia (the Presevo Valley), western Macedonia, and part of Montenegro, in order to keep all Albanians within ethnic borders. They were also anti-monarchist. In comparison to the Communists, the Balli Kombëtar was not as popular among Albanian society.

The Legaliteti (Legaliteti/Lëvizja e Legalitetit; eng. The Legality Movement) – was a monarchist resistance movement led by Abaz Kupi (also called Bazi i Canës).[11] This group declared its loyalty to King Zog. The Legaliteti formed in the northern part of Albania and largely consisted of Gegs (or Ghegs) guerillas[12]. Among the founders were also Muharrem Bajraktari, Fiqri Dine, and Cen Elezi.

The third group consisted of anti-Communist individuals from Kosovo and the northeast mountains of Albania led by Kosovo notables from the Kryeziu family of Gjakova: Said bey Kryeziu, Gani bey Kryeziu and Cano bey Kryeziu (the Kryeziu brothers). This group also fought against the German and Italian occupation forces. Its members were arrested by the German authorities in April 1941 in Belgrade and turned over to the Italians. After the capitulation of Italy in September 1943, they were released and returned to Kosovo, where along with Llazar Fundo, they took to the hills to begin armed resistance against the Germans. The Kryeziu brothers were in contact with the British mission in Albania. Said bey Kreziu was arrested for the second time by Albanian Communist partisans, but was released whereupon he left for Rome.[13]

Initially, these groups tried to cooperate with the Albanian Communists and fight on the side of the occupiers. However, they soon became rivals. In September 1942, the Communists organized a national conference in Peza to which they invited all Albanian resistance groups in order to establish one united front to fight fascism. At that conference the Albanians set up the General Council composed of seven Communists (among them was Enver Hoxha) and three nationalists: Abaz Kupi (who first led armed resistance against the Italians), Baba Faja Martaneshi and Myslym Peza. Moreover, Mehdi Frashëri (not to be confused with Mid'hat Frashëri) was elected honorary president of the conference.[14] This meeting led to the creation of the resist-

---

Frashëri wrote many of his articles under the following pseudonyms: Lumo Skëndo, Mali Kokojka, Ismail Malosmani, Hilë Lushaku, "Jeta e "gjeniut të kombit," Mithat Frashëri," *Tirana Observer*, 14.12.2012, http://www.tiranaobserver.al/jeta-e-gjeniut-te-kombit-mithat-frasheri/ (accessed 11 March 2015).

11 Robert Elsie, *Historical Dictionary of Albania*, 254; "Abaz Kupi: Orgaznizimi i rezistencës nga Legaliteti," *Gazeta 55*, November 6, 2005, 16–17.

12 There are two major subgroups of ethnic Albanians: the Gegs and the Tosks. They have distinct linguistic, cultural, and social characteristics. The Gegs live in the northern part of Albania while the Tosks live in the south part. The Shkumbin river is a natural border between these two groups, Elez Biberaj, *Shqipëria në tranzicion: rruga e vështirë drejt demokracisë: 1990–2010* (Tirana: AIIS, 2011), 42.

13 Robert Elsie, *Historical Dictionary of Kosovo* (Plymouth: Scarecrow Press, 2011), 106.

14 Mehdi Frashëri (1874–1963) was an Albanian politician, who served as Prime minister (1935–1936, 1943 – only for ca. two weeks). During his second term, he was the Prime Minister of Albania's

ance organization known as the National Liberation Movement (Lëvizje Nacionalçlirimtare, NLM).

Despite refusing to be part of that group, on 2 August 1943 Balli Kombëtar signed an agreement with the NLM, which is known as the Mukje Agreement (from the place where it was drafted – in the Kruja district). Ymer Dishnica, a member of the Political Bureau of the Central Committee, led the delegation of the National Liberation General Council. Both sides agreed to fight together against the Italian occupiers in order to establish a free, sovereign, and ethnic Albania. In addition, the meeting ended with the creation of the Committee for the Salvation of Albania that would coordinate their guerrilla operations. The agreement was signed by twelve representatives from each delegation.[15]

Kosovo remained the main point of contention between the two groups. The Communists who at that time also cooperated with the Yugoslavs advocated the idea that Kosovo should be part of Yugoslavia. However, this was not in accordance with the agreement reached by the Albanians in Mukje. The document stated that a plebiscite on the issue should be held in Kosovo once the war is over. Under Yugoslav pressure, the Albanian Communists immediately rendered the agreement invalid.

Instead of demanding that the Balli Kombëtar join the war against the occupiers, Ymer Dishnica and Mustafa Gjinishi agreed to the demagogic demands of the Balli Kombetar. These entailed the proclamation of independence and the overthrow of the fascist assembly of 12 April, in which almost all the Balli Kombetar chiefs had participated and which had never been recognized by the people. Ymer Dishnica and Mustafa Gjinishi accepted the 'ethnical Albania' hoax; a weapon of the fascists and reactionaries to beguile the Albanian people into forgetting their enemy was at that time and to stir up antagonism against the neighboring peoples. They accepted the proposal of the reactionaries to set up a 'Committee for the Salvation of Albania' with equal numbers of representatives from the Balli Kombëtar and the National Liberation Front. This committee was to be vested with the attributes of a provisional government. The General Council and the state power of the national liberation councils, which arose from the people's revolutionary struggle, were completely forgotten. Without any authorization from the General Council and the Central Committee of the Party, Ymer Dishnica and Mustafa Gjinishi approved the proclamation of

---

puppet government under Nazi Germany. See Bernd Jürgen Fischer, *Albania at War 1939–1945* (London: Purdue University Press, 1999), 223; Robert Elsie, *Historical Dictionary of Albania*, 148–149.
15 From the Balli Kombëtar: H. Dosti, M. Frashëri, Th. Orollogaj, Sk. Muço, Hysni Lepenica, Jusuf Luzaj, Kadri Cakrani, Major Raif Fratari, Nexhat Peshkëpija, Halil Mëniku, Ismail Petrela, Vasil Andoni; from the National Liberation Movement: N. Kolonel Jahja Çaçi, Myslim Peza, Abaz Kupi, Ymer Dishnica, M. Gjinishi, Omer Nishani, Sulo Bogdo, Shefqet Beja, Medar Shtylla, Stefan, Haki Stërmilli, G. Nushi, Marenglen Kasmi, "Marrëveshja e Mukjes dhe qëndrimi i Ballit Kombëtar gjatë pushtimit gjerman," *Dita*, August 1, 2014, http://www.gazetadita.al/marreveshja-e-mukjes-dhe-qendrimi-i-bal lit-kombetar-gjate-pushtimit-gjerman/ (accessed 12 March 2015); Nail Zhupani, *Marreveshja e Mukjes, shans i bashkimit dhe peng i trathtise*, http://www.lajmishqip.com/?p=12216 (accessed 14 March 2015).

the 'Committee for the Salvation of Albania', through which the people were informed of the Mukje decisions. They thus fell completely into the trap set by the reactionaries.[16]

Albanian Communists also considered taking part in a potential Balkan federation not to proclaim independence of Albania, but only to support the war against fascism. The refusal of the Communists to argue for the return of Kosovo to Albania made it impossible for the Balli Kombëtar to cooperate with the National Liberation Movement. From this time onwards, members of the Balli Kombëtar were treated as collaborators. In fact, some of them cooperated with the Germans, especially those from Kosovo. For them the real enemies were the Serbs (both Chetniks and Partisans), while their aim was freeing Kosovo from Yugoslavian rule.

In addition, the idea of creating an 'Ethnic Albania' was favored by the Second League of Prizren (Lidhja e Dytë e Prizrenit), an organization founded in mid-September 1943 by Albanians from Kosovo. Among the founding fathers were Bedri Pejani, Xhafer Deva, and Musa Shehut. They were supported by the German emissary Franz von Schweiger.[17] An executive committee was set up with Rexhep Mitrovica as its chair. However, because of the close cooperation between Albanian and Yugoslavian Communists, both Tito and E. Hoxha denied the Albanians living in Kosovo the right of self-determination.

After the Communists renounced Albania's claim on Kosovo, Abaz Kupi withdrew his support for the National Liberation Movement and established the royalist Legaliteti movement. Eventually, confrontation between the Communists, the Legaliteti, and Balli Kombëtar escalated rapidly and brought Albania into civil war. Over the next two years, the three major resistance groups spent most of their time fighting one another. Indeed, it is said that in World War II more Albanians fell fighting Albanians than opposing the Italians and Germans.

By the spring of 1944, the National Liberation Movement was marching to claim victory in Albania. There were approximately 70,000 partisans linked with the National Liberation Movement upon war's end. By contrast, other resistance groups consisted of no more than a few thousand members.[18] In the liberated town of Përmet (May 1944), the Communists held the first Anti-Fascist Congress for National Liberation. Enver Hoxha was elected head of the Anti-Fascist National Committee for National Liberation, a temporary government for the liberated territories.[19] In October 1944, a second congress declared the Anti-Fascist National Committee for National Liberation the democratic government of Albania and Hoxha became its president.

---

16 The Institute of Marxist-Leninist Studies at the Central Committee of the Party of labor of Albania, *History of the Party of Labor of Albania* (Tirana: The '8 Nëntori' Publishing House, 1982), 125–126.
17 Robert Elsie, *Historical Dictionary of Kosovo*, 251.
18 Tadeusz Czekalski, *The Shining Beacon of Socialism in Europe*, 23.
19 Richard J. Crampton, *The Balkans since the Second World War* (London/New York: Longman, 2002), 40–41.

After resisting a German offensive in May and June 1944, the Communists also managed to defeat both the Balli Kombëtar and the Legaliteti forces.

1.2 The aftermath of World War II

Many Albanians decided to leave the country once the Communists took power. Among them were not only collaborators but also prominent Albanian political figures and members of two main resistance groups, which were in conflict with the Communists. Unfortunately, there is only scarce data to assess the flow of Albanian migration at that time. Some Albanians emigrated to Western Europe (Italy, Greece, Great Britain, France), the United States, Latin America, Egypt (King Zogu lived in Alexandria at that time), Turkey, Syria and even Australia.[20] Among them were: Midhat Frashëri, who left the country not to save his life but to continue the fight for Albanian liberation; Ali bey Këlcyra, also known as Ali bey Klissura, a member of the Balli Kombëtar – he went to Italy[21]; Abaz Kupi, who together with his officers fled by boat from the coast of Mat to Italy in November 1944[22]; Muharrem Bajraktari, a member of the Legaliteti, who fled to Italy in 1944[23]; Xhafer Deva, who first went to Austria, then to Italy, in 1947 to Egypt and finally to Syria. In 1956 he left for the USA[24]; Ernest Koliqi, who fled to Italy; Kruja Mustafa, who also fled to Italy; Rexhep bey Mitrovica, who fled to Turkey; Baba Rexhepi, who fled Albania in 1944 because of his opposition to Communism. He found refuge in a DP camp in Italy, whereupon he then left for Egypt and eventually the United States; Ihsan Toptani, who in Octo-

---

[20] A small number of refugees from Albania, and especially Albanians from the Prespa region in southwestern Macedonia, were resettled in Australia. The majority of these, mostly Muslim Albanians, settled in Victoria, principally in Melbourne's industrial, working-class suburbs of Dandenong, Footscray, Yarraville, Altona, St Albans, Preston, Thomastown and Lalor, "After World War II," *Immigration Museum*, http://museumvictoria.com.au/immigrationmuseum/whatson/past-exhibitions/kurbet/after-world-war-ii/ (accessed 21 March 2015). After World War II, members of the Balli Kombëtar included: Petrit Kello, Ali Agushi, Said Demneri, Bahri Bregu, Hysni Cico, Halil Balla and Njazi Zeqo, see Kontributi i Shqiptarëve të Australisë, respektivisht i Ballit Kombëtar, në afirmimin e Shqipërisë Etnike, http://www.ballikombit.org/index.php?option=com_content&task=view&id=904&Itemid=9 (accessed 5 March 2015). For more on Albanian exiles in Australia, see Petrit Kello, *Emigrant në Australi* (London: Balli i Kombit, 2010).
[21] "Rikthehet në atdhe Ali Këlcyra, "armiku" i diktatorëve shqiptarë," *Tema*, April 3, 2014, http://www.gazetatema.net/2014/04/03/rikthehet-ne-atdhe-ali-kelcyra-armiku-i-diktatoreve-shqiptare/ (accessed 21 April 2015); Elsie, *Historical Dictionary of Albania*, 227–228.
[22] Abaz Kupi, along with other Albanians, drifted for six days without food and water. Finally, they were picked up by a Canadian minesweeper and taken to Brindisi (city in the region of Apulia). Kupi continued to organize anti-Communist resistance in Western Europe. In 1968 he moved to the United States. Elsie, *Historical Dictionary of Albania*, 254.
[23] Elsie, *Historical Dictionary of Albania*, 29.
[24] *Kush ishte Xhafer Deva, shtëpia e të cilit u dogj sot në Mitrovicë*, http://indeksonline.net/?FaqeID=2&LajmID=150972 (accessed 26 March 2015).

ber 1944 fled with Abaz Kupi to Italy and worked for *Newsweek* in Rome, along with Abas Ermenji, a member of the Balli Kombëtar.

Migration of the Jews in Albania in World War II is another interesting issue worth exploring. Albania was the only European country whose Jewish population after World War II was larger than before 1939. According to the Albanian census from 1930 there were only 204 Jews registered in Albania. Most of them lived in Kavaje, Vlora, Delvina, and in the southwestern part of the country. The Jewish population in Albania increased to 2,000 during World War II.[25] Many Jews came from Yugoslavia, Austria, Greece, and other parts of Europe to find a safe haven in Albania. For several of them, including Albert Einstein who became a citizen of Pogradec in 1931, Albania was the only place from which they could easily travel to other countries – especially the United States. Albanians saved many Jews from deportation to concentration camps by providing them with clothes, special papers stating that they were Albanian Muslims, and by hiding them in villages. Scholars have emphasized that one of the reasons why Albanians helped the Jewish community was rooted in a national creed called *besa* or *ndore* (the word *besa* means 'to keep a promise') or faith, whereby taking care of a guest in one's home and ensuring him protection, at all costs, is a must. Albanians were obligated to provide shelter and help anyone if there had been a promise to do so. Failure to act resulted in a loss of honor.

Some Jews were able to leave the country just before the Communists took power. Those who did not leave Albania in 1945 lived there until the early 1990s. Jews who survived World War II emigrated to Israel or the US.[26] Because of the communist regime, knowledge about Albanian heroism during the war was not known to the world before 1991. The Yad Vashem memorial has so far honored seventy-five Albanians as the "Righteous among Nations."[27]

Non-Communists who did not leave the country were put on trial for treason from December 1944. Many of them, including members of Balli Kombëtar, were sentenced at the trial that began on 1 March 1945 in the Kosovo cinema building in Tirana. From the sixty people who were put on trial, seventeen were sentenced to death (Fejzi Alizoti, Terenc Toçi, Aqif Përmeti, Gustav Mirdashi, Kostandin Kote, Hilmi Leka, Reshit Merlika, Beqir Valteri, Javer Hareshiti, Dik Cami, Ismail Golemi, Zef Kadarja, Tahsim Bishqeni, Shyqyri Borshi, Daut Çarçani, Kol Tromara, Bahri Omari, Qemal Vrioni, Tefik Mbroja, Koço Kota, Xhavit Leskoviku, Koço Tasi, Ibrahim Biçaku, Xhevat Korça, Rifat Begolli, Bajram Pustina, Shuk Gurakuqi). Some of them were executed in a ditch at Kodra e Priftit in Tirana. Another eight received life imprisonment (Sokrat Dodbiba, Mihal Zallari, Et'hem Cara, Ndoc Naraçi, Andon Kozmaçi, Lazër Radi, Sami

---

25 Shirley Cloyes DioGuardi, "Jewish Survival in Albania & the Ethics of 'Besa,'" *Congress Monthly*, (January/February 2006): 7.
26 Literature on the subject in English or any other language is scarce. In Albanian, there is Shaban Sinani's book *Hebrenjtë në Shqipëri: prania dhe shpëtimi: studim monografik* (Tirana: Naimi, 2009).
27 Righteous Among the Nations honored by Yad Vashem on 1 January 2017, http://www.yadvashem.org/yv/pdf-drupal/albania.pdf (accessed on 6 May 2018).

Koka, Sulejman Vuçiterni). The remaining ones served long-term prison sentences, ranging from three to thirty years.[28]

At the beginning of 1945, some Albanian non-Communists, still hidden in the mountainous area in the northern part of Albania, intensified their political activities. Supported by the West, an ever-increasing number of opponents to Communism planned to establish a united opposition. Among them were prominent Albanian intellectuals, including Sami Qeribashi, Qenan Dibra, Musine Kokalari, Shaban Balla, Profi Çokon, and Tut Maniku. They formed the Democratic Union (Bashkimi Demokratik) and demanded free elections, and the freedom of expression. However, members of that party were arrested in 1946 and a couple months later sentenced and imprisoned as the enemy of the people.[29] Albanian dictatorship did everything to eliminate opposition. In fact, Albanian Communists were effective in doing precisely that. There was no political opposition until the end of the 1980s.

According to the Albanian authorities, these trials served as a deterrent to other potential opponents who wished to seize power in Albania with American help. After the liberation of Albania in 1945, the American and British missions in Tirana were nothing more than centers of espionage, sabotage, and plots against the People's Republic of Albania. They became centers of meetings, contacts, organizations, and directives to all the enemies of the people's regime. The trials against the enemies of the people took place in the People's Republic of Albania.

1.2.1 The political situation in Albania after World War II

Albania was liberated by the National Liberation Movement (NLM) in November 1944. Communists officially took power after winning the parliamentary elections held on 2 December 1944. The NLM, succeeded by the Democratic Front (an umbrella organization led by the Communist Party of Albania[30]), won all seats in the Constituent Assembly. The People's Republic of Albania was proclaimed in January 1946. The new regime, headed by Enver Hoxha as the First Party Secretary, dominated the political landscape in Albania for more than forty-five years. He held this position until his death in 1985. Like in other Communist states in Eastern Europe, elections in Albania were bogus. It was in fact the politburo of the Party of Labor of Albania that acted as the real decision-making body of the state. The parliament solely approved decisions already made by the party.[31]

---

28 Admirina Peci, "Terrori komunist, dokumentet që botohen për herë të pare," http://shqiptarja.com/lajm/terrori-komunist-dokumentet-br-q-euml-botohen-p-euml-r-her-euml-t-euml-par-euml?r=pop5s (accessed 6 May 2018).
29 Peci.
30 The party changed its name to the Albanian Party of Labor in 1948.
31 Mirela Bogdani and John Loughlin, *Albania and the European Union: The Tumultuous Journey towards Integration and Accession* (London: Tauris, 2007), 22–23.

According to Mirela Bogdani and John Loughlin, Albania should be considered a unique case because of two main reasons: (1) it was the toughest dictatorship regime in the entire Communist bloc; (2) self-imposed international isolation.[32] The Albanian government was indeed one of the most repressive and oppressive Communist regimes. The Albanian Communist regime ignored the internationally recognized human rights such as the freedom of expression, movement, association, and religion. Albania was proclaimed the first atheist state in the world in 1967. The campaign against religion was thus launched. Religious worship was outlawed whereupon mosques and churches were closed, demolished, or converted into sports halls and storehouses.

According to the new constitution adopted in 1976, "the foundations of religious obscurantism were destroyed. The morality of the working man, his consciousness and his world outlook, are molded on the basis of the proletarian ideology, which has become the dominant ideology." Article 37 of the constitution states that "The state recognizes no religion whatsoever and supports atheist propaganda for the purpose of inculcating the scientific materialist world outlook in people."[33] Moreover, civil society in Albania did not exist and grass-roots organizations were banned. This was one of the reasons why the first organized oppositional political movement was not founded until December 1990, much later than in most other East European states. There is no doubt that one of the distinguishing features of Albanian Communism is the lack of a dissident movement. Under Hoxha's regime political opponents were either assassinated or given severe prison sentences for being "agents of imperialism or revisionism."[34]

As Hoxha's policy success grew, there was also considerable progress in education. Illiteracy was eliminated and the number of people in schools grew. Electricity was brought to almost every rural area and a healthcare system for all Albanians was introduced. Furthermore, there was a social change in the status of Albania women. They were encouraged to take up jobs outside the home. The Communist regime also tried to reduce the traditional North-South division (Ghegs-Tosks). One of the main successes of Albanian Communists was the maintenance of Albanian independence

---

32 Bogdani and Loughlin, 22–23.
33 In the new constitution the country's name was changed to the People's Socialist Republic of Albania. *The Albanian Constitution of 1976*, http://bjoerna.dk/dokumentation/Albanian-Constitution-1976.htm (accessed 25 April 2015). According to article 55 of the criminal code (1977), "Fascist, antdemocratic, religious, warmongering or anti-socialist propaganda, as well as the preparation, distribution or the possession for distribution of literature with such a content in order to weaken or undermine the state of the dictatorship of the proletariat are punishable by deprivation of liberty for from three to 10 years," "Albania: Violations of the Right to Freedom of Thought, Conscience and Religion," *A Preliminary Report of the Minnesota Lawyers International Human Rights Committee*, (August 1988): 6, http://www.theadvocatesforhumanrights.org/uploads/albania_-_violations_of_the_right_to_freedom_of_thought_conscience_and_religion_3.pdf (accessed 25 April 2015).
34 Fatos Tarifa, "Albania's road from Communism: political and social change, 1990–1993," *Development and Change* 26 (2005): 135.

and sovereignty. However, the negative aspects of the Hoxha period prevail and should not be forgotten.

Albanian foreign policy during Communism can be divided into four main periods.

The first period began in 1944 and lasted until 1948. It is characterized by attempts to maintain close relations with Yugoslavia as a major ally providing both economic and political support. In June 1946, Hoxha visited Belgrade where, together with Josip Broz Tito, he signed significant agreements on economic cooperation. Yugoslav specialists and experts came to Albania in order to boost cooperation between the two states. A treaty on friendship, cooperation, and mutual assistance was reached in July 1946. However, all the agreements signed by both sides subordinated Albanian's economy and turned this country into a Yugoslavian satellite. The Albanian-Yugoslavian friendship eventually ended after Soviet-Yugoslav relations broke off in 1948.

The second period encompassed the years between 1948 and 1961. Friendship with the Soviet Union (USSR) is the hallmark of this period. On an ideological level, Hoxha tried to strictly follow a Stalinist direction. Albania became a member of the Council for Mutual Economic Assistance (CMEA) in February 1949. In 1955 it joined the Warsaw Treaty Organization (Warsaw Pact). As a result, Albania became a Soviet satellite despite the fact that it was geographically far from the USSR. However, Hoxha denounced the Khrushchev leadership. From 1961 until the end of Communism, the relations with the Soviet Union were nonexistent.[35]

The third period began in 1961 and lasted until 1978. After breaking ties with the USSR, Albania decided to reorient itself towards the People's Republic of China. Both states shared a similar ideological stance to anti-imperialism and anti-revisionism. By improving ties with China, Hoxha also pursued his own vision of the Chinese Cultural Revolution. Furthermore, Albania decided to leave the Council for Mutual Economic Assistance (1962) and the Warsaw Pact (1968). However, in the 1970s, when China began to improve its relations with the US and Yugoslavia, the Sino-Albanian alliance started to weaken.[36] Albania eventually supported Vietnam, and, in its conflict with Beijing, China cut all political, military, and economic ties with Tirana.

The last period began in 1978 and ended in 1985. It was characterized by Albania's self-imposed isolation. Economic and political contacts with other countries, even Communist countries, decreased to a minimum after breaking off relations with China in 1978. Hoxha maintained only a semi-formal relationship with several Latin American and African Marxist-Leninist countries.[37] Albania was practically closed off to foreign influence. Scholars and journalists often compare Communist Albania with North Korea because of their isolation from other countries.

---

35 Anton Logoreci, "Albania: A Chinese Satellite in the Making?" *The World Today* 17 (May 1961): 200–202.
36 F. Stephen Larrabee, "Whither Albania?," *The World Today* 34 (February, 1978): 63–65.
37 Bogdani and Loughlin, 23.

1.3 Major migration streams from Albania during the Cold War

During Albania's socialist regime, emigration was non-existent. It was strictly regulated by the government and severely punished. The Albanian government heavily discouraged emigration by establishing political and legal barriers. According to Article 47 of the Albanian Criminal Code, leaving the country was considered an act of treason against the fatherland: "Escape outside the state, as well as refusal to return to the Fatherland by a person who has been sent to serve or has been permitted temporarily to go outside the state is a crime of treason which is punishable by a minimum sentence of ten years or even death."[38]

Albania was also closed off to foreigners. Both travel and visa restrictions made Albania one of the most difficult countries to travel from or to visit. Because of strict state control, Albanians were even afraid to converse with foreigners who had the opportunity to visit the country.

Communist Albania closed its borders to its neighbors in 1945. The border was made practically impassable in 1950. Albanian borders were protected by armed guards and high electric fences. Thousands of people died trying to escape the cruelty and brutality of life under the Communist regime. A high-voltage fence, with frequent sentry-posts, ran along the entire length of the land border with Greece and the former Yugoslavia. One of the former Albanian border guards recalled the different measures established by the authorities in order to prevent escapes from the country:

> An electrically-wired metal fence stands 600 meters to one kilometer from the actual border. Anyone touching the fence not only risks electrocution, but also sets off alarm bells and lights which alert guards stationed at approximately one-kilometer intervals along the fence. Two meters of soil on either side of the fence are cleared in order to check for footprints of escapees and infiltrators. The area between the fence and the actual border is seeded with booby traps such as coils of wire, noise makers consisting of thin pieces of metal strips on top of two wooden slats with stones in a tin container which rattle if stepped on, and flares that are triggered by contact, thus illuminating would-be escapees during the night.[39]

The Frontier Guards were subordinated to the Ministry of Internal Affairs until its abolition in April 1991 when they were subordinated to the Ministry of People's Defense.[40] They were responsible for protecting state borders and stopping Albanians from illegally leaving the country. Albania opened its first border crossing point with Greece in 1985.

---

38 James S. O'Donnell, *A Coming of Age: Albania under Enver Hoxha* (New York: Columbia University Press, 1999), 136.
39 O'Donnell, 137.
40 *Albanian Foreign Policy and National Security Yearbook*, vol. 1: *Strategic Information and Developments* (Washington: International Business Publications, 1999), 193.

The Sigurimi (State Security), whose primary aim was to prevent a revolution and to suppress the opposition, also played an important role in preventing Albanians from illegal emigration. It prevented Albanian citizens from leaving after having seen a much different world outside their borders (e.g. Greece or Italy). Sigurimi officers had a network of operatives, who collaborated with the Communist regime. Those collaborators were divided into four categories: (1) Residents – Communists or individuals otherwise trusted by the regime. They were responsible for collecting useful information for Sigurimi officers; (2) Agents, who were responsible for gathering information about the so-called enemies of the state – individuals suspected of having links with the bourgeois elite and those who were no longer supporters of the Communist regime; (3) Informers – low-level agents or ordinary spies who always worked undercover; (3) Receivers – individuals, usually communists, responsible for providing a secure space where Sigurimi officers could interrogate those under their surveillance.[41]

The Frontier Guards were effective in enforcing its closed borders although some Albanians still managed to escape. Many young people attempted to illegally cross Albanian borders and seek political asylum in Yugoslavia, Greece, and Italy. Unfortunately, only scarce data is available that would help track the extent of Albanian migration before the 1990s. Most Albanians left their country (during the Cold War) due to political factors, which included opposition to Communism and, in some cases, their collaboration with Italians and Germans during World War II.

It is unknown exactly how many people were killed at the Albanian border-by-border guards. According to a report published by *Muzeu i Memories*, during the forty-five years of Communism, there were a total 9,600 escape attempts, over 8,000 people managed to cross the border, approximately 6,000 people were killed by attempting to escape.[42] They were buried at the place where they were shot while 3,200 others were captured and imprisoned.[43] They were referred to as the "enemy of the country" and were severely punished. The labor camp in Spaç, located in the northern part of Albania, was the most known political prison in Albania[44]. Political prisoners were "the slaves of the state" who were forced to work without payment in the most difficult places and under the most severe conditions. Aside from being sen-

---

41 Aleksandra Bogdani, *Secrets and Lies: Victims of Albanian Communism Denied Closure*, http://www.balkaninsight.com/en/article/secrets-and-lies-victims-of-albanian-Communism-denied-closure (accessed 5 March 2015); Kastriot Dervishi, *Sigurimi i Shtetit 1944–1991. Historia e policisë politike të regjimit komunist* (Tirana: Shtëpia Botuese 55, 2012).
42 The Museum of Memory is a project designed by the Albanian Institute of Political Studies and supported by the Ministry of Culture, see: muzeuimemories.com (accessed 11 March 2015).
43 "Self-isolation," *Muzeum i memories*, http://muzeuimemories.info/self-isolation/ (accessed 08 March 2015).
44 Lee Stokes, *Stalinist Regime in Albania Keeps a Tight Rein on Its Citizens*, 24 May 1987, http://articles.latimes.com/1987-05-24/news/mn-2313_1_tight-rein (accessed 11 March 2015).

tenced to forced labor, they were tortured and many of them fell ill and died.⁴⁵ The property of the imprisoned was confiscated. Moreover, the state practiced collective punishment whereby an entire family or even far relatives of those who escaped or were caught escaping were considered enemies of the regime.

Arshi Pipa, an Albanian-American writer who managed to escape in 1957 to Yugoslavia from Albania, recalled in his book:

> An estimated 7–10 percent of Albania's population has been arrested, tortured, jailed, deported, interned during the fifteen years of Communist rule. Of this total, some 10,000 have been shot, hanged, killed by torture, or brought to death by diseases contracted in horrible jails or by inhuman labor conditions in camps. Only a very small part of these people (not more than one percent) were "collaborators with occupation powers" or "enemies of the people," as Communist propaganda has branded them. The bulk of them were nationally-minded people, from all regions and strata and conditions, who opposed Communism openly or clandestinely, by word or by gun, in individual rebellions or mass insurrections, for various reasons: religious, moral, intellectual, as well as political, social, economic. Among them were distinguished patriots belonging to this very Albanian extraction; and among them were also people whose only crime was their admiration for the United States.⁴⁶

It is still difficult to estimate the number of people who were executed during the Communist period as documents relating to this issue have been destroyed or lost. According to the Association of Albanian political Ex-prisoners (Asociacioni i ish të Burgosurve Politikë të Shqipërisë), from 1946 until 1991, approximately 5,577 men and 450 women were executed for political crimes.⁴⁷ Furthermore, in the forty-six years of the Communist regime, 5,037 men and 450 women were killed as political opponents, 16,788 men and 7,367 women were imprisoned for three to thirty-five years and 70,000 people were interned. As many as 354 foreign citizens were shot, among them were ninety-five Albanians from Kosovo.⁴⁸

In the belief that Albania was surrounded by "external enemies", Hoxha made a decision to militarize the Albanian landscape by building hundreds of thousands mushroom-shaped concrete bunkers. It was part of the plan to prepare for an attack from abroad.⁴⁹ Additionally, in a country of only around three million people, there were more than 700,000 bunkers throughout the country. There were three different

---

45 "Forced Labor & Works," *Muzeum i memories*, http://muzeuimemories.info/forced-labor-works/ (accessed 10 March 2015).
46 Arshi Pipa, *Albanian Stalinism...*, 6.
47 "Ish të burgosurit e komunizmit ndihen të tradhtuar," *Gazeta Jeta në Kosovë*, 10 October 2010, http://gazetajnk.com/?cid=1,4,3455 (accessed 11 March 2015).
48 "Vendimi i aleateve: Te terhiqet misioni prane Abaz Kupit," http://www.arkivalajmeve.com/Vendimi-i-aleateve-Te-terhiqet-misioni-prane-Abaz-Kupit.1047303035/ (accessed 11 March 2015).
49 Mirela Bogdani and John Loughlin, *Albania and the European Union: The Tumultuous Journey towards Integration and Accession* (London: Tauris, 2007), 24.

sizes of such bunkers: (1) small for individuals; (2) medium for small groups and; (3) large for groups of the most important military and political figures.⁵⁰

The Communist dictatorship not only prohibited free movement of people but also censored information (media, literature and art). Propaganda played a prominent role in preventing people from illegal emigration. The government portrayed emigration as a "wound of the past and the notion of *kurbet* was re-invoked and loaded with negative connotations of separation, suffering, loss and destruction."⁵¹ Albania was a closed country and media were used by the government to manipulate people. Until the end of Communism, there was only one channel on Albanian national television. It broadcast four hours per day, between 6 and 10 p.m. Albanians were permitted to watch only one film per week, "generally a repeat showing of an Albanian film, whose message was invariably political, patriotic and didactic and aimed primarily at indoctrinating audiences, rather than entertaining them."⁵² Occasionally, the government permitted the screening of films from other socialist countries or non-aligned countries that did not attack Marxist-Leninist ideology and Albanian culture. Italian television in Albania was not forbidden by law until 1973, but watching it was discouraged as an act of being under imperialist influence and could be punished as an attempt to spread subversive propaganda in Albania.⁵³ Thus, the Communist regime in Albania took every measure to prevent people from watching foreign television.

1.3.1 Albania's internal migration

Not only emigration but also internal migration was under government control during the Communist years in Albania. Citizens were generally allowed to move freely from one village to another. Marriage granted individuals, especially women, more mobility.

---

50 Jason Payne, "Projekti Bunkerizimit: The Strange Case of the Albanian Bunker," *Log*, 31, (Spring/Summer 2014): 161–162.
51 Julie Vullnetari, *Albania on the Move: Links Between Internal and International Migration* (Amsterdam: Amsterdam University Press, 2012), 65. "The emigration is known in the Albanian history and collective memory as *kurbet*. Originating from the Turkish *gurbet*, the word refers to the act of going away and being distant in a foreign land usually for work," Vullnetari, 59; The most common proverb about migration in Albania says that 'A man becomes a man out in the world (*kurbet*), a woman becomes a woman over the cradle' [literally: '*Kurbet* knows the man, cradle knows the woman'] (Al.: 'burrin e njeh kurbeti, gruan e njeh djepi'). Eckehard Pistrick, "Singing back the kurbetlli – Responses to migration in Albanian folk culture as a culturally innovative practice," *Anthropological Notebooks* 16 (2010): 30.
52 Nicola Mai, "Looking for a More Modern Life…': The Role of Italian Television in then Albanian Migration to Italy," *Westminster Paper in Communication and Culture* 1, (2004): 6.
53 Mai, 6.

Julie Vullnetari from the University of Sussex divides Albanian migration during the Communist period into two phases: 1945–1965 and 1965–1990. In the period between 1945 and 1965, there were large-scale internal movements, though centrally regulated and incorporating a high degree of urbanization. Most of these movements were intended only for supplying the much-needed labor for industrialization projects in the country.[54] The first movement was also influenced by agrarian reforms (First Agrarian Reform, 1945–1946)[55] through which Albanian government seized land from large landowners, religious institutions and foreign concerns and distributed it to landless peasants. The economic development of Albania after 1945 was centrally coordinated. The Communist leadership in Tirana made all decisions regarding economic planning and development.

At the same time, Hoxha set up an industrialization project, which required people to construct forty-one urban centers around areas, mainly in the northern part of Albania, where the government had decided to set up mines, factories. New schools and hospitals were also built and Albanians found new jobs.[56] The industry projects in Albania amounted to more than 50 percent of the PKB in 1960. Consequently, they significantly boosted the urban population although most Albanians continued to live in rural areas. (See Table 1.1)

Table 1.1: Albanian Population at Each Census, 1945–2001

Census	Total population	Average annual increase since the previouws census [%]	Rural [%]	Urban [%]
1945	1,122,000	0.7	78.7	21.3
1950	1,219,000	1.7	79.5	20.5
1955	1,392,000	2.7	72.5	27.5
1960	1,626,000	3.2	69.1	30.9
1969	2,068,000	2.7	67.7	32.3
1979	2,591,000	2.3	66.5	33.5
1989	3,182,000	2.0	64.5	35.5
2001	3,069,000	–	57.9	42.1

Source: Russell King and Julie Vullnetari, "Migration and Development in Albania, Working Paper," 11.

---

54 Julie Vullnetari, "Internal Migration in Albania: A Critical Overview," in Robert Pichler, ed., *Legacy and Change: Albanian Transformation from Multidisciplinary Perspectives* (Zurich: LIT, 2014), 48; *Migracioni në Shqipëri, Regjistrimi i popullsisë dhe i banesave 2001* (Tirana: Instituti i Statistikes, 2004), 10.
55 Adrian Civici, *100 vjet: Ekonomia shqiptare gjatë regjimit komunist (1945–1990), kolektivizimi integral i bujqësisë*, http://www.monitor.al/100-vjet-ekonomia-shqiptare-gjate-regjimit-komunist-1945-1990/ (accessed 8 April 2015).
56 Ilir Gedeshi and Elira Jorgoni, "Social Impact of Emigration and Rural-Urban Migration in Central and Eastern Europe," *Final Country Report Albania*, (April 2012): 5–6.

The second phase of Albanian internal migration can be characterized by stricter regulations in order to stop people from villages moving to towns, especially to Tirana. The capital city of Albania was the most desirable place for relocation especially to the younger generation. Rural-rural movement, which was not restricted, constituted around 60 percent of internal migration. Internal migration, both rural and urban, was also controlled and regulated by the government. Örjan Sjöberg, a Swedish professor, emphasized that the Communist regime introduced the "anti-migratory system" by addressing many restrictions in order to establish a legal prohibition on migration in Albania – including for instance: permission to change domicile, dwelling permission or *pasaportizi*.[57] Contrary to the first phase, there was minimal urbanization in the 1970s or 1980s. After relations with the Soviet Union and then with China broke down, Albania was left without the financial and technical help that was crucial for setting up other industrial projects in the country.

The positive rate of natural growth as well as the policy of not allowing people to freely choose where they would like to live and work had a great impact on the demographic city-countryside relationship. This remained relatively unchanged during the Communist period. After World War II, the population in Albania amounted to approximately 1,2 million people. Approximately 70 percent of Albanians lived in rural areas.[58] From the mid-1950s, the population grew at a constant of more than 2 percent, a rate higher than any other European country. In the late 1980s, the average population age was only twenty-six.[59] Albania was a unique example of an overwhelmingly rural country until the end of the Cold War.

1.3.2 The political activities of Albanian émigrés

Albanian emigration can be divided into anti-Communist groups, pro-Communist groups, and groups that are neither pro nor anti Communist. As previously mentioned, there were three main groups opposed to Communism that formed as a result of World War II: the Balli Kombëtar, the Legaliteti, and Albanians leaders from the northern part of Albania and Kosovo. Many of these group members them managed to emigrate and find a safe place to live and (in many cases) continue their political activity in different parts of the world.

Shortly after the end of World War II, the main anti-Communist groups undertook a number of measures to manifest their opposition to the new regime in Alba-

---

[57] Julie Vullnetari, "Internal Migration in Albania: A Critical Overview," 49.
[58] Sonila Papathimiu, "The demographic and economic development of Albania during and after the decline of Communist regime (1945–2010)," *Treballs de la Societat Catalana de Geografia* 73 (2012): 108–109.
[59] Russell King and Julie Vullnetari, "Migration and Development in Albania, Working Paper," Sussex Centre for Migration Research, Brighton (December 2003): 24, http://www.migrationdrc.org/publications/working_papers/WP-C5.pdf (accessed 21 April 2015).

nia. However, they presented different scenarios as to how Albanian's future should look. The royalist Legaliteti favored the return of Zog of Albania to the throne. King Zog also tried to play a role in integrating Albanian anti-Communists groups in exile, but with limited success. During the war, he even sent his representative, Peter V. Kolonia, to the United States. On 20 January 1943, he requested that the Department of State recognize King Zog as head of the Albanian government in exile.[60]

After the war, King Zog I once again, albeit unsuccessfully, proposed the unification of the Albanian diaspora by establishing a national liberation committee on condition that all concerned agree to the following three counts: (1) An institutional referendum preceded by explicit recognition by leaders of the three groups of the 1928 Albanian constitution, which established Albania as a monarchy; (2) That the leaders of all the groups would work toward settling Albanian refugees in other Eastern countries, pending the liberation of Albania; and (3) that anti-Zog propaganda among refugees be stopped.[61]

In order to achieve this goal, king Zog I invited many Albanian exiles to Cairo, where on 12 August 1948 he held a special meeting. Among the Albanians who went to Egypt were members of:

- The Legaliteti: Abaz Kupi, Hysen Selmani, Hiqmet Delvina, Sali Myftiu
- The Balli Kombëtar: Ali bey Këlcyra, Abaz Ermenji, Koço Muka
- The National Independent Block/The Independent Group (Partia Grupi Independent/Blloku Kombëtar Indipendent/Bloku Kombëtar i Pavarur): Mustafa Kruja, Ernest Koliqi, Nexhmedin Qerolli. Among the founders were also: Ismail Vërlaci, Kole Bibe Mirakaj dhe Ndue Gjomarkaj. The group was established on 6 November 1946 in Rome with Italian and the Vatican help.[62] Most of its supporters were Catholic Albanians from the northern part of Albania. Famous Albanian anti-Communist clan chieftain, Gjon Marka Gjonin (Gjon Markagjoni), who lived in Rome and also cooperated with the Independent Group[63].
- Partia Grupi i Kosovës (the name of the group was soon changed to Grupi i Kosovarëve and later into Partia Irendentiste) – Bajzit Buletini and Xhafer Deva who played a significant role in anti-Communist Albanians groups in exile. As

---

[60] On 1 May 1943 the Department sent to President Roosevelt for his signature a reply in which informed King Zog that "the occupation of his country makes it impractical to define our policy with respect to the future government of Albania beyond the broad outlines of the Secretary's statement of December 10." http://images.library.wisc.edu/FRUS/EFacs/1943v02/reference/frus.frus1943v02.i0005.pdf (accessed 21 April 2015).

[61] "Plan for Albania," 15 June 1949, Declassified and released by the Central Intelligence Agency (2007), 10–11, http://www.foia.cia.gov/sites/default/files/document_conversions/1705143/OBOPUS%20BG%20FIEND%20%20%20VOL.%201%20%28COUNTRY%20PLAN%20ALBANIA%29_0029.pdf (accessed 15 April 2015).

[62] Nafi Çegrani, "Emigracioni shqiptar dhe UDB!," *Bota sot*, January 20, 2011, http://botasot.info/opinione/99513/GPdmFBF/, (accesed: 25 April 2015).

[63] *Kapidan Ndue Markagjoni*, https://gjonmarkagjoni.com/kapidan-ndue-gjomarkaj/ (accessed 19 April 2015).

one of the Second League of Prizren founders, Xhafer Deva fled to Croatia in 1944 and then to Vienna where he joined other anti-Communist Albanian groups closely associated with Rexhep Mitrovica. Deva lived in Austria until 1947. He then moved to Italy and to Syria. In Damascus, he helped publish the newspaper *Bashkimi i Kombit* (Unity of the Nation). Deva emigrated to the United States in 1956. In the 1960s, he headed the Second League of Prizren, founded in New York. Its main goal was the liberation of Kosovo.[64]

During the meeting in Egypt, the Legaliteti, working for the restoration of the monarchy, proposed establishing an Albanian government in exile (Qeveria e Përbashkët Anti-komuniste në Emigracion, QPAE). They also advocated for the creation of a special military group (Krahë i armatosur ushtarak).[65] However, other Albanian groups were not so positive about these suggestions. The Balli Kombëtar in particular had a different plan regarding Albania's future, liberated from the Communists. They opted for referendum and regency representing each of the groups. The Independent Bloc was also in favor of that idea, despite its sympathy for the monarchy.[66]

Soon after the Cairo meeting, Midhat Frashëri resumed his attempts at unifying the Albanian diaspora. Albanians established the "Free Albania" National Committee (Komiteti Kombëtar "Shqipëria e Lirë", NCFA) on 26 August 1949 in Paris. Frashëri was elected the first chairman of the organization. Its international headquarters were opened on 17 July 1950 in New York. The "Free Albania" National Committee cooperated closely with the National Committee for Free Europe. The members of the Committee also maintained an office in Rome in order to stay in close contact with Albanians living in Albania. Members of the Committee also proposed setting up headquarters of the National Committee in Trieste and further branches in New York, Paris, Rome, Cairo, and Athens.[67]

---

[64] Xhafer Deva was undoubtedly a controversial Albanian political figure. During World War II, he openly declared his support for the Germans. Deva was appointed head of the local administration in Mitrovica, under German occupation. Moreover, he took part in establishing the Second League of Prizren, an Albanian organization whose aim was the creation of 'ethnic Albania.' See Robert Elsie, *Historical Dictionary of Kosovo*, 80–81.
[65] *Dështimi i "Krahut ushtarak" të "Ballit" dhe "Legalitetit" në ekzil, për rrëzimin e regjimit të Enver Hoxhës*, http://www.sot.com.al/dossier/d%C3%ABshtimi-i-krahut-ushtarak-t%C3%AB-%E2%80%9Cballit%E2%80%9D-dhe-%E2%80%9Clegalitetit%E2%80%9D-n%C3%AB-ekzil-p%C3%ABr-rr%C3%ABzimin-e-regjimit-t%C3%AB#sthash.BxDXsHpe.dpuf (accessed 19 April 2015).
[66] *Dështimi i "Krahut ushtarak"*.
[67] "Plan for Albania," 15 June 1949, Declassified and released by the Central Intelligence Agency (2007), 19, http://www.foia.cia.gov/sites/default/files/document_conversions/1705143/OBOPUS%20BG%20FIEND%20%20%20VOL.%201%20%28COUNTRY%20PLAN%20ALBANIA%29_0029.pdf (accessed 15 April 2015).

Once a month, the NCFA published its newspaper *Shqipëria* – an Albanian news bulletin for Albanians all over the world. Moreover, it also broadcasted on the Radio Free Europe and had its own clandestine radio station.[68]

The NCFA composed of the Executive Committee (Komiteti i Ekzekutiv) and the General Committee (Komiteti i Pergjitshem), which assisted the former.

Among the first members of the Executive Committee were:
- Midhat Frashëri – chairman
- Hasan Dosti – jurist, a member of the Balli Kombëtar. Imprisoned between 1932 and 1935 as an opponent of Ahmet Zogu. He was the Minister of Justice (1941–1943) during World War II[69]. On the eve of Communist victory, he moved to Italy and then to the United States.
- Abas Kupi – after World War II he helped direct the Committee's activities in Rome.[70] He was an effective leader of the guerilla against the Italians during the war. Kupi was one of the Legaliteti founders. In November 1944, when the Communists took power in Albania, Kupi along with his officers, fled by boat from the coast of Mat to Italy.[71]
- Said bey Kryeziu – As a cofounder of the Committee, he operated in its office in Rome. He was also a leader of the Albanian Agrarian Party (Lidhja Kombëtare e Fshatarëve). He moved to the United States in 1959.
- Zef Pali – an active and popular member of the Balli Kombëtar. He was forced to leave the country during World War II. Zef Pali became one of the members of

---

[68] *Voice of America's Albanian Services Celebrates its 70th Anniversary*, http://www.albertlulushi.com/2013/04/voice-of-americas-albanian-services.html (accessed 19 April 2015). The CIA also had an impact on the Voice of America. According to the Americans, that radio should prepare daily Albanian programes: 'To the extent possible, the programs should emphasize, in their reports of "news," the following lines: (1) how much the people of Albania have been betrayed by those whom they elected to office in 1945, (2) favorable reference to the activities of the committee itself (3) factual report of activities of resistance groups in Albania, sufficiently delayed after the fact to avoid jeopardizing the safety of these groups (4) the extent to which tan-Slavism is still alive outside Albania; (5) past and present evidences of US friendship for the Albanian people; (6) reference to "democracy" should be carefully defined, so as to avoid any possibility that the audience in Albania, which has been exposed to a good deal of propaganda about "new democracy", and which has not previously been accustomed to hearing the word, shall not become 'confused such other matters as may come up in the course of events and which can be used to keep the programs dynamic and encouraging to those who resist the Communists, "Plan for Albania," 15 June 1949, Declassified and released by the Central Intelligence Agency (2007), 20, http://www.foia.cia.gov/sites/default/files/document_conversions/1705143/OBOPUS%20BG%20FIEND%20%20%20VOL.%201%20%28COUNTRY%20PLAN%20ALBANIA%29_0029.pdf (accessed 15 April 2015).
[69] Robert Elsie, *Historical Dictionary of Albania*, 116.
[70] "The National Committee for a Free Albania," 28 November 1951, declassified and released by the Central Intelligence Agency, 2007, 1, http://www.foia.cia.gov/sites/default/files/document_conversions/1705143/OBOPUS%20BG%20FIEND%20%20%20VOL.%203%20%28OBLIVIOUS%20%20%20NATIONAL%20COMMITTEE%20FOR%20FREE%20ALBANIA%29_0001.pdf (accessed 19 April 2015).
[71] Robert Elsie, *Historical Dictionary of Albania*, 254.

the Paris Committee, a forerunner of the NCFA. Later, along with Abaz Ermenji, Hasan Dosti, and Vasil Andoni, he founded the Partia Agrarare Shqiptare. In Rome, Zef. Pali published the newspaper Flamuri.[72]
- Nuçi Kotta – An officer of the NCFA headquarters in New York and a member of the Legaliteti. He was responsible for the publication of the Committee's official mouthpiece, Shqipëria.[73]

The General Committee included[74]:
- Halil Maçi – member of the Balli Kombëtar
- Abas Ermenji – member of the Balli Kombëtar and a resistance fighter in World War II. In November 1939, he was arrested by the Italians. When the Communists took power in Albania, Ermenji emigrated first to Greece and then to France. In Paris (August 1954), together with Vasil Andoni, he established the anti-Communist National Democratic Committee for a Free Albania (Shqypnja e lire)[75]
- Vasil Andoni – member of the Kombëtar
- Gaçi Gogos (Gacio Gogo) – an independent
- Gani Tafili – member of the Legaliteti
- Asllan Zeineli – member of the Legaliteti
- Ihsan Toptani – an independent
- Muharrem Bajraktari – member of the Independent Fighting Group (Grupi Luftëtar i Pavarur). During the war he was one of the leading founders of the Legaliteti resistance movement. After the Communist takeover in 1944, Bajraktari fled to Italy where he worked for the NCFA.[76]
- Hysni Mulleti – member of the Agrarian League (Lidhja Agrare)
- Ekrem Telhai – an independent. He became member of the Peasant League (Lidhja Katundare)

---

72 Zef Pergega, *Profesor Zef Pali – flaka e pashuar e fjalës shqipe (1910–1977)*, https://www.balli kombetar.info/profesor-zef-pali-flaka-e-pashuar-e-fjales-shqipe-1910-1977/ (accessed 25 April 2015).
73 "The National Committee for a Free Albania," 28 November 1951, declassified and released by the Central Intelligence Agency, 2007, 2, http://www.foia.cia.gov/sites/default/files/document_conversions/ 1705143/OBOPUS%20BG%20FIEND%20%20%20VOL.%203%20%28OBLIVIOUS%20%20%20NA TIONAL%20COMMITTEE%20FOR%20FREE%20ALBANIA%29_0001.pdf (accessed 19 April 2015).
74 Rexhep Kastrati, *Aspektet programore tëdisa organizeve politike shqiptare të pasluftës së dytë botërore parë në kontekstin gjeopolitik të kohës*, http://www.shqiperiaetnike.de/html/body_rexhep_kas trati.html (accessed 25 April 2015).
75 Robert Elsie, 1983. "Abas Ermenji: Overthrowing the Communist Regime," http://www.alba nianhistory.net/1983_Ermenji/index.html (accessed 8 May 2018). After Frashëri's death, A. Ermenji became the leader of the Komitetit Kombëtar Demokrat "Shqipëria e Lirë" in Paris. This organization published the newspaper *Flamuri*, which was popular among the Albanian diaspora in Europe, the US, and Australia, *Abas Ermenji – apostull i bashkimit Kombëtar* http://www.ballikombit.org/index. php?option=com_content&task=view&id=980&Itemid=9 (accessed 21 April 2015).
76 Robert Elsie, *Historical Dictionary of Albania*, 29.

The NCFA included Albanians who resisted the Communist government in Tirana. Their primary aim was to work together for the complete restoration of independence, sovereignty and territorial integrity of the Albanian nation. In order to act effectively, Albanians needed to transcend political differences and act united against Hoxha's regime. However, not all emigrants wanted to cooperate with that organization. Among them were members of the National Independent Block and the Second League of Prizren. The first group did not want to take part in the Committee because of the presence of Albanians who cooperated with the Fascists during World War II. The Second League of Prizren was excluded from NCFA because of Xhafer Deva's collaboration with the Germans.[77]

Americans played a significant role in establishing the anti-Communist Albanian organization in exile. According to a report declassified by the Central Intelligence Agency (CIA): "The National Committee for Free Albania was created by the British and American Services in the summer of 1949 to serve as a front for covert activities and as a rallying point for anti-Communist elements among Albanian refugees and inside Albania."[78]

In June 1949, three months before establishing the Committee, the CIA even prepared an accurate list of Albanian refugees who were considered adequate for participation in that Committee. Among them were members of:
- The Balli Kombëtar:
  Midhat Frashëri (at that time he resided in Istanbul, Turkey)
  Abas Ermenji (Greece)
  Vasil Andoni (Rome, Italy)
  Vasil Dhimitraj (Rome, Italy)
  Stavro Skendi (New York, USA)
  Muharrem Bajraktari (Greece)
  Jani Dilo (Turin, Italy)
  Said Kryeziu (Rome, Italy)
  Hasan Dosti
- The National Independent Block:
  Ismail Vërlaci (Italy)
  Ali Vrioni (Italy)
  Gzon Markagjoni (Vatican)
  Ndue Markagjoni (Rome, Italy)

---

77 "Kubark-FPBERM Meeting in Belgrade on 16–17 February 1953," Declassified and released by the Central Intelligence Agency, 16, http://www.foia.cia.gov/sites/default/files/document_conversions/1705143/OBOPUS%20BFIEND%20%20%20VOL.%2024%20%28BGFIEND%20OPERATIONS%29_0028.pdf (accessed 24 April 2015).
78 Declassified and released by the Central Intelligence Agency, http://www.foia.cia.gov/sites/default/files/document_conversions/1705143/OBOPUS%20BG%20FIEND%20%20%20VOL.%203%20%20%28OBLIVIOUS%20%20%20NATIONAL%20COMMITTEE%20FOR%20FREE%20ALBANIA%29_0016.pdf (accessed 24 April 2015).

- The Legaliteti:
  Ferid Dervishi (Rome, Italy)
  Asaf Djadjuli (Ankara-Istanbul, Turkey)
  Abas Kupi (Cairo-Alexandria, Egypt)
  Caqo Gogo (Cairo-Alexandria, Egypt)
  Abdul Sula (Cairo, Egypt)
- Others:
  Tajar Zavalani (London)
  Ishan Toptani (Rome)
  Muredin Vlora (Rome)
  Asim Jakova (New York)
  Kristo Maloki (Graz, Austria)[79]

The CIA also prepared a list of Albanian exiles that were to be excluded from the activities of the Committee:
- From the Balli Kombëtar:
  Ali Klisura (at that time in Syria)
  Koco Muka (Egypt)
- The National Independent Block:
  Ernest Koliqi (Rome, Italy)
  Kol Bit Mirakaj (Rome, Italy)
- The Zogists (members of the Legaliteti or Zog supporters):
  Ahmet Zogu,
  Prenk Pervisi (Greece)
- Jake Koci (Tivoli, Italy)
  Zef Sereqi (Rome, Italy)
  Musa Juka (Cairo, Egypt)
  Hysai Dema (Greece)
- Others:
  Qazim Mulletti (Rome, Italy)
  Djafer Deva (Cairo, Egypt)
  Mehdi Frashëri
  Redjip Mitrovica[80]

The NCFA was composed of four main groups: the Legaliteti (in support of King Zogu), the Balli Kombëtar, the independent group of Muharrem Bajraktari, and the Agrarian Party of Said bey Kryeziu. Said bey Kryeziu was willing to cooperate with the Zogists despite the fact that King Zog had killed his eldest brother. The entire

---

79 "Kubark-FPBERM Meeting in Belgrade on 16–17 February 1953," 23.
80 "Kubark-FPBERM Meeting...," 24.

Kryeziu family lived in Yugoslavia under the protection of King Alexander when Ahmet Zogu ruled Albania.

King Zog I, who wished to come back to Albania and reestablish his throne, remained indifferent to the NCFA and to the Legaliteti as well. His primary aim was also the liberation of Albania. Ahmet Zogu at that time was still in favor of creating the government in exile with four or five ministers. However, neither the Committee nor the United States or Great Britain supported Zog's plan.

There was also another Albanian organization in the US with a similar name to the NCFA. It was Free Albania (Shqipëria e lirë) formed by Koste Çekrezi (also known as Kost/Kostandin/Constantine Chekrezi) in 1941. Along with Tajar Zavalani, he tried to establish the Albanian government in exile during the war and fight for integration of all ethnic Albanian territory in the Balkans. Çekrezi strongly opposed Greek policy toward the southern part of Albania.[81]

Both the NCFA and the Shqipëria e lirë concurred with other active Albanian associations in the United States, namely, the Vatra – the Pan-Albanian Federation of America, which was founded in 1912. Among its leaders were Sotir Peci, Fan Noli, Faik Konica, Christo Anastas Dako, Vasil Marko, Kristo Thanasi, Andoni Athanas, and Koste Çekrezi.[82] Vatra had its headquarters in Boston. After World War II, bishop Fan Noli, an outstanding leader of the Albanian American community, was still well-known in Albania even though he was not able to take any political action. He was in contact with Hoxha and was in favor of maintaining good relations with the Communist regime.[83] He tried to persuade the US government to recognized the Albania's communist regime.[84] In 1924, Fan Noli became the (leftist) Prime Minister of Albania. He was an opponent of Ahmet Zogu. Noli's government made the decision to establish diplomatic relations with the Soviet Union. Because of his leftist tendencies, Fan Noli was considered a "red bishop" and there were rumors that he received financial support from the Soviets. In addition, Vatra members had contacts with the Albanian representatives of the Communist government in the United Nations in New York (Albania became a member of the UN in 1955), which caused further polarization among émigré circles in the US.

Other Albanian organizations, which were active at that time, were:
- The Albanian Independent Democratic Group in Boston set up by Stavro Skendi. In July 1947, the group presented a five-point program to the Department of State. Skendi called for an independent Albania with a democratic government[85]

---

81 Hamit Kaba, *"Vatra" gjatë luftës së dytë botërore dhe luftës së ftohtë* in Roli i Mërgatës në Shtetformim (Prishtina: Ministria e Diasporës, 2012), 136.
82 Kaba, 135.
83 Kaba, 143.
84 Robert Elsie, *Historical Dictionary of Albania*, 331.
85 "Plan for Albania," 15 June 1949, Declassified and released by the Central Intelligence Agency (2007), 13, http://www.foia.cia.gov/sites/default/files/document_conversions/1705143/OBOPUS%20BG

- The Komiteti për Mbrojtjen e Integritrtit të Territoreve Shqiptare formed by Fred Kosta on 29 March 1946,
- Lidhja Progresive Shqiptaro-Amerikane[86]
- The Albanian-American National Organization (Organizatën Kombëtare Shqiptaro Amerikane) established in New York in 1946 in order to help Albanian exiles in finding new places of residence and jobs in the US.[87]

In summary, there was not one organization that represented all Albanian emigrants in the US.[88] During the Cold War Albanians remained divided and mutually antagonistic, despite sharing more or less the same opinion about fighting against the Communists and neighbors whose aim was the annexation of Albanian territory.[89]

Even the NCFA was not internally united. These divisions were even deeper after the death of Midhat Frashëri. He was the chairman of the NCFA for only three months. Frashëri died on 3 October 1949 in his room at the Winthrop Hotel in New York. After his death, Hasan Dosti became the new leader of the Committee, but he was also unsuccessful in uniting Albanian exiles. There was a split within the Balli Kombëtar in 1950 and the organization divided into:
- Balli i Ri Kobëtar, the left-wing faction, with Hasan Dosti as the leader, who decided to cooperate with the NCFA. After three months, Dosti changed its name to Balli Kombetar Agrarian (Partia Agrare Demokratike e Ballit Kombëta). Among its members were also Abas Ermenji and Zef Pali.
- The Balli Kombëtar Organization (Balli i Vjetër Kombëtar) was the more conservative faction under the leadership of Ali bey Këlcyra (also known as Ali Klissura). It refused to cooperate with the NCFA. After the split within Balli Kombëtar, Ermenji and Pali expelled two supporters of Ali bey Këlcyra from the NCFA Executive Committee and replaced them with Balli Kombëtar Agrarian members. Before World War II, Ali bey Këlcyra was a member of the Albanian parliament and a supporter of Fan Noli. After the fall of the Noli government, he fled the country and then headed the National Union (Bashkimi Kombëtar) – one of the Albanian organizations active abroad. The Zog regime sentenced him to

---

%20FIEND%20%20%20VOL.%201%20%28COUNTRY%20PLAN%20ALBANIA%29_0029.pdf (accessed 15 April 2015).
86 Kaba, 145.
87 *Histori e shkurtër e shqiptarëve në Amerikë*, http://www.proletari.com/histori-e-shkurter-e-shqiptareve-ne-amerike/html (accessed 5 April 2015).
88 The VATRA was also unable to unite Albanian emigrants in the United States (they lived in Boston, New York, Detroit, Chicago, Philadelphia, and Bridgeport), who numbered approximately 30,000 people. Most of them emigrated to the United States before 1939. Only a few of them were refugees from the Communist regime, Shyqyri Hysi, *Histori e trojeve dhe e diasporës shqiptare* (Tirana: Shtëpia Botuese e Librit Universitar, 2007), 36–37.
89 Kaba, 148.

death in absentia.⁹⁰ Moreover, A. bey Këlcyra was one of the leaders of the Balli Kombëtar, but as many other members of that organization, he was forced to leave the country in 1944 when Communists took power. He later broadcasted Albanian language news programs from the West.⁹¹ In July 1953, the Balli Kombëtar group, led by A. bey Këlcyra, merged with the National Independent Block and formed the Albanian Democratic Union led by Ismail Vërlaci (son of Shefqet Bey Vërlaci – the Italian's first puppet prime minister of Albania) and Nduc Marko Gjoni. This organization was known as the Balli of the Beys.⁹² A. bey Këlcyra died in Rome in 1963.

Eventually, thirty-four different groups and twenty-one parties emerged from the Balli Kombëtar. At that time, twenty-one other Balli Kombëtar groups were established in Italy, Greece, Germany, France, Great Britain, Egypt, Austria, Australia, and the US.

After Dosti, the next chairman of the Committee was Rexhep Krasniqi, a professor of history and geography, originally from Gjakova in Kosovo. After World War II, he left the country and travelled through Croatia moved to Austria then to Italy and finally to Australia, where he worked in the General Motor Factory. Krasniqi continued his political activity in exile. Along with Xhelal Mitrovica, he published the newspaper *Vatra shqiptare* and wrote papers on politics and history. He stayed in continuous contact with other Albanian emigrants. Between 1950 and 1951, Krasniqi corresponded with Deva with whom he exchanged opinions about the situation in the Balkans. At that time, Deva was part of NATO military exercises in Munich (West Germany). In his letters, he even tried to explain to Krasniqi how Albanians should fight in order to liberate Kosovo.⁹³

Krasniqi moved to the US in 1954. Two years later, he was elected head of the NCFA and decided to reorganize the organization in order to increase its effectiveness.⁹⁴ He also asked the Americans for financial support to reestablish the Albanian government in exile. Krasniqi launched many different initiatives. With US support, the NCFA was permitted 5,000 Albanian refugees live in camps in Yugoslavia, Austria, France, Italy, and go to the US. The organization also provided help to Albanian emigrants by finding them homes, employment and providing education. Krasniqi

---

90 *Rikthehet në atdhe Ali Këlcyra, "armiku" i diktatorëve shqiptarë*, "Tema" (April 3, 2014) http://www.gazetatema.net/2014/04/03/rikthehet-ne-atdhe-ali-kelcyra-armiku-i-diktatoreve-shqiptare/ (accessed 8 May 2018).
91 Robert Elsie, *Historical Dictionary of Albania*, 227–228.
92 Owen Pearson, *Albania in the Twentieth Century, A History*, vol. 3: *Albania as Dictatorship and Democracy, 1945–98* (New York: Tauris, 2007), 461.
93 Sejdi Peka, "Prof. Rexhep Krasniqi, kolos i madh i patriotizmit shqiptar," February 7, 2010, http://www.arkivalajmeve.com/Prof-Rexhep-Krasniqi-kolos-i-madh-i-patriotizmit-shqiptar.404865/ (accessed 6 May 2018).
94 Robert Elsie, *Historical Dictionary of Albania*, 249.

dismissed Communist propaganda assertions that Albanian emigration included collaborators with the Axis powers from World War II. He continually protested against Hoxha's repressive policy in Albania. Rexhep Krasniqi addressed an official protest letter to the general secretary of the UN and to the Human Rights Commission, asking them to "put an end to this strong prosecution of religious beliefs in Albania".[95] Moreover, Krasniqi also organized political meetings, conferences, and seminars on various Albanian cultural topics. Every year, the Committee sponsored and celebrated 28 November in honor of Albanian Independence Day. It was one of its most important activities.

Under the Krasniqi, the NCFA cooperated with ACEN, the Assembly of Captive European Nations (Asambleja e Kombeve Europiane të Robëruara), which sought to undermine Communist rule in Eastern Europe. From its inception, the ACEN comprised delegations representing Albania, Bulgaria, Poland, Czechoslovakia, Latvia, Estonia, Hungary, Lithuania, and Romania. In 1964 and again in 1970, Vasil Germenji[96], a prominent Albanian politician was elected president of the ACEN.[97] He became a member of the NCFA in 1953 and has since lived in New York. In 1939, after the Italian invasion, Germenji moved to France, where in 1941 he joined the French resistance movement. After World War II, Germenji published a newspaper, both in Albanian and French, entitled *Liberty of the Nation* (Liria e Kombit). Krasniqi headed the NCFA until it was disbanded in 1992. After forty-three years of intense political, cultural, and social activity, the Free Albania Committee recognized that its work was no longer needed.[98]

In the 1970s and 1980s, Albanian émigrés intensified their political activities not only in the US but also in Europe, especially in Belgium and France. At the beginning of the 1980s in these European countries, were ca. 5,000 emigrants, active in either the Balli Kombëtar, the Legaliteti or the National Block.[99] After the protests in Kosovo in 1981, the activities within the Albanian diaspora increasingly focused on the situation of Albanians living in Yugoslavia.

---

95 Nertila Haxhia Ljarjaa, "An Analysis of the Consequences of the Ideological and Cultural Revolution," *Sociology Study* 1, no. 6 (2011): 471.
96 Vasil Germenji was the nephew of Themistokli Germenji, the Albanian hero from Korça. In 1917, during the French occupation, he established the Republic of Korça, "Vasil Germenji (1908–1988), Germaine Germenji (1913–1988)," *Albanian Catholic Bulletin* 10, (1989): 177.
97 Frank Shkreli, *60-vjetori i themelimit të Asamblesë së Kombeve të Robëruara Europiane*, August 12, 2014, http://gazetadielli.com/60-vjetori-i-themelimit-te-asamblese-se-kombeve-te-roberuara-europiane/ (accessed 24 April 2015); Idriz Lamaj, "Vasil Gërmenji, nipi i Themistokli Germenjit, diplomat i shquar në kryqëzatën kundër komunizmit," *Dielli*, 10.09.2013, http://gazetadielli.com/vasil-germenji-nipi-i-themistokli-germenjit-diplomat-i-shquar-ne-kryqezaten-kunder-komunizmit-2/ (accessed 25 April 2015).
98 "Free Albanian Committee ends operations," *Albanian Catholic Bulletin* 13, (1992): 96.
99 After the two major events that took place in Kosovo in 1968 and 1981, more and more organizations were established by the Albanians who emigrated from Yugoslavia at that time, see: E. full name! Çeku, *Struktura politike e ilegales së Kosovës* (Tirana: Argeta-LMG, 2006), 71–78.

At that time, Zog's son, Leka, was also active in fighting for Albanians rights. King Zog I died at the 'Foch' Hospital in Paris, on 9 April 1961. He did not abdicate and after his death, Leka proclaimed himself King of Albanians.[100] The coronation ceremony took place on 15 April 1961 at the Hotel Bristol in Paris, in the Presence of royal Albanian parliament deputies and seventy selected delegates from the Albanian diaspora.[101]

Leka was well prepared to become the next king of Albania. He was educated in Egypt (Victoria College in Alexandria), Switzerland (Vilare Ailange College), England (Royal Military Academy at Sandhurst), and the University of Sorbonne in France, where he studied economics and political science. Just like his father, Leka also believed that one day Albania would be a free and democratic country.[102] Leka was also a supporter of the concept of an 'Ethnic Albania' and he continuously served for Albanians living not only in Albania, but also in Kosovo, Macedonia, and Chameria.

King Leka took action in order to unite all Albanian organizations. During his visit to the US in 1967, he tried to improve relations with different Albanian organizations in exile. King Leka paid his respects to Fan Noli and Faik Konica at their memorials and was greeted by members of the Balli Kombëtar, the Legaliteti, and the Vatra. His aim was also to forge ties with the US. King Leka even met with Ronald Reagan, the governor of California at that time.[103]

On 2–3 July 1972, King Leka took part in a conference in Madrid presided over by Deva, during which he also spoke with members of the *Balli Kombëtar, Partia Agrare Balli Kombëtar, Organizata Kombëtare Levizja e Legalitetit, Heroizma Shqiptare, Bashkimi Shqiptar, Lidhja e Prizrenit*, and *Komiteti "Shqipëria e lire"*. Undoubtedly, it was the first successful gathering of Albanian political and non-political communities under King Zog's slogan "Nation Above All"; a gathering against the Communist regime and in favor of creating a worldwide Albanian front. Leka once again emphasized that all groups should act together. All Albanian groups agreed to form a national force in order to secure national integration. First, the founding of an executive committee with nine members and an advisory committee made up of at least one representative from each Albanian organization was necessary.[104] King Leka was represented by Atanas Gega who ensured unification act and coordinated both political and diplomatic activities of Albanian emigrants. His activities also led

---

100 Sulejman Gjana, "Roli dhe Kontributi i Mbretit Leka në mërgim për lirinë e populit shqiptar dhe për çështjen kombëtare," in Roli i Mërgatës në Shtetformim (Prishtina: Ministria e Diasporës, 2012), 321.
101 *King Leka*, http://www.albanianroyalcourt.al/pages/Mbreti%20Leka%20I (accessed 19 April 2015).
102 Sulejman Gjana, "Roli dhe Kontributi i Mbretit Leka në mërgim për lirinë e populit shqiptar dhe për çështjen kombëtare," in Roli i Mërgatës në Shtetformim (Prishtina: Ministria e Diaspores, 2012), 321.
103 *King Leka*, http://www.albanianroyalcourt.al/pages/Mbreti%20Leka%20I (accessed 20 April 2015).
104 Sulejman Gjana, "Roli dhe Kontributi i Mbretit Leka në mërgim për lirinë e populit shqiptar dhe për çështjen kombëtare," in Roli i Mërgatës në Shtetformim (Prishtina: Ministria e Diasporës, 2012), 325.

to the creation of the Albanian Liberation Army (Ushtria Kmbëtare për Çlirimin e Shqipërisë Etnike), which Albanians would join voluntarily. Members of the army went through special training in Spain.[105] It was not random to choose Spain for establishing camps because during the 1970s, as a friend of General Franco, King Leka and his mother used to live in Spain. The aim of the army was the liberation of the country and the creation of an 'Ethnic Albania'.

King Leka also issued a special memorandum for the Conference on Security and Cooperation in Europe held in Helsinki in 1975 as a part of the ACEN to respect rights of the Albanian nation.[106] Two years later, he issued another memorandum showing his strong opposition to the idea of organizing a conference in Belgrade on 5 June 1977. Leka explained that such a conference was against Albanian interests.

In 1979, he was expelled from Spain for supporting subversive activities. Leka tried to explain that his "government-in-exile" was organizing guerrilla operations inside Communist Albania. After that controversial situation, he found refuge in South Africa.[107] However, King Leka always criticized the Communist regime in Albania. He never stopped believing that a monarchy could mean the end to the country's problems and he was ready to return to Albania should Albanians be in favor of a monarchy. On 24 November 1978, in an interview for *L'eventail*, King Leka argued that the Albanian nation should decide in referendum whether it wanted to be a republic or a constitutional monarchy.[108]

1.3.3 Covert operations in Albania during the Cold War

After World War II, the US and Britain pursued joint covert operations in Albania in order to overthrow the Communist regime.[109] Albania's relations with the West were hostile until the end of the Cold War. Despite the fact that on 10 November 1945 the Albanian government resumed diplomatic relations with the US, on 15 November 1946, the United States decided to withdraw its mission from Albania when the new government in Tirana refused to honor its prewar agreements.[110] The American Embassy building was left to the Italian government until 1991. During the Corfu Channel incident in October 1946, in which two British ships were hit by mines and

---

105 Gjana, 326.
106 Gjana, 325.
107 *Leka Zogu obituary*, http://www.theguardian.com/world/2011/dec/01/leka-zogu (accessed 20 April 2015).
108 Sulejman Gjana, "Roli dhe Kontributi i Mbretit Leka në mërgim për lirinë e populit shqiptar dhe për çështjen kombëtare," in Roli i Mërgatës në Shtetformim (Prishtina: Ministria e Diasporës, 2012), 327.
109 I use the terms "covert action" (a term of the 1970s) and "covert operations" (a 1950s term) synonymously.
110 American-Albanian diplomatic relations were established in 1922 but after Italy's invasion of Albania in 1939, the American legation in Tirana was closed, Robert Elsie, *Historical Dictionary of Albania*, 462.

sank (forty-four crew members died), the United Kingdom also broke off diplomatic ties with Albania.[111]

Overthrowing the Communist regime in Tirana and establishing a new democratic government was not the only reason for pursuing joint secret operations in Albania. The other reason, also extremely important, was the elimination of this country as a training and holding base for Greek insurgents and of depriving the USSR of an outpost in the Mediterranean.[112] Albania was perceived as an important Soviet satellite in the Balkans especially after the Tito-Stalin split in 1948. Western thinking assumed that since Albania was isolated from the Soviet bloc, a focused effort would be sufficient to topple the Communist regime. Albania was involved in the civil war in Greece whereby it provided military support to Greek guerrillas against the government in Athens.

After 1946, once the diplomatic ties with Albania had already been broken, both the Americans and the British began elaborating a covert plan in order to change the government in Tirana. First, they decided to support the anti-Communist forces among Albanian emigrants to establish the NCFA. The first paramilitary mission began in September 1946. Project 'Valuable' was a set of military operations of the Central Intelligence Agency (CIA), in collaboration with British agents and several Albanian exiles. The term 'Valuable' was used by the British and 'Fiend' was the codename used by the CIA.[113] According to Frank Gardiner Wisner, head of the CIA's Office of Policy Coordination (OPC) at that time, it was a "clinical experiment to see whether larger rollback operations would be feasible elsewhere."[114]

Albanians selected for the covert operation were recruited and trained in the use of weapons, codes, the techniques of subversion in different camps located in Cyprus, Malta (by British agents), and the Federal Republic of Germany (West Germa-

---

111 Elsie, *Historical Dictionary of Albania*, 459.
112 *Review of BGFIEND*, Declassified and released by the Central Intelligence Agency, http://www.foia.cia.gov/sites/default/files/document_conversions/1705143/OBOPUS%20BG%20FIEND%20%20%20VOL.%202%20%28PROJECT%20OUTLINED%20REVIEWS%20TERMINATION%29_0018.pdf (accessed 20 April 2015).
113 Other covert operations included: OBOPUS (formerly BGFIEND – 1949–58), OBDURATE (formerly OBSTACLE, Plan CHARITY – 1954–56), incorporated into OBLONG in 1956, OBHUNT (infiltration missions into Albania via airdrops or overland to organize underground resistance, establish safe houses, collect operational intelligence, and to spread propaganda). These missions were associated with Project BGFIEND; OBLIVIOUS (1949–55), formerly HTNEIGH and were part of OBOPUS/BGFIEND. OBLONG OBDURATE (formerly OBSTACLE, Plan CHARITY) (1954–56), OBSIDIOUS, For more information about the operation, see Albert Lulushi, *Operation Valuable Fiend: The CIA's First Paramilitary Strike Against the Iron Curtain* (New York: Arcade Publishing, 2014); Richard C.S. Trahair and Robert Miller, *Encyclopedia of Cold War Espionage, Spies and Secret Operations* (New York: Enigma Books, 2013); Keith Jeffery, *MI6: The History of the Secret Intelligence Service 1909–1949* (London: Crowd, 2010); Stephen Dorril, *MI6: Inside the Covert World of Her Majesty's Secret Intelligence Service* (New York: Touchstone, 2002).
114 William Thomas Smith, *Encyclopedia of the Central Intelligence Agency* (New York: Factson File, 2003), 8.

ny – by Americans agents).[115] They were then placed on Albanian territory where they stayed in contact with resistance leaders in the northern part of the country. Among those Albanian leaders were Gjergj Vata (Dukagjin), Martin Sheldija (Shkoder), Ndoc Mirakaj (Puka), Mark Bajraktari (Kashnjet), Ndue Bajraktari (Kushneni), Mark Bib Vokri (Fandi), Zef Preka (Zadrima), Bilal Kola (Mati), and Nik Sokoli (Nikaj).[116] All of them were willing to cooperate in order to topple down the Communist regime.

Despite many setbacks, covert operations continued from 1949 to 1954. Albanian security forces caught four émigrés in November 1950 and another twelve in July and October 1951.[117] However, the operation failed and most of the infiltrators were either captured or executed. It is estimated that several hundred Albanian exiles were killed during these operations. Eventually, in 1954, the CIA decided to end all infiltration operations in Albania and dismissed all agents already prepared and awaiting further operations in Greece. It is believed that project "Valuable" was betrayed by Kim Philby, a Soviet double agent, who worked as liaison officer in Washington for MI6 and the CIA. However, new research suggests that the main reason for the failure of the covert operation was the poor security surrounding recruitment and Hoxha's knowledge of the operation. The Albanian émigré community could have also leaked the information because it was divided. Moreover, there was no other real political alternative to the Party of Labor of Albania (the Communist Party of Albania from 1941–1948) and to Hoxha as a leader. The covert operation undertaken to influence the course of political events in Albania was unsuccessful. It also showed that even a preassembly weak regime is able to defend itself against insurgents supported from abroad.

1.4 Albanian migration since 1989

Enver Hoxha led Albania until his death in 1985. He was succeeded by Ramiz Alia. Alia sought to preserve the old regime while introducing gradual reforms, especially economic reforms in order to boost growth in the country. At the end of the 1980s, Albania faced a huge economic and social crisis and the government had to accept the centralized economic planning, which was ineffective especially in terms of providing adequate goods for consumers. The only solution was to end the era of isola-

---

115 "Declassified and released by the Central Intelligence Agency" 1–2, http://www.foia.cia.gov/sites/default/files/document_conversions/1705143/OBOPUS%20BGFIEND%20%20%20VOL.%2020%20%20%28BGFIEND%20OPERATIONS%29_0012.pdf (accessed 21 April 2015).
116 "Albania – 1949–1958," http://www.globalsecurity.org/intell/ops/albania.htm (accessed 21 April 2015).
117 Richard, C. Trahair, *Encyclopedia of Cold War Espionage, Spies, and Secret Operations* (New York: Enigma Books, 2012), 9.

tion and to open the country to the world market. The Party of Labor acknowledged that Albania needed international assistance.

When the Berlin Wall fell in 1989, Albania was still under Communism although different parts of Albanian society began to speak out against the regime. Among them were intellectuals, students, and workers. Although Alia was a more open-minded leader than Hoxha, he hesitated to introduce large-scale political liberalization. The Communist party did not want to compromise its monopoly in the country. However, the government came under increasing internal and external pressure to implement democratic reforms. Following massive students protests, Aliza decided to introduce changes by initiating several reforms that addressed long-standing problems such as the abolition of restrictions on religious worship, the liberalization of the justice system, and the right of criminal defendants to legal counsel.[118]

The Decree no. 7393 on the Issuance of Passports, dated 12 June 1990, is considered the first act of the Albanian authorities to ease restrictions on emigration.[119] After almost fifty years, Albanians received the right to choose their place of residence, to move freely within the country, and to emigrate. The liberalization of issuing passports caused a small-scale exodus that continue for the next few months.

Albanians immediately decided to enjoy their right of freedom of movement. The tragic exodus began on 2 July 1990 when approximately 5,000 of them entered embassies by force and sought political asylum, initially in German and then in other Western European embassies in Tirana (French, British, Italian, Spanish, Turkish).[120] Thousands of Albanians came to the capital city from every corner of the country in high hopes of entering one of the embassies. Others targeted the ships in the port of Durrës. Small-scale illegal emigration through the Adriatic Sea to the Apulian coast, across the narrow Corfu Strait was already underway. After a few weeks, some Albanians were given exile in various states of the European Union. As Pandeli Majko, the former Prime Minister of Albania, noticed, 2 July is celebrated in Albania as a day when the Albanian 'Berlin Wall' fell (ditën e rrëzimit përfundimtar të murit të Berlinit).[121]

The Albanian government wanted to prevent the illegal emigration of Albanians, for instance, by declaring refugees criminals and prohibiting them from seeking asylum in the embassies in the future.[122] In addition, Albanian authorities sent official

---

118 National Republican Institute for International Affairs, "The 1991 Elections in Albania. Report of the Election Observer Delegation," 4. http://www.iri.org/sites/default/files/fields/field_files_attached/resource/albanias_1991_parliamentary_elections.pdf (accessed 5 May 2018).
119 "Albania: Decree No. 7393 of 1990 on the Issue of Passports and Visas," http://www.refworld.org/docid/3ae6b54d4.html (accessed 5 May 2018).
120 Julie Vullnetari, "Albanian migration and development: state of the art review," IMISCO Working Paper (September 2007): 31.
121 Lediona Braho, "Majko: Sot, përvjetori kur shqiptarët rrëzuan "murin e Berlinit"" *Shekulli*, July 2, 2014, http://shekulli.com.al/50152/ (accessed 5 May 2018).
122 National Republican Institute for International Affairs, "The 1991 Elections in Albania. Report of the Election Observer Delegation," 4. http://www.iri.org/sites/default/files/fields/field_files_attached/resource/albanias_1991_parliamentary_elections.pdf (accessed 5 May 2018).

requests to the embassies as a form of reminder that Albanian citizens were prohibited from travelling abroad. Albanian security forces were also unable to stop illegal emigration from the country.[123]

At the same time, another thousands of Albanians tried to reach Greece through the dangerous mountain path.[124] Within a single night on the last day of 1990, an estimated 3,000 'refugees' were reported to have crossed the Albanian-Greek border. According to *the Associated Press*, Albanians wearing tattered clothes fled by the thousands into Greece on Tuesday, crossing snow-covered Mount Mourgana. Albanians braved freezing temperatures, snow and craggy terrain to cross through [Greece's] remote northwestern border outpost of Tsamandas. A police spokesman in nearby Filiates said more than 3,500 crossed the border overnight. The number could be higher, however, because police said many more refugees might not have reported to Greek authorities ... there were 4,000 refugees in [the] town ... of 5,000 ... the Albanians had no clothes, food or shelter and many were sleeping in muddy courtyards and on sidewalks.[125]

In December 1990 Greece accepted 3,000 ethnic Greek Albanians from southern Albania who sought political asylum. Greece accepted another 10,000 Albanians in the next three months. Albanians tried to reach Greece through five main crossings: at Bilisht (leading to Kastoria and Fiorina) and at Kakavi (leading to Ioannina). Albanian migration to Greece has followed three main routes since 1990:
- the short sea link from Sarandë to Corfu
- via southern Macedonia to Thessaloniki
- via mountain paths which cross the border in remote places[126]

Albanians from the central part of a country opted mainly for Italy as an emigration destination while Albanians from the southern regions, inhabited by a significant minority of Orthodox ethnic Greeks, chose Greece. Italy was the first choice of destination for those who lived in the coastal and center part of Albania. Between July 1990 and February 1991, around 20,000 Albanians left homeland.[127]

The next big exodus of Albanians took place after Albania's first democratic held on 31 March 1991, with later rounds on 7 and 14 April. The elections were the first

---

123 Russell King and Nicola Mai, *Out of Albania: From Crisis Migration to Social Inclusion in Italy* (London: Berghahn Books, 2008), 68.
124 Matilda Likaj, "*Migration as a Challenge for Albanian Post-Communist Society*," *Journal of Educational and Social Research* 4, no. 2 (2014): 143–144.
125 Erind Pajo, *International Migration, Social Demotion, and Imagined Advancement: An Ethnography of Socioglobal Mobility* (New York: Springer, 2008), 16.
126 Russell King, "Across the Sea and Over the Mountains: Documenting Albanian Migration," *Scottish Geographical Journal* 119, no. 3 (2003): 296–297.
127 "Skaneri i popullsisë, 32.5% e shqiptarëve jetojnë jashtë vendit," *Mapo*, 31.01.2013, http://www.mapo.al/skaneri-i-popullsise-32-5-e-shqiptareve-jetojne-jashte-vendit/ (accessed 6 May 2018).

multi-party elections since 1923.[128] As political chaos threatened and the economy collapsed, around 25,000 Albanians took boats and ships in order to get to Apulia (Italy), where they stayed for many days on the quays at Brindisi or in military accommodations.[129] All immigrants were dispersed in small groups all over the country. It was part of a strategy to diminish their disruptive potential and provide them with good chances of employment at the labor markets.[130]

Another exodus took place in August 1991 when approximately 20,000 Albanians escaped to Italy. Several ships from the main ports in Durres and Vlora carrying many Albanian migrants entered the port of Bari, Italy. However, this time, the Italian government's response was harsh. Most of the Albanians were detained at a sports stadium (La Vittoria Sports Stadium) without adequate food or water.[131] In order to resolve the problem of the massive number of illegal immigrants, the Italian authorities even decided to offer the Albanians 50,000 lire (40 US dollars) each and new clothes for returning home. Eventually, some were quickly repatriated. According to official statements made by the government in Rome, Albanians could no longer be treated as political refuges since democratic elections in Albania were held.

At the end of October 1991, Margherita Boniver, the Italian minister stated that of 24,157 Albanians, only 645 obtained political refugee status, 715 were sent back; 315 were expelled; 9,452 found jobs; 711 took vocational training courses; and approximately 8,000 had not yet found jobs. The rest became illegal immigrants. On behalf of the Italian authorities, the minister also added: "We were able to respond quickly to the dramatic events of last August. In the meantime, political conditions in Alba-

---

128 The R. Alia's policy did not convince the protesters. In December 1990 and January 1991 students led anti-government demonstrations in many Albanian cities. Eventually, they managed to force the government to democratic elections. In early December 1990, the ruling party allowed the formation of a multiparty system in Albania. The first formal opposition party, the Democratic Party, was established in 1990. The elections took place on 31 March 1991. However, the Communists won with a majority of 169 out of 250 seats in the parliament. One of the reasons for their victory was the fact that the Communists still controlled the media in Albania, which made it nearly impossible for the opposition to send its message to the society. The Democratic Party had even problems with publishing its mouthpiece, *Rilindja Demokratike* and *Republika*. However, demonstrations continued and led to the resignation of the Prime Minister, Fatos Nano, in June 1991. The Albanian President, R. Alia, replaced him with Ylli Bufi, a nonpartisan economist. The next parliamentary elections, held in March 1992, ended Albanian Communist rule. The Democratic Party won an overwhelming majority of the popular vote. The Communist era in Albania ended on 3 April 1992 when the newly elected Parliament chose the Democratic Party leader, Sali Berisha, as the country's president. He was Albania's first non-Communist president since the end of World War II. See Minton F. Goldman, *Revolution and Change in Central and Eastern Europe: Political, Economic and Social Challenges* (New York: M.E. Sharpe, 1997), 64–67; Tarifa, 146.
129 King and Vullnetari, "Migration and Development in Albania, Working Paper," 9.
130 King, "Across the Sea and Over the Mountains: Documenting Albanian Migration," 287.
131 Niels Frenzen, 29.07.2011, *20th Anniversary of the Arrival at Bari, Italy of 15,000 Albanian Boat People*, http://migrantsatsea.org/2011/07/29/20th-anniversary-of-the-arrival-at-bari-italy-of-15000-albanian-boat-people/ (accessed 8 May 2015).

nia changed as a democratic government was formed, which gave all the main political forces an opportunity to participate. By repatriating 17 476 Albanians from August 8–13, and another 3,400 (including 700 soldiers) on August 17, we were able to show respect to Law 39/90."[132]

However, Albanian illegal migration to Italy and Greece continued. In the mid-1990s, almost 20 percent of the working population, mostly young men, had emigrated.[133] Altogether, between 1991 and 1992, an estimated 200,000 Albanians left the country.[134]

In conclusion, the period between 1990 and 1993 should be recognized as a time of mass Albanian emigration whereby approximately 300,000 people tried to leave their homeland either with the help of the embassies or illegally. There is no doubt that due to the geographical and cultural proximity to both Italy and Greece, these countries were the most popular destinations among Albanian emigrants. From Italy, they tried to go to other western European countries, mainly Germany, Great Britain, and Switzerland.

1.5 Archives and Literature

Essential archival resources on Albanian emigration can be found in different archives and libraries in the Balkans, especially in Albania, Kosovo, and Macedonia. They include: the Albanian National Archives (Arkivi Qendror i Shtetit), the National Library of Albania (Biblioteka Kombëtare e Shqipërisë), the Archive of the Interior Ministry (Arkivi i Ministrisë së Brendëshme), the Institute for the Studies of Communist Crimes and its Consequences in Albania (Instituti i Studimeve për Krimet dhe Pasojat e Komunizmit), the Museum of Memory (Muzeu i Memories), the Museum of Memory in Shkodër (Muzeu i Kujtesës, Shkodër), the International Organization for Migration Mission (IOM), the South East European University (maced. Универзитет на Југо источна Европа, alb. Universitetit të Evropës Juglindore, SEEU) with the Max van der Stoel library, the National Library of Kosovo (Biblioteka Kombëtare e Kosovës "Pjetër Bogdani"), the Center for Albanian Studies (CAS), Vatra, the Pan-Albanian Federation of America Archive in New York, the "Free Albania" National Committee Archive (Arkivi i Komitetit "Shqipnia e Lirë"), and the Fan Noli Library at the Saint George Albanian Orthodox Cathedral in Boston.

Most of the Albanian archival records are kept at the National Library in Tirana and at the Albanian National Archives. The National Archive holds all original cor-

---

132 Giovama Campani, "Albanian Refugees in Italy," *Refuge* 12, no. 4 (October 1992): 9.
133 Sonila Papathimiu, "The demographic and economic development of Albania during and after the decline of Communist regime (1945–2010)," *Treballs de la Societat Catalana de Geografia* 73 (June 2012): 111.
134 Russell King, "Albania as a laboratory for the study of migration and development," *Journal of Southern Europe and the Balkans* 7, no. 1 (August 2005): 137.

respondence of the diplomatic activity of the Albanian state since 1912. All the original documents of bilateral and multilateral agreements signed by the Republic of Albania are also deposited in this archive. Albanian archives still contain documents that are either unexplored or explored only marginally.

The issue of Albanian emigration during the Cold War is not a topic of substantial research, commentary, or reflection in Albania. However, the analysis of documents and the review of hundreds of primary and secondary sources will eventually increase our understanding of the events and add to the body of knowledge about this period in Albanian history.

Many texts on Albanian migration (especially after 1991) have been written by Julie Vullnetari[135] and also Russell King[136]. Among other authors who wrote on this topic are: Shyqyri Hysi[137], Matilda Likaj[138], Giovama Campani[139], Sonila Papathimiu[140], Eckehard Pistrick[141], Nicola Mai[142], Fatos Tarifa[143].

---

[135] Julie Vullnetari, *Albania on the Move: Links Between Internal and International Migration*. Amsterdam: Amsterdam University Press, 2012; "Internal Migration in Albania: A Critical Overview," in Pichler ed., *Legacy and Change*.
[136] Russell King and Julie Vullnetari, "Migration and Development in Albania, Working Paper," University of Sussex, Development Research Centre on Migration, Globalisation and Poverty, Working Paper C5, http://www.migrationdrc.org/publications/working_papers/WP-C5.pdf; Russell King and Nicola Mai, *Out of Albania*...; King, "Across the Sea...," s. 283–309; King, "Albania as a laboratory...," 133–155.
[137] Shyqyri Hysi, *Histori e trojeve dhe e diasporës shqiptare* (Tirana: Shtëpia Botuese e Librit Universitar, 2007).
[138] Matilda Likaj, "*Migration as a Challenge for Albanian Post-Communist Society*," Journal of Educational and Social Research 4, no. 2 (2014): 143–149.
[139] Campani,7–10.
[140] Sonila Papathimiu, "The demographic and economic development of Albania during and after the decline of Communist regime (1945–2010)," *Treballs de la Societat Catalana de Geografia* 73 (Juny 2012): 101–118.
[141] Pistrick, 29–37.
[142] Mai, 3–22.
[143] Tarifa, 133–162.

2 Baltic States: Estonia, Latvia and Lithuania
Pauli Heikkilä

It is convenient to lump together Estonia, Latvia, and Lithuania given their size and their common history, especially during the Cold War. Although these countries are generally referred to as the Baltic States nowadays, the notion is not without its problems. Only Latvians and Lithuanians speak a Baltic language, while Estonian belongs to the group of Finno-Ugric languages. Politically, Lithuania has a long history as a Grand Duchy in the medieval times and during its union with Poland, whereas Estonia and Latvia were founded as political units in the aftermath of World War I. At that time, Finland and Poland as former parts of the Russian Empire, were also occasionally considered Baltic States. Finland was acknowledged as a Nordic country since the mid-1930s and remained unconquered during World War II.

The independent states created after World War I were relatively ethnically homogenous. The non-titular population consisted mainly of old German, Polish, and Jewish elites. In addition, there were Russian settlements in Estonia, mostly in the new Eastern territories, which were annexed back to Russia after World War II.

2.1 Regional migrations in historical perspective

These countries have a very different history, particularly of emigration. Estonian and Latvian migration in Tsarist Russia was directed mainly to the East and the South (Caucasus). There were approximately 30,000 Estonians living outside the Russian Empire before the World War I. At the same time, Catholic Lithuanians were prohibited from moving within the empire and thus Lithuanian colonies emerged in North America. Between 1899 and 1914, a quarter million Lithuanians immigrated to the US, especially to areas around Chicago and Cleveland.[1]

Emigration continued from the independent Lithuania in the subsequent period. In the 1920s, more than a hundred thousand citizens (102,461) left the country, mostly to the US and to South American countries. As traveling to the East, to the Soviet Union, became considerably more difficult, the direction of Latvian and Estonian emigrations shifted to the West but not in considerable numbers. During the interwar period, 16,000 Estonians left the country, creating Estonian colonies in South America. These young states did not want to support reducing their population since reconstruction required – and provided – necessary employment. The restrictions in

---

1 Alfonsas Eidintas, *Lithuanian Emigration to the United States 1868–1950* (Vilnius: Mokslo ir enciklopediju leidybos institutas, 2003); Tiit Tammaru, Kaja Kumer-Haukanõmm, and Kristi Anniste, "The Formation and Development of the Estonian Diaspora," *Journal of Ethnic and Migration Studies* 18 (2010): 1157, 1161–62; Raimo Raag, *Eestlane väljaspool Eestit: Ajalooline ülevaade* (Tartu: Tartu ülikooli kirjastus, 1999), 60.

the host countries, especially in the US, further slowed down emigration. Democratic constitutions were adapted in the new states, but they were rendered invalid; Lithuania in 1926, Estonia and Latvia in 1934. The new authorities opposed political extreme parties, including Communist and Fascist parties, so their supporters emigrated to Nazi Germany or the Soviet Union albeit in very small numbers.

In the aftermath of the Molotov-Ribbentrop Pact, these countries signed mutual assistance treaties with the Soviet Union in September and October 1939. The treaties allowed military bases in the Baltic States, which restricted significantly their independence but only next summer the Soviets orchestrated rigged elections. The new "parliaments" appealed for memberships in the Soviet Union, which were unsurprisingly granted in August 1940. In addition, after the Finno-Soviet Winter War (1939–1940), the territory of Karelia was annexed by the Soviet Union and the entire Finnish population of 410,000 was evacuated. Roughly, half of these people returned during the Finnish advance in summer 1941, only to leave the territory again in summer 1944.

Soviet administration and policy were implemented mercilessly in the new Soviet republics. In addition to agriculture, the economy was socialized without compensations. National organizations were replaced with all-union equivalents, including the army and security forces. The population was threatened with multiple mass deportations. The first deportation took place during the first Soviet year on 14 June 1941. The Operation *Priboi* in March 1949 was connected to collectivization and 95,000 people were deported from the Baltic States to Siberia. To provide just one example, a total of 128,000 (5 percent of the population) were deported to Siberia and Central Asia from Lithuania.[2]

2.2 The aftermath of World War II

The Baltic States were occupied by Nazi Germany between 1941 and 1944, and thereafter by the Soviets for 45 years. Having experienced Soviet rule for a year, massive migration to the west began. The exact numbers on the magnitude of refugees do not exist and estimation vary between 75,000 Estonians, 140,000 Latvians, and 65,000 Lithuanians (by Kasekamp) and 80,000 Estonians, 160,000 Latvians and 64,000 Lithuanians (by Plakans).[3]

---

2 Arvydas Anusauskas, "A Comparison of the Armed Struggle for Independence in the Baltic States and Western Ukraine," in *The Anti-Soviet Resistance in the Baltic States*, ed. Arvydas Anusauskas (Vilnius: Genocide and Resistance Research Centre of Lithuania, 2002), 63–70; Thomas Lane, *Victims of Stalin and Hitler: The Exodus of Poles and Balts to Britain* (Basingstoke: Palgrave Macmillan, 2004), 78–95; Andres Kasekamp, *A History of the Baltic States* (Basingstoke: Palgrave Macmillan, 2010), 145–146; Andrejs Plakans, *A Concise History of the Baltic States* (Cambridge: Cambridge University Press, 2011), 368.
3 Kasekamp, *A History of the Baltic States*, 139; Plakans, *A Concise History of the Baltic States*, 358.

After the siege of Leningrad ended in early 1944, Soviet troops began advancing westwards. Thanks to the Baltic recruits, the front was stopped at the (former) border. German defeat in both Operation Bagration and in Normandy resulted in reorganizing the defense and a less favorable situation for the Baltic States. Between July and October 1944, the Soviets conquered Vilnius (13 July), Tallinn (22 September), Riga (13 October), and reached Klaipėda (22 October), where the siege continued until January 1945. German troops in Courland, northwestern Latvia, were cut off and they remained isolated until the war ended in May 1945.

National armed resistance, the so-called 'Forest brothers,' emerged in each county. In Estonia *metsavennad* and in Latvia *meža brāļi* included 10,000 men at the peak of activity. In Lithuania, *miško broliai* grew to 50,000 members under a national central leadership. The activity ceased after the collectivization of agriculture, when partisans lost the support of the countryside. Many accepted the offered amnesty after Stalin's death in 1953, as hopes for Western intervention vanished. Nevertheless, few individual fighters remained in hiding for decades: the last known Lithuanian resistant fighter allegedly died in 1986.[4]

The explanation of the considerably smaller number of Lithuanians than that of other Baltic nations in the migration of late 1944, is that many of them were taken to Germany proper earlier. During the war, the Germans supported the transportation of Baltic population to Germany, where they could be put to work in the war industry. Once again, the exact numbers are unknown and estimates of Lithuanians living in Germany in October 1944 are as high as 300,000. Approximately 50,000 of them returned home (voluntarily or by force) already in 1945. A quarter million Latvians, that is 14 percent of the population, have been estimated to have fled the approaching the Soviet army, but half of them returned. Most of them did not reach Germany but turned back from Lithuania or Poland. Especially in comparison with neighboring Poland, Baltic refugees were more urban, better off, and had left almost exclusively for political reasons.[5]

Roughly speaking, a quarter of each Baltic nation perished during World War II. The ethnic map of the Baltic States changed dramatically. The Jewish population had consisted of almost 300,000 individuals but in 1945, only a few thousands were left. Likewise, the tiny Roma communities (about 3,000) were annihilated. Additionally,

---

[4] Kasekamp, *A History of the Baltic States*, 141–142; Plakans, *A Concise History of the Baltic States*, 360–362.
[5] Kim Salomon, *Refugees in the Cold War: Toward a New International Refugee Regime in the Early Postwar Era* (Lund: Lund University Press, 1991), 146, 148, 159–162; Mark Wyman, *DPs: Europe's Displaced Persons, 1945–1951* (Ithaca: Cornell University Press, 1998), 31–34; Emily Gilbert, *Changing Identities: Latvians, Lithuanians and Estonians in Great Britain* (Devon UK: Create Space 2013), 93–94, 103–113; Eidintas, *Lithuanian Emigration*, 207–208; Lane, *Victims of Stalin and Hitler*, 145–147; Kasekamp, *A History of the Baltic States*, 137, 139.

30,000 Baltic civilians perished under the Nazi occupation.[6] In fall 1940, as many as 14,000 Baltic Germans in Estonia and 52,000 in Latvia were called on to "return home." Germans were the ethnic majority of Klaipėda (Memel in German) and the whole population fled from the besieged city in January 1945. Almost all Estonian Swedes (7,000) left for Sweden. In the early 1920s, 115,000 Ingrian Finns used to live in the area around St. Petersburg including Eastern Estonia. Nearly all of them were deported in the next decades but they were allowed to resettle in the Estonian SSR since the 1950s. Due to border changes, Lithuania gained a Polish minority around Vilnius, whereas Russians began settling in Estonia and Latvia only from the 1950s onwards.[7]

2.2.1 Balts as Displaced Persons

Like other refugees, the Balts were placed in Displaced Persons (DP) camps in Germany after the war. Some found employment in Germany. Although the numbers vary, at the beginning of 1946, there were 57,495 Lithuanians, 94,730 Latvians, and 30,978 Estonians in West Germany. More than half of them resided in the US zone, 40 percent in the British zone, and 5,000 in the French zone. The number of Baltic refugees in other countries (Italy, Denmark, and Austria) was only a few thousand. The status of their state caused problems for the Baltic refugees. They were eventually considered citizens of United Nations member state and thus became eligible for assistance from the United Nations Relief and Rehabilitation Administration UNRRA. On the other hand, their states had ceased to exist, but they were not considered Soviet citizens, and consequently excluded from Soviet claims to repatriation. Very few repatriations took place – in the Estonian case only 479 – but it was constantly feared by Baltic refugees. Nevertheless, Soviet sources mention the figure of nearly 21,000, but this contain all the returnees, including those who had reached only Poland. To protect the Balts, some of the camps were intentionally misspelled for Disputed Persons and were hidden from the Soviet authorities. Furthermore, in the absence of a respective state, a special Baltic Welfare, Education and Employment Organization was created in summer 1946 to jointly deal with their social issues.[8]

---

6 Kasekamp, *A History of the Baltic States*, 135; Plakans, *A Concise History of the Baltic States*, 353–354.
7 Kasekamp, *A History of the Baltic States*, 126, 140.
8 Ferdinand Kool, *DP Kroonika: Eesti pagulased Saksamaal 1944–1951* (Lakewood: Eesti Arhiiv Ühendriikides, 1999); Tillman Tegeler, "Esten, Letten und Litauer in Nachkriegsdeutschland: Von rechtlosen Flüchtlingen zu heimatlosen Ausländern," in *Displaced Persons: Flüchtlinge aus den baltischen Staaten in Deutschland*, eds. Christian Pletzing and Marianne Pletzing (Munich: Martin Meidenbauer, 2007), 13–27, 18–23; Ieva Zaķe, *Nineteenth-Century Nationalism and Twentieth-Century Anti-Democratic Ideals: The Case of Latvia, 1840s to 1980s* (Lewinston: Edwin Mellen Press, 2008), 130–131; Kaja Kumer-Haukanõmm, "Eestlaste põgenemine Saksamaale," in *Eestlaste põgenemine läände teise maailmasõja ajal*, eds. Terje Hallik et al. (Tartu: Filiae Patriae, 2009), 17–29; Ilgvars

Suspicions and allegations of collaboration with the Nazi occupiers by the Balts started at the DP camps and continued throughout the Cold War. Approximately 19,000 Baltic DPs had been in the Wehrmacht, most of them in Baltic Legions within the German army since early 1944. Initially the Balts, who had joined voluntarily the German military, were ineligible for UNRRA assistance but those forced to enlist or work were assisted. Gradually and in the absence of evidence, the definitions were altered and in spring 1949, the International Refugee Organization IRO concluded that enlisting was no longer considered an act against the Allies but a contribution to the national cause. The criteria were relaxed further in 1951, when clear proof of criminal activity was required to exclude from assistance by the IRO.[9]

Besides emigration to Germany, another destination was Sweden across the Baltic Sea by boat. These trips were made either like traditional peasant sailing or, especially in 1944, as organized convoys. Many Estonians had fled to Finland (where 3,350 volunteered in the Finnish army), but after the truce in September 1944, Finland was no longer considered a safe country and they continued to Sweden. Eventually, approximately 30,000 Estonians, 5,000 Latvians, and few hundred Lithuanians arrived in Sweden. Approximately 1000 Estonians arrived later from the DP camps in Germany. They were also placed in DP camps but within a year, they had integrated into the Swedish job market.[10]

Sweden had political downsides. As a rare exception, Sweden had recognized the Soviet annexation in 1940 and was thus more inclined to comply with Soviet demands. In early 1945, Sweden deported 167 Baltic (mostly Latvian) soldiers of the Wehrmacht to the Soviet Union. This caused both domestic and international protests and many refugees decided to leave Sweden; the group of Latvian refugees thereby decreased by one third. Swedish refugee politics became less arbitrary in the following years, as it started to follow international law and regulations rather than ad hoc considerations, although even those pointed to Sweden's willingness to keep the Baltic refugees.[11]

Refugees in Sweden left for the US, mostly by small "Viking" boats barely adequate for an oceanic voyage. When they started to arrive on the US coast in Georgia

---

Veigners, *Latvieši Rietumzemē – un vēl dažās zemēs* (Riga: Drukātava, 2009); Salomon, *Refugees in the Cold War*, 66–70; Wyman, *DPs*, 38–65, 78; Eidintas, *Lithuanian Emigration*, 212–215; Lane, *Victims of Stalin and Hitler*, 148–178; Tammaru, Kumer-Haukanõmm and Anniste, "The Formation and Development," 6; Gilbert, *Changing Identities*, 117–143.

9 Ieva Zaķe, "'The Secret Nazi Network' and Post-World War II Latvian Émigrés in the United States," *Journal of Baltic Studies* 41 (2010): 1; Indrek Jürjo, *Pagulus ja Nõukogude Eesti: Vaateid KGB, EKP ja VEKSA arhiividokumentide põhjal* (Tartu: Tammerraamat, 2014), 197–198; Salomon, *Refugees in the Cold War*, 66–70; Wyman, *DPs*, 179–185; Lane, *Victims of Stalin and Hitler*, 48–55, 161–162; Tegeler, "Esten, Letten und Litauer," 18; Gilbert, *Changing Identities*, 94–103.

10 Raimo Raag, "Eestlaste põgenemine Rootsi teise maailmasõja ajal," in *Eestlaste põgenemine läände teise maailmasõja ajal*, ed. Terje Hallik et al. (Tartu: Filiae Patriae, 2009).

11 Cecilia Notini Burch, *A Cold War Pursuit: Soviet Refugees in Sweden, 1945–54* (Stockholm: Santérus Academic Press, 2014); Wyman, *DPs*, 64; Raag, "Eestlaste põgenemine Rootsi."

and Florida in January 1946, they were warmly welcomed and integrated into local communities. Although Estonians were initiators of this kind of emigration with thirty-four boats, more Latvians crossed the Atlantic in such a manner.[12]

The tales of these gallant journeys might have affected that when the US agreed to receive European refugees according to the DP Act of 28 June 1948, 40 percent allotted to the Balts. 23,150 Lithuanians, 37,500 Latvians and 10,500 Estonians were initially admitted. Their quotas were slightly increased during the next few years and the total number for Estonians was 12,629 and close to 30,000 for Lithuanians. Including the earlier emigration from the independent states, there were approximately 45,000 Latvians in the US in 1950; the respective figure for the Estonians was approximately 20,000.[13] In both cases, therefore, the majority of emigrants to the US had arrived after World War II.

Lithuanians, as noted earlier, already had a considerable colony in the US, which could assist people from the DP camps with their emigration to the US. They were thus not included in the official DP quotas. Lithuanian organizations in the US founded the Council of Lithuanian Americans (Amerikos Lietuviu Taryba) in August 1940 to coordinate efforts to restore Lithuanian independence. The major political parties were included, apart from the Communists, although the ruling fraction in Lithuania, *Tautininkai*, withdrew their cooperation in 1941 only to return in 1948. Practical funding was channeled through the United Lithuanian Relief Fund of America (Bendras Amerikos Lietuviu Fondas). Among other political activities, the journal *Lithuanian Bulletin* was published from 1944 onwards.[14]

Half of the Lithuanian refugees of World War II went to the US. Canada was also a popular destination country. Canada admitted 7,700 Lithuanians. Australia admitted 5,000, the UK admitted 3,000, Venezuela admitted 2,000, while the rest were scatted around the globe, mostly in South America. Close to 20,000 Balts remained in Germany; 7,550 Lithuanians, 4,167 Estonians, and the rest were Latvians. The US was the biggest destination for Latvians as well; 50 percent of all Latvians abroad in 1950 lived in the US.[15]

Canada permitted DPs to enter the country in order to ease the labor shortage especially in agriculture in November 1946. Canada eventually accepted more than 11,000 Estonian DPs, which contained 4,000 Estonians from Sweden. Including the DP program (1948–1951), 14,310 Estonians came to Canada after World War II.

---

12 *Estonians in America 1627–1975: A Chronology and Fact Book*, ed. Jaan Pennar (New York: Oceana, 1975), 29; Bernard John Maegi, *Dangerous People, Delayed Pilgrims: Baltic Displaced Persons and the Making of Cold War America, 1945–1952* (PhD diss., University of Minnesota, 2008).
13 Pennar, *Estonians in America*, 31, 132–133; Salomon, *Refugees in the Cold War*, 207–210; Wyman, *DPs*, 194–200; Raag, *Eestlane väljaspool Eestit*, 67; Eidintas, *Lithuanian Emigration*, 215–216; Maegi, *Dangerous People*; Kumer-Haukanõmm, "Eestlaste põgenemine Saksamaale," 42–45.
14 Eidintas, *Lithuanian Emigration*, 208–210.
15 Salomon, *Refugees in the Cold War*, 211–212; Eidintas, *Lithuanian Emigration*, 215, 218; Tegeler, "Esten, Letten und Litauer," 26.

Canada was initially considered a temporary location before moving forward to the US. However, many eventually decided to remain in Canada thereby making it a more common destination among Estonian refugees of World War II, although more Estonians lived in the US.[16]

The UK was the first European country to accept refugees. "Balt Cygnet" in July 1946 was a pioneering program that put 2,500 Baltic women to work in nurseries and hospitals. Once the program proved successful, it was implemented on a larger scale, and the "Westward Ho" was expanded to other ethnic groups as well. The women were soon followed by their families as well. The programs brought nearly 25,000 Balts to the UK; roughly one third of the total sum of refugees in the UK. Nevertheless, many Baltic people were not happy with the living conditions in the UK and once immigration policy was relaxed, they left for the US. The scale of this voluntary emigration is unknown, but it was a considerable blow to the remaining communities in the UK.[17]

Similar but more modest programs took Estonians to other European countries in the late 1940s, like Belgium, France, and the Netherlands. But like in the UK, the working conditions were not satisfying and most of them returned to Germany. Latvians and Lithuanians participated in similar programs but very few of them found permanent settlement in Western Europe.[18]

Baltic migration to more distant continents was rather marginal. Former Estonian emigrants founded a committee to assist Estonian DPs to arrive in Australia. It managed to procure approximately 3,000 immigration licenses. Australia eased emigration in 1948, which resulted in a total of 6,000 Estonians in Australia. A considerably larger group of Latvians arrived in Australia and few thousand Lithuanians, thus roughly amounting to 36,000 Balts in Australia. A few hundred Estonians arrived in New Zealand.[19] Estonian "Viking" ships took the direction also to South Africa and carried 70 Estonians there. Whilst a few thousand Latvians and Lithuanians found a new home in South America, only 617 Estonians left for South America.[20]

---

16 Karl Aun, *Political Refugees: A History of the Estonians in Canada* (Toronto: MacClelland and Stewart, 1985), 20 – 33; Salomon, *Refugees in the Cold War*, 213; Wyman, *DPs*, 190 – 191; Raag, *Eestlane väljaspool Eestit*, 67; Kumer-Haukanõmm, "Eestlaste põgenemine Saksamaale," 41 – 42.
17 Salomon, *Refugees in the Cold War*, 201 – 206; Wyman, *DPs*, 189; Lane, *Victims of Stalin and Hitler*, 190 – 197, 202 – 203; Kumer-Haukanõmm, "Eestlaste põgenemine Saksamaale," 30 – 34; Gilbert, *Changing Identities*, 145 – 185, 236 – 238.
18 Salomon, *Refugees in the Cold War*, 199 – 201; Kumer-Haukanõmm, "Eestlaste põgenemine Saksamaale," 34 – 38.
19 Leonid Rampe, "Eesti Abistamise Komitee ja Thirlmere Puhkekodu," in *Eestlased Austraalias I*, eds. Õie Haas and Voldemar Siska (Adelaide: Austraalia Eesti Seltside Liit, 1988), 137 – 139; Salomon, *Refugees in the Cold War*, 212 – 213; Wyman, *DPs*, 191; Raag, *Eestlane väljaspool Eestit*, 69, 72; Kumer-Haukanõmm, "Eestlaste põgenemine Saksamaale," 39 – 41.
20 Raag, *Eestlane väljaspool Eestit*, 71; Kumer-Haukanõmm, "Eestlaste põgenemine Saksamaale," 45 – 49.

Baltic literature does not document any clashes between the old emigrants and World War II refugees, which have been reported among other national groups. On the contrary there are cases of second generation groups helping the newcomers. The lack of disagreement may be due to the rather small size of previous colonies although the different development of the native language caused confusion. More significantly, earlier colonies also included Communists, who were avoided by Cold War refugees.[21] There were only sporadic defectors or refugees from the Baltic States after 1944.

2.3 Major migration streams during the Cold War

(For a general description of the legal framework and migration statistics please consult the chapter on the USSR)

The non-recognition of Soviet annexation of the Baltic States by the West is an exaggeration. Most of the Baltic legations had been closed due to occupations during World War II and the respective countries did not take initiative to reopen them. Without explicit decision they could conveniently emphasize either the Soviet (no diplomatic relations) or the Baltic (no official recognition) claim. In London, Baltic envoys were gradually degraded from the list of accredited diplomats and they could not prevent the transfer of Baltic assets to the Soviet Union in 1967. Argentina initiated diplomatic relations with the Soviet Union in 1946 and Brazil in 1961, recognizing the Baltic annexation and consequently Latvian and Lithuanian legations were closed. The same happened with the Estonian representative in Madrid in 1977. The notable exception was, of course, the US and for Lithuanians the Holy See, which had condemned the annexations in 1940. The US additionally allowed the representatives to use national assets; They were also permitted to finance diplomatic missions outside the US since 1951. Thanks to this funding, Estonia established new diplomatic representations with Western Germany, France, Spain, and Canada. Nevertheless, the title of "envoy" was prohibited from these representations. Even they withered away among the original representatives. Despite their limits to take action, the Baltic representations were constant reminders of the occupation of their countries.[22]

---

21 Wyman, *DPs*, 206; Raag, *Eestlane väljaspool Eestit*, 69; Eidintas, *Lithuanian Emigration*.
22 Ernst Jaakson, *Eestile* (Tallinn: SE&JS, 1995), 110–115; Laurynas Jonušauskas, *Likimo vedami: Lietuvos diplomatinės tarnybos egzilyje veikla 1940–1991* (Vilnius: Genocide and Resistance Research Centre of Lithuania, 2003), 253–265, 322, 326; Lauri Mälksoo, *Illegal Annexation and State Continuity: The Case of the Incorporation of the Baltic States by the USSR: A Study of the Tension between Normativity and Power in International Law* (Leiden: Martinus Nijhoff Publishers, 2003), 121; Tiina Tamman, *The Last Ambassador: August Torma, Soldier, Diplomat, Spy* (Amsterdam: Rodopi, 2011), 133–137, 164–166, 181.

2.4 Political activities in exile

Only one of the Baltic heads of state managed to escape to the West: Antanas Smetona of Lithuania fled to Germany and he was granted a visa for the US in September 1940. His entrance caused a stir among the diplomats and emigrated politicians, but the division was avoided when Smetona promised to stay out of political activities after his arrival in March 1941. He died in Cleveland, Ohio in 1944. Konstantin Päts of Estonia was taken to Russia in June 1940 and he was transferred between prisons and mental asylums until his death in 1956. Latvia's Kārlis Ulmanis died in prison in 1942.[23]

The foreign ministries of the independent Baltic States had not taken any precautions. On the contrary, they tried to comply with Soviet demands to every detail and not to give them excuses. It was only in May 1940 that the Latvian Foreign Ministry granted the chief of diplomatic corps to envoy Kārlis Zariņš in London. After his death in 1963, Arnolds Spekke, the head of Latvian legation in Washington, succeeded him. Spekke retired in 1970 and both positions were now given to Anatols Dinbergs. Similarly, Lithuanians appointed the envoy in Rome, Stasys Lozoraitis, as the chief of diplomatic corps in case of a catastrophe. After Lozoraitis' death in 1983, Stasys Antanas Bačkis (envoy in Washington DC) assumed this position.[24]

Estonia failed to deliver a decision on the leader among the diplomats, and, paradoxically, their smallest diplomatic representation, the Consulate General in New York, became the hub of Estonian diplomacy. It was first headed by Johannes Kaiv and after his death in 1965 by Ernst Jaakson. Jaakson died in the same post in 1998 at the age of 93. His 79 years of service in the Estonian foreign ministry famously make him the longest serving diplomat in the world.[25]

Another peculiarity of the Estonian case was the government-in-exile. A prominent group of politicians had declared the national government in Tallinn in September 1944 but only four of them escaped to Sweden. There were demands for an electoral body to elect the President-in-exile but in January 1953, the oldest surviving minister, August Rei, declared a new government and assumed presidential duties. It did not have the support of the entire Estonian diaspora and thus never played an active role. It merely preserved the continuity of the state in exile. This was carried

---

[23] Juozas Skirius, "Prezidento Antano Smetonos atvykimas į JAV 1941 metais ir išeivijos pozicija," *Lietuvos Istorijos Metraštis* 22 (2010): 2.
[24] Magnus Ilmjärv, *Silent Submission: Formation of Foreign Policy of Estonia, Latvia and Lithuania: Period from mid-1920s to Annexation in 1940* (Stockholm: Stockholm University, 2004), 482–489, 493, 520–521; Antonijs Zunda, "Lotewska służba dyplomatyczna i jej reprezentacja polityczna na uchodźstwie (1940–1991)," in *Rządy bez ziemi. Struktury władzy na uchodźstwie*, ed. Radosław Paweł Zurawski (Warsaw: Wydawnictwo DiG, 2014), 639; Jonušauskas, *Likimo vedami*, 43.
[25] Jaakson, *Eestile*.

out by appointing new Presidents and ministers until the symbols were returned to Tallinn in October 1992.[26]

Lithuanians had a similar incident with the Supreme Committee for the Liberation of Lithuania (Vyriausiasis Lietuvos išlaisvinimo komitetas, VLIK). It was founded in Nazi occupied Lithuania in 1943 as an underground movement. When its members fled to Germany in 1944, the VLIK resurfaced as a prominent exile organization. Although it had political prestige to perform as government-in-exile, the variety of opinions resulted in difficulties in decision-making. Additionally, it had unresolvable disputes with Lozoraitis and foreign countries were definitely unwilling to recognize it as a state organ. In 1955, the VLIK was moved to New York. Additionally, it reinstated the news service ELTA to provide information from Soviet Lithuania.[27]

The dilemma had the worst outcome for the Lithuanians in Germany. Estonia (Karl Selter) and Latvia (Robert Liepiņš) had a status of a special representative from the German foreign ministry, who was supported by their acknowledged diplomat in New York (Kaiv) and London (Zariņš) respectively. A similar Lithuanian nomination of Albertas Gerutis by Lozoraitis was contested by the VLIK and its unilateral appointment of Petras Karvelis. Eventually, since late 1954, Baltic activities were run by the joint Baltische Gesellschaft.[28] By the mid-1950s, the activity and role of diplomatic representations faded as they were eventually substituted with civic organizations in other countries.

The Lithuanian World Community (Pasaulio lietuvių bendruomenė, PLB) was founded in 1949 on the initiative of the VLIK as a federation of Lithuanian communities abroad. Avoiding political quarrels, the PLB concentrated on promoting Lithuanian culture and language abroad. Since 1958, the general council of the PLB came together every five years. Since 1997, the meeting has taken place in every three years in Vilnius.[29]

Like Lithuanians, soon after the Soviet annexation, Estonians founded an organization to coordinate the struggle for liberation, namely, the World Association of Estonians (Ülemaailmne Eesti Ühing). After World War II, several attempts were made to reorganize a similar global organization, but the federative Estonian World Council (Ülemaailmne Eesti Kesknõukogu) was founded in New York only in October 1955. Its biggest member organization was the Estonian National Committee in the United

---

26 Vahur Made, "The Estonian Government-in-Exile: A Controversial Project of State Continuation," in *The Baltic Question during the Cold War*, eds. John Hiden, Vahur Made, and David J. Smith (Abingdon: Routledge, 2008).
27 Kazys Bobelis and Jonas Aničas, *VLIK: Vyriausiasis Lietuvos išlaisvinimo komitetas 1943–1992* (Vilnius: Vaga, 2011).
28 Kristina Spohr Readman, "West Germany and the Baltic Question during the Cold War," in *The Baltic Question during the Cold War*, eds. John Hiden, Vahur Made, and David J. Smith (Abingdon: Routledge 2008), 105–113.
29 Vitalija Stravinskienė, *Pasaulio lietuvių bendruomenė 1949–2003* (Vilnius: Artlora, 2004).

States, which was founded in May 1952. The name was changed to the Estonian American National Council in 1972.[30]

The American Latvian Association (Amerikas latviešu apvienība) was founded in February 1951 as an umbrella organization for Latvian groups in the US. In October 1955, together with the Latvian Liberation Committee of the European Centre (Latvijas atbrīvošanas komitejas Eiropas centrs) and the Latvian Association of Australia (Latviešu apvienība Austrālijā), it founded the World Federation of Free Latvians (Brīvās pasaules latviešu apvienības). The Latvian National Association in Canada (Latviešu nacionālā apvienība Kanādā) and the Latvian Association of Brazil (Latviešu apvienība Brazīlijā) joined soon thereafter.[31]

American intelligence service created the Free Europe Committee to provide support for Eastern European emigrants in May 1949. Balts, who hadn't yet established political organizations in the US, were first excluded but individuals were invited to other Free Europe activities such as Mid-European Studies Center. In May 1951, extraordinary Consultative Panels were created for them, but the names were changed to National Committees for a free Estonia, Latvia and Lithuania in February 1952. Although the Baltic groups had now similar organizations as the other emigrants from Eastern Europe, the relevance of the committees remained rather marginal and caused more controversy than it fostered cooperation within the political diaspora. On the other hand, they were a Baltic channel to American politicians and other Eastern Europeans, which came together as the Assembly of Captive European Nations in 1954. Latvian Vilis Māsēns was the first chairman of this organization.[32]

The Baltic committees published individual national journals, including *Latvijas Brivibai* (For Latvia's Freedom), *Võitlev Eesti* (Fighting Estonia), and *Lietuva. Politikos žurnalas* (Lithuania. Political Journal). They also jointly published the *Baltic Review* until 1971. Radio programs in their respective languages by the Voice of America started in 1951. Two half-hour length broadcasts to the Soviet Union included daily news, commentaries, and reports on Baltic activities in exile. Broadcasts by Radio Free Europe were desired by the Baltic committees, but here the US non-recognition policy caused problems because the Americans (the FEC) could not sponsor the activities of independent states. It was only after the reorganization of the Radio Free

---

30 Marju Rink-Abel, "Lühiülevaade välisvõitlusest USA-s ning Eesti Rahvuskomitee Ühendriikides tegevusest," in *Sõna jõul. Diasporaa roll Eesti iseseisvuse taastamisel*, eds. Kristi Anniste, Kaja Kumer-Haukanõmm, and Tiit Tammaru (Tartu: Tartu ülikooli kirjastus, 2008); Pennar, *Estonians in America*, 24, 37–38, 40.
31 Ieva Zaķe, "Multiple Fronts of the Cold War: Ethnic Anti-Communism of Latvian Émigrés," in *Anti-Communist Minorities in the US. Political Activism of Ethnic Refugees*, ed. Ieva Zaķe (New York: Palgrave Macmillan, 2009), 132. For a more detailed study on Latvian Americans, see Ieva Zaķe, *American Latvians: Politics of a Refugee Community* (Piscataway, NJ: Transaction, 2010).
32 Jonathan L'Hommedieu, "The Baltic Freedom Committees: Politics and Policies of an Exile Community," in *The Inauguration of Organized Political Warfare: Cold War Organizations sponsored by the National Committee for a Free Europe / Free Europe Committee*, ed. Katalin Kádár Lynn (St. Helena: Helena History Press, 2013), 202–208.

Europe/ Radio Liberty that broadcasting in Baltic languages began in 1975. Other stations, such as the Vatican Radio, broadcasted regularly, especially in Lithuanian.[33]

Baltic emigrants also got involved with the European Movement. For the Estonians in particular, the unification of the continent signified the liberation of the homeland. The movement did not share the Estonian enthusiasm and a special Baltic Council of European Movement was created before national committees were admitted to the European Movement in January 1950. Like other emigrant groups, Baltic committees were sidetracked during the 1950s, but the Estonian committee repeatedly recruited the next generation thereby ensuring the survival of the organization until the Estonian re-independence in 1991.[34]

Estonians in Canada came together as the Estonian Federation in Canada (Eesti Liit Kanadas), which today consists of nearly 60 organizations. However, since half of Canadian Estonians resided in Toronto, the role of the central organization has been quite marginal, and the actual work was done within the member organizations. Political work was done via the Estonian Central Council in Canada (Eesti Kesknõukogu Kanadas), which was founded in 1954 as the Estonian Council for Political Action (Rahvusliku Välisvõitluse Nõukogu); the name was changed in 1974. As the Council was first a section in the Federation, its origin is most definitely linked to the foundation of the World Council, whose founding member it became.[35]

In the UK, the following national organizations were already founded in 1947: Association of Estonians in the UK (Inglismaa Eestlaste Ühing), Lithuanian Association in the UK (Didžiosios Britanijos Lietuvių Sąjunga), and Latvian Welfare Fund, which had already been established once in a POW camp in Belgium in 1945 and whose name (Daugavas Vanagi; Hawks of the river Daugava) in the English translation disguised its militaristic undertones. These organizations also formed the Baltic Council in the same year but very little is known about their activities. Like the diplomatic representations, the national associations faded out during the subsequent decades.[36]

Estonians in Sweden were divided into two groups, which characterized the division also globally. The Estonian National Council (Eesti Rahvusnõukogu) attracted liberal and socialist activist, whereas the World Organization of Free Estonians (Vabade Eestlaste Keskorganisatsioon), which was later reorganized as the Estonian National Congress (Rootsi Eestlaste Esindus, later Rootsi Eestlaste Liit) was an organization for conservatives. The latter joined in the Estonian World Council in 1955.[37]

---

33 Pennar, *Estonians in America*, 66; Zaķe, "Multiple Fronts of the Cold War," 140; L'Hommedieu, "The Baltic Freedom Committees," 219–224.
34 Pauli Heikkilä, *Estonians for Europe: National Activism for European Integration, 1922–1991* (Brussels: Peter Lang, 2014).
35 Aun, *Political Refugees*, 79–81; Stravinskienė, *Pasaulio lietuvių bendruomenė*, 239–253.
36 Lane, *Victims of Stalin and Hitler*, 204–223; Stravinskienė, *Pasaulio lietuvių bendruomenė*, 184–197; Gilbert, *Changing Identities*, 218–221, 247–248, 267–279.
37 Jüri Ant, *August Rei: Eesti riigimees, poliitik, diplomat* (Tartu: Rahvusarhiiv, 2012), 268–269, 287.

The Estonian National Fund (Eesti Rahvusfond) was also founded in Sweden and it began to live up to its official English name – the Estonian Information Centre. Its *Newsletter from behind the Iron Curtain* (also in German) and *East and West* were well received in the West. Similarly, the Latvian organizations in Sweden (Swedish Latvian National Council and Swedish Latvian Central Council) competed with each other. The Latvian Social Democrat Workers' Party was another separate political organization.[38]

Cultural and educational activities already began in the DP camps in the form of several publications and newspapers. Estonians in exile produced almost a thousand monographs, mostly fiction. Explicitly political literature was in the minority. In the early 1950s, they could boast having publishing more books than the Soviet Estonia even though they fell behind after destalinization. Nevertheless, their steady pace of publication was an accomplishment.[39]

As an extraordinary example, Baltic University opened in Hamburg on 14 March 1946. It had eight faculties ranging from technical subjects to philology and law. The facilities were located in the ruins of the city. Equipment was acquired from wherever possible; material stolen from Baltic universities by the Nazis were returned to the Baltic scholars. The university was meant to function as a place for Baltic students to complete their studies but also an ordinary university for research. However, the British authorities denied it the right to confer degrees and it was renamed the DP University Study Centre. It evolved into a center that prepared the transition of students from camps to accredited universities. More than a thousand students enrolled at the center. It was relocated to Pinneberg to former air force barracks in 1947 in anticipation of closing the institute as resettlements were underway. The move of the university to the US and even to Ethiopia was also discussed but the center was officially shut down on 30 September 1949.[40] Additionally, Baltic refugees reinstated vocational training. The Estonians set up an agricultural college and the Lithuanians established a maritime academy in Northern Germany.[41]

The most important Estonian newspapers, those which survived the Cold War, included *Teataja*, *Välis-Eesti* and *Stockholm Tidning Eestlastele / Eesti Päevaleht* in Sweden, *Vaba Eesti Sõna* in New York, *Meie Elu* and *Vaba Eestlane* in Toronto, and *Eesti Hääl* in London. They started either as daily or weekly publications and

---

38 Hain Rebas, "Sverigeesternas politiska verksamhet," in *Estländare i Sverige: Historia, språk, kultur*, eds. Raimo Raag and Harald Runblom (Uppsala: Centre for Multiethnic Research, 1988); Stravinskienė, *Pasaulio lietuvių bendruomenė*, 326–332.
39 Anne Valmas, *Eestlaste kirjastustegevus välismaal 1944–2000 I* (Tallinn: Tallinna pedagoogikaülikooli kirjastus, 2003), 146–173; Aun, *Political Refugees*, 90–119, 113–142; Wyman, *DPs*, 119–120, 161–167; Lane, *Victims of Stalin and Hitler*, 169–173; Raag, "Eestlaste põgenemine Rootsi"; Gilbert, *Changing Identities*, 127–134.
40 Wyman, *DPs*, 125–127; Eidintas, *Lithuanian Emigration*, 214; Tegeler, "Esten, Letten und Litauer," 20–21; Film maker Helga Merits made a documentary on the Baltic University, http://www.balticuniversity.info/index.html (accessed 3 May 2018).
41 Wyman, *DPs*, 102; Lane, *Victims of Stalin and Hitler*, 172.

in most cases their circulation decreased over the years. Additionally, there were numerous magazines for professional or local audience.[42]

Latvian newspapers included *Laiks* in the US and *Latvija Amerikā* in Canada. Worth mentioning is the literature magazine *Jaunā Gaita*. *Austrālijas Latvietis* was published in Australia, *Londonas Avīze* in the UK, and *Brīvā Latvijā* in Germany. Most of the Lithuanian newspapers in the US had started in the early years of the twentieth century and some of them changed their political affiliation under the new circumstances. *Nepriklausoma Lietuva* and *Tėviškės Žiburiai* were both published in Canada.[43]

2.4.1 The USSR and Baltic émigrés

Since the first years of the occupation of the Baltic States, the MGB/KGB aimed at infiltrating organizations in exile and the western intelligence network. Its goal was also to disorient and discredit communities in exile by providing false information. The Soviet embassies in the most relevant capitals had Baltic officers to survey their emigrants. Fictious organizations (for example the Supreme Committee for the Restoration of Lithuania vs. the actual Supreme Committee for the Liberation of Lithuania) were regularly used and they were quite successful. The British intelligent service in particular was convinced of counterfeited information on guerrilla warfare in the Baltic States to the extent that they sent agents to the region, who were captured on arrival. The hoax was eventually exposed and by 1956, all active Western espionage in the Baltic States ceased due to lost hopes for military intervention and positive impulses in international politics after Stalin's death.[44]

The thaw during the Khrushchev years brought increased tourism to the Soviet Union and this opened new opportunities for espionage and intelligence. Firstly, the Soviet Union initiated attempts at repatriation. The Committee for a Return to the Motherland was established in 1955 particularly for Baltic exiles in East Berlin.[45]

The call for permanent returns soon turned out to be a lost cause and the strategy was changed again. Tourism to the Soviet Union increased year after year and travel visas were expanded to emigrants in 1959. The opening of a direct ferry

---

42 Valmas, *Eestlaste kirjastustegevus välismaal*, 32–38, 88–90, 110–112, 141. Most of these newspapers are available online at *Digiteeritud Eesti Ajalehed* by the Estonian National Library http://dea.nlib.ee (accessed 3 May 2018).
43 Jonas Balys, "The American Lithuanian Press," *Lituanus* 22 (1976): 1.
44 Indrek Jürjo, "Operations of Western Intelligence Services and Estonian Refugees in Post-War Estonia and the Tactics of KGB Counterintelligence," in *The Anti-Soviet Resistance in the Baltic States*, ed. Arvydas Anusauskas (Vilnius: Genocide and Resistance Research Centre of Lithuania, 2002); Argita Daudze, "Latvian Exile Community in Sweden and Soviet Struggle against it in the 1970s and 1980s," in *The Occupation Regimes in the Baltic States 1940–1991*, ed. Daina Bleiere et al. (Riga: Institute of the History of Latvia, 2009), 731; Jürjo, *Pagulus ja Nõukogude Eesti*, 78–143.
45 Zaķe, *Nineteenth-Century Nationalism*, 131.

route between Helsinki and Tallinn in 1965 started an entire new chapter in personal contacts. The Baltic States could now be visited without first travelling to Leningrad or Moscow. This was accompanied by the establishment of cultural committees in various Soviet republics. In Latvia, it was called The Liaison Committee for Cultural Relations with Compatriots Abroad (Kultūras sakaru biedrība) and in Estonia The Commission for the Development of Cultural Ties with Estonians Abroad (Välismaaga Sõpruse ja Kultuurisidemete Arendamise Eesti Ühing); the latter was renamed to a Society for the Development of Cultural Ties with Estonians Abroad in 1976.[46]

The KGB wanted to recruit émigrés although it was aware of its slim chances because the organizations in exile were suspicious even towards the compatriots who had visited the Soviet Union. In the early 1960s, prominent cultural figures (e. g. Estonian composer Eduard Tubin) visited the Soviet republic for a shock for the emigrant communities. Only gradually they became commonplace. Newspapers to the emigrants, such as *Dzimtenes Balss* (Voice of Motherland) in Latvian and *Kodumaa* (Homeland) in Estonian, were started as well but with poor results. In the early 1980s, *Kodumaa* had 4,500 subscribers in the Western world. Radio programs were broadcasted from the eastern shore of the Baltic Sea in Swedish since the early Cold War.[47]

Undeniably, the committees had some success in tarnishing emigrant politicians, although they cannot be blamed for dividing the quarreling emigrant communities. They managed to recruit some individuals among the emigrants and to insert agents into their ranks, although these contacts remained sporadic. Furthermore, visits of promising individuals to the Soviet republics occasionally backfired, when they published critical reviews after their return.[48]

Increased tourism and the new Soviet strategy collided with the generation of children of the original refugees coming of age, and the Soviets tried to benefit from this natural gap. The young criticized the choices and attitudes of their parents and wanted to see the country, described so dearly by the old. Latvian youth decried the old generation as hypocrites, who approved collaboration with the Nazi Germany but condemned contacts with the Soviet. For Lithuania, opposition concentrated on the *Santara-Šviesa* organization. In the mid-1960s, three younger Estonians proposed a satellite status for the Baltic Soviet Republics in order to find a common ground

---

46 Lars Fredrik Stöcker, "Nylon Stockings and Samizdat: The 'White Ship' between Helsinki and Tallinn in the Light of Its Unintended Economic and Political Consequences," *Zeitschrift für Ostmitteleuropaforschung* 3 (2014): 390; Zaķe, *Nineteenth-Century Nationalism*, 138; Jürjo, *Pagulus ja Nõukogude Eesti*, 190–257.
47 Lilita Zalkans, *Back to the Motherland: Repatriation and Latvian Émigrés 1955–1958* (Stockholm: Stockholm University, 2014); Daudze, "Latvian Exile Community in Sweden," 730–731.
48 Jürjo, *Pagulus ja Nõukogude Eesti*, 190–257.

with Moscow and to support national tendencies in the Baltic. The initial reaction from the older generation was almost exclusively, at least publicly, hostile.[49]

The division of the Cold War and the dilemma of an appropriate attitude towards the Soviet-occupied homelands were also present among religious organizations. The Soviets nominated bishops for the Estonian and Latvian Lutheran churches, which were still represented in international contacts by their old leaders in exile, most significantly in the Lutheran World Federation. In the general rapprochement of 1960s, the World Federation called Soviet Lutheran bishops to their meeting for the first time in 1963 and later approved their congregations as members. Catholic Lithuania and its relations with the Holy See was a special case. Lithuanians could always rely on the papal anti-Communism.[50]

Visits to the old country were suspicious until the very end of Soviet rule.[51] Nevertheless, tourism increased and fostered connections across the Baltic Sea. This wasn't an even phenomenon, as in 1983, Estonia welcomed nearly 100,000 tourists, and the respective figures for Latvia and Lithuania were 16,000 and 6,000. Both sides of the Cold War used the visitors to gain information. Estonians created a smuggling network between Sweden and Estonia, but the KGB was fully aware of its scope and allowed it to operate until the members were arrested in 1983. Human right groups in the Baltic republics were also infiltrated by the KGB. Later, connections also emerged between emigrant and dissident movements in the Soviet Baltic republics. Lithuanians seems to be an exception as they explicitly favored cooperation. They were only strengthened during the Perestroika, when People's Fronts were established, and contacts to them added credibility to the emigrants.[52]

---

[49] Daiva Dapkute, "Between Organization and Informality: A few Pages from the History of Santara-Šviesa," *Lituanus* 52 (2006): 3; Lars Fredrik Stöcker, "Bridging the Baltic Sea in the Cold War Era: The Political Struggle of Estonian Émigrés in Sweden as a Case Study," in *The Baltic Sea Region and the Cold War*, eds. Olaf Mertelsmann and Kaarel Piirimäe (Frankfurt: Peter Lang, 2012), 113–114; Rein Taagepera, "Baltic Quest for a Hungarian Path, 1965," *Journal of Baltic Studies* 44 (2013): 1; Aun, *Political Refugees*, 153–158; Zaķe, *Nineteenth-Century Nationalism*, 132–146; Zaķe, "Multiple Fronts of the Cold War," 134–136; Zaķe, "The Secret Nazi Network."

[50] Mikko Malkavaara, *Kahtia jakautuneet Baltian luterilaiset kirkot ja Luterilainen maailmanliitto 1944–1963* (Helsinki: Suomen kirkkohistoriallinen seura, 2002); Jürjo, *Pagulus ja Nõukogude Eesti*, 144–168.

[51] Raag, *Eestlane väljaspool Eestit*, 107–108; Zaķe, "Multiple Fronts of the Cold War," 137–138.

[52] Juozas Banionis, *Lietuvos laisvės byla vakaruose 1975–1990: Istorinė apžvalga* (Vilnius: Genocide and Resistance Research Centre of Lithuania, 2002), 283, 285–287, 292; Helen M. Morris and Vahur Made, "Émigrés, Dissidents and International Organisations," in *The Baltic Question during the Cold War*, eds. John Hiden, Vahur Made, and David J. Smith (Abingdon: Routledge, 2008); Giedrius Janauskas, *Kongresinė akcija: JAV ir Kanados lietuvių politinis lobizmas XX amžiaus 6–9 desimtceciais* (Vilnius: Versus Aureus, 2009), 320; Jürjo, *Pagulus ja Nõukogude Eesti*, 182; Stöcker, "Nylon Stockings and Samizdat," 388–395.

2.4.2 Political cooperation among Baltic exiles

Lithuanian exiles had already been active during World War I in putting pressure on the US congress to recognize the independence of their native country.[53] During the Cold War, the first Baltic action towards the US congress was the so-called Kersten Committee to investigate Soviet domination in Eastern Europe. The result was a 678-page volume of reports and testimonies, but the effects were rather modest.[54]

Baltic diplomats had made appeals to the United Nations already in the founding conference in San Francisco in October 1945. Their membership in the preceding League of Nations had not been cancelled and thus they demanded representation in the new organization as well, but in vain. During the next decades, Baltic diplomats and organizations continued to send similar appeals, either individually or jointly, to the UN.[55]

The first joint Baltic organization was the Baltic Women's Council, which was already founded in DP camps in Germany in 1947. The council relocated to New York in 1950. Cooperation among the Balts also emerged in the field of sports and scouts. Sports competitions were organized annually in the DP camps in Germany and this tradition continued in North America in the form of Baltic Olympics in the 1960s. A similar but biennial event has been the Baltic Games in Australia since 1969. Baltic diplomats issued joint declarations in the early years of the exile, but this action came to a halt in the mid-1950s. This cooperation re-emerged, when the American Latvian Association, the Estonian American National Council, and the Lithuanian American Council founded the Joint Baltic American National Committee in 1961. It was not until 1965, partly due to the new generation coming of age, that new activism took shape within the Baltic Appeal to the United Nations (BATUN), which was renamed later officially as United Baltic Appeal Inc. Another example was the founding of the Association for the Advancement of Baltic Studies in 1968, which has subsequently promoted Baltic Studies in North America, for instance, by organizing bi-annual conferences. The cooperation expanded to a political level in November 1972, when the Estonian World Council, the VLIK, and the World Federation of Free Latvians signed the declaration of Baltic World Conference.[56]

---

[53] Gary Hartman, *The Immigrant as Diplomat: Ethnicity, Nationalism, and the Shaping of Foreign Policy in the Lithuanian-American Community, 1870–1922* (Chicago: Lithuanian Research and Studies Center, 2002).
[54] Zaķe, "Multiple Fronts of the Cold War," 136–137.
[55] Morris and Made, "Émigrés, Dissidents and International Organisations."
[56] Tiit Lääne, *Välis-Eesti spordielu 1940–1991 Austraalias ja Uus-Meremaal, Saksamaal, Rootsis, Kanadas, USAs ja teistes riikides* (Tallinn: Maaleht, 2000), 201–203; Eduard Selge, "Eesti sport Austraalias," in *Eestlased Austraalias I*, eds. Õie Haas and Voldemar Siska (Adelaide: Austraalia Eesti Seltside Liit, 1988), 192; Pennar, *Estonians in America*, 34, 53–54, 59–60, 70, 74; Wyman, *DPs*, 118–119; Zaķe, "Multiple Fronts of the Cold War," 141–142.

In 1961, Leonardas Valiukas founded the Americans for Congressional Action to Free the Baltic States to bring together the national groups and to propagate the common cause. Furthermore, this cooperation included California thereby filling a significant geographical gap, as the political campaigns were previously concentrated on the East coast. The action continued for a decade until new forms took over, and it was officially disbanded in 1981, when the Baltic American Freedom League took its place.[57]

Baltic cooperation emerged in other countries as well. Activists in Canada organized annual Baltic Evenings at the Parliament Buildings in Ottawa since February 1973. They benefited from Canadian aspirations to achieve a foreign political profile different from the US and to respect the multinationalism of the nation. Baltic activists could find various (family, ethnic, political) reasons to invite parliamentarians and the result was a wide array of decision makers favorable to the Baltic cause. Their longest lasting accomplishment with other Eastern European emigrants was the first Black Ribbon Day in 1986 to commemorate the Molotov-Ribbentrop Pact; Due to an international campaign, the European Union has made 23 Augustas the European Day of Remembrance for Victims of Stalinism and Nazism since 2009.[58]

National central organizations established the Baltic Council in Australia in March 1967. This was preceded by information centers all over the country and local cooperation had started earlier. The three emigrant groups were relatively small, and they had similar social and political programs, which were more practical when carried out together. The centers created contacts to the politicians in order to exchange information on the Baltic States and emigration. These meetings with the parliament became more regular since 1983 and culminated in the Baltic resolution in 1985.[59]

As children of refugees grew up in the US, some of them succeeded in getting positions in state administration and the Republican Party.[60] One of the successes of the Baltic American Freedom League was the proclamation of the Baltic Freedom Day by US President Reagan on 14 June 1983. The day was commemorated as a tribute to the continuing affirmation of the independent Baltic republics and US commit-

---

57 Arne Kalm, *Balti musketärid USA Kongressis* (Tallinn: Aade, 2015); Banionis, *Lietuvos laisves byla vakaruose*, 287–288; Janauskas, *Kongresine akcija*, 48, 54, 189–204; Zaķe, "Multiple Fronts of the Cold War," 141–142.
58 Milda Danyte, "The Baltic Evening in Parliament. How Canadian Lithuanians and other Balts lobbied for their Homelands during the Cold War Period," in *Beginnings and Ends of Immigration: Life without Borders in the Contemporary World*, ed. Milda Danyte (Vilnius: Versus Aureus, 2005); Aun, *Political Refugees*, 81; Janauskas, *Kongresine akcija*, 102–188.
59 Raivo Kalamäe, "Balti Nõukogu Austraalias," in *Eestlased Austraalias I*, eds. Õie Haas and Voldemar Siska (Adelaide: Austraalia Eesti Seltside Liit, 1988).
60 Banionis, *Lietuvos laisves byla vakaruose*, 285, 287; Zaķe, "Multiple Fronts of the Cold War," 142–144.

ment to pursue freedom of all people.⁶¹ A similar achievement was a declaration on Baltic States by the European Parliament in January 1983. It did not have the desired effect on the foreign policy of the member states, but the Baltic question was debated throughout the 1980s in the European Parliament and the Council of Europe.⁶²

The goals of the Conference on Security and Cooperation in Europe (CSCE) confronted the emigrant aspirations. Since its preparations in the late 1960s, the Baltic emigrants sent information to the representatives of their countries of residence and organized demonstrations in the location of the CSCE meetings. The most dramatic act of opposition was carried out by Latvian American Māris Ķirsons in Madrid in 1980, when he stepped on the Soviet flag and let the blood drip on it from his veins. Although initially perceived as a Soviet scheme to foster the post-World War II status quo, emigrants quickly discovered how the clauses on human rights in the Helsinki Final Act actually worked to their benefit.⁶³

Related to the 10th anniversary of the CSCE, Baltic emigrants organized the Baltic tribunal in Copenhagen in July 1985. The purpose was to look at the Soviet annexation of the Baltic States from legal point of view. Unsurprisingly a condemning verdict was reached by a panel of volunteer judges. After the tribunal, the Baltic Peace and Freedom Cruise toured around the Baltic Sea to campaign against the iron curtain dividing the body of water. The cruise lasted eight days and included approximately 400 emigrants and defectors. It ended in Helsinki and Stockholm, and featured seminars and lectures on Baltic history.⁶⁴

While the Baltic cooperation increased, national divergences were cast aside. Estonians organized Estofestivals every four years since 1972, which were prominently cultural events but also dealt with political questions that were discussed by the Estonian National Council and the Estonian World Council. The major Lithuanian organizations in exile (ALT, PLB, VLIK) had joint meetings since 1984. The World Federation of Free Latvians intensified its political action due to CSCE meetings since the late 1970s.⁶⁵

---

61 Banionis, *Lietuvos laisves byla vakaruose*, 288; Zaķe, "Multiple Fronts of the Cold War," 145; Janauskas, *Kongresine akcija*, 83–86.
62 William J.H. Hough, "The Annexation of the Baltic States and its Effect on the Development of Law Prohibiting Forcible Seizure of Territory," *New York Law School Journal of International and Comparative Law* 6 (1985): 302; Peter Kyhn, "Aspects of Recognition: Denmark's Relations to the Baltic States and Non-Recognition 1940–1991," in *Relations between the Nordic Countries and the Baltic Nations in the XX Century*, ed. Kalervo Hovi (Turku: University of Turku, 1998), 238, 245; Morris and Made, "Émigrés, Dissidents and International Organisations."
63 Morris and Made, "Émigrés, Dissidents and International Organisations"; Zaķe, "Multiple Fronts of the Cold War," 139.
64 Banionis, *Lietuvos laisves byla vakaruose*, 291–292; Morris and Made, "Émigrés, Dissidents and International Organisations"; Zaķe, "Multiple Fronts of the Cold War," 139.
65 Banionis, *Lietuvos laisves byla vakaruose*, 292.

2.5 Migration since 1989

After the Baltic States regained independence, there were only a few emigrants that returned to their home countries. Many visited their home country for the first time but were disillusioned with the changes brought about by the Soviet occupation. After decades in exile, they had put down new roots in the new country, which did not make resettling an easy option. During the first decade of independence, only a thousand Estonians returned from the West. In comparison, the number of Eastern returnees was 2,500. Notable exceptions of former DPs the returned to their home country include Valdas Adamkus (President of Lithuania 1998–2003, 2004–2009) and Vaira Vīķe-Freiberga (President of Latvia 1999–2007). In Estonia, Rein Taagepera made an unsuccessful run for presidency in 1993 and later transformed the Institute of Social Sciences at the University of Tartu into the leading institution in the Baltic States.[66]

2.6 Archives and Literature

The Baltic Heritage Network is a non-profit organization, which gathers information on the cultural heritage of the Baltic diaspora with the aim of ensuring access to the relevant archives. It functions as the meeting place between expatriates, archivists, and researchers. Their website provides the list of the most important archives. It also organizes conferences, summer schools, and seminars. The Baltic Audiovisual Archival Council is another international endeavor in the field.

The Baltic émigrés started to collect and preserve their cultural heritage in exile, fearing the total annihilation in the Soviet Union. The first of archival institutes was established in Sydney in 1952 and it was renamed The Estonian Archives in Australia in the late 1960s, when a proper building was erected.

After two decades in exile, other communities also started to organize their own material. The Estonian Archives in the US were opened in the early 1970s. The facilities were built within the Estonian House in Lakewood, New Jersey, in 1975, and expanded during the next decade, but eventually the space became too small. The solution was to send the material to the Immigration History Research Center Archives in, Minneapolis. Some material remained in Lakewood. The collection includes material of the largest Estonian DP camp in Geislingen and also on, for example, the BATUN, the Baltic American Freedom League, and the Baltic Women Council. In Canada, the Estonian Central Archive has collected material on the social and cultural

---

[66] Wyman, *DPs*, 10–12; Eidintas, *Lithuanian Emigration*, 219; Lane, *Victims of Stalin and Hitler*, 224–237; Daudze, "Latvian Exile Community in Sweden," 729; Tammaru, Kumer-Haukanõmm and Anniste, "The Formation and Development," 13; Plakans, *A Concise History of the Baltic States*, 409–410.

life of Estonian emigrants since 1961 and the Tartu Institute has sponsored education on Estonian topics. Both archives are located in Toronto.

The Swedish State Archives contain the so-called Baltic Archive (Baltiska Arkivet), founded in 1968, where personal collections of prominent Baltic – most of them Estonians – political and cultural figures are held. The archives of the most important Estonian organizations have been transferred to Estonia. The Estonian National Council has been divided into the Estonian State Archives (Eesti Riigiarhiiv) and the National Library (Eesti Rahvusraamatukogu) in Tallinn. The Estonian Literary Museum (Eesti Kirjandusmuuseum) in Tartu currently holds material by the Estonian Committee (Eesti Komitee), the main cultural and social organization in exile, and various personal archives. Several personal collections are held at the Library of the University of Tartu. The diplomatic collections of the government-in-exile, the Consulate General in New York and the Legation in London are in the State Archives. The State Archives also hold material donated by diplomat Kaarel Robert Pusta but the main part of this archive is at the Hoover Institution Archives at Stanford University. The Hoover Institution has also considerable Latvian and Lithuanian collections.

The Estonians in Sweden were divided during the Cold War and the same division remains in the archives. Estonian Nation Congress founded the Estonian Cultural Archives – nowadays Estonian Archives in Sweden – in November 1970 and are still in Stockholm.

Latvian exile material is collected in Riga either at the National Archives of Latvia (Latvijas Nacionālais Arhīvs), which has collections of the diplomatic representations, or in the Museum of the Occupation of Latvia (Latvijas Okupācijas muzejs), which concentrates more on the social aspect of the Latvian diaspora. The archives of the American Latvian Association in the US are available at the Historical Society of Pennsylvania in Philadelphia. The records are supplemented by a large quantity of periodicals, including many sample newsletters from local Latvian organizations and congregations. In the UK, the Latvian Documentation Centre is located in Catthorpe Manor in Leicestershire.

The Lithuanian Museum-Archives of Canada in Mississauga is the main archive of Lithuanians in Canada, which also holds the collection of the Baltic Federation. The American Lithuanian Cultural Archives (Amerikos Lietuvių Kultūros Archyvas) are in Putnam, Connecticut. The Lithuanian Research and Studies Center (Lituanistikos tyrimo ir studijų centras) in Chicago has valuable material, mostly from the US including the PLB and the local consulate, but also from the UK. Chicago is also a home to the Lithuanian World Center, which houses small archives and a library. The material of the Lithuanian diplomatic corps in exile is held at the Lithuanian Central State Archives (Lietuvos centrinis valstybinis archyvas) in Vilnius. The Lithuanian Emigration Institute (Lietuvių išeivijos institutas) at Vytautas Magnus University in Kaunas storages various collections of the Lithuanian diaspora. An extensive guide to Lithuanian sources at selected libraries, archives, and museums in the US has been written by Lee Burchinal.[67]

Even today, a quarter of a century after the Cold War, the contemporary works remain as the most congruous literature on Baltic emigrations. Works such as *Estonians in America 1627–1975: A Chronology and Fact Book* edited mainly by Jaan Pennar, Karl Aun's *Political Refugees: A History of the Estonians in Canada*, or Ferdinand Kool's *DP Kroonika: Eesti pagulased Saksamaal 1944–1951*, provide basic information but are distinctively part of political agitation and usually ignore the disputes within the emigration. Even the most significant books during the restored independence after 1991 are compiled by former activists and are usually either document collections or chronological reports rather than new academic research. Nevertheless, *Tõotan ustavaks jääda ... Eesti Vabariigi valitsus 1940–1992* edited by Mart Orav and Enn Nõu is a mandatory introduction to the Estonian government-in-exile. Likewise, it is impossible to study the Supreme Committee for the Liberation of Lithuania without *VLIK: Vyriausiasis Lietuvos išlaisvinimo komitetas 1943–1992* by Kazys Bobelis and Jonas Aničas or the Lithuanian World Community without Vitalija Stravinskienė's *Pasaulio lietuvių bendruomenė 1949–2003*. Most recently, Priit Vesilind's and Enn Kõiv's *Estonians in America, 1945–1995: Exiles in a Land of Promise* sheds new light on Estonian diaspora in the US.

To explore further on any aspects in the Baltic diasporas in English, for each country respectively, *Lithuanian Emigration to the United States 1868–1950* by Alfonsas Eidintas, *American Latvians: Politics of a Refugee Community* by Ieva Zaķe and the article 'The Formation and Development of the Estonian Diaspora' by Tiit Tammaru, Kaja Kumer-Haukanõmm and Kristi Anniste in the *Journal of Ethnic and Migration Studies* 18 (2010):1 are recommended.

Academic research on Baltic diasporas is slowly underway in all three countries although unevenly. For example, Laurynas Jonušauskas wrote a monograph on the Lithuanian Diplomatic Corps during the Cold War in Lithuanian. On the other hand, in the Latvian case, the same question is a topic of an article in Polish by Antonijs Zunda but the information on Estonian representation and diplomats is scattered throughout multiple publications. Lithuania has had a considerably larger emigration and the journals *Oikos* and *Lituanus* are specializing in publishing on these issues. Once the long-anticipated anthology on the BATUN and Joint Baltic American National Committee is published, the topic of the Estonian National Council will remain the largest gap in research. There are general studies on Baltic emigration to other continents, but research on political activities is concentrated in the US, and hardly anything is written on the political organizations in Canada or Sweden.

The overall problem in the research is still nationalism. In rare exceptions, researchers outside the Baltic States become interested in this region and reciprocally

---

[67] The directory of Lithuanian resources: http://www.lithuanian-american.org/m/wp-content/uploads/2012/04/archyvai_en.pdf (accessed 3 May 2018).

the conducted research rarely looks at the particular emigration within a larger context or compares it to similar phenomena elsewhere. The publications are categorically in the native language, Estonian, Latvian or Lithuanian. International cooperation both in exile and in the Soviet Union was undeniably vital in restoring the Baltic independences in 1991, but it is usually ignored in research. Even a research with "Baltic" in the title can refer to sources in only one of the three nations despite the significant differences between them.

3 Bulgaria
Detelina Dineva

3.1 Bulgarian migration in historical perspective

During Ottoman rule, there were periodical mass emigration waves of Bulgarians to the Danube principalities of Wallachia and Moldavia, as well as to Serbia and Austria-Hungary. Tens and even hundreds of thousands of Bulgarians also emigrated to Russia after the Russian-Turkish Wars of 1768–1774, 1787–1792, 1806–1812, 1828–1829, and 1853–1856.[1] According to data provided by the Association of Bessarabian and Tavrian Bulgarians in 1990, more than 300,000 Bulgarians emigrated to the Russian Empire in the eighteenth and nineteenth centuries. Recent studies show a greater number of about 400,000 Bulgarian immigrants there.[2] It should be noted that prominent figures of the Bulgarian National Revival and the resistance against Ottoman rule, like Georgi Sava Rakovski (1821–1867), strongly opposed this kind of population transfers that put Bulgarians under Russian rule and aided the de-Bulgarization of entire districts in the home country.[3]

The liberation of Bulgaria from Ottoman rule marked the beginning of a new period of migration. While the San Stefano Peace Treaty, signed on 3 March 1878, provided for a Bulgarian state encompassing the main parts of Moesia (the territory between the Danube, the Balkan Mountains and the Black Sea), Thrace and Macedonia, only a few months later, with the Treaty of Berlin, the ethnic Bulgarian lands were divided into several parts. The tributary Principality of Bulgaria, covering a territory of 64,000 square kilometers between the Danube and the Balkan Mountains, was placed under the suzerainty of the Ottoman Empire. The autonomous province of Eastern Rumelia, with a territory of 33,000 square kilometers between the Balkan Mountains, the Black Sea and the Rhodope Mountains, would be under direct Ottoman political and military rule.[4] Northern Dobrudzha,[5] together with the Danube

---

1 Vesselin Mintchev, "External Migration and External Migration Policies in Bulgaria," *South-East Europe Review for Labor and Social Affairs* 2, no. 3 (1999): 124.
2 Yanko Gochev, "Tragediyata na Tavriyskite balgari razbiva lazhata za ruskia i savetskia 'osvoboditel,'" *Faktor.bg*, 26 June 2015, http://www.faktor.bg/politika/na-vseki-kilometar/48749-tragediyata-na-tavriyskite-balgari-razbiva-lazhata-za-ruskiya-i-savetskiya-osvoboditel.html%7D (accessed 3 May 2018).
3 In many of his publications, including his pamphlet "Migration to Russia or Russian Murderous Policy for Bulgarians" (1861), Rakovski criticized the activities of Russian agents, aided by the Ottoman authorities, for attracting new Bulgarian settlers that he saw as implementation of Russia's aim at enslaving Bulgarians and eventually gaining dominance over their country. – Stefan Doynov, *Balgarite v Ukrayna i Moldova prez Vazrazhdaneto, 1751–1877* (Sofia: Marin Drinov, 2005), 151–153. Unless otherwise indicated, all translations into English from Bulgarian and Polish are mine.
4 Bulgaria united with Eastern Rumelia in 1885 and proclaimed full independence in 1908.

Delta, was given to Romania in compensation for its ceding southern Bessarabia to Russia. The districts of Niš, Pirot, and Vranje were given to Serbia. Macedonia and Eastern Thrace were returned to the Ottoman Empire.

The desire for uniting the ethnic Bulgarian lands and the brutal policies of the Ottoman authorities in Macedonia and Thrace sparked immediate resistance and led to organized efforts for liberation from Ottoman rule and uniting with Bulgaria. The struggle against the dictates of the Treaty of Berlin started almost straight away and every revolt against the Ottomans in Macedonia and Thrace, crushed with extreme brutality, was followed by mass emigration of the surviving population. This was the case with the Kresna-Razlog uprising (5 October 1878 – spring 1879) when 30,000 people escaped to Bulgaria,[6] and the failed Melnik (summer 1895) and Gorna Dzhumaya (autumn of 1902) revolts. The Ilinden-Preobrazhenie uprising (August 1903), in the course of which 4,694 men, women, and children were massacred, 201 villages and 12,440 houses were burnt, and 70,835 people were left homeless, was followed by the flight to Bulgaria of another 30,000 refugees.[7]

New refugee waves followed Bulgaria's defeat in the Second Balkan War and in World War I. Under the Treaty of Neuilly-sur-Seine (27 November 1919), Western Thrace was ceded to the Entente (and later awarded to Greece, thus depriving Bulgaria of a direct outlet to the Aegean Sea), the Western Outlands were ceded to the Kingdom of Serbs, Croats, and Slovenes, and the cession of Southern Dobrudzha to Romania was confirmed. Immediately after the end of World War I, a stream of refugees headed for the Bulgarian borders from Vardar Macedonia and especially from Aegean Macedonia, with this process continuing the following years and including more than 100,000 Macedonian Bulgarians.[8]

According to Carlile Aylmer Macartney, between 1878 and 1912, more than 250,000 Bulgarians, mostly from Macedonia and Thrace, entered Bulgaria, to be followed after the Balkan Wars by 120,000 Bulgarians from Thrace, Macedonia and Do-

---

5 For transliteration, the Streamlined System for the Romanization of Bulgarian is applied, with the exception of the names of several Bulgarian authors, transliterated differently in their publications in English.

6 Doyno Doynov, *Kresnensko-Razlozhkoto vastanie, 1878–1879* (Sofia: Balgarska akademia na naukite, 1979), 84.

7 Hristofor Tzavella, ed., *Dnevnik na kosturskiya voyvoda Lazar Kiselinchev* (Sofia: Makedonia Pres, 2003), 186.

8 The largest number of refugees from Aegean Macedonia and Thrace settled in the district of Burgas. In the south of Bulgaria, they started their lives anew in the towns of Svilengrad, Haskovo, Plovdid, Krumovgrad, Ivaylovgrad, Stara Zagora, Nova Zagora, Smolyan, and the villages near them, and in the northern parts of the country – in the Varna, Ruse, Gorna Oryahovitsa, Svishtov, Nikopol, Vidin districts. The capital city of Sofia also accepted its share of new settlers. Aleksandar Grebenarov, "Moderna balgarska darzhava (1878–1944)," in *Arhivite govoryat*, http://www.archives.bg/cgi-bin/e-cms/vis/vis.pl?s=001&p=0041&g= (accessed 3 May 2018).

brudzha, and by 180,000 more refugees from Western Thrace, Southern Dobrudzha, and the districts of Tsaribrod, Bosilegrad, Tran, and Kula after World War I.[9]

Given this influx of refugees, the Bulgarian governments had significant difficulties with settling them and providing them with the necessary means of existence.[10] While during the first decade of the twentieth century, with Bulgarian economy being on the rise,[11] refugees had the opportunity to successfully integrate into the economic life of the country it was not the case during the following decades. Resolved to cope with the problem of refugee settlement, the Bulgarian government took steps towards obtaining a refugee loan under the auspices of the League of Nations.[12] Thus in late 1926, large-scale activities for housing and land settlement of the refugees began. The General Directorate for Settlement of Refugees established in Bulgaria specifically for this purpose and a League of Nations Commissioner for Refugees were in charge of coordinating these activities. In less than five years, by mid-1931, more than 30,000 refugee families (over 200,000 people) had been allotted 1,090,323 decares (109,032 hectares) of arable land and given the opportunity to make a living. They had also received 24,359 heads of working cattle, 10,555 wagons, 10,042 plows, and 3,605 harrows. During this period, 10,262 houses for refugees were built in thirteen districts of the country, 127 villages with 10,570 refugee families in them were supplied with water, and a number of infrastructure projects were completed.[13]

The problem with the settlement of refugees during this period was exacerbated by the developments related to the different approaches to putting into practice the 1919 Convention for Emigration of Minorities between Bulgaria and Greece. According to the Convention, emigration was to be voluntary, but after Greece's defeat in the war with Turkey (1919–1922), the emigration of Bulgarians acquired a compulsory character. The Greek government sought to settle the vast number of Greeks from Asia Minor in the territories inhabited by Bulgarians. The 1924 Kalfov-Politis Protocol, signed in Geneva following the efforts of the League of Nations at regulating the minority problem between the two countries, did not fulfill its goal of protecting the minority rights, as the Greek Parliament refused to ratify it. The controversies concerning the scope of emigration were deepened by the problems related to the property rights and interests of the people concerned. The agreement signed in 1927 by the Bulgarian and the Greek Ministers of Finance, Mollov and Kafandaris, which dealt

---

9 Carlile Aylmer Macartney, *Refugees: The Work of the League* (London: League of Nations Union, 1931), 113. Bulgarian researcher Vesselin Mintchev gives the figure of 250,000 refugees coming to Bulgaria during the period 1912–1929. Mintchev, "External Migration," 124.
10 See Macartney, *Refugees*, 114–115.
11 The first twelve years of the century are considered to have been the "golden times" of economic growth in Bulgaria. – Martin Ivanov, Tsvetana Todorova and Daniel Vachkov, *Istoria na vanshnia darzhaven dalg na Bulgaria, 1878–1990* (Sofia: Balgarska Narodna Banka, 2009), Part 1, 149.
12 Ivanov, Todorova and Vachkov, Part 2, 60–72.
13 Ivanov, Todorova and Vachkov, Part 2, 78–79.

with the ways of compensating the emigrants from the two countries, as well as further discussions,[14] did not lead to compensation satisfactory to the Bulgarian side. Greece refused to pay what it owed, as specified by the Mollov-Kafandaris agreement. With about 90,000 Bulgarians involved (the Greeks applying for emigration were estimated to number about 46,000), it was not an insignificant matter.[15]

The Second World War brought the next wave of immigrants to the country. Following the signing of the Craiova Agreement of 1940 and the return of Southern Dobrudzha to Bulgaria, 61,537 Bulgarians resettled from Northern Dobrudzha. At the same time, under the obligatory population exchange clause, about 50,000 Romanians that had been settled in Southern Dobrudzha after the Second Balkan War emigrated to Romania[16].

The first large group of non-Bulgarian immigrants to settle in Bulgaria was the Armenian refugees fleeing persecutions and genocide in the Ottoman Empire. After the Hamidian Massacres of 1894–1896, nearly 20,000 Armenians emigrated to Bulgaria. The Bulgarian authorities set up special committees for meeting and aiding the settlement of the refugees, and the local Armenians sheltered many of their compatriots. Nevertheless, the new arrivals experienced many hardships. In 1922, the Bulgarian government opened the country's borders to a new wave of 25,000 Armenian refugees from the Ottoman Empire. In dealing with the problems of settling in Bulgaria, these immigrants received help from organizations already established by Armenians such as the Armenian Red Cross and the local chapter of the US-based Armenian Relief Society.[17]

Another large group of immigrants, numbering more than 20,000, arrived in the country after the defeat of the White Army in the Russian Civil War. The majority of them came from European Russia, followed by Ukraine and Romania (mostly Northern Dobrudzha and Bessarabia). Regarding the ethnic structure of this migration flow, it consisted mainly of Russians, but also included smaller ethnic groups such as Bulgarians, Jews, Tatars, Armenians, and others.[18] Macartney provides a larger

---

14 See Ivanov, Todorova and Vachkov, Part 2, 83–88.
15 Ivanov, Todorova and Vachkov, Part 2, 83–88; see Daniel Vachkov, "Makedonskite bezhantsi i tyahnoto nastanyavane v Bulgaria – finansovo-ikonomicheski aspekti na problema (1878 – 30-te godini na XX v.)," *Makedonski pregled* 1 (2016): 11–14. In the opinion of researchers, with the Mollov-Kafandaris agreement, the Bulgarian side de facto aided and recognized the de-Bulgarization of the territories in Greece inhabited by Bulgarians. Serious criticism evokes also the incapability of the Bulgarian government to defend the property rights of the Bulgarian emigrants. See Dimitar Sazdov and Pencho Penchev, "Angorskiyat dogovor i spogodbata Mollov-Kafandaris," *Sbornik Trakia*, vol. 1 (Haskovo: Trakiyski nauchen institut, 2001), 5–6, 25.
16 Mintchev, "External Migration," 124–125.
17 Evgenia Mitseva, *Armentsite v Bulgaria – kultura i identichnost* (Sofia: IMIR, 2001), 7, 90–91; "Armentsi," http://www.old.omda.bg/bulg/narod/armenians.html (accessed 3 May 2018).
18 See Penka Peykovska and Nina Kiselkova, "Ruskata imigratsia v Bulgaria spored prebroyavaniyata na naselenieto prez 1920 i 1926 godina," *Statistika* 3–4 (2013): 214, 221, 224–226.

number of emigrants from Russia and writes about Bulgaria "sheltering some 40,000 Russians."[19]

In terms of population leaving the country, beside the large groups of Romanians and Greeks that left Bulgaria in accordance with the Mollov-Kafandaris Agreement of 1927 and the 1940 Craiova Treaty, there was the case of Bulgarian Turks, whose emigration to the Ottoman Empire (later Turkey) between 1878 and 1944 was more or less a continuous process. According to data provided by researchers on Muslims leaving for Turkey between 1878 and 1944, 350,000 of them left between 1878 and 1912, 10,000–12,000 were leaving annually in the period 1913–1934, and about 15,000 left between 1940 and 1944.[20]

Bulgarian political emigrants to the Soviet Union represented a specific group of people leaving the country. About 400 Bulgarians went to Russia with the aim of aiding the Bolshevik Revolution and participating in the Russian Civil War. The bulk of the Bulgarian political emigration to the Soviet Union, however, consisted of participants in the failed September Uprising, an insurgency organized in 1923 by the Bulgarian Communist Party under pressure by the Communist International, and of people fleeing the authorities' measures following the 1925 St Nedelya Church assault.[21] A report presented in August 1989 to the Politburo of the Central Committee of the Bulgarian Communist Party states that about 1,200 insurgents were accepted into the Soviet Union. Bulgarian Communists continued emigrating to the Soviet Union, including a large part of the leaders of the Communist Party. Between 1923 and 1944, from nearly 130 members of the Central Committee, about 100 spent longer or shorter periods of time in the Soviet Union. Dozens of Bulgarians worked in Moscow for the Communist International, with two of them – Vasil Kolarov and Georgi Dimitrov, heading it. It was estimated that the Bulgarian political immigrants in the Soviet Union numbered approximately 3,000, family members included. Of these 3,000 people, about 1,000 became victims of Stalin's Great Purge. Of 868 Bulgarians persecuted in the repressions of the 1930s and the 1940s, 579 died, either shot or in prisons and concentration camps.[22]

Of significant dimensions was emigration to North America. It is impossible, however, to provide exact numbers for this emigration. Until 1899, Bulgarians did not figure as such in US statistical data, and between 1899 and 1920, they were

---

19 Macartney, "Refugees," 114.
20 Lidia Petkova, "The Ethnic Turks in Bulgaria: Social Integration and Impact on Bulgarian-Turkish Relations, 1947–2000," *The Global Review of Ethnopolitics* 4 (2002): 43.
21 On 16 April 1925, members of the Military Organization of the Bulgarian Communist Party blew up the roof of the St Nedelya Church in the center of Sofia during the funeral service of a general killed by the Communists two days earlier. One hundred and fifty members of the Bulgarian political and army elite were killed and about 500 people were injured.
22 Doklad za palno i poimenno reabilitirane na postradalite balgarski politemigranti ot represiite v SSSR. Prilozhenie kam Protokol No 170 na Politbyuro na TSK na BKP ot 25 i 29 avgust 1989 g. –Central State Archives, f. 1B, op. 68, a.e. 3735a, http://archives.bg/politburo/2013–04–24–11–12–48/dokumenti/1980–1989/1521–170–25–29–1989- (accessed 3 May 2018).

placed together in one group with Serbs and Montenegrins. Besides, nationality was judged by the type of passport carried by the immigrant, and it was not uncommon for a Bulgarian to land on American soil carrying an Ottoman, Serbian, Greek, Russian, or Austro-Hungarian passport. Taking into consideration various factors, Bulgarian researchers have assessed that by 1945 there were about 120,000 – 123,000 Bulgarian immigrants in North America, with one researcher estimating them as 230,000 in number.[23]

There is no specific data available on emigration during the Great Depression. According to researchers, just in the case of emigration to Canada approximately 8,000–10,000 Bulgarians emigrated there at that time.[24]

Within the framework of economic migration, Bulgarian gardeners present a very special case. The process of going abroad to garden for a living began as early as the end of the seventeenth and the beginning of the eighteenth century. In the first years of the twentieth century, between 12,000 and 17,000 Bulgarian gardeners went abroad annually for the gardening season. From the early 1930s until the outbreak of World War II, the annual average of gardeners leaving the country reached approximately 4,800 persons. They found employment mainly in Hungary, Austria, Czechoslovakia, Poland, and the Kingdom of Yugoslavia, with many among them gradually changing their pattern of migrating. Instead of travelling only for the gardening season, they chose to remain permanently in the countries of their employment.[25]

As we have seen, emigration may have been voluntary and motivated, for instance, by the desire for economic gain. We have also seen that in too many cases it was unavoidable, forced upon people against their own will. There was a period in Bulgarian history however when a population shift was prevented, thus saving tens of thousands of innocent lives. This special phenomenon concerns the fate of the Bulgarian Jews in the first half of the 1940s.

At that time, there were about 50,000 Jews living within the Bulgarian pre-World War II borders. About 14,000 more inhabited Aegean Thrace and Vardar Macedonia. On 22 February 1943, a secret agreement was signed between Theodor Dannecker, the German official in charge of the Final Solution in the Bulgarian territories and Alexandar Belev, the Bulgarian commissar for Jewish questions. The agreement dealt with the deportation of 20,000 Jews from the German-occupied "new" lands under Bulgarian administration. As there were no more than 14,000 Jews there, 6,000 to 8,000 Bulgarian Jews were to be included in the quota. When learning about the agreement, Dimitar Peshev, Deputy Chairman of the National Assembly,

---

23 Veselin Traykov, *Istoria na balgarskata emigratsia v Severna Amerika* (Sofia: Universitetsko izdatelstvo "Sv. Kliment Ohridski," 1993), 22–25; Nikolay G. Altankov, *The Bulgarian-Americans* (Palo Alto, California: Ragusan Press, 1979), 14.
24 Traykov, *Istoria na balgarskata emigratsia*, 25.
25 Marijana Jakimova, "Migration and Assimilation: The Case of the Bulgarian Gardeners in Austria," in *(Hidden) Minorities: Language and Ethnic Identity between Central Europe and the Balkans*, ed. Christian Promitzer, Klaus-Jurgen Hermanik and Eduard Staudinger (Berlin: Lit, 2009), 130–131.

threatened to propose a vote of no confidence to the government. With the support of many people, the Bulgarian Jews were saved on 9 March, just in time. The government, however, could not stop the deportation of 11,387 Jews (7,144 of them from Macedonia, 4,058 from Aegean Thrace, and 185 from the Pirot region) to Auschwitz and Treblinka. Further deportation plans, this time including all Bulgarian Jews, met with widespread opposition, and eventually fell through. The Bulgarian Orthodox Church headed by Stefan, Metropolitan of Sofia and Kiril, Metropolitan of Plovdiv, many MPs, King Boris III, and tens of thousands of ordinary Bulgarian citizens played an important role in saving Bulgarian Jews from death in the concentration camps.[26]

Throughout the war, Bulgarian Jews endured great hardships under the Law for the Protection of the Nation that deprived them of many constitutional rights. However, due to the efforts of the Bulgarian Orthodox Church, ordinary citizens, many politicians, and the Bulgarian King, they did not share the fate of the Jews in many other countries of Europe.

As a whole, it is considered that during the period between the Liberation of 1878 and the end of World War II, about 954,000 people emigrated from Bulgaria. More than half of them (574,000) were Muslims – Turks, Circassians and Tartars. Among the 806,000 people who settled in the country during the same period, there were 698,000 Bulgarians, 29,000 Russians, and 20,000 Armenians.[27]

3.2 The aftermath of World War II

Bulgaria's position during the Second World War was "paradoxical," to use the description provided by Bulgarian historians.[28] As a member of the Axis Alliance since 1 March 1941, Bulgaria declared a token war on the United States and the United Kingdom on 13 December of the same year (the UK had declared war on Bulgaria a day earlier and the US government took that step on 5 June 1942).[29] At the same

---

26 Ivan Bozhilov et al., *Istoria na Bulgaria* (Sofia: Izdatelska kashta "Hristo Botev," 1994), 710–714; Plamen S. Tzvetkov, *A History of the Balkans: A Regional Overview from a Bulgarian Perspective*, vol. 2 (New York: Edwin Mellen Press, 1993), 248–249. See Michael Bar-Zohar, *Beyond Hitler's Grasp: The Heroic Rescue of Bulgaria's Jews* (Holbrook, Massachusetts: Adams Media, 1998); John O'Rourke, "How Bulgaria Saved Its Jews: Hillel Exhibition Reveals Little-Known Piece of Holocaust History," 26 September 2012, https://www.bu.edu/today/2012/how-bulgaria-saved-its-jews (accessed 3 May 2018).
27 Mintchev, "External Migrations," 125.
28 According to Stoycho Grancharov, the country "did not have any motives of its own for declaring war on the United States," while "the Soviet Union's conduct was giving ground for breaking off diplomatic relations and declaring war on it." See Ivan Bozhilov et al., *Istoria na Bulgaria*, 705–706.
29 One of the consequences of this was the Allied bombing raids over Bulgarian cities and towns. They started as early as in April 1941, but the heaviest raids were carried out from mid-November 1943 until mid-April 1944.

time, Bulgaria maintained diplomatic relations with Moscow, refused to send troops to the Eastern Front, and on 26 August 1944 declared neutrality in the war between Germany and the Soviet Union. The latter, however, declared war on Bulgaria on 5 September 1944, and three days later Soviet troops entered Bulgarian territory.

With the Bulgarian government declaring war on Germany on 8 September 1944 and ordering the army to refrain from opposing the invading Soviet troops, the country found itself in the unique position of being in a state of war with the Allies and the Axis simultaneously.[30]

During the ensuing months, until the end of the war, the Bulgarian armies fought against Germany on Yugoslav, Hungarian, and Austrian soil, suffering losses of 31,360 killed and wounded.[31] Bulgaria, however, continued to be considered in a state of war against the Allies until the signing of the Paris Peace Treaty in 1947. Under the treaty, the country was restored to its borders of 1 January 1941, thus keeping Southern Dobrudzha, but having to return Vardar Macedonia to Yugoslavia and Eastern Macedonia and Western Thrace to Greece. Even earlier, together with the retreating Bulgarian troops and members of the administration, fearing repercussions and abiding by Article two of the Armistice Agreement,[32] tens of thousands of Bulgarians who in the previous years had returned to their places of birth in Vardar Macedonia, Western Outlands, and Aegean Thrace became refugees once more and fled to Bulgaria.[33]

The fate of some of the non-Bulgarians residing in the country was decided with the direct involvement of the Soviet-dominated Allied Control Commission.[34] In December 1944, the Bulgarian authorities were notified that all residents of German descent who held Hungarian, Czechoslovak, Yugoslav, or Romanian citizenship were to be sent to labor camps in the Soviet Union. Attempts were made on the part of the Bulgarian government to save some of these people, mostly either the spouses of Bulgarians or the children in mixed marriages. Some received certificates of being Czech or Jewish, but in the beginning of 1945, the Soviet Command expressed its displeasure at the Bulgarian government for having fulfilled only 28 percent of the quota of

---

30 Tzvetkov, *A History of the Balkans*, 261.
31 Joseph Rothschild, *East Central Europe between the Two World Wars* (Seattle/London: University of Washington Press, 1998), 353.
32 Article two stipulated that "the Bulgarian authorities must immediately take steps to withdraw from Greek and Yugoslav territory Bulgarians who were citizens of Bulgaria on 1 January 1941 (...)" *Department of State Bulletin*, October 29, 1944, Vol. XI, No 279 (Washington, DC: Government Printing Office, 1944).
33 For the Bulgarian administration in the "new lands" in the period 1941–1944 see Aleksandar Grebenarov and Nadya Nikolova (compilers), *Balgarskoto upravlenie vav Vardarska Makedonia, 1941– 1944* (Sofia: Darzhavna agentsia arhivi, 2012); Dimitar Yonchev, *Bulgaria i Belomorieto (oktomvri 1940 – 9 septemvri 1944 g.): Voennopoliticheski aspekti* (Sofia: Dirum, 1993).
34 Under the Armistice Agreement with Bulgaria (28 October 1944), the Allied Control Commission in the country was chaired by Marshal of the Soviet Union, Fyodor Tolbukhin and his deputy Colonel-General Sergey Biryuzov.

expected deportees. Consequently, those of German descent in mixed families were deported to the Soviet Union and their close Bulgarian relatives were interned by the authorities. The same fate – deportation and the hardships and death of the labor camps – was shared by people who had escaped from revolutionary Russia and found refuge in Bulgaria.[35]

Not only people of non-Bulgarian descent became victims of this policy. One of the cruelest acts of the Soviet Command in Bulgaria, with the collaboration of the Fatherland Front government led by Kimon Georgiev, was the deportation of the Tavrian Bulgarians to the Soviet Union in the spring of 1945. Tavrian Bulgarians were descendants of immigrants to Russia in the eighteenth and nineteenth centuries, who sought to escape the Ottomans. Through the years, they were the targets of forced Russification. After the Revolution of 1917, they were spared neither collectivization and dekulakization, nor the *Holodomor* (Great Famine) and Stalin's Great Terror. As a result, by the second half of the 1930s about 25,000 Bulgarian members of the intelligentsia – teachers, engineers, priests, agronomists, and students were murdered.[36]

In 1942, during the German occupation of the western territories of the Soviet Union, Tavrian Bulgarians asked the Bulgarian King Boris III to accept them in Bulgaria. Given permission to settle in the country of their ancestors, from late 1943 until mid-1944, at least 2,000 of them, or according to other sources, more than 3,000 (the exact number is probably never to be known), started their new lives in Dobrudzha and the Ludogorie region. The local people welcomed them as long-lost relatives, and the authorities allotted them land. But then, on 22 November 1944, the Soviets who occupied Bulgaria issued an order according to which Tavrian Bulgarians were to be treated as "traitors" of the Soviet Union. They were to be found, assembled, and deported. Soviet Army personnel, with the active participation of local Communist authorities, carried out this operation. Local Bulgarians tried to hide their Tavrian compatriots, and some of the latter changed their names, even their appearance. They were doing everything in their might to prove their Bulgarian ancestry and their Bulgarian citizenship, but to no avail. Quite a few of the Tavrian Bulgarians were murdered while still in Bulgaria. Almost nothing is known about the fate of the remaining Tavrian Bulgarians. Put on barges, they were either sent to Gulag camps after reaching Soviet territory or, as some contemporaries of the events later recalled, were drowned before their arrival.[37] During this time, the Tavrian Bulgarians in the

---

35 Tzvetkov, *A History of the Balkans*, 270–271.
36 Gochev, "Tragediyata na tavriyskite balgari"; Virzhinia Stoyanova, "Sofia nehae za tavricheskite balgari," Intervyu s d-r Vladimir Kaloyanov, *Standartnews.com*, 20 June 2005, http://paper.standartnews.com/bg/article.php?d=2005–06–20&article=10467 (accessed 3 May 2018).
37 Georgi Chunchukov, "Na Chervenata armia – proslava, a za ubitite ot neya balgari i tavriyski balgari – zabrava," https://demontirane.org/tag/таврийски-българи (accessed 3 May 2018); Gochev, "Tragediyata na tavriyskite balgari"; Atanas Markov, *Balgari v Tavria i tavriytsi v Bulgaria* (Dobrich: Matador 74, 2012); Petko Ogoyski, *Zapiski za balgarskite stradania 1944–1989*, vol. 3 (Sofia: Izdatelst-

Crimea, together with other minority groups, were put on trains and deported to the Central Asian steppes.[38]

A grave issue during the post-World War II period concerned Bulgaria's relations with Yugoslavia and the Soviet Union with regard to Macedonia. In its unique way, this was not a question of population transfer, but rather of ethnicity transfer.[39] In mid-September 1944, only days after the 9 September coup d'état in Bulgaria, the Yugoslav leader Josip Broz Tito sent emissaries to Sofia to demand the formation of a union of Pirin Macedonia with the newly created Democratic Federal Macedonia (later, People's Republic of Macedonia). The Bulgarian Communist leader, Georgi Dimitrov, who since the 1920s-1930s had favored the creation of Macedonian, Dobrudzhan, and Thracian nations with a view towards establishing a federation in the Balkans, was ready to collaborate on this project with Tito. Moreover, Dimitrov's willingness to do so was an act of compliance with Joseph Stalin's insistent demand that Bulgarians support the Yugoslav leader's policy on Macedonia and put their efforts into creating a Macedonian minority in Bulgaria.[40]

The idea of creating a Macedonian nation had started engaging Stalin's mind at least a decade earlier. In this respect, the Comintern had been a useful tool. Now, under the new circumstances, Stalin's order was as follows:

> "Cultural autonomy must be granted to Pirin Macedonia within the framework of Bulgaria. (…) Autonomy will be the first step towards the unification of Macedonia, but in view of the present situation, there should be no hurry on this matter. (…) That a Macedonian consciousness has not yet developed among the population is of no account. No such consciousness existed in Belarus either when we proclaimed it a Soviet Republic. However, later it was shown that Belarusian people did in fact exist."[41]

Following Stalin's dictate, at a party plenum in August 1946, the Bulgarian Communist leadership decided to announce the existence of an ethnic Macedonian minority in Bulgaria. To crush the resistance of the local population, the authorities declared all opponents of this policy "fascists" and "chauvinists" dreaming of a greater Bulgaria. As early as October 1944, more than 800 members of the Internal Macedonian Revolutionary Organization (IMRO) and the *Shar* student organization founded in the previous decade by refugees from Macedonia had already been arrested. Persecution

---

vo "Vulkan-4," 2000), 25, http://www.bosilkov.com/data/pages/files/1432115886.pdf. (accessed 3 May 2018)
38 Stoyanova, "Sofia nehae za tavricheskite balgari."
39 Chris Kostov uses the expression "shifts of the ethnic identity." Chris Kostov, *Contested Ethnic Identity: The Case of Macedonian Immigrants in Toronto, 1900–1996* (Bern: Peter Lang AG, 2010), 100.
40 Kostov, 96.
41 Kostov, 97; Dobrin Michev, *Makedonskiyat vapros i balgaro-yugoslavskite otnoshenia, 9 septemvri 1944–1949* (Sofia: Universitetsko izdatelstvo "Sv. Kliment Ohridski," 1994), 227–228.

involving consecutive mass arrests of activists continued. The most prominent among them were murdered and the rest were sent to prison and labor camps.⁴²

In December 1946, a national census was organized with the aim of showing that the majority of the people in Pirin Macedonia were ethnic Macedonians. Force and threats were resorted to in order to get the result of there being 252,908 ethnic Macedonians in the country. As the next step in Tito's plan for the unification of Pirin and Aegean Macedonia with the People's Republic of Macedonia, and Bulgaria eventually joining the Yugoslav Federation, between 1947 and 1948 the Yugoslav government sent teachers of the new Macedonian language and history to Pirin Macedonia. This was endorsed by Georgi Dimitrov.⁴³ It was only one of the measures directed towards creating a new identity for the local population, forced upon it with persisting zeal and mercilessness.⁴⁴

Pirin Macedonia and its population stopped being a pawn in Stalin's game only after his split with Tito. Eventually, the Macedonization of the Bulgarians in Pirin Macedonia was abandoned, but was briefly revived in 1956, this time on Nikita Khrushchev's demand. Gradually, however, the idea of a Macedonian minority in Bulgaria was left to die a natural death.⁴⁵ The whole venture, though, had lasting and often tragic effects on the lives of thousands of people. It also influenced the immigrant community abroad. In the words of Veselin Traykov, a researcher of Bulgarian emigration to the United States and Canada, decisions like the one of the Comintern about a separate Macedonian nation led to daily arguments among the immigrants, casting its shadow on the political life of their community.⁴⁶

3.3 Major migration streams during the Cold War

3.3.1 Migration policy

During Communist rule, as all kinds of mobility had been closely observed and controlled by the authorities, both the inflow and outflow of migrants were much more restricted. Anna Krasteva defines three types of outflows during that period in Bulgaria – ethnic, refugee, and labor ones, with the first type not encouraged, but tol-

---

42 Kostov, *Contested Ethnic Identity*, 97–98; Dobrin Michev, *Makedonskiyat vapros*, 238–240. Petko Ogoyski provides dozens of names of people convicted in the trials carried out between August 1945 and 1949. Ogoyski, *Zapiski za balgarskite stradania*, vol. 3, 22–23, 30; Petko Ogoyski, *Zapiski za balgarskite stradania 1944–1989*, vol. 2 (Sofia: IK Fenomen, 2008), 206–208, http://www.bosilkov.com/data/pages/files/1432115840.pdf (accessed 6 May 2018).
43 Kostov, *Contested Ethnic Identity*, 97–100.
44 About the denationalization of the Bulgarian population in Vardar Macedonia see Michev, *Makedonskiyat vapros*, 76–100.
45 Michev, 99–100.
46 Traykov, *Istoria na balgarskata emigratsia*, 255.

erated, the second – strictly forbidden, and the third – limited, but encouraged by the authorities.[47] While ethnic and labor migration occurred predominantly in accordance with bilateral agreements, emigration motivated by disagreement and refusal to live under the regime was severely punished.

In January 1945, the Council of Ministers adopted the Decree on Protection of People's Power, according to which Bulgarians in the country or abroad who led organizations acting to weaken, undermine, or overthrow the Fatherland Front, were liable to life imprisonment in close confinement or the death penalty. In 1948, the decree was included in the Penal Law, and under the new Article 155a, every person who left the country without permission was punishable by imprisonment in close confinement and a fine of 500,000 BGN. The same punishment awaited facilitators and persons disobeying an order to return to Bulgaria.[48]

Due to increased post-1947 emigration, in March 1948 a new Law on Bulgarian Citizenship was enacted. Under its Article 8, persons who left the country illegally or did not return within two months after being ordered to do so, would be forcibly stripped of citizenship and their property would be seized by the state. Later, in view of criticism from abroad, some changes were made in the Penal Law and the articles classifying illegal emigration as a crime against the People's Republic of Bulgaria were abrogated (1953).[49]

During this period, several amnesties were announced for emigrants, with the first Law on Amnesty being passed in late 1950. According to this law, persons liable to punishment under Article 155a of the Penal Law were amnestied provided they returned to the country within six months, had not committed treason, or carried out espionage activities. Announcements about amnesties were met with distrust by the emigrants, who considered them a sham.[50]

To prevent emigration, the authorities took special measures to reinforce the borders, especially those with Turkey and Greece. In August 1946, the Law for the Establishment of Border Militia (soon to be renamed Border Troops) was promulgated. It entrusted the Ministry of the Interior with guarding state borders. There were 440 frontier posts at the first line, 77 subsections at the second line, and 22 border sections at the third line. Submachine guns and 15,000 landmines (1951) were brought into use, and electronic equipment was installed in 1959. The intelligence-related tasks of the Border Troops included: organization and carrying out of intelligence activities within the border zones; reconnaissance on the territory of neighboring countries up to 25 kilometers from the border line; arresting offenders and conducting preliminary investigation of their cases. By the end of the 1950s, the inhabitants of

---

47 Anna Krasteva, "Bulgarian Migration Profile," in *Proliferation of Migration Transition: Selected New EU Member States*, ed. Felicita Medved (n.p.: European Liberal Forum, 2014), 191.
48 Elena Statelova and Vasilka Tankova, *Prokudenite* (Plovdiv: Zhanet-45 Publishing House, 2002), 22.
49 Statelova and Tankova, 23–24.
50 Statelova and Tankova, 24.

the border regions had been cleansed from "hostile elements" and concealers of underground groups had been turned into dedicated keepers of the frontier lines.⁵¹

It is interesting to note that in October 1978 in a document signed by the general commanding the Border Troops, a psychological profile of the illegal emigrant was presented, according to which that was a person between 18 and 26 years of age on average, lacking good education and upbringing. Such persons' reasons for escape would not often be politically motivated. In most cases, it was said, "adventurism" was at the root of their actions. According to that document, among the escapees there were many people doing their military service as well as criminals trying to avoid punishment.⁵²

A special category of border offenders presented citizens of other countries from the Eastern Bloc, having come to Bulgaria as tourists and attempting to get to the West by first illegally crossing Bulgaria's border mostly to Turkey and Greece. From 1973 to 1977, 382 citizens of Eastern Bloc countries tried to escape from Bulgaria to Greece, Turkey or Yugoslavia. Only 27 of them succeeded. Most of the attempts at escaping were carried out during the summer and early autumn, when the number of foreign tourists in Bulgaria was the highest.⁵³

3.3.2 Immigration

The case of the Greek political émigrés, as an example of inward migration, is noteworthy. Between 1948 and 1949, the Bulgarian government granted asylum to about 4,500 Greek participants of the Greek Civil War of 1946–1949. Considered to be "brothers in arms," fighting against capitalism, in Bulgaria these émigrés were provided with free health care and disability pensions, child care, preferential employment, housing, educational privileges, and help in reuniting family members. Since a considerable number of them were the children of Communists imprisoned in Greece, dormitories were built and special educational curricula were devised just

---

51 Ivan Gadjev, *Istoria na balgarskata emigratsia v Severna Amerika*, vol. 2: *Bulgaria, mashteha nasha, 1944–1989* (Sofia: Institut po istoria na balgarskata emigratsia "Ilia Todorov Gadjev," 2006), 95 ff; Boyko Kiryakov, "Bulgaria zad granitsa," in *Saprotivata sreshtu komunisticheskiya rezhim v Bulgaria 1944–1989: Sbornik materiali ot natsionalna nauchna konferentsia, NBU, 23–24 mart 2011 g.*, ed. Lachezar Stoyanov and Zhivko Lefterov, http://ebox.nbu.bg/anti (accessed 3 May 2018), 75–76; Introduction to *Darzhavna sigurnost i granichni voyski: Dokumentalen sbornik* (Sofia: Komisia za razkrivane na dokumentite i za obyavyavane prinadlezhnost na balgarski grazhdani kam Darzhavna sigurnost i razuznavatelnite sluzhbi na Balgarskata narodna armia / Committee for Disclosing the Documents and Announcing Affiliation of Bulgarian Citizens to the State Security and the Intelligence Services of the Bulgarian National Army /further cited as COMDOS/, 2014), 10–11.
52 *Darzhavna sigurnost i granichni voyski*, 11–12, 315–317.
53 *Darzhavna sigurnost i granichni voyski*, 320–321. Valuable information on the subject is presented in the documentary volume "State Security and the Tourism." – *Darzhavna sigurnost i turizmat: Dokumentalen sbornik* (Sofia: COMDOS, 2014).

for them.⁵⁴ Theodora Dragostinova, the author of *Between Two Motherlands: Nationality and Emigration among the Greeks of Bulgaria, 1900–1944*, discusses the "degree of differentiation" between the Greek immigrants and the local Greeks in light of the privileges granted to the new, left-wing arrivals. She speaks of the "political split that made any measure of national unity among the population impossible, as many local Greeks did not endorse the left-wing commitment of their newly arrived compatriots, refused to assist them financially, and kept apart from them in their communities".⁵⁵

Vesselin Mintchev provides a larger number of Greek immigrants to Bulgaria as a result of the Civil War – 7,000.⁵⁶ Another author, Aleksandar Grebenarov, notes that as many as 20,000 refugees came to Bulgaria after the Greek Civil War, "in order to save their Bulgarian names." Due to external influence, Bulgaria rejected most of them and sent them to the People's Republic of Macedonia. The Macedonian authorities were not willing to accept these refugees. As a result, they were forced to leave for countries in Central Europe and Central Asia. It was a time of hardship also for more than 17,000 children between the ages of two and fourteen, a significant part of them children of Macedonian Bulgarians. Taken out of the country by the Democratic Army of Greece across the borders with Albania, Yugoslavia, and Bulgaria, they were later sent to Hungary, Poland, Czechoslovakia, Romania, and the Soviet Union. Only 670 children remained in Bulgaria.⁵⁷

Another group of immigrants consisted of foreign university students who remained in the country after graduation. Also, as a result of marriages between Bulgarian citizens and citizens of the former Soviet Union and other Eastern Bloc countries, a large number of the latter chose to live in Bulgaria.

During the 1980s, in accordance with a bilateral agreement, Bulgaria accepted migrants from Vietnam. Most of them worked on construction sites. Together with the Vietnamese students who remained in Bulgaria after marrying Bulgarian citizens, they numbered approximately 15,000. The agreement was not renewed after 1990/1991. Presently the Vietnamese community in Bulgaria consists of about 1,500 members.⁵⁸

---

54 See Theodora Dragostinova, *Between Two Motherlands: Nationality and Emigration among the Greeks of Bulgaria, 1900–1949* (Ithaca/London: Cornell University Press, 2011), 255.
55 Dragostinova, 255–256.
56 Mintchev, "External Migrations," 126.
57 Aleksandar Grebenarov, "Balgarskata darzhava sled 1944 g." in *Arhivite govoryat*, http://www.archives.bg/cgi-bin/e-cms/vis/vis.pl?s=001&p=0064&g= (accessed 3 May 2018).
58 Evgenia Mitseva, "Vietnamtsi" in *Imigratsiyata v Bulgaria*, ed. Anna Krasteva (Sofia: Mezhdunaroden tsentar za izsledvane na maltsinstvata i kulturnite vzaimodeystvia, 2005), 68–69. See also *E-vestnik*, 30 July 2012, http://e-vestnik.bg/14682 (accessed 3 May 2018).

3.3.3 Emigration

Regarding outward migration, between 1946 and 1951, about 8,000 Armenians emigrated, mostly to Armenia. A little later, about 5,000 Russians and 4,000 people of other nationalities, mostly Czechs and Slovaks, left the country. Approximately 32,000 Jews left for Israel.[59] By 1956, 88.9 percent of Bulgarian Jews (as estimated in 1946), had emigrated, and in 1965, those remaining in the country numbered only 5,000.[60]

During the Cold War, there were three waves of Bulgarian Turks migrating to Turkey. The first one took place in 1950–1951, and was the result of the land expropriation in 1949 (the majority of the Bulgarian Turks were farmers) and the Bulgarian Communist Party's policy of fighting the "manifestations of nationalism and religious fanaticism among the local Turks." In December 1947, Georgi Dimitrov, then General Secretary of the Central Committee of the Bulgarian Communist Party and Chairman of the Council of Ministers, warned the Bulgarian Turks not to act as agents of the enemies of Bulgaria, referring to the soon-to-be NATO member state beyond the border. In a governmental note dated March 1951, Bulgaria accused Turkey of instigating the Bulgarian Turks to revolt. The number of Bulgarian Turks who left the country in the period 1950–1951 is estimated at approximately 154,000 people.[61]

The second emigration wave (1969–1978), following the signing of the Bulgarian-Turkish emigration agreement of 1968 for the reunion of divided families, involved 130,000 Bulgarian Turks.[62] The third mass emigration wave, following the name-changing campaign of 1984–1985,[63] resulted in about 311,000 Bulgarian Turks leaving the country between 3 June 1989 and 21 August of the same year,

---

59 Mintchev, "External Migration," 126.
60 Richard J. Crampton, *A Short History of Modern Bulgaria* (Cambridge: Cambridge University Press, 1987), 174.
61 Petkova, "The Ethnic Turks," 43–44; *Natsionalen doklad: Saglasno chl. 25, al. 1 ot Ramkova konventsia za zashtita na natsionalnite maltsinstva* (Sofia: Natsionalen savet po etnicheski i demografski vaprosi, 2001), 10. Richard Crampton, who sees the "sudden explosion of the emigration issue" as directly stemming from the collectivization measures, cites the number of 162,000 Turks having left Bulgaria by 1952. Crampton, *A Short History of Modern Bulgaria*, 174.
62 *Natsionalen doklad*, 11.
63 Discussing the "shifts" in the Bulgarian Communist leadership's policy in regard to the Bulgarian Turks, Vasil Paraskevov defines an "initial phase of relative 'toleration,'" then the "more integrationist policies of the 1960s and mid-1970s," and finally "the intense assimilation of the last phase of Communist rule." Speaking about the "broad consensus" among Bulgarian researchers regarding the interaction of domestic and external factors in shaping the Bulgarian Communist Party's approach to the Bulgarian Turks, he points that "several authors have recognized that the Cold War had an impact on minority policy but few have examined the relationship in any detail." – Vasil Paraskevov, "Insecurity and Control: Bulgaria and Its Turkish Minority," in *Ethnicity, Nationalism and the European Cold War*, ed. Robert Knight (London/New York: Continuum, 2012), 122.

when Turkey sealed its frontier with Bulgaria.⁶⁴ It should be noted that later nearly half that number, about 150,000 of them, returned to Bulgaria.⁶⁵

A special case in the pre-1989 period involved the government controlled outward labor migration. Thousands of Bulgarian medical doctors and nurses, engineers and other highly qualified persons worked in Third World countries under bilateral agreements, with the Bulgarian state taking a considerable part of their earnings.⁶⁶

3.3.4 Political emigration

Beside ethnic and labor migration, there was also a forbidden refugee outflow. There does not seem to be conclusive data about the scope of politically motivated emigration from Bulgaria. Nevertheless, some sources provide relevant information. Data from the Bulgarian Ministry of the Interior shows that between 1944 and 1949, 1,829 people left the country, with their number increasing to 4,542 in 1953.⁶⁷ According to the International Refugee Organization, during the 1950s in Western Europe and America the Bulgarian political emigrants did not exceed 8,000 people.⁶⁸ In a 1977 report to the Politburo of the Bulgarian Communist Party, the Bulgarian Minister of the Interior informed its members that 10,500 Bulgarian citizens had escaped from the country.⁶⁹ Other sources show that between the end of the 1950s and 1989, about 20,000 Bulgarians had arrived in other countries as refugees.⁷⁰ Additional research should lead to more conclusive numbers.

Several groups of people formed the Bulgarian emigration from the autumn of 1944 onwards. Among them were those who simply remained abroad – diplomats, students at foreign universities, and others who did not expect fair treatment upon returning home; then, there were the ones who left Bulgaria immediately after the Soviet Union declared war on Bulgaria (5 September 1944). These were mainly individuals involved, be it even only ideologically, with Nazism. Later, especially after the execution of Nikola Petkov (leader of the Bulgarian Agrarian National Union, co-founder of the Fatherland Front and – from the summer of 1945, leader of the anti-Communist opposition) in September 1947 and the dissolution of the opposition parties, members of the parties that had contributed to the Communist seizure of power and had subsequently declared themselves in opposition to the Communists,

---

64 See Petkova, "The Ethnic Turks," 47–49.
65 Krasteva, "Bulgarian Migration Profile," 196.
66 Krasteva, 192.
67 Vasil Paraskevov, "Small but Vociferous: Bulgarian Ethnic Anti-Communist Groups," in *Anti-Communism Minorities in the US: Political Activism of Ethnic Refugees*, ed. Ieva Zaķe (New York: Palgrave Macmillan, 2009), 153.
68 Mintchev, "External Migration," 125–126.
69 Statelova and Tankova, *Prokudenite*, 15.
70 Krasteva, "Bulgarian Migration Profile," 192.

left the country. This group also included intellectuals, owners of small businesses, and farmers whose land had been expropriated. Although many of them were not active in politics, they were still persecuted by the authorities. The outflow that started in the 1950s, intensified after the Hungarian Revolution of 1956.[71] Bulgarians continued to look for ways to illegally leave the country until the end of Communist rule and refugee migration is considered to have been relatively stable over the years at about 370 persons per year.[72] These numbers may seem small to an outside observer, but considering the measures taken by the authorities for reinforcing the country's borders, this should be no surprise.

Examining the social status of Bulgarian émigrés, Vasil Paraskevov concludes that officials of the previous regime formed the earliest post-1944 wave, while the ones leaving Bulgaria in the late 1940s were of peasant and petty bourgeoisie backgrounds. Consequently, among the leaders of exile organizations, there were lawyers, military officers, doctors, while their members were artisans and peasants. During Communist rule, mainly intellectuals emigrated, seizing the opportunity provided by the authorities' decision to increase contacts with the West in the 1960s.[73] This conclusion is rather at odds with the aforementioned psychological profile of the Bulgarian illegal emigrant.

3.3.5 The scope of Bulgarian migration and dominant settlement areas

The numbers of Bulgarian migrants in various countries and cities provided here come from research based on currently available sources. For even greater precision, however, the problem under consideration would require further research based on hopefully preserved and open-for-access sources. Most of the cited data on immigrant numbers does not cover the years beyond the late 1950s and early 1960s. However, by having a more or less accurate idea of the overall scope of Bulgarian emigration during the Cold War, a credible picture of its distribution can be drawn.

The prevailing majority of Bulgarian émigrés passed through refugee camps in Greece, Turkey, Italy, Austria, and Yugoslavia (after 1948). The time spent in camps lasted months and sometimes years and was, especially in Greece and Yugoslavia,

---

71 See Statelova and Tankova, *Prokudenite*, 14–15; Ogoyski, *Zapiski za balgarskite stradania*, vol. 2, 197–198; Kiryakov, "Bulgaria zad granitsa," 76–77; Boyka Vasileva, *Balgarskata politicheska emigratsia sled Vtorata svetovna voyna* (Sofia: Universitetsko izdatelstvo "Sv. Kliment Ohridski," 1999), 6.
72 Krasteva, "Bulgarian Migration Profile," 192.
73 Paraskevov, "Small but Vociferous," 153. On émigré intellectuals see Ogoyski, *Zapiski za balgarskite stradania*, vol. 3, 161.

one of deprivation, constant humiliation and demoralization, and in the case of Yugoslavia, often of brutality and torture.[74]

Among the terrifying testimonies of the treatment of Bulgarians in the Yugoslav concentration camp Gerovo, the one told by the survivor Blagorodna Bozhinova stands out. Blagorodna Bozhinova (1925–2000) was born in the village of Gega in the Petrich region. Her parents were from Strumica. Upon her graduation from the University of Skopje (she was among the 280 Bulgarian students in Yugoslavia – future builders of the new federation, or so they were told) Bozhinova was offered to declare herself an "ethnic Macedonian" and take Yugoslav citizenship. Her refusal led to her arrest and accusations of espionage on behalf of Bulgaria. After suffering from torment and cruelty at police stations and prisons, she was sent to the Gerovo concentration camp where in the course of sixteen months she, together with a large number of Bulgarian refugees, was subjected to inhuman torture. Surviving by miracle, she was able to return to Bulgaria in 1956 where she spent a long time in hospitals and sanatoria.[75] "At the time of Tito," Bozhinova writes, "more than 30,000 Bulgarians perished and over 200,000 passed through prisons and camps in Yugoslavia. In Vardar Macedonia the dictatorship was destroying everything that did not act the Serbian way, and everyone who dared call themselves a Bulgarian disappeared without a trace. The executioners were not interested whether you were a communist or a fascist. Since you were Bulgarian, you were the enemy."[76]

Upon release from the camps, larger numbers of Bulgarians went to West European countries – France, Germany, and others. Until the beginning of the 1950s, immigration to North America, Brazil, Australia, and other overseas countries was less intensive, with the trend reversing in later years.[77]

In Paris, an Association of Bulgarian Refugees in France was founded in November 1948. It took care of the new arrivals and maintained contact with various international organizations. According to the association's estimates, 2,159 Bulgarians arrived in France after World War II. The Bulgarian Legation provided similar data in 1950, namely 2,000 immigrants, but added that most of these people had come to the country before 9 September 1944 (the date of the coup d'état when the Kingdom of Bulgaria administration was replaced by a Fatherland Front government). Data for

---

74 Statelova and Tankova, *Prokudenite*, 16; Spas Raikin, *Politicheski problemi pred balgarskata obshtestvenost v chuzhbina*, vol. 2 (Sofia: Izdatelstvo "Damyan Yakov," 1993), 325; Gadjev, *Istoria na balgarskata emigratsia*, vol. 2, 66–68, 94; Ogoyski, *Zapiski za balgarskite stradania*, vol. 2, 198–199.
75 Tsocho Bilyarski, "Blagorodna Bozhinova – edna balgarska svetitsa," *Site balgari zaedno*, http://www.sitebulgarizaedno.com/index.php?option=com_content&view=article&id=340%3A2011-10-04-16-59-43&catid=29%3A2010-04-24-09-14-13&Itemid=61 (accessed 3 May 2018).
76 Blagorodna Bozhinova, *Zhertveno pokolenie* (Sofia: Bulgarika, 1996), 5–6.
77 Statelova and Tankova, *Prokudenite*, 17.

the period between 1948 and 1954 shows that the number of Bulgarian immigrants to Paris constantly increased.[78]

In the first post-war years, the Bulgarian refugee community in Germany became smaller due to the difficult economic conditions and uncertain political situation. Then, in the late 1940s and early 1950s, new emigrants from Bulgaria began to arrive.[79] There are indications that in February 1952 the Bulgarian community in Germany numbered 500 members. A company of 200 Bulgarian volunteers served as part of the American military forces in West Germany in Germersheim.[80]

According to incomplete data cited by Boyka Vasileva, in Austria after the war, there were 530 Bulgarians in the Soviet occupation zone and a total of 270 in the American, British, and French zones. Among them, there were about 500 gardeners and 170–180 students. More than 300 of them did not wish to return to Bulgaria.[81] Recent research on Bulgarian gardeners in Austria shows that 4,064 persons were members of the Vienna branch of the Society of Bulgarian Gardeners from 1939 to 1944. During the war years, Bulgarian gardeners used to replace their German colleagues who were conscripted into the army for which the Bulgarian post-war authorities accused them of having collaborated with the Nazis.[82] In view of this, their unwillingness to return to Bulgaria is easily understood. Apart from Vienna, there were Bulgarian groups in Graz, Klagenfurt, Innsbruck, and Leoben. In the beginning of the 1950s, there were about 100 Bulgarians in the refugee camp in Salzburg.[83]

In Italy, unlike in other countries, the majority of Bulgarian immigrants lived in camps – in Capua, Udine, Trieste, Salerno, and Aversa. Initially, there were about 300 of them, but their number grew with the arrival of refugees from the camps in Yugoslavia in 1955. There were 600 Bulgarian immigrants in Italy in 1956; most of them were sent to the camps.[84]

As far as other European countries and cities are concerned, Madrid was known as the place of residence of the young Bulgarian Tsar Simeon II (nine years old when exiled in 1946), the circle around him and his mother. Research shows that in 1959 the entire Bulgarian community in England numbered approximately 160 immigrants, with 75 of them residing in London. From about 25–30 political immigrants, 15–20 had come to the country either before or during World War II. Only ten of them came after 9 September 1944.[85]

---

[78] Statelova and Tankova, 17, 223–224. Bulgarian historian Boyka Vasileva gives the number 300–400 for the Bulgarian political immigrants in France in the post-World War II years. Vasileva, *Balgarskata politicheska emigratsia*, 90.
[79] Statelova and Tankova, *Prokudenite*, 17.
[80] Vasileva, *Balgarskata politicheska emigratsia*, 117–119.
[81] Vasileva, 125.
[82] Jakimova, "Migration and Assimilation," 132–133.
[83] Vasileva, *Balgarskata politicheska emigratsia*, 125.
[84] Vasileva, 61–62, 65.
[85] Vasileva, 134.

The United States was an attractive destination for a number of the Bulgarian post-World War II emigrants. As in the case with other countries, the exact number of the immigrants cannot be assessed. In his study on Bulgarian immigration, Veselin Traykov suggests, based on various data, that between the end of World War II and 1975, at least 7,000 – 8,000 Bulgarians emigrated to North America.[86] This number might call into question the previously cited statement of the Bulgarian Minister of the Interior that about 10,500 Bulgarian citizens escaped from the country before 1977, as that would leave less than 4,000 Bulgarian emigrants for the rest of the world. For a more precise and fully convincing assessment, however, further research and more sources are needed.

In earlier periods, Bulgarian immigrants used to settle in the American Midwest and the Northeast. Preferred cities were: Philadelphia, Pennsylvania; Cleveland and Dayton, Ohio; Chicago, Illinois; Detroit, Michigan; St. Louis, Missouri; and New York City. A smaller number of Bulgarians settled in the West and Northwest. Other cities in which larger numbers of Bulgarians lived included: Gary, Fort Wayne, and Indianapolis, Indiana and Los Angeles, California.[87] The "new" post-World War II immigration is concentrated mostly in the states of New York, Illinois, Ohio, and California.[88]

Regarding the factors that stood behind the inflow and outflow of people during the period discussed, they could be defined roughly as internal and external, frequently intertwined. The internal factors had to do with the ideology of the Communist regime and the realities of life under it. The external ones stemmed from the multifaceted manifestations of the confrontation between the two key adversaries in the Cold War. Both ideological reasons and foreign-policy considerations stood behind the Bulgarian government's decision to accept the Greek political emigrants and help them start new lives in Bulgaria. The realities of life under Communism and the existence of another system on the opposite side of the Iron Curtain predetermined the flight from the country of the Bulgarians for whom it was impossible to live or even survive under the rules enforced by the Communist state. The Bulgarian Turks left the country both because of the hardships forced upon them by the authorities – expropriation of their land, forceful change of their names, and the power play between the two sides in the Cold War confrontation. Part of the reason behind the Bulgarian authorities' desire to quickly homogenize Bulgarian society by changing the Turkish and Arabic names of the Bulgarian Turks sprang from fear of the influence the NATO member across the border could exert on them. The result for the country was the loss of bright and independent minds as well as of a hard-working population that could have been instrumental to shaping a different future for it.

---

86 Traykov, *Istoria na balgarskata emigratsia*, 26.
87 "Bulgarian Emigration," Bulgarian-American Community Portal, http://dirbg.us/bg-history/bulgarian-emigration (accessed 3 May 2018). For detailed information about Bulgarians' places of settlement see Traykov, *Istoria na balgarskata emigratsia*, 37–59.
88 Traykov, *Istoria na balgarskata emigratsia*, 26.

3.4 Political activities in exile

Bulgarian émigrés came from the entire political spectrum – left, center, and right. Among the larger émigré organizations, the Bulgarian National Front (both its wings) and the Bulgarian Provisional Representation shared right-wing ideas. The Union of Free Bulgarians, the *Balgarsko ognishte* circle, and the Free Bulgarian Center were ideologically rather center-oriented. The Bulgarian National Committee "Free and Independent Bulgaria," the Bulgarian Liberation Movement, the Bulgarian Agrarian National Union *Vrabcha 1* and the political formations of the social democrats and the anarchists belonged to the left-wing part of the spectrum.[89]

Researchers differentiate two stages in the development of émigré organizations. During the first stage, involving the establishment of the organizations, their leaders were political emigrants forced to leave Bulgaria out of fear for their lives. This period ended about the time of Georgi Mihov Dimitrov's death in 1972. He was known as *Gemeto* and was one of the most prominent figures of Bulgarian emigration. The second stage, covering the period from the early 1970s to the early 1990s, was characterized by the emergence of new leaders, either raised and educated in the West, or newly-emigrated from Bulgaria.[90]

Among the Bulgarian émigré organizations, two unquestionably stood out as the major and most enduring ones, namely, the Bulgarian National Committee for a Free and Independent Bulgaria (BNC) and the Bulgarian National Front (BNF). The rest of the formations, to use the words of the editors of the documentary volume on Bulgarian "hostile" emigration, either gravitated around them, or acted as their divisions.[91]

With the exception of the BNC's prototype, created much earlier, in 1941, in Cairo,[92] perhaps the earliest formation was the short-lived (16 September 1944–10 May 1945) Bulgarian government-in-exile in Vienna. It was headed by the leader of the National Social Movement and former Prime Minister Aleksandar Tsankov. De-

---

89 Statelova and Tankova, *Prokudenite*, 5.
90 Introduction to *Darzhavna sigurnost i vrazheskite emigrantski organizatsii, 1945–1989: Dokumentalen sbornik* (Sofia: COMDOS, 2014), 13.
91 *Darzhavna sigurnost i vrazheskite emigrantski organizatsii*, 13. Information as well as documents about formations like the Council of One Hundred (Savet na stote), the Bulgarian Provisional Representation (Vremenno balgarsko predstavitelstvo), Organization of Free Bulgarians (Organizatsia na svobodnite balgari), American-Bulgarian League (Amerikano-balgarska liga), Bulgarian Anti-Bolshevik Union (Balgarski protivobolshevishki sayuz) – later developed into BNF, All-Bulgarian Union for National Salvation (Obshtobalgarski sayuz za natsionalno spasenie), Bulgarian League for Rights of Exiled Persons (Balgarska liga za pravata na choveka v izgnanie), Bulgarian Liberation Movement (Balgarsko osvoboditelno dvizhenie) – created after the decline of the BNC, and about the Bulgarian collaboration with the American Slav Committee can be found in the vast work of the chronicler of the Bulgarian immigration to North America Ivan Gadjev. – Gadjev, *Istoria na balgarskata emigratsia*, vol. 2, 203–264, 311–324.
92 Gadjev, *Istoria na balgarskata emigratsia*, vol. 2, 188.

vised as a counterpoint to the newly established (9 September 1944) Fatherland Front government in Bulgaria, it did not outlive Germany's defeat in the war.[93]

Naturally, there existed emigrant organizations founded long before the Communist takeover of Bulgaria, which had their own agenda and position about post-World War II developments. In this respect, of interest are for instance the activities and relationship between the Macedonian Patriotic Organization (MPO) and Ivan (Vancho) Mihaylov (1896–1990), the longstanding and widely revered leader of the Internal Macedonian Revolutionary Organization (IMRO).

The efforts of Macedonian-Bulgarian associations in North America, dating back to the late 1890s and early 1900s, to unite the Bulgarian immigrants resulted in the foundation of the Macedonian Patriotic Organization (until 1952 named Macedonian Political Organization) in 1922 in Fort Wayne, Indiana. During the 1920s conflict between the *Mihaylovists* and *Protogerovists* in the old country, the MPO, described by Dr. Ilia Gadjev as the largest and strongest organization of Bulgarian immigrants, maintained a neutral position, but it took Ivan Mihaylov's side in 1930.[94] Completely different was the organization's position concerning the Bulgarian-Macedonian National Union. The latter was strongly criticized by the MPO for its Comintern-inspired stand on the existence of a separate "Macedonian nation."[95]

From the late 1940s onwards, Ivan Mihaylov, in exile in Italy since 1944, maintained close contact with the MPO, taking the position of ideological leader of the Macedonian liberation movement despite the IMRO's inactivity. Between the 1950s and the 1970s, he wrote his memoirs, which were published by the Central Committee of the MPO in four volumes.[96]

Due to the change in governmental policy towards Macedonia in the 1960s, contacts developed in the 1970s and 1980s between the MPO and Bulgarian scholarly and patriotic circles. After the disintegration of Yugoslavia, the MPO, similarly to the Bulgarian government, provided help to the newly announced Republic of Macedonia.[97]

---

[93] On Tsankov's activities after the 9 September 1944 coup in Bulgaria see Gadjev, 141–159.
[94] Gadjev, 330.
[95] Trendafil Mitev, "MPO in the United States, Canada and Australia," http://macedonia.kroraina.com/en/mpo (accessed 3 May 2018).
[96] Mitev.
[97] Mitev. Until recently, due to the dispute with Greece over the use of the name "Macedonia," the country was being accepted in international organizations under the provisional description "Former Yugoslav Republic of Macedonia." After the Prespa agreement, signed by Greece and Macedonia on 17 June 2018, a referendum in the latter is expected to decide whether it would adopt the name "Republic of North Macedonia."

3.4.1 The Bulgarian National Committee and the Bulgarian National Front

Both émigré organizations were founded in 1948. What they had in common besides the time of their establishment, was their firm stand against Communism and the desire to change the political system in post-1944 Bulgaria. While the Bulgarian National Committee (BNC), led by Dr. Georgi Dimitrov, had its political base in an alliance of agrarians, democrats, social democrats, anarchists, and independents – all having opposed the pre-World War II political system in Bulgaria, the Bulgarian National Front (BNF) under Ivan Dochev and Hristo Statev united former participants and supporters of the previous regime. It included adherents of the Union of the Bulgarian National Legions, former diplomats and army officers, intellectuals as well as followers of organizations such as Ratnik, Stozher, and Otets Paisiy. The BNF criticized the BNC for the Bulgarian Agrarian National Union's earlier collaboration with the Communists in the Fatherland Front. The BNC on its part could not agree with the BNF's stand on the question of "monarchy or republic," being a firm supporter of the latter.[98]

Within the BNF itself, the question of collaborating with the former Tsar Simeon Saxe-Coburg-Gotha and his Madrid circle caused disagreement that led to the organization's split in 1959. It was divided into the BNF *Svoboda* (Freedom) under Hristo Statev that firmly supported the former monarch's initiative of drawing émigrés closer to himself in a Provisional Bulgarian Representation, and Ivan Dochev's BNF *Borba* (Struggle), part of whose members were inclined to collaborate with other parties and groups, including the anti-monarchist BANU. "We did not break openly with the tsar and the palace," reminisces BNF activist prof. Spas Raikin, "but we did not tolerate being treated as mute letters." He admits that he and his associates had to overcome serious difficulties since many of their co-members were inveterate monarchists and for them the Tsar's crown shone more brightly than the arguments in favor of upholding the independence of their organization.[99]

Both the BNC and the BNF had branches they could rely on in many West European countries, the United States, Canada, Australia, and South America. They participated in international organizations, such as the Assembly of Captive European Nations (ACEN) and the International Peasants' Union (where the BNC was active) as well as the Anti-Bolshevik Bloc of Nations (ABN) and the World Anti-Communist

---

98 See Ogoyski, *Zapiski za balgarskite stradania*, vol. 2, 200; Ogoyski, *Zapiski za balgarskite stradania*, vol. 3, 159–161; Paraskevov, "Small but Vociferous," 153–155; Maria Kokoncheva, "Democracy in Exile: The Bulgarian National Committee and G.M. Dimitrov," in *The Inauguration of "Organized Political Warfare": Cold War Organizations Sponsored by the National Committee for a Free Europe/Free Europe Committee*, ed. Katalin Kádár Lynn (Saint Helena, CA: Helena History Press, 2013), 371–376; Gadjev, *Istoria na balgarskata emigratsia v Severna Amerika*, vol. 2, 118, 279, 289.
99 Spas Raikin: *Politichesko pateshestvie sreshtu vetrovete na XX vek*, vol. 7 (Sofia: Pensoft, 2004), 2–3; Paraskevov, "Small but Vociferous," 154. A detailed account of the split in the BNF is given in Gadjev, *Istoria na balgarskata emigratsia v Severna Amerika*, vol. 2, 281–287.

League (WACL) of which the BNF was a member. They published their own periodicals, as well as other material and tried to convince Western policy makers and public opinion that harder measures were needed for the liberation of the Eastern Bloc countries from Communist oppression. The activities directed towards Bulgarians at home included active participation of the Bulgarian immigrants in the work of the Western radio stations with broadcasts for the countries behind the Iron Curtain.[100]

A matter of grave importance was the support, both financial and political, for émigrés' activities, which largely depended on their relations with the governmental institutions of their host countries, mainly the United States which they regarded as the foremost force in the struggle against Soviet domination in East-Central Europe.[101] The better the leadership of an émigré organization was received by these institutions, the more aid it could rely on. This inevitably stirred up rivalry and caused displeasure among the less fortunate émigré leaders and organizations.

One of the reasons for contention between the BNC and the BNF was the relations with the National Committee for a Free Europe (later known as Free Europe Committee), founded in March 1949 in New York with the task of spreading US influence in Europe as a counteraction against Soviet leverage there. The most substantial part of the funding for the FEC came from the Central Intelligence Agency (CIA).[102]

It was natural for the BNC to be chosen as the Bulgarian partner of the Free Europe Committee. As Jordan Baev points out, for the CIA and the State Department, it had been the main target group among the Bulgarian political emigrants and contacts with Dr. G.M. Dimitrov and his associates had already been established during the war.[103]

The BNC was involved in the CIA's first covert operation against Bulgaria QKSTAIR, later renamed BGCONVOY (1950–1955).[104] CIA officers maintained confidential connections with Dr. Georgi Dimitrov in Washington, D.C. and New York, his representatives, Tsenko Barev and Slavi Neykov, in Western Europe, and with

---

100 See the documentary volume about the Bulgarian State Security and the "hostile" radio stations. – *Darzhavna sigurnost i "vrazheskite" radiostantsii* (Sofia: COMDOS, 2014).
101 About Bulgarian émigrés' contacts with the Americans, "whom they saw as the most effective opponent of the Soviet Union," see Paraskevov, "Small but Vociferous," 155–156. According to Anna Mazurkiewicz, who also remarks upon the fact that the political immigrants "invariably recognized the United States as their most powerful ally in the struggle for the liberation of their fatherlands," it is doubtful whether "in the late 1940s any of the European states was ready to support such a wide representation of immigrants on its soil, clearly opposing the maintenance of the *status quo* of the division of Europe and at the same time incurring the high costs (political and financial) connected with this." – See Anna Mazurkiewicz, *Uchodźcy polityczni z Europy Środkowo-Wschodniej w amerykańskiej polityce zimnowojennej 1948–1954* (Warsaw: Instytut Pamięci Narodowej; Gdańsk: Uniwersytet Gdański, 2016), 474, 476.
102 Mazurkiewicz, *Uchodźcy polityczni z Europy Środkowo-Wschodniej*, 210, 213–214, 477.
103 Jordan Baev, "BGCONVOY: Parvata tayna operatsia na TSRU v Bulgaria," *Geopolitika* 6 (2016): 151.
104 About the operation see Baev, "BGCONVOY," 149–158.

Stratia Skerlev in Turkey. Not long after the start of the operation, however, disagreement arose between the BNC leader and the Americans over the "Bulgarian" operation. A large part of the problem was Dr. Dimitrov's "dictatorial" behavior towards the rest of the Bulgarian émigré groups, his unwillingness to build a broader political basis for the BNC, and his insistence on maintaining control over the agents involved.[105]

Concerning the Free Europe Committee's attitude to the other main Bulgarian émigré organization, the BNF, while staunchly anti-Communist, was in a rather precarious position due to its leadership's wartime relations to Nazi Germany. Moreover, Dr. Dimitrov was firmly against any dealings with the BNF. Despite repeated protests on the part of the BNF's leaders, the Committee was not allotted official funding from the FEC. However, CIA representatives held confidential meetings with Ivan Dochev, the leader of the BNF. In 1951, the BNF leadership sent a letter to the Supreme Allied Commander Europe General Dwight Eisenhower and the Chief of Staff, Supreme Headquarters Allied Powers Europe General Alfred Gruenther. It proposed that BNF volunteers be trained on US bases in Greece and Turkey for clandestine crossing into Bulgaria in the case of a surprise attack by the Soviet Bloc. Not wanting to be considered foreign agents, the authors of the letter insisted that the training be carried out under the "united defense of Europe" slogan. In time, the BNF was allotted certain funds for its activities and Ivan Dochev, who was included in the CIA's next operation in Bulgaria, ZRNAUNTLE (1956–1958), was given a monthly payment. In later years, however, things changed, and Ivan Dochev blamed the CIA for having contributed to the split in the BNF.[106]

Discussing the situation in Bulgaria, the authors of a 1955 US intelligence analysis conclude that, until 1952, the BNC had been the most authoritative among the émigré organizations, but that its influence had later decreased. The most prominent Bulgarian émigré leader, Dr. Dimitrov, it was said, was incapable of improving the situation. It was considered highly unlikely that organized resistance in the country could be built up under such conditions.[107]

After Dr. Dimitov's death in 1972, controversies surfaced within the organization about its leadership and future policy. For a short time, the BNC was headed by Nikola Petkov's nephew, Dimitar Petkov Kravarev, and thereafter by Iskar Shumanov, who became the main BNC figure in the United States. In Paris, Tsenko Barev was at the helm of the organization. Divisions within the organization led to his founding the Bulgarian Liberation Movement in 1963.[108]

---

[105] Baev, "BGCONVOY," 151–152.
[106] Baev, "BGCONVOY," 153–154; Mazurkiewicz, *Uchodźcy polityczni z Europy Środkowo-Wschodniej*, 305–306, 398.
[107] Baev, "BGCONVOY," 152.
[108] Ogoyski, *Zapiski za balgarskite stradania*, vol. 2, 202; Ogoyski, vol. 3, 160.

George Paprikoff succeeded Ivan Dochev as BNF leader in 1981. Since then, until his death in 2005, Dochev was honorary chairman of the organization.[109]

3.4.2 Unfulfilled hopes and disappointment

Unfortunately, the consolidation of the Bulgarian émigré organizations proved to be an impossible mission. The efforts of the US hosts could not convince Dr. Dimitrov to reorganize the Bulgarian National Committee. Ideally, in addition to the already existing participants (eight representatives of BANU's left wing, two social democrats, two representatives of the *Zveno* political circle, and two non-party members), it would also include at least three representatives of BANU's right wing, two democrats, as well as persons from the cultural, academic, and religious circles, thus acquiring a more representative character. According to these plans, no political group was to dominate the Committee, which was to declare itself a non-partisan democratic organization. After more than two years, facing Dr. Dimitrov's unyielding opposition to these demands, the CIA and the FEC decided to cease the attempts at reorganizing the BNC and instead try to organize a group of young émigrés who could serve US interests.[110]

It seems that Bulgarian émigré leaders were incapable of putting behind old grievances and party loyalty in the name of the greater goal. Instead, personal ambitions intervened and political games were played that only deepened the division. Both political activists' complaints and observations by representatives of US institutions present the picture of mutual accusations, arbitrarily taken decisions, threats of deportation, and violence towards Bulgarians in refugee camps in Europe where followers were recruited. Examining this problem, Anna Mazurkiewicz notes that this kind of behavior among the Bulgarian émigrés was unusual even in comparison with other émigré groups.[111]

However, besides divisions among Bulgarian émigrés, including ones within the particular organizations, there was another serious problem recognized by at least some of the politically active immigrants. They were disappointed and frustrated with what they judged to be a lack of tangible, consistent support from the West for the nations suffering under Communist rule. A case in point here are the thoughts voiced by the history professor Spas Raikin (1922–2014), who as a young man escaped from Bulgaria in 1951 and settled in the United States. Raikin, an active member of the Bulgarian National Front until 1964 and Secretary General (1960–1962) of the

---

109 Gadjev, *Istoria na balgarskata emigratsia v Severna Amerika*, vol. 2, 289.
110 Mazurkiewicz, *Uchodźcy polityczni z Europy Środkowo-Wschodniej*, 309–313; Baev, "BGCONVOY," 151–152.
111 Mazurkiewicz, *Uchodzcy polityczni z Europy Srodkowo-Wschodniej*, 305–312; See also Gadjev, *Istoria na balgarskata emigratsia*, vol. 2, 188, 190–196, 205–207, 260–261, 279, 289, 305–311, 326–327, 330–338; Ogoyski, *Zapiski za balgarskite stradania*, vol. 2, 200.

American Friends of the Anti-Bolshevik Bloc of Nations[112], recalls the time of his defection to Greece and the offers to remain in Bulgaria as a guerilla fighter against the Communists,

> The British and the Americans hid in mouse-holes and no one could see them anywhere. Oh, they gave speeches, they cursed Communism, they shouted on the radio what great evil Communism was, how the Communists were enslaving and robbing the poor people, as if these people were not experiencing the Communists' cruelties and terror every day, that they, from thousands of kilometers away, had to remind them of that, to incite them to rise against their oppressors (...) without lifting a finger to help them.[113]

Prof. Raikin saw the reasons for the demoralization among the émigré circles not only in the lack of a democratic spirit and the excessive ambitions for leadership, but also in the policy pursued by the foreign agencies:

> These agencies not only 'inform' the Bulgarian people about the developments in the world. They seek ways to 'form' the public opinion in Bulgaria. Millions of dollars and pounds are paid by foreign governments for this 'formation' of the public opinion in Bulgaria. (...) If the interests of these foreign powers require Bulgaria to remain under Communist rule or the Bulgarian people to stay docile, the 'formation' of the public opinion will follow in that direction. (...) If these interests require the demoralization of the Bulgarian emigration, they will demoralize it; if these interests require the weakening of the resistance movement in Bulgaria, they will weaken it; if these interests require the kindling of the resistance movement in Bulgaria, they will kindle it; if these interests require the elimination of certain ideological trends among the Bulgarian émigrés, they will eliminate them; if these interests require the elimination of certain Bulgarian groups or prominent Bulgarian leaders in emigration, they will eliminate them; if these interests require the promotion of certain groups and certain leaders in emigration or in the opinion of the Bulgarian people, they will promote them.[114]

Naturally, Prof. Raikin's comments might be seen as an overstatement or they might be ascribed to his former affiliation with a less privileged émigré organization. Nevertheless, they exemplify the bitter realization of the realities of foreign policy.

Lack of unity and insufficient help from the West were not the only issues Bulgarian political emigrants faced. Throughout the entire period between 1944 and 1989 they had a strong adversary to be wary of – the Bulgarian State Security.

---

112 On Spas Raikin see Detelina Dineva, "The 'Master of Several Trades' and the Historian: The Stories of Two Exiled Bulgarian Intellectuals during the Cold War Years," *Bulgarian Historical Review* 3–4 (2014): 220–230.
113 Spas Raikin, *Politichesko pateshestvie sreshtu vetrovete na XX v.* vol. 1: *Sinya i chervena Bulgaria* (Sofia-Moskva: Pensoft, 2000), 352.
114 Spas Raikin, *Politicheski problemi pred balgarskata obshtestvenost v chuzhbina*, vol. 2, 239–240.

3.4.3 Bulgarian State Security and émigré organizations

A lot can be said about the activities of the State Security directed towards "hostile émigrés," as the Bulgarians abroad who protested against the regime in the country and engaged in fighting against it were called in the documents of the Bulgarian State Security. Substantial resources were used for gaining control over emigration leaders and for generating and aggravating the already existing conflicts among the émigrés on both a personal and an organizational level.[115]

The State Security Service (from 1952, State Security Committee) was established in 1947, with some of its directorates engaged solely in fighting against "hostile emigration." Initially, measures against the émigrés were the domain of the foreign intelligence service (from 1970, First Main Directorate). The counterintelligence service, the Second Main Directorate also played an important role in this. In 1968, a special unit, the Sixth Directorate, was set up to fight the "centers of ideological subversion on capitalist territory." Reorganization within the committee led in the late 1970s to the creation of an operational group that combined senior members of the First, Second, and Sixth Directorates, whose task was to organize and coordinate the operational work on immigration in the Western countries.[116]

Operations against the "hostile emigration" intensified during the mid-1970s. According to researcher Jordan Baev, a likely reason for that may have been the intelligence received about the efforts for uniting political emigrants and for starting actions against Bulgarian missions abroad. The organizations under greatest suspicion were the Bulgarian Liberation Organization led by Tsenko Barev and Ivan Dochev's Bulgarian National Front. Following a Politburo decision, in the spring of 1978, the Minister of the Interior signed an order envisioning activities on the part of the State Security directed towards the "political, ideological, and organizational demoralization, discrediting and isolation of Bulgarian enemy emigration."[117]

Documents in the collection *The State Security and Hostile Émigré Organizations, 1945–1989*, published by the COMDOS, give evidence of the role played by the State Security in corroding relations among émigré groups. They show the "sheer scale of State Security resources and manpower invested to control émigré leaders and implant suspicion in their midst." It is in these types of activities of the State Security that researchers see one of the main reasons for the lack of unity and more effective cooperation among Bulgarian political emigration circles. The conclusion reached is

---

115 Introduction *Darzhavna sigurnost i vrazheskite emigrantski organizatsii*, 13.
116 Jordan Baev, "Bulgarian Regime Countermeasures against Radio Free Europe," in *Cold War Broadcasting: Impact on the Soviet Union and Eastern Europe: A Collection of Studies and Documents*, ed. A. Ross Johnson and Russell Eugene Parta (Budapest – New York: Central European University Press, 2010), 260–261.
117 Baev, "Bulgarian Regime Countermeasures against Radio Free Europe," 268–269.

that the State Security "successfully eliminated the émigré threat, and thus fulfilled its primary mission."[118]

In hindsight, it could be said that the active measures of the State Security against political emigration (sometimes even including kidnappings abroad and assassinations[119]), together with the lack of consistent, sufficient support from the West, defined the ineffectiveness of the émigré organizations' fight against the regime in the home country.

3.5 Migration since 1989

It is difficult, if not impossible, to assess the loss of human potential for Bulgaria resulting from emigration. Certain assessments can be made only with regard to the economy and only in relation to a short period. Thus, according to one of the estimates made so far, in the period between 1986 and 1992, the human resource exported amounted to 19.6 million years of life and 11.4 million years of labor.[120]

Lack of access to reliable up-to-date data about population flows is a grave problem for researchers, who point to the fact that Bulgaria is the only EU member state that does not have comparable annual statistics on migration processes.[121]

Census data (2011) shows that, since the early 1990s, Bulgaria has been a net emigration country. According to estimates, in the course of twenty years, starting from 1992, "emigration represented a six percent loss in the total population, and a ten percent loss considering only the active population."[122]

In contrast to the period under Communist rule, when in the words of Bulgarian researcher Anna Krasteva there was minimum migration and maximum migration policy in Bulgaria, the post-1989 period was characterized by minimum migration policy and maximum migration.[123] Krasteva discerns three characteristics and three periods in the Bulgarian post-1989 migration policy. The first period, starting in the 1990s, was a time of withdrawal of the state from problems related to migration. From a top priority during Communism, migration became a minor political issue, to be dealt with by no other specialized institutions than the Agency for Bul-

---

118 Introduction to *Darzhavna Sigurnost i vrazheskite emigrantski organizatsii*, 13.
119 See Hristo Hristov, "Prestapleniyata po vreme na komunisticheskia rezhim i opitite za tyahnoto razsledvane sled 10 noemvri 1989 g.," http://www.decommunization.org/Articles/Hristov4.htm (accessed 3 May 2018).
120 Mintchev, "External Migration," 134.
121 See Georgi Angelov and Zvezda Vankova, "Aktualni tendentsii v transgranichnata migratsia ot i kam Bulgaria spored drugi pokazateli," in *Tendentsii v transgranichnata migratsia na rabotna sila i svobodnoto dvizhenie na hora – efekti za Bulgaria: Doklad*, ed. Ivanka Ivanova (Sofia: Institut "Otvoreno obshtestvo," 2010), 52–55; Krasteva, "Bulgarian Migration Profile," 189–190, 195.
122 OECD, *International Migration Outlook 2012* (Paris: OECD Publishing, 2012), 216, https://doi.org/10.1787/migr_outlook-2012-en.
123 Krasteva, "Bulgarian Migration Profile," 192–193.

garians Abroad and the State Agency for Refugees. Krasteva describes the political discourse during this period as "concerned with the brain drain and the massive emigration of young Bulgarians," but with no appropriate policies developed or applied.[124]

The second period (the beginning of 2000–2007) was one of institutionalization, "built on two main pillars: Ministry of the Interior – Directorate of Migration and Ministry of Labor and Social Policy." With the beginning of the third period in 2007, greater importance began to be placed on migration policy.[125]

As far as the characteristics of Bulgarian post-1989 migration policy are concerned, they were as follows: late inclusion of migration policy in government priorities; very quick acceleration of the process of strategic vision development; and a redefinition of the major priorities of migration policy. While economic emigration and the integration of foreign citizens into Bulgarian society were the focus of the 2008 strategy, in later times, the stress shifted to security issues.[126]

3.6 Archives and Literature

Multifaceted sources on migration to and from the country are kept in several rich archival collections in Bulgaria. Valuable data for the Cold War period both from the point of view of internal migration-related problems and external developments related to them can be found in the collections of the Bulgarian Central State Archives, and especially in the BCP Funds (the archives of the Bulgarian Communist Party).

Of particular significance for the researchers of Bulgarian emigration during the period between the 9 September 1944 coup d'état and the end of 1989 are the collections of the Centralized Archives of the Committee for Disclosing the Documents and Announcing Affiliation of Bulgarian Citizens to the State Security and the Intelligence Services of the Bulgarian National Army (cited in this publication as COMDOS). Especially important here are the archives of the National Intelligence Service (Fund 2: Investigation Files on Persons, and Fund 4: Institution Files) and of the Ministry of the Interior.

While the archives of the Bulgarian Communist Party and particularly the documents of its Central Committee and Politburo throw light on the information presented to the party leadership and expose the decision-making process in relation to both the internal and the foreign policy during the period examined, the collections of the COMDOS show how the decisions with regard to what used to be defined as "hostile

---

[124] Krasteva, "Bulgarian Migration Profile," 202.
[125] Krasteva, "Bulgarian Migration Profile," 203.
[126] Krasteva, "Bulgarian Migration Profile," 203–204.

émigrés" and "hostile émigré organizations" were implemented in practice. The latter collections also provide information about the Bulgarian political emigration.

In recent years, the Bulgarian Historical Archives at the Saints Cyril and Methodius National Library have been enriched with the personal archives of prominent Bulgarian political emigrants. They contain information about the activities of immigrant organizations in Europe, the United States, Canada and other countries. Among these organizations are the Bulgarian Free Centre, Bulgarian Jurists in Exile, the Bulgarian Immigrant Society in France, and the Bulgarian Immigrant Society in Spain.

A case of special interest to the researcher is the extensive private collection of Dr. Ivan Gadjev (1937–2017) dedicated to the preservation of the memory of the Bulgarian immigrants to North America.[127] Dr. Gadjev, who escaped from Bulgaria in 1968 and built a new life for himself in the United States, brought to Bulgaria and housed in a specially constructed building in the town of Gotse Delchev tens of tons of books, archival material, photographs, and tapes. His collection of more than a million pages contains private archives of Bulgarian immigrants to the United States and Canada, documents, journals and newspapers of Bulgarian émigré organizations, as well as recorded reminiscences of immigrants, many of whom are no longer alive.

Of the foreign archives, of special interest to the researcher are the collections kept at the Hoover Institution at Stanford University. The Spas Raikin Papers, those of Kyril Drenikoff and Dora Gabensky, as well as other material, contain important information about the life and activities of Bulgarian political emigrants.

During the pre-1989 years, both inward and outward migration was usually a topic of research as part of broader studies on particular events and processes in the history of Bulgaria. As far as publications on Bulgarian political emigration are concerned, they were sparse not only due to ideological reasons, but also due to the inaccessibility of the archives of the Ministry of the Interior, Ministry of Foreign Affairs, and the collections of the (then) Central Communist Party Archives until the end of 1989. Émigré periodicals at the National Library were classified as sensitive and were thus inaccessible to researchers. An attempt in the mid-1980s for compiling emigration-related material by a specially created unit at the Bulgarian Academy of Sciences was quickly terminated.[128]

Only two pre-1989 works dealt with the problems of Bulgarian emigration. One of them, *Bulgarians in Australia*, written by Simeon Damyanov and Lyuben Berov after a brief visit to Australia in 1984, was published in 300 copies "for official use."[129] The other one was Boyka Vasileva's study on *The Bulgarian Political Emigration after*

---

[127] http://www.bgemigration.org (accessed 3 May 2018).
[128] Statelova and Tankova, *Prokudenite*, 6; Vasileva, *Balgarskata politicheska emigratsia*, 5.
[129] Simeon Damyanov and Lyuben Berov, *Balgarite v Avstralia* (Sofia: Izdatelstvo na BAN, 1986).

9 September 1944.¹³⁰ It is mostly based on information from émigré periodicals kept at the BDIC – Nanterre. Both publications are ideologically colored.¹³¹

Earlier, outside Bulgaria, Nikolay Altankov published his study on *The Bulgarian-Americans*¹³² and George Paprikoff published a bibliography of the publications of Bulgarian emigrants.¹³³

Since the early 1990s, an increasing number of publications about Bulgarian emigration and its activities have been appearing.¹³⁴ Noteworthy scholarly works include Elena Statelova's and Vasilka Tankova's monograph about the political organizations of the Bulgarian emigrants *The Banished*¹³⁵ and the earlier publication by Boyka Vasileva, *The Bulgarian Political Emigration after the Second World War*.¹³⁶ The latter work, however, lacks the scope and depth of the former. Impressively well researched, based on a number of publications both by émigrés and researchers and on material from the State Central Archives, is Boyko Kiryakov's study *Bulgaria Abroad*.¹³⁷

A number of publications by prominent political emigrants: Ivan Dochev, Tsenko Barev, Spas Raikin, Ivan Gadjev, Panayot Panayotov, Stefan Gruev, Toncho Karabulkov, and many others, provide the opportunity of looking at the their lives and activities as well as the attitude towards them by authorities both in Bulgaria and abroad.¹³⁸

Three books by investigative journalist Hristo Hristov examine the operations of the State Security against the political emigrants, with two of them investigating the murder of Georgi Markov: *State Security against the Bulgarian Emigration, Kill 'Wan-*

---

130 Boyka Vasileva, "Balgarskata politicheska emigratsia sled 9 septemvri 1944 g.," in *Izvestia na Balgarskoto istorichesko druzhestvo*, vol. 39 (Sofia: BAN, 1987), 257–288.
131 See Statelova and Tankova, *Prokudenite*, 6–7.
132 Altankov, *The Bulgarian-Americans*.
133 George I. Paprikoff, *Works of Bulgarian Emigrants: An Annotated Bibliography* (Chicago: Stanka K. Paprikoff, 1985).
134 A survey of the works about the organizations of Bulgarian émigrés published until 2002 is given in the monograph *The Banished* – Statelova and Tankova, *Prokudenite*, 6–12. Both earlier and more recent publications are briefly commented on by Boyko Kiryakov in his study "Bulgaria Abroad." Kiryakov, – "Bulgaria zad granitsa," 78, 81–83, 91–93, 95, 98, 102–103, 105.
135 Statelova and Tankova, *Prokudenite*.
136 Vasileva, *Balgarskata politicheska emigratsia sled Vtorata svetovna voyna*.
137 Kiryakov, "Bulgaria zad granitsa".
138 Ivan Dochev, *Shest desetiletia borba protiv komunizma za svobodata na Bulgaria* (Plovdiv: Pigmalion, 1995); Tsenko Barev, *S pero v izgnanie*, book 1–3 (Sofia: Robinzon, 1993); Spas Raikin, *Politichesko pateshestvie*; Spas Raikin, *Politicheski problemi pred balgarskata obshtestvenost v chuzhbina*; Ivan Gadjev, *Istoria na balgarskata emigratsia*; Panayot Panayotov, *Moyat zhiteyski pat: Misli za Bulgaria* (Sofia: Gutenberg, 2002); Stefan Gruev, *Moyata odiseya* (Sofia: Obsidian, 2002); Toncho Karabulkov, *Za da ne izchezne nashiyat svyat s nas: Spomeni na edin politicheski emigrant* (Paris/Sofia: Svetat utre, 1999).

derer': *The Bulgarian and British State Policy on the 'Georgi Markov' Case*, and *The Double Life of Agent 'Piccadilly'*.[139]

Document collections of great value to researchers have been published. *The Other Bulgaria, 1944–1989* contains documents of nine émigré organizations.[140] The COMDOS has published (in Bulgarian) the following documentary volumes: *The State Security and the Hostile Émigré Organizations, 1945–1989* (2014), *State Security and the Hostile Radio Stations* (2014), *State Security and Border Troops* (2014), and *State Security and Minorities* (2015).

In recent years, post-1989 migration has been the topic of serious research. Among the publications worth mentioning are Anna Krasteva's *Bulgarian Migration Profile* and *The Balkan Migration Phenomenon* as well as Evelina Staikova's *Emigration and Immigration: Bulgarian Dilemmas*.[141] Two possible directions for further research may include: characteristics, national peculiarities, and external determinants of émigré activities in a comparative perspective; and political emigrants during the post-1989 years (activities and reflections).

---

139 Hristo Hristov, *Darzhavna sigurnost sreshtu balgarskata emigratsia* (Sofia: Izdatelska kashta "Ivan Vazov," 2000); Hristo Hristov, *Ubiyte "Skitnik": Balgarskata i britanskata politika po sluchaya "Georgi Markov"* (Sofia: Siela, 2005); Hristo Hristov, *Dvoyniyat zhivot na agent "Pikadili"* (Sofia: Ikonomedia, 2008).
140 Elena Statelova et al., *Drugata Bulgaria: Dokumenti za organizatsiite na balgarskata politicheska emigratsia 1944–1989* (Sofia: Anubis, 2000).
141 Krasteva, "Bulgarian Migration Profile"; Anna Krasteva, "Balkanskiyat migratsionen fenomen," https://annakrasteva.wordpress.com/2016/01/08/balkan-migration-phenomenon (accessed 3 May 2018); Evelina Staikova, "Emigration and Immigration: Bulgarian Dilemmas," *SEER Journal for Labor and Social Affairs in Eastern Europe* 16 (2013): 403–415.

4 Czechoslovakia

Michael Cude and Ellen Paul

4.1 Migrations in historical perspective

Émigré communities heavily influenced the history of former Czechoslovakia. Prior to its creation in 1918, the lands that would become Czechoslovakia saw the migration of over a million individuals to Western Europe, Russia, and the United States. This population shift was largely driven by economics, as individuals and families looked for new opportunities not comparably available in their homelands, to own property or gain employment within industrial workforces. A political component piggybacked on this migration, with individuals migrating to escape restrictions on national activities in former Austrian-Hungary. This was particularly relevant for the less populous ethnic minorities, such as the Slovaks and Rusyns, where immigrant communities developed particularistic national identities in some respect more cogently than many had within the homeland before World War I.

World War I would see the political component take prominence in the exile movement led by Tomáš Masaryk and others, which established the First Czechoslovak Republic in 1918. Masaryk's organization relied heavily on support from existing immigrant communities, who provided material and symbolic support in the effort to gain Western recognition of the new state. The creation of Czechoslovakia and changes in US immigration laws caused a decline in migration rates during the interwar period. In 1938, the fall of the First Republic, and the subsequent breakup of Czechoslovakia, gave rise to new political exile movements organized by former political leaders, notably former President Edvard Beneš. Beneš's movement eventually garnered support from the Allied leaders during World War II, producing the postwar Third Czechoslovak Republic until its fall after the February 1948 Communist coup.[1]

---

[1] Victor S. Mamatey, *The United States and East Central Europe, 1914–1918: A Study in Wilsonian Diplomacy and Propaganda* (Princeton: Princeton University Press, 1957). Otakar Odložilík, "The Czechs," and Victor S. Mamatey, "The Slovaks and Carpatho-Ruthenians," in *The Immigrants' Influence on Wilson's Peace Policies*, ed. Joseph P. O'Grady (Lexington: University of Kentucky, 1967), 224–249. Victor S. Mamatey and Radomir Luža, eds. *History of the Czechoslovak Republic, 1918–1948* (Princeton: Princeton University Press, 1973). Zbyněk Zeman, *The Masaryks: The Making of Czechoslovakia* (New York: Harper and Row, 1976). Igor Lukeš, *Czechoslovakia Between Stalin and Hitler: The Diplomacy of Edvard Beneš in the 1930s* (New York: Oxford University Press, 1996). Marian Mark Stolarik, "The Slovak League of America and the Canadian League in the Struggle for the Self-determination of the Nation, 1907–1992," *Slovakia* 39, 72 and 73 (2007): 7–35. Charmian Brinson and Marian Malet, eds. *Exile in and from Czechoslovakia during the 1930s and 1940s* (Amsterdam: Rodopi, 2009). Michael Cude, "The Imagined Exiles: Slovak-Americans and the Slovak Question during the First Czechoslovak Republic," in *From Exsilium to Exile: Coercion in Migration, Studia Historica Gedanensia*, vol. 5, ed. Anna Mazurkiewicz (Gdańsk: Wydawnictwo Uniwersytetu Gdańskiego, 2014), 287–305.

The experience of Communist-era exiles from Czechoslovakia differed from the prior generations of exiles. This period of exile lasted much longer, from roughly 1945 to 1989, and did not result in the exile movements establishing a new government with Western support. It also differed in that it included different stages of exiles, with separate groups leaving in 1945, 1948, and 1968. Each group fled Czechoslovakia under different circumstances and with different objectives and goals for anti-Communist activities. While national divisions had challenged the previous exile movements in important ways, the memory of World War II and the breakup of the First Republic caused even more acrimony and division among Cold War exiles, particularly between the Czechs and the Slovaks and Sudeten Germans.

The historiographical concerns surrounding the Cold War exiles from Czechoslovakia largely fall into three main categories: 1) debates over the effectiveness of the exile organizations, 2) debates over how to interpret competing national organizations, and 3) debates over the value of Western government support.

This chapter will show how much of the historiography is consistent when interpreting the effectiveness of exile organizations, including a mix of criticism and sympathy. Most historians judge the organizations as well intended, but undermined by long-standing political and personal rivalries among the individuals involved and by a sense of hopelessness with the West's de-facto acceptance of the Iron Curtain over the region. Igor Lukeš, for example, argues that the exile leaders "were honest, patriotic and thoroughly decent people who were no more infallible and charismatic as leaders in exile than they had been as politicians in Czechoslovakia. They were capable party administrators, not men that others would follow through thick and thin," along with being far away from home, with no access to events there, and little money with which to work. The individual leaders differed in outlook and personality, and many cooperated solely based on the common trait of being an anti-Communist exiles. They made a noble effort to organize themselves to inform the world about the problems of Czechoslovakia under communism but were undermined by these factors.[2] Scholars more laudatory of the exile organizations, such as Francis Dostál Raška, likewise argue that the exiles' support for refugees and involvement in international organizations proved to be their most effective activities. Most historians also credit the exiles' political activities in the late Cold War, after 1968, to have been much more effective than in the early Cold War.[3]

---

[2] Igor Lukeš, "Czechoslovak Political Exile in the Cold War: The Early Years," *The Polish Review* 47, no. 3 (2002): 332–343. Martin Nekola provides a similar, albeit more laudatory, interpretation. Martin Nekola, "Petr Zenkl: The Leader of the Czechoslovak Exile in the United States," in *East Central Europe in Exile: Transatlantic Identities*, vol. 2, ed. Anna Mazurkiewicz (Newcastle upon Tyne: Cambridge Scholars, 2013), 169–176.

[3] Francis D. Raška, "History of the Council of Free Czechoslovakia," in *The Inauguration of Organized Political Warfare*, ed. Katalin Kádár Lynn (Saint Helena, CA: Helena History Press, 2013), 71–120; Francis Dostál Raška, *Fighting Communism from Afar: The Council of Free Czechoslovakia* (Boulder:

The most disputed postwar issue continues to be the treatment of Czechoslovakia's ethnic minorities. This chapter will show how nationality questions sharply divided the exile movements during the Cold War. The same arguments continue to bleed into the current historiography. This is the area where the historical scholarship is most highly politicized and remains rancorous at its extremes. Perspectives on the nationality questions differ radically based on national and political orientation. Czech and Czechoslovakist scholars tend to absolve the Czechoslovak organizations on the nationality questions and consistently disparage minority group activities not affiliated with the Czechoslovak organizations. Scholars sympathetic to groups such as the Slovak autonomists or the Sudeten Germans tend to be much more critical of Czechoslovak organizations for what they perceived as unfair treatment of national minorities.[4]

Additionally, Western government support for exiles is a topic of scrutiny. Most historians criticize the West's treatment of Czechoslovakia's exiles. They present this support as, generally, meager and underutilized. These historians make this criticism even though they openly recognize that there was little real possibility to reverse the Communist domination of Czechoslovakia. In contrast, the Western governments, particularly the United States, did provide resources that expanded exile activity, including their early support for refugees and the later involvement in Cold War Radio. They did so despite ample reason not to, given the internal dysfunction among Czechoslovakia's Cold War exiles.[5]

East European Monographs, 2008); Francis D. Raška, *Long Road to Victory: A History or Czechoslovak Exile Organizations after 1968* (Boulder: East European Monographs, 2012).
4 For a good overview of these divides, see: Prokop Tomek, "The Highs and Lows of Czech and Slovak Émigré Activism," in *Anti-Communist Minorities in the US: Political Activism of Ethnic Refugees*, ed. Ieva Zaķe (New York: Palgrave Macmillan, 2009), 109–126. Scholarship that better mediates between these conflicts, and that shows the arguments of each side more judiciously, is the most needed update to the historiography. The tendency of works on exile from Czechoslovakia is to focus on groups within certain categories and to dismiss as irrelevant, villainous, or domineering any group representing an alternate perspective. This tendency betrays the complex realities of the broader exile movements.
5 Petr Prokš, *Československo a Západ, 1945–1948: vztahy Československa se Spojenými státy, Velkou Británií a Francií v letech 1945–1948* (Prague: ISV, 2001). Igor Lukeš, *On the Edge of the Cold War: American Diplomats and Spies in Postwar Prague* (Oxford: Oxford University Press, 2012), 203–215. While Western governments certainly may have done more, it is doubtful what they could have done that would have radically changed the outcome of Cold War Czechoslovakia. The area where the United States government may be open to the most criticism was its ham-handed approach to the minority questions. US officials often exacerbated those issues despite their attempts to ease tensions.

4.2 The aftermath of World War II

From 1948 to 1989, an estimated 3.5 percent of the population of Czechoslovakia left the country. In total, roughly 550,000 Czechs and Slovaks emigrated. Of these, around 250,000 fled between 1968 and 1989. In the Czech case specifically, there were three key streams of emigration: 1) the *utíkali*, those who left after the Communist takeover in February 1948, believing that Communism was destined to fail, 2) the *vycestovali*, those who left after the 1968 Soviet invasion, who were the "forever gone," and 3) the *vypařily*, those who "evaporated" during "normalization" after 1970.[6] These numbers do not include the more than 3 million Sudeten Germans forced out of the country after 1945. Not surprisingly, some of the Czechs and Slovaks who had returned after liberation in 1945 were forced to leave again after the coup in 1948. Between 1948 and 1950, about 60,000 Czechs and Slovaks left the country. In 1950, fleeing the country became a criminal act. Czechoslovak State Security (Státní bezpečnost, StB) closed the border to prevent further escapes in 1951. These numbers fell to 300 per year afterwards. Over 100 people were killed trying to escape. Most of the 1948 generation—those who left after the Communist coup—tended to be professionals or factory owners and, generally, among the most skilled and educated Czechs and Slovaks. In exile, many worked to fight Communism and return Czechoslovakia to democracy.[7]

In contrast, the failure of the Prague Spring reforms spurred thousands more to flee. Nearly 100,000 people left Czechoslovakia by the end of 1969.[8] Although the working class also emigrated, most of these exiles were part of the intelligentsia and had more university education than the average Czechoslovak. Of the scholars who fled between 1952 and 1992, roughly half had been members of the Czechoslovak Academy of Sciences, heading for the United States, Sweden, Denmark, and Switzerland. In addition, among the one-fifth of émigrés who reportedly fled for political reasons after 1968, many of them were disillusioned Communists. Indeed, many of the 1968 generation seemed initially united in their belief in the program of "socialism with a human face." From 1970 to 1989, in the era of "normalization," out-migration continued, though at a slower pace. Statistics of Communist-era Czech and Slovak émigrés show that of the close to 250,000 who fled between 1968 and

---

[6] While the historians of Czech and Slovak exiles broadly recognize the different generations, particularly the two from 1948 and 1968, the above, specific, categorization derives from: Madeleine Hron, "The Czech Émigré Experience of Return after 1989," *The Slavonic and East European Review* 85, no. 1 (Jan. 2007): 54.
[7] Jiři Pehe, "Czechoslovakia. Émigrés in the Postcommunist Era: New Data, New Policies," *Report on Eastern Europe* (26 April 1991): 11–15.
[8] According to Antonín Kostlán and Soňa Štrbáňová, "…thanks to temporarily more benevolent political leadership and more relaxed passport control." Antonin Kostlán and Soňa Štrbáňová, "Czech Scholars in Exile, 1948–89," in *In Defense of Learning: The Plight, Persecution, and Placement of Academic Refugees, 1933–1980s*, Proceedings of the British Academy, vol. 169, eds. Shula Marks, Paul Weindling, and Laura Wintour (Oxford: Oxford University Press, 2011), 247.

1989, most ended up in North America and Europe.[9] In the early 1970s, Radio Free Europe (RFE) editor Karel Jezdinský noted that "the criminal practice of the Communist regime ... made mere economic emigration turn into an integral part of political exile."[10]

4.3 Major migration streams during the Cold War

World War II and the Communist takeover spurred a major refugee crisis from Central and Eastern Europe in the 1940s that lasted into the early 1950s as governments struggled over how to respond. The Western support to exiles and refugees from Czechoslovakia was mixed. Former political and cultural leaders were given preferential, expedited treatment and thus experienced an easier adjustment than did most general refugees from Czechoslovakia. These leaders reestablished at their new homes in exile, while most of their compatriots remained in refugee camps.

While the British did comparatively little to help the escape of political leaders from Czechoslovakia, French Intelligence helped some individuals, notably Czech National Socialist politician Hubert Ripka. The US embassy also aided several escapees, mostly friends of US officials or individuals who had supplied information to U.S. intelligence in Czechoslovakia. The most notable example was the arranged escape of Czech National Socialist politician Petr Zenkl, who the US embassy staff intended to establish as the leader of the Czechs and Slovaks in exile. Many other escapees had to flee on their own, usually with the aid of sympathetic Czechoslovak security agents or police officers. For example, National Socialist General Secretary Vladimír Krajina escaped by pretending to be a skier, while National Socialist Minister of Agriculture Ladislav Feierabend fled with his family hidden on a riverboat. Many prominent Czech exiles, such as Zenkl, received temporary lodging at the "Alaska House" near Frankfurt am Main, run by Czech-American military intelligence agent Colonel Charles Katek, before being relocated to Britain, France, or the United States. It fast-tracked their travel and visa processing. The US government accepted them as a symbolic statement against Communism, but also as sources of

---

9 Kostlán and Štrbáňová, "Czech Scholars," 248–251. Milos Calda, "Demographic Slump vs. Immigration Policy. The Case of the Czech Republic," The Center for Comparative Immigration Studies, University of California, San Diego, Working Paper 127 (Nov. 2005), 5, fn. 9, https://ccis.ucsd.edu/_files/wp127.pdf; Raška, Long, 168; Pehe, "Czechoslovakia," 14.
10 Tomáš Vilímek, "Exile and emigration in 1968–1989," in *Vzkazy domů/Messages Home: Stories of Czechs who went abroad (Emigration and Exile 1848–1989)*, ed. Lucie Wittlichová (Prague: Labyrint, 2012), 271. Josef Škvorecký notes the following: In the Czech lands "*exile* is associated with the catastrophe of 1620, when the Czech Protestant armies were decimated in the Battle on the White Hill near Prague, and the...kingdom of Bohemia...became for three hundred years an oppressed province of the Austrian Empire of the Catholic Habsburgs." Interestingly and perhaps related to that past, the Czechoslovak Communist Party press "referr(ed) to them never as exiles but always only as emigrants," Josef Škvorecký, "Bohemia of the Soul," *Daedalus* 119, no. 1 (Winter 1990): 112.

information. Not all received this treatment. For example, General František Moravec was turned away even though his daughter was a US citizen.

In contrast, most everyday refugees from Czechoslovakia, about 24,000 in total in the late 1940s, were stuck in refugee camps in Western occupied Austria and West Germany, with smaller numbers in other countries. Much of the 1948 generation remained interred in these camps for up to three years until western officials organized their permanent relocation. The majority eventually emigrated to the United States or Canada, while others remained in various countries in Western Europe. Most western countries were initially hesitant to accept them, requiring refugees to prove an ability to find employment quickly, usually based on education or a trade skill.

Czech- and Slovak-Americans played an active role fundraising and pursuing legal options to aid these refugees. The former Czechoslovak Ambassador to the United Nations, Ján Papánek, founded and organized the American Fund for Czechoslovak Refugees (AFCR), with ample support from the former US Ambassador from Czechoslovakia Juraj Slávik and the Czechoslovak National Council of America. Along with extensive fundraisers and charity work, the AFCR coordinated with the US government on the legwork to get the refugees legal entry into the United States. It also helped arrange employment for them and paid the cost of their travel. These organizations also played a key role in lobbying for the passage of the 1948 Displaced Person's Act, which temporarily lifted US immigration quotas to accommodate postwar refugees. The AFCR kept its organization separate from the Council of Free Czechoslovakia, to assure it remained detached from the political disputes of that organization. In 1952, the State Department organized the United States Escapee Program to provide financial support to voluntary refugee aid organizations and actively supported the Czechoslovak programs. The Czech Refugee Trust Fund and the Czechoslovak Relief Committee for Political Refugees, the latter formed by Vladimir Ležák-Borin in 1946 in London, did the same for those moving to England. The Anglo-Czechoslovak Refugee Welfare Organization also helped bring many exiles to Britain, although the British government cut their agreed quota short. The International Refugee Organization also contributed and improved conditions in the camps when it took over their management in 1948.[11]

The Slovak League of America (SLA), the largest Slovak-American fraternal organization, also worked to get Slovaks to North America, although the US government, influenced by Czechoslovakist groups, refused to recognize separate Slovak refugee institutions. The Slovak League of America and the Slovak League of Canada nevertheless helped arrange Red Cross packages for Slovak exiles through the US

---

11 Lukeš, *On the Edge*, 203–215; Lukeš, "Czechoslovak Political Exile," 240–342. Vojtěch Jeřábek, *Českoslovenstí uprchlíci ve studené válce: dějiny American Fund for Czechoslovak Refugees* (Brno: Stilus, 2005). Petr Koura, "My conscience does not allow me to spread such lies: Czech exiles between February 1948 and August 1968," in *Vzkazy domů/Messages Home: Stories of Czechs who went abroad (Emigration and Exile 1848–1989)*, ed. Lucie Wittlichová (Prague: Labyrint, 2012), 202–215; Raška, *Fighting*, 18, 139–153; Raška, "History," 113–115. Tomek, "Highs and Lows," 113–115.

Army. They also convinced the International Refugee Organization in Switzerland to accept as refugees Slovak exiles linked to the wartime Slovak state, who fled the Communists in 1945. This included recognizing Jozef Kirschbaum, who had served as Slovak Charge d' Affairs in Switzerland for most of the war, as the League's official overseas delegate from 1946 to 1948. The Slovak Leagues also dedicated many resources to helping these exiles reestablish in North America, raising money and petitioning US and Canadian immigration agencies to arrange their entry. While these efforts were successful in gaining entry of some Slovak academic leaders into the United States, attempts on behalf of former politicians were largely ineffective. The upper leadership of the wartime Slovak state, including its president, Jozef Tiso, was captured in Austria and repatriated to Czechoslovakia where most were executed. The SLA attempted to gain entry of other politicians, such as Karol Sidor and Kirschbaum, to the United States, although Washington rejected them. They were later accepted into Canada.[12]

4.3.1 Czech/Czechoslovak organizations

The early attempts at organization by Czech and Czechoslovak political exiles occurred mostly in Western Europe, due to the slower process of migration to North America. Representatives of the four primary non-Communist parties exiled from the Third Czechoslovak Republic, the National Socialists, Social Democrats, People's Party, and Slovak Democrats, met in Paris and London in 1948 to try to organize a common front. Social Democrat politician Blažej Vilím organized a meeting of former Czechoslovakia Parliamentarians in May 1948 in London. Another group of politicians organized in Paris, led by Hubert Ripka. The Paris group also included political parties from the pre-World War II First and Second Republics that the postwar National Front had banned from political participation, including the Republicans (former Agrarians), National Democrats, and Smallholders. In the United States, displaced diplomats, including Ján Papánek and Juraj Slávik, and interwar diplomat Štefan Osuský, held a meeting in June 1948 to form a US-based organization.

---

[12] Despite having been expelled from the wartime government for challenging Nazi prerogatives, former Slovak Foreign Minister Ferdinand Ďurčanský was sentenced to death in absentia by the Czechoslovak government for his role in the creation of the Slovak state during World War II. Washington attempted to capture Ďurčanský until the late 1940s, but eventually gave up. Ďurčanský eventually settled in Munich. Washington eventually allowed former wartime Slovak officials such as Sidor and Ďurčanský to enter the US on temporary visas. Marian Mark Stolarik, *Where is my Home? Slovak Immigration to North America (1870–2010)* (Bern: Peter Lang, 2012), 74–81, 94–95. Michael Cude, "Transatlantic Perspectives on the Slovak Question, 1914–1948" (PhD diss., University of Colorado-Boulder, 2013), 260–261; Stolarik, "Slovak League," 28–29. Gilbert Oddo, *Slovakia and Its People* (New York: Robert Speller & Sons, 1960); Charles Murin, "In Honor of Joseph M. Kirschbaum," in *Slovak Politics: Essays on Slovak History in Honor of Joseph M. Kirschbaum*, ed. Stanislav J. Kirschbaum (Cleveland: Slovak Institute, 1983), xii–xviii.

It would take over a year before the different exile branches settled on a common organization. The individuals involved debated over who should participate and who should take positions of leadership. On 25 February 1949, they officially formed the Council of Free Czechoslovakia (CFC) in Washington, D.C. The Council purchased a house in Washington for its base of operations but maintained its branches in London and Paris. Its first official declaration, written by journalist Ferdinand Peroutka, condemned the Communist domination of Czechoslovakia and vowed to speak for those left silenced there and to aid them in their fight for liberty. Twenty-one countries, including the United States, Britain, and France, tacitly recognized the organization. Almost every key political figure in exile from the Third Republic, and many exiled cultural leaders, participated in the organization in some capacity, as did several individuals from the First Republic. In its initial structure, the Council's chair became Czech National Socialist politician Petr Zenkl, with Slovak Democrat Jozef Lettrich and Czech Social Democrat Václav Majer as vice-chairs. It also included a presidium of twelve members selected by an executive committee of thirty, with many other individuals given consultative roles. Zenkl was placed into leadership as the most experienced politician and out of respect for his past as a concentration camp survivor during World War II.[13]

Dominated by exiles from the Third Republic, the CFC allowed only a few leaders from the pre-1945 political parties to participate and limited their role in the organization. It also excluded many figures. These included leaders of national minority groups from Czechoslovakia as well as World War II Czech and Slovak exiles who had challenged Edvard Beneš's vision for postwar Czechoslovakia, most of whom were political conservatives. Prominent among these figures were the supporters of a Central European Federation. Former Agrarian Prime Minister Milan Hodža initially led this movement, as an alternative to Beneš's organization during World War II, and Czech General, and Christian activist, Lev Prchala maintained it in the postwar period after Hodža's death. Prchala founded the Czechoslovak National Committee and presented a federal model as a means of common security against the Germans and Soviets and as a solution to minority questions in Central Europe. Prchala received support from conservative Czechs, Sudeten Germans, and Slovak autonomists, among others. The Czechoslovak organizations such as the CFC, however, con-

---

[13] Several of the sources cited in this paper provide detailed lists of participants in the CFC and lists of positions held at various stages in the Council's life. There are few English language biographies of exiled leaders, but Czech and Slovak scholars have given them some biographical consideration. For examples, see: Slavomír Michálek, *Ján Papánek: politik, diplomat, humanista, 1896–1991*(Bratislava: Veda, 1996); Slavomír Michálek, *Diplomat Štefan Osuský: 1889–1973* (Bratislava: Veda, 1999); Pavel Kosatík, *Ferdinand Peroutka: pozdější život, 1938–1978* (Prague: Paseka, 2000); Vladimír Goněc, *Za sjednocenou Evropu: z myšlenek a programů Huberta Ripky* (Brno: Vyd. Masarykova univerzita v Brně, 2004); Slavomír Michálek, et al, eds. *Juraj Slávik Neresnický: od politiky cez diplomaciu po exil 1890–1969* (Bratislava: Prodama, 2006); Nekola, "Petr Zenkl," in *Iave*, 169–176. Martin Nekola, *Petr Zenkl: politik a člověk* (Prague: Mladá Fronta, 2014).

demned the federalists as "neo-Monarchists," suggesting they wanted to reestablish the Habsburg Empire.[14]

The North American branch of the Council of Free Czechoslovakia became the dominant one and held regular meetings through the 1950s. While the US branch of the CFC remained active, its impact early on was limited because it lacked financial support. The European branches wilted away, due to many members relocating to North America. It is also unclear how much popular support the organization had among the general Czech and Slovak exile communities. Additionally, internal politics weakened the organization. For example, Hubert Ripka was voted out as the chair of the Paris branch in early 1950. The Paris branch subsequently split into two parts and never recovered. The Council's central organization also remained wracked by internal disputes. In the early Cold War, the organization remained in seemingly perpetual gridlock from issues ranging from leadership, organizational structure, and sources of funding, to the language of texts produced. This conflict made it difficult for the CFC to function. It reorganized on several occasions in the 1950s and 1960s, and saw many individuals leave the organization. For example, after a dispute Peroutka removed journalist Pavel Tigrid from his position at RFE in Munich as well as from control over published materials at the CFC. Long-standing political and ideological rivalries drove most of these disputes, as did a multitude of personality conflicts between members over leadership. The Czech National Socialists dominated the organization, and the other groups never fully trusted them. Interpretations of the 1948 coup also divided the different factions, which regularly blamed one another for the Communist takeover. The use of the Third Republic political parties to guide leadership also angered those Czechs and Slovaks who were not members of those parties and who remained on the outside of the organization's leadership.

The Council of Free Czechoslovakia splintered on several occasions. The first such division came in 1951, shortly after its foundation. Feuds between its Chair, Zenkl, and first deputy, Lettrich, and between Zenkl and Peroutka were at the center of this split. Zenkl became a target of accusations, as many members accused the Czech National Socialist leader of controlling the organization from the top down. This sentiment was fed by Zenkl's regular intransigence on important matters, a trait that proved common among exile leaders from Czechoslovakia regardless of political persuasion. Reformers in the organization called for the creation of rotating leadership positions and term limits but were resisted by those who wanted the positions fixed based on past political party agreements or on leading "personalities." This debate ultimately led to the removal of Zenkl, who, with other National Socialist leaders, left the organization in protest and formed a new organization, the National

---

14 Raška, *Fighting*, 1–28; Raška, "History," 71–76; Koura, "Conscience," 202–215; Slavomír Michálek, "Rada slobodného Československa, 1949–1960," *Historický Časopis*, 4 (1999): 327–344; Lukeš, "Czechoslovak Political Exile", 333–335; Igor Lukeš, "Československý politický exil za studené války: první roky", *Střední Evropa* 119 (February 2004): 1–13; Tomek, "Highs and Lows", 109–126.

Committee of Free Czechoslovakia. The US government's National Committee for a Free Europe (NCFE), which funded the organization, threatened to withdraw its support due to the dispute and mediated efforts to reconcile the competing camps. It insisted on the need for a united Czechoslovakia movement and this pressure led the divided Council to reconcile and reunify in January 1952. It reorganized again along party lines, with Zenkl as chair of the executive committee and Osuský as chair of deputies for a new 110-member assembly that would provide additional oversight. They agreed in principle to term limits, although the Council never put them into effect.

Feuds nevertheless continued to divide the organization through the next fifteen years. Younger members increasingly expressed frustration over the situation and called for representation that was more democratic and that allowed more opposition voices within the exile movement. Efforts at reconciliation were unsuccessful. National Socialist politician and math professor Václav Hlavatý proposed reforms to eliminate the political parties in favor of a new, two-party system and to weaken the executive committee, which many members still believed ruled without consent of the Council's other bodies. When several parties, notably the National Socialists, rejected this proposal, Agrarian politician Miloslav Rechcígl stepped in. Rechcígl called for further decentralization of leadership, as well as an increased involvement of non-politicians in the organization. Rechcígl's efforts saw the implementation of some reforms, including two-year term limits, and a rotating president and vice-president of the executive council. The reforms also established new political and working committees to oversee political affairs, led by Lettrich and former diplomat Arnošt Heidrich. The reforms changed little else and did not solve the disputes. The new bodies in the Council feuded with one another over roles and influence. Ultimately, the older organization and leadership maintained its control. The Council of Free Czechoslovakia's inability to function cooperatively led the NCFE to pull its support for the organization in the late 1950s. The Council saw a final split in 1961, when the political committee came into disagreement with the executive committee over a lack of Slovak representation in leadership and a dispute over the role of members who had taken up new citizenship and given up their "exile" status. The political committee ended up splitting into a separate organization, the Committee of Free Czechoslovakia, and replaced the Council of Free Czechoslovakia (CFC) on the Assembly of Captive European Nations (ACEN).[15]

This division and distrust caused Czechoslovak exile political activities to decline precipitously in the 1960s, although the Council of Free Czechoslovakia survived. The CFC supported the development of "reform Communism" in Czechoslovakia during the 1968 Prague Spring in the hope that such reforms would lead to an

---

15 Raška, *Fighting*, 29–106, 155–173. Raška, "History," 76–83; Boris Čelovský, *Politici bez moci: první léta exilové Rady svobodného Československa* (Šenov near Ostrava: Tilia, 2000), 8–171; Michalek, "Rada," 327–344; Lukeš, "Czechoslovak Political Exile," 332–343; Nekola, "Petr Zenkl," 171–173.

overthrow of Communism. The passive response by Western governments to the Soviet invasion and the start of "normalization" almost led the Council to disband in frustration. Zenkl, however, rallied to save the organization. He called for the election of a new executive council and for reforms to try to draw in a younger generation, as much of the old leadership had passed on. In November 1972, the Council undertook internal reforms, notably getting its members to abandon the old political parties that had driven past conflict and were relevant only as relics of a bypassed era. The Council likewise chose to narrow its focus to be a voice on behalf of those left in Czechoslovakia. It also abandoned any plans of recreating the old political order in Czechoslovakia. In 1973, after Zenkl begrudgingly gave up the reigns, the Council elected a new, younger leadership including Mojmír Povolný as Chair and Slovak Democrat politician Martin Kvetko as vice-chair.

By the late Cold War, however, the CFC was a secondary body, supporting newer, more effectual organizations. The Council of Free Czechoslovakia's most notable effort during this period was to build more links with other Czechoslovak groups, including the Czechoslovak Society of Arts and Sciences (SVU) and the Czechoslovak National Council of America (CNCA), a Czech-American organization founded during World War I. The organization also began cooperating with groups in Europe again. These groups included the Czechoslovak Advisory Committee in Western Europe, headed by Czech journalist and politician Edmund Řehák, and the Free Central European News Agency in London, headed by Czech journalist Josef Josten. After the failed 1968 Prague Spring, the Council faced the decision whether to include the new exiles, many of whom were reform Communists who had helped to destroy democracy in postwar Czechoslovakia.

Roughly 138,000 fled Czechoslovakia in the early stages of post-1968 "normalization" in Czechoslovakia, before the Communist government once again cracked down on the border in 1971. Generally united in their support for the Prague Spring and "socialism with a human face," these new exiles started their own organizations and publishing companies, with thirty-five new publishing houses founded in exile after 1968. They also had connections with the dissidents in Czechoslovakia. Two very influential organizations founded by reform Communists were the *Listy Group*, formed by Jiří Pelikán, and Palach Press, founded by Jan Kavan. Pelikán had directed Czechoslovak television in 1960s and fully embraced the Prague Spring. He sought asylum in Italy in 1969 after the Soviet crackdown against the reform movement. As an exile, he published the magazine *Listy*, which helped foster connections between exiles and dissidents in Czechoslovakia. Kavan was a student leader in the Prague Spring and left Czechoslovakia shortly after the Soviet invasion. In exile in the United Kingdom, he founded and edited several publications through Palach Press, a press agency which helped supply the West with news and writings of Czechoslovak dissidents.

Initially, the Council of Free Czechoslovakia resisted these new exiles due to their Communist affiliations. Younger leaders, such as Czech historian Radomír Luža and political scientist Mojmír Povolný ultimately decided to reach out to them. Although

Povolný failed in his goal of bringing these diverse groups under the common umbrella of the Council, they did cooperate and coordinate activities. The Council thus continued to function, although it struggled with limited funding and a lack of permanent central organization outside of those who volunteered their time. It continued to produce statements to world leaders and participate in summits, and it began a new newsletter in 1976, the *Czechoslovak Newsletter,* published quarterly out of New York City. The post-1968 organizations, such as *Listy Group* and Palach Press, however, came to drive the exile agenda, due to better connections with the dissident movements within Czechoslovakia. Although decentralized in organization, this variety of groups became much more coordinated during the late Cold War, as older rivalries became less prominent and the embrace of détente between East and West allowed some coordination with activist organizations within Czechoslovakia. Czechoslovak organizations accordingly built common messages surrounding international agreements such as the Helsinki Accords.[16]

Along with politicians and journalists, many cultural and intellectual figures fled Czechoslovakia. In 1958, Jaroslav Němec convinced Václav Hlavatý and 200 other artistic, academic, and intellectual exiles to form the Czechoslovak Society of Arts and Sciences (Společnosti pro vědy a umění, SVU). Němec was adamant that the Society remain apolitical. Despite an increase in its stature, the apolitical nature of the Society led to animosity from exiled politicians in its early years, who regarded the group with suspicion. In 1962, the Society established its reputation with its First World Congress in Washington D.C. The biennial conferences featured scholarly presentations from nearly all major fields of intellectual endeavor and complemented other activities of the Society, such as its regular news bulletin, *Zpravý SVU,* and the scholarly quarterly *Promeny* ("Metamorphosis"). By 1966, membership had grown to one

---

16 Raška, *Long,* 13–110. Raška, "History," 83–113; Mojmír Povolný, *Zápas o lidská práva: Rada Svobodného Čeakoslovenska a helsinský process, 1975–1989* (Brno: Stilus Press, 2007); Neil Stewart, "We Do Not Want an Émigré Journal: Pavel Tigrid and *Svědectví,*" in *The Exile and Return of Writers from East-Central Europe: A Compendium,* eds. John Neubauer and Borbála Zsuzsanna Török (Berlin: de Gruyter, 2009), 243–275. Vilímek, "Exile," 270–285. Francesco Caccamo, *Jiří Pelikán a jeho cesta socialismem 20. Století* (Brno: Doplněk, 2008); Milada Polišenská, *Zapomenutý 'nepřítel' Josef Josten: Free Czechoslovakia Information na pozadí československo-britských diplomatických styků 1948–1985* (Prague: Libri, 2009); Kate Connelly, "Jiri Pelikan," *The Guardian,* 29 June 1999, http://www.theguardian.com/news/1999/jun/30/guardianobituaries.kateconnolly (accessed 3 May 2018); Jana Ciglerova, "Who is Jan Kavan? A profile of controversial Czech politician Jan Kavan," *The Guardian,* 9 February 2003, http://www.theguardian.com/world/2003/feb/09/theobserver (accessed 3 May 2018); Jo Glanville, "'Godot is here' how Samuel Beckett and Vaclav Havel changed history," 15 September 2009, http://www.theguardian.com/culture/2009/sep/15/vaclev-havel-samuel-beckett-catastrophe (accessed 3 May 2018); Alice Lovejoy, "'Video Knows no Borders': Samizdat Television and the Unofficial Public Sphere in 'Normalized' Czechoslovakia," in *Samizdat, Tamizdat, and Beyond: Transnational Media During and After Socialism,* eds. Friederike Kind-Kovács and Jessie Labov (New York: Berghahn, 2013), 206–217; Jacques Rupnik, "The Legacies of Dissent: Charter 77, the Helsinki Effect, and the Emergence of a European Public Space," in *Samizdat, Tamizdat...,* 316–332.

thousand including many regional branches. The 1968 Fourth World Congress in Washington D.C. was the first to invite scholars and scientists from Czechoslovakia, but the timing of the conference, a mere nine days after the Soviet invasion, limited their attendance. The most active European chapter was in Switzerland, and in 1976, the Swiss hosted the first European Congress on the meaning of Czech and Slovak history. This event featured scholars living in Western Europe, such as Milan Hauner (London), Milan Ďurica (Padova), Karel Hruby (Basel), and Pavel Tigrid (Paris). From its inception, the Czechoslovak Society of Arts and Sciences attracted intellectuals from wide-ranging fields and promoted collaboration among exiled Czechs and Slovaks from around the world. After 1989, the Society's mission expanded from "supporting and coordinating the educational, scholarly, literary and artistic endeavors of the Czechoslovak intelligentsia abroad" to also being "a bridge between Czech and Slovak professionals and those in other countries."[17] The Society's history shows extensive collaboration between Czech and Slovak exiles, unlike relations among politicians.

4.3.2 Slovak organizations

While there were Slovaks and Slovak groups involved in the broader Czech and Czechoslovak organizations, there was also a large political movement separate from these groups. The Slovaks abroad generally split into three broad categories. The smallest of these groups were the Czechoslovakists, who wanted a close, non-differential linkage with the Czechs, such as diplomats Ján Papánek and Juraj Slávik. Another faction of moderate nationalists pursued cooperation with the Czechs but wanted recognition of separate Slovak identity and political autonomy within the exile organizations. These included figures such as Štefan Osuský, whom Beneš had ostracized from the postwar government for resisting the Czech president's leadership, as well as many Slovak Democrat Party members sent into exile in 1948, such as Jozef Lettrich and Fedor Hodža. Most of the former two groups came from Slovakia's Lutheran minority. The Slovak autonomists, who were predominantly Catholics, were the most controversial. They had abandoned the Czechoslovak project and supported Slovak independence. This latter group was the first to go into exile, fleeing persecution by the returning Czechoslovak government and the Red Army in 1945. Many were academics and journalists, such as historians František Hrušovský and Konštantín Čulen, poet Mikuláš Šprinc and journalist Jozef Paučo. They also included former politicians and diplomats from the World War II Slovak state, such as Jozef Kirschbaum, Karol Sidor, and Ferdinand Ďurčanský. While some Slovak nationalist

---

17 Miloslav Rechcígl, "Milestones in the History of the Organization: Historical Overview," *Czechoslovak Society of Arts and Sciences*, https://www.svu2000.org/about/historical-overview/ (accessed 3 May 2018); Rechcígl, "Jaroslav Němec (1910–1992)," *Remembering, Czechoslovak Society of Arts and Sciences*, http://www.svu2000.org/remembering/jaroslav-nemec/ (accessed 3 May 2018).

academics entered the United States, politicians mostly emigrated to Canada, where they had an easier time gaining entry. The exact numbers of Slovaks within these three groups is unknown, although membership rates in Slovak autonomist groups, which included Slovak-Americans as well as exiles, exceeded the Czechoslovakist organizations.

These divisions left the Slovaks in exile sharply divided. Most of the Slovak exiles from the 1948 generation remained supporters of a Czech-Slovak state, albeit with Slovak autonomy upheld. They collaborated with the Council of Free Czechoslovakia, although the Slovak question remained a source of tension. Figures such as Lettrich and Osuský feuded with Czechoslovakist leaders over Slovak autonomy, demanding separate recognition of the Slovaks in the CFC and parity in its leadership. The Czechoslovakists such as Zenkl and Papánek tried to subdue such appeals, arguing that they sowed dissent and threatened their mission of recreating the common Czechoslovak state. Czech parties such as the National Socialists and Social Democrats also openly rejected Slovak quotas. The Slovak question contributed to the division of the Council. The first reconciliation in 1952 attempted to address this issue by giving the Slovaks separate recognition with separate votes on programs within the CFC. In 1960, the moderate nationalists in the Council formed the Permanent Conference of Slovak Democratic Exiles and formally split from the CFC to join other Czech dissenters in the formation of the Committee of Free Czechoslovakia. The Czechoslovakists remained involved in the Council and in its 1973 reorganization, the body established Czech-Slovak parity in its leadership.

In turn, the Czechoslovakists and moderate nationalist Slovaks despised the Catholic nationalist exiles for their connections to the Slovak state and their continued appeals for independence. They condemned anti-Czechoslovak mentalities as undemocratic and accused the autonomist leaders of trying to reestablish a fascist system over the Slovak people, continuously reminding them of the state's wartime cooperation with Nazi Germany. The Catholic nationalists in turn condemned the moderate nationalist exiles for having sold out the Slovaks to Communist oppression. They defended the Slovak state as a rational decision made for national survival. As a small nation in a volatile region, the Slovaks were the victims, and Prague's poor treatment of national minorities should receive the blame for the wartime breakup of Czechoslovakia. The Czechs were now duping the world, using the claim of Slovak fascism as a masquerade to justify domination over Slovakia. The two sides thus remained in a perpetual tit-for-tat to equate each other to the opposing totalitarian systems of the twentieth century.[18]

---

[18] Stolarik, *Where*, 78–80, 275–279; Stolarik, "Slovak League," 28–29; Štefan Polakovič and František Vnuk, *Zahraničné' akcie na záchranu o obnovenie slovenskej samostatnosti (1943–1948)* (Lakewood-Hamilton: Slovak Research Institute of America, 1988); Jozef Špetko, *Líšky kontra ježe: slovenská politická emigrácia 1948–1989* (Bratislava: Kalligram, 2002); Marek Junek, "Slovenská redakce Rádia Svobodná Evropa," in *Svobodně!: Radio Svobodná Evropa 1951–2011*, ed. Marek Junek, et al. (Prague: Radioservis, 2011), 60–68; Cude, "Transatlantic," 260–263, 281–282, 305–306, 338–341;

The Catholic nationalist organizations also lacked unity in the early Cold War. Peter Prídavok, a wartime exile prohibited from the Third Republic, joined former politician and World War II diplomat Karol Sidor in founding the Slovak National Council Abroad (SNCA) in 1948, based in North America. Alternatively, former Slovak foreign minister Ferdinand Ďurčanský founded the Slovak Action Committee (SAC) in 1946 in Europe. The SNCA and the SAC were similar in purpose, promoting anti-Communism and the reestablishment of an independent Slovakia. However, they became rival organizations due to a personal competition between Sidor and Ďurčanský over leadership of the Slovaks in exile.[19] The rivalry eventually ended when the two organizations merged in 1960 into the Slovak Liberation Council.

The Slovak-American organizations welcomed the participation of Catholic exiles, as the Slovak League of America and the Slovak League of Canada each set up a system where a Slovak-American would serve as president and an exile as secretary in their organizations. Nevertheless, there remained regular tensions between Slovak-Americans and new exiles, as the latter moved into leadership positions long held by Slovak-American leaders. The factional differences among the Slovaks in exile also caused concern to the point that the League sent former SLA president Peter Hletko to Europe to mollify these divisions before they spread to America. The Slovak Leagues formally supported the SNCA over the SAC in the early Cold War. Despite these concerns, Slovak exiles quickly merged into the existing Slovak-American political and cultural institutions, becoming leaders in publishing, cultural development, and political activism. Slovak nationalism had long been popular among Slovak-Americans and was the dominant view in both the American and Canadian Slovak Leagues, the largest North American political organizations.

The period from the late 1940s through the 1960s proved the most prolific period of publishing by Slovaks in America. Publication topics ranged from history, politics, and culture to anti-Communism. Among these publications were several academic histories of the Slovaks and Slovak-Americans and the founding of the academic journal *Slovakia* in 1951. In 1952, Abbot Theodore Kojiš founded the Slovak Institute at the St. Andrew's Abbey in Cleveland as a center and repository of Slovak culture and an archive of the experiences of the Slovaks in America. Two exile historians, Hrušovský and Čulen, served as its first two directors. The exiles also emboldened Slovak-American support for Slovak independence, interjecting concepts and interpretations linked to their first-hand accounts of Slovakia's brief period of independ-

---

Čelovský, *Politici*, 88–101; Raška, *Fighting*, 11–12, 59, 107–117; Lukeš, "Czechoslovak Political Exile," 339; Tomek, "Highs and Lows," 109–126.
19 The primary difference between the two organizations was that the SNCA conceptualized itself as new organization, whereas the SAC presented itself as the legal continuation of the World War II Slovak Republic.

ence during the war. These Slovak organizations also held numerous conferences and public events to promote an independent Slovak identity, culture, and politics.[20]

The best attempt to unite the Slovaks came with the creation of the Slovak World Congress (SWC) in June 1970 by Canadian Slovak businessman Stephen Roman. The SWC brought together Slovak organizations from North and South America, Western Europe, and Oceania, absorbing many of the existing organizations, including Catholic, Lutheran, and Greek Catholic organizations, émigré and Slovak-American organizations, and individuals ranging from Osuský to Ďurčanský, as well as 1968-generation Slovak socialists such as Eugen Löbl and Dušan Tóth. They unified in a common mission of resisting Communism in the name of democracy, religious freedom, and Slovak self-determination. The Slovak World Congress was somewhat successful in uniting the Slovaks abroad, although the Czechoslovakists and many of the moderate nationalists refused participation due to the involvement of Catholic autonomist leaders. The organization began to decline after Roman's death in 1988, as he had personally bankrolled the organization. It officially supported the Velvet Revolution and organized many visits and programs in Slovakia after 1989. The SWC increasingly came into conflict with the new Czechoslovak government over Slovak autonomy, which it still vigorously supported. After the Velvet Divorce in 1993, its functions declined, with its most notable achievement being to convince the US and Slovak governments to allow dual citizenship. By 2000, the SWC was functionally gone. The Council of Free Czechoslovakia continued to function after 1989 but renamed itself the Czech and Slovak Solidarity Council to reflect a new focus on Czech-Slovak unity.[21]

4.3.3 Sudeten Germans, Rusyns, Hungarians, and other ethnic minorities

Like the Slovaks, the other ethnic minorities from Czechoslovakia had issues with the broader Czechoslovak organizations. The different nationalities in Czechoslovakia, according to Ieva Zaķe, largely "identified with the national political agendas of

---

20 Polakovič and Vnuk, *Zahraničné' akcie*; Jozef C. Trubinsky, *Slovenský exil za suverenitu a štátnosť slovenského národa* (Martin: Matica slovenská, 2003); Špetko, *Líšky*; Stolarik, *Where*, 158–162, 274–278; Stolarik, "Slovak League," 28–32; Cude, "Transatlantic," 261–263, 339–340; Bonaventure S. Buc, "The Role of Emigrants in Slovak Nationalism," *Slovakia* 9, no.4 (March 1959), 44–46; Oddo, *Slovakia*, 340–341; Joseph M. Kirschbaum, "Dr. Paučo's Writings and the History of American Slovaks" *Furdek* 13 (1974): 75–80; Joseph Paučo, "Twenty Years of the Slovak Institute in Cleveland" *Slovakia* 23, no. 46 (1973): 16–21.
21 Joseph M. Kirschbaum, ed., *Slovakia in the 19th & 20th Centuries*, Proceedings of the Conference on Slovakia held during the General Meeting of the Slovak World Congress on June 17–18, 1971 in Toronto, Ontario, Canada (Toronto: Slovak World Congress, 1973); "The Slovak World Congress and American Slovaks," in *Slovaks in America: A Bicentennial Study*, ed. Joseph C. Krajsa, et al (Middletown, PA: Slovak League of America, 1978), 437–457; Stolarik, "Slovak League," 30–31, 33–34; Stolarik, *Where*, 279–296; Raška, *Long*, 46.

their pre-World War II countries" and saw themselves as political refugees with the legitimate and noble goal of restoring their nation's independence.[22] While the Slovak question remained muddled, due to the conflicting views over Slovak identity, the Sudeten German question was much more transparent. The Nazi occupation of the Czech lands during World War II and the subsequent forced expulsion of three million Sudeten and Carpathian Germans by the Czechoslovak government during the Third Republic created seemingly irreparable divides between Czechoslovakia's Czech and German populations, as well as desires for retribution, and serious questions of human rights. As historian R.M. Douglass noted, "any discussion of the expulsions immediately brings to the fore a host of deeply uncomfortable and—still—highly contentious and divisive questions."[23]

In the immediate aftermath of the expulsions of Germans from across Central and Eastern Europe, a variety of organizations arose among the Sudeten Germans in the western zones of Germany. Although the occupation governments discouraged unsanctioned political mobilization of any kind, expellee heritage societies or homeland societies (*Landsmannschaften*), began to emerge. By the mid-1950s, there were twenty *Landsmannschaften* with 1.3 million members. Initially, the groups were fueled by anger and the desire for revenge for the injustices committed against them during the expulsions, by individuals, misguided mobs, and by the Communist Czechoslovak government. The Sudeten German political organizations despised the Czechoslovak organizations, particularly the Council of Free Czechoslovakia and the National Socialists linked to Edvard Beneš, whom they blamed for their expulsion. While broadly anti-Communist in sentiment, the Cold War remained only a tertiary concern for the Sudeten Germans as they focused most of their effort on drawing attention to their forced expulsion. They blamed the exiles from the Czechoslovak Third Republic not only for the postwar ethnic cleansing, but also for helping the Communists takeover Czechoslovakia in 1948.

The hope of returning home unified their efforts and a variety of West German politicians encouraged and even exploited this sentiment for political gain. In the early 1950s, West German chancellor Konrad Adenauer successfully exploited the homeland dream to cultivate Sudeten German support.[24] Like the Slovak organizations, the Sudeten movement involved figures previously involved in wartime nation-

---

[22] Ieva Zaķe, "Experience of Political Exile and the Nature of Ethnic Prejudice," in *East Central Europe in Exile: Transatlantic Identities,* vol. 2, ed. Anna Mazurkiewicz (Newcastle upon Tyne: Cambridge Scholars, 2013),153.
[23] Ray M. Douglas, *Orderly and Humane: The Expulsion of the Germans after the Second World War* (New Haven/London: Yale University Press, 2012), 3. For more on the population transfers of Germans and Hungarians from Czechoslovakia, see: Matthew Frank, *Making Minorities History: Population Transfer in Twentieth-Century Europe* (Oxford: Oxford University Press, 2017), 265–355
[24] Pertti Ahonen points out the West German leaders' "tactical opportunism, telling expellees...what they wanted to hear, with scant regard for existing realities or possible long-term consequences." Pertti Ahonen, *After the Expulsion: West Germany and Eastern Europe 1945–1990* (Oxford: Oxford University Press, 2003), 278.

alist political institutions, such as the Expellees' and Disenfranchised People's Bloc (*Block der Heimatsvertriebenen und Entrechteten*) led by nationalist Waldemar Kraft, a former member of the SS with a questionable wartime record. Another early lobbying group was the Association for the Protection of Sudeten German Interests (AG) formed in 1947 by Walter Becher, Hans Schütz, and Richard Breitzner. Such groups garnered minimal political support from their Sudeten German constituents in the long term. The AG ceased functioning in 1952. Alternatively, Adenauer defused the growing political representation of expellee groups, absorbing the Sudeten Germans as a constituency of his Christian Democratic Party. While he expressed nominal sympathy to their goals to reverse the postwar ethnic reorganization of Czechoslovakia, he also worked to accommodate them into West German society. In 1952, he passed "expellee-friendly" legislation which "created an off-budget fund" entitling many to compensation, loans, and even pensions. A year later, Adenauer invited several prominent Sudeten German representatives such as Kraft, Theodor Oberlander, and Hans-Christoph Seebohm to serve in his cabinet, thereby linking the bloc to his policies. The success of capitalism, aka the Miracle Years, in West Germany also helped neutralized the bitterness of the expellees. Although these efforts motivated many to accept their new lives in West Germany, the memory of resentment, and even the hope of returning to the Sudetenland remained prominent through the early Cold War.

In turn, like their counterparts in Czechoslovakia, many Czechs in exile never forgave the Sudeten Germans for their role in the 1938 Munich Agreement and for the collective guilt placed on the Sudeten Germans for the years of Nazi occupation that followed. In addition, many exiled Czechoslovak leaders had helped organize the expulsion of the Sudeten Germans from Czechoslovakia during the Third Republic. Most officials in the Council of Free Czechoslovakia held no remorse for the expulsion, perceived it as historical justice and as permanent, and refused to give in to demands to apologize for it. Throughout the Cold War, they turned the topic of Germans expelled after the Second World War into a taboo. Lev Prchala's organization was the notable exception. He organized a "joint committee" that welcomed Sudeten German participation, along with participants from almost every ethnic group from Czechoslovakia.

After the 1950s, public discourse on the postwar expulsions of Germans from Central and Eastern Europe virtually ceased, even in the West. It was only after 1968 that discussion of the *odsun* (evacuation) was kept alive in samizdat publications and exile circles. Although Sudeten German refugee associations existed in West Germany, they ceased having any political influence by the 1970s.[25] In Commu-

---

[25] Matěj Spurný claims that despite this decline in prominence in the late Cold War, "the discourses through which this notion found expression were preserved in refugee circles, very much as if in a hall of mirrors, where un-interrogated images of the past could proliferate unhindered by any exterior influences." Matěj Spurný, "Czech and German Memories of Forced Migration," *Hungarian Historical Review* 1, no. 3–4 (2012): 355.

nist Czechoslovakia, the government tried unsuccessfully to "expunge all knowledge of the Germans and the expulsions from historical consciousness" because memories cannot simply be erased. Those publications significantly contributed to discussions of the subject after 1989. For over a decade beginning in the early 1990s, and especially in the early 2000s as the Czech and Slovak Republics sought membership in the European Union, the issues of the tumultuous postwar period, i.e. expulsions, amnesties, decrees, and losses of property and citizenship, were intensely debated among politicians and in the media and constitutional courts.[26]

The Council of Free Czechoslovakia was also limited in its acceptance of other ethnic minorities. Although most North American organizations of the postwar Subcarpathian Rusyn/Ruthenian exiles were indeed anti-Communist and many initially voiced their hopes of returning "home," much of their focus was on preserving their language and culture. With their prewar populations divided among multiple countries, including Czechoslovakia, and with the Soviet Union's annexation of the majority of Czechoslovakia's Rusyn territories after the war, only a small portion of the Rusyn populations abroad specifically identified as part of Czechoslovakia. Paul Robert Magocsi notes that the year 1939 ended "the natural evolution of the discussion of a Rusyn identity—stifled by state intervention." This came about due to the Hungarian fascist takeover of Subcarpathian Rus' in Slovakia (Prešov Region), the General Government of Germany that ruled the Lemko Region of Poland, and the Soviet rule after 1945, due to a 1925 decision by Communists in Ukraine declaring all Rusyns Ukrainians. The Sub-Carpathian Rusyn population in Czechoslovakia, like the Slovaks, divided between support for the broader Czechoslovak State and their hopes for national self-determination and political autonomy with Czechoslovakia. While there was constant talk of possibly including the Rusyns in the Council of Free Czechoslovakia, only one organization received a limited participatory role, namely, the Council of Free Sub-Carpathian Ruthenia, which was organized in 1951 in Hamilton, Ontario, Canada.[27]

---

26 Douglas, *Orderly*; Ahonen, *After the Expulsion*; Jan Křen, *Češi-Němci-odsun* (Prague: Academia, 1990); Radomír Luža, *The Transfer of the Sudeten Germans: A Study of Czech-German Relations, 1933–1962* (New York: New York University Press, 1964); Gilad Margolit, "The Foreign Policy of the German Sudeten Council and Hans-Christoph Seebohm, 1956–1964," *Central European History* 43 (2010): 464–583; Spurný, "Czech and German Memories," 353–367; Arnold Suppan, "Austrians, Czechs, and Sudeten Germans as a Community of Conflict in the Twentieth Century," Working Paper 06–1, *CAS Working Papers in Austrian Studies*, Center for Austrian Studies, University of Minnesota (October 2006), 37–39; Raška, *Fighting*, 117–138; Čelovský, *Politici*, 88–101; Lukeš, "Czechoslovak Political Exile," 339–3340; Tomek, "Highs and Lows," 111–112; Arch Puddington, *Broadcasting Freedom: The Cold War Triumph of Radio Free Europe and Radio Liberty* (Lexington: University Press of Kentucky, 2000), 75–78.
27 Paul Robert Magocsi, *Of the Making of Nationalities There is No End* (New York: Columbia University Press, 1999), 145–146; Paul Robert Magocsi, "Magyars and Carpatho-Rusyns: On the Seventieth Anniversary of the Founding of Czechoslovakia," *Harvard Ukrainian Studies* 14, no. 3 (December 1990): 442–457; Raška, *Fighting*, 117–138.

The Magyar (Hungarian) minority in Slovakia received similar treatment to the Sudeten Germans, although on a lesser scale, with about a third of their population expelled or voluntarily relocated to Hungary during the Third Republic. After the Communist takeover in Hungary and Czechoslovakia, many of the Magyars from Slovakia fled abroad. The Magyar minority from Slovakia also had a small, but active, organization in exile, the National Committee of Hungarians from Czechoslovakia. The Committee campaigned for the overthrow of Communism and for national self-determination for Slovakia's Magyars. These Magyars were not considered for membership in the larger Czech or Slovak organizations due to the mutual national animosity, although both Magyar and Rusyn organizations participated in Prchala's Czechoslovak National Committee.[28]

4.4 Czech and Slovak political activities in exile

4.4.1 Early Cold War

The Council of Free Czechoslovakia pursued a steady program of anti-Communist propaganda, ran campaigns to gain support from Western leaders and populations, and released regular publications, including political pamphlets, histories, and serials, such as the *Council of Free Czechoslovakia Rapporteur,* and the *Voice of Czechoslovakia.* Most of these serials did not last long. The journal *Svědectví* ("Testimony"), under the direction of Pavel Tigrid and published from 1956 to 1992, was arguably the most influential publication, with its widest readership not only among exiles but also within Czechoslovakia. In 1960, Tigrid moved his operations from New York to Paris. Through creative distribution methods, the publication made its way into a variety of Czechoslovak hands, with some addressees even being chosen at random. Among the information published were the plenary meeting proceedings of the Communist Party. The journal promoted Tigrid's theory of gradualism to begin the dismantling of Communism. To that end, the journal attempted to keep open the lines of communication with the Communists inside Czechoslovakia, especially in the years and months leading up to the Soviet invasion in August 1968 in order "to improve relations with the people back home and encourage gradual liberalization of the political system."[29] Some historians consider Tigrid a proponent of "democratic humanism" reminiscent of Czechoslovakia's first president Tomáš Masaryk. Tigrid advocated for national reconciliation and wanted his publication to be known as a Czechoslovak one, not simply as one that was anti-Communist or just

---

28 Magocsi, *Of the Making;* Magocsi, "Magyars and Carpatho-Rusyns," 442–457; "National Committee of Hungarians from Slovakia," *Hungarian American Coalition,* http://www.hacusa.org/en/member-organizations/26 (accessed 3 May 2018); Raška, *Fighting,* 117–138.
29 Stewart, "We Do Not Want" 249. True to Tigrid's vision and purpose, the journal ceased publication only after the breakup of Czechoslovakia in 1992, not after the fall of Communism in 1989.

for exiles. According to Neil Stewart, Tigrid dismissed the exile community's complaints about "a lack of unity and authoritative organization. What others bemoaned as ideological fragmentation that would weaken Czech exiles, Tigrid celebrated as modern pluralism that attested to its democratic culture."[30]

Scholars have consistently shown how the CFC's most successful effort was its contribution to Radio Free Europe (RFE). Peroutka became the head of the Czechoslovak Division from 1951 to 1976. His writings and broadcasts to Czechoslovakia provided reports on international events from a Western and exile perspective and encouraged anti-Communist resistance. The CFC initially received funding from the US government through the National Committee for a Free Europe (NCFE). It was also involved in many international organizations and conferences. The Council also participated in broader anti-Communist organizations such as the Assembly of Captive European Nations (ACEN). Osuský headed the first Czechoslovak delegation to the ACEN and was an active contributor to its meetings and programs, as were other CFC leaders such as Ripka and Lettrich.[31]

Beyond support for refugees, Western support for exile activities remained limited. Western containment policy rested on the premise of containing Communism within Eastern Europe to prevent its spread to the West. Having conceded the region, efforts to change the situation in Communist East Central Europe, including Czechoslovakia, did not develop much further than anti-Communist propaganda.[32] In Britain, former World War II exile defense minister Sergej Ingr arranged a meeting with Winston Churchill. The former Social Democrat General Secretary Blažej Vilím had connections to the Labor government, but neither he nor Vilim were able to parlay this into any concrete support. Neither the British nor the French governments were willing to fund the European branches of the Council of Free Czechoslovakia. Initially, the US government was hesitant, as the State Department did not want to sponsor an exile government. It did eventually push for the creation of the CFC as a means of coordinating exile activity. Czech and Slovak groups would sometimes get token hearings from US leaders, including a Czechoslovak National Council of America meeting with President Truman in 1949, but these rarely led to concrete policy. Some US politicians gave rhetorical support, such as Congressman Charles J. Kersten's resolution of support for Czechoslovakia in July 1951, or the statements of sym-

---

30 Stewart, "We Do Not Want," 249, 243–275
31 Raška, *Fighting*, 29–106, 155–173; Raška, "History," 76–83; Čelovský, *Politici bez moci*, 8–171; Michalek, "Rada," 327–344; Lukeš, "Czechoslovak Political Exile," 332–343; Nekola, "Petr Zenkl," 171–173.
32 Bennett Kovrig, *Of Walls and Bridges: The United States and Eastern Europe* (New York: New York University Press, 1991), 1–102; Slavomír Michálek, *Nádeje a vytriezvenia: československo-americké hospodárske vzťahy v rokoch 1945–1951* (Bratislava: Veda, 1995); Prokš, *Československo a Západ*; Ronald R. Krebs, *Dueling visions: US strategy toward Eastern Europe under Eisenhower* (College Station, TX: Texas A & M University Press, 2001); Milada Polišenská, *Diplomatické vztahy Československa a USA 1918–1968* (Prague: Libri, 2012); Lukeš, *On the Edge*.

pathy by the Eisenhower administration for the "captive nations." Practical support was limited to a few areas.

In the 1950s, the Council received financial support from the US Central Intelligence Agency (CIA) through the National Committee for a Free Europe, a nominal non-profit organization used as a staging operation for the funding of exiles from the Communist Bloc. It provided stipends to individual exile leaders as well as monthly payments of $8,900 to the CFC, although the source of the funding was unknown to most members. The other major collaborative area for Czech and Slovak exiles was Cold War radio. Many countries set up Czech and Slovak broadcasts, utilizing exile support, including the British Broadcasting Corporation (BBC), Radio France Internationale, Deutsche Welle, Radio Canada International, and Vatican Radio. The American international broadcaster, Voice of America, also employed exiles for Czech and Slovak broadcasts, although this station focused on disseminating the official stance of the US government on world affairs.[33]

More prominently, Czech and Slovak exiles were given an active role in Radio Free Europe. RFE's first official broadcast was made to Czechoslovakia on 4 July 1950, and it began regular broadcasting in May 1951. Ferdinand Peroutka initially led the agency's programming for Czechoslovakia. He and Pavel Tigrid produced these early broadcasts, calling for the people of Czechoslovakia to stand up against Communism, in part by exposing Communist collaborators for public condemnation. The Voice of Free Czechoslovakia at RFE also related stories of those who escaped and defected to the West: a train engineer who barreled through a checkpoint into West Germany in 1951, or a pilot who escaped to Austria. It encouraged others to do the same, particularly disaffected government officials. In response to the 1953 riots in Pilsen, RFE pushed Czechoslovak police and military to avoid targeting their own people and encouraged workers to stand up against the regime. It also encouraged young people to learn how to use firearms, while promising a future of political freedom and an opportunity to buy luxury goods not available to them under Communism. This participation in RFE assured that an exile anti-Communist perspective reached Czechoslovakia. RFE broadcasts were the most popular foreign broadcast in Czechoslovakia, as they ran with more consistency. Broadcasting for shorter time blocks, VOA and the BBC were the next most popular, although the smaller broadcasters (French and Canadian) could oftentimes slip through the cracks when the larger stations received attention from Czechoslovak jamming.

RFE also organized Operation Winds of Freedom to drop propaganda material via balloons into the Eastern Bloc, including Czechoslovakia, coordinated with RFE broadcasts. In the three separate operations, this propaganda campaign called for people to hold out hope and continue to resist domination. Operation Prospero in

---

33 Lukeš, "Czechoslovak Political Exile," 334–336; Raška, *Fighting*, 2–5, 9, 33–36; Raška, "History," 72–77; Tomek, "Highs and Lows," 115–123; Michael Nelson, *War of the Black Heavens: The Battles of Western Broadcasting in the Cold War* (Syracuse, NY: Syracuse University Press, 1997), 13, 55, 107–115, 132–134.

1953 launched 6,500 balloons in 4 days, with 12 million leaflets. It encouraged workers to imitate the East German uprising and for farmers to resist paying collectivization quotas. It also included replicas of the new Czechoslovak currency, targeting an unpopular currency reform, with stamps of "All Czechs and Slovaks for Freedom— All the Free World for Czechs and Slovaks." Operation Veto in 1954 dropped 41 million leaflets. A bit tamer, this campaign focused on promoting social democracy and working within the system to gradually reform away from Communism. It promoted basic concepts such as secret ballots, running for local elections, the organization of Western styled labor unions, and better pay. It also encouraged voters in the upcoming parliamentary elections to cross out all the candidate names, as a statement rejecting one-party rule.

RFE and US officials generally saw its programs as a success and a propaganda coup during the Cold War. While difficult to verify, RFE used recent escapees to gauge its effectiveness, and many escapees claimed to have heard broadcasts directly or from friends and family. In retrospect, most historians accredit RFE as the one area where Czech and Slovak exiles pursued an effective program that gradually undermined the Communist regime. Some historians, such as Igor Lukeš and A. Ross Johnson suggest that these positive accounts are overblown, with preventative jamming limiting the program's success. Muriel Blaive also argues that RFE and its supporters misunderstood its possible influence in the 1950s, hoping it could spark dissent and uprising, without having enough knowledge of events in Czechoslovakia to apply a truly effective program.[34]

The debates over nationality questions also spread to Radio Free Europe, where Slovaks regularly complained about the organization not giving them proper access. Washington embraced the Council of Free Czechoslovakia as its main source for policy advice and initially let the exile group guide hiring, which limited Slovak access only to those supportive of Council objectives. American officials in turn actively dismissed Slovak autonomists, expressing a desire to avoid any organization that confused the objectives of the CFC. As a result, almost all the Slovaks working at RFE were Lutherans or Jews, with only a few token Catholics, even though most Slovaks were the latter.

---

34 Lukeš, "Czechoslovak Political Exile," 334–336; Tomek Prokop, "Radio Svobodná Evropa a jeho československá redakce," and "Balony svobody nad Československem" in *Svobodně!: Radio Svobodná Evropa 1951–2011*, ed. Marek Junek, et al. (Prague: Radioservis, 2011), 16–36, 154–169; Tomek, "Highs and Lows," 115–123; Čelovský, *Politici*, 47–73; Raška, *Fighting*, 70, 122–123, 127–133; Raška, "History," 72–82, 90. Raška, *Long*, 111–118; Nelson, *War*, 46, 68–69, 190–192; Puddington, *Broadcasting*, 50–51, 61–84; A. Ross Johnson, *Radio Free Europe and Radio Liberty: The CIA Years and Beyond* (Washington DC: Wilson Center Press, 2010), 58, 155–157, 223; Muriel Blaive, "The Danger of Over-interpreting Dissident Writing in the West," in *Samizdat, Tamizdat...*, 137–155; Richard H. Cummings, *Cold War Radio: the Dangerous History of American Broadcasting in Europe, 1950–1989* (Jefferson, NC: McFarland, 2009), 16.

The Slovak League of America (SLA), the largest Slovak-American political organization, pushed Washington to allow a separate Slovak division at Voice of America and RFE, although the Czechoslovak organizations blocked it. When complaints from Slovaks continued to hit the desks of RFE officials, RFE released a report in 1961 reaffirming that it would never start a separate Slovak desk because it was committed to Czech-Slovak unity. The Slovak autonomists received some symbolic support from some members of US Congress, especially senators with large Slovak constituencies such as Representative Ray J. Madden from Indiana. Later, RFE tried to accommodate the Slovaks by creating parity in employment and implementing a balance between Czech and Slovak specific programs. These efforts and the appointment of a Slovak, Samuel Belluš, as manager of Czechoslovak Broadcasting helped ease tensions during the late Cold War. These debates nonetheless never subsided completely. The CFC, for example, protested fiercely when the US Department of State allowed a Slovak-American autonomist to attend the Madrid CSCE meeting and tried to have her expelled from participation.

The nationality issue, like the Slovak question, spread to Cold War activities. The Council received pressure from the National Committee for a Free Europe, which hoped to appease the Sudeten Germans because they had become an important voting bloc in support of Adenauer, a key Cold War ally of the United States. Like the Slovak autonomists, the Sudeten Germans made Radio Free Europe a target. RFE almost considered blocking any discussion of Beneš to ease tensions but decided against it after extensive Council protests. Nevertheless, RFE officials made sure that the Czechoslovak programs at a minimum did not provoke the issue. Some Czech and Slovak leaders began to change their tune by the mid-1950s and called for reconciliation with the Sudeten Germans. Most notable in this regard was Peroutka, who worked closely with the NCFE on the issue. The Council, however, rejected these appeals.[35]

The National Committee for a Free Europe (NCFE), Radio Free Europe, and the US government also asserted themselves regarding the Council of Free Czechoslovakia. To ease tensions, they occasionally pressured the Czech organization to relax its stance on the Sudeten Germans and autonomist Slovaks, including the discouragement of hagiographical presentations of figures such as Beneš, about whom the Slovaks and Sudeten Germans had negative views. The nationality questions among Czechoslovak exiles also became caught up in the anti-Communist fervor of the 1950s. Figures such as Ripka and Peroutka received sharp scrutiny from congression-

---

35 Stolarik, *Where*, 78–80, 275–279; Stolarik, "Slovak League," 28–29; Polakovič and Vnuk, *Zahraničné' akcie*; Špetko, *Líšky kontra ježe*; Junek, "Slovenská redakce Rádia Svobodná Evropa," in *Svobodně!: Radio Svobodná Evropa 1951–2011*, ed. Marek Junek, et al. (Prague: Radioservis, 2011), 60–68; Cude, "Transatlantic," 260–263, 281–282, 305–306, 338–341; Čelovský, *Politici*, 88–101; Raška, *Fighting*, 11–12, 59. 107–138; Lukeš, "Czechoslovak Political Exile," 339–340; Tomek, "Highs and Lows," 109–126; Puddington, *Broadcasting*, 37, 75–78, 128–129; James F. Brown, *Radio Free Europe: An Insider's View* (Washington, DC: New Academia, 2013), 14, 87–88.

al anti-Communist investigations, in large part spurred by autonomist Slovaks, Sudeten Germans, and conservative Czechs, who pointed out their past support for socialism and their willingness to ally with the Communists in the Third Republic. Several members of the CFC came to resent NCFE involvement in its affairs. Papánek, for example, blamed the organization and RFE for causing their internal disputes. The NCFE eventually pulled its support in 1957 in frustration over the internal squabbling and clear lack of effectiveness of the Council. The CFC never again received equivalent financial aid, despite efforts by its well-connected members to cultivate support from US officials. RFE's Czechoslovakia branch was also considered for elimination in 1960, due to debates over its effectiveness. The State Department even considered offering a deal with the Czechoslovak government to end the program in exchange for an end to the jamming of VOA. The CIA defended the program and it survived.[36]

Czech and Slovak exiles also supported western military activities and espionage in the early Cold War. The US Army temporarily accepted a Czechoslovak guard group, led by Major Karel Černý, designated to serve as military advisors and the start of a potential Czechoslovak force in case of an outbreak of war. Ultimately, this unit only participated in labor service and did not last beyond the late 1940s. Several Czechs and Slovaks worked as spies for the CIA, led by Czech-American Colonel Charles Katek in Germany. Oftentimes these agents tended to be American citizens of Czech and Slovak heritage rather than political exiles. Some former military leaders did aid Western intelligence efforts in Europe such as General Ingr and General Moravec, the latter heading the CFC intelligence services and collaborating with American, British, and French intelligence agencies. They recruited refugees to serve as couriers, who travelled along the Czechoslovak border and provided information. They also aided counter intelligence efforts, helping debrief new refugees to try to smoke out spies. The Slovak White Legion (Biela légia), led by Jozef Vicen, also organized in Austria as a Christian anti-Communist organization. Supporting the US Army's Counter-Intelligence Corps, it sent couriers into Czechoslovakia and produced early radio broadcasts into Slovakia. Communist infiltration undermined this operation, including the capture of Vicen in Vienna in 1957. These espionage efforts did not seem to provide much useful information and petered off by the late 1950s. The start of détente in the 1960s allowed access to new sources within Czechoslovakia who could provide better information.[37]

The Czechoslovak government in turn attempted to counteract these efforts. The Communist government was initially happy to see many of the exiles flee the country, although Czechoslovak State Security (StB) saw them as a threat and undertook

---

36 Lukeš, "Czechoslovak Political Exile," 334–336; Tomek, "Radio," and "Balony" 16–36, 154–169; Tomek, "Highs and Lows," 115–123; Čelovský, *Politici*, 47–73; Raška, *Fighting*, 70, 122–123, 127–133; Raška, "History," 72–82, 90; Raška, *Long*, 111–118; Nelson, *War*, 46, 68–69, 190–192; Puddington, *Broadcasting*, 50–51, 61–84; Johnson, *Radio*, 155–157, 223.
37 Tomek, "Highs and Lows," 115–123; Vladimír Varinský, *Jozef Vicen a Biela légia* (Banská Bystrica: Univerzita Mateja Bela, 2003); Stolarik, *Where*, 94; Cummings, *Cold War Radio*, 51–56.

its own preventive measures even before it closed the border in 1951. Some escapees did not avoid capture, notably People's Party leaders Jan Šrámek and František Hála, who were captured as French intelligence tried to help them flee Czechoslovakia. The StB also organized an elaborate ruse program (Operation KÁMEN), where its agents pretended to be acting for the United States, and instead led would-be escapees to fake guard stations where they would be arrested. This entrapment plan led to the capture of Air Force General Karel Janoušek. This program ended after a short run when the US Embassy in Czechoslovakia exposed it. The Czechoslovak government also tried to claim ownership over Red Cross funds organized by the Czechoslovak American Fund but was unsuccessful. It likewise organized its "Action for Reparation" program in the early 1950s to try to get non-political refugees to return to Czechoslovakia as a symbol of the improved situation there, although few accepted. Where possible, Czechoslovak security captured exiles to be held for treason. For example, Štefan Kiripolský fled Czechoslovakia in 1951, and helped debrief escapees from Czechoslovakia for RFE and US military intelligence in Austria. Soviet agents later captured him in Vienna and sentenced him to life in prison.

The StB's main effort was to marginalize exile propaganda. The Czechoslovak government was the first to protest RFE, condemning the Voice of Free Czechoslovakia as interference in its domestic affairs. The US government simply denied involvement, stating that it was a privately-run organization acting on the will of the American people. Listening to foreign broadcasts remained legal in Czechoslovakia, but officials used rumors about political retribution to discourage listening. Czechoslovakia began jamming Western radio in February 1952. The Czechoslovak government in turn tried to stop the balloon program by shooting down the balloons, using police forces to collect the material, and instigating a media blitz that ordered people to turn over the propaganda. The Czechoslovak government also falsely blamed a plane crash in January 1956 near Levoča, Slovakia on the balloons. The Communist security agencies otherwise worked to smear and discredit exiles. Through its operation "Active Measures" (*aktivní opatření*), the StB published propaganda hit-pieces against Czech and Slovak exile leaders, usually by condemning them as traitorous agents of Czechoslovakia's enemies in the capitalist West. The Czechoslovak Communist press disparaged Zenkl and his "mercenaries" almost daily in the early Cold War. It also threatened to harm exiles' family members still living in Czechoslovakia. Communist propaganda made hay with exile disunity, drawing attention to it in mockery of the exile organizations. The stationing of RFE in Munich was a sore spot for the Czechs. Communist propaganda exploited this, regularly calling it "Munich Free Europe," claiming that the organization was a collaboration of Western capitalists and Neo-Nazis. Claims of involvement with exiles and foreign intelligence were also used to attack victims of the 1950s Stalinist show trials in Czechoslovakia. After Czechoslovak State Security cracked down on the border again in 1971, they renewed threats to target family members of exiles to discourage people from fleeing the country, as well as threats of stripping them of their citizenship to prevent their future return.

The number of those who fled in such a short period consumed their operations, as StB efforts to verify and address those who escaped lasted until the late 1970s.

Czechoslovak State Security (StB) was also active in espionage against exile organizations. The StB First Directorate in the 1950s tried to recruit spies by threatening their family members in Czechoslovakia. Most targets ignored the threats and reported the activities to Western security agencies. Czechoslovak agents had infiltrated RFE and émigré groups to some extent, where they collected information and tried to sow discord within the exile movements. One StB agent, for example, infiltrated the Committee for the Defense of the Unjustly Prosecuted in London, and after becoming its treasurer, absconded with much of the organization's funds. The primary focus of this espionage, however, was in press agencies such as RFE, which StB perceived as the exiles' only threatening function. Several spies infiltrated RFE's Munich office, where they stole information on RFE and émigrés in West Germany and tried to intimidate employees with threats of violence or by vandalizing their property. The most famous example of this type of espionage was Pavel Minařík, who infiltrated RFE in the 1970s. Minařík smuggled out many photocopies on RFE's organization and reported on gossip and possible sources of infiltration among exiles. He later proposed to bomb the organization, although the StB rejected this plan. Minařík's biggest success was as a propaganda symbol; the government praised him as a hero upon his return to Prague in 1976. The CIA used double agents to root out espionage. Notably, a US double agent Iva Havlík exposed an StB plot in 1959 to poison RFE employees via saltshakers in the cafeteria. It is unclear if this espionage had any impact on exile activities, but it seems likely that sabotage was unnecessary, as the exiles did more to hamper their own efforts through their internal discord.[38]

4.4.2 Era of *détente*

The adoption of *Ostpolitik* and détente in the late 1960s made a difference in exile activities. These bridge-building policies between the East and West increased access between the dissident groups in Czechoslovakia and exile organizations, which allowed them to coordinate activities and share material.[39]

---

38 Prokop Tomek, *Československé bezpečnostní složky proti Rádiu Svobodná Evropa "Objekt ALFA"* (Prague: Úřad dokumentace a vyšetřování zločinů komunismu, 2006); Tomek, "Highs and Lows," 113–114, 120–124; Lukeš, *On the Edge*, 217–221; Lukeš, "Czechoslovak Political Exile," 340–341; Raška, *Long*, 39–40, 117–122; Raška, *Fighting*, 71, 145, 150; Koura, "Conscience," 202–215; Vilímek, "Exile," 270–285; Nekola, "Petr Zenkl," 173; Puddington, *Broadcasting*, 47, 74–75, 227; Cummings, *Cold War Radio*, 39–44, 51–56, 198–207; Tony Sharp, *Stalin's American Spy: Noel Field, Allen Dulles and the East European Show Trials* (London: Hurst, 2014), 275–283; Nelson, *War*, 43–44, 61–63, 172.
39 Kovrig, *Of Walls*, 103–363; Günter Bischof, et al, ed. *The Prague Spring and the Warsaw Pact Invasion of Czechoslovakia in 1968* (Lanham: Lexington, 2010); Polišenská, *Diplomatické*.

The signing of the Helsinki Final Act on 1 August 1975 in many respects streamlined Czechoslovak exile activities, as they zeroed-in on promoting general human rights in line with the Helsinki Process. In fact, the primary role of political exiles in the late 1970s became drawing attention to the persecuted reform movements within Czechoslovakia, such as Charter 77 and the Committee for the Defense of the Unjustly Prosecuted. They worked to expose how the Czechoslovak government's oppression of these groups violated the Helsinki terms, to which Czechoslovakia and the Soviet Union had agreed, and demanded a system of enforcing compliance. Many exile organizations contributed to this effort. The CFC aligned itself with the ideals stated in Charter 77's founding charter and disseminated Charter 77's texts to the Western press, world leaders, and international organizations, aided by translations by the Czechoslovak National Council of America. The CFC also began a formal collaboration with the Polish Exile Government in 1986. In 1979, Josten founded the UK Committee for the Defense of the Unjustly Prosecuted (CDUP), including many East European dissidents and British personalities, to draw attention in the United Kingdom to Human Rights violations in the Communist bloc. Exile nuclear physicist František Janouch organized fundraising through his Charter 77 Foundation, based out of Stockholm. Janouch went into exile in 1974, when he fell out of political favor after the Prague Spring. Janouch was a friend of Václav Havel and encouraged his political activism. A member of the *Listy Group*, Janouch supported Czechoslovak and other dissidents (such as Andrei Sakharov), and promoted human rights. Figures such as Řehák, Pelikán, Kavan, and exiled Charter 77 member and Voice of America Broadcaster Ivan Medek were critical for keeping in touch with events in Europe and Czechoslovakia and for informing exiles of activities there, coordinating exile campaigns with reformers within Czechoslovakia, and spreading materials through the samizdat underground distribution network. These connections later included film. *Videomagazín*, produced in the 1980s by exile Czech Journalist Karel Kyncl, spread through Czechoslovakia as a samizdat publication. It included clips from Western television as well as interviews and statements by important exile figures and Czechoslovak dissidents. *Originální videojournal*, made in Czechoslovakia in the late 1980s by a group of amateur filmmakers called Čeněk and funded by Charter 77, filmed accounts of events in Czechoslovakia detached from the "official" sources that they sent abroad to inform exiles.

Although decentralized in organization, these groups became much more coordinated during the late Cold War. Czechoslovak exile groups regularly petitioned to world leaders and international organizations, such as the Commission on Security and Cooperation in Europe (CSCE) and the United Nations, working jointly with Charter 77 and other reform groups to present a common drumbeat on human rights from both within and outside of Czechoslovakia. The CFC gave testimony on Helsinki violations in Czechoslovakia at the CSCE Belgrade meeting from October 1977 to March 1978. The Council followed up the next year with a petition (*Petition '78*) to the UN Human Rights Committee, demanding international organizations to condemn and sanction the Czechoslovak government for human rights violations. A group of twenty-one Czechoslovak organizations in North America, Europe, and Oceania, then produced a document condemning persecution of Charter 77 for the 1980 Madrid meeting of the Commission on Security and Cooperation in Europe and again for the CSCE's 1985 meeting on human rights in Ottawa. At the opening of the CSCE's Vienna meeting on 3 November 1986, Povolný organized protests joined by several East European exile groups. They focused on demands such as the removal of Soviet troops from Czechoslovakia and recognition of Charter 77 as a non-government monitoring organization for human rights under the terms of the Helsinki Act. By November 1989, during the Velvet Revolution, this internal and external pressure led the Communist government to step down. The CFC praised the end of Communist oppression in Czechoslovakia and the return of Czechoslovakia to the community of democratic nations. It also supported the accession of Václav Havel to the presidency.[40]

The Slovak World Congress organized regular anti-Communist propaganda campaigns in the late Cold War, held scholarly conferences and cultural festivals on Slovakia, and contributed to the protest movements in the 1980s. The SWC gained much support from the Vatican under Pope John Paul II and Slovak clergymen in Rome, such as Cardinal Jozef Tomko. It played a key role in getting the Vatican to create an independent archbishopric and church province for Slovakia. It also aided in getting the Pope to proclaim Cyril and Methodius as co-patron saints of Europe in 1980. Collaborating with figures such the hockey player Marián Šťastný and the Čarnogurský family, who were leading members of the organization, the SWC organized overseas protests in conjunction with the candlelight protests in Bratislava on 25 March 1988 to promote religious freedom. In July of that year, they also participated in the Matica Slovenská Institute for Slovaks Abroad held in Bratislava. The following year, it held its Fourth Slovak World Youth Festival in Semmering, Austria, to draw attention to events in Slovakia, including statements from many Slovak dissidents.[41]

Radio Free Europe continued to play an essential role. RFE actively supported the 1968 Prague Spring, as well as the goals of reform Communism in Czechoslovakia. Given the memory of the false hopes spread by RFE in the 1956 Revolution in Hungary, the Czechoslovak branch was careful simply to encourage reforms without provoking beliefs of unrealistic support from the West. Voice of Free Czechoslovakia gave passive praise of Communist First Secretary Alexander Dubček and supported gradual reforms for more decentralization. It did not promote more aggressive re-

---

40 Raška, *Long*, 13–110; Raška, "History," 83–113; Povolný, *Zápas o lidská práva*; Stewart, "We Do Not Want," 243–275; Vilímek, "Exile," 270–285; Caccamo, *Jiří Pelikán*; Milada Polišenská, *Zapomenutý 'nepřítel' Josef Josten*; Connelly, "Jiri Pelikan"; Ciglerova, "Who is Jan Kavan?"; Glanville, "Godot is here"; Lovejoy, "Video Knows no Borders," 206–217; Rupnik, "Legacies of Dissent," 316–332.
41 "Slovak World Congress," in *Slovaks in America*…, 437–457; Stolarik, "Slovak League," 30–31, 33–34; Stolarik, *Where*, 279–296; Raška, *Long*, 46.

forms, such as multi-party elections or an independent foreign policy for Czechoslovakia. To placate the Slovaks, RFE also emphasized Dubček's Slovak heritage and embraced the plans for federalized Czech and Slovak lands. RFE was particularly careful not to hint at intervention and promoted non-violence. Historians note that RFE was more timid than even official Czechoslovak Radio during the Prague Spring, as the Americans hoped to avoid a Soviet intervention and a reversal of détente. RFE focused on objective and general reporting, with little commentary other than a simple condemnation of the invasion and statements of sympathy for the Czech and Slovak people. Afterwards, Radio Free Europe went back to its focus of simply providing news not otherwise received in Czechoslovakia and continued to support the goals of reform Communism in its broadcasts. Most historians praise Radio Free Europe's approach to the Prague Spring as its most effective period.

This approach, however, spurred frustration among the older generation of exiles, who criticized RFE's timidity, complicity with reform communism, and demanded a return to a more aggressive platform. When RFE began hiring post-1968 exiles, mostly experienced radio personalities placed in key roles, this sentiment spread. Older émigrés bemoaned how Communists had taken over the station. During détente, Czechoslovakia limited jamming in return for US limiting of broadcast wattage. Although jamming of RFE continued, Czechoslovakia halted jamming of the BBC and VOA in 1963, and by the late 1980s, VOA became the most popular international station in Czechoslovakia. As détente prioritized more cultural bridge building, RFE added more theater, music and literature to the content of its programs, which focused predominantly on politics and news. It hoped to use culture as a political weapon by drawing attention to the lack of cultural diversity in the Communist bloc. Initially, these programs focused on Czech and Slovak culture from before Communism, utilizing exiled actors and musicians from the First Republic. By the late 1960s, RFE shifted more toward popular culture, particularly jazz and rock music, to make their broadcasts more attractive to young people in Czechoslovakia. To that end, RFE utilized entertainment disk jockeys such as Honza Douba (Jan Měkota) and Rozina Jadrná-Pokorná. Their personalities and programming became so popular with Czechoslovak youth that Radio Prague eventually decided to compete with a similar line up in the same afternoon timeslot.

In the final years of the Cold War, Radio Free Europe gained more access to information, including interviews with dissidents in Czechoslovakia such as Václav Havel. American broadcaster Jolyon Naegele served as East European Correspondent for the Voice of America in the 1970s and 1980s and helped undermine the credibility of Communist leaders and influenced many people in Czechoslovakia in the lead up to the Velvet Revolution. The same was true for musician, journalist, and Charter 77 signatory Ivan Medek, who became an influential broadcaster at VOA in Vienna after his exile in 1978, providing news reports on Czechoslovakia from a Western perspective. In 1988, jamming of RFE ended, making its programs more accessible in Czechoslovakia. Some of its Czech employees, including Pavel Pecháček, were allowed into Czechoslovakia, where they recorded and broadcast events such as the demonstrations at Wenceslas Square in 1989. Radio Free Europe also received and broadcast incoherent ramblings of then new First Secretary Miloš Jakeš, which quickly spread around Czechoslovakia in mockery of the Communist leader. The Slovak World Congress also coordinated its plans for the Candlelight Vigil with RFE, VOA, and Vatican Radio to broadcast the event. A false report by RFE and VOA that police in Prague had killed a student also helped spark the protests in November 1989, thus beginning the Velvet Revolution. After the fall of Communism, RFE relocated from Munich to Prague.[42]

The exile organizations also received increased rhetorical support from Western officials during this time. The Council of Free Czechoslovakia rebuilt linkages with the US State Department's Czechoslovakia Desk and the US Congressional Committee for the Commission on Security and Cooperation in Europe (CSCE), and with Canadian Parliamentary officials, who offered support for the objectives of the Helsinki Program. US Congressional leaders played a key role in getting human rights violations in Eastern Europe recognized, despite attempts to minimize such rhetoric in the name of détente by the administration of US President Jimmy Carter and by West European leaders. Reform Communist exiles from 1968 frequently got along well with and received support from West European socialists. For example, Jiří Pelikán was elected to the European Parliament in 1979. Although Pelikán unsuccessfully pushed for support for Helsinki compliance monitoring within the body, he managed to get the parliament to condemn persecution of Charter 77. Eventually, Jimmy Carter reversed his approach, condemning the treatment of Charter 77 in Czechoslovakia on the fourth anniversary of the Helsinki Act. In the 1980s, the Ronald Reagan administration became staunch supporters. For example, Secretary of State George Schultz regularly mentioned Charter 77 in condemnation of human rights violations in Eastern Europe, and President Reagan made a similar statement on the twentieth anniversary of the Prague Spring. Other leaders in the West such as Margaret Thatch-

---

42 Prokop Tomek, *Nejlepší Propaganda je Pravda: Pavel Pecháček v Československém Rozhlase, v Hlasu Ameriky a ve Svobodné Evropě* (Prague: Nakladatelství Lidové noviny, 2014), 58–182; Prokop Tomek, "Radio Svobodná Evropa a jeho československá redakce"; Marek Junek, "Program na vlnách Rádia Svobodená Evropy"; Vladimír Just, "Svobodná Thálie Svobodné Evropě"; Filip Pospíšil, "Hudební vysílání Svobodné Evropy," in *Svobodně!: Radio Svobodná Evropa 1951–2011*, ed. Marek Junek, et al. (Prague: Radioservis, 2011), 33–49, 74–147; Raška, *Long*, 111–118; Alan L. Heil, Jr., "The Voice of America: A Brief Cold War History," in *Cold War Broadcasting: Impact of the Soviet Union and Eastern Europe* (Budapest: Central European University Press, 2010), 43–44; Puddington, *Broadcasting*, 142–152, 265, 301–302; Brown, *Radio*, 21–26; Nelson, *War*, 116, 137, 184–186; Johnson, *Radio*, 158–167, 223; Stolarik, *Where*, 283; Jan Čulík, "Pár poznámek k historii Svobodné Evropy," *Britský Listy*. 24 October 2011, http://www.blisty.cz/art/60713.html#sthash.UYSvPvWp.dpuf (accessed 3 May 2018); Chris Johnstone, "Legendary Radio Broadcaster Remembered," *Radio Praha*, 7 January 2010, http://www.radio.cz/en/section/curraffrs/legendary-czech-broadcaster-ivan-medek-remembered (accessed 3 May 2018); Radko Kubičko, "Honza Douba on the road again," *Český rozhlas*, 10 April 2015, http://www.rozhlas.cz/plus/nazory/_zprava/radko-kubicko-honza-douba-on-the-road-again-1477068 (accessed 3 May 2018).

er and Pope John Paul II also made statements of support for Czechoslovak organizations, as did other East European exile groups, all of whom drew attention to human rights issues in Czechoslovakia and Eastern Europe broadly. In 1987, US congressional leaders nominated Charter 77 for a Nobel Peace Prize. This support remained primarily rhetorical but corresponded with the broader objective of Cold War exiles to advocate for human rights.[43]

4.5 Migration since 1989

Of the roughly half million Cold War-era Czech and Slovak émigrés, only a small percentage became involved in anti-Communist movements and political organizations. Particularly after 1968, émigrés overwhelmingly turned their energies to heritage preservation or to the daily exigencies of family, social integration, and professional success in their new homes. After the fall of Communism in Czechoslovakia, many exiles went back to their homeland as consultants to the new democracy or as benefactors and fundraisers helping to update the material and intellectual resources of institutions such as libraries, hospitals, scientific academies, archives, and university curricula. Some became politicians, even ministers and close advisors to President Václav Havel (1989–1992, Czechoslovakia, and 1993–2003, Czech Republic). For example, Tigrid was the Minister of Culture from 1994 to 1946. Returning home from Vienna, Ivan Medek was invited by Havel to serve in the office of the president beginning in 1993, eventually becoming the chancellor. Jan Kavan returned to Czechoslovakia and in the early 1990s, he was elected to a seat in the Federal Czechoslovak Assembly. Kavan later had posts in the Czech Senate and Chamber of Deputies. He also served as Minister of Foreign Affairs (1998–2002) and President of the United Nations General Assembly (2002–2003).

Nevertheless, former exiles faced a challenging process when they returned to Czechoslovakia in the early 1990s. After the fall of Communism, the new democratic Czechoslovak government worked quickly to create laws intended to welcome exiles from abroad, keep re-citizenship paperwork to a minimum, and return lost property.[44] The excitement of homecoming was soon beset by a degree of resentment, by unexpected social and cultural assumptions, particularly around what life abroad was really like, and by bureaucratic difficulties, such as the requirements for citizen-

---

43 Raška, *Long*, 27–31, 36–44, 113–116; Raška, "History," 95–97, 100–107; Stolarik, *Where*, 283.
44 Citizenship was usually required for former exiles to request former property. In 1994 a new law made it easier to reclaim revoked citizenship. "These restitution laws brought back many wealthier citizens often with capital and business expertise. Nevertheless, numerically their numbers are very small." Claire Wallace and Andrii Palyanitsya, "East-West Migration and the Czech Republic," *Journal of Public Policy*, 15, no. 1 (Jan–Apr 1995): 89–109: 106.

ship or the recovery of confiscated property in 1948.[45] Resettling in Czechoslovakia after the Velvet Revolution was even more complicated for minority groups that were forced out after the Second World War. In the Sudeten German case, according to Katherine Vadura, "the cut-off date in an otherwise generous restitution law was chosen to preclude the Sudeten Germans from claiming back their property, as did the new citizenship and residency requirements."[46] By 1991, only 10,000 émigrés had resettled in Czechoslovakia, but 20,000 more were predicted to resettle by 1996. Generally, returning exiles did not receive the welcome they had expected, and the process was fraught with misunderstanding, prejudice, and red tape.[47]

4.6 Archives and Literature

There are several important archives in various locations beyond the larger national archives. In the Czech Republic, there is the Center for the Study of Czechoslovak Exiles (Centrum pro československá exilová studia) at the Univerzita Palackého in Olomouc, and in Slovakia, there are the Matica slovenská and the Slovak National Library in Martin. In Vienna, the Research Center for the History of Minorities (Forschungszentrum für historische Minderheiten) houses papers of the Czech Social Democratic Party of Austria which had connections with many who fled Czechoslovakia, especially after the Prague Spring, and the collection of Viennese Czech Ludwig Kolin, who supported escapees from Czechoslovakia. Two important collections on the Sudeten Germans are at the Federal Archives (Bundesarchiv) in Koblenz, Germany: The Bundeskanzleramt records and the records of the Bundesministerium für Vertriebenen, Flüchtlinge und Kriegsgeschädigte. Additionally, the Sudetendeutsches Archiv in Munich maintains collections on many Sudeten German leaders and organizations. The United States is home to numerous collections of papers of individual Czech and Slovak exiles and their organizations. The East European Collection at the Hoover Institute in Stanford, California includes papers from the following: Czech novelist Josef Škvorecký, Slovak Diplomat Štefan Osuský, Czech historian and Czech journalist and former chief of Czechoslovak Desk at Radio Free Europe Vilém Prečan, and Slovak diplomat Juraj Slávik. The Immigration History Research

---

45 One scholar connects the resentment and misunderstandings with the lack of evidence of personal suffering in the novels of Czechoslovak exiles. See: Hron, "The Czech Émigré Experience."
46 All political parties agreed on the following "…with some even wanting to prevent Sudeten Germans from returning," Vadura notes that 1995 was a turning point toward reconciliation between the Czechs and the Sudeten German exiles. Katherine Vadura, "Exile, Return and Restitution in the Czech Republic," *Portal* (January 2005): 19–20.
47 Pehe, "Czechoslovakia," 14. Zuzana Habšudová, "Returned Pianist Feeling Shunned by Compatriots," *The Slovak Spectator*, 13 August 2001, http://spectator.sme.sk/c/20007807/returned-pianist-feeling-shunned-by-compatriots.html (accessed 3 May 2018); Zdeněk Nešpor, "The Disappointed and Disgruntled: A Study of the Return in the 1990s of Czech Emigrants from the Communist Era," *Czech Sociological Review* 38, no. 6 (2002); 789–808; Suppan, 37–40.

Center in Minneapolis, Minnesota houses a wide range of documents: writings of Slovak activist Adam Podkrivacký, records for the American Fund for Czechoslovak Refugees, and papers from Czech politician and editor for RFE, Miloslav Rechcígl, Sr., as well as many Czech and Slovak publications from America. The Historical Society of Pennsylvania, formerly the Balch Institute, has records on many individuals, such as Slovak politician Edward J. Behuncik and diplomat and historian Vladimir Hurban. The University of Nebraska-Lincoln Czech Heritage Collection maintains collections of several Czech exiles including politician Petr Zenkl and journalists Rudolf Kopecký and Josef Josten. The Archives of Czechs and Slovaks Abroad at the University of Chicago and the National Czech and Slovak Museum and Library in Cedar Rapids, Iowa, house material on many organizations and individuals, including papers from the Czechoslovak National Council of America and a fine collection of oral histories. The papers of Slovak diplomat and lawyer Ján Papánek are housed at the New York Public Library. There are also several sources specifically devoted to the Slovaks. The Slovak Institute in Cleveland, Ohio has documentation and publications from many Slovak groups such as the Slovak World Congress and the Slovak League of America, as well as documents on many Slovak exiles, including politicians Karol Sidor and Ferdinand Ďurčanský, and historian Konštantín Čulen. Indeed, the Slovak Institute has the largest collection of Slovak immigrant and émigré publications, and there is a sizeable collection of Slovak publications at the Jankola Library in Danville, Pennsylvania. Generally, there are no shortages of published memoirs, political, historical, and cultural writings of exiles.[48]

In addition, there are many recent valuable historical works on the topic of Cold War exiles from former Czechoslovakia. Francis Raška has written prolifically on the topic of Czech and Czechoslovak organizations, particularly the Council of Free Czechoslovakia.[49] Other scholars have also produced works on the topic, including Boris Čelovský, Igor Lukeš, Slavomír Michálek, Mojmír Povolný.[50] There are also many recent biographical works of important exile leaders.[51] Regarding the Slovaks specifically, M. Mark Stolarik is the preeminent scholar on Slovak immigration to North America, and recent works by Jozef Špetko and Jozef C Trubinsky have expanded upon the Slovaks in exile.[52] Paul Robert Magocsi has written prominentely on the Subcarpathian Rusyn.[53] Pertti Ahonen and R. M. Douglas are some of many scholars

---

[48] For a more comprehensive list of Czech and Slovak Archives in the United States, see: Miloslav Rechcígl, Jr. *Czechoslovak American Archivalia* (Olomouc-Ostrava: Repronis, 2004).
[49] Raška, *Fighting Communism from Afar*; Raška, *Long Road to Victory*.
[50] Čelovský, *Politici bez moci*; Lukeš, "Czechoslovak Political Exile"; Michalek, "Rada"; Povolný, *Zápas o lidská práva*.
[51] Michálek, *Ján Papánek*; Michálek, *Diplomat Štefan Osuský*; Kosatík, *Ferdinand Peroutka*; Goněc, *Za sjednocenou Evropu;* Nekola, *Petr Zenkl.*
[52] Stolarik, *Where is my Home?*; Stolarik, "Slovak League"; Jozef C. Trubinsky, *Slovenský*; Špetko, *Líšky.*
[53] Magocsi, *Of the Making*; Magocsi, "Magyars and Carpatho-Rusyns." The situation of exiles from the smaller minorities, such as the Rusyn and Czechoslovak Hungarians, is one area needing much

who have produced new research on the Sudeten Germans.⁵⁴ Lukeš and Prokop Tomek, among others, have contributed with works focusing on Czech and Slovak involvement in Cold War espionage and organizations such as Radio Free Europe.⁵⁵ Other works include those analyzing the return of exiles after the fall of Communism in 1989.⁵⁶ There are many collected works that address Czechoslovakia as part of broader examinations of Cold War exile movements from Central and Eastern Europe.⁵⁷

---

more research to contribute to the expanding literature on the Czech, Slovak, and Sudeten German exiles.
54 Ahonen, *After the Expulsion*; Douglas, *Orderly*; Margolit, "Foreign Policy of the German Sudeten Council"; Spurný, "Czech and German Memories."
55 Lukeš, *On the Edge*; Tomek, *Československé bezpečnostní*; Tomek, *Nejlepší Propaganda je Pravda*; Vojtěch Jeřábek, *Československi uprchlici ve studene valce. Junek, Marek et al. eds. Svobodně!: Radio Svobodná Evropa 1951–2011* (Prague: Radioservis, 2011).
56 Hron, "The Czech Émigré Experience"; Vadura, "Exile, Return and Restitution."
57 Anna Mazurkiewicz, ed. *East Central Europe in Exile: Transatlantic Identities* (Newcastle upon Tyne: Cambridge Scholars Publishing, 2013); Katalin Kádár Lynn, ed. *The Inauguration of Organized Political Warfare* (Saint Helena, CA: Helena History Press, 2013); *Samizdat, Tamizdat...*, *passim*; Ieva Zaķe, ed. *Anti-Communist Minorities in the US: Political Activism of Ethnic Refugees* (New York: Palgrave Macmillan, 2009).

5 Germany
Bethany Hicks

5.1 German migration in historical perspective

In post-Napoleonic Europe, migration into, from, and within the territories that would eventually become the German Empire was influenced largely, but not exclusively, by socio-economic factors. As political upheaval, the second Industrial Revolution, and the rhetorical beginnings of ethnic nationalism began to reshape Europe, migration – both out of choice and necessity – became increasingly common. In the aftermath of the German revolutions of 1848–1849, tens of thousands of "Forty-Eighters," emigrated to the United States, the United Kingdom, Switzerland, and the Ottoman Empire.[1] While the emigration of German nationals to the United States peaked after 1848, over three million arrived between 1871 and 1920, with a significant number settling in the burgeoning cities of the American Midwest.

Although the burgeoning mining centers and industrial cities of within the western Ruhr Valley attracted considerable population growth in the late nineteenth and early twentieth century, previously established migratory patterns were largely maintained until the First World War.[2] Even as net overseas immigration continued to rise, seasonal migration of young men and women from rural to urban areas during agricultural down periods saw an increase as rail networks became more dense, while traditional circular migration patterns dictated by seasonal planting and harvest schedules of asparagus, sugar beets, and hay remained important.[3]

Nationalism also heavily influenced emigration patterns after 1848. Although periodic westward movements of German-speaking populations have been documented as far back as the eighth century, in the nineteenth century ethnic nationalist organizations began to actively encourage further *Ostsiedlung*, with the goal to Germanize the ethnically Slavic provinces of the new empire. Despite support from pan-German nationalist organizations such as the Alldeutscher Verband, who saw further German settlement in the East as a means to "raise German national consciousness," this drive was largely offset by internal migration from the rural south to newly industrializing areas in the western empire.[4]

---

[1] Heléna Tóth, *An Exiled Generation: German and Hungarian Refugees of Revolution, 1848–1871* (Cambridge: Cambridge University Press, 2014).
[2] James Harvey Jackson, *Migration and Urbanization in the Ruhr Valley, 1812–1914* (Boston: Brill, 1997).
[3] Steve Hochstadt, *Mobility and Modernity: Migration in Germany 1820–1989* (Ann Arbor: University of Michigan Press, 1999).
[4] Henry Cord Meyer, *Drang nach Osten: Fortunes of a Slogan-Concept in German-Slavic Relations, 1849–1990* (Bern: Peter Lang, 1996).

The First World War saw the disruption of many previously entrenched migration patterns. The mass mobilization of German soldiers, as well as the development of wartime industrial production centers meant that more people were on the move (both voluntarily and involuntarily) than in any previous period in human history. Despite the devastating territorial, economic, and social consequences of its defeat after 1945, Germany became the primary destination in Europe for political refugees (primarily from the Russian Civil War), persons displaced as a result of the state building process set in motion by the Paris Peace Conference.[5]

The terms of the Treaty of Versailles ceded a large section of the former German Empire to reconstituted Poland, including Posen, West Prussia, and Upper Silesia. Fear of a mass expulsion of ethnic Germans by the ethnically Polish population and the revival of the eugenic concept of *Lebensraum* by the National Socialist Party and other opponents of the Weimar government were used as a political tool to draw public attention to the alleged threat posed to the survival of the German nation. After the National Socialists seized power in 1933, the goal to protect Germans already in the East became secondary to the idea to obtain, occupy, and ethnically cleanse Eastern Europe for the future development of an Aryan population under the banner *Heim ins Reich*. From 1939 through 1944, approximately 867,000 ethnic Germans were transferred from lands occupied by the Soviet Union because of the Molotov-Ribbentrop pact (the Baltics, western Ukraine, and Moldova), as well as from South Tyrol and Slovenia, primarily to the newly formulated *Reichsgaue* and the Protectorate of Bohemia and Moravia.[6]

Between 1933 and 1939, legal and illegal migration of Jewish and other persecuted groups under the Nazi regime became a major complication in both domestic and international terms. Domestically, the movement and livelihoods of Jewish inhabitants of Germany were increasingly restricted as laws mounted to deprive individuals of the right to practice professions, attend school, operate, or patronize businesses, and to own property or possess wealth. As argued by Marion Kaplan, the removal of Jews from society facilitated mass deportation to Jewish ghetto districts in the East, as a transit station before their eventual deportation to death camps.[7]

For Jews who did possess property and acted early enough, emigration in the early years of the Hitler regime was possible. Out of approximately 523,000 Jews living in Germany in 1933, around 40,000 migrated immediately or shortly after the appointment of Hitler as Chancellor. The majority of those who emigrated during this period went to neighboring European countries including France, Belgium, and the Netherlands, with many becoming subject to racial policies after Nazi occupa-

---

5 Jochen Oltmer, *Migration und Politik in der Weimarer Republik* (Göttingen: Vandenhoek & Ruprecht, 2005).
6 Klaus J. Bade and Jochen Oltmer, "Deutschland," in Klaus J. Bade et. al. *Enzyklopädie Migration in Europa. Vom 17. Jahrhundert bis zur Gegenwart* (Munich: Schöningh, 2007), 1041–1070.
7 Marion A. Kaplan, *From Dignity to Despair: Jewish Life in Nazi Germany* (Oxford: Oxford University Press, 2005).

tion. Although emigration was officially encouraged by Hitler's regime until 1941, internal policies became more restrictive, it became harder to leave the country, with limits put in place to restrict wealth taken out of the country, and prohibitively high costs of exit visas. In addition, especially after the pogroms of 1938, many destination countries, including Cuba, the United States, and Canada, actively denied or retracted entry to Jewish refugees.[8]

As with the First World War, the transition to wartime industry and production in preparation for the World War II meant a previously unprecedented volume of people on the move. An estimated 12.5 million soldiers mobilized for the German military during the course of the war. In addition, labor migration – both voluntary and involuntary, accounted for a considerable volume of movement both eastward and westward into various manufacturing centers. The resumption of mining and industrial production in the Ruhr by the Nazi regime, in defiance of the terms of the Treaty of Versailles in 1935, resulted in a drastic reduction in unemployment and a westward demand for German labor. However, unlike other wartime labor mobilization efforts, the Nazi regime resisted large-scale participation of women in the domestic labor force until nearly the end of the war. As wartime demand outweighed available workers, the Nazi regime relied heavily on the forced labor of occupied peoples. According to Ulrich Herbert, there were an estimated 7.8 million foreign forced laborers in the Reich and the occupied territories in January 1944, with most having been relocated to or near worksites. In addition to the forced labor carried out by prisoners of concentration and extermination camps, foreign workers can be divided into three categories: *Zivilarbeiter*, primarily Poles paid low wages from the General Government, *Ostarbeiter* – Soviet and Polish workers imprisoned in camp and given minimal rations, and *Militärinternierte* – (primarily Soviet) prisoners of war.[9]

5.2 The aftermath of World War II

5.2.1 Migration and mobility in occupied Germany, 1945–1949

As the Second World War came to a close, Allied gains and Axis retreat meant the start of an intensely chaotic period of mass migration. In Central Europe, many different populations were set into motion as Allied forces first moved in first to occupy, and then to stabilize the territories of the former Third Reich. Between 1945 and 1949, an estimated 30 to 35 million individuals in the territory of the former Third Reich (out of a total population of 65 million) were at one time defined as either a displaced

---

[8] Dirk Hoerder, *Cultures in Contact: World Migrations in the Second Millennium* (Durham: Duke University Press, 2002), 458–459.
[9] Ulrich Herbert, *Hitler's Foreign Workers: Enforced Foreign Labor in Germany under the Third Reich* (Cambridge: Cambridge University Press, 1997).

person, evacuee, expellee, or refugee.[10] By 1947, the initial division of Germany and the city of Berlin into four Allied sectors had cemented into a permanent division, as the western sectors (British, American and French) united to create a trizonal authority in exclusion of the Soviet occupation zone. The ways that the Western and Soviet occupation regimes defined and managed the practical and political aspects of migration during this period reflected the structural and ideological goals of each occupation regime.

The label "displaced person" (DP), referred specifically to foreign nationals who found themselves in German territory at the end of the war, including those who had been forced to labor for the Nazi regime, prisoners of war, and concentration camp survivors.[11] Even before the war ended, measures were taken to prepare for the inevitable population crisis that would erupt on the European continent at the conclusion of the war. In 1943, a 44-nation conference led by the United States was held in Washington D.C. to establish the United Nations Relief and Rehabilitation Administration (UNRRA). With the assistance of the four Allied authorities and the International Red Cross, the UNRRA took the lead in facilitating the repatriation of approximately 12 million DPs in the three western zones immediately after the German capitulation in May 1945. Four months after the end of the war, approximately 6 million DPs had been successfully repatriated from the western occupation zones; by the end of 1946, only 500,000 remained.[12] While the majority of DPs returned to their countries of origin, the UNRRA arranged for those who were unable or unwilling to be repatriated to settle in one of the charter nations, or in the case of many Jewish survivors, to emigrate to the United States or Israel.[13]

In the Soviet occupation zone, repatriation was handled much differently than in the three western zones. Although the Soviet Union had been a founding member of the UNRRA, the agency was not invited to administer DPs in the Soviet occupation zone after the war. In contrast to the repatriation options available to many DPs in the western zones, compulsory repatriation under Soviet authority was mandatory. As reported by historian (and former DP) Eugene Kulischer, those who refused to return to their home country were "assumed to be collaborationists, Nazi helpers, or quislings, and therefore should be extradited to their legal governments as war criminals."[14] This policy was so effective that the Soviet occupation regime was able to

---

10 Klaus J. Bade, *Europa in Bewegung: Migration vom späten 18. Jahrhundert bis zur Gegenwart* (Munich: C.H. Beck), 284–297.
11 As of October 1944, there were more than 8 million forced laborers in Germany. This number includes 6 million civilian laborers and 2 million prisoners of war from over 20 different countries. Klaus J. Bade and Jochen Oltmer, "Deutschland," in Bade et. al., *Enzyklopädie Migration in Europa. Vom 17. Jahrhundert bis zur Gegenwart* (Munich: Schöningh, 2007), 158.
12 Bade and Oltmer, "Deutschland," 159.
13 UNRRA countries with the highest labor shortages accepted the largest number of DPs from Belgium, the United Kingdom, Canada and Australia. Bade and Oltmer, "Deutschland," 158.
14 Eugene Kulischer, "Displaced Persons in the Modern World," *Annals of the American Academy of Political and Social Science* 262 (1949): 170.

declare in January 1947 that "no single displaced citizen of an Allied nation remains in the USSR or in the Soviet occupied countries."[15]

The Soviet regime also insisted upon universal repatriation of their citizens from Allied occupied territories; an expectation legitimized with the inclusion of a mutual repatriation policy signed by the Americans, British, and Soviets at Yalta in February 1945.[16] With the cooperation of the UNRRA in the western zones, two million pre-war Soviet citizens were subjected to compulsory repatriation.[17] Targeted groups included POWs and former forced laborers, as well as politically persecuted groups who had fled the Soviet Union immediately before or during the war. Upon repatriation, many were convicted of either having fought for the German forces or otherwise collaborated with the enemy, including approximately 1.5 million Red Army soldiers taken by the Germans as prisoners of war who were sentenced to the Gulag upon their return to Soviet soil.[18]

Germans who had been displaced from their homes as a result of the war were a further category of migrants. The intensification of the air war against Germany in late 1944 and early 1945 resulted in the mass evacuation of over six million urban citizens. By the end of the war, an estimated 25 percent of all housing available in 1939 had been destroyed. However, in some large cities such as Cologne, Würzburg, and Dresden, the totality of Allied bombing campaigns had made a majority of buildings unsuitable for habitation.[19] In contrast with the comparatively quick administrative action mobilized to manage displaced persons, a lack of organization, resources, a weakened labor pool, and competition for housing with other displaced populations slowed down the resolution for evacuees.

In the Soviet zone, a preoccupation with reparations hindered the reconstruction of usable housing facilities. At Yalta, the Soviets had proposed to take $10 billion in reparations from their occupation zone, a proposal that was not accepted by the western powers. According to the Potsdam Agreement, occupation powers were to prioritize stabilizing their respective zones before allocating resources for reparation, which the Soviets readily ignored. Quickly following the establishment of the Soviet Occupation Authority, military and state industries, as well as those owned by Nazis

---

15 Mark Elliot, "The United States and Forced Repatriation of Soviet Citizens," *Political Science Quarterly* 88 no. 2 (Spring 1973): 258.
16 According to Kulischer, "(Yalta) provided compulsory repatriation of Soviet citizens (from the pre-war USSR territory not including the Baltic States, eastern Poland and Bessarabia) who were: (1) captured in German uniforms, (2) members of the Soviet Armed Forces, or (3) found on the basis of reasonable evidence to be collaborators with the enemy." Kulischer, "Displaced Persons in the Modern World," 170.
17 Kulischer, "Displaced Persons in the Modern World," 172.
18 Ulrike Goeken-Haidl, *Der Weg zurück: Die Repatriierung Sowjetischer Zwangsarbeiter während und nach dem zweiten Weltkrieg* (Essen: Klartext Verlag, 2006), 258.
19 Jeffery Diefendorf, *In the Wake of the War: The Reconstruction of German Cities after World War II* (New York: Oxford University Press, 1993), 125–127.

and war criminals were confiscated.[20] These industries amounted to approximately 60 percent of the total industrial production in the Soviet zone. In addition, the Soviet Union claimed heaviest industrial production outright as reparation. Soviet joint stock companies were formed to manage and trade these commodities directly out of the occupation zone and to send the proceeds back to Moscow. In contrast to the situation in the western zones, very little native capital was put towards reconstruction. Housing, however, especially in urban areas, remained in low supply for all Germans in the immediate occupation period.[21] As late as April 1947, an estimated three to four million evacuees remained displaced across the four occupation zones. Although as local administrations were re-establish some local capital was put into the rehabilitation of housing stocks, in the western zones would not occur until the currency union and arrival of Marshall Aid in mid-1948.[22]

Although DPs and evacuees were prominent in the immediate post-war period, ethnic German expellees made up the largest migrant population in all four occupation zones. Between 1944 and 1949, over 14 million ethnic Germans living east of the Oder-Neisse line were displaced, initially fleeing the advancing Soviet Red Army or later resettled by local authorities of the reconstituted Czechoslovak state.

By 1949, a total of 12.5 million expellees had been registered as refugees in occupied Germany.[23] Although the Potsdam Agreement had stipulated that expellees should be distributed equally among the four occupation zones, the actual settlement was unevenly distributed. Approximately 4.3 million expellees were resettled in the Soviet occupation zone, while 8 million refugees were spread across the three western zones. The vast majority of expellees who ended up in the West were registered to the British and American authorities, with only 1 percent ending up in the French occupation zone.[24]

For expellees who arrived in the western occupation zones, the immediate post-war years were chaotic and difficult. From 1945 to 1948, expellees faced dire material shortages as they competed for resources with other migrant populations. Expellees in both East and West were settled in rural areas. However, as with policies regarding evacuees, the coordination of resources and policy was minimal in all four zones until after the formation of the two Cold War German states in 1949.[25]

---

20 US Department of State, *The Soviet Note on Berlin: an analysis* 6757, no. 52 (1959), 26.
21 Stephen R. Burant, *East Germany: A Country Study* (Washington D.C.: Library of Congress, 1988), 44.
22 Gregory F. Schroeder, "Ties of Urban Heimat: West German Cities and Their Wartime Evacuees in the 1950s," *German Studies Review* 27 no.2 (May 2004): 308.
23 According to Bade and Oltmer, 500,000 expellees settled in Austria, 300,000 were repatriated to the USSR and hundreds of thousands did not survive the initial journey. Bade and Oltmer, "Flucht und Vertreibung nach dem zweiten Weltkrieg," 158.
24 Gerhard Reichling, *Die Deutschen Vertriebenen in Zählen: Umsiedler, Verschleppte, Vertriebene, Aussiedler, 1940–1985* (Bonn: Kulturstiftung der Deutschen Vertriebenen, 1995), 17.
25 Philipp Ther, "The Integration of Expellees in Germany and Poland after World War II: A Historical Reassessment," *Slavic Review* 55, no. 4 (1996): 789.

5.3 Major migration streams during the Cold War

5.3.1 German migration before the Berlin Wall, 1949–1961

With further ideological entrenchment caused by the Soviet blockade of West Berlin following the currency union of the three western zones in June 1948, and the failure of that blockade to force West Berlin to adopt the Soviet issued *Ostmark*, the momentum toward separate German statehood increased. As each state established its own structures and policies to deal with migration, reconstruction, resettlement, employment and other related issues, sharper legal categories began to be drawn in order to define immigration as legal or illegal, and to determine to which benefits (if any) certain migrant groups were entitled.

The Federal Republic of Germany (FRG) was founded in May 1949, uniting the three western occupied zones under one independent German government. The new state was initially concerned with managing the large number of German expellees who continued to enter the Federal Republic throughout the 1950s, and to mitigate the competition that had developed between groups (evacuees, expellees, GDR-refugees) who required aid from the economically fragile West German state.

The foundation of the German Democratic Republic (GDR) on 9 October 1949 would transfer responsibility for the regulation and definition of migration and migrants from Soviet occupation forces to the new regime headed by the Socialist Unity Party (SED). Although emigration would prove to be the most pressing issue, other migratory concerns surrounding refugee populations, repatriation, contract workers, and internal migration were prominent as well. As a whole, migration during this period reflected political, economic and social conditions within the state, as well as policy enacted in both Cold War German regimes. As the population and labor needs of both German states shifted, so too did the political, legal, social and cultural attitudes toward migration. After the construction of the Berlin Wall in 1961, the massive emigration of the young and educated from the GDR, which had been the primary concern of the state, stabilized. New energy was afterward put into publicizing repatriation and using those who wished to emigrate as political capital to trade for Western currency and commodities.

One strategy employed in the West to combat population concentration was to settle expellees in rural areas. Klaus Bade and Jochen Oltmer identify three main "expellee-states" in the West. By the mid-1950s, Schleswig-Holstein had received 837,500 expellees (31.6 percent of the population), 1,475,500 expellees were settled in Lower Saxony (22.9 percent of the population), and Bavaria had received 1,657,800 expellees (18.4 percent of the population).[26]

---

26 Klaus J. Bade and Jochen Oltmer, "Einführung: Einwanderungsland Niedersachsen – Zuwanderung und Integration seit dem Zweiten Weltkrieg," In *Zuwanderung und Integration seit dem Zweiten Weltkrieg*, ed. Klaus J. Bade and Jochen Oltmer (Osnabrück: Universitätsverlag Rasch, 2002), 14.

Rural areas were attractive resettlement areas due to slow pace of reconstruction and limited resources in urban areas. The British military authority, in an attempt to avoid a concentration of refugees in the eastern half of the state, transported expellees to more sparsely populated districts in Lower Saxony, as well as to the northern East Frisian Islands. In the case of expellees who were transported to Lower Saxony, the eastern side of the state was preferred by expellee farmers who favored the dry fields of the East over the swamps of the Emsland, as well as by workers who hoped to find work in the industrial districts of Hanover.[27] The greater difficulty of integration in rural areas contributed to the tendency for expellees to migrate again within West Germany. While rural areas were targeted for resettlement because of the lower population density, employment and housing were in short supply.[28]

In contrast to the situation in the Federal Republic, the Soviets targeted the presence of the "resettler" (*Umsiedler*) population as justification for the redistribution of housing and land.[29] With the establishment of the Central Office for German Resettlers (Zentralverwaltung für deutsche Umsiedler) in September 1945, the Soviet authorities pursued an aggressive policy of population redistribution. As was generally true regarding the distribution of resources across the population of the East German state, working age expellees received priority assistance, leaving a large older population with substandard housing and little access to resources.[30] The lack of opportunity for social mobility and the closed nature of the SED party system made nonprofessional expellees more or less a permanent underclass in the GDR. These factors all contributed to a high number of expellees emigrating to West Germany throughout the 1950s.

In the Federal Republic, the legal definition and reception of incomers changed according to the development of various political and economic realities during the 1950s. In the initial months after being founded, the Federal Republic offered aid to all ethnic Germans – those with evidence of German ancestry, regardless of whether they came from the former eastern Reich or the German Democratic Republic. The term *Vertriebene* (expellee) came into use in the West only after the adoption of the Federal Law on Expellees in January 1953, to refer to those who had been forced

---

27 Bernhard Parisius, "'und ahnten, dass hier die Welt zu Ende ist.' Aufnahme und Integration von Flüchtlingen und Vertriebenen im Westen Niedersachsens," in *Zuwanderung und Integration ...*, 41.
28 Daniel Levy, "Integrating Ethnic Germans in West Germany: The Early Postwar Period," in *Coming Home to Germany? The Integration of Ethnic Germans from Central and Eastern Europe in the Federal Republic,* ed. David Rock and Stefan Wolff (Oxford: Berghahn Books, 2002), 27.
29 The Soviet Occupation Authority and the East German regime did not use the term *Vertriebene* to refer to ethnic German refugees. Instead, they chose to use the more neutral term *Umsiedler* (resettler) to avoid addressing the issue of German victimhood at the hands of the Soviet Army. Ian Connor, *Refugees and Expellees in Post-War Germany* (Manchester: University of Manchester Press, 2007), 22.
30 Esther Neblich, "Das Umsiedlerproblem der Jahre 1945–1955 in der SBZ/DDR am Beispiel des Oberen Vogtlandes," in *Agenda DDR-Forschung,* ed. Heiner Timmermann (Berlin: LIT Verlag, 2005), 248.

to leave their homelands as a result of the territorial reconfiguration in the aftermath of the war.[31]

In 1950 and again in 1951, the West German government instituted "emergency procedures" to legally differentiate between *Vertriebene* and *Sowjetzonenflüchtlinge* (SBZ-refugees) – Germans who had come to the West from the German Democratic Republic. In order to qualify for emergency refugee status as a SBZ-refugee, one had to first present themselves at a refugee camp for registration and to provide evidence that they faced imminent danger of political persecution. Due to the stringency of these requirements, many SBZ-refugees lived in a legally grey area, as it was very difficult to gain a refugee permit under the emergency law if they initially sought shelter with a relative in the West, or if the individual could not produce documentation of a specific political threat from the state.[32]

Despite the barriers to legal status in the West, the numbers of those "fleeing the Republic" (GDR) for the FRG steadily increased in the decade before the construction of the Berlin Wall. A 1953 report in the West German newsmagazine *Der Spiegel* points to a distinct pattern of emigration that was directly related to Soviet and East German attempts at social and economic reorganization:

> From 1945 to 1947, it was mostly owners of large businesses and industries, deposed by Soviet reorganization, which came. In 1948, smaller business owners and light industrialists, especially from Saxony and Thuringia, after the hunt for capitalists, were revived by textile commissioner Fritz Lange. Numerous owners of large commercial firms came in 1949, after the creation of national wholesale head offices for the retail trade. In 1950, many fallen ministers of the SBZ people's parties, Eastern CDU ministers, district administrators and mayors … in 1951 and 1952, an increasing number of physicians was counted, who had been obligated to give up their private practices in favor of public health centers. Likewise, pharmacists whose pharmacies had also been nationalized, and owners of theatres, who saw their theatres communalized. By the end of the year, the exodus of the farmers had begun. The iron stirring the cauldron of the transformation had now reached the depths of the social pyramid.[33]

While political and economic grounds were often entwined, there were several other non-material motives for emigration. A pamphlet published by the West German Agency for Refugee Matters (Westdeutscher Senat für Flüchtlingsfragen) reported an increase in the number of males between the ages of 14 and 24 appearing at refugee camps in West Berlin by 37.5 percent after the implementation of compulsory military service in the East German *Volksarmee* or labor duty in the Soviet Union.[34]

The age distribution of emigrants in this period was also very pronounced and had significant impact on the development of East German social structures and re-

---

31 Connor, *Refugees and Expellees*, 22.
32 Helge Heidemeyer, *Flucht und Zuwanderung aus der SBZ/DDR: Die Flüchtlingspolitik der Bundesrepublik Deutschland bis zum Bau der Berliner Mauer* (Düsseldorf: Droste, 1994), 53–58.
33 "Sowjetzonen-Flüchtlinge: Reine Torschlusspanik," *Der Spiegel*, 18 February 1953.
34 Senate of Berlin, ed. "Refugees Flooding the Island of Berlin: Senate of Berlin Report" (Berlin: Senate of Berlin, 1953), 84.

gional productivity. While the gender balance remained around 50/50 (with females outnumbering males (approximately 52 percent to 48 percent), between 1949 and 1961 more than 75 percent of all migrants were under the age of 40. In addition, more than 30 percent of those who emigrated between 1949 and 1953 were classified either as homemakers or dependent children.[35]

While the reasons for emigration could be seen as fundamentally material, the consequences for the GDR of the continued emigration of the most productive parts of its population to the FRG were certainly political on both sides. In the GDR, migrants were portrayed as *Republikflüchtlinge*, enemies of the state who had fled the GDR either by choice or by force. In the early 1950s, the SED went to great lengths to discourage the general population from considering fleeing to the FRG. In 1952, the greater inner German border was militarized, creating a 500 m protected strip and evacuating or severely restricting communities within five km of the border. After the completion of this project, German-German emigration shifted almost exclusively to the border between East and West Berlin.

Propaganda was also utilized in order to discourage potential emigration. In 1953, Gerhard Eisler, SED Commissioner for *Republikflucht*, toured several major East German cities with a dozen repatriates. As he described in an interview given to *Der Spiegel*, the purpose of the tour was to show GDR citizens that the grass was not greener on the other side of the border:

> These people have come back. They lost their heads, but they realized quite quickly that only the castoffs of the GDR collect themselves in West Berlin, those who have not heard the call of the hour to fight for Germany. It will be for all of those who flee, like their predecessors, the Russian Kulaks, spies, and cowards. They will end up in the bordellos, penitentiaries, and foreign legions of Western Europe. Restless, they will roam from miserable quarter to miserable quarter, always moving further westward.[36]

While the SED tried its hardest to discourage its citizens from even thinking about leaving, the western German economy began to grow under the support of Marshall Aid and the recovery of key industries. The passage of the Federal Refugee Law (Bundesvertriebenengesetz, BvG) on 15 May 1953 reaffirmed the West German commitment to defend the "right to return" to areas of previous residence (which had been first established under Article 116 of the Basic Law), while simultaneously relaxing the conditions under which GDR citizens could emigrate to the Federal Republic. While the previous statute defined the parameters for refugees from the Soviet Zone (*SBZ-Flüchtlinge*), the BvG made no distinctions between refugees, effectively lumping *Vertriebene* and *SBZ-Flüchtlinge* into the same category.

---

[35] Statistisches Bundesamt Deutschland. *Statistisches Jahrbuch für der Bundesrepublik Deutschland –1965* (Wiesbaden: Statistisches Bundesamt, 1964), 98–117.
[36] "Sowjetzonen-Flüchtlinge: Reine Torschlusspanik."

This softening of the West German legal framework was tested just two months later as migration from east to west again surged after Soviet forces assisted the SED regime in the suppression of a worker's protest in Berlin on 17 July 1953, and again after the Hungarian Uprising of 1956. In the following years, as material conditions in the west continued to improve and tensions with the GDR increased, the phenomenon of east-west migration became an increasingly important political discourse in the escalating climate of the Cold War.

The year 1957 was as a turning point on both sides of the Cold War divide. As the West German regime renewed its rhetorical push for eventual unification after the Hungarian Uprising, it became increasingly important to publicly stress the political illegitimacy of the regime in the GDR. According to historian Volker Ackermann, this impulse began to recast which populations were believed to have legitimate grounds for refugee status. While in the past the *Vertriebene* population tended to be privileged over *SBZ-Flüchtlinge*, the increased migration from the GDR now became politically important as proof of a repressive and illegitimate regime. In March 1957, the West German government tried to suppress the publication of study conducted by the private firm Infratest in the West German newspaper *Frankfurter Allgemeine Zeitung* that indicated that most who fled the GDR upon arrival, gave non-political grounds for their flight (*unpolitische Fluchtgründe*). Furthermore, that 29 percent of those who came, did so to "improve their economic situation."[37]

This trend was also reflected in changes to the legal frameworks surrounding refugee status. In July 1957, an amendment to the BvG expanded the grounds for flight to include a 'serious conflict of conscience.' Three months after the amendment to the BvG, the GDR voted a passport requirement into law (*Passgesetz*). In addition to increasingly restrictive visa requirements and the introduction of educational and economic punitive measures for the relatives of those who "fled" the republic, formally outlawed *Republikflucht*, the law increased punishment for those who had been caught and it introduced measures to facilitate the confiscation of property of those who emigrated illegally. The passage of this law contributed to the reduction of east-west migration by one-third between 1957 and 1958. However, legislation did not get to the root of the problem – the porous border between East and West Berlin, which would not be closed until the construction of the Berlin Wall in 1961.[38]

---

[37] Volker Ackermann, *Der "echte" Flüchtling: Deutsche Vertriebene und Flüchtlinge aus der DDR, 1945–1961* (Osnabrück: Universitätsverlag Rasch, 1995), 35.

[38] As investigated by historian Corey Ross, many East Germans, especially members of the intelligentsia, used the possibility of emigration as leverage for gaining better employment, housing, automobiles etc. "The success or failure of using the open border to one's advantage depended very much on the person doing it. Emigration of members of the intelligentsia, especially those in scientific and technical fields, as considered no less than 'a great danger to society,' and they, more than any other segment of the population, were well placed to exploit the situation. Although the criminalization of *Republikflucht* under the 'Passport Law' of December 1957 put a swift end to open threats of leaving for the West, the possibility of leaving the GDR remained an implicit part of the equation." Corey

Although the massive flight from the GDR to the FRG tends to dominate the historical narrative of this period, a considerable number of FRG citizens chose to move to the GDR each year. From 1950 to 1961, approximately 400,000 people migrated from the FRG to the GDR. These migrants were very important as tools of propaganda for the SED. In addition to taking migrants who had been "repatriated" on a public speaking tour, the GDR also issued periodic press releases detailing the numbers of migrants and the reasons for their defection.[39]

In 1960, *Der Spiegel* reported on the outrage of the West German media over reports in the *New York Times* and the *New York Daily Mail* concerning the increase in the number of West Germans defecting to the GDR. Although the article emphasized the propaganda that had been dealt out by the SED in order to make the movement appear larger than it actually was, the report did concede that there were a total of eight reception centers in the GDR which were designed to receive western "refugees," including a special center for members of the intelligentsia.[40]

Despite the measures taken to outlaw *Republikflucht* in 1957, and the energy put into creating propaganda that showed people moving in the opposite direction, illegal migration to the FRG continued to be a real concern. Indeed, stopping the "bleeding out" of the GDR became the key to stabilizing the country internationally, economically, and socially. In June 1961, the West German government made an additional amendment to the BvG, officially recognizing economic reasons as grounds for flight. This removed the final real barrier to emigration and East to West defection quickly resumed to pre-1958 levels.

By 1960, the working age population in the GDR was reduced to 61 percent of its total population; a loss of almost 10 percent since the end of the Second World War. The loss was disproportionately heavy among professionals: engineers, technicians, physicians, teachers, lawyers, and skilled workers. On 12 August 1961, SED Chairman Walter Ulbricht signed the orders to start the construction on the Berlin Wall – a bid to halt the brain drain once and for all.[41]

The construction of the Berlin Wall and the sealing off of West Berlin from the surrounding GDR was highly successful in dramatically reducing the volume of illegal emigration. Nevertheless, an average of 20,000 GDR citizens a year managed, either through legal or illegal channels, to migrate to the FRG in any given year. While the dramatic loss of young, skilled, professionals out of the GDR had stopped, emigration became even more political. Western politicians and the media used it as evi-

---

Ross, "Before the Wall: East German Communist Authority and the Mass Exodus to the West," *The Historical Journal* 45, no. 2 (Spring 2002): 462–469.

39 The official West German figure for this time period (~400,000) differs from those reported by the statistical office of the German Democratic Republic (~600,000).
40 "Zonenflucht: Es stand in der Welt," *Der Spiegel*, 10 September 1958.
41 Alan Dowty, *Closed Borders: The Contemporary Assault on Freedom of Movement* (Binghamton: Vail-Ballou Press, 1987), 122.

dence of the sub-modern conditions in the East. The closing of the border cemented the place of the *Umsiedler* in West German public discourse.

5.3.2 German migration after the Berlin Wall, 1961–1989

The sealing of the German-German border also intensified the need for labor in the advancing industrial economy in the West. Although the FRG gained industrial jobs in the northwest as a result of the post-war economic revival, interregional migration in West Germany from the end of the war through the 1960s consisted both of interregional migration from the north to the south, as well as intraregional urban to suburban movement. From 1955 to 1973, West German citizens moved away from urban center to new suburban settlements. In 1967, for example, the total volume of internal migration in West Germany (interregional plus intraregional) equaled 4.3 percent of the population. Of these migrants, 1.7 percent moved to another state, with the majority to the south.[42] Ironically, despite the concentration of employment growth in the industrial centers of the northwest, the majority of the internal migration of Germans trended southward. This pattern was to accelerate after the onset of the global oil crisis in 1973, as unemployment grew in the heavy industrial areas of the northwest, and as a new high-tech industrial center merged in the states of Bavaria and Baden-Württemberg.[43]

Changes in migration to West Germany after the war helped to shape the need and nature of labor migration. Until 1961, the majority of vacancies had been filled by migrants from the GDR, as well as small-scale contract labor from Italy. The construction of the Berlin Wall in 1961, however, cut off the stream of labor migrants from the GDR that had been arriving steadily since the war. Although the rate of growth of the post-war German economy would have required an investment in international labor without closing the border, the sudden halt of an average of 300,000 migrants from the East exacerbated the situation. Although there were more than one million unemployed workers in Germany, most were "unable or unwilling" to move to the new industrial centers, to do the hard labor required of the new industrial economy.[44] In order to fill labor needs, the FRG had, since its first bi-lateral labor contract with Italy in 1955, recruited *Gastarbeiter* (guest workers) in order to fill vacancies in the growing industrial labor force. In 1960, further contracts were signed with Spain and Greece. Between 1961 and 1968, contracts were signed with Turkey, Morocco, Portugal, Tunisia, and Yugoslavia. From the construc-

---

[42] Richard K. Vedder, Lowell E. Gallaway, and Gene L. Chapin, "The Determinants of Internal Migration in West Germany," *Weltwirtschaftliches Archiv* 106, no. 2 (1967): 315.
[43] Jörg Decressin, "Internal Migration in West Germany and Implications for East-West Salary Convergence," *Review of World Economics* 130, no. 2 (1994): 161.
[44] Deniz Götürk, David Gramling, and Anton Kaes, *Germany in Transit: Nation and Migration, 1955–2005* (Berkeley: University of California Press, 2007), 10.

tion of the Wall in 1961 until the end of foreign recruitment in light of the worldwide oil crisis in 1973, the FRG brought more than 14 million foreign *Gastarbeiter* to Germany.[45]

The recruitment ban instituted in the wake of the worldwide oil crisis in 1973 ended the notion that *Gastarbeiter* were only mere "guests" who would come and go according to the needs of the Federal Republic. Of the 14 million who came between 1961 and 1973, approximately 11 million returned to their country of origin, leaving approximately three million migrants to settled permanently in Germany, with many choosing to bring their families as well. At the time of the recruitment halt a total of 605,000 Turks resided in Germany, already making up the largest foreign population in the country. Thus, Germany was faced with the very real problem of a large number of non-Germans as long-term residents, despite declarations to the contrary that Germany was "no country of immigration" (*kein Einwanderungsland*).[46] As Rita K. Chin described the situation, "Germany had to figure out how to deal with being a non-immigration country with a whole lot of immigrants."[47]

The refusal to officially recognize the reality of immigration resulted in contradictory and confused policies that made any efforts toward integration sporadic and generally unsuccessful. For example, family unification laws were relaxed in 1974, which resulted in a mass of family members migrating to Germany. Nevertheless, throughout the 1970s and 1980s, the right to family unification was paired with (largely unsuccessful) incentive programs for returning to one's country of origin. One such measure, the "Act to Promote the Preparedness of Foreign Workers to Return," was passed in 1983 with the support of all the major political parties. Only 500,000 of 4,500 who were included in this measure accepted the offer.[48] The political tension between attempts to relax citizenship requirements and to implement measures toward integration on one hand and the denial of the reality that Germany was indeed an "immigration country" on the other impeded integration and contributed to the stark divide between the *Einheimische* (native born) and *Ausländer* (foreign born) which persists to the present day.

As the industrial economy began to grow, the GDR came to rely upon *Vertragsarbeiter* (foreign contract workers) to fill increasing industrial labor shortages. Beginning in 1966, *Vertragsarbeiter* from the socialist countries of Vietnam, Mozambique, and Cuba were employed in light and heavy industry. By 1989, over 90,000 foreign

---

45 Klaus J. Bade and Jochen Oltmer, "Mitteleuropa: Deutschland," in *Enzyklopädie Migration in Europa: vom 17. Jahrhundert bis zur Gegenwart*, ed. Pieter C. Emmer, Leo Lucassen, and Jochen Oltmer (Munich: Schöningh, 2007), 164.
46 A phrase first attributed to Chancellor Helmut Kohl in 1982. Ulrich Herbert, *Geschichte der Ausländerpolitik in Deutschland: Saisonarbeiter, Zwangsarbeiter, Gastarbeiter, Flüchtlinge* (München, C. H. Beck, 2001), 249.
47 Rita C. K. Chin, *The Guestworker Question in postwar Germany* (Cambridge: Cambridge University Press, 2007), 100.
48 Chin, *The Guestworker Question in postwar Germany*, 128.

workers were employed in the GDR. Unlike the *Gastarbeiter* in West Germany who experienced widespread, yet informal, segregation, *Vertragsarbeiter* were separated from the general population by the state, controlled and under strict supervision. Contact with people outside the workplace was only allowed under special circumstances. Workers were housed in company barracks and not allowed to leave the premises without permission. Violating these rules would have serious consequences. A worker who became pregnant, for example, would be subject to immediate deportation. In addition, contracts were negotiated between the East German state and government representatives of the sending state, not the workers themselves. Pay was frequently withheld until all work had been completed in order to ensure compliance of the worker.[49]

Another development that helped to reinforce the legitimacy of ideological grounds within the phenomenon of east-west migration was the practice of *Freikauf* (ransom). The institutionalization of ransom action came about as a combination of efforts from private citizens and those from the Evangelical Lutheran Church (EvKD) between 1949 and 1962 to free individuals who were convicted and imprisoned for political or ideological crimes in the GDR. Although both the Catholic and Protestant churches had negotiated for the individual release of prisoners from late 1949, the institutionalization of ransom as a regular mechanism for emigration did not develop until the early 1960s. In the summer of 1962, the Lutheran church negotiated an exchange of the release of over 100 political prisoners for a shipment of various commodities.[50]

In August 1964, the two German states negotiated the first mass release of prisoners. Laundering money through the Catholic charity organization *Caritas*, the West German government turned payments to *Caritas* for "medical" equipment into currency and commodities demanded by the SED state. In this first mass action, 884 prisoners were set free; most had either been in prison a long time, had long prison sentences forthcoming, were labelled as a head of household, or had the "greatest human need". In return, the West German government (through *Caritas*) provided foodstuffs, especially citrus fruits, cocoa, butter, and other goods, which amounted to a total value of 35.32 million DM.[51]

Between 1964 and 1989, the West German government ransomed 33,755 individuals from East German prisons. In addition, the West German government also facilitated the emigration of 215,019 individuals on the grounds of "family reunification" with relatives in the West. Officially, a total of 3.43 billion DM in cash and goods were

---

49 Jeffrey Peck, Mitchell Ash, and Christian Lemke, "Natives, Strangers and Foreigners: Constituting Germans by Constructing Others," in *After Unity: Reconfiguring German Identities*, ed. Konrad Jarausch (Providence: Berghahn Books, 1997), 88–90.
50 "Heikle Linie," *Der Spiegel*, 24 October 1983.
51 Jan Philipp Wölben, "Die Entstehung des "Häftlingsfreikaufs" aus der DDR, 1962 – 1964," *Deutschland Archiv* 41 (June 2008): 1032–1035.

exchanged for the release of these individuals.⁵² For the West German state, it provided a way to secure the release of political prisoners, especially West Germans who had been convicted and imprisoned for smuggling in the West. It also allowed for the development of relations and an instrument of stabilization through the transfer of subsidies.

For the GDR, the stakes and rewards were much higher. Negotiating ransom gave the GDR access to Western commodities it could not access on the open market. In addition, the monthly ransom schedule also gave a predictable outlet for the release of political agitators and potential destabilizing elements to the West. A safety valve, it provided a covert avenue for the state to silence critics of the regime, while still maintaining a strong outward appearance of unity.

Over time, however, it can be argued that the ransom program did more to destabilize the population. Alongside the dissidents and destabilizing "asocials," who the state gladly sent west, went intellectuals, skilled professionals, doctors, lawyers and academics who were needed to build and maintain a strong civil society. By the mid-1980s, as the ransoming scheme had become relatively common knowledge, prisoners would often inquire as to how much they bring on the ransom market. Beginning in 1984, a sharp increase in "family reunification" migration began to signal a more significant shift. The emigration of young workers and potential young workers be families, threatened the viability of the East German state itself.

Combined with the growth of internal opposition within the GDR in the mid-1980s, the practice of prisoner ransom compromised the ability of the state to maintain itself. As the strength of the borders began to crumble in the late 1980s, it was the same populations that had contributed to the increase in ransom transfer that would risk going west via Eastern Europe or, after the Wall came down, to move an existing business, practice or office in the West. Although it cannot be separated from structural and geopolitical factors, the impulse of certain populations to move, and the inability of the East German regime not only to control this movement, but also to solve the issues that compelled people to move, undermined the integrity of the state itself.

5.3.3 Migration and the Peaceful Revolution of 1989

While the summer of 1989 is typically referred to as the date from which mass emigration from the GDR took hold, an increase in emigration can already be seen in late 1988. Several factors, both internal and external, coincided to result in an increased rate of emigration from the GDR. The GDR granted exit visas not only to retirees, but also to known political dissidents as an "internal safety valve" which func-

---

52 Enquete Kommission, *Aufarbeitung von Geschichte und Folgen der SED-Diktatur in Deutschland: Widerstand, Opposition, Revolution*, (Berlin: Suhrkamp Verlag), 326–329.

tioned to quell domestic unrest.⁵³ As applications for exit visas dramatically increased in the 1980s, especially amongst the young professionals whom the GDR so desperately needed to retain, it became increasingly difficult to control dissent through controlled emigration.

The inability to effectively curb unrest contributed to an increase in the frequency and size of mass protests throughout the GDR in the late 1980s. Protest movements were primarily organized through the Evangelical Church. Although the Church and its members had initially faced harsh repression, the SED tolerated its existence after the formation of the Bund der Evangelischen Kirchen (BEK) in 1969. Under the BEK, churches in the GDR formally broke away from Western organization while formally acknowledging the limited role of the "Church in Socialism."⁵⁴ The church retained a degree of autonomy from the state unparalleled by any other organization. As a result, the BEK emerged as the center of dissident activity in the GDR during the 1970s and 1980s.

The organization of these dissident movements culminated in the *Montagsdemonstrationen* (Monday Demonstrations), which began on 4 September 1989 at the Nikolaikirche in Leipzig as a meeting offering a "prayer for peace." Weekly meetings quickly evolved into peaceful mass protest for extensive reforms including freedom of speech and above all, the end to travel restrictions. Fueled by word of mouth and reports broadcast on West German television, the movement quickly grew. On 9 October, over 70,0000 people filled Karl Marx Square in Leipzig; two weeks later the number surpassed 300,000 and mass protests were held in large cities throughout the GDR. These protests climaxed on 4 November, just five days before the fall of the Berlin Wall, when over 500,000 people gathered on Berlin's Alexanderplatz to hear speeches by leading intellectuals including writers Christa Wolf and Stefan Heym calling for extensive democratic reforms. However, it was clear that democratic reforms at this point did not mean the abandonment of the GDR in favor of an open call for unification, especially not on the terms dictated by West Germans. In fact, the speeches at the Alexanderplatz demonstration reflected the urgency of the problem of mass emigration and its consequences for the effectiveness of the people to enact reform. Christa Wolf, in particular, called for people to stay and help forge the path towards the "third way," a reform of socialism within the GDR:

---

53 The most famous case is the expulsion of folk singer and artist Wolf Biermann from the GDR in 1976. An outspoken critic of the SED, Biermann was branded a "class traitor" in 1965 and subsequently banned from public performance in the GDR. In 1976, Biermann's GDR citizenship was revoked while on tour in the Federal Republic. Many prominent GDR intellectuals and artists, including author Christa Wolf and popular actor Manfred Krug, openly criticized Biermann's expulsion.

54 The BEK was most active in protests against compulsory military training and in environmental causes. For a detailed accounting of the evolution of church organization, in regards to the formation of dissident movements, see Karl Cordell, "The Role of the Evangelical Church in the GDR," *Government and Opposition* 25, no. 1 (Winter 2007): 48–59. Also see Steven Pfaff, "The Politics of Peace in the GDR: The Independent Peace Movement, the Church, and the Origins of the East German Opposition," *Peace and Change* 26, no. 3 (Summer 2002): 280–300.

Indeed, the language is bursting out of the bureaucratic and newspaper German in which it has been wrapped for so long, and recalling its emotional, expressive vocabulary. One such word is "dream." Let us dream with an alert sense of reason: Imagine there was socialism and no one ran away! But we continue to see pictures of those leaving, and we have to ask ourselves, "What is to be done? And the answer echoes – "Do something!" It is a start when demands become rights – and obligations. Fact-finding committees, constitutional court, administrative reform. There is a lot to be done, and all of it during our spare time. We still need time to read the newspaper! We won't have any more time to pay official homage or to attend prescribed demonstrations.[55]

Ultimately, neither East German intellectuals nor West German politicians could prevent mass emigration. To summarize, internal political and economic instability in the GDR, combined with increasingly frequent mass demonstrations created an atmosphere that promoted mass emigration. However, it was an eternal factor – the withdrawal of external military and border support of the Eastern Bloc by the Soviet Union, which turned the trickle of people going over the border into a tidal wave. GDR citizens applied for asylum at the West German embassies in Prague, Warsaw, and Budapest. In August 1989, Hungary declared the withdrawal of patrols from the Austrian border. Within two weeks, 13,000 GDR citizens travelled through Austria into the Federal Republic via Hungary. In addition, 15,000 GRD citizens were released into West German custody after negotiations with the Hungarian government.[56]

The increasing numbers of emigrants seeking shelter in West Germany overloaded the reception centers for GDR refugees, ethnic German refugees, and asylum seekers. On the eve of the fall of the Berlin Wall, 86 *Notaufnahmelager* (official emergency accommodation centers) had been established throughout West Germany.[57] While there were a small number of previously established refugee reception centers in operation from the early days of the Cold War, most emergency accommodations were quite informal. Tent cities were erected on the outskirts of Munich. In each of the eleven western federal states, hotels, gyms, schools, and apartments were cleared out in order to make room for the new arrivals.

In terms of refugee reception, each of the West German federal states were obligated to take on a percentage of all refugees according to their relative population size. However, how this obligation was fulfilled was not federally administrated

---

55 "Christa Wolf, Christoph Hein, and Steffi Spira at the Berlin Demonstration, November 4, 1989," in *United Germany: Documents and Debates, 1944–1993*, ed. Konrad Jarausch and Volker Gransow (Providence: Berghahn Books, 1994), 70–71.
56 Evron M. Kirkpatrick, "A Chronology of Events: The Collapse of the German Democratic Republic and steps toward German Unity: May 1989 – January 1991," *World Affairs* 152 (1990): 195.
57 There were two main official refugee reception centers. The *Notaufnahmelager Marienfelde*, near the Tempelhof district in Berlin opened in 1953 and operated until 2003 when it was turned into a museum site. The other official center is the *Notaufnahmelager Gießen* in the state of Hesse, which was opened in 1946 and is still currently in operation for international refugees.

and as a result, each state was left to decide how to accommodate newcomers.[58] In addition to housing, many states also offered immediate financial assistance to GDR emigrants. For example, in Berlin each refugee was given a stipend of 15 DM a day. In North Rhine-Westphalia, emigrants were given a one-time payment of 500 DM. Bavaria provided 200 DM per person while Schleswig-Holstein gave emigrants 100 DM per child and 150 DM per adult.[59]

As late summer turned into fall, the number of GDR refugees arriving in West Germany continued to climb, in addition to the arrival of increasing numbers of ethnic Germans from Eastern Bloc countries. On the afternoon of 8 November, the *Hamburger Abendblatt* described emergency camps in many areas of the Federal Republic as "bursting at the seams." The situation was worst in Bavaria, which served as the primary reception site for those arriving via Eastern Europe because of its borders with Austria. Space quickly became sparse, as reported of one Bavarian camp: "The situation became so precarious that new arrivals had to switch places over and over again. Some had beds to lie in while others had only chairs. A good portion of the refugees had no choice but to stand."[60]

Such situations increased after the opening of the border, which exacerbated conflicts between refugees and native inhabitants. Before the fall of the Berlin Wall, refugees from the GDR were generally well received; many West Germans answered the call for donations of material goods or even opened up their homes to help support these emigrants. However, at the same time, there was also an increase in the number of ethnic German migrants from Eastern Bloc countries, particularly from Poland and the Soviet Union. As was the case in the immediate post-war period, this led to tension between GDR and ethnic German refugees as they competed for the same resources.

Although GDR refugees and ethnic German refugees both had a legal "right to return" as outlined in the Basic Law, they were not considered in the same manner. In a near mirror image to the refugee situation in the 1950s, GDR refugees often held an advantage over ethnic Germans in terms of allocation of donations and supplies. In Hamburg-Eidelstedt, although both GDR refugees and ethnic German refugees were housed together in the same camp, partly as an attempt to prevent the so-called "ghettoization" of emigrants, clear preference was given to GDR refugees in terms of donations and housing. As reported in *Die Zeit:* "In order to avoid the wrangling at the entrance, the Samaritan Alliance advised the donors to select the specific families they want to help. This created bad blood [between the GDR refugees and the ethnic German refugees] because many donors expressly wanted to give items

---

58 "Lastenausgleichsgesetz in der Fassung der Bekanntmachung vom 2. Juni 1993," *Bundesgesetzblatt* 845 (1995): 248.
59 "Unterbringung ist vorläufig gesichert," *Hamburger Abendblatt*, 12 September 1989.
60 "Notaufnahmelager überfüllt."

"only for use by GDR refugees." This preference also extended to housing allocation – with GDR refugees being granted access to the few apartments available.[61]

This explicit hierarchy of preference contributed to conflict between the refugee groups, with the perception that GDR refugees were given priority access to aid over ethnic Germans and other asylum seekers. One representative of the aid agency Samaritan Alliance perceived the imbalance to be so great between the two groups that, "for the amount the GDR refugees receive as gifts during their first fifteen days, emigrants from Poland and the Soviet Union must work for years."[62] While this statement may seem hyperbolic, any pretence of preference was to end after the opening of the Berlin Wall in November 1989.

Although the sheer volume of migration that had been steadily on the rise from the time the Hungarian government dismantled its militarized border with Austria in August 1989, no one could predict the complete opening of the border between East and West Berlin on the evening of 9 November 1989. As late as January 1989, Erich Honecker boasted that "The Wall will still be standing in 50 and even in 100 years – if the reasons for it have not been removed by then." In the eyes of the regime, the situation only had the potential to change with the removal of the external threat of so-called "Western corruption."

As the events of the summer unfolded, however, it became obvious that the biggest threat to the Berlin Wall and the larger border it symbolized would be a lack of support from Communist allies and the power of the East German people to continue to "vote with their feet." After it became clear that the Soviet Union was unwilling to use force to keep the East German people in the GDR, Hungary, Czechoslovakia, or in East Berlin, it also became increasingly evident that the power of the SED itself was in jeopardy. On 18 October, just eleven days after observing in a speech celebrating the GDR's 40th anniversary, and partially pressured by hosting reticent Soviet Premier Mikhail Gorbachev, Erich Honecker was forced to resign his post as head of the SED and step down as head of state.[63]

The turning point in the history of the East German collapse would come just a few weeks later in a rapid series of dramatic events. A combination of the growing strength of popular protest, epitomized by the Alexanderplatz demonstration on 4 November and the instability within the ruling apparatus itself, forced the resignation of the government on 7 November. This was followed by the resignation of the entire Politburo on 8 November. Unable to devise a way to quell the increasingly popular unrest and emigration, the newly appointed Politburo, under new General Secretary Egon Krenz, decided to allow limited border crossings with permission in the form of a visa on 10 November. However, when party official Günter Schabowski, who had not been informed of the plan beforehand, was handed a note during a live press

---

[61] Jens Glüsing, "Deutsche unter sich: Aus- und Umsiedler schätzen einander nicht," *Die Zeit*, 13 October 1989.
[62] "Halle-Budapest-Bremen-wieder da!" *taz-bremen*, 3 October 1989.
[63] "Der Geduld ist zu Ende," *Der Spiegel*, 9 October 1989.

conference stating that private travel to the West would be allowed, he read the note aloud. When pressed by journalists, he added that this would be "effective immediately" (not at 4 a.m. the next morning as the Politburo had intended). He also confirmed that the Berlin border crossings were included in the order.

A mixture of chaotic euphoria followed shortly thereafter as thousands of East and West Berliners streamed to the wall and many crossed the border for the first time in their lives, or at least for the first time in forty years. However, as the euphoria from the moment of transgression passed, uncertainty and discomfort began to set in. Face to face meetings between West and East German relatives were tinged with awkwardness, as many had only had contact through yearly letters and *Westpakete* – parcels containing with western coffee, chocolates and other goods sent by West Germans to their East German relatives, usually around the holidays. As the West German government offered *Begrüßungsgeld*, welcome money of 100 DM to every GDR citizen who visited the West for the first time. West Germans, in particularly those living in border areas, quickly began to tire of the endless stream of *Trabis* with their characteristic cloud of exhaust as well as the seemingly backward spending habits of the *Ossis*.[64]

However strange the behavior of East Germans seemed in the first weeks after the opening of the border, for West Germans the immediate concern in the period between the fall of the wall and the vote for unification was the continued emigration of East Germans to the FRG. In November alone, close to 150,000 GDR citizens registered in the West. Although the number fell significantly to just under 65,000 in December, an average of 50,000 people a month arrived to stay from December 1989 through March 1990.[65]

The continual arrival of East German refugees after the border was opened had a significant and rapid impact on their reception in the West. Whereas just a few months before West Germans had been happy to donate and find space for a GDR family, in the months after the Berlin Wall fell, the welcome had decidedly cooled down. In March 1990, residents of Bremen refused to allow their neighborhood sports hall to be converted into another shelter for GDR refugees. As reported in *Die Zeit*,

> The mothers could not believe their eyes when they dropped their children off at the Fröbelstraße Gymnasium in Bremen-Vegesack: Craftsmen were in the process of moving chipped boards onto the parquet. 'Not anymore!' they told the surprised women and children, 'GDR-refugees will soon arrive.'[For the parents] ... this was the last straw, and the protest began: Angry

---

64 *Trabi* is a reference to *Trabant*, the East German state manufactured automobile. *Ossi* is a derogatory slang term used to refer to an "Easterner." After unification, the term was often used as part of the phrase *Jammerossi* to refer to the perception of the complaining nature of East Germans. Its counterpart, *Besserwessi* was used by Easterners to describe the "stuck-up" nature of the common Westerner.

65 Siegfried Grundmann, *Bevölkerungsentwicklung in Ostdeutschland: Demographische Strukturen und räumliche Wandlungsprozesse seit 1945* (Opladen: Leske und Büdrich, 1998), 170–174.

parents, pedagogues and sportsmen took up residence in the sport hall – a measure of self-help by residents frustrated by the loss of the use of their own public facilities.[66]

In Saarland, accommodation and resources were so sparse that an agreement was reached by the city council of Lehrbach to transport and house 250 GDR refugees in an immigrant district of Farébersviller, a small industrial town in the neighboring French province of Lorraine. Here again there is a clear change of tone both in the behavior of officials and the nature of the report. Before opening of the borders, it was likely that an appeal to ethnic German solidarity would have been made to make room for our "brothers from the East." After the fall of the wall, however, it was now "perfectly justified" to send GDR refugees to France in order to establish "... a German colony in the midst of a *cité* where one hears no German, rather Arabic, Turkish or French."[67] Ethnic solidarity gave way to the need to manage the problem of GDR refugees, a tense situation that began to wear on the native population of Lehrbach as well as among the refugees. Despite the prospect of moving into a mixed community of immigrants in France, GDR refugees seemed eager to apply: "In Lehrbach, many GDR refugees have announced that they are ready for relocation. Life in the mass emergency shelters tugs at the nerves ... The partitions between the beds offer no private sphere. On the other hand, Farébersviller lures with furnished twin-bedded rooms and communal kitchens."[68]

Turks, Moroccans, Sicilians, and Poles had first settled in the area surrounding Farébersviller in the 1960s and 1970s when housing was quickly constructed for workers in local coal plants. By the 1980s, however, the coal supply had been nearly exhausted, and now much of the housing lay empty, as workers had moved on. Because of the multicultural composition of the living quarters, refugees were not assigned to relocation at whim. There were strict precautions taken to screen out "alcoholics or asocials" who might not fit into the largely immigrant neighborhood. As reported in *Die Zeit*, Red Cross reception assistants described the situation as tense: "The French are anxious to avoid aggravating the newcomers. News has travelled ahead of the GDR refugees that they are [prejudiced] against Poles and Turks."[69] In response, the French Mayor of Farébersviller requested that Red Cross assistants in Saarland "screen the Germans [for potential problems] before their arrival ... The choice criteria: They must be athletic and have no problems with alcohol ... as the mayor hopes that a [predisposition] to 'sport will eliminate all prejudice.'"[70]

This screening process is important not only because the French reception center demanded it of the Germans, but also because it reflects the general sense of how GDR refugees were portrayed. Whereas before conflicts between GDR refugees and

---

66 "Armut und Enge," *Die Zeit*, 16 March 1990.
67 "Raus aus den Hallen: Das Saarland schickt Übersiedler nach Lothringen," *Die Zeit*, 2 March 1990.
68 "Raus aus den Hallen: Das Saarland schickt Übersiedler nach Lothringen."
69 "Raus aus den Hallen: Das Saarland schickt Übersiedler nach Lothringen."
70 "Raus aus den Hallen: Das Saarland schickt Übersiedler nach Lothringen."

ethnic German refugees were chalked up to competition between two foreign groups, between the collapse of the inter-German border in November 1989 and German unification in October 1990, GDR refugees were often pitted against "native" West Germans. Very soon after the collapse of the border, distinctions in the press between the "good" and "bad" GDR refugees became common with the implication that the "good" refugees had tended to come before the fall of the Berlin Wall and that the "bad" population flooded in after the border was open. In Lehrbach, this distinction was especially made explicit: "Recently, the police have increased patrols in the area. Employees complain that many alcoholics as well as criminals, have come in the last wave [of emigration]."[71]

The continuing stream of GDR citizens emigrating to the West overwhelmed attempts at emergency accommodation, straining relationships both inside camps and within local communities. In addition to increasing social pressure caused by the simultaneous influx of ethnic German refugees and asylum seekers, GDR refugees, while previously supported by the West German public, were increasingly portrayed not as "brothers from the East," but rather as a parasitic strain on West German society. As a result, the emigration problem became a focus of local politics in major receiving areas. In April 1990, for example, Hamburg halted the allocation of apartments to GDR refugees and took an increasingly hard line against those trying to cheat the system. As reported in *Der Spiegel*, The Hamburg Social Service office wants to deal with GDR refugees [trying to cheat the system] drastically, especially those trying to be clever. The Hanseatic town wants to give neither bed nor butter bread to those who have kept their apartments in the East as a sort of safety net to fall back on. According to Brigitte Eberle of the Social Service office, "[If one is caught retaining a residence in the East] ... then he will just have to lie out on the street – Bam!"[72]

While city councils such as Bremen-Vegesack described earlier in this chapter supported citizens' protests against the allocation of public facilities to house and supply GDR refugees, states also quickly entered pleas to reduce or halt acceptance and aid to emigrants from the GDR. Bremen started refusing to accept GDR refugees in the middle of March 1990. Instead of receiving accommodation and support, prospective GDR refugees were instead greeted with "one red slip of paper informing the newly arrived in a friendly, but certain manner ... that Bremen cannot take up their care. The homeless refugees are simply advised to return to the GDR." In the Saarland, the federal state that had arranged to send GDR refugees to France, from April 1990 new arrivals were "given just one more free ticket, one way, second class back to the GDR."[73]

---

71 "Raus aus den Hallen: Das Saarland schickt Übersiedler nach Lothringen."
72 "Schluß mit lustig," *Der Spiegel*, 26 March 1990.
73 "Schluß mit lustig."

The refugee problem figured significantly on the national political stage as well. The year 1990 was a national election year in West; emigration and unification quickly emerged as the focus of the election. The ruling Christian Democrats (CDU), led by Helmut Kohl, was convinced of the benefit of speedy unification and did not want to undertake any measures that might alienate a future electorate in the East. The opposition Social Democrats (SPD), on the other hand, found itself firmly on the other side of the issue, calling to end gifts and benefits to GDR refugees in order to stem the seemingly relentless in-migration.

Unsurprisingly, the fight in the Bundestag to end benefits for GDR refugees was led by the representatives of the states that had already undertaken measures to stop reception. Oskar Lafontaine, Prime Minister of the Saarland and Klaus Wiedemeier, Prime Minister of Bremen, spearheaded the campaign to cut off incentives for further immigration from the East. In a speech to the Bundestag in January 1990, Lafontaine, the SPD candidate for Chancellor in 1990, proclaimed the views of his electorate: "The population increasingly feels that it is socially unfair that GDR citizens, without having paid one Mark here [in the West] in social insurance fees or taxes, can simply come over and fully enjoy all of these social benefits."[74] Calling for a slow approach to unification, Lafontaine was blasted in the press and by the opposition party as "an enemy of the Germans" as well as the "Schönhuber" of the SPD while the CDU campaigned on a political and emotional platform of reuniting two peoples that should have been one all along.[75] Elections in both the GDR and the FRG would ensure the CDU vision of unification would be victorious. The first and only free election in the GDR was held on 18 March 1990 and resulted in a coalition victory for the East German faction of the CDU. With its position in favor of speedy unification confirmed, the CDU passed a law just two days after the election that would end benefits to GDR refugees by 1 July, the date of the currency reform.[76]

The path to unification after the free elections in the GDR was swift. Although there were several political parties in the GDR that called for unification via the drafting of a new constitution taking into account both Germanies, the victory of the CDU on 18 March was a vote for a more rapid path toward unification. In August 1990, the Volkskammer voted for unification with the West under Article 23 of the Basic Law, which instead of a renegotiation resulting in a new constitution simply extended the structures and laws of the Federal Republic eastward to cover the territory of the GDR. The Unification Treaty signed on 31 Augustdesignated that the five newly formed federal states of the former GDR would become states of the Federal Republic

---

[74] Klaus-Peter Schmidt, "Falscher Neid: Nur wenige Rentner aus der DDR belasten bisher die Rentenversicherung der Bundesrepublik," *Die Zeit*, 26 January 1990.
[75] "Schluß mit lustig." A reference to right wing politician Franz Schönhuber, former SS officer and founder of the populist *Die Republikaner* party.
[76] Deutscher Bundestag, *Entwurf eines Gesetzes zur Aufhebung des Aufnahmegesetzes* (Bonn: Deutscher Bundestag, 1990).

of Germany. On 12 September, the Allies officially signed off on unification with the "two plus four" treaty. Germany was formally unified on 3 October 1990.

5.4 Political activities in exile

Unlike other Cold War Soviet satellite states, the political activities of East Germans in exile were minimal. Before the construction of the Berlin Wall in 1961, the presence of exiles in the West served to legitimize the Federal Republic and to establish East Germany as a successor to the prior Nazi totalitarian state. However, even at this time, exiles did not organize as a group or act outside of the direction of the West German government in order to challenge East German policies or practices.

Although there were a few high-profile exiles who continued political activity in the West after the construction of the Berlin Wall, (the artist Wolf Biermann and the author Rudolf Bahro) the normalization of citizen ransom between the two German states kept exile activity in the margins. Although an occasional op-ed penned by an ex-GDR citizen, or, more likely, by a political activist currently in country appeared in national magazines or newspapers, exile activism did not exist in a tangible manner in the two German states during the Cold War.

5.5 Migration since 1989 – during and after unification

After forty years on opposing sides of the Iron Curtain, East and West Germans officially became *ein Volk*. However, the quick transfer of Western political and economic structures to the East did not easily solve the problems that had taken hold in the eleven months between the fall of the Berlin Wall and formal unification. While politicians and the public alike had seen rapid unification as a remedy to increasing civil unrest caused by the continuing influx of GDR refugees, political unification halted neither migration nor social conflict. Even after the formal right to benefits and shelter was removed, thousands continued to move from the former GDR into the West as the eastern economy faltered and unemployment soared.

Although the five new eastern states were officially joined to the eleven western states as one nation, the eastern German region was, from many perspectives, still perceived as another country. The negative western perceptions concerning the backwardness of East Germans continued to evolve as more and more West Germans travelled to the eastern states, witnessing first-hand the dilapidated infrastructure and poor air and water quality that had come with decades of a focus on heavy industry in the GDR. The neglected condition of the landscape itself was often blamed on the East German people – further evidence that the *Ossi* simply did not possess the same professional drive, personal accountability and moral compass that had emerged as a characteristic of the *Wessi* in the economic miracle and recovery of the post-war West.

These experiences and attitudes contributed to a discourse of difference between East and West Germans that painted the former citizens of the GDR as a different people altogether; a pseudo-German group that lacked the defining qualities of a "true" German; namely ambition, cleanliness, orderliness and common sense. The remainder chapter will examine the intersection between the redefinition of German identity and patterns of internal migration between the eleven "old" western federal states and the five "new" eastern states from unification in October 1990 to the end of economic privatization with the closure of the Treuhandanstalt in 1994.[77] While the initial economic shock caused by the wholesale restructuring of the "employment society" of the GDR to fit the West German "capitalist risk" model resulted in widespread unemployment in each of the five new eastern states, it was portrayed as a temporary situation that would be remedied once the economy in the East had stabilized.

However, the "blossoming landscapes" promised by Helmut Kohl on 1 July 1990 never materialized and the market did not grow as predicted. When it became clear that there would be no "economic miracle in the East," the combination of this initial displacement of workers and a continued lack of new opportunities fueled a continuing emigration of skilled workers from the East well into the twenty-first century.[78]

The loss of a high proportion of the most productive portion of the population resulted in a skill gap that further discouraged investment possibilities in the eastern states long after the initial period of high emigration. In addition, a considerable percentage of westward migrants were both young and female, which according to demographic research, has been a major factor in the decline in the birth rate, especially in rural areas. The effect of the prolonged emigration of productive females over the last two decades has contributed to the perpetuation of structural weakness and demographic decline in the eastern states that has in turn prevented growth and made the region unattractive for both domestic and foreign investment.[79]

Patterns of internal migration in the last twenty years reflect the long term economic instability and unemployment in the eastern states caused by rapid and wholesale structural transformation. Rather than a unification of two halves into a new unified whole, western systems were transferred to the new eastern states. Because the East was simply remade in the image of the West, this transformation

---

[77] The Treuhandanstalt (Treuhand) was the government agency responsible for selling public land and assets in order to restructure and privatize more than 8500 state owned enterprises. Initially founded by the GDR Volkskammer on 17 July 1990, oversight was transferred to the united German government upon unification.
[78] Kohl's famous prediction of "blooming landscapes" in the East as a result of unification first aired in a television interview on 1 July 1990. "Fernsehansprache von Bundeskanzler Kohl anlässlich des Inkrafttreten der Währungs-, Wirtschafts- und Sozialunion," 1. Juli 1990," *Konrad Adenauer Stiftung*, http://www.helmutkohl.de/index (accessed 3 May 2018).
[79] Steffen Kröhnert and Reiner Klingholz, *Not am Mann: Von Helden der Arbeit zur neuen Unterschicht?* (Berlin: Berlin Institut für Bevölkerung und Entwicklung, 2007).

made the qualifications of entire sectors of the eastern workforce obsolete and resulted in a large eastward migration of western expertise to fill the gap. While this seemed to initially compensate for the displacement of East German professionals, the majority of these western managers did not move house and family to settle in the east. Therefore, this west to east migration did not compensate structurally for the loss in the native eastern productive population.

After unification, patterns of internal migration became even better defined in terms of both age and gender. There was a much higher rate of labor market participation among women in the GDR (nearly 83 percent in 1990) than in West Germany, where the participation rate hovered between 56–60 percent upon unification.[80] After unification, privatization and structural transfers disproportionately affected female workers, who were more likely than men to become unemployed. In addition, women also lost state support for child rearing and publicly funded childcare, which had both been introduced in the GDR in the 1960s and 1970s to support women's participation in the labor market.

Without state support, women of childbearing age began to look westward in order to remain in the labor market, or were forced out of the job market altogether. In these terms, East German women were often portrayed as more flexible in terms of their attempts to stay in the labor market in comparison to East German men. However, they were often portrayed as being less of a woman because of the perception that they lacked proper maternal emotionality. The perceived unwillingness to mother their own children in favor of putting them in a crèche tied the behavior of East German women to damage done to the East German family structure under socialism. As seen through western eyes, this dysfunction within the home was tied to a moral breakdown within East German society, rooted in the experience of life in the GDR, which served to further separate the East Germans from the so-called "real Germans."[81]

In addition to the consequences on population structure, the distinct age structure of both eastward and westward migration after unification continued to be significant after privatization in 1994. The lack of investment in the East further encouraged the young and the talented to look toward the West in terms of their futures. As a new generation came of age in the late 1990s, a cultural generation gap opened up in the East between the younger generation, which had largely either gone West tem-

---

80 Gerd Wagner ed., "An der Schwelle zur Sozialen Marktwirtschaft: Ergebnisse aus der Basiserhebung des Sozio-ökonomischen Panels in der DDR im Juni 1990." Beiträge Aus der Arbeitsmarkt- und Berufs Forschung 143 (1991): 43, https://www.iab.de/179/section.aspx/Publikation/i910516d14 (accessed 31 August 2018).
81 Hannelore Scholz, "East-West Women's Culture in Transition: Are East German Women the Losers of Unification?" *Journal of Women's History* 5, no.3 (Summer 1994): 109–116; Eva Kolinsky and Hildegard Maria Nickel, ed., *Reinventing Gender: Women in Eastern Germany since Unification* (Portland: Frank Cass, 2003).

porarily or permanently for training, university or work, and the older generation which had been socialized in the GDR and remained in the East.

Although migration declined significantly from its peak in from August-November 1989, the refugee problem from the East was not solved with legal unification. While a mixture of political and economic factors influenced the mass emigration from the GDR during the Cold War, the collapse of the East German economy resulted almost immediately in the creation of a large wage gap and high unemployment between the eastern and western states. These immediate shocks, combined with the long-term processes of the deprofessionalization of GDR qualifications and the privatization of native industries to create economic depression in the eastern states throughout the 1990s. As a result, migration rates to the western states remained significant after unification. The volume of westward migration is especially significant when comparing the total volume of emigration with the declining population in the East. While the total population in united Germany grew from 79,365,000 in 1990 to 81,422,000 in 1994, the population in the eastern states fell from 16,111,000 to 15,564,000 during the same period.[82]

Part of the appeal of going west to look for work was the continuing wage imbalance between East and West. Although the decision to go with a 1:1 conversion rate was made in order to keep labor in the East, the fluctuations caused by rapidly converting the market created more long-term structural problems than they solved.[83] While the currency union had been proposed in order to quickly increase wages in East Germany to western standards and to boost the value of individual savings of East German citizens, in actuality, it precipitated the demise of native industry. From July to December 1990, the total net industrial production in the former GDR dropped by almost 50 percent.[84] This left many factories fully staffed, but without any production orders. Thus, many former GDR companies were faced with a choice of either participating in labor rental schemes from which they profited from the labor of their employees, or going out of business altogether.

The role played by the federal government in the liquidation of former GDR state assets and industries further destabilized the employment situation in the eastern states. The privatization process was initiated when the first freely elected government of the GDR enacted the *Treuhandgesetz* (Trust Agency Law) on 17 June 1990. Under this law, privatization was meant to occur as "quickly and comprehensibly

---

[82] Statistisches Bundesamt Deutschland, "Bevölkerungsentwicklung," Statistisches Jahrbuch für die Bundesrepublik Deutschland – 2002 (Wiesbaden: Statistisches Bundesamt, 2001), 76–82.
[83] George Akerlof, et. Al., "East Germany in from the Cold: The Economic Aftermath of the Currency Union," *Brookings Papers on Economic Activity* 1 (1991): 62–80.
[84] Christoph Buechtemann and Jürgen Schupp, "Repercussions of Unification: Patterns and Trends in the Socio-Economic Transformation of East Germany," *Industrial Relations Journal* 23, no. 2 (Spring 1992): 91.

as possible."[85] Formal privatization began with a monetary union on 1 July 1990. All publicly owned entities became companies and those companies were in turn under the ownership of the Treuhand. The Treuhand was entrusted with the responsibility of preparing companies for sale (or if they were not competitive or saleable, liquidating them) and vetting potential buyers. Under the terms of the unification treaty, the Treuhand was transferred to the control of the united government of the FRG.

The organization and administration of the Treuhand influenced the development of internal migration in both directions after unification. A lack of desire in the East for eastern goods, out of date equipment, inadequate telecommunications and outdated infrastructure, combined with the collapse of the largest potential export market in Eastern Europe, attracted far fewer investors than had been predicted. This contributed to the massive loss of employment in the eastern states, which hovered at around twice the rate in the West throughout the 1990s. In August 1992, an article in *Die Zeit* reported that the number of jobs in the East German economy had fallen by 64 percent between 1989 and 1992.[86]

While the attractive force of higher wages and employment in the West fueled westward migration, the selective selling of former GDR companies to West German investors encouraged the eastward migration of West German professionals, managers and entrepreneurs. While the Treuhand focused on modelling the East German economy in the image of the West, little was being done to encourage the formation of the middle-sized businesses that had been the core of West German post-war economic success.[87] The simultaneous shrinking of the size of the East German managerial class combined with the growing West German influence resulted in a more permanent displacement of native professionals. Early retirement schemes, in particular, permanently decreased the number of older managers in the workforce. Economist Heinrich Best estimated that from 1990 to 1995, around two-thirds of the leadership positions that had existed in the GDR in 1989 had been eliminated. Furthermore, of the total number of managers left in the eastern states in 1995, as many as 25 percent had lived in West Germany before 1990.[88] The combination of the decrease in mean retirement age for East German managers with the decrease in available management positions due to privatization resulted in a firm Western hold on management and decision making in eastern Germany in the aftermath of unification.

The persistence of this wage imbalance coupled with the reduction in the East German labor force capacity as a whole resulted in unemployment rates that were

---

[85] "Gesetz zur Privatisierung und Reorganisation des volkseigenem Vermögens (Treuhandgesetz)," *Bundesgesetzblatt* 1471 (1990).
[86] "Wirtschaftsbericht," *Die Zeit*, 7 August 1992.
[87] Jörg Roesler, "Privatization in Eastern Germany, Experience with the Treuhand," *Europe-Asia Studies* 46 no. 3 (Summer 1994): 510.
[88] Heinrich Best, "Cadres into Managers: Structural Changes of East German Economic Elites before and after Unification," *Historical Social Research* 30, no. 2 (Spring 2005): 18.

both higher and more enduring than previously expected. In addition, wage and employment differences continued to support the maintenance of a high east to west migration rate even as privatization wound down. The consequences, political, economic, social, and demographic, of the maladaptation of East German structures to the Federal German system have proven to be long lasting. More than 25 years after German unification, the five eastern states still lag behind most of their western counterparts in terms of economic production, higher unemployment rates, and the persistence of gender imbalance as a consequence of the young, female driven migration streams of the early 1990s.

This regional imbalance has manifested itself not only politically and economically, but also socially and culturally through the phenomenon of *Ostalgie* in the early 2000s and the return to popularity of eastern products, ceremonies, and other reminders of life under the GDR, treasured by those not old enough to have lived under the system itself. Understanding the history and nature of various ways that migration has developed and had been controlled and defined is important. It not only helps to understand the various factors which influence movement in times of political duress, but can also be useful in uncovering the political and economic intricacies of both the eastern and western systems through the Cold War and the transition to unification.

Although the broad outlines of the migration streams have been determined, the largest gaps in research regarding East German emigration concern the reception and integration of GDR emigrants into West German society, as well as the relationship between migration, institution, policy and the experience of living out these tensions before and after unification. Suggestions for further research include:
- Formal orientation and reception by state and private institutions
- Social integration and adaptation, especially regarding family reunification
- The role of non-state/non-profit agencies in facilitating emigration
- The larger role of protestant Evangelical church organizations (GDR and FRG) in negotiating and facilitating legal and illegal emigration
- The relationship between developing discourses surrounding migration and the agendas of dissident movements in the 1970s and 1980s.

5.6 Archives and Literature

Archival resources in the Federal Republic of Germany are varied and relatively easy to access. The lifting of the 30-year classification on most general documents in the GDR archives has opened up the possibility for more detailed research. However, any files relating to individual persons are still under the 30-year restriction. Examples of the most important archival repositories in Germany include:

Central Archives: Central Archives of the German Evangelical Church (Evangelisches Zentralarchiv Berlin); German Federal Archives – GDR Section (Bundesarchiv, Abteilung DDR, Berlin); Political Archives of the Foreign Office – Berlin (Politisches

Archiv des Auswärtigen Amts, Berlin); Central Archive for the Ministry for State Security (MfS) – Berlin (Die Bundesbeauftragte für die Unterlagen des Staatssicherheitsdienst der ehemaligen Deutschen Demokratischen Republik (BStU) – Zentralstelle Berlin, Abteilung Archivbestände); Foundation for the Archives of the Parties and Mass Organizations of the GDR/SAPMO (Stiftung Archiv der Parteien und Massenorganisationen der DDR im Bundesarchiv – Berlin).

Regional and Specialized Archives: Regional archives located in Chemnitz, Dresden, Erfurt, Frankfurt/Oder, Gera, Halle, Leipzig, Magdeburg, Neubrandenburg, Potsdam, Rostock and Schwerin. Regional Lutheran Church Office Archive – Hannover (Landeskirchliches Archiv Hannover); Regional Church Archive of Berlin-Brandenburg (Landeskirchenarchiv Berlin-Brandenburg, Berlin); Robert Havemann Archive (Robert Havemann-Archiv in der Robert-Havemann-Gesellschaft – Berlin); Archive of the Citizens' Movement (Archiv-Bürgerbewegung E.V. – Leipzig); Central Archive for Empirical Social Research – University of Cologne (Zentralarchiv für empirische Sozialforschung – Universität Köln).

For an overview of German internal international migration streams within a historical European context, see Klaus J. Bade (ed.) *The Encyclopedia of Migration and Minorities in Europe: From the 17th century to the present*.[89] Dirk Hoerder's *Cultures in Contact: World Migrations in the Second Millennium*, incorporates discussion of various relevant German historical migrations within global frameworks.[90] Jochen Oltmer's *Migration und Politik in der Weimarer Republik* provides a detailed study of various migrant populations and issues from the end of the First World War to the Nazi seizure of power in 1933, whereas Ulrich Herbert's *Hitler's Foreign Workers: Enforced Foreign Labor in Germany under the Third Reich* remains the definitive study of the effect of Nazi policies on migration and labor during the Second World War.[91] Ulrike Goeken-Haidl's *Der Weg zurück: Die Repatriierung Sowjetischer Zwangsarbeiter während und nach dem zweiten Weltkrieg* examines the various repatriation experiences of Soviet forced laborers in detail.[92]

For a more detailed treatment of major migration issues to, from, and within German speaking lands between 1949 and 1989 see chapters by Patrice G. Poutrus, Frank Wolff, and Monika Mattes in Jochen Oltmer (Ed.) *Handbuch Staat und Deutschland seit dem 17. Jahrhundert*.[93] Volker Ackermann's *Der "echte" Flüchtlinge: Deutsch-*

---

[89] Klaus J. Bade et. al., *The Encyclopedia of Migration and Minorities in Europe: From the 17th century to the present* (Cambridge: Cambridge University Press, 2011).
[90] Dirk Hoerder, *Cultures in Contact: World Migrations in the Second Millennium* (Durham: Duke University Press, 2002).
[91] Jochen Oltmer, *Migration und Politik in der Weimarer* ... Ulrich Herbert, *Hitler's Foreign Workers: Enforced Foreign Labor in Germany under the Third Reich* (Cambridge: Cambridge University Press, 2007).
[92] Goeken-Haidl, *Der Weg zurück.*
[93] Patrice G. Poutrus, "Zuflucht im Nachkriegsdeutschland," in *Handbuch Staat und Migration in Deutschland seit dem 17. Jahrhundert*, ed. Jochen Oltmer (Oldenbourg: De Gruyter, 2015), 853–894. Frank Wolff, "Deutsch-deutsche Migrationsverhältnisse: Strategien staatlicher Regulierung, 1945–

er Vertriebene und Flüchtlinge aus der DDR, 1945–1961 and Helge Heidemeyer's *Flucht und Zuwanderung aus der SBZ/DDR: Die Flüchtlingspolitik der Bundesrepublik Deutschland bis zum Bau der Berliner Mauer* provide complementary treatments of Soviet Zone/East German migration before the construction of the Berlin Wall in 1961.[94] Ian Connor's *Refugees and Expellees in Post-War Germany* and *Coming Home to Germany? The Integration of Ethnic Germans from Central and Eastern Europe in the Federal Republic*, edited by David Rock and Stefan Wolff, are the best English-language treatments of migration from East Germany, East/East-Central/Southeastern Europe, and the Soviet Union into West Germany/the Federal Republic before and after unification.[95]

1989," in *Handbuch Staat und Migration in Deutschland...*, 773–814. Monika Mattes, "Wirtschaftliche Rekonstruktion in der Bundesrepublik Deutschland und grenzüberschreitende Arbeitsmigration von den 1950er bis zu den 1970er Jahren," in *Handbuch Staat und Migration in Deutschland...*, 815–852.

94 Volker Ackermann, *Der "echte" Flüchtlinge: Deutscher Vertriebene und Flüchtlinge aus der DDR, 1945–1961* (Osnabrück: Universitätsverlag Rasch, 1995); Heidemeyer, *Flucht und Zuwanderung.*

95 Connor, *Refugees and Expellees*; Rock and Wolff eds., *Coming Home to Germany?*

6 Hungary

Katalin Kádár Lynn

6.1 Hungarian migration in historical perspective

During what has become known as the Great Migration, beginning in 1861 and ending in 1913, Hungary, like many of the agricultural, semi-feudal countries of Central and Eastern Europe, experienced a mass exodus to the West of its unskilled and agricultural work force. Hungary was part of the Austro-Hungarian Monarchy during that period and was geographically two-thirds larger than its present territory. The United States was the principal destination for some 1.8 million of Hungary's economic migrants, with the majority of them arriving there after 1899.[1] The number of immigrants from the entire Austro-Hungarian Monarchy during this same period, according the numbers registered by the US Office of Immigration, was 3,765,381. Hungarians made up but a portion of the large flow of migrants emanating from nations such as Ireland and Italy but also from the Scandinavian countries of Sweden, Norway, and Finland as well as en masse from Russia, in response to the opening of the West and the labor opportunities the New World provided.[2]

After the peace treaties of the Great War were concluded and the postwar economies were no longer as robust, demand for unskilled immigrant labor diminished worldwide, including in the United States, where, by 1924, the economic circumstances, the labor movement, and the nativist movement were pressuring the US Congress to pass that year's Immigration Restriction Act. This act set quotas based on the numerical representation of a given nationality in the 1890 US Census. At the height of the worldwide depression, Congress was further pressured to pass the Quota Act of 1931, which set the annual number of immigrants from a given group at 3 percent of that group's population in the United States in 1910. These changes in US immigration policy precipitated a marked decline in migration from Central, Eastern, and Southern Europe to the United States.[3]

In 1920, after signing the Treaty of Trianon, Hungary lost two-thirds of its territory and 60 percent of its population. Its 1921 United States quota was 5,757; the 1924 Act reduced that number to 473, and the 1927 revision to the quota system increased it to 869.[4] The tightening of US immigration laws made labor migration from Hungary to the United States virtually impossible. Instead, seasonal laborers sought work in the mines of Belgium and the agricultural sectors in Germany and France.

---

[1] Julianna Puskás, *Ties that Bind, Ties that Divide: 100 Years of Hungarian Experience in the United States* (New York: Holmes & Meier, 2000), 21.
[2] Puskás, 21.
[3] Puskás, 190.
[4] Puskás.

In the latter part of the 1920s, migration opportunities did emerge in Canada and Latin America, but with the onset of the Great Depression, those options soon ceased to exist. Even with the small numbers dictated by restrictive US quotas, the majority of Hungarian migrants to the United States continued to be from the working class, with only 5.6 percent of them classified as white-collar workers.[5] The Great Depression caused a decrease in international migration throughout the world, and during the period from 1929 to 1934, more persons returned from the United States to Europe than migrated in the other direction. Only 130 Hungarians emigrated from Hungary to the United States in 1935.[6]

A demographic change in the migrants from Hungary came with the end of the 1930s and the rise of Nazism in Germany, because of its threat to the small nations of Central Europe, coupled with support within Hungary to accede to German pressure to pass anti-Semitic legislation. In 1938, almost half the emigrants from Hungary reported that they were Jewish, and only 8.1 percent were blue-collar workers. This constituted the first major shift in the demographic composition of immigrants to the U.S in the 20th century. US immigration authorities registered 1,348 Hungarians in 1939 and 1,902 in 1940. During World War II, the United States considered Hungary to be an enemy combatant and shut down immigration almost completely – the records show that 198 emigrants from Hungary were admitted between 1941 and 1947.[7] Only after this period, two years after the end of World War II hostilities did the migration pattern from Hungary change dramatically from its earlier composition.

6.1.1 The aftermath of World War II – the refugee crisis

The end of World War II saw over sixty million persons displaced from their homelands in Europe, precipitating a refugee crisis of epic proportions – ten times as many refugees as World War I produced.[8]

It is important to note the distinction between migrants and refugees. Malcolm Proudfoot, quoting Sir John Simpson, points out in his seminal book *European Refugees* that the refugee "is distinguished from the ordinary alien or migrant in that he has left his former territory because of political events there, not because of economic conditions or because of the economic attractions of another territory."[9] This indeed was the situation in which the Western Allies and the European governments found themselves at the end of the war. The over sixty million displaced persons living outside their homelands were not economic migrants, as during the Great Migra-

---

5 Puskás, 193.
6 Puskás.
7 Puskás, 195.
8 Malcolm J. Proudfoot, *European Refugees –1939–1952: A Study in Forced Population Movement* (Evanston: Northwestern University Press, 1956), 21.
9 Proudfoot, 22.

tion, but primarily political refugees – a great percentage of whom were fleeing or anticipating the occupation and takeover of their homeland by the Soviet Union.

The various waves of migration from Hungary during and after World War II mirrored those from the other small countries of Central and Eastern Europe. Both internal and external factors motivated these migrations, but the predominating factors differed within the period in question. However, there is no question that the immediate prewar and postwar immigrations were motivated by politics or that they were political in nature. Each of these migrations had its own unique demographic characteristics with a different composition of social status, education, financial status, and political orientation.

While political events may have been the root cause for Hungarians to leave their homeland permanently, the war and the devastation it wreaked should not be underestimated as an influence and driver of postwar migration. Emigration was also compounded by the alteration of Hungary's borders after World War II. A portion of the territory that Hungary lost after World War I was returned to it in the First (1938) and Second (1940) Vienna Awards, but these awards were reversed at the end of World War II. Hungary lost the region of Sub-Carpathia, which was returned to Czechoslovakia, and portions of Transylvanian Maramures and Crisana, which were restored to Romania. The Hungarian population from the Bukovina and Moldova regions (of Romania) that had been re-settled into the Bácska region then had to relocate to southwestern Hungary when the Bácska again became part of Yugoslavia.[10] At war's end over 100,000 ethnic Hungarians fled Romania for Hungary, distorting population figures even more.[11] The forced movement of Hungarian populations within and from these regions motivated the refugees to consider not only emigration into postwar Hungary proper but also provided incentive to flee to the West.

Another factor motivating Hungarians to choose to leave their homeland was that even before Soviet forces entered Hungary, Hungarians recognized that Soviet occupation was likely. Most Hungarian adults had experienced the six-month rule in 1919 of Béla Kun, who was returned to Hungary by the Soviet Union after he had been radicalized as a POW in Russia during World War I. Those who remembered that period for its chaos and brutality, especially the professional and upper classes, were enormously fearful of the consequences of a Soviet occupation and were thus strongly motivated to join the exodus. The movement of this population was coupled in December 1944 with an order by the Hungarian government forcing all members of the pro-fascist Hungarian government of Ferenc Szalási to evacuate to its temporary headquarters in Sopron, Kőzseg, and Szombathely in western Hungary. Number-

---

10 Puskás, *Ties that Bind*, 261.
11 Anne Applebaum, *Iron Curtain: The Crushing of Eastern Europe 1944–1956* (New York: Doubleday, 2012), 133.

ing about half a million persons, by mid-spring of 1945, a great portion of these populations of displaced Hungarians had moved into Austria and Germany.[12]

Shortly after the arrival of the Soviet Army in Hungary, the occupation that had been feared became reality. The period between 1945 and 1947 saw more Hungarians fleeing to the West. The next external force was the actual Soviet takeover, in the spring of 1947 While long anticipated, it was fought against without success by various Hungarian political entities. The takeover motivated the departure of yet another wave of Hungarians into exile.

The Hungarian Revolution of 1956 precipitated the last and most well-known of the Hungarian migrations. This was also a politically motivated exodus, but the resulting emigration had a unique composition. As Julianna Puskás describes it: "An inseparable intertwining of the political and economic factors can be seen in the 1956 refugee movement for the first time."[13]

6.1.2 Post-World War II Hungarian policy related to migration

Despite the Hungarian government having set policy regarding migration, it could control little at war's end. The chaos of the period resulted in population movement that was unprecedented under such extremely difficult conditions. This situation was exacerbated by the Szálasi government's self-imposed December 1944 evacuation order to its temporary headquarters in western Hungary, putting this group at the forefront of the huge migration to the West, ahead of the advancing Russian troops. The government "ordered the evacuation of all important state administrative officers, members of the Arrow Cross [the Hungarian fascist party] and the semi military formations of young people. Hungarian military units were directed west by the German commanders, in addition, alongside those under military service with the Germans who were retreating from the Russian Army, masses of civilians fled west out of Hungary."[14] A quarter of a million civilian refugees and at least an equal number of Hungarian Royal Army members were said to have left Hungary during early April 1945. The Hungarian government itself left for Austria in the last days of March 1945, with some of the key leadership members seeking refuge on German soil shortly thereafter.

There was little or no control of population movement as the Szálasi government and the enormous waves of émigrés moved westwards through territories controlled by various militaries. The movement was made possible by leaky or virtually non-existent border control, but it was nevertheless highly dangerous between 1944 and 1947.

---

12 Gyula Borbándi, *A magyar emigráció életrajza: 1945–1985* (Bern: Európái Protestáns Magyar Szabadegyetem, 1985), 8–9.
13 Puskás, *Ties that Bind*, 275.
14 Puskás, 261.

However, by mid-1947, when control of Hungary was permanently taken over by interests allied with the Soviets, the border crossings were strengthened and the barriers to both entry and exit were made virtually impenetrable. The government of Hungary controlled ingress and egress in the most severe manner, instituting a thirty-kilometer-wide no man's land on its western border and a similar fifteen-kilometer-wide barrier on the southern border.

The Hungarian Revolution of 1956 began on 23 October and briefly brought Imre Nagy's more moderate government to power, a situation that the Soviet Union could not tolerate – and which provoked the Soviets to send tanks rolling into Budapest on 4 November. At that point, Hungarians began to flee by the thousands to the west into neighboring Austria and south into Yugoslavia. During November and December, when the borders could be only partially secured, "many of them crossed into Austria without seeing any guards or troops and without interference. Others met border guards who in general were sympathetic."[15] Nonetheless, the crossing was extremely dangerous. A clampdown at the borders occurred after the Soviet military re-established control by means of controlling the leadership of the Hungarian communists, led by Janos Kádár. There has always been speculation that the Kádár government intentionally left the borders open long enough to rid itself of a disaffected element of the population that could trigger future unrest. By leaving the borders open (whether intentionally or by circumstance), the tension that had been building up in Hungarian society since the communist takeover in 1947 eventually found release.[16] The borders were again fully secured by the end of January 1957.

On 16 December 1956, the first death sentence – for hiding weapons – was pronounced against a participant in the Revolution, and by mid-1957, the trials of the revolutionaries had begun. Imre Nagy and his co-defendants, the principal government officials during the Revolution, were executed on 18 June 1958. With these actions, the Soviet-controlled Hungarian government made the consequences of dissent clear to Hungarians and the international community.[17] After the Hungarian Revolution was suppressed, tight border controls and repressive exit policies were restored. They remained in place throughout the Cold War until a turn toward détente was taken by the Kádár regime in 1960. Kádár famously pronounced: "he who is not against us is with us"; thus paralleling the movement toward rapprochement between the Soviet Union and the United States. Hungary was granted Most Favored Nation Status by the United States in 1978, which had been held up until then because the Jackson-Vanik amendment, which had been added to the US MFN law,

---

15 Puskás, 270.
16 Andreas Gémes, "Deconstruction of a Myth? Austria and the Hungarian Refugees of 1956–1957," in *Time, Memory and Cultural Change*, ed. S. Dempsey and D. Nichols. *Institute for Human Sciences, Vienna, Austria. IWM Junior Visiting Fellows' Conferences* 25, http://www.iwm.at/iwmauthor/andreas-gemes/ (posted 6 November 2009, accessed 1 September 2015).
17 György Litván, ed., *The Hungarian Revolution of 1956: Reform, Revolt and Repression 1953–1963* (London: Longman, 1996), 188.

stipulated a right to emigration, which was not granted to citizens of Iron Curtain nations. By 1978, there was some official emigration from Hungary, but most migrants still found a less than official path for their exit, be it by vacationing in Yugoslavia and then finding a way to cross the border into Italy or by accepting an officially sanctioned job abroad and then asking for asylum. These migrants regarded themselves as dissidents; the Hungarian government called them defectors.

6.2 Major migration streams

Each succeeding Hungarian emigration stream/wave had not only a different demographic mix but also a different motivation for migration. Puskás observes that, "Voluntary migration is motivated by attraction, while forced migration is motivated by repulsion."[18] The former describes the Hungarian emigration of the Great Migration while the latter characterizes the migrations of the Cold War period. It is only after the onset of détente and the granting of Most Favored Nations Status to Hungary that one can say that Hungarian migration was once again motivated by "attraction."

Under pressure from Germany, increasingly repressive anti-Jewish laws were passed by the Hungarian government in 1938 and 1939. These followed the *Numerus Clausus* ('closed number') rulings of the 1920s, which limited university enrollment of Jewish students to 6 percent. Because of the clearly anti-Semitic stance of the Hungarian government of the 1930s, over half of the then-emigrants from Hungary were Jews.[19] The looming war motivated those who had the means to leave to do so and changed the patterns of migration – these refugees went directly to Latin America and the United States rather than remaining in Western Europe.

6.2.1 1944–1945: the "45-ers"

The bitter and hard fought battles of the Budapest Offensive, which began in October 1944 and pitted the Soviet and Romanian armies against the German and Hungarian armies, ended with the fall of Budapest on 13 February 1945. The decisive victory of the Soviet Army ensured the USSR's control in Central Europe. The Allied occupation force in Hungary consisted of Soviet troops – and while ostensibly it was a joint occupation by the Allied Control Commission, only the USSR's forces were on site. This was the period when the 45-ers left their homeland.

The war's physical and economic devastation wrecked Hungary, particularly the capital city, Budapest, the siege of which has been characterized as "one of the

---

[18] Puskás, *Ties that Bind*, 277.
[19] Puskás, 195.

bloodiest city sieges" of the entire war.[20] This motivated a continuing flood of Hungarian refugees, including "involuntary refugees," such as members of the retreating Hungarian Army and former concentration camp survivors, that swept a half million Hungarian citizens into Western Europe. A European exodus of such proportions was unprecedented in modern times.

On 30 September 1945, there were officially 122,182 Hungarian refugees in the West. Of this number, 95,904 were in Germany and an additional 17,855 in Austria. Other countries where Hungarians sought refuge were France (6,525) and Switzerland (966). Italy and Norway received a smattering. Hungarians comprised 6.5 percent of the displaced persons (DPs) recorded in Western Europe on that date. In comparison, by far the largest number of refugees, 1,888,401 came from Poland, comprising 56 percent of the total.[21] These statistics did not include ethnic Germans from Hungary, whose numbers were substantial. German nationals were also not included in the statistics.

The Western Allies, overwhelmed by the flood of refugees into the West, began an aggressive repatriation plan by September 1945. Hungarians numbering in the hundreds of thousands were officially repatriated, including the involuntary exiles from the government administration and the military. They were joined by civilians who felt that Hungary's postwar coalition government would accord them fair treatment. Thus they had nothing to fear and could take their chances returning to their homeland.[22]

Many of these refugees were initially convinced that their stay in the West was temporary and they would soon be able to return to Hungary. However, the consolidation of power by the Soviets and the takeover of the government by Soviet quislings eventually disabused them of that idea. The lengthy amount of time that the 45-ers spent in the DP camps, many having been in them since 1945, convinced them that their only option was to leave Europe. By 1947, DPs were opting for any opportunity to overcome their unsettled situations and leave the camps. Many chose to emigrate to regions willing to welcome new settlers, including Latin America and Australasia, with a sizeable number of the refugees relocating to Brazil, Bolivia, Peru, Argentina, and Venezuela. Many also left for Australia, New Zealand, and Canada. Of the 62,001 Hungarian refugees that were placed through PCIRO and IRO between 1 July 1947 and 31 December 1951, 45,284 went to these nations. Palestine and, after its formation, Israel accepted 7,191 Hungarian Jews during the same period. The United States at this time was accepting only a minimal number of refugees – having accepted just 6,141 of the Displaced Persons resettled from West Germany in 1946.[23]

---

20 Krisztián Ungváry, *The Siege of Budapest: 100 Days in World War II* (New Haven: Yale University Press, 2002), 374.
21 Proudfoot, *European Refugees*, 238–239.
22 Steven Béla Várdy, *The Hungarian Americans* (Boston: Twayne Publishing, 1985), 116.
23 Proudfoot, *European Refugees*, 294, 296.

Those who decided not to return to Hungary became known as the 45-ers. Their number is estimated at about 120,000 – in line with Malcolm Proudfoot's statistics.[24] This group included former members of the upper- and mid-level social and political elites, members of the former professional officer corps, the gendarmerie, and the conservative or rightist political parties. While 45-ers were statistically an older group than those who had emigrated earlier in the 20th century, by no means was this group "old" – 23.4 percent of them were under 19 years of age and 70 percent were under 40 years of age.[25] Families formed a large component of this migration. Puskás writes of descriptive literature that emphasized that the 45-ers were from "middle and higher social groups and had higher education almost without exception," which set this group apart from the older economic migrants from Hungary. "Political views and ideology differentiated the new arrivals both from their predecessors and among themselves even more than class structure did."[26]

Even in the devastating circumstances in which Hungary found itself, attempts to normalize the situation continued. Elections were held in November 1945, with the Smallholders Party enjoying a comfortable 57 percent win at the polls. Ferenc Nagy was elected Prime Minister and the process of rebuilding began. Implementing plans, they had formulated prior to their "occupation" of Hungary, the Soviets dominated the work of the Allied Control Commission operating in Hungary and strategically placed their own people in positions that controlled public safety, the police, and the military. Hungarian communists returned from exile in the Soviet Union and were put in positions of power. The systematic takeover of Hungary began, using what Mátyas Rákosi, the Hungarian communist leader, later referred to as "salami tactics."[27]

6.2.2 The 1947 exodus: the "47-ers"

The consolidation of Soviet power and the takeover of the Hungarian government were effectively finalized in mid-1947, when Hungarian Prime Minister Ferenc Nagy and the speaker of the Hungarian Parliament, Msgr. Béla Varga, were forced to flee to the West. During the period of this exodus, James McCargar, a US intelligence officer posted in Budapest, was responsible for exfiltrating seventy-four Hungarian political figures and diplomats – all of whom were successfully spirited across the

---

24 Proudfoot.
25 Puskás, *Ties that Bind*, 264.
26 Puskás, 265.
27 "Hungary: Salami Tactics," *TIME*, 14 April 1952. The phrase refers to an interview Rákosi gave in Hungary in February 1952 in which he candidly outlined how the communists marginalized the opposition in Hungary by "cutting them off like slices of Salami." (accessed 14 February 2016). http://content.time.com/time/magazine/article/0,9171,857130,00.html.

border to Austria.[28] From 1946 to 1950 (principally in 1946–1947), the Hungarian refugees of the first wave who remained in the West were augmented by approximately 40,000 additional refugees.[29]

How did the 47-ers differ from the 45-ers? Primarily in their political outlook and by the fact that the 1947 emigration was a "democratic emigration" and the 1945 emigration was a "national emigration," as identified by Puskás. The departure date from Hungary was a reliable indicator of a Hungarian refugee's political views.[30]

The US Congress passed the first Displaced Persons Act in 1948, followed by the 1950 Displaced Person Act (amended in 1953 to admit former military combatants). Passage of these urgently needed changes to the US nationalities quota system became necessary in order to accommodate the flood of refugees from Central and Eastern Europe after the fall of the Iron Curtain.

The victorious Allies had neither anticipated the onslaught of millions of refugees nor developed a way to cope with it; nor, at the conclusion of the war, did they intend to loosen or change their immigration policies in order to accommodate the refugee populations. Rather, repatriation was their main goal. Approximately 11,078,000 persons required repatriation by war's end.[31] There were 10,054,000 Europeans who were officially repatriated in the seven months between 1 March and 30 September 1945.[32]

The United States – émigrés' first choice of destination – found it could no longer maintain a hard line on immigration quotas. The onset of the Cold War and the waves of liberal and democratically elected officials arriving from all the countries of Central and Eastern Europe after their Soviet occupation forced the US to rethink its immigration policy. From Hungary these were the 1947 refugees. With the passage of the 1948 Displaced Persons Act, the United States created a path thanks to which both the 1947-ers and the larger group of 1945-ers had an opportunity to immigrate to the US. The United States admitted 16,718 Hungarians between 1 July 1947 and 31 December 1951.[33]

Only a trickle of people found their way out of Hungary after the fall of the Iron Curtain. Obstacles of every sort were placed in the way of anyone who entertained the idea of emigrating legally. After the Iron Curtain came down in 1947 and foreign travel was restricted, no one under 65 years of age was allowed to leave Hungary to join family members who had emigrated previously. This restriction persisted until

---

[28] Katalin Kádár Lynn, "The Hungarian National Council 1947–1972," in Katalin Kádár Lynn, ed., *The Inauguration of Organized Political Warfare: Cold War Organizations Sponsored by the National Committee for a Free Europe, Free Europe Committee* (St. Helena: Helena History Press, 2013), 240.
[29] Várdy. *The Hungarian Americans*, 116.
[30] Puskás, *Ties that Bind*, 265.
[31] Proudfoot, *European Refugees*, 189.
[32] Proudfoot, 228.
[33] Proudfoot, 427. Steven Béla Vardy cites 26,532 Hungarians entering the USA between 1945 and 1956, *The Hungarian Americans*, 118.

September 1956, when two sons of a DP couple were reunited with their parents after a nine-year separation.[34] Those few who left Hungary officially were considered suspect by their countrymen who had emigrated earlier and were seen as "fellow travelers" (meaning they were suspected of being communist plants or operatives sent abroad on assignment and not true refugees from the communist system).

6.2.3 The 56-ers: emigration after the Hungarian Revolution of 23 October – 10 November 1956

After the brief, failed Hungarian revolution was suppressed by Soviet troops, over 200,000 Hungarians left their homeland for the West. The unique characteristic of these refugees was their age – two-thirds were under 30 years of age and they were predominantly male, 60 percent had a profession. However, a substantial number of teenagers also exited Hungary alone.[35]

As a consequence of the 1956 Revolution, the next Hungarian refugee influx to the United States occurred between 1956 and 1960. Over 38,000 Hungarians were admitted immediately after the revolution and later another several thousand, 47,643 by the end of the decade. That still left over 150,000 Hungarian refugees seeking refuge somewhere in the world. By 1959, Canada had accepted 25,513, Great Britain 20,690, France 12,700, Germany 15,500, Switzerland 12,000, and between Belgium, Holland and Sweden about 10,000. Australia accepted 11,000 and South Africa took 1,300.[36]

The situation of the 1956 émigrés, or Freedom Fighters as they came to be called by the media, stirred greater worldwide sympathy than did any of the prior Hungarian immigrations, except perhaps that of Kossuth's followers in the mid-19th century. Unlike the postwar immigrants, who received a less than enthusiastic reception, the 56-ers were lauded as heroes; theirs was the first such international humanitarian crisis to appear on television. It was headline news throughout the world.

6.3 Repatriation

6.3.1 Repatriating the Hungarian postwar exodus: 1945–1951

Hungarians who found themselves in the West at the end of World War II lived in an environment completely controlled by the Allies. Many Hungarians who sought greater security in the West – including the general population, former concentration camp inmates, and members of the Hungarian Army – could best be characterized as

---

34 "Sons Rejoin Parents Here After 9 Years," *San Mateo [CA] Times*, 17 September 1956, 1, section 1.
35 Puskas, *Ties that Bind*, 271.
36 Borbándi, *A magyar emigráció életrajza*, 242.

involuntary refugees. Most were repatriated to Hungary within two years after the end of the war, as they could be characterized as those "who had little to fear and who felt that the postwar coalition governments afforded them enough assurance of fair treatment that they could take their chances."[37]

In the fall of 1945, when the period of mass repatriation ended, it was clear that an international agency would need to be established to deal with the refugees who could not or would not return to their homelands. As a great percentage of the refugees were from countries that were "claimed by the Soviet Union and its satellites, the matter was one of considerable political difficulty and it was accordingly approached with care by the international community."[38]

The refugee question was listed as agenda item 17 at the first session of the General Assembly of the United Nations; then, in January 1946, it was referred to a committee dealing with social, humanitarian, and cultural questions. The issue was debated, but the urgency of the question meant that a short resolution was presented to and passed unanimously by the General Assembly by 12 February 1946.[39] Referring to the mission of the new refugee organization (to be named the International Refugee Organization or IRO), the resolution stated that it was not to resettle the refugees and displaced persons but was to "encourage and assist in every way possible their early return to their countries of origin."[40] There was no explicit plan in the document regarding a resettlement program for the DPs and refugees. However, the resolution did state that "no refugees or displaced persons, who have finally and definitely, in complete freedom and after receiving full knowledge of the facts, including adequate information from the Governments of their countries of origin, expressed valid objections to returning to their countries of origin ... shall be compelled to return to their country of origin."[41] By the end of 1946, the General Assembly approved the IRO Constitution and an initial annual budget of 161 million dollars for its operation.

While the Western nations approached the challenge of the refugee situation with the view that repatriation should be voluntary and that the alternative of resettlement should be offered to those who found themselves outside their homelands, the Soviet bloc policy advocated forcible repatriation and resettlement only for those declared stateless. The UN rejected this view, but the Soviet bloc continued to stress that Western policy violated the Soviet's sovereign right to control its own citizens. Further complaints included the fact that the refugee camps were providing refuge for war criminals and traitors and that they had become centers of anti-Communist propaganda. Because of the Soviet view, from its onset, the IRO was "entirely an in-

---

37 Várdy, *The Hungarian- Americans*, 116.
38 Proudfoot, *European Refugees*, 399.
39 Proudfoot, 399.
40 Proudfoot. 399–400.
41 Proudfoot, 399–400.

strument of the West, and from the first to last the opposition of the Soviet bloc to the IRO was bitter and uncompromising."[42]

At the end of the war, 303,000 Hungarians had officially been recorded as requiring repatriation, although several authoritative sources say the unrecorded count may have been twice that number.[43] The official numbers included 235,000 in the Supreme Headquarter Allied Expeditionary Force (SHAEF) area, 50,000 in the Soviet-controlled zone, 17,500 in France, and 1,000 in various other European countries.[44] Under the SHAEF plan, low priority was given to repatriation of the ex-enemy Hungarian nationals, but as 137,700 were in the zones of Austria under the control of the Western powers, it was deemed practical to begin their repatriation immediately. Repatriation began on 25 June 1945 and continued throughout the summer and into the fall. The Soviets stopped the repatriation of Hungarians by September 1; it was not resumed until 19 December. By October 1946, 223,787 Hungarians had been officially repatriated from West Germany (125,158) and Austria (96,629).[45] Proudfoot notes that over 100,000 Hungarians unofficially repatriated themselves from Austria and West Germany.

Statistics related to postwar refugee counts are notoriously unreliable. Some sources, among them Puskás and Borbándi, quote numbers of refugees that are a half million in excess of official SHAEF, IRO, and UNRRA (United Nations Relief and Rehabilitation Administration) statistics. Records for the Soviet Zone are unavailable. Based on the statistics given by researchers dealing with the Hungarian migration, it is clear that while the SHAEF numbers are the only reliable count of refugees who registered with the Allies, many hundreds of thousands of persons were not represented in these official statistics. Proudfoot notes this in his research as well. Statistics citing refugee numbers should be regarded as consistently underestimated.

By 1947, as indicated by the IRO PCIRO statistics, Hungarian repatriation slowed tremendously, totaling just 1,608 refugees in the five-year period from 1946 to 1951. From 1 July 1947 to 30 June 1948 1,118 Hungarians were repatriated and 318 in the following twelve months. The flow was reduced to a trickle by 1951, when the number was 12 for the entire year.[46] Although ostensibly a voluntary choice, repatriation was

---

42 Proudfoot, *European Refugees*, 401.
43 Proudfoot notes that the German newspaper *Der Tagesspiegel* (Berlin, US Zone) from 6 June 1946 reported that by the end of April, 137,000 Hungarians had been repatriated from the US Zone of Germany, 80,000 from the US Zone of Austria, and 20,000 were in transit from Western European countries, for a total of 287,000. The *Wiener Zeitung* reported on 16 January 1947 that after 1 October 1945, 540,000 Hungarians had returned to Hungary from Austria. Proudfoot notes also that Jacques Vernant suggests in his book *The Refugee in the Post-War World* (Edinburgh: T. & A. Constable, 1953) that a million Hungarians may have been repatriated from West Germany and Austria after the war. Proudfoot, *European Refugees*, 285.
44 Proudfoot, 227.
45 Proudfoot, 285.
46 Proudfoot, 416.

encouraged by the homeland, with Hungarian agents operating within the DP community and every effort being made to encourage return. Remaining in the West was a particularly difficult choice for the elderly and for fragmented families. It was also difficult for those who had fled without any personal documents in their possession, for they could not provide proof of professional certification, degrees, or even basic information about themselves.[47]

As can be seen from the above statistics, repatriation was virtually non-existent after the Hungarian borders were under the firm control of the Hungarian People's Republic, regardless of the efforts of its assigned agents to encourage refugees to return to their homeland.

6.3.2 Repatriation after the 1956 Hungarian Revolution

The United Nations High Commissioner for Refugees (UNHCR) statistics indicate that 17,000 persons who fled to the West after the 1956 Revolution were repatriated to Hungary.[48] Borbándi sets the number at 8,300.[49] The Hungarian Foreign Ministry reported that 13,000 refugees had returned by January 1958.[50] Repatriation efforts on the part of the Hungarian commissioners in the Austrian camps were very aggressive, as in the immediate postwar period, and caused enormous friction within the bilateral commission composed of Hungarian and Austrian representatives that had been established in January 1957 at the request of the Austrian government to the United Nations High Commissioner. "The Hungarians having proclaimed an amnesty to all those willing to return, declared they had information about thousands of Hungarian refugees wanting to return to their homes. The Austrian authorities, they claimed, prevented this and forced the refugees to emigrate to other countries."[51] Indeed, a propaganda offensive in support of the Hungarian position was mounted by the other members of the Eastern bloc. The press in these countries painted a picture of horrific conditions in the Austrian camps, terming it virtual imprisonment, and alleging that the Hungarians "were being sold as slaves to mines and plantations or were being recruited for the Foreign Legion."[52]

---

[47] Proudfoot, 416.
[48] "Refugees," *United Nations High Commissioner for Refugees: Yearbook 1958*, Chapter 10, 235, http://www.unhcr.org/cgi-bin/texis/vtx/home/opendocPDFViewer.html?docid=4e1ee774d&query=hungary%201956%20repatriation (accessed 9 January 2015).
[49] Borbándi, *A magyar emigráció életrajza*, 242.
[50] Andreas Gémes, "Deconstruction of a Myth?".
[51] Andreas Gémes, "Deconstruction of a Myth?".
[52] Andreas Gémes, "Deconstruction of a Myth?". There was an element of truth to the accusation that young Hungarian refugees were joining the French Foreign Legion even if out of necessity rather than by force. Hungarian historian Béla Nové is the expert on this topic, having researched it for more than a decade. His book on the Hungarian Legionnaires *Patria Nostra*, published in 2016, is available

6.4 Hungary's minorities: Motivations for emigration

6.4.1 Hungarian Jews

It was clear to Hungarian Jews who survived the horrors of World War II that migration was by far their most desirable option. Estimates of surviving Hungarian Jews vary widely. Anne Applebaum, in her highly regarded history of Eastern Europe, places the range at 143,000 to 260,000, and notes that the long tradition of "assimilation, intermarriage, and conversion" makes it difficult to pinpoint the numbers more accurately.[53] Those who did survive were predominantly Jewish residents of Budapest, as the mass deportation of Hungary's Jews that began in March of 1944 was concentrated on the Jewish populations in Hungary's provinces. Applebaum goes on to note, "Within the city [Budapest], which then had about 900,000 inhabitants, Jews were a very visible and vocal minority. With their families and professional networks intact, the Hungarian Jewry quickly began to play an important role in public life."[54]

However, postwar Hungarian government policy turned from support for its Jewish population to antagonism when the newly created state of Israel refused to align its foreign policy with that of the Soviet Union in 1948. While many wished to emigrate to Western Europe and the United States, immigration opportunities were limited by restrictive policies in both those destinations. Ultimately, the USA admitted the largest number – 105,000 – of Jewish refugees from Europe during the immediate postwar period of 1946 to 1950, and Canada took in 19,697. From 1 January 1946 to 14 May 1948, 4,713 Hungarian Jews emigrated to Palestine.[55] From 15 May 1948 – the day after Israel was established – to December 1951, 14,301 Hungarian Jews emigrated to Israel.[56] When Israel became a nation, the American Jewish Joint Distribution Committee paid the Hungarian government a million dollars to expedite the departure of 3,000 Hungarian Jews to Israel.[57] After 1951, the exit visas required to emigrate from Hungary became increasingly expensive and restrictive. In 1951 only 1,273 Jews we allowed to leave the country.[58]

---

online as *Patria Nostra*, Budapest, Balassi Kiadó Kft. 2016, disszertacio.uni-eger.hu/17/13Nóve_Béla_-tézisek_angol.pdf (accessed 22 February 2018).
53 Applebaum, *Iron Curtain*, 136.
54 Applebaum, *Iron Curtain*, 136.
55 Proudfoot, *European Refugees*, 356.
56 Proudfoot, *European Refugees*, 359.
57 Applebaum, *Iron Curtain*, 142.
58 Applebaum, *Iron Curtain*, 360.

6.4.2 The ethnic German minority

The history of Hungary's ethnic German population cannot be assessed accurately without mentioning not only that population's transfer to the West but also its deportation to the Soviet Union as slave laborers at the end of World War II. In mid-1944, Hungary had a population of approximately half a million ethnic Germans. Some were serving in the Hungarian army – the estimate is about 30,000, from a civilian population of ethnic Germans of about 470,000. A population transfer of 169,000 ethnic Swabians to the Soviet Zone of Germany (later East Germany, officially the German Democratic Republic) by 1 January 1947 reduced the ethnic German population substantially. An additional 42,000 ethnic Germans from Hungary were living as refugees in Bavaria immediately after the end of the war, further reducing the total remaining in Hungary.[59] Hungary, like Romania, paid its war reparations to the Soviet Union in the form of labor. Additional research is needed to estimate the ethnic German population remaining in Hungary when deportations to the USSR began in January 1946. A provision of the peace treaties ending World War II stipulated furnishing labor to the Soviet Union to compensate for its manpower losses incurred during the war. However, persecution of the Hungarian Germans began much earlier, on 22 December 1944. On Soviet orders, all Germans in Hungary were ordered to the front lines as forced laborers.[60] In Hungary, all able bodied men and single women of German extraction aged 17–44 (men) and 18–30 (women) were to be mobilized by the Red Army and sent to the Soviet Union. The ethnic German classification was somewhat of a ruse because, in order to fulfill quotas, laborers who could not prove German ancestry were also sent. The estimated numbers of those sent vary widely – from 160,000 (Bardi/Szarka) to about 31,000 according to recently opened Soviet archives.[61] If we use the Hungarian census of 1941 and its count of the German population in Hungary, the number is substantially under a half million. The number of ethnic Germans in the census was 302,198.[62] However, in the same census, the

---

[59] Applebaum, *Iron Curtain*, 376. Puskas claims that 250,000 Hungarian Germans sought refuge in Germany at the end of the war, but statistical proof needs to be found to establish that this was the case. In his essay "Population Movements in the Carpathian Basin" Tamás Stark states that Hungary succeeded in deporting 160,000 of its ethnic German population to the Soviet Zone of Germany by the time the campaign was stopped on 15 June 1948, which corresponds to the Proudfoot statistic. In *Minority Hungarian Communities in the 20th Century*, Nándor Bárdi, Csilla Fedinec, László Szarka (eds.), (Boulder: Social Science Monographs, Atlantic Research and Publications, 2011), 688–689.
[60] Applebaum, *Iron Curtain*, 125.
[61] Steven Béla Várdy and Agnes Huszár Várdy, *Stalin's Gulag: The Hungarian Experience* (Naples: Universita degli Studi di Napoli L'Orientale, 2007), 55.
[62] Tab. 14.1. Population by ethnic minorities and main age groups, 1941, 1980–2001 in Hungarian Central Statistical Office, Népszámlálás [Population Census] 24 (2001): http://www.nepszamlalas2001.hu/eng/volumes/24/tables/load1_4_1.html (accessed 7 November 2015). See also Tab. 1.6. Population by knowledge of languages (most commonly used in Hungary) and sex, 1930–1960,

number of respondents in the population reporting that German was their "mother tongue" was 553,179.[63] It is in all probability the classification of who was considered "German" that causes the statistical confusion about the number of Germans emigrating, being sent to the Soviet Union in labor battalions, and/or being re-located to Germany, thereby making an accurate assessment of the remaining German population in Hungary in the immediate post-war years virtually impossible.

As a result of the huge postwar influx of Germans from all over Europe to Germany's four Allied Occupation Zones, 18.1 percent of Germany's population was soon composed of ethnic German refugees. This stretched that region's already impoverished resources to the limit.[64]

6.4.3 Hungary's Roma

In the scholarly works examined by this author to date, there is little or no mention or analysis of the Hungarian Roma population in relation to migration of any sort – yet we know some Roma must have been part of the emigration. This topic calls out for further and more in-depth research. The 1941 Hungarian census puts the Hungarian Roma population at the rather low number of 27,033. In 1949, the count of Hungarian Roma was 37,598 despite the loss of population during World War II and the Hungarian Arrow Cross government's deportation of between 28,000 and 33,000 Hungarian Roma. Whether this reflects the result of population transfer from surrounding countries cannot be determined. However, it is unclear whether the 1941 statistic included the ethnic Hungarian populations returned by the First and Second Vienna Awards, making the census numbers substantially higher. This points to substantial undercounting of the Roma population.[65] Indeed, the trajectory of the Roma population out of Hungary into Western Europe or elsewhere in the world is difficult to track.[66]

1980–2001 in Népszámlálás (2001), http://www.nepszamlalas2001.hu/eng/volumes/24/tables/load1_6.html (accessed 1 September 2018).
63 Népszámlálás (2001).
64 Proudfoot, *European Refugees*, 378–379.
65 Proudfoot, *European Refugees*, 54.
66 Following the democratic transitions in Central and Eastern Europe, some extremely well-researched scholarship regarding Roma migration has been published, including: Zsuzsanna Vidra, ed., *Roma Migration to and from Canada: The Czech, Hungarian and Slovak Case* (Budapest: Central European University Press, 2013). In this volume, the chapter "Roma Migration Trends Before and After EU Accession" (Table 1, page 6) notes that Roma migration out of Hungary prior to EU Accession was "non-significant." More specific data are not included.

6.4.4 Resettlement and Supporting Organizations

The Hungarians whose immigration was handled by the IRO were resettled in twenty-one countries between 1 July 1947 and 31 December 1951. The greatest number emigrated to the United States, followed by Australia, Canada, and Israel. The Latin American countries of Argentina, Bolivia, Brazil, Chile, Paraguay, Peru, Uruguay, and Venezuela all accepted refugees. New Zealand did as well. Belgium, France, the Netherlands, Norway, Sweden, and the UK all accepted refugees from Hungary. Other parts of the world that accepted refugees included French Morocco and Turkey.[67]

6.5 Political activities in exile

Hungarian refugees, even while in the displaced persons' camps, began to organize along religious, professional, and political lines. When the refugees arrived in their new homelands, the organizations they created continued to serve them. Later, larger institutions, many of them not-for-profit organizations, were established worldwide. This section mentions only the organizations that continued to operate once Hungarians reached their place of exile – their host countries. Hungarian organizations included several large veterans' organizations, including military and gendarmerie. Religious, cultural, and social groups reflecting the refugees' values and political orientations were also established.

6.5.1 The 45-ers' organizations

The early organizations of the 1945-ers in exile were organized by and represented the interests and political views of the supporters of the old regime in Hungary. These included the Fraternal Organization of Hungarian Veterans (Magyar Harcosok Bajtársi Közössége, MHBK). The MHBK was founded in 1947 by General András Zákó with the intention of representing Hungarian professional military officers. As, over time, Hungarians were dispersed throughout the world because of immigration, the MHBK became more of a social organization and its membership represented the most prominent refugees in some dozen countries. It was estimated to have between 15,000 and 20,000 members – perhaps 60,000 to 80,000 if one includes family members. It had hundreds of branches that perpetuated the conservative values of the Horthy regime in Hungary. Although its central leadership remained in Germany, over the years, as members emigrated, its funding shifted to the United States.[68]

---

67 Proudfoot, *European Refugees*, 427.
68 Vardy, *The Hungarian Americans*, 123–124.

The Hungarian Movement for Freedom (Magyar Szabadságmozgalom), another military organization, was founded in Germany in 1946 by General Ferenc Kisbarnaki-Farkas. He had been elected regent on 20 August 1947 at a Parliament-in-Exile held by Hungarian exiles in Altötting, Germany. He was to succeed Regent Horthy, who had fallen out of favor with the exiles because he was increasingly lending his support to Otto von Habsburg's bid for leadership. Historian Béla Vardy reports that the Kisbarnaki-Farkas organization numbered "21,268 members in 108 local chapters in 32 countries" by 1953.[69] By all accounts, at the height of the Cold War, both this organization and MHBK had large memberships and were influential among their émigré communities worldwide.

There were other military-based organizations, such as the Hungarian Gendarmerie Benevolent Aassociation (Magyar Királyi Csendőr Bajtársi Közössége, MKCSBK], which also had an association for family members, and the Familial Association of Hungarian Gendarmerie (Magyar Csendőrok Családi Közössége, MCsCSK]. Neither of these organizations had the membership numbers or the influence of the two major military organizations.

There were other organizations formed during this period, which historians Gyula Borbándi and Béla Vardy both explore fully in their works. Most were based or initiated in the centers of Hungarian immigration, for example, in Cleveland, Ohio, in the United States. Vardy aptly describes their efforts: "The 45-ers also established a host of other associations, few of which were free from unrealistic and basically unattainable political goals."[70] However, these organizations were also founded to provide cultural and social life for the newly arrived Hungarian émigrés. In many cases, access to those benefits made it possible for the émigrés to thrive and prosper for decades.

In addition to these conservative mainstream organizations, there were also extreme right organizations that attempted to establish a following in the West immediately after World War II. The most prominent among them was the Hungarist movement led by General Árpád Henney. The Hungarists were the successors during 1946–1948 to the Arrow Cross (Hungarian Nazi) movement. They founded organizations in Germany and Austria immediately after the war, but since most of the Arrow Cross leadership (or even its members) did not succeed in emigrating to North America, their activities shifted to Latin America and Australia. As the movement was associated with ideas rejected by both the Eastern and Western powers, their influence was limited and was closely monitored by Western intelligence.

---

69 Vardy, *The Hungarian Americans*, 123–124; Borbándi, *A magyar emigráció életrajza*, 39–40.
70 Vardy, *The Hungarian Americans*, 124.

6.5.2 The 47-ers' organizations

The organizations the 45-ers formed at the end of World War II received little or no support or recognition from the Allied Powers. However, by the time the Iron Curtain fell and a relatively smaller group of Hungarians – including a large contingent of Hungarian political figures – began to flee Hungary, the Western powers, especially the United States, stepped up with financial and organizational support. By far the most important among the newly established organizations was the Hungarian National Council (Magyar Nemzeti Bizottmány, HNC). It was founded in 1947 with the support of the US Department of State moved under the umbrella of the National Committee for a Free Europe, Inc., (NCFE, later renamed the Free Europe Committee) when the NCFE was established in 1949.

The Hungarian National Council was founded by Hungarian political leaders who were deemed acceptable by the US government, all of them recent arrivals in the United States. The only member of the HNC executive committee who did not arrive with the 47-ers was former Smallholder Party leader Tibor Eckhardt. He had traveled to Washington, D.C., on an ill-fated mission for the Hungarian government in 1941 and stayed there in self-imposed exile. Eckhardt was charged by the US Department of State with the formation and establishment of the HNC. He wrote the organization's mission statement and became its public voice during its first few years. The other founding members, also members of the executive committee, were Ferenc Nagy, Prime Minister of Hungary until 31 May 1947, Msgr. Béla Varga, speaker of the Hungarian Parliament until 31 May 1947, Dezső Sulyok and Zoltan Pfeiffer. Msgr. Varga served as the organization's chairman until it was disbanded in 1971, when its patron, the United States, revised its foreign policy goals and its stance with regard to the Soviet-satellite countries of Central and Eastern Europe.[71]

During the height of the Cold War, the NCFE sponsored many other international organizations that served to represent the interests of the United States in world forums. In several of them, members of the Hungarian émigré community held leadership positions. The sponsored organizations included the International Peasant Union, representing the interests of agrarian, peasant citizens behind the Iron Curtain, which was brought into the NCFE fold in 1950, and in which Ferenc Nagy was active. Another "international" supported by the United States was the International Center of Free Trade Unionists in Exile, established in Paris in 1947. It represented exiled prewar trade unionists of Poland, Hungary, Romania, Yugoslavia, Bulgaria, Lithuania, Latvia, Estonia, and Ukraine. It was initially funded by the Free Trade Union of the American Federation of Labor (AFL) and from 1951 onwards by the NCFE. The third NCFE-supported international was the Christian Democratic Union of Central Europe (CDUCE), which came into being in 1950 when the exiled representatives of the Christian Democratic Parties began their activities in the

---

71 Kádár Lynn ed., *Inauguration of Organized Political Warfare*, 241.

West.⁷² In all of these organizations, the exiled political leadership of the Central and Eastern European nations worked collaboratively and effectively together.

6.5.3 The 56-ers' organizations

The aftermath of the 1956 Revolution generated an exodus of an entirely different group of refugees out of Hungary, the great majority of them: young single men. The organizations they formed were related to their fight for freedom. They had lived under Stalinist communism since 1947. Those nine years had made a profound difference in their outlook and political views. The staid HNC or the American Hungarian Federation, the umbrella organization of Hungarian groups that was founded in 1906, were not for them; they formed their own groups, the most successful of which was the Hungarian Freedom Fighters Federation (HFFF), which was an outgrowth of an organization established by General Béla Kiraly in 1957. The most influential of the post-1956 groups, it splintered into several factions by 1958, of which it and the Hungarian Freedom Fighters Movement (HFFM) were the largest that remained. Vardy observes that they were much stronger in Europe, "for the more conservative Hungarian Americans generally view them as cryptocommunists 'who have no place in Hungarian American life'."⁷³

There were many other organizations in which Hungarian refugees participated; some of them global in their outlook, many simply local and regional. As was the case with émigrés of other nationalities, there was little interaction between the organizations of the newly arrived refugees and those of the earlier Hungarian American arrivals. The mainstay organizations that belonged to the American Hungarian Federation, for example, had memberships that reflected primarily the Great Migration arrivals, although some of the 45-ers (on the whole a conservative constituency) did have some cross over with them. The 47-ers and 56-ers had virtually no cross over at all. In fact, the 47-ers' Hungarian National Council, established with US support, was characterized by Béla Vardy as an organization of "heads without bodies," implying that they represented no one but themselves and did not represent the Hungarian American emigration.⁷⁴

---

72 Kádár Lynn ed., *Inauguration of Organized Political Warfare*, 55–56.
73 Vardy, *The Hungarian Americans*, 130.
74 Vardy, *The Hungarian Americans*, 111.

6.5.4 Hungarian cooperation with other émigré political, cultural, artistic, and scientific groups

It was in exile that the recently arrived national political leaders from Central and Eastern Europe came to know and respect each other and recognize that they served a common cause by working together. These political leaders met informally at first, through the so-called Tuesday Panel, which started meeting in 1947 and was organized by former Foreign Minister of Romania Gregoire Gafencu, and then later at two conventions, one in Philadelphia (11 February 1951) and a later in Williamsburg (12 June 1951). At these conventions 195 exiled national leaders from behind the Iron Curtain were represented – including Alexander Kerensky, head of the Russian Provisional Government of July–November 1919.[75] In September 1954, the Assembly of Captive European Nations (ACEN) was established with the support of the National Committee for a Free Europe. It served as a permanent forum for the exiled leadership.

The Hungarians were represented in all of these bodies and held leadership positions in some of them. All of the ACEN members provided the Hungarian National Council (HNC) with significant support in its attempts after the Hungarian Revolution to censure both the Soviet Union and Hungary at the United Nations. ACEN members and even countries that were not members of ACEN lent their support to the HNC-organized protests. The HNC files contain hundreds of letters and telegrams from every major and minor ethnic group, all in support of the Hungarian Revolution and the Hungarians' right to self-determination. Cooperation, in support of the Hungarian refugees arriving in the West after the Hungarian Revolution, came not only from the Hungarian organizations but also from many other nationality groups.[76]

6.5.5 Infiltration: communist actions against émigré groups and leaders

There is ample evidence of infiltration of émigré groups by agents of their former homelands or by agents from other Soviet satellites. In research related to this author's biography of Tibor Eckhardt, the inter-war Hungarian political leader who emigrated to the United States in 1941, archival evidence was found showing that during World War II the American Hungarian Federation Executive Committee was infiltrated to the point that word for word minutes of their closed session meetings were provided to Soviet intelligence operatives. John Radzilowski, in his essay "Ethnic anti-Communism in the United States," writes about the infiltration of ethnic organizations by Soviet agents by 1943, arguing that "there is now ample evidence that they were not only deeply interested in overseas ethnic communities but expended

---

75 Kádár Lynn, *Inauguration of Organized Political Warfare*, 47–48.
76 Kádár Lynn, *Inauguration of Organized Political Warfare*, 279–280.

considerable resources to monitor, infiltrate and influence immigrant communities. In other words, when community newspapers like *Svoboda* complained about Communists in their own ranks, they were essentially correct."[77]

In the postwar era, and more intensely after the onset of the Cold War, the concerted disinformation campaign waged by the USSR's propaganda apparatus against nationalist leaders in the West was mirrored by campaigns mounted by the satellite nations themselves after their own national security services were established following communist takeovers. In many cases, sowing the seeds of dissent within and among the exile communities was where these campaigns proved most effective. Campaigns against nationalist, military, and religious leaders, as well as against prominent dissidents in exile, were vicious, ongoing, and relentless. They included any number of attempts to liquidate the targets, as in the case of the aborted attempt by Romanian intelligence operatives in New York in 1951 to take the life of Msgr. Béla Varga, the leader of the Hungarian National Council.[78] Earlier operations included the assassination of Attila Kovacs, operations head of the MHBK, in broad daylight on 21 January 1949, by Hungarian Katpol agents (Katonapolitikai Osztály – Military political department of the Hungarian Ministry of Defense) in Innsbruck, Austria.[79] Hungarian Security Archives provide evidence of over 123 agents being deployed abroad to deal with the "removal" of former Hungarian military personnel. Hungarian intelligence had at least 800 agents actively deployed in the West, many in neighboring countries but some posted as far away as the United States.[80]

After the Soviet consolidation of power within Hungary, the long arm of ÁVO – Államvedelmi Osztály –the Hungarian state security forces – reached into the immigrant communities, causing considerable dissent and fear amongst the émigrés. The head of the MHBK, General András Zákó was targeted for abduction from his home in Innsbruck by the Hungarian State Security forces. While that plan was never implemented, bold action by the Hungarians Soviet allies enabled them to kidnap Attila Dósa, the head of the MHBK intelligence network headquartered in Vienna. Having been lured to the Soviet Zone, he was tortured, tried, and then returned to the Hungarian intelligence authorities for trial and subsequent execution. Dósa's flatmate, István Feherváry, was also seized in Vienna, tried in the Soviet Zone, and then shipped to Hungary to be tried again and sentenced to twenty years' imprisonment. Fe-

---

[77] John Radziłowski "Ethnic anti-Communism in the United States," in *Anti-Communist Minorities in the US: Political Activism of Ethnic Refugees*, ed. Ieva Zake (New York: Palgrave Macmillan, 2009), 13–14.
[78] "Red plot to kill Msgr. Varga seen: warned of liquidation," *New York Times*, 3 April 1951, 10, http://timesmachine.nytimes.com/timesmachine/1951/04/03/81772069.html?pageNumber=10. (accessed 19 March 2015).
[79] Library and Archives of Canada, Rakoczi foundation MG 28 V 162, Volume 12, folder 12, jpg. 3527.
[80] Ildikó Zsitnyányi, Egy Titkos Háború Természete. A Magyar Harcosok Bajtársi Köszöszége tagjaival szemben lefolytatt internalási és büntetőeljarási gyakorlat 1948–1950. Hadtörtenelmi Közlemények 115. évf. 4. Sz. (2002). http://epa.oszk.hu/00000/00018/00022/pdf (accessed 30 January 2018).

herváry's autobiography provides us with a first person account of the brutal mistreatment and torture émigrés faced who dared to maintain relationships and mount any form of resistance in Hungary.[81] Such tactics employed by the intelligence agencies in the Soviet satellites extended well into the era of détente, as in the case of Georgi Markov, a Bulgarian dissident author who defected to the United Kingdom in 1969 and was employed by the BBC World Service. He was considered a "traitor to the fatherland."The Bulgarian Secret Police eventually succeeded in assassinating him (third attempt) in September 1978.[82]

6.6 Hungarian migration until 1989

To complete the history of Hungarian migration up to the regime change of 1989 and the fall of communism, one would have to include the history of the "forgotten" generation of migrants – those who left Hungary in the decades following the resettlement of the 1956 exodus. George Lázár, an independent scholar, has begun to study the departure of this smaller, better-educated group, focusing on those who migrated to the United States. Lázár observes that these forgotten migrants received little or no support for resettlement and "many of them felt neglected or sometimes misunderstood by the Hungarian-American community, and they harbored conflicted feelings about the Kádár-regime. They had to fight various additional obstacles, among them, Socialist Hungary's ongoing legal and political maneuvers to convince (or force) them to return to Hungary."[83]

Little research has been done about the Hungarian migration of this period. Lázár notes that some of the issues with which this group had to contend, including the pressure to return to Hungary, were also experienced by the earlier migrants. However, the paucity of US government support was a result of détente and normalization of relations between the countries that were still Soviet satellites. Members of this group had to find their way in their new homeland on their own. Although their numbers were much smaller than after 1956, their story and struggle deserve further scholarly attention in order to complete the history of Hungarian migration up to the year 1989.

The various waves of emigration from Hungary had many of the same characteristics as those from the other countries of Central and Eastern Europe. Prewar emigration from Hungary was perhaps not as large as that from countries that had al-

---

[81] István Feherváry, *The Long Road to Revolution: The Hungarian Gulag 1945–1956* (Santa Fe.: Pro Libertate Publishing, 1989).
[82] Vasil Paraskevov, "Small but vociferous: Bulgarian ethnic anti-Communist groups," in Ieva Zake, ed., *Anti-Communist Minorities in the US*, 161.
[83] George Lázár, *The Forgotten Generation – Hungarian Refugees in the US 1960–1989*, Paper presented at the American Hungarian Educators Association Conference, College Park, MD, 28 April 2016.

ready been impacted by German occupation or aggression. Postwar emigration, if we consider the 45-ers and 47-ers as a percentage of the total Hungarian population, was perhaps greater, but it is difficult to establish accurate statistics, as the territories restored by the Vienna Awards – and then lost – and the loss of additional territory to Romania make it hard to accurately pinpoint the origin of refugees. The available statistics are not completely accurate and should be considered guidelines rather than facts.

The migration of Hungarians from 1938 until the mid-1970s was characterized by distinctly different demographic and political groups. Due to the constraints of length, this essay has focused on the emigration to North America, yet Hungarians are scattered throughout the entire world and the bibliography reflects some of the excellent sources that deal with scholarship related to the entire diaspora.

There was little interaction between the disparate Hungarian migrants that arrived in the West, as each of the émigré groups had its distinct demographic composition, economic, educational, and cultural background, and each group arrived with its own hopes and dreams of what to expect from their lives in exile. Their reasons for making the profoundly difficult decision to abandon their homeland for a life of exile were also different. Nearly all the early émigrés of the turn of the 19th century were economic migrants. The interwar period brought political migrants and Jews escaping the Nazi onslaught; the immediate post-World War II emigrants were, on the whole, political émigrés of the middle and upper middle class and were generally of a conservative and anti-Communist bent. The 1947-er's were also political émigrés, but were liberals who thought that they could find rapprochement with their Soviet occupiers, but eventually learned that power sharing was not a concept the Soviets could accept. The refugees of the 1956 Revolution were both economic and political refugees. The later, smaller, and more intermittent migrant groups were diverse in their composition but their members tended to come from the professional classes, whose ambitions were economic betterment and political freedom.

Regardless of the level of diversity of these migrant groups, each of them contained Hungarians of talent and accomplishment who, in countless ways, enriched the nations that became their new homelands.

6.7 Archives and Literature

Archival material as it relates to the pre and post-World War II Hungarian migration is fragmentary and widely dispersed. No one repository has sizeable enough holdings to be considered the main repository for research on this topic. The principal archives that house the papers of some of the key figures of the Hungarian migration are the Hoover Institution Archives at Stanford University in California, and the Bakhmeteff Archives at Columbia University. The Immigration History Research Center at the University of Minnesota, Minneapolis MN holds the archives of the Assembly of Captive European Nations (ACEN) amongst other materials, which provide an overview of the political life and organizations of the émigrés.

The challenge for any researcher is to access the various international archives that have holdings related to the Hungarian migration. Amongst them are: The American Hungarian Foundation Library and Archive in New Brunswick, NJ and the American Hungarian Library and Historical Society in New York City. In Hungary, the Open Society Archives, the National Archives of Hungary – Magyar Országos Levéltár (MOL) and the Széchenyi National Library Archives (OSZK) all located in Budapest. Additionally, in Budapest the Historical Archives of the State Security Services: (ÁBTL) in Budapest holds valuable source material as do the archives of the Hungarian Central Statistical Office (HSCO).

In the United Kingdom, the National Archives at Kew, Greater London have extensive holdings related to Hungarian immigrants to the British Isles as do the National Archives of Canada in Ottawa for the Hungarian immigrants to Canada.

Literature related to the Hungarian migration is extensive, but verifiable official statistics related to the Hungarian migration are hard to come by. In all instances in this article, the choice was made to use official statistics such as those gathered by the International Refugee Organization (IRO) United Nations Relief and Rehabilitation Administration (UNRRA) avoiding data without verifiable sources to support it. The research of geographer Malcom Jarvis Proudfoot (*European Refugees 1939 – 1952: A Study in Forced Population Movement*) a Lt. Colonel in the Division of Supreme Headquarters Allied Expeditionary Force where his duties involved working with refugee and displaced persons populations is particularly useful for examination of the chaotic period at the end of WWII and holds up under scrutiny.

Several authors have written comprehensive works on Hungarian migration or topics related to Hungarian migration. Key among them are: Julianna Puskás' *Ties that Bind, Ties that Divide: 100 Years of Hungarian Experience in the United States*, Gyula Borbándi, *A magyar emigráció életrajza: 1945 – 1985 (The history of the Hungarian Emigration: 1945 – 1985)* and Steven Béla Vardy, *The Hungarian Americans*.

Sources for research regarding the Hungarian emigration to Latin America, Australia, as well as the emigration resulting from the failed 1956 Hungarian Revolution can be found in the bibliography. Oral history has taken an increasingly important role in the documentation of Hungarian post-war migration. In 2015 documentarians Réka Pigniczky and Andrea Lauer Rice initiated the Memory Project, a nonprofit documentary venture, the purpose of which was to conduct in-depth interviews of Hungarians émigrés, both from the DP generation and from the 1956 generation in order to create a visual history archive. The Memory Project is ongoing and continues to add interview subjects to the video database providing scholars an opportunity to study a wide demographic range of Hungarian émigrés of the period. www.memory-project.online.

7 Poland
Sławomir Łukasiewicz

While migration is a phenomenon that affected all the countries of Europe in the twentieth century, World War II and its aftermath have already been branded 'the dark decade', as most migration at the time occurred as a result of coercion. It has been estimated that from the beginning of World War II roughly thirty million people were on the move in East-Central Europe.[1] Some were evacuated, some deported, and some fled war and its atrocities. The population movements that occurred in the Polish territories contributed immensely to that number. Dariusz Stola estimated that since the middle of the nineteenth century, different types of migrations in and out of Poland alone could have represented the shared experience of as many as twenty million people. According to his estimation, the 1939–1948 period was the peak of coercive migration flows of Polish citizens, while "4.5 million Polish nationals were forced to go abroad" during the war, and "more than 4 million inhabitants of Poland's post-war borders had to leave between 1945 and 1948."[2]

The end of fighting in 1945 did not ease the migration crisis. Some Eastern Europeans were faced with changed borders, which resulted in expulsion and/or loss of citizenship. Certain regions and countries were subjected to programs of ethnic homogenization, which resulted in massive population transfers. In the case of Polish citizens, the altered borders made it impossible for many of them to return to their ancestral homes in the eastern lands of pre-war Poland. Furthermore, not many of those who had left the USSR for the 'free world' were willing to risk return to a Poland controlled by the Soviets. As a result, by the end of 1945, the new Polish diaspora in the West reached a number of five hundred thousand.

The size of this group, as well as its impact and achievements abroad, which are yet to be fully assessed, prompted Polish historians to call it the Second Great Emigration.[3] This term is a reference to the Polish exiles of the nineteenth century, whose

---

[1] Krystyna Slany, *Między przymusem a wyborem. Kontynentalne i zamorskie emigracje z krajów Europy Środkowo-Wschodniej (1939–1989)* (Kraków: Wydawnictwo Uniwersytetu Jagiellońskiego, 1995), 90; Heinz Fassmann and Rainer Munz, "European East-West Migration, 1945–1992," *International Migration Review* 28, no. 3 (Autumn 1994): 520–538.
[2] Dariusz Stola, "Poland," in *Patterns of Migration in Central Europe*, ed. Claire Wallace and Dariusz Stola (New York: Palgrave, 2001), 176; Dariusz Stola, *Kraj bez wyjścia. Migracje z Polski 1949–1989* (Warsaw: Instytut Pamięci Narodowej, 2010), 10.
[3] This term first appeared in the three-volume publication by Andrzej Friszke, Rafał Habielski, and Paweł Machcewicz under common title *Druga Wielka Emigracja* (Warsaw: Biblioteka Więzi 1999): Andrzej Friszke, *Życie polityczne emigracji* (Warsaw: Biblioteka Więzi 1999); Paweł Machcewicz, *Emigracja w polityce międzynarodowej* (Warsaw: Biblioteka Więzi 1999); Rafał Habielski, *Życie społeczne i kulturalne emigracji* (Warsaw: Biblioteka Więzi 1999).

departure is commonly referred to as the Great Emigration.⁴ However, the post-World War II migration was much bigger and can be considered 'great' not only due to the far bigger number of people who ended up in the West, but also because of the significance of its political representation in the globalising world. The Polish post-war political diaspora could reach the cabinets of the main world powers and lobby for certain policy positions – at times quite efficiently – not on behalf of the Polish state, but claiming to represent the Polish *raison d'etat*. At the same time, the state – namely the People's Republic of Poland – attempted to neutralize the émigrés' efforts and carry out plans, which were principally dictated by Moscow.

The Polish post-World War II migration was definitely political in nature. Therefore, in accordance with the classification used by social sciences, it should be classified as coerced. Its core was made up of émigrés who had served in the Polish Armed Forces in the West during the war, or who had taken part in organizing Polish governmental and institutional structures abroad. They were joined by former soldiers of the Polish underground state and their families, who left the country as the Red Army moved in and the new regime was being installed. At the time, the alternative to emigration was to remain and adapt to the new political reality of an undemocratic Soviet-controlled regime. For those who found themselves abroad during the war, a possible return to Poland often meant victimization, as was well portrayed by Janusz Wróbel in his book *At the Crossroads of History*.⁵ There were also naturally many instances of other, personal reasons for remaining aboard, such as there being no remaining family members to go back to, or war-time marriages with foreigners.⁶

Thus far, researchers have been unable to provide an estimate of exactly how many of the Cold War-era migrants were motivated by political factors. Whereas non-political motivations were not ignored, scholars are still searching for other categories that could represent the essential character of the Polish Cold War emigration. For example, Adam Walaszek uses the concept of the 'diaspora of victims' developed by Robin Cohen, or the 'diaspora of fighters' proposed by Mekuria Bulcha.⁷ However, in the case of the Poles, the politically motivated émigrés were numerous and recognizable enough to clearly dominate the character of the migration of that period.

---

4 This term refers first to the political and cultural importance of this wave, though it was also 'great' in numbers. According to estimates by Dariusz Stola "at least 3,5 million people left the Polish lands before 1914". A further "2 million emigrated between 1919 and 1939." Dariusz Stola, 'Poland', in *Patterns of Migration in Central Europe*, 176.
5 Janusz Wróbel, *Na rozdrożu historii. Repatriacje obywateli polskich z Zachodu w latach 1945–1949* (Łódź: Instytut Pamięci Narodowej, 2009).
6 Czesław Łuczak, *Polacy w okupowanych Niemczech 1945–1949* (Poznań: Pracownia Serwisu Oprogramowania, 1993), 28. See also Janusz Wróbel, "Geografia, demografia i profil społeczny polskich skupisk emigracyjnych w okresie powojennym," in *Polska emigracja polityczna 1939–1990. Stan badań*, ed. Sławomir Łukasiewicz (Warsaw: Instytut Pamięci Narodowej, 2016), 15.
7 Adam Walaszek, "Polska diaspora," in *Polska diaspora*, ed. Adam Walaszek (Kraków: Wydawnictwo Literackie 2001), 8–11, 23–26.

7.1 World War II and Polish migration

The key to understanding the Polish diaspora during the Cold War lies in the events and decisions of September 1939.[8] Faced with a dual invasion, the Polish government decided that its priority was to maintain the legal continuity of the state authorities. The country's president Ignacy Mościcki, in accordance with his prerogatives as listed in the 1935 constitution, nominated Edward Rydz-Śmigły as his successor and Chief Commander of the Polish Armed Forces. However, both leaders, along with the prime minister and members of the cabinet, were interned by the Romanian government at the Polish-Romanian border while attempting to evacuate the government to France. On 25 September 1939, while incapacitated, the president nominated Bolesław Wieniawa-Długoszowski as his successor. The nomination decree was dated 17 September 1939, as if it had been issued in Poland. At the time, the nominee was the Polish ambassador in Rome, renowned for his faithful service as aide-de-camp to the late Marshal Józef Piłsudski. However, due to the overly political nature of this nomination, this move did not resolve the issue. Both the French and the anti-Pilsudski-ite Poles objected. Under pressure, Mościcki changed his decision and nominated Władysław Raczkiewicz, a former member of the cabinet, speaker of the Polish Senate, president of the Global Union of Poles Abroad (Światpol), and governor of a number of voivodeships in Poland. This decision, linked to Wieniawa-Długoszowski's resignation, was accepted by all the interested parties, even though Raczkiewicz's affiliations with Piłsudski's followers were well-known at the time.

On 30 September 1939, Mościcki resigned and Raczkiewicz became Poland's president in exile in Paris. On the same day, Prime Minister Felicjan Sławoj-Składkowski also resigned, and by a decision of the new president, a new cabinet was to be formed by General Władysław Sikorski. The general, who was an anti-Pilsudski-ite politician and a supporter of Ignacy Paderewski (who was a Christian Democrat), took over the post of prime minister as well as the portfolios of military affairs, internal affairs and (from 16 October) also the ministry of justice. Furthermore, on 7 November he became the chief commander and accumulated an enormous amount of both civilian and military power in an unprecedented way. He remained prime minister and commander in chief until his tragic death in a plane crash on 4 July 1943.

---

[8] After aggression against Poland in 1939 waged by German and Soviet armies, the Polish government attempted to rally the support of the Polish diaspora in the West. The communities of Polish economic migrants in the West had previously enthusiastically responded to calls for support on behalf of Poland during World War I. This time however, despite the mission of Gen. Józef Haller and Ignacy Paderewski to the United States, no comparable military or financial support was in sight. See: "Sprawozdanie Józefa Hallera z przebiegu prac Misji Dobrej Woli do Stanów Zjednoczonych Ameryki i Kanady," in *Archiwum polityczne Ignacego Jana Paderewskiego*, vol. 6 *1915–1941*, ed. Marian Marek Drozdowski (Warsaw: Wydawnictwo DiG, 2007), pp. 295–310.

In sum, the events of September 1939 set the stage for decades of Polish political presence in the West. On the one hand, the international recognition of the Polish governmental authorities was sustained; on the other, the circumstances surrounding the nominations paved the way for future debates on their legality. The latter exploded in full force after Raczkiewicz's death in June 1947.

The relocation of the Polish state authorities to Western Europe, which coincided with the evacuation of a considerable number of Polish soldiers, shaped an entirely new set of circumstances. Polish army troops assembled in Angers, a town in northeastern France; then, following the fall of France in the spring of 1940, its remnants were transported to Great Britain. There, in Scotland, the First Polish Corps was created, including special parachute and armoured brigades. In cooperation with the British Special Operation Executive (SOE), the Poles created special paratrooper units called 'the silent unseens' (*cichociemni*), trained for special actions and parachuted over occupied Poland to join the resistance units.[9] Great Britain became a key ally of the Poles, both military and political, as it hosted the Polish troops, the country's government-in-exile, and many exiled political and intellectual leaders.

In July 1941 the Polish Prime Minister Sikorski signed an agreement with the Soviet diplomatic envoy to Great Britan (Ivan Mayski) reinstating the bilateral relations which had been broken at the time of the Soviet attack on Poland in September 1939. This agreement included a provision for the creation of a Polish army in the Soviet Union. These military units were led by General Władysław Anders and consisted of Poles who had been deported to the USSR. These military units, later named the Polish Second Corps, made their way through the Middle East, via Africa to Italy, accompanied by many civilians who had managed to leave Soviet Russia with the soldiers. Polish soldiers courageously fought their way back to Europe, but at the end of the war, most of them still resided in Great Britain, unwilling to risk a return to their homeland, which had been overtaken by the Communists.

British policy during and after the war had a tremendous influence on the decisions taken by both the Polish state and the Polish exiles. The historians' debate on Churchill's attitude towards Poland, his true intentions, and the actual room for manoeuvre in his talks with Stalin continues. It is common in Poland to refer to the Yalta conference as a betrayal of a faithful wartime ally. Representatives of the Polish government-in-exile were not invited to the San Francisco conference devoted to the founding of the United Nations in spring 1945. No Polish soldiers were present during the victory parade in London. Given their wartime sacrifice, including during the Battle of England, they justifiably considered this a dishonor.[10] At the same time, these

---

[9] Recent work on *cichociemni*: Jędrzej Tucholski, *Cichociemni. Historia legendarnych spadochroniarzy* (Wrocław: Wydawnictwo Dolnośląskie, 2010). One of the first accounts on this topic: Józef Garliński, *Politycy i żołnierze* (London: Odnowa, 1968).

[10] The fate of the Polish Armed Forces in the West after the war is the subject of Mieczysław Nurek, *Gorycz zwycięstwa. Los Polskich Sił Zbrojnych na Zachodzie po II wojnie światowej. 1945–1949* (Gdańsk: Wydawnictwo Uniwersytetu Gdańskiego, 2009).

exiles were exposed to agitation by the newly installed Communist regime in Poland, which proclaimed its will to facilitate the return of the soldiers who had served in the Polish armed forces in the West.

Regardless, Great Britain became home to the single largest post-war Polish exile community. London remained the seat of the Polish president in exile and the Polish National Council until the 1990s. It was in the British capital that key Polish émigré social and political party organizations were located. Without British hospitality and the informal protection it extended to Polish exiles, their organizations would not have lasted. London decided to create the Polish Resettlement Corps, which aimed at the demobilization and assimilation of the soldiers who had served in the Polish Second Corps. Despite rough conditions in the camps, this program provided the opportunity for many to begin (albeit slowly and not without problems) civilian life on the British Isles.

However, the essential theme in the Polish presence in the West remains the political continuity of the state in exile.[11] Because of the peculiar character of the post-World War II migration, its main aim was to ensure the continued existence of the country's authorities and the functioning of its key political groups. The patterns and traditions were derived from the interwar period and World War II. These produced an impression of legitimacy for this continuum on both the symbolic and practical/institutional levels.

In order to characterize Polish migration during the Cold War, it is essential to explain the major population shifts that had occurred during the Second World War. These happened in a couple of discernible stages and followed varied routes.[12]

7.1.1 Evacuations and escapes

Following the Nazi aggression signifying the outbreak of World War II, Soviet troops marched into Poland on 17 September. The first wartime migration stream was the evacuation of the Polish state and the country's political, military elites during the first months of the Nazi and Soviet occupation. In the period 1940–1945, soldiers, their families, and other special emissaries left the country clandestinely. People sought to escape occupied country by heading south to the mountainous regions,

---

[11] There are numerous editions of primary source materials that deal with the post of the President and the cabinet in exile. One of the earliest was *Wybór dokumentów do dziejów polskiego uchodźstwa niepodległościowego 1939–1990*, ed. Andrzej Suchcitz, Ludwik Maik, Wojciech Rojek (London: Polskie Towarzystwo Naukowe na Obczyźnie, 1997); *Dzienniki czynności Prezydenta RP Władysława Raczkiewicza 1939–1947*, ed. Jacek Piotrowski, vol. 1–2 (Wrocław: Wydawnictwo Uniwersytetu Wrocławskiego, 2004); Kazimierz Sabbat, *Polska na drodze do wolności i niepodległości. Pisma polityczne*, ed. Wanda K. Roman (Toruń: Wydawnictwo Adam Marszałek, 2009).

[12] Hubert Orłowski and Andrzej Sakson, *Utracona ojczyzna: przymusowe wysiedlenia, deportacje i przesiedlenia jako wspólne doświadczenie* (Poznań: Instytut Zachodni, 1996).

hoping to get to safety via Romania and Hungary, or north via the sea, to the Scandinavian countries.

There were also extraordinary cases of emigration, such as the odyssey of several thousand Polish Jews who were rescued by the Japanese consul Chiune Sugihara. They managed to escape the war-ravaged country via the Trans-Siberian railroad, safely reaching the countries of the Far East, principally Japan. However, these extemporaneous migrations were limited in number and pale in comparison with the population transfers caused by the two occupying powers.

The consequence of the German-Soviet pact signed on 23 August 1939 was the partition of Poland into two spheres of influence. The entire Polish territory was divided into two equal parts, although the majority of population (almost 63 percent, i.e. c. 22,140,000 people) was concentrated in the lands occupied by Germans.[13] Moreover, although the legal Polish authorities still existed and there was no international recognition of the occupation, this situation has complicated the possible estimations of how many people exactly left Polish territory. For example, the total number of Polish soldiers imprisoned by the occupying powers does not provide us with any precise information as to where they were captured or how they moved later. Piotr Eberhardt estimates that around 700,000 soldiers and hundreds of thousands of civilians left their former places of residence.[14]

The number of Polish citizens (within the borders of the pre-war Second Republic of Poland) who were deported to Nazi Germany or the Soviet Union against their will is staggering. Deportations, arrests, expulsions, and the forced labor drain displaced 2,841,500 Polish citizens forced into the Third Reich and 1,782,000 into the USSR. Overall, the Second World War resulted in the forced migration and wartime exile of 5,423,500 Polish citizens.[15]

7.1.2 Population transfers by the Nazis

The expulsion of Poles from the territories seized by the Third Reich lasted for the entire duration of World War II and constituted a part of the General Resettlement Plan (Generalsiedlungsplan). The beginning of the war mostly saw escapes and 'wild' expulsions, followed by fully organized deportations serviced by resettlement centers (in Poznań, Łódź, Gdańsk) and smaller units – that is, camps. Some areas of occupied Poland, like Greater Poland (which the Nazis called Reichsgau Warthe-

---

[13] Piotr Eberhardt, *Migracje polityczne na ziemiach polskich: 1939–1950* (Poznań: Instytut Zachodni, 2010), 30.
[14] Eberhardt, *Migracje polityczne na ziemiach polskich*, 49.
[15] Andrzej Gawryszewski, *Ludność Polski w XX wieku* (Warsaw: Instytut Geografii i Przestrzennego Zagospodarowania, 2005). Robert Rauziński, "Migracje zagraniczne Polaków w XX i XXI wieku w świetle badań demograficznych," in *Emigracja jako problem lokalny i globalny*, ed. Lipski Aleksander and Walkowska Wiesława (Mysłowice: GWSP, 2010).

land), Pomerania, Silesia, as well as areas around Łódź and Zamość were subjected to particularly harsh eviction policies. There were several categories of Poles that were removed from the occupied territories: prisoners of war, forced laborers (in Germany and Austria, as well as in the occupied countries such as France, Belgium, Norway) and Poles who were conscripted into the Wehrmacht.[16]

Citizens of Poland were terrorized by the system of labor, concentration and death camps. The fate of the Polish Jews stands out as the greatest atrocity the world had ever seen up to that time.[17] The plan to integrate formerly Polish territories into the Reich included the removal of Poles from the incorporated territories and the planned settlement of Germans in these areas. Polish citizens were persecuted both in the occupied territories and in the Reich proper. Piotr Eberhardt estimates the number of Poles living in the latter territories just after the initial attacks at 10,568,000.[18] During wartime, more than 900,000 were permanently removed.[19] Hitler's plan included the eventual complete removal, even if by physical extermination, of 'non-Aryans' in the territories of the defeated Republic of Poland (Lebensraum, Generalplan Ost). Warsaw was the site of the two most dramatic acts of resistance: the Ghetto Uprising (1943) when the Jews forced into inhumane conditions in a restricted area resisted further deportation to the death camps; and the Warsaw Uprising of 1944. Both resulted in mass executions of civilians and the latter was followed by the war's last major expulsion of Poles – as forced laborers, concentration camp and POW camp inmates, displaced persons transferred to other occupied areas outside of Warsaw. The organized expulsions of Polish citizens from the Nazi-occupied territories affected about two million citizens of Poland.

Finally, it should be mentioned that at war's end there were approximately 150 – 260,000 representatives of the so-called 'old Polish diaspora' in occupied Germany, as well as about 100,000 pre-war migrants. The wartime group – forced laborers, prisoners of war, and concentration camp inmates – numbered as many as 2.8 million people.[20] This group was dominated by Poles. The number of Poles who found themselves in Germany during the war should be further expanded by 16,000 soldiers and officers, who served in the Allied armies, as well as Poles, who were coerced to enlist in the Wehrmacht. There were also 150 – 200,000 Polish children who had been abducted for adoption by German families.[21]

---

[16] Eberhardt, *Migracje polityczne na ziemiach polskich*, 50 – 59, 75 – 142.
[17] Timothy Snyder, *Black Earth: The Holocaust as History and Warning* (London: Vintage, 2016).
[18] Eberhardt, *Migracje polityczne na ziemiach polskich*, 24.
[19] Czesław Łuczak, *Polityka ludnościowa i ekonomiczna hitlerowskich Niemiec w okupowanej Polsce* (Poznań: Wydawnictwo Poznańskie, 1979), 136; See also Piotr Eberhardt, *Migracje polityczne na ziemiach polskich*, 56.
[20] Jerzy Kozłowski, "Polska diaspora w Niemczech," in *Polska diaspora*, ed. Walaszek, 246 – 249; See also Eberhardt, *Migracje polityczne na ziemiach polskich*, 88.
[21] Dariusz Stola, "Forced Migrations in Central European History," *International Migration Review* 26, no. 2 (1992): 333.

7.1.3 Population transfers by the Soviets

From the attack of 17 September 1939 until the outbreak of the Soviet-German war in June 1941, around 600,000 Polish citizens were relocated under political pretexts. Of this number around 330,000 were moved into special labor camps and kolkhozes in remote regions of the Soviet Union (Northern Russia, Siberia, Kazakhstan).[22] People who lived on the Soviet-occupied territories were categorized into several types of 'enemy of the people' and then usually arrested and deported. Of these 63.6 percent were Poles (including those who had fled the Nazi invasion), 21.2 percent Jews, 7.6 percent Ukrainians and 6 percent Belarusians. There were also small numbers of Lithuanians, Germans, and Russians. The main phases of deportation took place in February, April and June 1940, and May–June 1941.

Almost 60,000 Polish citizens were exterminated. Just after September 1939, more than 200,000 Polish soldiers were imprisoned. Some of the privates were later released or drafted into the Red Army, while the number of those who escaped remains difficult to assess. At least forty thousand were taken to POW camps. The most tragic part of this history was the fate of fifteen thousand Polish officers (mainly professionals and intellectuals) who were inmates of the POW camps in Kozielsk, Starobielsk, and Ostaszków. On 5 March 1940, the decision was taken to kill them all; 21,857 persons were executed and dumped into mass, unmarked graves. In literature this incident is referred to as the Katyń forest massacre.[23]

It was from within these ranks that the Polish Armed Forces in the East, under the command of General Władysław Anders (hence the alternative name of the 'Anders Army') was created in summer 1941. Based on the aforementioned Sikorski-Mayski agreement (30 July 1941), 116,543 Polish citizens (90 percent of whom were Poles) were evacuated from the Soviet Union, including 78,631 soldiers.[24] They reached the countries of the Middle East and regrouped to enter the Western war theatre in Europe (in Italy). Thus, by 1943 they had joined the Polish Armed Forces in the West, who numbered over 100,000 soldiers. Because of the new rupture in diplomatic re-

---

22 These numbers are based on Eberhardt, *Migracje polityczne na ziemiach polskich*, 62–71; Artur Patek move to end of footnote gives slightly different numbers of deportees: 320,000 Polish citizens, two thirds of whom were ethnic Poles. He estimates that during the whole war there were 6–7 million Poles on Soviet territory. Artur Patek, *Polska diaspora w Rosji radzieckiej i Związku Socjalistycznych Republik Radzieckich*, in *Polska diaspora*, ed. Walaszek, 302, 304.

23 There are more than 600 publications on the topic. One of the most famous studies was written by Janusz Zawodny, *Death in the forest: the story of the Katyn Forest Massacre* (University of Notre Dame Press, 1962). More recent ones include Eugenia Maresch, *Katyn 1940: the documentary evidence of the West's betrayal* (Stroud: Spellmount, 2010) and *Zbrodnia katyńska: w kręgu prawdy i kłamstwa*, ed. Sławomir Kalbarczyk (Warsaw: Instytut Pamięci Narodowej, 2010).

24 Zbigniew Wawer, "Formowanie sił zbrojnych poza granicami kraju," in *Władze RP na obczyźnie podczas II wojny światowej*, ed. Zbigniew Błażyński (London: Polskie Towarzystwo Naukowe na Obczyźnie, 1994), 521; See also Magdalena Hułas, *Goście czy intruzi. Rząd polski na uchodźstwie wrzesień 1939 – lipiec 1943* (Warsaw: Instytut Historii PAN, 1996), 203–204; Gawryszewski, *Ludność Polski*, 436.

lations between the Polish government-in-exile and the USSR, caused by the discovery of mass graves in Katyń, the further exit of Polish citizens from the Soviet Union was halted. The Soviets had their own idea of using the Poles as part of their war and propaganda effort. Stalin agreed to the creation of a Polish infantry division under the auspices of the Polish Communist puppet group in the USSR (the Union of Polish Patriots). With this military establishment, soon to be called the Polish First Division (commanded by General Zygmunt Berling, though staffed largely by Soviet officers), almost 95,000 Polish citizens returned to Poland.[25] As the Red Army entered the prewar Polish territories occupied by the Third Reich, the Polish underground units rose up as part of the Home Army's plan to initiate an open battle for Poland's liberation (under the codename *Burza* [tempest]). The Poles fighting against the Germans in the Eastern theatre in 1944 to 1945 were interned and deported by the Soviets, or forcibly incorporated into the army of General Berling.[26]

7.1.4 German expellees

The defeat of the Third Reich affected the Germans who lived on former Polish territories under German occupation during the war, but also the territories which had been German until 1939 and became Polish after the decisions taken by world leaders in Yalta and Potsdam (such as Western Pomerania, Prussia and Silesia). Eberhardt states that almost 8,890,000 citizens of the Third Reich had lived in these areas although the total number of Germans living in the formerly occupied territories of Poland was uncertain, as the figure may take into account the Germans colonists in the Zamość region, among others.[27] With the decisions reached at the Potsdam conference, the remaining Germans were to be resettled from the 'Polish-administered territories.' The new borders of Poland imposed by the Big Three meant that the country shifted about 200 kilometeres westward. Given these circumstances, some Germans decided to flee in fear of the arrival of the Red Army, while others sought to be evacuated by land or sea. Still others fell victims to 'wild' expulsions and/or evacuations. The number of Germans displaced at war's end may number at least 5 million people, although the total number could be even higher, as many as 6–7 million.[28]

---

[25] Gawryszewski, *Ludność Polski*, 437. Henryk Stańczyk and Stefan Zwoliński states that in July 1944 around 101,400 soldiers had been enlisted into those forces. Henryk Stańczyk and Stefan Zwoliński, *Wojsko Berlinga i Żymierskiego* (Warsaw: Rytm, 2015), 131.
[26] Eberhardt, *Migracje polityczne*, 165 ff.
[27] Eberhardt, *Migracje polityczne*, 127.
[28] Eberhardt, *Migracja polityczne*, 137; Heinz Fassmann and Rainer Munz estimate that 7 million "ethnic Germans and former German citizens" had been expelled from Poland between 1945 and 1950 on the basis of the Potsdam decisions. Fassmann and Munz, 'European East-West Migration, 1945–1992, 521–522. They cite Stola, "Forced Migrations,": 324–341.

7.1.5 Post-war returns and arrivals to Poland

Many of the citizens of pre-war Poland found themselves outside the boundaries of the country now reshaped by the war. Some were able to return home without any additional support. Others awaited assistance. However, there was a group that had to decide whether it wished to stay abroad or return home, which was now outside Polish territory. This would mean either accepting Soviet citizenship or choosing a brand new location within the new Poland.

In cooperation with the new Polish authorities and the authorities of the Socialist Soviet Republics of Byelorussia, Lithuania and Ukraine, the Soviet authorities initiated 'repatriation' programs as a result of the Yalta and Potsdam decisions. The so-called population exchanges of 1944–1948 resulted in 1,517,983 people being resettled to Poland.[29] Between 1942 and 1959, as many as 2,207,716 Polish citizens left the Soviet Union although only half of the people who had been forcefully transported to the USSR were able to return.[30]

As for the Polish citizens in the West, their arrivals were also conditioned by Soviet domination over post-war Poland. As Andrzej Gawryszewski writes, "in the final stages of World War II, there were 3.4 million Polish citizens in Western Europe, in particular on the former territories of the Third Reich."[31] Of the 2.5 million Polish citizens resident on the territory of Germany (divided into four occupation zones) between 1945 and 1950, around 1,640,000 people took advantage of the organized return/arrival to Poland.[32] Around 350,000 Poles from the western zones of occupied Germany refused to leave and decided to stay in the West. Between July 1947 and December 1949 357,635 such DPs were resettled to the USA (110,566), Canada (46,961), Australia (60,308), Palestine/Israel (54,904); many others went to non-European countries such as Brazil, Argentina, Paraguay and Venezuela. Others were relocated to other European countries, mainly the United Kingdom (35,780), France (11,882), Belgium (10,378), and the Netherlands (2,969).[33]

---

[29] Eberhardt, *Migracje polityczne*, 148; See also Jan Czerniakiewicz, Monika Czerniakiewicz, *Przesiedlenia ludności w Europie 1915–1959* (Warsaw: Wydawnictwo Wyższej Szkoły Pedagogicznej TWP, 2005); Gawryszewski, *Ludność Polski*, 460 ff.

[30] Eberhardt, *Migracje polityczne*, 153; See also Stefan Banasiak, *Działalność osadnicza Państwowego Urzędu Repatriacyjnego na Ziemiach Odzyskanych w latach 1945–1947* (Poznań: Instytut Zachodni, 1963), 151.

[31] Gawryszewski, *Ludność Polski*, 449.

[32] Eberhardt, *Migracje polityczne*, 161. On the basis of Krystyna Kersten, *Repartiacja ludności polskiej po II wojnie światowej (studium historyczne)* (Wrocław: Ossolineum, 1974); Anna Jaroszyńska-Kirchmann, referring to data from UNRAA, states that "between November 1945 and June 1947, some 549,998 Polish DPs were repatriated to Poland from the three Western occupation zones of Germany, and 11,676 from Austria." Anna Jaroszyńska-Kirchmann, *The Exile Mission. The Polish Political Diaspora and Polish Americans, 1939–1956* (Athens: Ohio University Press, 2004), 61.

[33] Jaroszyńska-Kirchmann, *The Exile Mission*, 105–108; See also Jerzy Kozłowski, "Polska diaspora w Niemczech," in *Polska diaspora*, ed. Walaszek, 246–249.

Most of the displaced Poles in the West left for Poland after the war. Gawryszewski assessed that the number might be as high as 2.1 million.[34] Including the Polish citizens who returned from the settlements in the Middle East, Africa, or Latin America, this number can be increased to anywhere from 2.4 to 2.6 million.[35] For these expatriates, the decision whether to return to the reshaped Communist-dominated country was especially difficult as they had well-founded reasons to fear the new regime – especially if they had served in the Polish Armed Forces in the West (250,000).[36]

However, any approximate number of the citizens of pre-war Poland who decided to remain in the West is very difficult to assess. Although scholars disagree, Janusz Wróbel presented the most precise data. He estimated that at war's end, within the new borders (which automatically led some of the displaced Poles in the Third Reich to reside within the country), the number of Polish citizens in Western Europe was 2,450,000. Already by 1950 fewer than half still resided west of the Oder-Neisse line (1,200,000). This number includes the 'old Polonia' – the pre-war migrants of North Rhine-Westphalia, Belgium, and northern France. Once these groups are deducted, the number of wartime migrants can be assessed at 600,000.[37] Most of them were men of fighting age, which had a significant impact on the émigré community. Rafał Habielski estimated that as many as 70 percent of the exiles were men.[38]

Only within this context can an overview of the Cold War-era migrations be provided. The Communist regime imposed on Poland by a foreign power obliterated the nature of Polish migrations. The economic, ethnic, national and religious motivations became secondary to the fact that Poland had not regained its freedom as an outcome of the war. Thus all of those motivations were mixed with an overwhelming political motivation – even decisions of an economic character had their political dimension. This is why the Cold War emigration from Poland was at the same time economic and political.[39]

---

34 Gawryszewski, *Ludność Polski*, 450.
35 Habielski, *Życie społeczne i kulturalne emigracji*, 5–21.
36 Nurek, *Gorycz zwycięstwa*, 623; Eberhardt, *Migracje polityczne*, 156.
37 Wróbel, *Na rozdrożu historii*, 561, table 4. The most common estimate in literature of the number of Polish exiles who stayed in the West is 500,000.
38 Habielski, *Życie społeczne i kulturalne emigracji*. See also Wróbel, *Na rozdrożu historii*, 30.
39 Marcin Kula, 'Emigracja z realnego socjalizmu: ekonomiczna i polityczna zarazem,' *Sprawy Narodowościowe. Seria Nowa* 4, no. 2 (1995): 142–146; See also Stola, *Kraj bez wyjścia*, 13.

7.2 Major emigration streams, 1945–1989

7.2.1 Post-war standstill

Based on the Yalta (and Potsdam) agreements, the Polish people were to choose their government in 'free and unfettered' elections. An interim coalition government was formed in June 1945. In the meantime, the leaders of the Polish underground were abducted by the Soviets, and the government included only representatives of the Polish Communists and a few pro-Western politicians such as the former prime minister Stanisław Mikołajczyk, who arrived in Poland from London. The lure of free elections (which were eventually organized in January 1947) convinced some independent-minded and anti-Communist Poles to return and attempt to enter the political and cultural life of the war-ravaged country. In the aftermath of the rigged elections, many of the politicians, intellectuals, professionals who had been part of the democratic opposition decided to flee the country, some for the second time. Mikołajczyk left with the clandestine support of Western embassies in November 1947.

Janusz Wróbel characterized the post-war illegal border crossings westward as a migration stream that consisted of "members of the military underground as well as anti-Communist dissenters fearing persecution, family members of the soldiers and politicians who decided not to return. The exodus also encompassed former political elites, wealthy landowners, professionals, entrepreneurs who saw grim future prospects in the Communist dominated country."[40] This was the first Cold War migration stream from Poland. Soon enough, the country borders were sealed tight, prompting Stola to call the Poland of the next decade "the no-exit country."[41]

Fortified borders guarded by the military, the tight system of passport control, and severe penalties for illegal border crossings put strict limitations to international travel. This clearly marked an unprecedented period in the history of Poland.[42] The traditional migration patterns from the Polish lands, which had existed since the mid-nineteenth century, were now cut off. At the same time, Poland was undergoing forced industrialization and urbanization, which meant increased levels of internal migration. They included disturbing cases of the forcible removal of ethnic and national minorities and their planned resettlement in the 'recovered territories', as the Communist regime referred to the formerly German.[43] Such transfers, dictated by the border changes between 1945 and 1946, affected many of Poland's minorities, such as the Ukrainians (481,183), Byelorussians (36,393), Lithuanians (c. 1,000).[44] Many

---

40 Wróbel, *Na rozdrożu historii*, 21–22.
41 Stola, *Kraj bez wyjścia*, 46.
42 Jarosław Molenda, *Ucieczki z PRL* (Warsaw: Bellona, 2015).
43 As an example see the fate of the Ukrainian forced resettlement: Jan Pisuliński, *Akcja specjalna "Wisła"* (Rzeszów: Libra, 2017).
44 Krystyna Iglicka, *Poland's post-war dynamic of migration* (Aldershot: Ashgate, 2001), 17.

representatives of those minorities escaped to the West, strengthening their own diasporas.[45]

According to Krystyna Iglicka, the most important elements of the post-1945 patterns of direct migration were "the repatriation of Poles from the USSR, the migration of ethnic Germans from Poland under intergovernmental agreements, and emigration by people of Jewish origins."[46] She also defined certain crucial subperiods: 1945–1960, 1960–1980 and the 1980s.[47] These outflows and phases deserve separate attention although they were definitely of a different character than wartime migration.

7.2.2 Emigration of Jews from Polish People's Republic

A separate issue was the postwar Aliyah of Polish Jews. Of the estimated 3,350,000 Polish Jews in 1939, fewer than 10 percent survived World War II.[48] The Polish Communist regime initially tolerated the activities of associations promoting Jewish emigration to Palestine (after 1948 to Israel). Between 1944 and 1948, about 140,000 (almost half) of Poland's remaining Jews left the country bypassing official procedures. As reasons for leaving Poland, these émigrés cited war-trauma, or 'the inability to live on a graveyard', the desire to reconnect with dispersed family members, Zionism, as well as feelings of insecurity fueled by acts of aggression and anti-Semitism.[49]

After a brief interruption resulting from the worsening of Soviet-Israeli relations between 1948 and 1949, the Warsaw government signed an agreement with Israel in 1949 that provided for the 'release' of the Jews from Poland in return for a trade surplus in bilateral exchanges (the 'Israeli option'). The 28–29,000 people who decided to take advantage of this opportunity to leave the country were stripped of Polish cit-

---

45 Janusz Wróbel, "Geografia, demografia i profil społeczny polskich skupisk emigracyjnych w okresie powojennym," in *Polska emigracja polityczna 1939–1990. Stan badań*, ed. Sławomir Łukasiewicz (Warsaw: Instytut Pamięci Narodowej 2016), 21. There is no comprehensive synthesis of the history of Ukrainian emigration; an attempt was made by Andrzej A. Zięba, "Ukraińcy i Karpaccy Rusini," in *Polska diaspora*, ed. Walaszek, 447–459. In the case of the Belorussians, the book by Jerzy Grzybowski should be noted *Pogoń między Orłem Białym, Swastyką i Czerwoną Gwiazdą. Białoruski ruch niepodległościowy w latach 1939–1956* (Warsaw: Bel Studio, 2011).
46 Iglicka, *Poland's post-war dynamic of migration*, 13.
47 Iglicka, *Poland's post-war dynamic of migration*, 15.
48 The main statistics can be found, for example, in Eberhardt, *Migracje polityczne*, 97–107; 193–194.
49 Bożena Szaynok states that by June 1946 around 50,000 Jews left; from July to December 68–71,000, and by September 1949 around 30,500. Bożena Szaynok, "Raport o stanie badań na temat emigracji z Polski Żydów obywateli polskich po II wojnie światowej (1944–1989)," in *Polska emigracja polityczna 1939–1990. Stan badań*, ed. Sławomir Łukasiewicz (Warsaw: Instytut Pamięci Narodowej, 2016), 400–406.

izenship, which meant that in practice this was a one-way passage.⁵⁰ This migration stream was stopped in February 1951. Only 1,100 Jews left Poland in the next four years.⁵¹ The government in Warsaw reinstated the provisions enabling emigration to Israel by the mid-1950s. As many as 50,000 Jews left the country. These included some of the 13–14,000 Jews who had arrived ('returned') in Poland from the USSR.

All three aforementioned migration streams resulted in a significant reduction in the number of Polish Jews to 30,000 in 1967⁵² – one-hundredth of the pre-war Jewish population in Poland. Following another rift in diplomatic relations with Israel in 1968, the Polish Communist government (following the Soviet lead) launched an anti-Semitic campaign. Another exodus of Polish Jews took place as a result of political, social, and economic pressure. The Warsaw government offered similar conditions: the permission to leave for Israel in exchange for surrendering Polish citizenship. Declining the right to return, 13,000 mostly well-educated citizens (engineers, doctors, economists, humanists, journalists, academic teachers, scientists, actors, artists) as well as some Communist bureaucrats (apparatchiks) left Poland. This was probably the single most important exodus of professional cadres in the history of the People's Republic of Poland. Interestingly, only 28 percent of these migrants actually went to Israel; most of them sought to re-establish their lives in Scandinavia or North America.⁵³

7.2.3 The emigration of Germans from People's Poland

The other special case in the outward migration from Poland was the German minority. Between 1945 and 1949, around 3.1 million Germans were removed from Polish territory within the framework of an officially organized resettlement under the auspices of the Allied Control Council for Germany.⁵⁴ Together with expulsions and population transfers, only about 100,000 ethnic Germans remained within the boundaries of the new Poland. However, if their children and grandchildren are added, as well as people who claimed German ancestry (or wished to claim German citizenship), the number could be as high as one million.⁵⁵ From February 1950 to March 1951, another migration stream moved Germans from Poland to both West and East Germany. Within the framework of the program Aktion Link, approximately

---

50 Szaynok, "Raport o stanie badań," 408.
51 Szaynok, "Raport o stanie badań," 409.
52 Stola, *Kraj bez wyjścia*, 219 ff.
53 Stola, *Kraj bez wyjścia*, 221–223; See also Szaynok, "Raport o stanie badań," 415–416.
54 Eberhardt, *Migracje polityczne*, 187; Iglicka gives the number of people who left Poland between 1945 and 1950 at 4,092,200. Iglicka, *Poland's post-war dynamic*, 17.
55 See also Gawryszewski, *Ludność Polski*, 466; Stola, *Kraj bez wyjścia*, 67.

75,000 people were resettled to Germany.[56] This was also called 'repatriation.' Exit visas were again being granted by 1954.

Interestingly, allowing the Germans to leave Poland did not cause a significant decrease in the number of Polish citizens who claimed German ancestry. Between 1956 and 1958, another major program aiming at reconnecting separated family members was initiated. As a result of this peculiar 'migration fever' between 1955 and 1959, about 275,000 people left the country.[57] In the period 1960–1968, over 100,000 persons emigrated to West and East Germany.[58]

Even before the agreement signed between Federal Republic of Germany and the Polish People's Republic in 1970, around 120,000 people had applied for resettlement from Poland to Germany. The main official motivation was the reunion of families, although it should be emphasized that for most of them the reasons were predominantly economic. Approximately 50,000 emigrated in the early 1970s.[59] However, the emigration wave was stopped because the motivations of the Warsaw government were also economic. The authorities of People's Republic made their consent for the release of the Germans conditional on the German government making repayments for wartime losses as well as loans.[60] Finally, a specific agreement combining emigration and a financial settlement was reached in 1975, providing for family reunification programs and resettlements that were to encompass as many as 130,000 people.[61] Some citizens of Poland married German citizens during their short-term visits to West Germany, and/or were denied returns for political reasons. Despite the major exit streams between 1960 and 1968 and 1975 to 1979, the number of applications from people who wanted to move to Germany continued to increase, which meant that ethnicity and the opportunity to move to an attractive destination country were important factor in emigration. Therefore, even after the collapse of the Polish People's Republic, when the next wave of 600,000 migrants was absorbed into Germany, around 300,000 Polish citizens still declared themselves as belonging to the German minority.[62]

7.2.4 Repatriation campaigns and migrations after 1956

The regime's migration policy changed by the mid-1950s. The returns of Polish citizens deported to the Soviet Union during and after the war were now permitted.

---

[56] Stola, *Kraj bez wyjścia*, 71.
[57] Stola, *Kraj bez wyjścia*, 125.
[58] Stola, *Kraj bez wyjścia*, 257.
[59] Stola estimates that the different types of migrations to Germany (also illegal) between 1955 and 1974 eventually covered around 460,000 people. Stola, *Kraj bez wyjścia*, 248, 441.
[60] Stola, *Kraj bez wyjścia*, 244.
[61] Stola, *Kraj bez wyjścia*, 248.
[62] Stola, *Kraj bez wyjścia*, 257.

In just four years (1955–9), about 250,000 people, including those released from Soviet prisons and forced labor camps, arrived in Poland.[63]

On the other hand, the Warsaw government initiated the so-called 'repatriation campaign' targeting the centers of the Polish diaspora in the West. However, the main goal of this policy was to neutralise the threat posed by the émigré political activities in the West, and to disrupt the work of the old and new cultural and social organizations, most of which were staunchly anti-Communist. In order to connect with Poles abroad, a new organization was established under the telling name of *Polonia Society* for *Liaison with Poles Abroad*. Under the guise of cultural and economic exchange, the Warsaw government tried to win some recognition and support among Poles abroad by offering tourist visas. This caused friction among the expat communities. These efforts were successful to a certain extent. Some Poles were tired of life among foreigners and accepted the promise of a safe return to their homeland at face value. However, for the regime, the true assets were the prominent diaspora leaders who decided to return, including members of the government-in-exile such as the Prime Minister Hugon Hanke (retuned in 1955) and his predecessor Stanisław Mackiewicz (who returned to Poland in 1956).[64]

Nevertheless, the Polish Communists suffered serious defeats as well. Some of them were caused by the fact, that the US launched a campaign aiming at encouraging escapes from behind the Iron Curtain. Pilots, naval officers, diplomats and bureaucrats of the regime, including high-ranking security force officials, fled Poland, thus discrediting the regime and ridiculing its attempts to lure Poles to return. These so-called defectors and escapees were eagerly engaged by Western propaganda.[65] This was illegal migration caused mostly by political factors. Among the most famous people who worked for the security apparatus and decided to stay in the West during an official trip there were Józef Światło in 1953 (described below) and Marceli Reich-Ranicki (later a famous German literary critic). Not only did Communist officials use this way to leave the country, but ordinary citizens did so as well. Between 1955 and 1959, the total number of such escapes reached 14,000. Together

---

63 Stola, *Kraj bez wyjścia*, 81.
64 See also Sławomir Cenckiewicz, 'Geneza, działalność i udział rozgłośni "Kraj" w akcji reemigracyjnej (1955–1957). O nowych metodach walki bezpieki z emigracją i Polonią,' in Sławomir Cenckiewicz, *Oczami bezpieki. Szkice i materiały z dziejów aparatu bezpieczeństwa PRL* (Łomianki: LTW, 2012), 35–138; Jan Lencznarowicz, 'Rola Towarzystwa "Polonia" w polityce PRL wobec Polonii w krajach zachodnich,' *Przegląd Polonijny* no. 1(1996): 43–60; Paweł Ziętara, *Emigracja wobec Października. Postawy polskich środowisk emigracyjnych wobec liberalizacji w PRL w latach 1955–1957* (Warsaw: LTW, 2001), 39–66; Krzysztof Tarka, *Mackiewicz i inni. Wywiad PRL wobec emigrantów* (Łomianki: LTW, 2007), 9–88.
65 Anna Mazurkiewicz, *Uchodźcy polityczni z Europy Środkowo-Wschodniej w amerykańskiej polityce zimnowojennej 1948–1954* (Warsaw: Instytut Pamięci Narodowej; Gdańsk: Uniwersytet Gdański, 2016), 452–460.

with the Jewish and German waves described above, legal and illegal emigration during this period amounted to a total of 350,000 persons.⁶⁶

By many counts, the year 1956 marked a watershed year in the history of East-Central Europe and Poland. The major change regarding migration was the relative relaxation of international travel. Trips abroad became possible in various contexts: tourism, contracted labor, education, sport, or cultural exchanges. More family reunions were allowed as well. Finally, by the 1960s, Poles were allowed to officially apply for permits to leave in order to settle in another country. Over half a million people took advantage of this option. The 1960s and 1970s were the peak period for short-term migration. Most of the people who left Poland at this time (70–80 perrcent) were allowed to visit other countries in the Socialist bloc. The number of travellers continued to increase, both privately and on work-related visits to the West. Many could be categorized as economic or seasonal emigrants. The legal flow between 1960 and 1980 comprised at least 480,000 persons, most of whom moved to one of the German states (66 percent), with a clear preference for West Germany (58 percent), whence they sought entry to the USA (14 percent), Israel (5 percent), Canada (5 percent) and Australia. However, many of these 'tourists' decided not to return home, which resulted in illegal emigration of between 67,000 and 112,000 people. This is why Dariusz Stola estimates the total number of clear migrants at anywhere between 550,000 and 590,000.⁶⁷

7.2.5 The 'Solidarity' period

The last major migration stream from Poland is often referred to as the 'Solidarity-era' migration. It occurred at the beginning of the 1980s and still remains the least researched of all the Cold-War Polish migrations. It can be divided into several phases. The first coincides with the birth of the Solidarity independent self-governing trade union – the first workers' organization of its kind in the entire Communist bloc. The 'carnival of freedom' – as the brief period from Solidarity's recognition by the Communist government to the imposition of martial law is called – prompted the emergence of an unprecedented relaxation of foreign travel from post-war Poland. The majority of emigration at this time was economically motivated. Both blue-collar laborers as well as politically motivated union activists could travel abroad. This is why this migration stream is so hard to characterize despite deriving its name from a political context (*Solidarność*).

Scores of ordinary men and women decided not to go back once they had left the country, either as tourists, short-time visitors or on private or business trips. The number of illegal departures increased shortly before the imposition of martial

---

66 Stola, *Kraj bez wyjścia*, 100.
67 Stola, *Kraj bez wyjścia*, 179, 218.

law. Fourteen times the attempts to hijack airplanes took place (3 of which were successful). The number of Polish asylum-seekers in Austria reached 29,000 in 1981. They were particularly visible at the refugee camp in Traiskirchen. They treated this country as a transit point to other destinations – Canada (on the basis of a special program, East European Self-Exiled Persons, initiated at the time), Australia (which accepted mostly skilled professionals), the USA, New Zealand, and South Africa (which recruited likely immigrants while they were still in Austria).[68]

The most decisive moment affecting this emigration stream occurred on 13 December 1981, when martial law was introduced in Poland, immediately closing cross-border traffic. Polish migration levels reverted to those of the 1950s. The complete closing of the country's borders trapped around 150,000 Polish citizens abroad. Among them there were 500 diplomats (including the ambassadors in Washington and Tokyo), 500 seamen, as well as artists and plane crews. Many Poles tried to cross the border illegally, also by hijacking airplanes; four such attempts were successful. About 50,000 citizens of Poland asked for asylum in Austria, West Germany, and the United States, taking advantage of the previous relaxation of the foreign travel regulations.[69]

The immediate return was not possible for many, and for some – mostly leaders of the opposition – unwelcome by the regime. One such case was that of Seweryn Blumsztajn who in 1985 took a plane back to Warsaw from Paris, but was turned away and had to return to France. The case of Kornel Morawiecki in 1988 was similar.[70] At the same time, the regime agreed (and even propagated this solution) to issue one-way tickets to dissenters and unionists who preferred emigration to internment or life in a country led by a military junta. The inspiration for this action was the Cuban *marielitos* – some people deemed undesirable by the regime were let out on the basis of a 'travel document' rather than a passport. On this basis, 8,333 persons received consent to travel after 1982 although eventually only 4,400 left.[71]

For most Poles, the new migration policy was yet another piece of evidence against the oppressive Communist regime. It also prompted the creation of political structures aboard, namely, the 'Solidarity diaspora.' It actively supported the dissenters operating illegally (underground) in Poland by sending (smuggling) them financial and material support from the West and by lobbying on behalf of Solidarity abroad. These activities helped to mobilize the 'old Polonia' in the West and public opinion across the world. The West's support for Solidarity in the 1980s was almost

---

[68] Stola, *Kraj bez wyjścia*, 309–310.
[69] Stola, *Kraj bez wyjścia*, 312–314.
[70] Patryk Pleskot, *Emigracja polityczna z Polski w latach osiemdziesiątych XX wieku. Stan badań, perspektywy i trudności*, in *Polska emigracja polityczna 1939–1990. Stan badań*, ed. Sławomir Łukasiewicz (Warsaw: Instytut Pamięci Narodowej, 2016), 90; Stola, *Kraj bez wyjścia*, 317.
[71] Stola, *Kraj bez wyjścia*, 315–322.

unanimous, as was the contempt for Gen. Wojciech Jaruzelski's crackdown on the Polish democratic opposition.[72]

In terms of migration policy, more restrictions on legal emigration were introduced. The years 1982 to 1987 were characterized by a reduction in the numbers of family members granted permission to join their relatives (mostly residing in West Germany), as well as by discrimination in the migration policies in favor of skilled professionals. Illegal emigration was still very important. Besides family members, the country saw the departures of sportsmen and women, sports fans, merchant sailors, airplane and ship crews, passengers on the ferries (as in the notorious case of the *Rogalin*, a ferry running between Świnoujście, Copenhagen and Travemünde which routinely came back to Poland with 10 to 50 percent of its passengers missing), as well as diplomats, bureaucrats and others.[73] However, at the same time, this temporary migration was not brought to a complete halt. Approximately one million passports, mostly for private trips, were issued by the end of 1982. During subsequent years, this number rose, from 3.3 million passports in 1985 to 7 million in 1988. Official statistics registered about 19.3 million departures in 1989, 4–6 million of them to the West. Not surprisingly, many of these passports were used to emigrate permanently.[74]

In the face of the further dramatic worsening of the economic situation in Poland, the entire decade of the 1980s was marked by a steady increase in the number of Poles who openly declared that they wished to leave the country. Based on the public opinion research carried out at the time, 80 percent of Poles working in the state-owned industries wanted to leave 'for some time.' For the country's intellectuals, the number was as high as 75 percent and 70 percent for young people with at least a high school diploma.[75] Poor economy was not the only factor affecting their willingness to emigrate. Other motivations included the fact of friends and family members living abroad, improved understanding of the vast discrepancy in the quality of daily life between Poland and the West, increased levels of education, the attraction of better-quality consumer goods compared to those available in the Socialist bloc, and the economics of earning 'hard cash' abroad and its especially high value in the crisis-ridden economy of Poland. All of these motivations contributed to the exceptional, possibly record-high readiness of Poles to emigrate.[76]

---

[72] The best description of this phenomenon is given the book *Za naszą i waszą Solidarność. Inicjatyw solidarnościowe z udziałem Polonii podejmowane na świecie (1980–1989)*, ed. Patryk Pleskot, vols. 1–2 (Warsaw: Instytut Pamięci Narodowej, 2018).
[73] Stola, *Kraj bez wyjścia*, 350 ff.
[74] Stola, *Kraj bez wyjścia*, 342–343.
[75] Stola, *Kraj bez wyjścia*, 332.
[76] See also Patryk Pleskot, *Emigracja polityczna z Polski w latach osiemdziesiątych XX wieku. Stan badań, perspektywy i trudności*, in *Polska emigracja polityczna 1939–1990. Stan badań*, ed. Sławomir Łukasiewicz (Warsaw: Instytut Pamięci Narodowej, 2016), 90.

Not surprisingly, between 1983 and 1989, the number of short-term trips abroad from Poland to the West reached 5.7 million. Of these 'tourists' (visitors, but also short-term laborers, peddlers, smugglers, potential emigrants) about 530,000 did not return home. Others did return, but after prolonged stays abroad, in most cases to work illegally. Mary P. Erdmans referred to them as '*wakacjusze*' (vacationers).[77] Such experience produced the know-how, networks, and – of course – the 'hard' cash essential for surviving the economic crisis in Poland. By the end of the 1980s, these factors turned out to be of key importance for many Poles hoping to start a private business in non-Communist Poland. During the same decade, legal emigration was only possible for 83,000 people. Regardless, the 1980s saw the greatest (and mostly illegal) outflow of citizens from the People's Republic in its entire existence. Scholars estimate the total number to be 1.2 million citizens of Poland.[78] About 100,000 of them came back, although this process may still not be complete.

During the forty years from 1949 to 1989, about 2.1 to 2.3 million people left Poland for good. It must be added, however, that as with any country with 'no exit', the sudden opening of borders resulted in a skyrocketing number of foreign trips. Stola states that during the *annus mirabilis* 1989 alone about 19.3 million Poles went abroad. In other words, half of the country's citizens wanted to see and experience the world abroad.[79]

7.2.6 Spatial distribution

It is extremely difficult – and yet essential – to describe the spatial distribution of the Polish diaspora in order to understand the peculiar nature of emigration patterns from Poland. The outflows of ethnic Germans, Jews, Ukrainians and others described above very rarely empowered the Polish communities outside Poland. They became a part of their own ethnic diasporas and for this reason a separate comprehensive approach towards them is necessary. This aim is partly covered by other texts in this volume. When discussing spatial distribution, we focus mostly on those migration outflows, which identified themselves as 'Polish', despite being fully aware how imprecise such approach is. Their shape and possibilities were largely influenced by pre-existing diaspora centers in the West, the so-called 'Polonia.' Regardless of its character (peasant, skilled, political or economic), it could potentially play the

---

[77] Mary Erdmans, *Opposite Poles: Immigrants and Ethnics in Polish Chicago, 1976–1990* (University Park, PA: Penn. State University Press, 1990).
[78] I hereby refer to the corrected numbers listed by Barbara Sakson and Marek Okólski, cited in Stola, *Kraj bez wyjścia*, 355. They differ from the official data listed by the Central Statistical Office of Poland used by Andrzej Gawryszewski, *Ludność Polski*, 477. Krystyna Iglicka gives the following numbers: 1,073,000–1,317,000 long-term migrants and 1,028,000–1,132,000 short-term migrants. Krystyna Iglicka, *Poland's post-war dynamic*, 25.
[79] Stola, *Kraj bez wyjścia*, 342–343.

role of a safety net for the new arrivals, as well as a basis for political lobbying in the host country. Despite regional differences, Great Britain, the United States, and France serve as excellent examples of such models.

As Janusz Wróbel writes, up to 1939, the Polish diaspora was most numerous in Europe (Germany, France, Belgium and Denmark) and the Americas (the United States, Canada, Brazil and Argentina). This pattern changed dramatically with the outbreak of World War II. The Polish émigrés of the early months of the war congregated mostly in France, a Polish ally. After the fall of France in spring 1940, most Poles moved from France to Great Britain. Undoubtedly, it was the British Isles that, over the next sixty years, had the biggest post-World War II concentration of Polish émigrés. Of course, it was not the only one; groups of Polish political exiles were temporarily detained in Romania and Hungary.[80] The people who had escaped a country occupied by two totalitarian aggressors, as well as those who were rescued from Stalin's wrath, awaited war's end together with Gen. Anders' soldiers in remote locations in Africa – North, East and South, the Middle East (Iran, Palestine), India, Shanghai, New Zealand (Pahiatua) and Mexico (Santa Rosa). Some of these locations were selected and sponsored by agreements signed by the Polish government-in-exile and the British and/or American authorities, with the consent of the local administrations.[81]

The Polish government-in-exile considered wartime migration both coerced and temporary. The Polish political leaders abroad planned the return of these displaced persons as soon as Germany was defeated and a peace treaty was signed. However, the final settlement was far from Polish expectations. Due to the decisions made by the Big Three, Poles abroad remained dispersed – mostly in Great Britain, France, Germany, and Italy (where Gen. Anders' Second Corps fought alongside the Western Allies). Some Poles stayed in Scandinavia. Some decided to go back to the newly reshaped Poland, where they had to undergo special security screenings.[82] Others looked for opportunities to leave Europe and rebuild their lives in the Americas (in the US, Canada, Argentina, Brazil and other locations). At the same time, the Polish settlements in Africa, the Middle East and India broke up. After 1950, key migration streams of war-displaced Poles led them to the well-developed countries of Western Europe, including Austria and Scandinavia; North America, but also Australia and

---

80 Florin Anghel, Jerzy Bednarek et al., eds. *Polscy uchodźcy w Rumunii 1939–1947. Dokumenty z Narodowych Archiwów Rumunii / Refugiaţii polonezi în România 1939–1947. Documente din Arhivele Naţionale ale României*, vol. 1, part 1 and 2 (Warsaw/Bucharest: Instytut Pamięci Narodowej/Arhivele Naţionale ale României, 2013).
81 Robert W. Kesting, "American Support of Polish Refugees and Their Santa Rosa Camp," *Polish American Studies* 48, no. 1 (Spring 1991): 79–90; See also Elżbieta and Janusz Wróbel, *Rozproszeni po świecie: Obozy I osiedla uchodźców polskich ze Związku Sowieckiego, 1942–1950* (Chicago: Panorama, 1992); Jaroszyńska-Kirchmann, *The Exile Mission...*, 43.
82 Janusz Wróbel, *Na rozdrożu historii. Repatriacja obywateli polskich z Zachodu w latach 1945–1949* (Łódź: Instytut Pamięci Narodowej, 2009).

the Union of South Africa. As mentioned before, in the mid-1950s, the Polish Peoples' Republic slightly relaxed its strict passport policies, which allowed some citizens to leave the country. Their destinations were mostly the Federal Republic of Germany, the United States, Israel, Canada and Australia.[83]

One has to agree with Janusz Wróbel that it is a great pity that the atlas of the Polish diaspora envisioned by the late Wojciech Wrzesiński in the 1980s has not been created.[84] This would greatly enhance scholars' ability to assess the numbers of Poles abroad. The basic statistics collected for the *Polska diaspora* volume yield the following data.

As mentioned above, the major center of Polish post-war diaspora was in Great Britain. By war's end there were approximately 90 to 95,000 Poles there.[85] Given the fact that there was no visible and active 'old' (i.e. prewar) Polish diaspora in the British Isles, the number of Poles who came there in the brief period of crisis is significant. Due to the relocation of the Polish Armed Forces in the West in 1949, the number of Poles in Great Britain rose to about 160,000. In the following years, this number fell from 127,846 in 1961 to 110,925 in 1971. By the early 1980s the figure was 93,364.

Unlike the British Isles, France was a traditional hub for Polish economic (and earlier, also political) migrants. It was in France that the Polish government sought refuge in 1939 and where the Polish army in the West was regrouped. The figures reached 80,000 soldiers, 50,000 of whom were Polish pre-1939 immigrants in France. Poles took an active part in the defense of France. It was only after its capitulation in spring 1940 that many of them (about 24,000) were evacuated to Great Britain. Some Poles who stayed behind took part in French underground operations and established their own spy networks. At the war's end, there were 100,000 Poles in France who could be categorized as wartime exiles. Almost 80 percent of them decided to repatriate. Moreover, some Poles who had settled in France before the war decided to return to Poland (between 51,000 and 78,000).[86] During the Cold War, several distinctly political migration streams reached France from Poland: about 6000 in the aftermath of 1956, two thousand after 1968, and about 1500 within the so-called 'Solidarity wave' between 1980 and 1981. They blended in with the Polish economic mi-

---

83 Stola, *Kraj bez wyjścia*, 179; Wróbel, *Na rozdrożu historii*, 22.
84 Janusz Wróbel, "Geografia, demografia i profil społeczny polskich skupisk emigracyjnych w okresie powojennym," in *Polska emigracja polityczna 1939–1990. Stan badań*, ed. Sławomir Łukasiewicz (Warsaw: Instytut Pamięci Narodowej, 2016), 26.
85 Tadeusz Radzik, "Polska diaspora w Wielkiej Brytanii," in *Polska diaspora*, ed. Walaszek, 152.
86 Ewa Nowicka and Hanna Firouzbakhch, eds., *Homecoming. An Anthology of Return Migrations* (Kraków: Nomos, 2008). Rare cases of Polish migrants returning to Poland for ideological reasons were analyzed by Aneta Nisiobęcka in her doctoral dissertation *Reemigration of Poles from France and their adaptation in People's Poland in 1945–1950* (PhD diss., University of Warsaw, 2015).

grants in France. Wiesław Śladkowski estimated that the latter group did not exceed 150,000.[87]

A relatively large number of Poles settled in Belgium and Holland after the war. Wiesława Eder estimated that the number of Poles there was between 72,000 and 74,000 by the 1990s. There were 60,000 of them in Belgium alone. These postwar migrants were soldiers, including about 500 men who had served under Gen. Stanisław Maczek (First Armored Division), prisoners of war and DPs (27,000). These numbers decreased as the migrants left for other countries and continents. In the 1980s, the Polish diaspora in the Benelux increased with the arrival of the 'Solidarity wave' (about 5,000).[88]

As mentioned before, one of the most important European destinations for Poles was West Germany. Before World War II there were numerous and influential Polish organizations in the country, such like the Union of Poles in Germany. As a consequence of all the processes described above between 1939 and 1949, around 120,000 Polish Displaced Persons remained in West Germany. Most of them adopted German citizenship. In addition to the migration caused by the border changes and the family reunions, there were also economic and political migrants. A single migration stream consisting of the latter arrived in 1981–1990 during the Solidarity period, bringing no less than 300,000 Polish immigrants to Germany. Taking all these streams together, by 1990 the number of Poles who had migrated to Germany since the end of the war was over 2.5 million.[89]

Approximately 12,800 Polish soldiers had been interned in Switzerland in 1940. After the war most of them chose to be repatriated, leaving only 800 men behind. By 1950 the entire Polish community in this country (civilians included) did not exceed 4000 persons.[90] In 1945 in Austria there were about 80,000 Poles – mostly prisoners and forced laborers who received DP status. Three years later only 23,700 remained, as most of the forced migrants decided to return to Poland or leave Europe for other continents upon liberation. It was not until 1981 that a single migration stream brought 30,000 Poles asking for political asylum. It is estimated that in the 1990s there were 45,000 persons of Polish origin living in Austria.[91]

Interestingly, despite its many ties to Poland, Italy was not a prime destination for Polish migrants. Although Polish soldiers of the 2nd Corps were stationed in

---

[87] Wiesław Śladkowski, "Polska diaspora we Francji 1871–1999," in *Polska diaspora*, ed. Walaszek, 187–188.
[88] Wiesława Eder, "Polska diaspora w Belgii i Holandii," in *Polska diaspora*, ed. Walaszek, 201–202; See also Wiesława Eder, "Belgia," in *Akcja niepodległościowa na terenie międzynarodowym 1945–1990* ed. Tomasz Piesakowski (London: Polskie Towarzystwo Naukowe na Obczyźnie, 1999), 280–296; Idesbald Goddeeris, *Polonia w Belgii w pierwszych latach po II wojnie światowej* (Warsaw: Wydawnictwo Naukowe Semper, 2005).
[89] Jerzy Kozłowski, "Polska diaspora w Niemczech," in *Polska diaspora*, ed. Walaszek, 246–249.
[90] Halina Florkowska-Frančić, "Polska diaspora w Szwajcarii," in *Polska diaspora*, ed. Walaszek, 215–216.
[91] Władysław S. Kucharski, "Polska diaspora w Austrii," in *Polska diaspora*, ed. Walaszek, 255–257.

Italy alongside the Western allies in 1943, after the fighting was over most of the soldiers (including Gen. Anders) left the Apennine Peninsula. While most went to Great Britain, some looked for another location that they found more appropriate for continued activities on behalf of their homeland. Such was the case of two former soldiers, Jerzy Giedroyc and Józef Czapski, who went to France. In Maisons-Laffitte (near Paris) they established the Literary Institute (see below). Some demobilized soldiers stayed in Italy and enrolled in schools there. There were about 2,000 Poles in Italy by 1948. The next arrivals of significance occurred in the 1980s but most of these were temporary. The estimated number of Poles in Italy at that time was between 1,500 and 4,000.[92]

There were also Poles in Spain and Portugal after World War II. Their numbers were not significant (150 persons in Spain and 200 in Portugal) but some of them, like Józef Łobodowski, the poet, publicist, and co-founder of the Polish Section of Radio Madrid, were essential to the activities of Polish exiles. By the 1980s the number of Poles residing on the Iberian Peninsula had increased, but in Spain the total number did not exceed 600 immigrants.[93]

By war's end there were also 10,000 Polish exiles in Denmark. Most of them were repatriated to Poland; only 800–900 persons remained behind. However, due to the close geographical proximity to the Eastern Bloc, this number increased by 4,000 between 1969 and 1974; of these, 3,000 were Polish Jews. Between 1982 and 1990 another 4,000 Poles arrived as part of the so-called 'Solidarity wave'; most of these were economic migrants.[94]

Sweden had not been a traditional destination for Polish migrants before 1939. It was estimated that in 1945 about 138,000 Poles arrived, but most of them did not stay. Four years later there were only 3,500 left. After 1956 there were about 500 new arrivals. In the first decades of the Cold War, however, Sweden was a stopover on the Polish migrant path to the West. In 1968 it received about 5,000 Polish Jews. This migration was followed by an increased number of emigrants. The number of Poles living in Sweden reached 20,000 by 1980. These numbers have not decreased since then. By 1985 there were 28,000 Polish immigrants. In 1990 that figure was 32,000 and on the rise.[95]

---

[92] Stefan Bielański, "Polska diaspora we Włoszech," in *Polska diaspora*, ed. Walaszek, 359–360.
[93] Danuta Bartkowiak, "Polska diaspora w Hiszpanii i Portugalii," in *Polska diaspora*, ed. Walaszek, 198–199; Paweł Libera, "Józef Łobodowski i polska audycja Radia Madryt (1949–1975)," in *Polska a Hiszpania. Z dziejów koegzystencji dwóch narodów w XX wieku*, ed. Marek Białokura and Patrycja Jakóbczyk-Adamczyk (Toruń: Duet, 2012), 156–187.
[94] Elżbieta Later Chodyłowa, "Polska diaspora w Skandynawii," in *Polska diaspora*, ed. Walaszek, 222; See also Edward Olszewski, *Emigracja polska w Danii 1893–1983* (Warsaw-Lublin: IS PAN, 1993).
[95] Chodyłowa, "Polska diaspora w Skandynawii," 227–228; See also Arnold Kłonczyński, *My w Szwecji nie porastamy mchem...: emigranci z Polski w Szwecji w latach 1945–1980* (Gdańsk: Wydawnictwo Uniwersytetu Gdańskiego, 2012).

At war's end, Poles did not constitute any major diaspora in Finland. The number of Polish emigrants there began to increase slowly in the 1960s, reaching about a thousand persons by the 1990s.[96] In Norway, however, there were 20,000 Poles at war's end. Of them 12,500 were Poles who had been forced to serve in the Wehrmacht. Due to repatriation, their numbers fell significantly; by 1950 only 900 persons remained. Norway's restrictive immigration laws prevented many Poles from seeking refuge in this country. It was not until the 'Solidarity wave' that 4,000 Poles arrived in Norway.[97]

The United States was among the top destinations for Poles during the Cold War. Between 1939 and 1956 about 140,000 Polish political refugees chose to be resettled there from Western Europe. From 1948 to 1990 the total number of Poles who arrived in the US was 435,000 immigrants and 1.2 million visitors (regular tourists as well as 'vacationers') and refugees.[98]

During World War II, Canada accepted 800 Polish refugees, three-quarters of whom were skilled technicians. It was not until the final months of 1946 that the arrival of the demobilized soldiers from the Polish Armed Forces in the West began. The number of these Polish post-war immigrants in Canada was 55,000 by 1952. A similar number of Poles came from Communist-dominated Poland between 1953 and 1971. They were followed by a further 8000 in the 1970s before the 'Solidarity wave' increased the number of Poles in Canada by 80,000 persons (1981–1991). More came in the 1990s. In the Canadian census of 1996, more than a quarter of a million citizens of Canada listed Polish ancestry. Half a million mentioned Polish ancestry as one of their many origins.[99]

In the case of the Latin American countries, the distribution of Poles was rather unequal. By the 1990s, the biggest Polish diaspora was located in Argentina (170,000). The other countries hosted no more than a few thousand Poles (Paraguay 10–13,000; Uruguay 8–10,000; Mexico 3–4,000; Venezuela between 2,000 and 2,500; Colombia 1,500; and even fewer in Peru, Chile, Ecuador and other countries of the region).[100] Brazil became a temporary home to wartime refugees, accepting more than 7,000 Polish DPs after the war. The total number of Polish immigrants to Brazil remains very difficult to assess; scholars estimate it must have been somewhere between 10,000 and 20,000 persons.[101]

---

96 Chodyłowa, 224.
97 Chodyłowa, 225–226.
98 Stanisław A. Blejwas, "Polska diaspora w Stanach Zjednoczonych," in *Polska diaspora*, ed. Walaszek, 93; See also Erdmans, *Opposite Poles* ...
99 Anna Reczyńska, "Polska diaspora w Kanadzie," in *Polska diaspora*, ed. Walaszek, 30–32.
100 Krzysztof Smolana, 'Polska diaspora w Ameryce Południowej, Środkowej i Meksyku' in *Polska diaspora*, ed. Walaszek, 135.
101 Zdzisław Malczewski, *Polacy i osoby polskiego pochodzenia w Brazylii. Zarys historyczny i współczesność Polonii brazylijskiej*, http://www.kurytyba.msz.gov.pl/pl/polonia_w_brazylii/polonia_w_brazyli (accessed 19 December 2016).

On the Pacific, the most popular destination for Poles was Australia. According to the country's 1947 census, there were 6,500 Polish-born inhabitants. By 1948, this number increased due to the arrival of 1,500 Polish soldiers. They were joined soon thereafter by 60,000 Polish DPs relocated there between 1949 and 1951. Australia received not only the resettled Poles but also these who wanted to immigrate in order to join their family members or friends (at least 5,000). A group of 11,000 emigrants arrived after 1956, followed by 25,000 of the Solidarity migrants during the 1980s.[102]

The Cold War presence of the Polish diaspora in Asia, the Middle East and Africa must also be noted, both in regards to war-time displacement as well as the numbers of Poles who arrived in countries of these regions in the 1980s. In South Africa alone there are at least 30,000 Poles who had settled there during the Cold War.[103]

7.3 Political activities in exile

7.3.1 The main political power structures

During the war, the Polish political power centers in exile mostly clustered around the four major political parties: the Polish Christian Labor Party (Stronnictwo Pracy, SP),[104] the Polish Socialist Party (Polska Partia Socjalistyczna, PPS),[105] the People's Party (Stronnictwo Ludowe, SL),[106] and the National Party (Stronnictwo Nar-

---

102 Jan Lencznarowicz, "Polska diaspora w Australii," in *Polska diaspora*, ed. Walaszek, 399–400, 406.
103 Krzysztof Sawicki ed., *Raport o sytuacji Polonii i Polaków za granicą*, (Warsaw: Ministerstwo Spraw Zagranicznych, 2009), http://www.msz.gov.pl/resource/c7694f2f-843d-4386-ac09-0ebaf40387db:JCR (accessed 28 March 2018).
104 Janusz Zabłocki, *Chrześcijańska demokracja w kraju i na emigracji 1947–1970* (Lublin, Ośrodek studiów polonijnych i społecznych PZKS w Lublinie, 1999); See also Paweł Ziętara, "Konrad Sieniewicz w dokumentach bezpieki' *Pamięć i Sprawiedliwość* no. 1 (2010): 89–110; Piotr Stanek, 'Figurant "Tybr". Nieudany werbunek niedoszłego ministra' *Pamięć i Sprawiedliwość* no. 1 (2010): 117–138. Cf. volume recently edited by Piotr Kosicki and Sławomir Łukasiewicz, *Christian democracy across the Iron Curtain. Europe Redefined* (Palgrave Macmillan, 2018).
105 Dorota Urzyńska, *Polski ruch socjalistyczny na obczyźnie w latach 1939–1945* (Poznań: Instytut Historii UAM, 2000); Anna Siwik, *Polska Partia Socjalistyczna na emigracji w latach 1945–1956* (Kraków: Księgarnia Akademicka, 1998); Anna Siwik, *Polskie uchodźstwo polityczne. Socjaliści na emigracji w latach 1956–1990* (Kraków: Abrys, 2002); Andrzej Friszke, "PPS na emigracji. Spory o strategię polskich socjalistów (1945–1980)," in *Polska Partia Socjalistyczna. Dlaczego się nie udało? Szkice – polemiki – wspomnienia*, ed. Robert Spałek, (Warsaw: Instytut Pamięci Narodowej, 2010), 275–312.
106 See also Roman Buczek, *Stanisław Mikołajczyk*, vol. 1–2 (Toronto: Century Publishing Company, 1996); *Polski ruch ludowy na emigracji. Dokumenty i materiały*, part 1: *1944–1954*, part 2: *1954–1968*, part 3: *1968–1991*, ed., Romuald Turkowski (Kielce-Pińczów: Wyższa Szkoła Umiejętności Zawodowych, 2005–2007); *Stanisław Mikołajczyk w dokumentach aparatu bezpieczeństwa*, vol. 1–3, ed., Witold Bagieński et al. (Łódź/Warsaw: Instytut Pamięci Narodowej, 2010).

odowe).¹⁰⁷ These were the historical political factions active in exile party politics during World War II, participating in the governments of Gen. Władysław Sikorski, Stanisław Mikołajczyk, and Tomasz Arciszewski. Their members were also represented in the émigré National Council. Their cooperation was not easy. From July 1941 to November 1944, the SN opposed the government, mostly due to its disapproval of the Sikorski-Mayski agreement. The SL suffered an internal divide as some of its members disapproved of Prime Minister Mikołajczyk's decision to resign his post (in autumn 1944) and join the talks with the Soviets leading to the creation of a coalition government. During the war, however, not a single party organization represented the milieu of the followers of the late Marshal Pilsudski (the Pilsudski-ites). There were some informal groupings and prominent individuals from within this group that were represented in the governments-in-exile (including August Zaleski).¹⁰⁸ In addition, this panorama of the parties would be incomplete without mentioning the Democratic Party (Stronnictwo Demokratyczne, SD), although it was rather small compared to the four parties mentioned above.

After the war, the émigré parties and groupings were an important element of the political system in exile. They carried on the Polish political tradition and maintained the historical arrangement of the political stage. This gave them legitimacy, as the organization of any electoral process in a Communist-dominated Poland and from afar was out of the question. There were attempts to organize elections in exile in order to seek legitimacy from the Polish diaspora, but these were unsuccessful. The first such attempt was organized by the government led by Stanisław Mackiewicz in the mid-1950s. The second attempt was undertaken by the political representations gathered under the umbrella of the Provisional Council of National Unity in 1962. Finally, elections to the National Council were announced after the re-unification of the Polish political groups in exile in the 1970s. Regardless, the key argument for the legitimacy of the actions carried out by the exiled politicians was grounded in their 'historicity'.

The party formations in political exile that emerged abroad after the war were much more complex in nature. Some, like the League for Independent Poland

---

[107] In the original émigré documents, the abbreviation SN can also refer to *Skarb Narodowy* i.e. the National Treasury. In this text, SN refers to *Stronnictwo Narodowe*, i.e. the National Party. See also Stanisław Kilian, *Myśl społeczno-polityczna Tadeusza Bieleckiego* (Kraków: Wydawn. Naukowe Akademii Pedagogicznej, 2000); Wojciech Turek, *Arka Przymierza. Wojciech Wasiutyński 1910–1994. Biografia polityczna* (Kraków: Arkana, 2008); Jan Żaryn, *"Taniec na linie, nad przepaścią": Organizacja Polska na wychodźstwie i jej łączność z krajem w latach 1945–1955* (Warsaw: Instytut Pamięci Narodowej – Komisja Ścigania Zbrodni przeciwko Narodowi Polskiemu, 2011).
[108] Arkadiusz Adamczyk, *Piłsudczycy w izolacji (1939–1954). Studium z dziejów struktur i myśli politycznej* (Warsaw: Instytut Józefa Piłsudskiego; Bełchatów: Związek Strzelecki 'Strzelec', 2008); Jacek Piotrowski, *Piłsudczycy bez lidera* (Toruń: Adam Marszałek, 2003).

(Liga Niepodległości Polski, LNP)[109] aspired to 'historicity' since they carried on the Pilsudski tradition. However, Polish Freedom Movement "Independence and Democracy" (Polski Ruch Wolnościowy "Niepodległość i Demokracja," PRW NiD)[110] and the Independent Social Group (Niezależna Grupa Społeczna)[111] were composed of émigré youth, who could hardly relate to the system of traditional party arrangements. The problems facing the political splinter groups, politicians who broke away from the Labor, Peasant or Socialist parties, were different in their turn.

The continued operation of the President, the government, and the National Council in exile had its symbolic significance, but it did not satisfy all the needs of the politically active diaspora. This led to complications in the political system. The power structure, united and initially gathered around the President in exile, gradually disintegrated into parallel power centers. One early example was the emergence of the Democratic Concentration and the Coalition of the Democratic Parties in 1947, which resulted from uncertainty regarding the succession to the late President Władysław Raczkiewicz.

These cleavages had a tremendous impact on the political structure of the Polish émigré community in the coming years. Further splits resulted in the Polish government in the West being split three ways by 1950. Besides the government and the President there were two more political centers, the Political Council (Rada Polityczna led by Tomasz Arciszewski) and the Polish National Democratic Committee (Polski Narodowy Komitet Demokratyczny led by Stanisław Mikołajczyk). The emergence of these councils and committees resulted from the Cold War policy of the US, as represented in the creation of the National Committee for a Free Europe (1949). Many prominent exiles considered moving to Washington or New York as they became convinced that the center of world power had shifted to the United States. Since crucial decisions regarding the world, Europe and Poland were taken there, post-World War II exiles attempted to enlist Polish-American support for their lobbying efforts. The most important political outlet for the old Polish diaspora in the United States was the Polish American Congress led by Karol Rozmarek from 1944 to 1968. Paradoxically, American policy fostered the mobilization of the Polish political groups in many European countries, including France (the *Kultura* milieu), Germany (the Polish section of Radio Free Europe), and Italy (the Christian Democrats).

---

109 Piotrowski, *Piłsudczycy bez lidera*...; Adamczyk, *Piłsudczycy w izolacji* .... The latter particularly (16 ff) emphasized those features of the Piłsudski-ites' camp, which made them resemble a political party.
110 Sławomir Łukasiewicz, *Partia w warunkach emigracji. Dylematy Polskiego Ruchu Wolnościowego "Niepodległość i Demokracja"* (Lublin/Warsaw: Instytut Pamięci Narodowej, Instytut Studiów Politycznych PAN, 2014).
111 Walery E. Choroszewski, "Niezależna Grupa Społeczna. Zarys historii," in *Kierownictwo obozu niepodległościowego na obczyźnie 1945–1990*, ed., Aleksander Szkuta (London: Polskie Towarzystwo Naukowe na Obczyźnie, 1996), 411–437.

The year 1954 represented a watershed in émigré politics. The groups questioning the legacy of the actions taken by President-in-exile August Zaleski formed an alternative structure, the so-called unity camp (obóz zjednoczenia): the Provisional Council of National Unity (Tymczasowa Rada Jedności Narodowej, TRJN), the Council of the Three (Rada Trzech, i.e. Tomasz Arciszewski, Gen. Władysław Anders and Count Edward Raczyński) and the Executive of National Unity (Egzekutywa Zjednoczenia Narodowego, EZN). The TRJN acted as a quasi-parliament, Rada Trzech as a type of collective presidency, while the EZN resembled a government body. The TRJN dropped the adjective 'Provisional' from its name in 1962. About the same time, a Federation of Democratic Movements was established as a form of opposition within the unity camp. As we now know, this organization was infiltrated largely by Communist intelligence. Ten years later, when Zaleski passed away, the Polish political diaspora was able to reunite, at least partially. The one important political party that was absent was the National Party, which was made up of the Polish National Union (Polskie Zjednoczenie Narodowe) and the remnants of the PRW "NiD". Nevertheless, this attempt at political unification among the émigrés was by far the most successful to date. Though additional complications were caused by the fact that there was a presidential usurper, Juliusz Sokolnicki, who claimed the right to take over the presidency. While ephemeral, his arrogated service as president continues to produce discord to this day, as Sokolnicki unlawfully distributed a number of state honors and recognitions.

The Polish feud over émigré claims to legitimacy within their representation in exile requires further commentary as it distinguishes the Polish diaspora from the other East-Central European nations. One of the most interesting studies of the legal complexities involved was published in London in 1959 by Jerzy August Gawenda.[112] The author, a Polish exile himself, offered definition of legalism understood as "the continuity of state power in exile in accordance with the provisions of the Constitution. In this regard, it means formal compliance of the actual state of political affairs with the legal order." Gawenda adds: "This implied the continuation of the legitimate authority of a given nation up to the point of its liberation."[113] Indeed, this remained one of the key definitions of the largely symbolic power that the Polish president-in-exile and the government-in-exile held until 1990. According to Gawenda, "its essence focused on the defense of completeness and the integrity of the legal order of the Polish state, which were guaranteed by the sovereign nation and its legitimate government. What is more, it lies in the legal continuity of the institution of the state itself."[114] This stance emphasized the legitimacy of the émigré governments and at the same time undermined the legitimacy of the Warsaw regime. Consequently, as Gawenda argued, during the change in the international balance of power, one

---

[112] Jerzy A. Gawenda, *Legalizm Polski w świetle Prawa Publicznego* (London: White Eagle Press, 1959), 5–6.
[113] Gawenda, 6.
[114] Gawenda, 6–7.

should expect that the Warsaw regime will lose recognition. And the legitimate authorities in exile will regain this recognition without any political or legal doubts.[115] There were only three cases that could terminate the legitimacy of operations of the government-in-exile: a return to the home country for the sake of reinstating power based on the principle of continued constitutional order; the legal authorities abroad ceasing to operate due to formal-legal reasons; or the exiled government ceasing to operate due to the will of the sovereign nation (material and formal reasons).[116] In fact, on 22 December 1990, the last President in Exile, Ryszard Kaczorowski, symbolically bequeathed the presidential insignia to Lech Wałęsa, recognizing in him the legal continuation of the émigré authorities.

Throughout the Cold War the Polish state authorities in exile in London remained an important point of reference for the Polish diaspora despite their limited resources and capabilities. The government-in-exile played a pivotal role in assisting Poles abroad as well as helping Poles in Poland. However, their existence remained largely symbolic on the international political scene. Regardless of the legal disputes, the contested claims to legitimacy and unresponsiveness to the changes occurring in Poland deprived the Polish émigré politicians of credibility in the eyes of their West European partners.

7.3.2 Social and political life in exile

An important role in terms of maintaining the social and political functions was played by diaspora community organizations and institutions. First and foremost, it was the demobilized soldiers who initiated the process of self-organization of the post-war émigrés. The veterans' and combatants' organizations (Polish Ex-Combatants Association, Stowarzyszenie Polskich Kombatantów, SPK)[117] and the Polish Home Army Ex-Servicemen Association (Związek byłych Żołnierzy Armii Krajowej) attracted many former soldiers scattered around the world. Their membership was a subject of heated rivalry among various emigrant parties since their wartime role, opinions and numbers were fundamental to the post-World War II émigré ethos. The politicians were also interested in gaining control of their assets in the West. Besides the veterans' organizations, there were also civilian organizations such as the Association of Polish War Refugees (Zjednoczenie Polskiego Uchodźstwa Wojennego), which not only had a sizeable membership but also considerable assets.

---

115 Gawenda, 26.
116 Gawenda, 120. See also Dariusz Górecki, *Polskie naczelne władze państwowe na uchodźstwie w latach 1939–1990* (Warsaw: Wydawnictwo Sejmowe, 2002).
117 See also Tadeusz Kondracki, *Historia Stowarzyszenia Polskich Kombatantów w Wielkiej Brytanii 1946–1996* (London: Zarząd Główny SPK w Wielkiej Brytanii, 1996); Piotr Kardela, *Stowarzyszenie Polskich Kombatantów w Stanach Zjednoczonych w latach 1953–1990* (Olsztyn/Białystok: Instytut Pamięci Narodowej, 2015).

Émigré daily life looked different in all the host countries. Their political activities were also subject to different treatments by the host governments. This was largely influenced by the number of émigrés and their activities, and the presence or absence of the so-called 'old Polonia.' For example, in accordance with a 1938 law, any activity carried out in the United States on behalf of a foreign organization (such as the Rada Polityczna or the subsequent Tymczasowa Rada Jedności Narodowej) had to be registered with the Department of State as a 'foreign agent,' which was obliged to submit special reports and submit any materials distributed within the country with the annotation that they had been prepared by a 'foreign agent.'[118]

However, for many émigrés, finding a way to obtain means to support themselves in a foreign land remained a basic problem. Earning a livelihood, finding a job, learning a new profession, or obtaining a professional degree became vital issues to be resolved before any political action could be planned.

The British government tried to organize help for the demobilized Polish troops that had congregated in the Isles at war's end. To this end, the Polish Resettlement Corps was organized with the task of facilitating the soldiers' entry into civilian life. While not as smooth as initially envisioned, the integration nevertheless took place. The Polish veteran community in Great Britain tried to organize itself independently of that of the British. For example, the Polish ex-Combatants Association proved to be very successful as it accumulated a number of homes and other assets, which helped it carry out many of its social, cultural, and political activities. Various army formations had their own, distinct associations – the air force, the navy, and the veterans of the Home Army.

Moreover, the Poles in Great Britain established the Federation of Poles in Great Britain (Zjednoczenie Polskie w Wielkiej Brytanii), which aimed at uniting smaller organizations in order to coordinate their activities. On the educational front, post-war groups joined forces to complement the British education system with a Polish institution of higher learning, the Polish University Abroad in London (Polski Uniwersytet na Obczyźnie, PUNO).

It was quite a different story on the other side of the Atlantic, where the six million-strong Polish diaspora offered a solid base to build upon. Still, even in the United States, new cultural and political institutions were founded by the World War II migrants. Among such institutions were the Polish Institute of Arts and Sciences in America and the Pilsudski Institute of America in New York. Moreover, the situation of the veterans was more complex in comparison with their colleagues in Great Britain. World War II soldiers who had served in the Polish Armed Forces in the West, and Polish Home Army veterans who came to America, had to negotiate their place and position with the older organizations of Polish war veterans from World War I. The latter had already established the Polish Army Veterans Association of America (Stowarzyszenie Weteranów Armii Polskiej w Ameryce, SWAP), while the

---

118 Mazurkiewicz, *Uchodźcy...*, 122.

former created their own organization called the Polish Ex-Servicemen's Association (Stowarzyszenie Polskich Kombatantów, SPK).[119] In many regards, the organization of the post-World War II Polish diaspora was more complicated in the vast American territories that allowed for a wider dispersion of people than was the case in the British Isles.

In France, traditionally there were many Polish cultural and veterans' associations to integrate the community. There was also one particular organization called the Committee of Naturalized Poles in France (Komitet Polaków Naturalizowanych we Francji) whose *spiritus movens* was Jerzy Jankowski. Essentially, its activities consisted of mobilising anti-Communist Poles in France to take advantage of their French citizenship and participate in municipal elections.[120]

As most of the Polish diaspora was Catholic, the role of the parishes cannot be omitted when discussing their social and cultural organization. Many émigré activities – meetings, private and official celebrations, as well as political discussions and protests – were organized by parish organizations and communities. In addition to the grassroots level activities, there were special Polish Catholic missions, for example, in London and Paris. At the top level of the hierarchy of the Polish Catholic Church during the Cold War, the Holy See assigned a special position (delegating the competences of the Primate of Poland, who was unable to operate freely in a foreign environment) of Spiritual Protector of the Polish Émigré community. Archbishop Józef Gawlina, Cardinal Władysław Rubin, and Archbishop Szczepan Wesoły held this post successively. The religious life of the Polish émigré community underwent a significant revival when the cardinals in Rome elected Cardinal Karol Wojtyła as the new Pope John Paul II in 1978.

As previously mentioned, Jews were one of the largest groups that left Poland after the war. While many maintained contact with their fellow Poles in exile, many also chose to create their separate communities. The picture of Polish religiosity would also be incomplete without mentioning other groups of citizens of pre-war Poland, namely Polish Protestants[121] or the Christian Orthodox, the Ukrainians and the Byelorussians, who observed religious traditions in exile as well. The recreation of the complex ethnic and religious relations among the citizens of pre-war and wartime Poland in exile is a fascinating topic, which merits further research.

Another important feature of the Polish political emigration after 1945 was the widespread usage of national culture abroad for the mobilization of the diaspora. It was prompted by the fact that many prominent writers and artists lived abroad; Gustaw Herling-Grudziński, Marian Hemar, Józef Czapski, Melchior Wańkowicz, Witold Gombrowicz, Czesław Miłosz (winner of the Nobel Prize for Literature in

---

119 Kardela, *Stowarzyszenie Polskich Kombatantów w Stanach Zjednoczonych*.
120 Florence Vychytil-Baudoux, "Le Comité électoral des Polonais naturalisés (1953–1976). Une expérience *polonienne* en France," *Relations internationales* no. 141 (2010): 65–81.
121 Jarosław Kłaczkow, *Na emigracji. Losy polskiego wychodźstwa ewangelickiego w XX wieku* (Toruń: Wydawnictwo Adam Marszałek, 2013).

1980). It was no accident that Jerzy Giedroyc called his journal *Kultura*. It was a clear indication of the fact that the main political battle with the ideology and system dominating Poland was to be fought in the field of national culture. Through the promotion of the highbrow and high-quality culture, the people would continue to operate open-minded in spite of regime's controls. *Kultura* was one of the most influential magazine of émigré cultural activity, although it was certainly not alone in this regard.

The many publications, émigré press, and journalistic activities were decisive in terms of maintaining and enriching Polish national culture from abroad. The spread of émigré literature and the demand for it had a pivotal impact on the emergence of the cultural centers in the West, such as the Literary Institute in Maisons-Laffitte. Titles like *Kultura*, *Wiadomości Literackie*, *Merkuriusz Polski*, followed by *Zeszyty Literackie* and *Aneks* set a very high standard for émigrés' literary endeavors. The free press market offered room for émigré newspaper publications as well. Each of the major political parties published its own flagship paper. For example, the PPS published *Światło*, the SN *Horyzonty*, the PSL *Jutro Polski*, and the PRW 'NiD' published *Trybuna*. In addition, there were also titles that had a broader and more universal outreach, such as *Dziennik Polski i Dziennik Żołnierza*, *Orzeł Biały*, *Syrena* and *Rzeczpospolita Polska*, the latter serving as the official press organ of the Polish government-in-exile.

Besides the press, an increasingly important role was played by the radio. Polish journalists, writers, artists and politicians alike worked for Western radio stations that targeted audiences behind the Iron Curtain. These included the Polish section of the BBC,[122] the Polish Section of Radio Free Europe (which was particularly important for the preservation of Polish culture),[123] the Voice of America, Radio France Internationale, but also Radio Madrid.[124] In terms of American-led initiatives, it is safe to say that the support for the émigré activities resulted from the national program of psychological warfare planning.[125] The National Committee for a Free Europe, the

---

122 Krzysztof Pszenicki, *Tu mówi London: Historia Sekcji Polskiej BBC* (Warsaw: Rosner & Wspólnicy, 2009).
123 See also Violetta Wejs-Milewska, *Radio Wolna Europa na emigracyjnych szlakach pisarzy: Gustaw Herling-Grudziński, Tadeusz Nowakowski, Roman Palester, Czesław Straszewicz, Tymon Terlecki* (Kraków: Wydawnictwo Arcana, 2007); Lechosław Gawlikowski, *Pracownicy Radia Wolna Europa. Biografie zwykłe i niezwykłe* (Warsaw: Instytut Studiów Politycznych Polskiej Akademii Nauk; Naczelna Dyrekcja Archiwów Państwowych, 2015); *Rozgłośnia Polska RWE 1952–1975*, ed. Paweł Machcewicz and Rafał Habielski (Wrocław: Zakład Narody im. Ossolińskich, 2018).
124 Magdalena Bogdan, *Radio Madryt 1949–1955: powstanie, organizacja oraz funkcjonowanie polskiej sekcji Radio Nacional de España w pierwszym okresie działalności* (Łomianki/ Warsaw: Wydawnictwo LTW/Uniwersytet Kardynała Stefana Wyszyńskiego, 2011).
125 Mazurkiewicz, *Uchodźcy...*, 33–36.

printing of many of the journals, the creation of the Congress for Cultural Freedom,[126] and the printing and smuggling of books across the Iron Curtain[127] were all elements of the Cold War confrontation, which was at times described as the *Cultural Cold War*.[128] Equally important, yet very difficult to assess directly, was the Polish input into many disciplines of science across the world.

7.3.3 The government-in-exile's international position

The international position of the Polish government-in-exile was peculiarly difficult in relation to the major Western powers, as they had withdrawn their recognition from it in the mid-1940s.[129] Nevertheless, some countries did continue to maintain their diplomatic relations with the Polish government operating in London on the basis of the 1935 Constitution of Poland. In the late 1940s these included Spain, Ireland, Lebanon and Cuba. The Vatican continued to recognize the government in London as the legitimate Polish authority up until the late 1950s.[130]

The withdrawal of diplomatic recognition from the exiled Polish government did not terminate the émigrés' diplomatic activities. Western governments, though not recognizing the Polish government-in-exile, have been inviting its representatives, of course unofficially. Such was the case of former Polish ambassadors: Józef Potocki in Madrid, Kazimierz Papée in Vatican, Kajetan Morawski in Paris, and Jan Wszelaki (unlike the others, not a former ambassador) in Washington, and the diplomats Juliusz Łukasiewicz and Józef Lipski. Apart from the informal representatives of the government, individual exiles such as Count Edward Raczyński and Kajetan Morawski provided a working connection with foreign policy makers at the Foreign Office and the Quai d'Orsay. Moreover, Poles actively participated in foreign and international organizations and institutions. Examples of such participation include

---

126 Mirosław A. Supruniuk, *Przyjaciele wolności. Kongres Wolności Kultury i Polacy* (Warsaw: DiG, 2008); Pierre Gremion, *Intelligence de l'antiCommunisme: le Congrès pour la liberté de la culture à Paris (1950–1975)* (Paris: Fayard, 1995).
127 Alfred A. Reisch, *Hot Books in the Cold War: The CIA-Funded Secret Western Book Distribution Program Behind the Iron Curtain* (Budapest/New York: Central European University Press, 2013).
128 Frances Stonor Saunders, *The Cultural Cold War: CIA and the World of Arts and Letters* (New York/London: The New Press, 2001).
129 The best interpretation of the Polish government-in-exile's international legal status was given by Robert Zapart, "Służby informacyjne władz II RP na uchodźstwie po zakończeniu II wojny światowej. Szkic historyczno-prawny," in *Służby wywiadowcze jako narzędzi realizacji polityki państwa w XX wieku. Wybrane zagadnienia*, ed. Leszek Pawlikowicz and Robert Zapart (Rzeszów: Wydawnictwo Uniwersytetu Rzeszowskiego, 2014), 75–102.; See also Górecki, *Polskie naczelne władze państwowe...*; Krzysztof Tarka, *Emigracyjna dyplomacja* (Warsaw: Rytm, 2003).
130 See also Zapart, "Służby informacyjne...," 77; Tarka, *Emigracyjna dyplomacja...*, 25–26.

Roman Michałowski's role in the preparatory phase of the NCFE[131], Jan Kułakowski's position as secretary-general of the World Confederation of Labor, Prof. Jerzy Łukaszewski's service as rector of the Collège d'Europe in Bruges (1972–1990), and Jerzy Rencki's role in various European institutions. Rencki was the director of the General Directorate for Regional Development Policy (1977–1988) and later also the director of the Directorate-General XVI – Formulation and Implementation of Regional Policy. Many of them worked as informal or formal advisers for governmental, parliamentary, or other organizations within their host countries, although it is hard to assess the role they played for maintaining international interest in Poland. The most impressive career was that of Zbigniew Brzeziński (son of a Polish diplomat), who achieved a strong and independent position within the decision-making process of US foreign and security policy, despite being a US citizen of Polish origins.

Moreover, as the government was losing international recognition, the new Polish bodies in exile – the Political Council, the Polish National Democratic Committee and the Provisional Council of National Unity – were able to count on various forms of international support. A significant source of backing emerged in the United States in 1949, in the form of the National Committee for a Free Europe (NCFE), better known as the Free Europe Committee. It sponsored individual political leaders as well as parties and organizations, including party internationals in which Poles actively participated.[132]

The émigrés used their networks to organize international lobbying carried out in many countries of the free world. These can be divided into three major categories: activities carried out in the countries of residence (UK, USA, France etc.), undertakings targeting international forums like the United Nations or the Council of Europe, and actions undertaken in close cooperation with other East-Central European diasporas.

Some of the projects carried out in cooperation with other East-Central Europeans were of bilateral character, such as the Polish-Czechoslovak Study Committee in the 1950s, which resulted in the joint publication *The Central European Federalist*. Other forms of joint political action included supranational party structures such as the International Peasant Union, the Christian Democratic Union of Central Europe, the Socialist Union of Central Eastern Europe, and the Liberal-Democratic Union of Central Eastern Europe, in which Poles played prominent roles.[133] The

---

131 Sławomir Łukasiewicz, *Third Europe: Polish Federalist Thought in the United States – 1940s–1970s* (Budapest: Helena History Press, 2016).
132 Mazurkiewicz, *Uchodźcy...*, 358–406.
133 Mazurkiewicz, *Uchodźcy...*; Łukasiewicz, *Third Europe...*; Józef Łaptos, *Europa marzycieli: wizje i projekty integracyjne środkowoeuropejskiej emigracji politycznej 1940–1956* (Kraków: Wydawnictwo Naukowe Uniwersytetu Pedagogicznego, 2013), 84 ff. Even the émigrés analyzed this phenomenon: Zygmunt Nagórski Jr., "Liberation Movements in Exile," *Journal of Central European Affairs* 10, no. 2 (July 1950): 128–144; Feliks Gross, "Political Emigration from Iron Curtain Countries," *The Annals of the American Academy of Political and Social Science* 271 (September 1950): 175–184.

best-known regional lobby of political exiles, which brought together prominent prewar and wartime politicians from East Central Europe, was the Assembly of Captive European Nations (ACEN). This organization was established in 1954 in New York by representatives of nine countries (Albania, Bulgaria, Czechoslovakia, Estonia, Hungary, Latvia, Lithuania, Poland and Romania) under the aegis of the US-founded NCFE. Its charter listed the organization's key aims as lobbying for the withdrawal of Soviet troops and free elections in East-Central Europe.[134] Among the prominent Polish exiles involved in the work of the ACEN – both in their American offices and in the regional bureaus – the following politicians of diverse political backgrounds should be listed: Stefan Korboński, Stanisław Mikołajczyk, Otto Pehr, Feliks Gadomski, Karol Popiel, Bolesław Biega, Adam Niebieszczański, Stanisław Olszewski, Stanisław Bańczyk.[135] This transnational forum for many journalists resembled an alternative United Nations, with representatives of those whose authentic voice had been silenced. It continued its operations until 1989. After 1972, it functioned without the support of the then-terminated Free Europe Committee.[136]

7.3.4 Political thought in exile

The development of political ideas complemented and often replaced the political actions that were severely limited in exile. Émigré political thought was the key weapon, the use of which led not only to political schisms but also to the advancement of ideas, analyzes and plans that were presented not only within the diaspora but also to the leaders of the free world. Apart from the discussions regarding the legitimacy of political activities in exile (see above), émigré political thought was formulated on the basis of the diaspora's relation to the home country, the strategic role to be played by exiled politicians, Poland's geopolitical location, and the role it played in international relations within certain alternative alliances to Soviet domination. Naturally, the US government – the main adversary of the USSR – was seen as

---

134 Anna Mazurkiewicz, "Assembly of Captive European Nations: 'The Voice of the Silenced Peoples,'" in *Anti–Communist Minorities: The Political Activism of Ethnic Refugees in the United States*, ed., Ieva Zaķe (New York: Palgrave Macmillan, 2009), 167–185.
135 Anna Mazurkiewicz, "The Schism within the Polish Delegation to the Assembly of Captive European Nations 1954–1972," in *The Inauguration of "Organized Political Warfare" – The Cold War Organizations Sponsored by the National Committee for a Free Europe / Free Europe Committee*, ed. Katalin KádárLynn (Saint Helena: Helena History Press, 2013), 323–361; Piotr Stanek, *Stefan Korboński (1901–1989): działalność polityczna i społeczna* (Warsaw: Instytut Pamięci Narodowej. Komisja Ścigania Zbrodni przeciwko Narodowi Polskiemu, 2014); Feliks Gadomski, *Zgromadzenie Europejskich Narodów Ujarzmionych: krótki zarys* (New York: *Nowy Dziennik* Bicentennial Publishing Corporation, 1995).
136 Anna Mazurkiewicz, "The Little U. N. at 769 First Avenue, New York (1956–1963)," in *East Central Europe in Exile. Transatlantic Identities*, ed. Anna Mazurkiewicz (Newcastle upon Tyne: Cambridge Scholars Publishing, 2013), 227–245.

a key ally. When asked for assistance, most Polish exiles did not refuse cooperation with the Americans. On many levels, the interests of the Americans and Polish exiles were the same. At times, however, as was the case with the Oder-Neisse border, they proved to be divergent in reference to the relations with West Germany and the Soviet Union. The émigrés strongly defended the border arrangement, even though, on the one hand, this collided with Germany's interest (supported at that time by the Americans), and on the other hand, it made the Soviet Union the only guarantee of this frontier.

The Polish borders of 1945 were also the subject of yet another stream of political thought in exile focused on Poland's neighborhood. Polish intellectuals centerd around *Kultura* in Paris and widely discussed Poland's Communist-imposed renunciation of Wilno (then in the Lithuanian Soviet Socialist Republic) and Lwów (in the Ukrainian Soviet Socialist Republic). For many Polish émigrés, whose origins lay in the Eastern territories of pre-war Poland, any debate on this issue was too controversial a topic to begin with. The *Kultura* milieu – including Włodzimierz Bączkowski, Józef Łobodowski and Juliusz Mieroszewski – managed to open a discussion which was rooted in the past but offered solutions for the future, with the hope of fostering the emergence of a friendly international environment for a Poland which had been pushed into a new geopolitical context. This also included issues pertaining to reconciliation.[137]

The latter notion obviously also applied to the debates on Polish-German relations. These were not only centered on border issues, but also on dealing with wartime trauma. Some Polish groups in exile, such as the Christian Democrats (Stanisław Gebhardt), federalists (Jerzy Jankowski), and publicists (Aleksander Bregman), worked towards reconciliation and future cooperation, even though for many members of wartime diaspora these efforts were premature. *Kultura* took on an active role in these discussions, thus preparing its audience for groundbreaking events: the letter of the Polish Bishops to their German peers and German reunification.

Understandably, one of the key areas in Polish political thought in exile was anti-Communism. It must be remembered that in 1939 Poland fell victim to two aggressors – the National Socialists and the Communists – only one of which had been defeated during the war. The anti-Communism of Polish exiles operated on three levels – political thought, their relationship to the homeland and the international operation of the émigré organizations. Furthermore, two main streams of anti-Communism must be distinguished here.

The first, basic stream meant that all matters related to the imposition of the Communist regime in Poland, the USSR and the countries of the Eastern Bloc, as

---

137 See, for example, *Wizja Polski na łamach Kultury 1947–1976*, vols. 1–2, ed. Grażyna Pomian (Lublin: UMCS, 1999); Jerzy Giedroyc, *Emigracja ukraińska. Listy 1950–1982*, ed. Bogumiła Berdychowska (Warsaw: Spółdzielnia Wydawnicza Czytelnik, 2004).

well as the ideology itself, were to be confronted and eradicated. This was evident during public anti-Communist rallies, and the participation in organized campaigns targeting Communist ideals and practices. Some Poles took part in organizations sponsored by the CIA, which operated in many countries around the world, using the exiles to promote anti-Communism. For example, Stanisław Grocholski and Jerzy Jankowski participated in a movement called *Paix et Liberté* whereby they were provided with resources to publish the journal under the same title in order to mobilize the Polish diaspora in France to counteract Warsaw's propaganda.[138] However, the CIA was not the only agency sponsoring the exiles' political activities in the West.[139]

The second form of Polish anti-Communism in exile was academic in nature. Polish thinkers and scholars in exile criticized Marxism and Communism on philosophical and ideological grounds. Drawing upon Polish academic achievements in Sovietology during the interwar period, they pointed out Communism's weaknesses and its incompatibility with the values of Western culture. The key critics of Marxism and Communism among the Polish émigrés were Father Józef Innocenty Maria Bocheński, Zbigniew Jordan, and Wiktor Sukiennicki. In 1968, the exiled Polish intellectuals were joined by a renowned expert in the field – Leszek Kołakowski. Marian Kamil Dziewanowski, a scholar of Polish Marxism and the Communism, should also be mentioned in this group.

An equally important part of Polish political thought in exile was focused on European integration. While practically unknown and unrecognized by the Polish People's Republic, the input of Polish émigré thinkers was significant. Historians (Oskar Halecki, Piotr Wandycz, Wiktor Sukiennicki)[140] and journalists (Aleksander Bregman, Zdzisław Najder) devoted immense attention to European integration. This in turn prompted many exiles to join various initiatives aiming at unification. In 1949 the Polish community abroad established the Polish Federalists' Association (Związek Polskich Federalistów), affiliated with the Union Européenne des Fédéralistes. Prominent émigrés formed the Polish Section of the European Movement inspired by Józef Rettinger. They were joined by prominent politicians like Edward Raczyński and Jan Pomian (Bławdziewicz). The Polish Section of Radio Free Europe also broadcast a

---

138 Bernard Ludwig, "Paix et Liberté: A Transnational Anti-Communist Network," in *Transnational anti-Communism and the Cold War: agents, activities, and networks*, eds. Luc van Dongen, Stéphanie Roulin, and Giles Scott-Smith (Basingstoke: Palgrave Macmillan, 2014), 81–95. For the Polish section, see Sławomir Łukasiewicz, *Partia w warunkach emigracji. Dylematy Polskiego Ruchu Wolnościowego "Niepodległość i Demokracja"* (Lublin: Instytut Pamięci Narodowej; Warsaw: Instytut Studiów Politycznych Polskiej Akademii Nauk, 2014), 538–542.
139 Stephen Dorril, *MI6. Inside the covert world of her Majesty's secret intelligence service* (New York: Simon & Schuster, 2002).
140 Łukasiewicz, *Third Europe…*; also *Towards a United Europe: An Anthology of twentieth-century Polish thought on Europe*, ed. Sławomir Łukasiewicz, transl. Robert Looby (Warsaw: Ministry of Foreign Affairs of the Republic of Poland, 2011).

program on European integration.¹⁴¹ Józef Retinger, while not strictly a political thinker, he played a fundamental role in the early stages of European integration.¹⁴²

Taking all this into consideration, while absent from the debates in the People's Republic (at least before the development of a regular opposition in the 1970s), Polish political thought in exile was of the utmost importance for the free Poles and confirmed the role which the émigrés had to play.

7.3.5 The People's Republic and the Polish diaspora

The political system of the Polish People's Republic (as Poland was officially called after 1952) did not envision independent political parties. The state authorities stripped many Polish émigrés of their citizenship in absentia. This affected such distinguished persons as General Władysław Anders, President August Zaleski, and later Stanisław Mikołajczyk.¹⁴³ The return of leading political figures from exile was highly unlikely due to the oppressive nature of the system and the inability of the Communist regime to accommodate such powerful symbols of the country's true sovereignty. Émigrés were thus considered grave enemies of the regime (which indeed they were). They were also commonly accused of cooperating with foreign intelligence services, which made them appear even more dangerous. On the other hand, the exiled Poles routinely emphasized that the Warsaw regime was temporary and that its rule would be immediately terminated once free and unfettered elections were held.

To begin with, the Soviet-installed regime first had to deal with the domestic legal opposition, such as the peasant and labor parties, by forcing them into exile. Throughout the first post-war decade, the militant underground (and the imagined enemies of the state) was tracked by the Communist security forces within the country. Some dissenters were accused of maintaining contacts with leaders abroad. This charge was then extended to working for foreign intelligence services. Andrzej Friszke neatly summarized the importance of émigrés: "From the late 1940s to the birth of the democratic opposition in the country, the People's Republic of Poland considered émigrés to be the only center of the organized anti-Communist center. Consequently, attempts were made to break it or even weaken it."¹⁴⁴ The state's se-

---

141 Andrzej Borzym and Jeremi Sadowski, *Polscy ojcowie Europy* (Warsaw: Wydawnictwo Trio, 2007).
142 Bogdan Podgórski, *Józef Retinger: prywatny polityk* (Kraków: Universitas, 2013); Mieczysław B. B. Biskupski, "Spy, Patriot, or Internationalist? The Early Career of Józef Retinger, the Polish Patriarch of the European Union," *Polish Review* 43, no. 1 (1998): 23–67.
143 On the basis of a law enacted by the Provisional Government represented by Edward Osóbka-Morawski in September 1946, and later on. See also Maciej Szczurowski, "Sprawa obywatelstwa polskiego generałów i oficerów, którzy wstąpili do Polskiego Korpusu Przysposobienia i Rozmieszczenia w świetle dokumentów Urzędu Rady Ministrów w Warszawie," *Teki Historyczne* 23 (2004); Władysław Anders, *Bez ostatniego rozdziału* (Newtown: Montgomeryshire Printing Co., 1949).
144 Friszke, *Życie polityczne emigracji*.

curity service, intelligence, and counter-intelligence (civilian and military) were used to discredit the activities of the political exiles in the eyes of their countrymen and disrupt the ties between them.[145] There were also attempts to infiltrate the émigré organizations and compromise their information sources.

Among the most spectacular Cold War spy games involving Polish émigrés, two cases are worthy of mention. The first one was called the Berg affair.[146] The Communists infiltrated and took over the courier network located in Berg near Munich used by the leaders of the émigré Political Council (Rada Polityczna) to contact the underground in Poland. In the second operation, code-named *Cezary*, Warsaw's counterintelligence infiltrated the headquarters of the political underground movement, specifically the so-called 5th Command of the Freedom and Independence organization (Wolność i Niezawisłość, WiN). The Communist Ministry of Public Security was able to fool the émigrés and western intelligence agencies into believing that a firm connection to the Polish underground had been established. They thereby embezzled considerable sums of money sent from the West. This was such a success that the case was later used by the Communist regime for the training of future agents.[147]

The regime also suffered some significant loses. The most irksome to the Communists were the defections of high-ranking regime officials.[148] The best-known defection, which had a tremendous impact both in Poland and abroad, took place in December 1953 when Józef Światło, the deputy director of the 10th Department with-

---

145 Sławomir Łukasiewicz, "Wywiad cywilny PRL wobec polskiej emigracji na Zachodzie – przegląd struktur i kierunków działania do początku lat sześćdziesiątych," in *Tajny oręż czy ofiary zimnej wojny? Emigracje polityczne z Europy Środkowej i Wschodniej*, ed. Sławomir Łukasiewicz (Lublin/Warsaw: Instytut Pamięci Narodowej, 2010), 154–161. An updated overview of the activities of the Communist intelligence against Polish émigrés can be found in Witold Bagieński, *Wywiad cywilny Polski Ludowej w latach 1945–1961*, vol. 2 (Warsaw: Instytut Pamięci Narodowej, 2017), 11 ff.

146 Anna Siwik, "Sprawa Bergu. Współpraca emigracyjnej Rady Politycznej z zachodnim wywiadem," *Studia Historyczne* 2 (2001): 267–288; Rafał Wnuk, 'Dwie prowokacje – Piąta Komenda Zrzeszenia "WiN" i Berg,' *Zeszyty Historyczne* no. 141 (2002): 71–112.

147 Jan Łabędzki and Marian Strużyński, *Z doświadczeń pracownika operacyjnego SB. Sprawa kryptonim "Cezary"* (Warsaw: Departament Szkolenia i Doskonalenia Zawodowego MSW, 1972).

148 One of the first high-ranking defectors was Gen. Izydor Modelski in 1948. From 1946, he worked in the US as a military attaché and was instructed by his supervisors (including the chief of military intelligence Wacław Komar) on how to organize a network of military intelligence residences with the aim of infiltrating the émigré and *Polonia* communities. After his defection, he revealed all the details of his mission, handing over documents and naming other Communists involved in the spy network. See also *Documentary testimony of Gen. Izyador* [sic] *Modelski, former military attaché of the Polish Embassy, Washington D.C. Hearings before the Committee on un-American activities*. House of Representatives. Eighty-First Congress. First Session. March 31 and April 1, 1949 (Washington: Government Printing Office, 1949). There were more defections over the next ten years, most notably those of Michał Goleniewski and Paweł Monat. See also Leszek Pawlikowicz, *Tajny front zimnej wojny. Uciekinierzy z polskich służb specjalnych* (Warsaw: Rytm, 2004); Christopher Andrew, Vasili Mitrokhin, *The Sword and the Shield: The Mitrokhin Archive and the Secret History of the KGB* (New York: Basic Books, 1999).

in the Ministry of Public Security, fled to the West.¹⁴⁹ For the Polish state security, the work of destroying opposition forces abroad was relatively easier in Europe than in the US for logistical and financial reasons. However, it was carried out on a global scale.

The list of anti-émigré activities should also include the so-called repatriation campaigns, which attempted to lure Poles into returning to their Communist homeland. In effect in 1955, some prominent leaders such as Stanisław Mackiewicz and Melchior Wańkowicz did return from exile.¹⁵⁰ The campaign also had another angle – it provided for the expansion of the informant networks within the émigré centers. Among the most valuable human assets obtained by the Polish Communist intelligence were the politician and journalist Klaudiusz Hrabyk, the former prime minister of the government-in-exile; Hugon Hanke, a high-ranking member of the Peasants' Party in exile; Adam Bitoński, one of the most dangerous agents who used the pseudonyms 'Beatrice' and 'Carmen'; Witold Olszewski, the editor of the émigré journal *Horyzonty*; and Bolesław Świderski, an émigré publisher and book seller. Many of them eventually returned to People's Poland.

The second half of the 1950s and the following decade were a period of wide-ranging and systematic monitoring of the Polish diaspora. In accordance with the instructions issued by successive interior ministers, émigré centers were surveilled by departments I and II of the interior ministry. In 1958, the minister Mieczysław Moczar (previously the deputy minister for intelligence and counterintelligence) issued a special instruction in which émigré centers of interest to him were listed with all the émigré power centers (such as 'the London government') and the political parties in exile. Additionally, the ministry was also interested in reports concerning the Free Europe Committee, Radio Free Europe (Munich),¹⁵¹ General Anders and his Second Corps, and social and cultural associations including historical research centers in London like the Polish Institute and Sikorski Museum and the Józef Piłsudski Institute in London. This operation resulted in the lengthy report on the Polish political diaspora, which was printed ('for internal use only') in 1962.¹⁵²

The results of the Polish state's intelligence operations were a variety of operations targeting the above-listed centers, each of them under a separate code name. Individual exiles were also subject to Communist operations. They were spied on and agents were placed within their milieus in order to report and disrupt their activities. The so-called 'illegal agents' were a separate category. They operated under deep cover within the exile community, usually under so-called "legalization" names

---

149 Andrzej Paczkowski, *Trzy twarze Józefa Światły. Przyczynek do historii komunizmu w Polsce* (Warsaw: Prószyński i S-ka, 2009); See also Mazurkiewicz, *Uchodźcy...*, 457–460.
150 See also Tarka, *Mackiewicz i inni*.
151 Paweł Machcewicz, *Monachijska menażeria. Walka z Radiem Wolna Europa 1950–1989* (Warsaw: Instytut Pamięci Narodowej; Instytut Studiów Politycznych PAN, 2007).
152 Cenckiewicz Sławomir (ed.), *Polska emigracja polityczna. Informator (reprint of 1962 edition)*, (Warsaw: Adiutor and Instytut Pamięci Narodowej, 2004).

(i.e. names adopted especially for intelligence operations).¹⁵³ The post-war diaspora, the emigration streams of 1968 and the 'Solidarity wave' were monitored by Warsaw's security forces. When a Polish émigré travelled to Poland (like Czesław Miłosz's visit in June 1981), the whole procedure was closely monitored and 'protected' by the domestic security forces, to assure maximum exploitation for intelligence purposes.

The archives of the former security apparatus (today in the archives of the Institute of National Remembrance, IPN) contain numerous examples of heroic efforts to prevent Communist agents from penetrating the diaspora, and of individuals avoiding any contacts and escaping the traps set up by Warsaw's agents. There are also files that document unintended cooperation between the émigrés and the regime. Some exiles (other than the willing agents mentioned before) were unaware that they were providing information and access that resulted in substantial damage. Due to the recent release of formerly classified archival collections by the IPN, this field is currently of great interest to Polish scholars.¹⁵⁴

The systematic political and propaganda campaign against the émigré community was carried out throughout the entire existence of the Polish People's Republic with the aim of effectively delegitimising the political émigrés. As early as the 1960s, though, its security apparatus assumed that the role of the organized political diaspora was diminishing. The Communists believed that this was due to the passing of the old generation of leaders, the loss of financial support from the western governments, as well as successful efforts to discredit some organizations and people carried out by Communist agents. This is why by the end of the 1960s Department I of the interior ministry decided to focus its attention on the so-called ideological subversion and its main centers, namely Radio Free Europe (Munich) and *Kultura* (Paris). Within the next decade it became obvious that the major source of worry for Polish Communists would be domestic dissent and the birth of a democratic opposition by the end of the 1970s. Émigré centers were mainly of interest to the extent they maintained contact with the dissenters in Poland (finances, resources, exchange of information).

7.3.6 Interactions with the home country

In the 1940s and early 1950s the Polish political diaspora attempted to maintain their ties to the Polish underground. These contacts were of various nature; personal and/

---

153 See also Władysław Bułhak and Patryk Pleskot, *Szpiedzy PRL-u* (Kraków: Znak Horyzont, 2014).
154 See also *Aparat bezpieczeństwa wobec emigracji politycznej i Polonii*, ed. Ryszard Terlecki (Warsaw: Instytut Pamięci Narodowej 2005); Machcewicz, *"Monachijska menażeria"*; Cenckiewicz, *Oczami bezpieki*; Tarka, *Mackiewicz i inni*; Krzysztof Tarka, *Emigranci na celowniku. Władze Polski Ludowej wobec wychodźstwa* (Łomianki: LTW, 2012); Tarka, *Jest tylko jedna Polska*; *Tajny oręż czy ofiary zimnej wojny? Emigracje z Europy Środkowo-Wschodniej*, ed. Sławomir Łukasiewicz (Lublin/Warsaw: Instytut Pamięci Narodowej, 2010).

or political and included military and intelligence operations that were supported by western powers. The latter ceased with the realization that the Communist security apparatus had not only penetrated the transnational networks but also ruthlessly destroyed the last vestiges of dissent within the country. The former contacts were somewhat enlivened with the thaw of 1956. Some exchanges became possible again as the passport policies were relaxed. At the same time, the 'thaw' prompted a heated debate over whether the economic and social changes occurring in Poland should be supported from abroad. Upon Władysław Gomułka's return to power in October 1956, the Polish political diaspora split into two groups: the supporters of the liberalising trends (who trusted Gomułka), and the sworn enemies backing any leader whom they saw as a Communist puppet steered from Moscow. Despite the relatively swift realization that Gomułka was not a true reformer, the division within the Polish diaspora into the so-called 'pro-country' and 'steadfast' groups prevailed. As it appears today, the former group maintained ties with Warsaw, with some of its members actually being financed by the Polish regime.[155]

The schism within the Polish diaspora, despite efforts at re-unification in 1954 and 1972, did not foster coherent and well-planned political operations. These were replaced by dispersed individual or group initiatives, which had various outcomes. Against this background, the achievements of *Kultura* in Paris and the broadcasts of Radio Free Europe must be emphasized. The unceasing flow of books, émigré journals and radio broadcasts to Poland, all supported to various extents by the Free Europe Committee, had a pivotal impact on the prevalence of hope for a better future and the strengthening of domestic dissent in Poland.[156] It may be said that their impact was greater than that of the perseverance of the legal Polish authorities in exile, who were driven by conflicts over legitimacy (see above). As the post-war political diaspora was losing its energy and potential by the 1970s, the Polish state's security services focused their attention on Maisons-Laffitte and Munich, as well as the 1968 wave of migrants from Poland, whom they also treated as great political danger. At the same time, the citizens of Poland dreamt of leaving the country and the Western powers were using the potential of the émigrés to realize their psychological warfare goals of weakening the Communist grip. Naturally, the Communists called it 'ideological sabotage' serving 'western imperialism'.

In sum, the Polish political diaspora in the 'free world' was divided over the issue of how to respond to the changes occurring in Communist Poland. The most difficult question they were faced with was how the apparent changes were permanent and did they herald an evolutionary liberalization of the regime's grip. Those émigrés who believed in permanence of changes considered returning to Poland in the hope they could contribute to the rebuilding of the country, albeit within a So-

---

[155] See also especially the works cited by Krzysztof Tarka and Paweł Ziętara.
[156] Reisch, *Hot Books...*; *Cold War Broadcasting: Impact on the Soviet Union and Eastern Europe*, ed. A. Ross Johnson and Eugene Porta (Budapest/New York: CEU Press, 2010); Mazurkiewicz, *Uchodźcy...*, 472–479.

cialist framework. Other exiled Poles either did not give in to the lure, or had no choice in the matter as they had been deprived of their citizenship. Many Polish émigrés adopted the citizenship of the country of their residence, thus accepting the notion that their stay abroad could be permanent. Regardless of their individual decisions, the imposition of martial law in Poland on 13 December 1981 mobilized and solidified the Polish diaspora around the world, whose unanimous voice on behalf of the terrorized Poles was unprecedentedly loud and persuasive.[157]

The emergence and pivotal impact of Solidarity in the early 1980s, followed by the profound political transition of 1989, prompted questions about the feasibility and need for the continued maintenance of the Polish political diaspora in the West. Some émigrés, based on the lessons of 1956, did not initially believe that the Round Table process could bring about any lasting change. Even Jerzy Giedroyc was skeptical at first. With the first fully free and unfettered (presidential) elections in Poland in 1990, political emigration symbolically lost its rationale. Government-in-exile did respond to the election of Lech Wałęsa by symbolically marking the end of its mission while President-in-exile Ryszard Kaczorowski returned Poland's presidential insignia to Warsaw in December 1990. The last meeting of the Polish National Council took place a year later. Its operations concluded with the establishment of the Liquidation Commission, whose task it was to administer the funds of the government-in-exile, for example, by directing them to historical research. Several political parties continued to exist for several more years; the PRW 'NiD' ceased its activities in 1994. However, these activities had no immediate impact on political life in Poland.

The question of the role émigré Polish politics played in Poland remains yet to be answered. Some exiled Poles did return to Poland and played important roles in diplomacy, such as Jan Kułakowski, the first ambassador of Poland to the European Union, or Jerzy Łukaszewski, who became Polish ambassador to France. However, it is yet to be assessed whether the intellectual and networking potential was utilized during the period of the Polish transformation, and if so, to what extent. Despite numerous attempts to (re)introduce the Cold War Polish migration to mainstream historical education and the contemporary public debate, as the Second Great Migration, the Polish memory of the émigrés remains frail.[158]

---

[157] See also album *Wasza solidarność – nasza wolność. Reakcje emigracji polskiej i świata na wprowadzenie stanu wojennego*, eds. Agnieszka Jaczyńska, Sławomir Łukasiewicz, and Patryk Pleskot (Lublin/ Gdańsk: Instytut Pamięci Narodowej/Europejskie Centrum Solidarności, 2017).
[158] Sławomir Łukasiewicz, "Polska emigracja polityczna w XX wieku i pamięć historyczna," *Przegląd Zachodni* no. 1 (2007): 63–76.

7.4 Migration since 1989

In 1989 only some of the Poles living abroad decided it was safe and rational for them to return. This was not the first time in the history of Poland that émigrés had returned to the country. This return migration was not on a mass scale, but had its own peculiar character. Among the returnees there were intellectuals, scholars, business investors, small entrepreneurs, young graduates of foreign universities – all in all between about 1,500 to 4,000 people annually. Within a decade (1990 – 2000), about 75,500 people had come to Poland. 14 percent of them were returnees from the United States, 50 percent from European countries (more than half from Germany). Not all of them moved to Poland indefinitely, although they did bring with them the greatly needed economic, cultural, and social assets. In this way they did contributed to the Polish transformation.[159] Within that same time, however, 240,000 Poles emigrated.

Emigration from a free and independent Poland must be understood in the context of the very uncertain economic transformation.[160] There was no precedent to reversing a Communist state-controlled economy back to the free market after almost fifty years of economic restrictions. In the 1990s, migration was perceived as a way of coping with the crisis. There were multiple push factors (e.g. unemployment, income diversification), combined with relaxed laws on foreign travel and the emergence of companies seeking short-term contract laborers. Legal work opportunities were particularly attractive in Germany, where annually 200 – 300,000 Poles found temporary employment. Between 1989 and 2004, when Poland joined the European Union, legal migration to the European Community was possible thanks to the bilateral agreements Poland had made with Germany, France, Luxembourg and Belgium. Within their contractual terms, 400,000 Poles found legal employment abroad. An additional 100 to 150,000 were illegally employed in Western Europe. All in all, about half a million Poles had been working there before Poland's accession to the European Union in 2004.

What happened after this date should come as no surprise. The liberalization of travel and the attractive labor opportunities brought yet another great exodus. In 2004 alone, one million people left Poland temporarily. Since 2006, this number has fluctuated at around 2 million. Of the 2 million, almost 78 percent, (over 1.5 million people in 2011) were long-term migrants – they stayed abroad longer than a

---

[159] *Migracje powrotne Polaków. Powroty sukcesu czy rozczarowania?*, ed. Krystyna Iglicka (Warsaw: Instytut Spraw Publicznych, 2002); See also Krystyna Iglicka, "Mechanisms of migration from Poland before and during the transition period," *Journal of Ethnic and Migration Studies* 26, no. 1 (2000): 61 – 73.
[160] Lena Kolarska-Bobińska ed. *Emigrować i wracać. Migracje zarobkowe Polaków a polityka państwa* (Warsaw: Instytut Spraw Publicznych, 2007).

year.[161] This time, in contrast to the Polish history of migration, it was not coerced, not political and not one-way – and hence not definitive. With the free market and the free flow of goods and capital came freedom of human movement within Europe, such as had been unheard of under Communism.

7.5 Archives and Literature

One of the undisputed achievements of the post-World War II Polish diaspora was the establishment of lasting social, cultural and academic institutions that collected archival sources and artefacts of essential value to Polish twentieth century history, including the history of the Polish diaspora since 1939. Many of these are private and some are specialized such as the archives of former combatants' associations, the Polish Catholic Missions (e. g. in London, Paris, Munich and Rome) or Polish parishes around the world.

The most important Polish institutions abroad that hold collections essential for research on Cold War migration include:
– in Great Britain (London): Polish Institute and Sikorski Museum, Polish Library, Polish Underground Movement Study Trust (Studium Polski Podziemnej), Józef Piłsudski Institute;
– in France: La Société Historique et Littéraire Polonaise et Bibliothèque Polonaise à Paris [Polish Historical and Literary Association, Polish Library in Paris], Instytut Literacki [Literary Institute] (Maisons-Laffitte);
– in the United States (New York): Józef Piłsudski Institute of America, Polish Institute of Arts and Sciences of America.

Similar institutions with fonds on the post-1939 Polish diaspora were established in Italy, Germany, Sweden, Canada, and Australia. Among the archives that hold collections related to the activities of Polish exiles, the Hoover Institution Archives in California stands out for its many collections of individual papers (as well as the corporate files of the Free Europe Committee). Otherwise, the legacy of individual exiles and the organizations they formed remain scattered. However, since the 1990s, tireless efforts are being made to locate as many of the émigré collections as possible and return them to Poland (even as copies). Many of them are currently located in Warsaw (Central Archive of Modern Records, National Library), Wrocław (Ossoliński National Institute), Lublin (Catholic University Library), Kraków (the library of Jagiellonian University), Toruń (Emigration Archive at the Copernicus University), and Opole (University Library).

---

[161] Główny Urząd Statystyczny, "Informacja o rozmiarach i kierunkach emigracji z Polski w latach 2004–2012," (Warsaw: GUS, 2013), http://stat.gov.pl/cps/rde/xbcr/gus/L_Szacunek_emigracji_z_Polski_lata_2004-2012_XI_2012.pdf (accessed 13 April 2018).

Scholars of migration should also consult the collections available from the state authorities in the countries of settlement, such as the National Archives and Record Administration in Washington and the British National Archives in Kew, as well as migration research centers like the Immigration History Research Center (Minneapolis). In addition, we should remember the archival collections of the People's Republic of Poland, specifically the security services (today in the possession of the Institute of National Remembrance), as well as the collections of the Ministry of Foreign Affairs in Warsaw and the Association for Liaison with Poles Abroad "Polonia" (Towarzystwo Łączności z Polonią Zagraniczną "Polonia") in Pułtusk.

Researchers will appreciate the edited collections of documents available both in print and online.[162] Among the latter, the following offer impressive collections for free: the Polish State Archives digital project,[163] *Kultura*,[164] and the Józef Piłsudski Institute of America.[165]

Archival material on the post-World War II diaspora is dispersed, with no central register and – most troublingly – with many individual and organizational collections still in private hands. Some have already been lost forever often due to carelessness or a lack of appreciation by the immediate family members. Others, preserved in the forms of memoirs and diaries, have sometimes been published both in Poland and abroad.

The following look at recent publications in the field of the Polish Cold-War diaspora must be considered a cursory survey. Within the past two decades, available literature on Polish migration has increased significantly. It is an ongoing process. However, what is already available may be considered solid background, or a cornerstone for future generations of researchers. In the 1990s two syntheses of Polish Cold War exile history were published, notably one in London, the other in Warsaw. The eight-volume collective work "*Materiały do dziejów polskiego uchodźstwa niepodległościowego*" published in London contains texts written by both émigrés and his-

---

[162] A perfect example is the correspondence between Jerzy Giedroyc and outstanding émigré intellectuals like Konstanty Jeleński, Jan Nowak-Jeziorański, Juliusz Mieroszewski, Czesław Miłosz, Zbigniew Siemaszko and many others. There are separate series on the peasants' movements: *Stanisław Mikołajczyk w dokumentach aparatu bezpieczeństwa*, vol 1–3, eds. Janusz Gmitruk et al. (Warsaw/Łódź: Instytut Pamięci Narodowej, 2010); *Polski ruch ludowy na emigracji. Dokumenty i materiały*, part 1: *1944–1954*, part 2: *1954–1968*, part 3: *1968–1991*, ed., Romuald Turkowski (Kielce: [s. n.], 2005–2007). As part of the special documentary program financed by the Polish Ministry of Science, Rafał Habielski is currently working on as selection of documents from the Polish Section of RFE. Within the same program, Rafał Stobiecki and Sławomir Nowinowski are working on a selection of texts and correspondence by historians from the *Kultura* milieu. They are also the editors of a recently published selection of correspondence between Władysław Pobóg-Malinowski and Wacław Jędrzejewicz, prominent émigré historians: *Listy 1945–1962* (Warsaw: Instytut Pamięci Narodowej, 2016).
[163] szukajwarchiwach.pl (accessed 4 August 2018).
[164] kulturaparyska.com (accessed 4 August 2018).
[165] http://www.pilsudski.org/portal/pl/ (accessed 4 August 2018).

torians who attempted to summarize the actions, achievements, and legacy of the post-1939 Polish migrants. The volumes deal with wartime Polish authorities in exile, the political activities of Polish émigrés after 1945, the leaders and centers of the Polish political diaspora after World War II, the international activities of the exiles, the assistance extended to Poles, and the final phases of political diaspora in the face of the dismantling of Communism in Poland. The last two volumes contain a selection of documents and appendices.[166] The three-volume synthesis published in Warsaw was entitled *The Second Great Emigration*, and was written by three Warsaw-based authors: Andrzej Friszke, Paweł Machewicz, and Rafał Habielski. Each author focused on a different area of émigré experience. Friszke wrote on political life, Machcewicz on the international context of the émigrés' political activities, and Habielski on social, cultural, and scientific life in exile.[167] Since the publication of this work, no comprehensive approach to the question of post-1939 migration from Poland has been undertaken even though numerous new primary sources have become available.

A comprehensive approach to Polish migration and diaspora in general, including during the Cold War, was presented in two seminal works published in the first decade of this century: a volume called *Polish Diaspora*, edited by Adam Walaszek, and Dariusz Stola's *The No-Exit Country*, both published in Poland.[168] The first covers a geographic overview of the Polish diaspora. Classified region by region and country-by-country, it contains important information related to post-1939 émigrés. Stola's work is the first thorough overview of migrations affecting the People's Republic of Poland. This chapter has been based on the information contained in all of the above-mentioned works.

The other source of information and scholarly expertise used herein was the group of academics gathered under the aegis of the IPN's 'Polish Political Emigration 1939–1990' Central Research Program. The author of this chapter served as the program's coordinator from its beginnings in 2011 until 2015. Moreover, he edited a volume containing scholarly reports on the current state of research on Polish political emigration since 1939, which was published in 2016.[169] However, an abbreviated English-language version was also published as a special volume of *Polish-American Studies* (Fall 2015). It contains five reports (on the political system, émigré ties to the homeland, the 'Solidarity' migration, and East-Central European migrations) selected from the fourteen published in the Polish volume. Another research panora-

---

[166] Leonidas Liszewicz et al., eds. *Materiały do dziejów polskiego uchodźstwa niepodległościowego*, vol. 1–8 (London: Polskie Towarzystwo Naukowe na Obczyźnie, 1994–1996).
[167] Andrzej Friszke, Rafał Habielski, and Paweł Machcewicz *Druga Wielka Emigracja*; Friszke, *Życie polityczne emigracji*; Machcewicz, *Emigracja w polityce międzynarodowej*; Habielski, *Życie społeczne i kulturalne emigracji*.
[168] *Polska diaspora*, ed. Walaszek; Stola, *Kraj bez wyjścia*.
[169] *Polska emigracja polityczna 1939–1990. Stan badań*, ed. Sławomir Łukasiewicz (Warsaw: Instytut Pamięci Narodowej, 2016).

ma, based on different theoretical approach, was presented in the volume edited by Grzegorz Babiński and Henryk Chałupczak[170].

Any scholar interested in the demography of post-World War II migration should consult the latest works by Piotr Eberhardt (for the period 1939–1949) and Dariusz Stola (for the post-1949 period). Very often they provide up to date estimates. Supplementary information can be found in elder works by Andrzej Gawryszewski, Krystyna Iglicka, and Marek Okólski (mostly on the recent, post-1989 migration, also in the regional context).[171] Polish Cold War migration in the regional context is the research focus of Krystyna Slany.[172]

In terms of particular areas of émigré experience during the Cold War, there is an obvious discrepancy of scholarly interest. There is a multitude of works related to Polish political affairs in exile – from works on the functioning of the Polish government-in-exile to the fate of demobilized Polish soldiers in the West.[173] The ties between the Cold War diaspora and the People's Republic have been thoroughly examined by Paweł Ziętara, Krzysztof Tarka, and Sławomir Cenckiewicz.[174] Important works on Solidarity-era migrants have recently been written by Marcin Frybes, Magdalena Heruday-Kiełczewska, and Partyk Pleskot.[175] The international context of political activities in exile was provided by such authors like: Józef Łaptos, Krzysztof Tarka, Paweł Machcewicz, Sławomir Łukasiewicz, and Anna Mazurkiewicz. The biggest concentration of Poles abroad (USA) and its peculiar role during the Cold War

---

170 Grzegorz Babiński, and Henryk Chałupczak, eds., *Diaspora polska w procesach globalizacji. Stan i perspektywy badań* (Kraków: Komitet Badania Polonii PAN 2006).
171 Andrzej Gawryszewski (*Ludność Polski w XX wieku*, (Warsaw: Instytut Geografii i Przestrzennego Zagospodarowania, 2005); Krystyna Iglicka (*Poland's post-war dynamic of migration*, VT: Ashgate, 2001); Marek Okólski ed., European Immigrations: Trends, Structures and Policy Implications (Amsterdam: Amsterdam University Press, 2012).
172 Slany, *Między przymusem a wyborem*.
173 Górecki, *Polskie naczelne władze państwowe*; Romuald Turkowski, *Parlamentaryzm polski na uchodźstwie 1945–1972 w okresie rozbicia emigracji politycznej w Londonie* (Warsaw: Wydawnictwo Sejmowe, 2001); Romuald Turkowski, *Parlamentaryzm polski na uchodźstwie 1972–1991 po zjednoczeniu emigracji politycznej w Londynie* (Warsaw: Wydawnictwo Sejmowe, 2002); Nurek, *Gorycz zwycięstwa*; Kondracki, *Historia Stowarzyszenia Polskich Kombatantów w Wielkiej Brytanii*.
174 *Aparat bezpieczeństwa wobec emigracji politycznej i Polonii*, ed. Ryszard Terlecki (Warsaw: Instytut Pamięci Narodowej 2005); Machcewicz, "*Monachijska menażeria*; Cenckiewicz, *Oczami bezpieki*; Tarka, *Mackiewicz i inni*; Tarka, *Emigranci na celowniku*; Krzysztof Tarka, *Jest tylko jedna Polska. Emigranci w służbie PRL* (Łomianki: LTW, 2014); *Tajny oręż czy ofiary zimnej wojny? Emigracje z Europy Środkowo-Wschodniej*, ed. Sławomir Łukasiewicz (Lublin/Warsaw: Instytut Pamięci Narodowej, 2010).
175 Marin Frybes, 'Społeczne reakcje Zachodu na fenomen "Solidarności" i rola emigracyjnych struktur związku 1980–1989' in *NSZZ "Solidarność" 1980–1989*, vol. 2: *Ruch społeczny*, ed. Łukasz Kamiński and Grzegorz Waligóra (Warsaw: Instytut Pamięci Narodowej, 2010); Magdalena Heruday-Kiełczewska, "*Solidarność*" *nad Sekwaną: działalność Komitetu Koordynacyjnego NSZZ "Solidarność" w Paryżu 1981–1989* (Gdańsk: Europejskie Centrum Solidarności, 2016); Patryk Pleskot, *Solidarność na Antypodach. Inicjatywy solidarnościowe polskiej diaspory w Australii* (Warsaw: Instytut Pamięci Narodowej, 2014).

was described by Joanna Wojdon in a recently published monograph in English.[176] Rafał Habielski, Wioletta Wajs-Milewska, and Ewa Rogalewska have written on the cultural life in exile.[177] Jan Draus and Rafał Stobiecki examined scientific life of émigrés.[178] Émigré artists have been presented in the numerous works of Jan Wiktor Sienkiewicz.[179] The topic of the daily lives of émigrés during the Cold War remains one of the most significant research gaps even though several scholars have now began researching/examining it.

This brief essay was meant to provide preliminary insight into the literature. For anyone interested in finding out more, there are numerous useful internet sites, some of which offer bibliographic overviews, including: the Bibliography of Polish History,[180] the general index of Polish academic journals, as well as foreign Polonica available through the National Library's website,[181] or the central catalogue of Polish libraries.[182]

---

[176] Joanna Wojdon, *White and red umbrella: The Polish American Congress in the Cold War era, 1944–1988* (Reno, NV: Helena History Press, 2015).
[177] *Powrześniowa emigracja niepodległościowa na mapie kultury nie tylko polskiej: Paryż, London, Monachium, Nowy Jork*, eds. Violetta Wejs-Milewska and Ewa Rogalewska (Białystok: Trans Humana, 2009); vol. 2: Białystok: Instytut Pamięci Narodowej/Uniwersytet w Białymstoku, 2016). Write out seperately Athough published in 1960 the following two-volume work is still worth consulting: *Literatura polska na obczyźnie 1940–1960*, ed. Tymona Terleckiego (London: B. Świderski, 1964–1965).
[178] Jan Draus, *Nauka polska na emigracji w latach 1945–1990* (Warsaw: Instytut Historii Nauki PAN/ASPRA-JR, 2015); Rafał Stobiecki, *Klio na wygnaniu: z dziejów polskiej historiografii na uchodźstwie w Wielkiej Brytanii po 1945 r.* (Poznań: Wydawnictwo Poznańskie, 2005); Rafał Stobiecki, *Klio za wielką wodą: polscy historycy w Stanach Zjednoczonych po 1945 roku* (Warsaw: Instytut Pamięci Narodowej, 2017).
[179] Jan Wiktor Sienkiewicz, *Artyści Andersa: continuità e novità* (Warsaw/Toruń: Polski Instytut Studiów nad Sztuką Świata/Tako, 2016).
[180] http://www.bibliografia.ipn.gov.pl/ (accessed 4 August 2018).
[181] http://www.bn.org.pl/katalogi-i-bibliografie (accessed 4 August 2018).
[182] English-language version: http://nukat.edu.pl/search/query?locale=EN&theme=nukat (accessed 4 August 2018).

8 Romania
Beatrice Scutaru

Ultimul care pleacă stinge lumina! [The last one to leave must turn off the lights!] was one of the jokes that Romanians used to make during the Communist era.[1] Beyond its humorous intentions, this witty joke reveals the important place held by the idea of immigration in the Romanian mentality.[2] Due to the strict limitations imposed by the totalitarian regime, only a handful of people were granted permission to travel outside the country.

The migration of Romanian citizens is, however, not a new phenomenon. After a brief historical overview of Romanian migration before (8.1) and after the Second World War (8.2), which will enable a better understanding of the international migration of Romanians on a long-term basis, this chapter presents the evolution of the Romanian migration during the Cold War and explains its determining factors (8.3). Several emigration waves can be identified before 1989, influenced both by the transformations underwent by the Romanian state and by the different geopolitical changes. The specific features of this migration phenomenon had certain consequences for the emigrants' living conditions. Part of this study therefore presents the lives of Romanian emigrants and focuses on the financial aspects as well as their political, cultural, and civic mobilization (8.4). It is only in the 1990s that the situation began to change: after half a century of restrictions, Romanians embarked on discovering the Europe they had dreamed of and idealized during Communist times.[3] The fifth section of this chapter will explore the characteristics of this migration during the first years following the fall of the Communist regime. Finally, the last part consists of a brief overview of the main resources available for studying/researching Romanian migration during the second half of the twentieth century.

8.1 Romanian migration in historical perspective

Due to frequent territorial changes Romania was, during the nineteenth century and the first part of the twentieth, mainly a country of emigration. Members of ethnic minorities were among the most mobile populations. In 1859, through the unification of the principalities of Moldavia and Wallachia, located in the east and the south of the

---

[1] Călin-Bogdan Ștefănescu and Mihai Pop, *10 ani de umor negru românesc: jurnal de bancuri politice* (Bucharest: Metropol-Paideia, 1991), 38.
[2] Several academic studies have analyzed the political and linguistic aspects of Romanians' sense of humour during the Communist period. See: Călin-Bogdan Ștefănescu, *Umorul român in faza terminală a socialismului* (Bucharest: Paideia, 2014); Marie-Viorica Constantin, *Umorul politic românesc in perioda comunistă. Perspective lingvistice* (Bucharest: Editura Universitatii din Bucuresti, 2012).
[3] Caherine Durandin, *Europe: l'utopie et le chaos* (Paris: Armand Colin, 2005).

Carpathian Mountains respectively, Romania emerged as a state (The Old Kingdom) that, along with Transylvania (1918), became The Greater Romania.[4] A significant number of inhabitants of Transylvania, Bukovina, and Banat started migrating across the territory of The Old Kingdom, which had become very attractive due to the modernization measures that had been implemented, as well as the numerous large areas of agricultural fields that had been made available.[5] Thus, between 1880 and 1890, approximately 50,000 inhabitants from Transylvania migrated to the territory of The Old Kingdom. Many more left towards the New World, especially the United States and Canada and, to a lesser extent, South America.[6]

Between 1896 and 1919, approximately 320,000 inhabitants of Transylvania – 6 percent of a total population of 4.8 million in 1900 – emigrated to the United States of America. Most of them were of German ethnicity.[7] The first wave of Romanian emigration to Canada started in 1880, but the numbers were significantly lower. Before World War I, around 8,000 Romanians emigrated to Canada; by 1921, their number increased to roughly 30,000. Most of them came from Bukovina.[8] Other communities took part in this phenomenon, like the Muslim community of Dobruja, whose members emigrated to present-day Turkey. The Jewish population, due to their emigration to Argentina or to the USA, took part in the important emigration wave through which populations from East-Central Europe moved to the other side of the ocean.[9] From 1882 onwards, a segment of this population decided to relocate to Palestine. Approximately 140,000 Jews left the territory between 1896 and 1914.[10]

The end of World War I and national unity (1918) determined new population movements. Since Transylvania was now part of The Greater Romania, a part of the population of Hungarian ethnicity sought refuge in the territories under Hungarian administration; 197,000 people relocated between 1918 and 1922, out of a total population of 1.6 million Hungarians in Transylvania.[11] Moreover, despite the improvement

---

[4] Florin Constantiniu, *O istorie sinceră a poporului român* (Bucharest: Editura Univers Enciclopedic, 1997).
[5] Ionuț Muntele, "Migrations internationales dans la Roumanie moderne et contemporaine," in *Visibles mais peu nombreux ... Les circulations migratoires roumaines*, ed. Dana Diminescu (Paris: Éditions de la Maison des sciences de l'homme, 2003), 35.
[6] Bénédicte Michalon and Mihaela Nedelcu, "Histoire, constantes et transformations récentes des dynamiques migratoires en Roumanie," *Revue d'Études Comparatives Est-Ouest* 4 (2010): 6. This decision was mainly due to overpopulation and the pull emigration factors from across the Atlantic.
[7] Istvan Horvath, "Country profile: Romania," 9 (2007): 2, http://focus-migration.hwwi.de/Romania.2515.0.html?&L=1c (acessed 23 November 2017).
[8] Irina Culic, "One Hundred Years of Solitude: Romanian Immigrants in Canada," *Studia UBB Sociologia* 2 (2011): 33. See also GJ Patterson, "Romanians," in *Encyclopedia of Canada's Peoples*, ed. Paul Robert Magocsi (Toronto: University of Toronto Press, 1999).
[9] Muntele, "Migrations internationales dans la Roumanie moderne et contemporaine," 35.
[10] Istvan Horvath, "Migrația din România și Republica Moldova de la mijlocul secolului XIX pâna în present, cu accent pe migrația minorităților," *Working Papers in Romanian Minority Studies*, Cluj Napoca: Institutul Pentru Studierea Problemelor Minoritatilor Nationale 40 (2011): 11.
[11] Horvath, "Migrația din România și Republica Moldova," 12.

of living conditions for Romanians in Transylvania, relocations to North America continued, especially for economic reasons. Also, approximately 64,000 young people who had emigrated to America returned to Romania in the 1920s.

According to a 1940 American census, 270,000 inhabitants of Romanian ethnicity were identified; one third of them were Jewish, 20 percent were Saxons from Transylvania and 6 percent Hungarians.[12] Another important destination for Romanians – especially for intellectuals – was France, a tradition that went back to the nineteenth century. Romanian intellectuals used to travel and study abroad, especially in France.[13] Among those who studied in Paris were the young Romanians who in 1848 tried to bring major change to the principalities by means of a revolution.[14]

8.2 The aftermath of World War II

World War II brought new significant changes for European populations, especially in the eastern part of the continent. From 1940 to 1944, Romania lost and won back several territories, which resulted in major relocations, mostly imposed by force. Minorities were particularly affected. In 1940, Romania had to cede the north of Transylvania, Bessarabia, and the *Cadrilater*[15] to Hungary, the Soviet Union, and Bulgaria respectively. Following a treaty between the two states, 220,000 Romanians left the territory newly annexed by Hungary and 160,000 Hungarians made the opposite journey. A different treaty was signed with Bulgaria, which determined that approximately 61,000 Bulgarians had to leave Romania. It also led to the migration of 100,000 Romanians.[16] In addition, 70,000 inhabitants of Bessarabia requested repatriation to Romania, along with the 100–150,000 Romanians who chose to leave the Soviet-occupied territories. Following the German invasion of the Soviet Union in June 1941, Romania regained these territories. Numerous refugees thus returned to their homes.[17] A different treaty signed in 1940 between Romania and Germany occasioned the repatriation of around 66,000 citizens who were members of the Ger-

---

[12] Michalon and Nedelcu, "Histoire, constantes et transformations récentes des dynamiques migratoires en Roumanie," 6.
[13] Lucian Boia, *La Roumanie. Un pays à la frontière de l'Europe* (Paris: Les Belles Lettres, 2003), 253.
[14] Ion Heliade Rădulescu, Ion Ghica, C. A. Rosetti, Ncolae Bălcescu, A. G. Golescu, Mihail Kogalniceanu. See: Ruxandra Ivan, *La politique étrangère roumaine (1990–2006)* (Brussels: Éditions de l'Université de Bruxelles, 2009), 64. See also Mihaela Nedelcu, "Des 'ennemis du people' aux 'Roumains de partout'. Le role de l'État d'origine dans la mobilisation transnationale de ses ressortissants," in *Les migrations internationals: enjeux contemporains et questions nouvelles*, eds. Cédric Audebert and Emmanuel Ma Mung (Bilbao: Université de Deusto, 2007), 41.
[15] Southern part of Dobruja, the border area between Romania and Bulgaria, West form the Black Sea.
[16] Dariusz Stola, "Forced Migration in Central European History," *International Migration Review* 26 (1992): 332.
[17] Mihai Gribnicea, *Basarabia în primii ani de ocupație sovietică 1944–1950* (Cluj-Napoca: Dacia, 1995) 19.

man minority. Another 73,000 joined the Waffen-SS in 1943; very few of them returned to Romania after the war. "The most severe case of forced migration" of this period concerned the Jewish and Roma minorities.[18] The deportation of Jews from Romania started in 1941 and reduced their number by half, from a total of 780,000.[19] At least 25,000 Roma were deported by force to Transnistria.[20] Most of them did not survive the war.[21]

On 23 August 1944, Romania joined the Allied forces and declared war on Germany. Subsequently, the country became part of the Soviet sphere of influence. A part of the Red Army, which had entered the territory on 20 August, remained and started taking control of the territory.[22] The end of the war once again resulted in the relocation of numerous populations: Romania regained the north of Transylvania but lost Bessarabia, the north of Bukovina and the southern part of Dobruja. Around 15,000 ethnic Hungarians decided to settle in Hungary. In 1944, over 200,000 ethnic Germans left the country along with the German troops. The same year, numerous Romanians accompanied the withdrawing Romanian troops from Bessarabia.[23]

8.3 Major migration streams across "the nylon curtain"

I borrowed György Péteri's expression of the "nylon curtain" because I believe it best describes the Cold War era which saw plenty of connections over the East-West divide. The "alternated periods of increased isolation, regimentation, and terror, and periods of 'Thaw', increased openness, emulation, and the softening of Iron into Nylon."[24]

The end of World War II marked the beginning of a new stage in Romania's history. The country had suffered important human and financial losses, with 1 million people dead, missing or displaced (e. g. prisoners, minorities) and damages of 3.7 billion dollars (at the exchange rate of 1938). Furthermore, the country's territory, even after having regained the north of Transylvania, represented only 80.5 percent of that

---

18 Vladimir Solonari, *Purificarea națiunii: dislocări forțate de populație și epurări etnice în România lui Ion Antonescu, 1940–1944* (Iasi: Polirom, 2015).
19 Liviu Rotman, *Evreii din România în perioada comunistă. 1944–1965* (Iasi-Bucharest: Polirom, 2004).
20 Out of a total of 200,000–300,000 Romanian Roma, 25,000 were deported. Transnistria is a province situated at the eastern border between today's Moldova and Ukraine. It was under Romanian control at the time.
21 Viorel Achim, ed., *România și Transnistria: problema Holocaustului. Perspective istorice și comparative* (Bucharest: Curtea Veche, 2004).
22 Ioan Scurtu, *Istoria contemporană a României (1918–2001)* (Bucharest: Editura Fundatiei Eomania de Maine, 2002) 106–112.
23 Horvath, "Migrația din România și Republica Moldova," 7.
24 Péteri, György, "Nylon Curtain – Transnational and transsystemic tendencies in the cultural life of state-socialist Russia and East-Central Europe,"*Slavonica* 2 (November 2004): 113–122.

of 1938; the total population figures decreased from 20 million to a little more than 15 million in 1945. The Soviet political system was installed at the end of 1947 when, after having forced King Michael to abdicate and leave the country, Romania was declared a People's Republic on 30 December 1947. The implementation of this totalitarian regime had a significant impact on all aspects of social life[25] and represented the beginning of a new phase in the history of Romanian migration. Relocations became more difficult but were not impossible. In other words, the Iron Curtain was permeable.[26]

8.3.1 Choosing freedom over security

After the end of World War II, many Romanians chose to try and find their "freedom in the West."[27] Leaving meant losing their jobs, their possessions, and their social and political status. By abandoning their home country and exposing themselves to the dangers and hardships of exile, migrants made an important statement: their situation in Romania was worse than what might await them abroad. Therefore, by questioning the legitimacy of the Communist regime, immigration could become an act of resistance.[28]

Those who decided to live on the other side of the Iron Curtain became spokesmen for their fellow citizens still living in Romania. Émigrés claimed they represented the "authentic" Romania and Romanian nation. A distinction was then made between the nation, the people and the state: the nation was in exile, thus no longer under the authority of the state. By challenging the home state and denying its legitimacy, exiles' actions led to what Stéphane Dufoix called exo-polity, a "political space and time both national and transnational." This induced a situation where émigrés had cut all ties with the state but maintained continuity with it through the actions they implemented.[29] Because they saw themselves as the guardians of national sov-

---

[25] Bogdan Murgescu, *România și Europa. Acumularea decalajelor economice (1500–2010)* (Iasi: Polirom, 2010) 333–336.
[26] On connections and relationships over the East-West divide see: Simo Mikkonen and Pia Koivunen, eds., *Beyond the Divide. Entangled Histories of Cold War Europe* (New York, Oxford: Berghahn Books, 2015).
[27] Sanda Stolojan, *Au balcon de l'exil roumain à Paris avec Cioran, Eugène Ionesco, Mircea Eliade, Vintilă Horia* (Paris: l'Harmattan, 1999), 345.
[28] Frithjof Trapp, "L'exil en tant que résistance. Ébauche d'une typologie," in *Exil et Résistance au National-socialisme 1933–1945*, eds. Krebs, Gilbert and Gérard Schneilin (Paris: Université de la Sorbonne Nouvelle, Publications de l'Institut d'allemand, 1998), 45.
[29] Stéphane Dufoix, "Sertorius ou Prospero?," *Socio-anthropologie* 9 (2001): 3, https://journals.openedition.org/socio-anthropologie/8 (accessed 5 September 2017). For more information on this topic see Robert Waldinger, *The Cross-Border Connection: Immigrants, Emigrants, and Their Homelands* (Cambridge and London: Harvard University Press, 2015).

ereignty, the real voice of the people, they felt their actions were justified.³⁰ In 1972, Constantin Cesianu (1913–1983) argued that "the only privilege exiles ha[d was] being able to show the world the reality, the truth that their fellow citizens could not express. It [was] a duty they needed to accomplish because this way they defended Romania's superior and permanent interests."³¹ As a former member of the Romanian National Liberal Party and political prisoner, Cesianu was allowed to leave Romania in 1967. He chose to move to France where he became an active member of the Romanian exile until his death.

8.3.2 Restricted freedom of movement

Mass migration was thought to discredit the regime both within and outside national borders. By leaving their country, Romanians indeed "voted with their feet" against the Communist regime, bringing about a political significance to their act.³² Romania – as other Communist countries – exercised very restrictive exit policies.³³ By limiting the number of departures, the leaders hoped to reduce the risk of their legitimacy being challenged. Travelling and even migrating was, however, possible during this period, as Bucharest's purpose was not preventing all type of migration, but rather controlling the flux. While limiting most citizens' access to international mobility, the regime granted certain groups the right to leave. These actions were meant to limit the number of Romanians applying for asylum abroad, which would not benefit the country's international image.³⁴

However, Romanians were not free to have a passport. In order to obtain a travel document, each citizen needed approval from the authorities. It was very difficult to obtain an exit visa as the whole process was strictly controlled by the Romanian Ministry of Internal Affairs and by the *Securitate* (Romanian political police). Each applicant had to go through a long series of ordeals when dealing with the administration. This was the general procedure: 1) each citizen had to submit an application to the police; 2) the passport was provided only if the visa was granted; 3) the passport had

---

30 Emmanuelle Loyer, "Exile," in *The Palgrave Dictionary of Transnational History*, ed. Akira Irie and Pierre-Yves Saunier (Hampshire: Palgrave Macmillan, 2009), 369.
31 Beatrice Scutaru, "La Roumanie à Paris: exil politique et lutte anti-Communiste," *Histoire@Politique. Politique, culture, société* 23 (2014): 4, https://www.histoire-politique.fr/index.php?numero=23&rub=autres-articles&item=83 (accessed 12 February 2018).
32 Scutaru, "La Roumanie à Paris," 1. See also Magdolina Barath, "Attempts to create unity in Hungarian political emigration after the 1956 revolution," in *Anti-Communist Resistance in Central and Eastern Europe*, ed. Peter Jasek (Bratislava: Ustav Pamati Naroda, 2011), 798.
33 Carol Mueller, "Escape from the GDR, 1961–1989: Hybrid Exit Repertoires in a Disintegrating Leninist Regime," *The American Journal of Sociology* 105 (1999): 702.
34 Mueller, "Escape from the GDR, 1961–1989," 697–735.

to be returned to the police at the end of each trip.³⁵ Many testimonies depict what this process entailed: the endless queues, the hopeless waiting, the need to pay bribes, to be placed under surveillance and have each aspect of one's life thoroughly analyzed.³⁶ It is therefore safe to say that obtaining a passport was not a right, but a privilege only few enjoyed.³⁷ Moreover, the privilege of obtaining a passport sometimes came with a high price: e.g. the obligation to collaborate with the *Securitate*, to give information on Romanians or foreigners met abroad, being vulnerable to other forms of blackmail and having to pay bribes. Thus the passport could be either a reward or a penalty.³⁸

When applying for a visa, the first step was paying 25 lei (in the 1970s the average salary was of 2000 lei/month) for an eight-page long passport application and answering numerous questions about the applicant's personality, his/her acquaintances, relatives and in-laws to the third and fourth degree. Several restrictions limited Romanian citizens' possibility of travelling abroad as, for example, the requirement of not having had access, three years prior to applying, to state secrets. Furthermore, a decision taken in April 1970 by the Council of Ministers prohibited citizens to travel abroad for personal matters more than once every two years, except if one had a foreign currency account. Since Romanians were not allowed to be in possession of foreign currency, this was a rare occurrence.

Once this step validated, the completed application was sent to the Securitate for investigation. Afterwards, if everything checked out, the applicant's employer was requested to express his or her opinion on the employee and the trip he/she wanted to take. Only after several months of waiting, when all these steps were complete, did the applicant receive an answer. Very often, however, the first request was denied. Such was the case for Dinu Zamfirescu, an opponent of the Communist regime, who had to present his application several years in a row (23 applications) before receiving a positive answer. Because of his attitude towards the regime and connections to the former Liberal and Peasant Parties, he only managed to leave the country after his family from France "bought" him.³⁹ This was not without precedent. Money was however more often used as a means to accelerate the proceedings of ethnic migration. Those who presented an economic and political interest for the Romanian government had the hardest time leaving the country.

---

35 Istvan Horvath, "Migratia internationala a cetatenilor romani dupa 1989," in *Inerție și schimbare. Dimensiuni sociale ale tranziției în România* ed. Traian Rotariu and Virgil Voineagu (Iasi: Polirom, 2012), 201.
36 Virgil Târău, ed., *Invățând istoria prin experiențele trecutului: Cetățenii obișnuiți supravegheați de Securitate în anii 70–80* (Bucharest: CNSAS, 2009), 142, 149.
37 Smaranda Vultur, "Pentru un dicționar al lumii comuniste," *Colloquium politicum* 2 (July-December 2010): 104.
38 Târău, *Invățând istoria prin experiențele trecutului*, 149.
39 Beatrice Scutaru, "Les relations entre les sociétés française et roumaine des années 1960 à 1995: un atout pour l'ancrage de la Roumanie à l'Europe? " (PhD diss., University of Angers, 2013), 255–256.

The situation became even more complicated following the signing of the Helsinki Final Act. On 1 August 1975, the representatives of thirty-five states, including Communist ones, signed an agreement committing to respect and apply its principles. Freedom of movement was one of them.[40] Surprisingly, despite Helsinki's Final Act third basket – stating that all signatory countries must encourage people's circulation and facilitate their citizens' departure abroad – leaving Romania or travelling outside the country became even more difficult than before. If until then the two years' rule for travelling abroad had not always been applied, following the signing of the Act there were no more exceptions. Furthermore, while Romanian authorities used to ask for the employer's opinion on his/her employee's passport application, they were now requesting a guarantee that the employee would return to Romania when the trip came to an end. Employers were made responsible for their employees' actions and were thus determined to perceive their employees' mobility as being fraught with risk.

In this regard, the French ambassador in Bucharest mentioned the following in his report to the Ministry of Foreign Affairs: "there are practically only two legal ways of emigrating: marriage and family reunification." Nonetheless, marriage with a foreign partner required approval from the State Council. Concerning family reunification, an authorization from the passport processing service of the *Miliția* (State Police) was compulsory, which in turn required prior approval from the People's Council of the applicant's place of residence. In the past, applicants would normally receive a positive answer after one year, but after August 1975, Romanian authorities toughened their procedures.[41]

Authorities, however, did not limit their actions to the legal aspects. Other means were also used in order to limit the number of departures. Those applying as emigrants had their social and economic rights revoked and were harassed by the authorities.[42] They had to face pressure both in their personal life and at work. Some had to accept work below their qualifications, while others even lost their jobs. According to the International Helsinki Federation for Human Rights, some even risked going to prison for wanting to move to another country.[43] Moreover, propaganda was very active, trying to prevent both legal and illegal migration. Plays, movies, and articles were used to propagate the image of a decadent Western society and to convince Romanians that there was no better place than home. Several writers who held important political positions, published articles and poems praising the qualities of their motherland: Dumitru Popescu, secretary of the Central Committee of PCR

---

40 Ana-Maria Cătănuș, "Disidență și represiune în epoca Nicolae Ceaușescu. O analiză comparativă: Paul Goma-Vlad Georgescu," in *Forme de represiune în regimurile comuniste* ed. Cosmin Budeanca and Florentin Olteanu (Iasi: Polirom, 2009), 257.
41 Scutaru, "Les relations entre les sociétés française et roumaine," 257.
42 Horvath, "Country profile: Romania," 1.
43 International Helsinki Federation for Human Rights, *Violations of the Helsinki Accords: Romania* (November 1986), 2–8.

(Romanian Communist Party) and President of the Council for Education and Socialist Culture; Vasile Nicolescu, director of the Cultural, Literary and Artistic Publications (that is to say in charge of censorship); the novelist Eugen Barbu, substitute member of the Central Committee and editor of the weekly magazine *Săptămana* (The Week), to name only a few. They depicted "the exiles' moral hell" – exiles whom they described as the "country's traitors" – and highlighted the suffering they had experienced themselves when abroad.[44] Those who had managed to flee the country were seen by the Communist regime as spies, manipulated by obscure forces or opposing groups from abroad, and therefore put under surveillance.[45]

The wish to renew the Most Favored Nation (MFN) clause given by the USA was one of the few factors which had an impact on Romania's emigration policies. Romania was awarded this status in 1975, in order to encourage its "independent" politics with the USSR. From that year on, the products imported from Romania benefitted from the same facilities as the products of Western European economic partners. In 1983, Romania and Hungary were the only two countries among the members of the Warsaw Pact that were given this advantage. The article 402 of the Jackson-Valik Amendment was the only major limitation; according to it, the MFN preferential rates were conditioned by the respect of certain humanitarian and emigration policies. The article stipulated that the MFN clause could not be granted to countries that prevented their citizens from emigrating or required excessive amounts of money for emigration procedures. As a result, the American Congress started discussing Romania's emigration policy on a yearly basis. In order to maintain the MFN clause, Ceaușescu would regularly make efforts during the months prior to the discussions; afterwards, the situation would become "the same as before or worse," according to the US Helsinki Watch report.[46]

In consequence, the USA hesitated between the wish to maintain economic relations with Romania and the desire to ensure that human rights were respected. In addition, on 1 November 1982, Romania adopted a decree that imposed a tax on education for emigration applicants. If they had studied for more than the minimum and compulsory period of ten years, the latter had to reimburse the Romanian state for the amounts of money spent on their education. The required sums could amount to 40,000 dollars in the case of medical studies. The debt had to be paid in foreign currency, although the vast majority of Romanians were not allowed to possess such currency. The only citizens who were capable of paying were the ones who had relatives abroad. In a way, this represented the formalization of an older practice used in the migration process of Jewish and German minorities. In May 1983, after sev-

---

44 Dumitru Popescu, "Țara," in *Un om în Agora* (Bucharest: Editura Eminescu, 1972), 182; Adrian Păunescu, "Aici e țara," *România Liberă* (December 1975); Eugen Barbu, "'Mămica' Lovinescu față cu refugiații,' *Săptămâna* (December 1975).
45 Vultur, "Pentru un dicționar al lumii comuniste," 103.
46 US Helsinki Watch Committee, *Romania: Human Rights in a "Most Favored Nation"* (New York, Washington, June 1989), 1–7, 10–13.

eral meetings between the representatives of the USA and Romania, the latter declared that this tax would no longer be in force. Following this declaration, President Reagan announced the renewal of the MFN clause. Economic interests thus outweighed the wish to limit emigration. For Romania, the loss of the MFN clause meant the loss of roughly 250,000,000 dollars, which the country could not afford.[47]

8.3.3 Migration streams: an overview

Despite all these restrictions, Romanians still managed to leave the country. In fact, Ionel Muntele estimated that Romania had a negative migration rate of 789,578 people from 1948 to 1989.[48] Migratory flows were closely connected to changes in domestic and international politics. The publications that dealt with this topic established a distinction between literary and political exile, hence proposing different chronologies. The first periodization – conceptualized by the literary critic Laurențiu Ulici and later reused in the exact same form by Eva Behring – identified three consecutive waves: 1940–1950, 1960–1970 and the 1980s.[49] Another literary critic, Ion Simuț, suggested a different chronology, one aiming to be "more precise, more connected to the realities and the phases of the Communist politics." The first stage runs from 1941 to 1947. Due to the closing of borders that followed the abdication of King Michael and the proclamation of the Romanian People's Republic, emigration was practically impossible until 1964. Numbers of emigrants increase progressively, especially after 1971 and during the 1980s.[50] Monica Lovinescu, a prominent figure of the Romanian exile in Paris, proposed a slightly different chronology, which she connected to the identification of three categories of exiles: political (1946–1956), economic (1956–1970) and those associated with human rights movements (the 1970s and 1980s).[51] In fact, she was not the first one to make a distinction between the first and the second wave of emigrants. For example, Mircea Eliade was particularly critical of those who had migrated in the 1970s, whom he perceived as being interested solely in the occidental way of living (à la manière occidentale).[52] The analysis of these different chronologies reveals the existence of four main phases in Romanian emigration.

---

47 Scutaru, "Les relations entre les sociétés française et roumaine," 373–374.
48 Muntele, "Migrations internationales dans la Roumanie moderne et contemporaine," 36.
49 Eva Behring, *Scriitori români din exil, 1945–1989* (Bucharest: Editura Fundației Culturale Române, 2001) 23–44.
50 Ion Simuț, "Cronologia exilului literar postbelic," *România literară*, 23 (June 2008).
51 Monica Lovinescu, "Dialoguri pe unde scurte," in *Incursiuni în literatura diasporei și a disidenței* ed. Gheorghe Glodeanu (Bucharest: Libra, 1999), 303–314.
52 Mircea Eliade, quoted in Teodora and George Șerban-Oprescu, "Overview of Romanian Emigration to America during Communism and PostCommunism: Cultural Dimensions of Quality of Life," *International Journal of Humanities and Social Science* 23 (December 2012): 47.

The first wave – from 1940 to 1956 – consisted mainly of people who were fleeing Communism. A significant migration wave took place between 1944 and 1946 and involved mainly ethnic Germans from Banat, Jews, and ethnic Hungarians and, for the first time, a substantial contingent of Romanians who were apprehensive about the effects of Soviet occupation.[53] They were joined by former prisoners of war who, once liberated by the Allies, refused to return to Romania and decided to settle in the West. Furthermore, after the abdication of King Michael, the new political regime requested that all Romanian citizens who were abroad return to Romania. Many of them refused and decided to stay in the West. They were mainly intellectuals, students, and politicians. This first wave of emigration also comprised of Romanians who, having a compromised background of collaboration with regimes in favor of Nazi Germany, chose exile.[54] Members of the Iron Guard emigrated to Austria, Germany, France, and Spain by the thousands.[55] The victims of nationalization and collectivization policies also tried to move to the West.[56] Certain members and leaders of former political parties that bad been dissolved and banned by the Communist regime – *Partidul Național Liberal* (National Liberal Party), *Partidul Național Țărănesc* (National Peasant Party), *Partidul Social Democrat* (Social Democrat Party) – followed a similar path.

The Hungarian Revolution and its defeat (1956) marked the end of this first phase. Romanians started understanding that Sovietization was a long-term phenomenon and Western countries would not take action to liberate the East European states. Thus, the exiles had no other option than to start picturing their exile and fight against Communism in the long term.[57] Prior to this, every New-Year's-Eve celebration in Paris would end with the invariable "Next year in Bucharest!" as they were all certain the return was near.[58] Up until that moment, migrants were living in the hope that their exile would be short, that they would somehow be allowed to return to Romania thanks to foreign intervention.[59]

---

53 Muntele, "Migrations internationales dans la Roumanie moderne et contemporaine," 36.
54 Antoine Marès, "Exilés d'Europe centrale de 1945 à 1967," in *Le Paris des étrangers depuis 1945* ed. Antoine Marès, Pierre Milza (Paris: Publications de la Sorbonne, 1994), 140–141.
55 Founded by Corneliu Zelea Codreanu, the Iron Guard is the name most commonly given to the far-right movement and political party in Romania from 1927 to the early part of World War II. It is also known as the *Legiunea Arhanghelului Mihai* (Legion of the Archangel Michael) or the *Mișcarea Legionară* (Legionnaire Movement). See Radu Ioanid, "The Sacralised Politics of the Romanian Iron Guard," *Totalitarian Movements & Political Religions* 4 (2004): 419–453; Mihai Chioveanu, *Faces of Facism* (Bucharest: University of Bucharest, 2005).
56 Gail Kilgman and Katherine Verdery, *Peasants Under Siege: The Collectivization of Romanian Agriculture, 1949–1962* (Princeton: Princeton University Press, 2011).
57 Behring, *Scriitori români din exil*, 29.
58 Ion Calafeteanu, *Politică și exil. 1946–1950. Din istoria exilului românesc* (Bucharest: Editura enciclopedica, 2000) 24.
59 Bogdan Barbu, *Vin Americanii! Prezența simbolică a Statelor Unite în România Războiului Rece* (Bucharest: Humanitas, 2006).

The second half of the 1960s saw a reorientation in Romania's foreign policy, consisting of a detachment from the USSR and an increased rigour in domestic affairs.[60] Although Communist authorities had taken measures to limit the emigration of Romanian citizens, which had gradually become more significant since 6 March 1945 – when the first Communist government was established – hence threatening to turn into an actual exodus, certain agreements concluded between Romania and Israel allowed the relocation of the Jewish people. This explains the fluctuation in the departures recorded from the end of the 1950s until 1964, as illustrated by the following chart. The latter concerns official, legal relocations that took place after the first emigration period discussed in this paper:

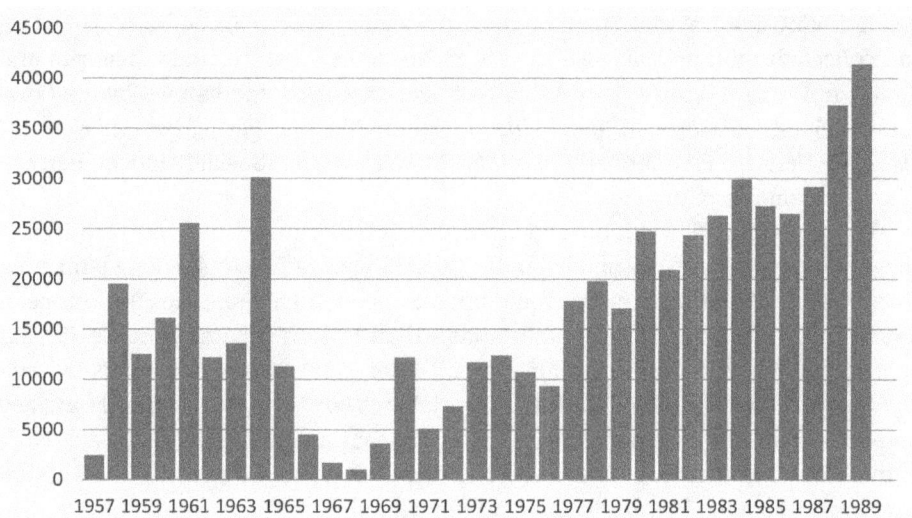

Chart 8.1: Evolution of Romanian legal migration between 1957 and 1989
Source: Istvan Horvath and Remus Gabriel Anghel, "Migration and Its Consequences for Romania," *Südosteuropa* 57 (2009): 387.

The emigration phase that lasted until the mid-1960s is more difficult to define. According to Monica Lovinescu, it consisted mainly of Romanians who would leave the

---

60 Dan Cătănuș, "Divergențele româno-sovietice din CAER și consecințele lor asupra politicii externe a României, 1962–1963," *Arhivele totalitarismului*, 46–47 (2005), 68. A more recent article offers a new perspective on Romania's progressive detachment from the URSS during the second half of the 1950s, emphasizing that the origins of the shift in relationships "were to be found in the soviet injunctions against Romanian leaders in the summer of 1953." Irina Gridan, "Le 'nouveau cours' des relations roumano-soviétiques (années 1950): un assouplissement consenti ou octroyé depuis Moscou?," *Relations internationales* 2 (2015): 111–124.

country for economic reasons, wishing to rebuild their lives in the West.[61] Nonetheless, it can be difficult to make a clear distinction between "political" emigration, which originated from exile, and the "economic" one. Several studies have shown it is entirely possible that the exiles' initial stance would change over time.[62] On the one hand, exile can politicize one's life: immigrants who are perceived as "economic" can start becoming involved in the anti-Communist fight after their arrival in the West.[63] On the other hand, once settled in the West, certain political activists chose to give up the fight: "The refugees' relationship with politics is neither compulsory nor static or predictable."[64]

Following this fluctuating development, which involved a significant number of departures, the second half of the 1960s saw a decrease in numbers of emigrants, determined by the strict control of the population as well as by the illusion that the regime would become more liberal. This gave people hope. In 1958, Gheorghe Gheorghiu-Dej (1901–1965) succeeded in having the troops of the Red Army leave the territory. Moreover, in order to get more support from the Romanian people, he decided to appeal to their sense of national pride and make use of Romania's long-standing anti-Sovietism. The dissemination of Russian culture was slowed down and the Russian language ceased to be compulsory in schools, while learning languages "of universal circulation" was encouraged.[65] The streets and the institutions that had been named after leading Russian figures were renamed.[66] Another means used to attract popular support was the improvement of living conditions by giving access to consumer goods, dwellings, and even holidays.[67]

On 22 April 1964, the Romanian People's Republic (RPR) adopted the *Declarația cu privire la politica Partidului Muncitoresc Român in problemele mișcării comuniste și muncitorești internaționale* [The Declaration concerning the politics of the Romanian Workers' Party with regard to the issues of the international Communist and working movement] – viewed by many as a declaration of independence – which laid the foundations for national Romanian Communism.[68] This document was in accord-

---

61 Lovinescu, "Dialoguri pe unde scurte," 303–314.
62 Trapp, "L'exil en tant que résistance. Ébauche d'une typologie," 51.
63 Loyer, "Exile," 368; Geneviève Dreyfus-Armand, *L'exil des républicains espagnols en France de la guerre civile à la mort de Franco* (Paris: Albin Michel, 1999), 424.
64 Ioana Popa, "Dépasser l'exil. Degrés de médiation et stratégies de transfert littéraire chez les exilés de l'Europe de l'Est en France," *Genèses* 38 (2000): 32.
65 Irina Gridan, "Du Communisme national au national-Communisme. Réactions à la soviétisation dans la Roumanie des années 1960," *Vingtième siècle. Revue d'histoire* 109 (January–March 2011): 118–119.
66 Steven D. Roper, *Romania: The Unfinished Revolution* (Amsterdam: Harwood Academic Publishers, 2000), 37.
67 Murgescu, *România și Europa. Acumularea decalajelor economice (1500–2010)*, 132.
68 Ruxandra Ivan, "Între internaționalismul proletar și național-comunismul autarhic. Politica externă sub regimul Communist," in *Transformarea socialistă. Politici ale regimului Communistântre ideologie și administratie* (Bucharest: Polirom, 2009), 120.

ance with the national interest of that time as it associated the RPR with the Romanian fight for independence, thus reinforcing its frail legitimacy. However, the declaration was not followed by any democratization or liberalization of the regime on the domestic front; for this reason, certain historians stated that "the declaration of April 1964 was PMR/PCR's declaration of independence from the Romanian people."[69] Initiated by Dej, this direction was adopted and developed by his successor, Nicolae Ceaușescu (1918–1989). The latter's disapproval of the invasion of Czechoslovakia also helped create a positive image for the new leader. Ceaușescu criticised the invasion, invoking the principle of non-interference in a state's domestic affairs. Following this declaration, the menace of an USSR military intervention in Romania worked as an enhancing factor for Romanian nationalism as well as a means to legitimate the regime.[70] In addition, Romania received visits from important Western heads of state, such as Charles de Gaulle (1968)[71] or Richard Nixon (1969).[72] At that point, Ceaușescu's popularity reached its climax, both in Romania and abroad.

Many Romanians, however, still wanted and managed to emigrate. Among them were several former political prisoners who, once liberated, left Romania and settled in the West. They were joined by the Jews whose migration, although temporarily interrupted, would occasionally recommence. In 1971, Nicolae Ceaușescu started introducing changes meant to harden the country's internal politics. On 6 June 1971, he declared that the control exercised by the Party over the actions of intellectuals – who worked in contact with the people and who had to be actively involved in the development of the new man, the *homo sovieticus* – would be reinforced.[73] This change determined a new increase in the number of emigrants.

The fourth phase started in the 1970s; the number of emigrants increased progressively and reached its peak in the 1980s. Given the restrictions imposed by the Romanian regime, the number of applications for asylum filed by Romanian citizens was constantly increasing.[74] Nonetheless, as indicated in the chart, the signing of the Helsinki Final Act did not help improve the situation. On the contrary, after 1975 it became even more difficult than before to leave the country. Emigrating turned into a complicated obstacle course. However, Romanian citizens did not give up on the idea of living in the West. They simply decided to circumvent the official system

---

69 Dinu Giurescu, "Cu patru decenii în urmă 'Declaraţia' din aprilie 1964," *Dosarele istoriei* 4 (2004): 16.
70 Gridan, "Du Communisme national au post-Communisme," 113–127.
71 Dan Constantin Mâţa, "Relaţiile franco-române în perioada 1964–1968. Dialog în anii destinderii" (PhD diss., Universitaty "Al. I. Cuza," 2011).
72 Gabriel Stelian Manea, "O lovitură de imagine pentru Nicolae Ceaușescu. Vizita președintelui Richard Nixon la București, 2–3 august 1969," *Studii și materiale de istorie contemporană* 1 (2012): 170–183.
73 Tiberiu Troncota, *România comunistă. Propagandă și cenzură* (Bucharest; Tritonic, 2006) 176–177. See also: Bogdan Ficeac, *Cenzura comunistă și formarea "omului nou"* (Bucharest: Nemira, 1999).
74 United Nations High Commissioner for Refugees, *Asylum Applications in Industrialized Countries: 1980–1999*, (Geneva, November 2001).

and the attempts to illegally cross the borders multiplied. The number of departures became more and more significant, taking into consideration the citizens of German ethnicity and the dissidents who were allowed to leave the country. The emigration of the latter can be better understood in connection with the multiplication of the dissident movements that emerged in all Eastern European countries between 1975 and 1989. They were meant to ensure the respect of the regulations adopted in 1975 as well as of other internal (Constitution) or international documents that the Communist countries had undertaken to respect.[75] In order to contain the effects of the dissident movements that emerged on its territory, the Romanian Government chose to allow – and sometimes even to compel – the emigration of the regime's opponents.

8.3.4 Who, how and where?

But what travelling opportunities did Romanian citizens have? Two main classifications can be identified: 1) temporary travels and migration as well as permanent migration and 2) legal and illegal migration. Temporary travels abroad were generally reserved for a rather privileged minority. They could take place for personal (e.g. tourism, visiting a friend or a family member) or professional reasons (e.g. training, temporary work assignment, participating in a demonstration). During the first years of the Communist regime, travelling abroad was very difficult. Things started to change from the first half of the 1950s, especially after the Decree no. 548 of 1957 was adopted, which facilitated temporary travels abroad. Romanians started spending their holidays abroad more often. From the 1960s, the regime initiated measures aimed at developing individual tourism. At first, the preferred destinations were the USSR, Bulgaria, Czechoslovakia, Poland, Hungary, or the Federal Republic of Germany. At the end of the 1960s and in the ensuing years, the destinations became more diversified, including non-socialist countries as well, such as Austria, France and even Japan.[76] As indicated in the following chart, the transformations that took place in Romania's politics and legislation resulted in a significant increase in the number of tourists travelling abroad.

---

75 Cătănuș, "Disidența și represiune în epoca Nicolae Ceaușescu," 258.
76 Adelina Oana Ștefan, "Between Limits, Lures and Excitement: Socialist Romanian Holidays Abroad during the 1960s–1980s," in *Mobilities in Socialist and Post-Socialist States: Societies on the Move*, eds. Kathy Burrell and Kathhrin Hörschelmann (Hampshire/New York: Palgrave Macmillan, 2014), 87, 91, 93.

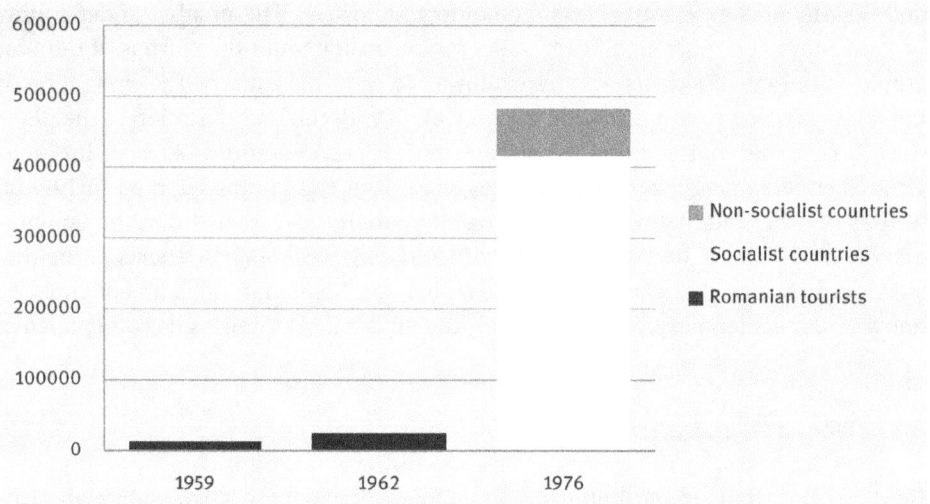

Chart 8.2: Romanian citizens travelling abroad
Source: Adelina Oana Ştefan, "Between Limits, Lures and Excitement: Socialist Romanian Holidays Abroad during the 1960s-1980s," in *Mobilities in Socialist and Post-Socialist States: Societies on the Move*, eds. Kathy Burrell and Kathhrin Hörschelmann (Hampshire/New York: Palgrave Macmillan, 2014), 93.

Despite these extensive travels, a more profound analysis of the tourists' profiles reveals that the average Romanians had only limited access to trips in the non-socialist countries; these still seemed reserved to intellectuals, artists, doctors or politicians. By contrast, the destinations most frequently chosen by the workers were the neighboring countries, the "fraternal countries."[77]

Unlike tourist stays, temporary migration entailed a change of residence for a certain period of time. Most often, these mobilities took place in a strictly regulated bilateral framework. This form of migration encompassed a variety of social categories, from students to professionals, including university professors of Romanian language or the employees of various Romanian institutions located abroad (e.g. embassy, tourist office). With the intention of improving relations between the Western countries and Romania, the latter began signing a series of agreements that would allow its citizens to go abroad for a specific period of time. The first agreement of this sort was signed with France in 1959, followed by one with the USA only a year later.[78] As it was rather difficult for the average Romanian to go abroad, receiving a grant was sometimes their only opportunity to travel to Western countries.

Most scholarships, internships, or training programs were carried out through official exchange agreements. For instance, the Franco-Romanian Cultural Agreement signed in Paris in 1965 stated that a program of cultural, scientific, and technical ex-

---

77 Ştefan, "Between Limits, Lures and Excitement," 95.
78 Barbu, *Vin Americanii!*, 233.

changes would be organized every two years. In this particular framework, several types of exchanges were possible, not only short-term programs, but also grants and specialized scholarships that extended for a longer period of time. Different types of grants were offered based on the status of the scholar in question. For example, the Association for Technical Internships in France (ASTEF) organized internships mostly for experienced researchers and specialists, with financial expenses divided between the two countries.

Exchanges also took place outside the official bilateral agreement, like the special agreements between French and Romanian institutions, or the one between the French National Centre for Scientific Research (CNRS) and the Academy of the Socialist Republic of Romania. Institutions from different fields – such as nuclear energy, information technology, radio, and television – developed bilateral agreements/regulations for exchanging scholars. Private or semi-public institutions, such as the *Alliance française*, also offered scholarships to Romanian students. These exchanges were highly desired by France since they provided real contacts between the two countries, with all the aspects that this entailed. While Romanians sought the scientific and technical contacts and cooperation that were made possible through academic exchanges, they also dreaded them for the very same reason.[79]

The Communist regime wished to limit the mobility of its citizens also for fear that they would decide not to return and temporary travels would turn into permanent migrations. If they wanted to settle abroad, Romanians had two options: the legal or the illegal way. It was long and complicated for Romanians to get the right to settle permanently in a different country. Moreover, it almost always meant they would not be allowed to return or maintain any connection with their friends and family and would lose their social, political, and professional status as well as all their possessions.

Since it was so difficult to emigrate legally, Romanians were forced to find illegal and dangerous ways of leaving the country. Numerous Romanians used to take advantage of a trip abroad to claim political asylum and stay in the West. Such was the case of the dancers of the National Opera House of Bucharest who first sought refuge in Greece in 1970 with the intention of moving to West Germany at a later time. It is worth mentioning one of the most surprising asylum requests of that time, namely one filed by Victor Dumitriu, Romania's former ambassador to France (1964–1968). In 1970, he joined a group of five Romanian tourists who, during their stay in Paris, sought political asylum. If this were to happen, the Romanian trip organizers did not hesitate to put pressure on the asylum seekers in order to convince them to return to Romania. An anonymous source of AFP informed that one of the Roma-

---

[79] Beatrice Scutaru, "French-Romanian Academic Exchanges," in *Beyond the Divide: Entangled Histories of Cold War Europe*, eds. Mikkonen and Koivunen, 124–128, 133. On the French-Romanian exchange of language teachers see Beatrice Scutaru, "Ambassadeurs en pays étranger: la place des lecteurs dans la dipomatie culturelle franco-roumaine (années 1960–1970)," *Valahian Journal of Historical Studies* 20 (2013): 169–185.

nian citizens tried to commit suicide twice in his hotel room, as he refused to return to Romania. Certain athletes, who were in tournaments abroad, decided against returning to Romania at the end of the competition. From 1 to 5 August 1976, during the Montreal Olympic Games, five Romanian athletes (their names were not revealed) along with the soviet diver Serguei Nemtsanov and an Ethiopian journalist filed requests for political asylum to the Canadian Ministry of Immigration.[80] Throughout the Communist era and especially during the last years of the regime, Romania was an important source country of asylum seekers. Besides, as they were coming from a Communist country, their requests had high chances of being successful.[81] For this reason, the Romanian government took utmost interest in the surveillance of the citizens who were abroad for temporary stays.

For instance, the Romanian Embassy in Paris was responsible for maintaining contact with the grant recipients while they were abroad as well as for ensuring that they respected the schedule established prior to their departure. The Embassy maintained continuous contact with most of them, both through correspondence and visits that selected diplomats would pay to students in Grenoble, Strasbourg, and Lyon. For reasons of proximity, students in Paris were contacted more often by the embassy and were sometimes supposed to participate in monthly information sessions. As expected, their actions were also closely monitored. They were even briefly disciplined if their extracurricular activities took up too much of their time. Although most of the scholars were "well-behaved," on some occasions, the Romanian Embassy paid special attention to certain students. For example, the student Alexandru A. was said to maintain very irregular contacts with the embassy, spending most of his time in theatres or visiting museums and exhibitions. He obviously wanted to take advantage of this opportunity and visit Western Europe: besides France, he travelled to Germany and Italy. He even suggested to the Romanian Embassy officials that his mother could come to see him in Paris. The embassy staff firmly "explained" to him that this was not the reason of his being in France and "encouraged" him to behave.[82]

Apart from deciding not to return from abroad, another option was leaving the country illegally, which was a complicated and very dangerous undertaking. Crossing the borders was possible with the help of a people smuggler who generally lived close to the frontier. Most of them were Hungarian or Serbian citizens and they charged substantial amounts of money for their services. The smugglers were also supposed to help the fugitives after they reached the other side of the border. Another means of illegal immigration was trying to cross the borders by speeding up one's car despite the soldiers shooting at it. Some Romanian citizens who were farming in the area took advantage of the custom officers' temporary inattention and crossed

---

80 Scutaru, "Les relations entre les sociétés française et roumaine," 258.
81 Reginald Appelyard, "International Migration Policies: 1950–2000," *International Migration* 39 (2001): 7–20.
82 Scutaru, "French-Romanian academic exchanges in the 1960s," 179–180.

the borders in their agricultural vehicles. There is also mentioning of people attempting to cross the borders by boat or swimming as well as hiding on international trains.[83]

It is difficult to calculate the success rate of this method. According to various researchers, only 10 percent of them managed to leave the country illegally in the 1940s.[84] They exposed themselves to major risks. If caught, they were subject to prosecution under article 245 of the Romanian Penal Code and could face a punishment ranging from six months to three years of imprisonment. In its 1988 report, Amnesty International presented the case of two Romanian citizens, Marin Istoc and his cousin Mihai Bogonaș. For several years, they had tried to join their family in Canada by legal means. Their efforts were interrupted after Romanian authorities threatened to imprison them if they filed more emigration requests. Hence, they decided to leave the country illegally with their families. They were arrested as they were trying to cross the border with Yugoslavia. The two men received a sentence of two years in prison plus a fine that had to be paid throughout the period of their imprisonment. The women and children were set free.[85]

One of the most highly publicized defections of the end of the decade was Nadia Comăneci's, a former star of Romanian gymnastics. When she was only fourteen years old, she achieved the first 10 (the maximum possible score) in the history of gymnastics, thus becoming "the hero of the Montreal Olympic Games." Since then, Nadia Comaneci has inspired entire generations of Romanians and even today she is a very prominent figure in Romania. Her image was skillfully and continuously exploited by the Ceaușescu couple to benefit the regime.[86] On 28 November 1989, she left the country clandestinely, in the company of six other people and helped by a smuggler; she first sought refuge in Hungary and then went to New York. The fleeing of this athlete who was so often associated to the success of the regime represented yet another hard blow to Ceaușescu's image.

Given how extensive illegal emigration was, it is difficult to give the accurate figures concerning Romanian migration. According to an article published in the *New York Times* at the beginning of 1948, there were approximately 300,000 Romanian exiles across the globe.[87] These figures, which concern the whole Romanian population, most probably also take into account the Jewish citizens who left Romania. An article published in *Deutsches Ostdienst,* in 1960, entitled "Das deutsche und das rumänische Volk. Das rumänische Exil heute" [The Romanian and the German people. The Roma-

---

83 Ilarion Tiu, "Migrația ilegală a românilor în anul 1989. Aspecte socio-demografice," [The illegal migration of Romanians in 1989/ Socio-demographic aspects] *Sfera politicii* 166 (2011): 118–119.
84 Horvath, "Migrația internaționala a cetățenilor români după 1989," 201.
85 Amnesty International, *Amnesty International. Rapport 1999* (Paris: Les éditions francophones d'Amnesty International, 1989), 251.
86 Bela Karoly and Nancy Anna Richardson, *Feel no Fear: The Power, Passion and Politics of a Life in Gymnastics* (New York: Hyperion, 1994).
87 *The New York Times,* 6 March 1948.

nian exile today], stated that, compared to the emigration from other Eastern European countries, Romanian exiles represented "a relatively small group." The article referred to approximately 15,000 immigrants, half of them living in Europe, particularly in France, Germany, Italy and Spain. As far as their political orientation was concerned, roughly one third of them (5,000) presumably were former legionnaires. Despite these modest figures, the German publication estimated that the influence of Romanian exile was much more important than what the numbers seemed to imply.[88] In the *Opisul emigrației politice* [The register of political emigration], Mihai Pelin quoted a document that belonged to the *Securitate* and presented the statistics regarding the illegal Romanian emigration between 1941 and 1982. A total of 42,262 Romanians left the country illegally and settled abroad: 3,509 after work-related travels, 31,664 after personal trips and 7,089 crossed the borders illegally.[89]

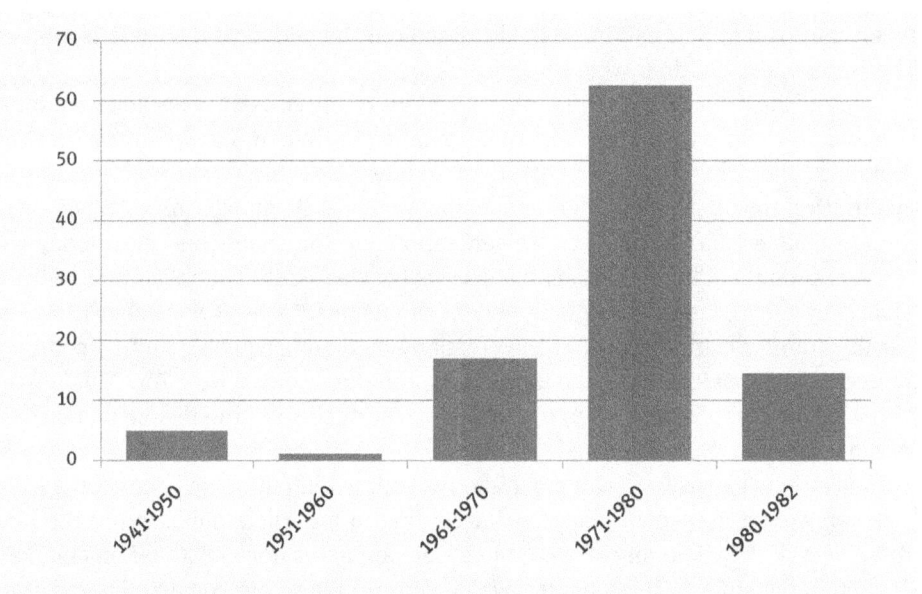

Chart 8.3: Illegal migration of Romanians from 1941 to 1982 (percentage)
Source: Mihai Pelin, *Opisul emigrației politice: destine în 1222 de fișe alcatuite pe baza dosarelor din arhivele Securității* [The index of political emigration: destinies in 1222 sheets composed by the Securitate archives], (Bucharest: Compania, 2002), 7.

---

[88] "Das deutsche und das rumänische Volk. Das rumänische Exil heute," *Deutsches Ostdienst*, 31 August 1960. Quoted in Calafeteanu, *Politică și exil*, 31.
[89] Mihai Pelin, *Opisul emigrației politice: destine în 1222 de fișe alcătuite pe baza dosarelor din arhivele Securității* (Bucharest: Compania, 2002), 7.

The last decade of the regime saw an increase in the number of illegal border crossings. This can be correlated with the economic crisis that Romania was going through at the time. According to the statistics provided by the border police of *Județul* Timiș [the Timiș county, in the southwest of Romania], the number of people who risked their lives trying to cross the frontier with Yugoslavia rose from 913 in 1980 to 2,483 in 1989.[90] The situation was even more dangerous than before, since in the 1980s, in order to contain the phenomenon, custom officers became increasingly violent. According to some sources, they would sometimes open fire on groups of fugitives without warning. This situation turned into a European level issue by the end of 1988 when Hungarian and German newspapers depicted in detail cases of Romanian citizens who were shot mercilessly by custom officers as they were trying to cross the borders. According to the West-German newspaper *Niedersächsische* from 30 December 1988, the Romanian-Yugoslavian frontier was "the bloodiest of Europe": during the year that was about to end, 400 fugitives were presumably shot dead and many others drowned in the Danube. These publications also mentioned the numerous citizens who had managed to leave the country. Roughly 4,000 Romanians arrived in Hungary in 1988 alone.[91] In 1989, the Federal German statistical Bureau registered 8,287 Germans fleeing Romania illegally, having illicitly crossed at least one border. Sometimes, they had to bribe Romanian authorities in order to get to the other side of the border. Others were caught by Yugoslavian authorities and were kept in camps in appalling conditions. Several even died there before they could be sent back to Romania.[92] As indicated by the following chart, ethnic migration prevailed throughout the final decade of the regime.

---

[90] Johann Steiner and Doina Magheti, *Mormintele tac: relatări de la cea mai sângeroasă granița a Europei* (Iasi: Polirom, 2009), 21.
[91] Tiu, "Migrația ilegală a românilor în anul 1989," 116–117.
[92] Vultur, "Pentru un dicționar al lumii comuniste," 102–103.

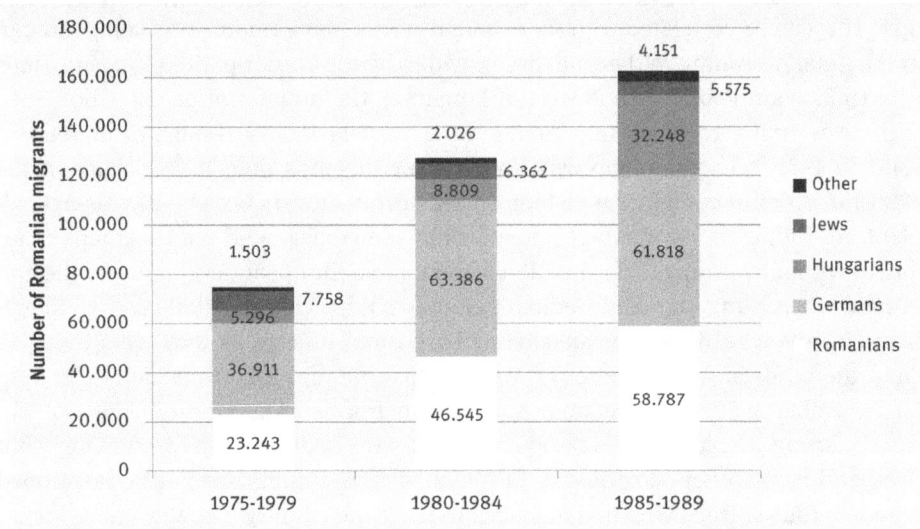

Chart 8.4: Evolution of Romanian migration according to the citizens' ethnic origin (1975–1989)
Source: Ionuț Muntele, "Migrations internationales dans la Roumanie moderne et contemporaine," in *Visibles mais peu nombreux ... Les circulations migratoires roumaines*, ed. Dana Diminescu (Paris: Éditions de la Maison des sciences de l'homme, 2003), 41.

Romanians of German descent represented the largest percentage of immigrants, followed closely by Romanians. While the Hungarian population reached its emigration peak in 1985, the number of Jewish emigrants is the only one that decreased during this time, especially since the former communities had almost completely disappeared. These relocations were made possible thanks to agreements made between Romania and the USA, Germany, Israel and Hungary. These states became the main destination countries, followed by France, Austria, Canada, and Australia. Nonetheless, according to Ion Calafeteanu, from a political point of view, the Romanian exile was present mainly in the USA, especially in Washington and New York, and secondly in France, particularly in Paris. According to the retrospective statements made by certain exiles, the decision to emigrate to the USA was the result of a strategic and geopolitical choice. Given the country's stance on the conflict with the Soviets and the fact that Europe had lost its influence on the matter, by coming to settle in the USA the Romanian migrants were hoping to have a direct influence on American citizens. France, especially Paris, ranked second in terms of its importance for the Romanian political exile. A report of the Romanian Legation in Paris (14 March 1951) stated that the City of Lights played the part of a "filtering unit"; there were journalists, politicians, teachers, military men, former war prisoners, business men, etc. who arrived in Paris. Some of them managed to settle in France and its capital city, whereas others moved further, seeking asylum elsewhere.[93] Moreover, France was the preferred destination of Romanian writers from 1941 to 1989 (60), followed by Germany, the USA, and Israel (30 writers in each country).[94]

8.3.5 A new form of migration: international adoptions

In 1990, following the shock of the "live" Romanian revolution, the world discovered in horror the situation of the Romanian institutionalized children. Images of abnormally thin children living in appalling conditions became known around the world and raised social awareness in Romania. Thus, Romania started receiving support and donations from abroad. Another way of trying to save these children was through international adoption. An adoption is qualified as international when the adopted child's nationality differs from the one of the adoptive parents. This practice started developing in the 1960s and since then it became an international social phenomenon.[95]

Although the adoption of Romanian children after 1990 was a widely publicized topic, it is less known that such international adoptions also took place during Communist times, especially in the 1980s.[96] This brief review of the above-mentioned phenomenon aims to show how this singular migration evolved and in what way the issues related to it differed, before and after 1989. Indeed, until the fall of the Communist regime, international adoption of orphan children was part of Ceaușescu's foreign policy with regard to the West.[97] Beginning in the 1990s, the situation changed dramatically and Romania no longer seemed capable of controlling its international adoption policy, which resulted in the intervention of the European Union (EU).[98]

Since his coming to power, Nicolae Ceaușescu prohibited abortion through the Decree no. 777 of 1966, which was maintained until the fall of the regime. In addition, the state encouraged women to have children, banned all contraception methods,

---

[93] Calafeteanu, *Politică și exil*, 32, 33, 38.
[94] Ion Simuț, "Comentarii critice: Cronologia exilului literar postbelic (II)," *România literară* 24 (2008), http://www.romlit.ro/index.pl/cronologia_exilului_literar_postbelic_ii?caut=cronologia%20exilului (accessed 10 January 2018).
[95] Yves Denéchère, *Des enfants venus de loin. Histoire de l'adoption internationale en France* (Paris: Armand Colin, 2011).
[96] Beatrice Scutaru, "Images d'enfants roumains et médias occidentaux. La construction d'une cause (1989–1990)," *Relations internationales* 161 (2015): 99–112.
[97] Yves Denéchère, "L'adoption des "enfants de Ceaușescu": un fait social au cœur des relations franco-roumaines," *Cahier d'Histoire Immédiate* 44 (2013): 171.
[98] Yves Denéchère and Beatrice Scutaru, "International adoption of Romanian children and Romania's admission to the European Union (1990–2007)," *Eastern Journal of European Studies* 1 (June 2010): 136.

and even ensured regular gynecological check-ups at the workplace.[99] The goal of these pro-birth policies was to increase the Romanian population (25 million inhabitants in 1990 and 30 million in 2000) and thus improve the country's international status.[100] Although at first there was an increase in the number of births, this success also determined an increase in illegal abortions as well as in the occurrence of abandonment and placement of children.[101] For this reason, the government adopted the law no. 3 of 1970 concerning the protection of minors: the state had to look after institutionalized children.[102]

Researchers at The Institute for the Investigation of Communist Crimes and the Memory of the Romanian Exile (IICCMER) estimated that in 1990 there were 125,000 children in the Romanian state placement "system."[103] In numerous situations, the family still held rights concerning the children's upbringing; they were not really considered orphans, hence they could not be adopted. The children who entered the state system of social protection were sent, according to their age and status, to different types of institutions. After time spent in the *leagăne* (from 0 to 3 years old), four options were available for them: returning to their families, adoption or being placed in *case de copii* (children's homes) and *cămine-spital* (children's medical homes). *Casele de copii* were institutions for minors in difficulty: i.e. orphans, abandoned children, minors whose parents were no longer able or allowed to look after them. There was also a category of minors seen as "beyond help." They had physical or mental disabilities and were placed in *cămine-spital*.[104] There were two types of adoption: 1) national (limited to only 450 adoptions per year) and 2) international. For the latter, the procedure was very restrictive, as the Decree no. 137 stated that adoption requests filed by foreign citizens could only be authorized by the state's highest institutions. A case study of the adoption of Romanian children in France will allow us to depict more accurately the issues related to international adoptions under Ceaușescu's rule. Moreover, to our knowledge, there are no

---

99 Gail Kilgman, *Politica duplicității. Controlul reproducerii în Romania lui Ceaușescu* (Bucharest: Humanitas, 2000). See also: Corina Palasanu, "Caracterul restrictiv al politicii pronataliste în Romania comunistă (1966–1989)," in *"Transformarea socialista." Politici ale regimului Communist între ideologie și administrație*, ed. Ruxandra Ivan (Bucharest: Polirom, 2009), 148–174.
100 Peter J. Gloviczki, "Ceaușescu's Children: The Process of Democratization and the Plight of Romania's Orphans," *Critique: A Worldwide Journal of Politics* (2004): 117–123.
101 Several movies address this issue, including Florin Iepan's documentary, *Nascuți la comandă. Decrețeii* (Born on Command: Children of the Decree), 2005, 68 min, and Cristian Mungiu's drama, *4 luni, 3 săptămâni și 2 zile* (4 months, 3 weeks and 2 days), 2007, 113 min.
102 Beatrice Scutaru, "Du droit de protection à la protection des droits des enfants: acteurs et processus réformateur en Roumanie (1995–2004)," in *Droits des enfants au XXe siècle. Pour une histoire transnationale*, eds. Yves Denéchère and David Niget (Rennes: Presses Universitaires de Rennes, 2014), 83.
103 Luciana M. Jinga, "Concluzii," in *Politica pronatalistă a regimului Ceaușescu*, 2nd vol., *Instituții și practici*, eds. Luciana M. Jinga and Florin S. Soare (Iasi: Polirom, 2001), 248–249.
104 Luciana M. Jinga, "Abandon familial. Ocrotire. Distrofici," in *Politica pronatalistă a regimului Ceaușescu*, 194–229.

other studies that address this topic from the point of view of Romania's bilateral diplomatic relations during the Communist era.

While Romania had a substantial number of institutionalized children in the 1970s, in France there was a shortage of adoptable children. In addition, the improvement of means of communication facilitated cross-border adoption. These two factors facilitated the development of the adoption of Romanian children in France and French citizens adopted approximately 500 Romanian children in the 1980s. Although in 1981, with 145 adopted children, Romania is the fourth source country (after South Korea, India and Colombia), in 1982 a first significant decrease was recorded. Due to the slow pace of the procedures as well as the limited number of granted requests (only 1 out of 10), the French Ministry of Social Affairs concluded that "the Romanian government is officially opposed to the adoption of [Romanian] children by foreign citizens" and thus tried to encourage adoptions from other countries. This situation was also related to the degradation of the Franco-Romanian relations. That very year, François Mitterrand cancelled his state visit and criticized Romania for its disrespect of human rights. As a reaction to this state of affairs, the adopting families started rallying and putting pressure on their elected representatives to improve the situation. Therefore, every time a French minister came to Romania or vice versa, requests would be made to simplify the adoption procedures and unblock the ongoing applications. France started "playing the part of the supplicant, while putting pressure on the Romanian regime." As stated by the French historian of international adoptions, Yves Denéchère, "adoption was a very singular aspect of the Franco-Romanian relations and one working rather to Ceaușescu's advantage."[105]

Despite the rallying, the number of Romanian children adopted in France continued to decrease (92 in 1983, 70 in 1984, only 41 in 1985 and 30 in 1987), reaching zero in February 1989, when Franco-Romanian relations were at their worst.[106] During these last months of the Ceaușescu regime, hundreds of families waited to no avail for the Council of State to authorize children, whom they had known (in certain cases, for years), to join them. The new authorities allowed the children whose files were complete to go to France only after the fall of the communist regime. On 6 January 1990, sixty-three children joined their adoptive families in France, followed by those who had been waiting to go to Italy, Belgium and Switzerland. After the departure of these children, which in a way marked the end of the Ceaușescu era, Romania opened its borders for international adoption (law 11/1990).[107] Following the abrogation of the Decree no. 137 of 1966, there were no more limitations on international adoption. In 1990, most of the adopted children went to the United States (914), followed by the UK (600), Italy (520), Canada (400), France (311), and Greece (200). From January to June 1991, the number of adoptions increased significantly: the

---

[105] Denéchère, "L'adoption des 'enfants de Ceaușescu'," 172–184.
[106] Denéchère, "L'adoption des 'enfants de Ceaușescu'," 178.
[107] Scutaru, *Les relations entre les sociétés française et roumaine*, 486, 545.

USA was at the top of the ranking with 2,594 adoptions (28 percent were children adopted abroad by American citizens), in Italy there were 1,009 adoptions recorded and only 688 in France. In 1990 and 1991, according to UNICEF, 10,000 Romanian children had been adopted.[108]

Adoption requests continued to increase. The abuses were numerous. The dubious conditions in which certain adoptions were fulfilled, going as far as acts of trading children, and their coverage in the media led the Romanian authorities to impose a moratorium in 1991 (law 48/1991). Adoption procedures resumed in 1992. From 1992 to 1996, the Romanian legislation was gradually reviewed in order to ensure that adoptions were appropriately regulated.[109] Despite all these measures, abuses were still common. Romania came under a lot of pressure and international adoptions became an important issue in terms of the country's accession to the European Union. While the European Union, through the actions of Baroness Nicholson, took measures to ensure an improved control and a decrease in the number of adoptions, the different states tried to protect their national interests. For this reason, Romania imposed a new moratorium in 2004, putting an end to the international adoption of its children. The actors of this singular type of adoption, the adopted children, have by now become adults and have started writing a new page in the history of international adoptions. Some have organized in groups and associations, wishing to maintain a contact with Romania and search for their origins.

8.4 Political activities in exile

Once Romanians overcame all the obstacles and managed to emigrate, they had to face new challenges.[110] After leaving everything behind, they had to rebuild their lives by finding employment and a place to live. Although this is characteristic of all types of migration – both older and more recent – the context of the Cold War and the fact that returning to Romania was virtually impossible put extra pressure on those who had to start anew in a new country with a language and culture other than their own.

8.4.1 Building a new life on the other side of the Iron Curtain

Most emigrants were confronted, at least during the first years, with a particularly difficult financial situation. According to Ion Calafeteanu, there were also rich people

---

108 Peter Selman, "Intercountry Adoption in Europe (1998–2006): patterns, trend and issues," paper presented at the Annual Conference of the Social Policy Association (Edinburgh, June 2008).
109 Denéchère, Scutaru, "International adoption of Romanian children," 138–141.
110 Anca Baicoianu, "Exile and Identity Reconfiguration," *Journal of World Literature* 3 (2018): 10–22.

among the exiles, but they were not directly involved in the fight against the regime. Some of them would offer financial support for anti-Communist activities and occasionally help certain exiles. The personal accounts of numerous Romanians depict their permanent financial issues and the constant fear of being left without money. Even the Romanian Legation in Paris mentioned in 1952 the "particularly difficult" material situation with which most exiles were confronted.[111] Virgil Tănase (1945-), who had been living in France since 1977, gave a detailed account on this topic:

> To make ends meet, I had all sorts of small jobs...I worked for a small TV-repairing company in Montrouge. I put fliers in mailboxes. In 1980, a bit before Alexandre – my second son – was born, I worked as a janitor to manage the extra expenses [...]. A Romanian poet, who had written twenty volumes of poetry and started being published by Gallimard Jeunesse, had the best job in the building – at the parking area – his main mission being to get the tips. Another Romanian, with a PhD in philosophy, along with a painter, was the doorman.[112]

This Romanian author had his first novel published by an important French publishing house in 1976 without the agreement of the Ceausescu regime, which was considered an offence.[113] He was granted permission to go abroad for the launch of this book. He stated that the Romanian authorities had advised him to stay in the West for as long as possible in order to avoid imprisonment. He thus started a long alternation between small jobs and literary activities. The "ideal" solution for him, as well as for other authors, that would allow him to dedicate himself entirely to writing, was a scholarship for a PhD thesis or from a foundation like Ford. However, these sources of funding were scarce and hard to find. Coping strategies had to be found: some worked for publishing houses writing reviews of foreign books, others worked as journalists for the print media or the radio, or even as chess teachers like the writer Dumitru Țepeneag (1937-). Oftentimes, those who had a pre-established immigration project, such as building a literary career in France, accepted to live in these precarious conditions. They agreed to scarify their status hoping they would achieve their goal in the future.[114]

Many of these immigrants were also involved in numerous political and cultural activities aimed at creating a community and preserving Romanian culture, language, and traditions despite the lack of a direct contact with their homeland. This approach is not intended as an exhaustive monographic overview of the exile's organizations,

---

111 Calafeteanu, *Politică și exil*, 29.
112 Blandine Tézé-Delafon and Virgil Tănase, *Ma Roumanie: Entretiens avec Blandine Tézé-Delafon* (Paris: Ramsay, 1990), 157. See also Elena Botezatu, "Fragmente de 'destin'. Dramaturgi români din diaspora de limbă franceză," *Comunicare interculturală și literatură* 1 (2017): 94–106.
113 Virgil Tănase, *Portrait d'un homme à la faux dans un paysage marin* (Paris: Flammarion, 1976).
114 Swanie Potot, "Migrations et construction indentitaire: le cas des Roumains en France," in *Identifications ethniques. Rapport de pouvoir, Compromis, Territoire*, ed. Hélène Bertheleu (Paris: Armand Colin, 1995), 96.

associations and leading figures, but as an attempt to depict, through a series of examples, the variety of the activities in which Romanian migrants were involved. Their choices allowed me to identify the main forms of organization as well as the functions of this migration during the Cold War. As mentioned before, the most important political actions were organized in the United States and in France. The majority of the examples quoted in this chapter will therefore refer to individuals and groups established in these two countries.

8.4.2 Political mobilization: between democratic tradition and anti-Communist fight

During the Communist period, the political mobilization of Romanian exiles gave way to several forms of dissidence against the regime albeit without managing to change the course of history. Some of the Romanian migrants felt they had to show Western citizens what they thought to be the truth about the Romanian regime. When asked why he decided to act against the Romanian regime and not just enjoy his life as a free man, Ion Dumitriu (a Romanian in exile in Western Germany) stated that it was because of "the commitment towards [his] friends [...] to be the massager of their cry of despair and the tragic reality they were living."[115] By founding organizations and newspapers, writing literary reviews, publishing articles in well-known Western newspapers and taking a public stand, they continued to fight the Ceaușescu regime. They insisted on the gap between the perception and the reality of the Romanian regime. These actions were aimed at Romanians living in Romania, Romanians living abroad, host countries, and the political representatives of host countries.

Unfortunately, until the mid-1970s, their actions were unsuccessful. For example, in June 1970, right before Nicolae Ceaușescu's visit to France, a group of former Romanian political leaders, exiled in Paris, sent the French president and selected French newspapers a file criticizing the Romanian leader and the country's situation. I could access the file at the archives of the French Ministry of Foreign Affairs. However, there was no official reaction from the president and the newspapers did not mention the information provided by the exiles. The end of the 1960s and the beginning of the 1970s are Ceaușescu's moment of glory at an international level. His stand during the Prague Spring and Charles de Gaulle's and Nixon's visits to Romania created the myth of an "independent" Communist leader, a key element for the *Détente* process. Even if Western policy-makers were aware of the reality of the Romanian Communist regime, it was more difficult to change the public's perception. A shift can be observed in the second half of the 1970s, following the publication of Alexandr Solzhenitsyn's book, *The Gulag Archipelago*, and the signing of the Helsinki Final Act. From 1975 onwards, several protest movements were born in Eastern Europe, which started receiving broad media coverage. Criticism developed against all the members

---

115 Titu Popescu, *Convorbiri despre exil și literatură* (Bucharest: Jurnalul literar, 2001), 60.

of the Warsaw Pact mainly concerning human rights violations. More and more articles began to be published on this subject and Romania was no exception. Political actions initiated by Romanian migrants can therefore be divided in two main periods: 1) before the signing of the Helsinki Final Act exiles strongly mobilized but the success of their actions was very limited; 2) after 1975, the geopolitical context legitimated the movements in favor of human rights.[116]

Romanians created national and international associations and organizations in all the countries in which they settled.

The Romanian National Committee was the government of the "democratic parties in exile" after 1945. It was founded in New York on 6 April 1949 and recognized by King Michael. It was composed of ex-officials of the National-Peasant Party and the Liberal Party. They were charged with "representing the Romanian nation until liberation" and with fighting "for the independence of Romania and restor[ing] the human rights and fundamental freedoms destroyed by the Bucharest puppet government at the dictation of Moscow." They collaborated with the National Committee for a Free Europe and the US State Department. The frictions inside the organization caused a double rupture before 1955, attracting Americans' disapproval. It had to dissolve in 1972 as it lacked external financial support.[117] In the 1980s, there was an attempt to recreate the Committee. Negotiations were complicated, especially due to differences of opinion between representatives of the Romanian exile in the UK (Ion Rațiu) and France (Radu Câmpeanu). The new organization was founded in 1984 and took the name Free Romanians' World Union.

In the Federal Republic of Germany, one could mention the Free Romanians' Associations from RFG, the Romanians' Association from Southern Germany, the Society for Human Rights from Frankfurt, the Anti Yalta League or the National Front for Romanians' Union created in Freiburg.[118] In the United Kingdom, the first Romanian initiative dates back to 1940, with the Free Romanians' Movement. Virgil-Viorel Tilea (1896–1972), one of the initiators of this project, was a Romanian diplomat and ambassador in the UK during World War II. He refused to return to Romania in 1940 and became one of the main figures of Romanian exile in the UK. This association is also known as the Romanian National Committee from England. One of the members of the Movement was Ion (Iancu) Rațiu (1917–2000) who played an essential role among the Romanian community from England. In 1940, when King Carol I fled Ro-

---

[116] Nicoleta Şerban, "Românii din exilul American și poziția lor față de proiectul de sistenatizare rurală," *Studii și Materiale de Istorie Contemporană* 15 (2016): 80–92.
[117] Marius Petraru, "The Romanian Government in Exile in the United States: 1947–1975," in *The Inauguration of "Organized Political Warfare": The Cold War Organizations Sponsored by the National Committee for a Free Europe/Free Europe Committee*, ed. Katalin Kádár Lynn (Saint Helena: Helena History Press, 2013), 121–198.
[118] Sorin Gabriel Ioniță, *Publicațiile românești din exil despre problematica respectării drepturilor omului în România, 1975–1989* (Bucharest: Institutul Național pentru Memoria Exilului Românesc, 2009) 74–75.

mania and this led to the formation of the National Legionary State, Ion Rațiu resigned and asked for asylum in the UK. He was, at that time, a counsellor at the Romanian Legation in London. Rațiu continued living in London even after the Communists came to power and became involved in the fight against totalitarianism. He contributed regularly to the BBC Romanian services, Radio Free Europe (RFE) and the Voice of America.[119] He was one of the initiators of the British-Romanian Association (ACARDA) in 1956. Very active in the 1970s, this association advocated for the organization of exile based on democratic principles.[120] ACARDA was the most important exile organization in the UK but its impact was more limited than that of the League for the Defense of Human Rights of Romania in Paris.[121]

As already mentioned, Romanian exiles in France were very active in the fight against the Communist regime. The Association of the Former Political Prisoners in Romania (1977) and the Group from Paris (1982) were among the associations and organizations created in France.

One of the most effective organizations in the fight against Communism was the League for the Defense of Human Rights of Romania in Paris. Following the signing of the Helsinki Final Act, Paul Goma initiated the first human rights protest in Romania (1977). Paul Goma (1935-) is a Romanian writer and a leading anti-Communist dissident. In 1971, following the publication of his novel *Ostinato* in Western Germany, he was expelled from the Communist Party he had joined in 1968. In 1977, his public letter calling for respect for human rights in Romania and for Romanians to sign Charter 77 was read on Radio Free Europe. As a result, he was expelled from the Romanian Writers' Union and arrested by the *Securitate*.[122] The Romanian regime reacted rapidly, trying to contain the spread of this action and most of the internal and international media coverage.[123]

In order to inform the international public opinion about the goals of this movement and the reaction of the Romanian regime towards its members, by February 1977, the founding of a Committee for the defense of Human Rights seemed necessary. Soon thereafter, other cases of persecution perpetrated by the Socialist Republic of Romania came to the Committee's attention. These concerned the miners' strike in the Jiu Valley that took place in 1977, the persecution of Romanian citizens for their religious beliefs and of the members of the Free Trade Union of the Working People in Romania (1979). It was also during 1979 that the Committee changed its status and became the League for the Defense of Human Rights in Romania (LDHR). This choice was meant to provide the organization with a clearer

---

119 Andrei Catalin Galița, "Instituții ale exilului românesc din Franța și Marea Britanie. O abordare comparativă" (M. A. diss., University of Bucharest, 2014), 81–83.
120 Nedelcu, "Des 'ennemis du people' aux 'Roumains de partout'," 43.
121 Galița, "Instituții ale exilului românesc din Franța și Marea Britanie," 117–121.
122 Ana Cătănuș "Paul Goma Scriitorul devenit dissident," in *Paul Goma și exilul etern*, ed. Liliana Corobca (Oradea: Ratio et Revelatio, 2016), 62–76.
123 Liliana Corobca, *Paul Goma și exilul etern*.

legal status. The League's main goal was to collect and communicate information on human rights violations perpetrated by the Romanian Communist regime to international organizations and the media. The League wanted to emphasize the gap between Romania's international image and the realities of its domestic politics.[124]

Several Romanians living in France and some French citizens interested in the realities in Eastern countries were members of the League. The most active ones included Constantin Cesianu, Mihai Korne, Mihnea Berindei, Sanda Stolojan, Maria Brătianu, Marie-France Ionesco, Dan Bosnief-Paraschivescu, Anne and François Planche. Anne Planche had studied in Cluj in the 1950s. During her stay with a peasant family from Ardeal, the central region of Romania, she witnessed the collectivization of agriculture. Upon her return to France, she continued to show interest in Romania's evolution and played an active part in anti-Communist movements.[125] The others were well-known members of the Romanian diaspora in Paris. Constantin Cessianu was a former political prisoner who came to France in 1967. Soon after settling in, he initiated a series of actions against the Romanian Communist regime. Mihai Korne fled the country in 1949. He was known to the *Securitate* for spreading hateful pamphlets about the Socialist Republic of Romania. Maria Brătianu came from a very famous and old family of liberal politicians and victims of the Communist regime. Marie-France Ionesco is the daughter of Eugen Ionesco, the well-known playwright living in Paris.[126] Sanda Stolojan came to France in 1961 and was the interpreter to the French president. She even accompanied Charles de Gaulle in his official trip to Romania in May 1968.[127]

The main human right violations against which the League fought included the lack of freedom of association, the existence of political prisoners, the obstruction of family reunification, the disappearance of dissidents and the development of repressive legislation. One of the League's first important actions took place in 1980 during the Madrid Second Follow-Up Helsinki Act Conference. It was the first time the LDHR got involved in an international action. The League intervened in order to obtain the release of those who had been unjustly arrested or committed to a mental institution and for those who wished to receive the right to leave the country. First, the League's members prepared files on Romanian legislation, the Free Trade Union of the Working People from Romania, on political prisoners and against labor camps, the abusive practice of psychiatry, the lack of freedom of movement and religious persecution. These files were sent to all the main Western heads of state present at the conference. The file also included a letter demanding the creation of a commission to investigate the complaints regarding human rights violations in Romania, which

---

[124] Beatrice Scutaru, "The Romanian Anti-Communist Resistance: The League for the Defense of Human Rights of Romanian from Paris (1979–1989)," in *Anti-Communist Resistance in Central and Eastern Europe*, ed. Peter Jasek, 843.
[125] Vasile Paraschiv, *Lupta mea pentru sindicatele libere din România* (Iasi: Polirom, 2005), 67.
[126] Scutaru, "The Romanian Anti-Communist Resistance," 844.
[127] Pelin, *Opisul emigrației politice*, 309–310.

would put pressure on Romanian authorities. Secondly, the LDHR organized a press conference during which files were given to media representatives. The League also spoke against the idea of holding the next conference in Bucharest. In February 1981, right before the end of the Madrid Conference, a paper entitled *Bucharest should not be the next Helsinki Review Conference* was written by Helsinki Watch. It read: "we strongly oppose this choice of location. A conference in Bucharest would appear to condone or minimize the manifold violations of human rights that exist in Romania [...] it would virtually eliminate any opportunity for the kind of active citizens' participation that has characterized the conference in Madrid."[128] Romania's image was affected by this event and the conference did not take place in Bucharest. Helsinki Watch was convinced by the information provided by the LDHR. However, it is important to emphasize that the general context made this success possible. Indeed, by the beginning of the 1980s, Romania's and especially Nicolae Ceaușescu's image abroad had greatly changed. More and more criticism became public and actions like the one organized by the League were convincing.

Besides the desire to help the victims and force the Communist regime to change its actions, this constant pressure and struggle to prove human rights abuses in Romania was also intended to provide Bucharest with proof of international monitoring. Criticism against Ceaușescu and his regime intensified year after year until it reached a point of no return at the end of the 1980s.

8.4.3 The mission to inform

Ever since the end of the Second World War, Romanian exiles tried to show Westerners the truth about the Communist regime's domestic policy. Exiles acted both individually and collectively. They gathered and disseminated information on the situation in Romania in matters related to human rights violations, the country's economic situation, living and working conditions, and Ceaușescu's frenzied cult of personality.

There were different means of obtaining information on Romania's latest developments: by reading Romanian newspapers, listening to national radio broadcastings and watching national TV, talking to family members and friends living in Romania, meeting with Romanians visiting France. Sometimes Romanians contacted Romanian migrants they knew or whom they thought influential in order to inform them of their actions. Indeed, for dissidents, being known on the other side of the Iron Curtain was a guarantee of safety. It was more difficult for the regime to make them disappear without arousing any reaction from the West. Their aim was to create enough contacts among well-known and influential Romanian immigrants

---

128 Scutaru, "The Romanian Anti-Communist Resistance," 851–852.

and Western citizens who could put international pressure on the Romanian government in case something happened to them.

This information was then forwarded to newspapers, radios, international organizations (Amnesty International, International Federation for Human Rights, Helsinki Watch), and governments. Émigrés attempted to raise awareness on human rights violations in Romania through press releases and press conferences, articles in newspapers, radio or TV shows, letters to policy-makers and street protests. Some exiles worked for Western newspapers, public service broadcasting (BBC, Reuters), or radios (Radio Free Europe). Prior to ministerial or even presidential visits to Romania, exiles had made a habit of sending files on human rights violations in Romania to delegation members requesting their intervention on behalf of individuals who were detained or missing (e.g. Caliciu Dumitreasa, Vasile Paraschiv, Doina Cornea). They also reacted to public statements made by politicians. For example, in April 1977, Maria Brătianu sent a letter to French president Valéry Giscard d'Estaing in response to an interview in which he spoke about the dissidents' situation in Eastern Europe and the Soviet Union. After presenting the situation of Paul Goma, she asked the president to intervene for his release because "France must report [human rights violations] and help those brave men" who fight for respect.[129]

It was indeed difficult for Romanians to make their protest known on the other side of the Iron Curtain. There were no foreign media representatives in Romania and few Western journalists were able to enter the country, compared to other European Communist states. Their visibility on the other side of the Iron Curtain depended almost exclusively on personal or occasional links with foreign countries and their access to radio stations such as RFE, Voice of America, or the BBC.[130]

RFE, considered "the most influential politically oriented radio station in history,"[131] acted as a "surrogate domestic broadcaster."[132] Among all the national Departments, the Romanian one had the biggest number of listeners. This is partly because Romania was the first country to stop jamming in 1963. RFE was therefore listened under better conditions than in other countries. This success could also be attributed to the popularity and professionalism of Noël Bernard (1925–1981), considered to be the best director of the Romanian Department.[133]

---

129 Scutaru, "The Romanian Anti-Communist Resistance," 849.
130 Comisia prezidențială pentru analiza dictaturii comuniste din România, *Raport final* (Bucharest, 2006) 367, https://www.wilsoncenter.org/sites/default/files/RAPORT%20FINAL_%20CADCR.pdf (accessed 25 July 2018).
131 Arch Puddington, *Broadcasting Freedom: The Cold War Triumph of Radio Free Europe and Radio Liberty* (Lexington: The University Press of Kentucky, 2000), ix.
132 Michael Nelson, *War of the Black Heavens: The Battles of Western Broadcasting in the Cold War* (London: Brassey's, 1997), xiv.
133 Ioana Macrea-Toma, *Radio Free Europe in Paris: The Paradoxes of an Ethereal Opposition* (M.A. diss., Central European University, 2008), 49–50.

The total broadcasting time of the Romanian Department was eighty hours a week. The most appreciated programs seemed to be – as in the case of the other departments – the "News" program, the "Political Program," "Censored News from the Press of R.S.R.," "Talking to the Listeners," the "Editorial of the Week," "The Occident seen by the Romanians." "American Actuality," "Women Chronicle," or "Music" – mass culture programs – were less known but played the role of widening the listener's horizons and attracting them to the political ones. Monica Lovinescu's programs "lie at the intersection between coverage of the West and criticism of the East, between literary reviewing and political indictment. She analyzes events, organizes round tables and insures the lobby for the dissidents, everything being done from Paris, not from Munchen." Monica Lovinescu (1923–2008) was already living in Paris – having received a scholarship from the French Cultural Institute – when the Communists came to power in Romania. She then decided to stay abroad and soon became involved in the fight against the Romanian regime.[134] Her programs summed a total of one hour and twenty minutes of weekly transmission since 1967. She is often considered "the second most important editor after Noël Bernard."[135] According to Iulia Vladimirov, she was "for hundreds of thousands of Romanians, [...] the voice which dares to present [...] the true face of Communist Romania."[136]

Another important role played by RFE was that of "constructing 'cases' of dissent." A case like that of Goma, "constructed by multi-level activism," is a perfect illustration:

> RFE reads Goma's censored novels, broadcasts Goma's declarations, mediates the dialogue between the signatories and keeps them informed about each other, participates (as a witness endowed with "doubtful subjectivity") to the manifestations held in Paris in favor of liberating Paul Goma, obtains legitimating testimonies from prominent French intellectuals and, last but not least, insures multi-faceted concentrated coverage of the event.[137]

Moreover, the importance of Goma's action is emphasized by RFE by the doubling of the moral capital of his action with an aesthetic dimension, by Monica Lovinescu's defense of the artistic quality of his work. After Goma is expelled from the Romanian Writers' Union and his skills as a writer are thus contested, RFE felt it had the duty to

---

134 Édith Lhomel, "Monica Lovinescu, la force d'une voix," *Le Courrier des pays de l'Est* 1067 (2008), 109. See also Iulian Boldea, "Exilul literar românesc. Dileme și trauma identitare," *Comunicare interculturală și Literatură* 21 (2014): 59–69.
135 Macrea-Toma, *Radio Free Europe in Paris*, 56–57.
136 Iulia Vladimirov, *Monica Lovinescu în documentele Securității. 1949–1989* (Bucharest: Humanitas, 2012) 9, 18. See also Dumitru-Mircea Buda, "Două jurnale din exil în lecture contemporane," *Studia Universitatis Petru Maior* 10 (2011): 109–119.
137 Macrea-Toma, *Radio Free Europe in Paris*, 68–69.

defend him.¹³⁸ Indeed, Lovinescu considered ethics an essential requirement for a writer working in a totalitarian regime.¹³⁹

8.4.4 Culture as resistance

As seen on the political level, very rapidly upon their arrival abroad, Romanians organized themselves and sometimes even reproduced structures and communities they had known at home. The same happened at the cultural level. One of these actions was the recreation of the Charles 1st Romanian University Foundation in Paris on 8 December 1950.¹⁴⁰ This decision was taken in order to safeguard the freedom of expression and thought that had been eliminated by the Communist regime. Besides promoting Romanian culture and identity in the West, the foundation also aimed at "uniting all free Romanians," meaning those living outside national borders. To attain this goal, it supported and encouraged all forms of cultural and artistic expression. Its members were also continuously monitoring the way Romania was referred to in French media. If and when they thought the coverage did not reflect reality, they did not hesitate to contact newspapers, radio, and TV stations asking for rectification. Unfortunately, these initiatives were not very successful.¹⁴¹

The foundation also supported the publication of books and journals in both Romanian and French. Publications in French (e. g. *Bulletin scientifique roumain, Études roumaines*) aimed to raise awareness and spark interest in the situation of Romanian citizens among Westerners. In order to allow exiled writers the possibility to express themselves in their mother tongue, the foundation also supported publications in Romanian, such as the journal *Ființa Românească* (The Romanian Being). This is not something new. The first journal published by the members of the Romanian diaspora dates back to 1850 (*România viitoare* [Future Romania]), in the United States. These publications were initially aimed at soothing nostalgia.

After the Communists came to power, many publications in exile became explicitly anti-Communist. Romanians founded journals in nearly all the countries in which they settled: England, Germany, Belgium, Canada, Argentina, Australia, Italy, Finland, the Soviet Union, and Yugoslavia. The most important and varied journals could be found in the United States where researchers have identified more than 180 publications between 1900 and 1989. The numerous Romanian writers living in

---

138 Ioana Macrea-Toma, "Între politică și morală. Percepția drepturilor omului la Radio Europa Liberă prin cazul lui Paul Goma," in *Paul Goma si exilul etern*, ed. Liliana Corobca, 35–51.
139 Oana Fotache, "Troubled Heritage. Monica Lovinescu and the Aestretical Tradiction in Romanian Literary Historiography," *Studia UBB Philologia* 2 (2012): 53–61.
140 Florin Manolescu, *Enciclopedia exilului literar românesc 1945–1989. Scriitori, reviste, instituții, organizații* (Bucharest: Compania, 2003), 323. The Foundation had to stop its activities in 1974 due to financial problems.
141 Scutaru, "La Roumanie à Paris," 6.

Paris also published a great number of journals.¹⁴² Romanian exiled writers formed an "intellectual international network." Authors such as Mircea Eliade, Virgil Ierunca, and Vintilă Horia kept in touch, launched new journals, and helped each other publish in the publications existing in their countries of residence.¹⁴³ However, if the large number of publications is a sign of cultural effervescence, it also shows the lack of unity, the divisions, and power struggles, which characterized Romanian exile.

These publications helped maintain a connection among the Romanians living abroad and provided information on various events taking place in Romania and abroad. Just as the migration of exiles, the existence of these publications – even those with no political agenda – can also be regarded as a form of anti-Communist existence and a form of resistance to censorship.¹⁴⁴ As the publications were mostly published in Romanian, they were aimed especially at Romanians in exile. Their influence on Western societies was very limited.¹⁴⁵

Some exiles established good connections with the citizens and institutions of their host country. For example, Leonid Mămăliga (1921–2001) built solid relations with publishers, members of ministries and other institutions with whom he came in contact through his professional activity.¹⁴⁶ For this reason *Securitatea* considered him the Romanian migrant with the best professional and economic situation, "the Romanian magnate from Paris." It is also true that from time to time he helped newly arrived Romanians who found themselves in difficult financial situations.¹⁴⁷ However, he is mostly known for his cultural activity. In 1954, he began organizing monthly literary cenacles at his house where texts in Romanian were read. Romanian writers living in France, many of them involved in anti-Communist activities, participated regularly in these meetings. Sometimes non-exiled writers visiting Paris were also invited to read passages from their work. The readings were followed by discussions of Romanian literature and cultural policy (censorship).¹⁴⁸

One unique initiative – also in Paris – is that of Dumitru Țepeneag (1937-) who wanted to create "an international literary journal in Paris." In 1975, he launched

---

142 Ilie Rad, ed., *Jurnalism românesc in exil și diaspora* (Bucharest: Tritonic, 2012), 31–54. See also Mihaela Albu, "Presa literară din exil – Mijloc și sursă de continuitate a culturii românești" (Luceafărul. Paris, 1948–1949), *Studii de Știința și Cultură* 3 (2009): 72–77. Confusing footnote. Difficult to say what belongs where

143 Mihaela Albu and Dan Anghelescu, *Luceafarul – o reconstituire* (Bucharest: Ideea Europeană, 2009), 60.

144 Nicoleta Sălcudeanu, "The Cultural Cold War in Romania," *Studia Universitatis Petru Maior* 12 (2012): 30–35.

145 Luciana Radut-Draghi, "'Luceafarul' et 'Kultura', deux premises de modèles de pratiques diasporiques parisiennes," *Revista comunicare* 27 (2012): 174–175.

146 Between 1953 and 1976, Leonid Mamaliga was a sales manager for Colos Rex Rotary, a Duch company selling typewriters, computers, and scanners.

147 Manolescu, *Enciclopedia exilului literar românesc*, 57–59.

148 Scutaru, "Les relations entre les sociétés française et roumaine," 263–264.

Cahiers de l'Est whose objective was to present the Western public with "real" Eastern literature, taking into consideration only aesthetic and not political selection criteria.[149] This is something that had never been done before: for the first time a citizen who was not an exiled, legally residing in France, launched a journal independent of the Romanian regime in a Western country. Indeed, Dumitru Țepeneag had always stated that he never contemplated permanently leaving Romania in order to live in France. He actually wished to be able to move back and forth between the two countries so he could benefit from both influences in his writing. It is also the first journal launched by East-Central European migrants to be published in French and aiming to play the role of a common "platform." The 20 numbers published between 1975 and 1980 featured Polish, Romanian, Hungarian, Bulgarian, Czech, Serbian, and Croatian authors. Polish literature was, by far, the most represented, followed by Romanian texts, while Bulgarian texts were the least represented. However, despite the declared wish to choose the authors published in the journal only based on cultural and not political criteria, this proved to be impossible. Indeed, given the geopolitical context, politics could not be completely absent. Beginning in 1977, the numbers became increasingly politicised: the double number 9–10 was dedicated to the fight for human rights especially in Czechoslovakia and Romania. This gravitation towards a more political character is confirmed in the following numbers where political essays started becoming more numerous and the percentage of literary texts decreases.[150]

8.5 Migration since 1989

In 1990, after almost forty-five years of confinement, Romania re-enters the international migration flow. One of the first measures undertaken by the new government was granting free access to passports. Leaving the country became possible and free from obstacles. Therefore, as passport administration and international travel were relaxed, new possibilities were created for Romanian citizens. From 1990 to 2007, when Romania became a member of the EU, scholars identify three periods of the Romanian migratory movement: 1990–1995, 1996–2001, and 2002–2006.[151] In 1990, emigration reached its peak, with 95,000 Romanians moving abroad.[152]

---

149 Radut-Draghi, "'Luceafarul' et 'Kultura'," 176.
150 Catherine Durandin, Le Paris de Paul Goma," in *Le Paris des étrangers depuis 1945*, eds. Antoine Marès and Pierre Milza, 183.
151 Diminescu, *Visibles mais peu nombreux...*, 46.
152 Horvath, "Country profile: Romania," 3

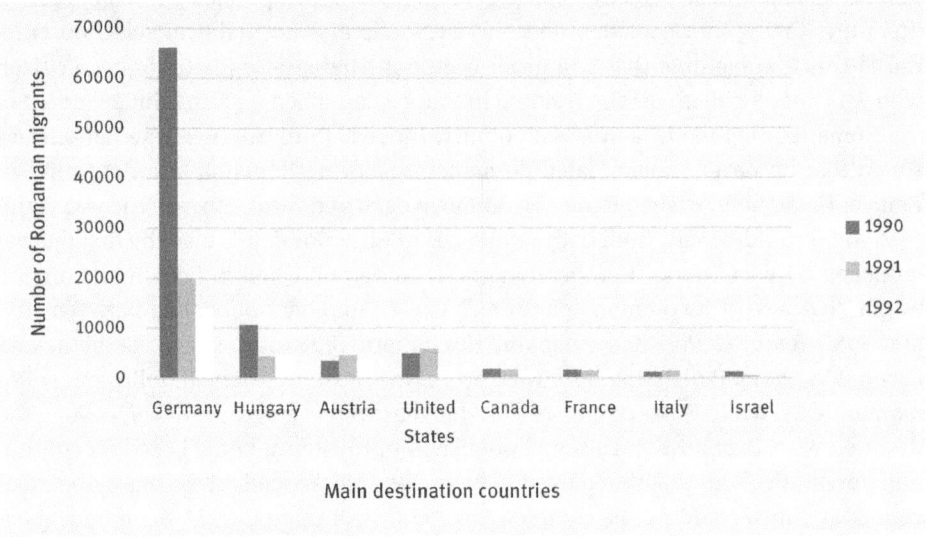

Chart 8.5: Evolution of Romanian migration in the main destination countries (1990–1992)
Source: Eurostat, Monographie par pays. Roumanie 1995 (Luxembourg: Eurostat, Office statistique des Communautés Européennes, 1995), 42.

This migration was the result of both the reintroduction of free movement and the turbulent economic and political situation in the country. Between 1990 and 2002, the process of transition and the restructuration of Romania's economy caused the loss of more than 3.5 million jobs (44 percent), the most dramatic decrease being registered in industry (only half of the jobs survived).[153] An equally important attraction factor was the Romanians' long-lasting fascination with Western societies and ways of life. During the Communist period, fleeing to the West was perceived as "the first step towards freedom and prosperity."[154] This migration was also a reaction to the hardships and deprivations that Romanians had to endure during Communism. The liberalization of travel opened a window of opportunity and many seized it in search of a better life abroad.[155]

---

[153] Sebastian Lăzăroiu, "Romania: More 'Out' than 'In' at the Crossroads between Europe and the Balkans," in *Migration Trends in Selected EU Applicant Countries* (Vienna: IOM, 2004). See also Dumitru Sandu, ed., *Locuirea temporară in străinătate. Migraţia economică a românilor 1990–2006* (Bucharest: Fundaţia pentru o Societate Deschisă, 2006).
[154] Adrian Cioroianu, *Pe umerii lui Marx. O introducere în istoria comunismului românesc* (Bucharest Curtea Veche, 2007), 86–87.
[155] Valeriu Rusu, *Migraţia forţei de muncă în Europa* (Bucharest: Arvin Press, 2003), 40–41. See also Dana Diminescu, "Deplasările oşenilor în străinătate, un nou model de migraţie," *Revista de Cercetări Sociale* 2 (1996): 16–32.

Table 8.1: Main Romanian ethnic groups' migration (1990–1992)

Ethnic groups	1990		1991		1992	
Romanians	23,888	25.15%	19,307	45.57%	18,104	59.40%
Germans	60,072	63.23%	15,567	36.74%	8,852	29.04%
Hungarians	11,040	11.62%	7,494	17.69%	3,523	11.56%
Total of migrants	**95,000**	**100%**	**42,368**	**100%**	**30,479**	**100%**

Source: Eurostat, *Monographie par pays. Roumanie 1995* (Luxembourg: Office statistique des Communautés européennes, 1995), 42.

Germany was the favorite destination country from 1990 to 1992. With 66,23 percent of the legal migration directed to Germany during the first year alone, it is safe to say that ethnic migration became dominant once again. The first to leave Romania were members of ethnic minority groups.[156] In the case of ethnic Germans, migration was encouraged by the assistance offered by the Federal Republic of Germany. *Aussiedler* policy stated that ethnic Germans from East-Central Europe and the former Soviet Union were welcome to return to Germany and reclaim their citizenship.[157] *Aussiedlers* are members of the ethnic Germans whose families have lived for generations in the eastern part of Central Europe, in Eastern and South-Eastern Europe and who decided to move back to Germany.

As the table shows, the number of ethnic Germans diminished rapidly (divided by four between 1990 and 1991) and became less important than that of the "Romanians." However, Germany continued to be the privileged destination country. Attracted by the *Aussiedler* policy, even Romanians who were not ethnic Germans decided to try their luck in this country. Roma were also part of this migration. Their mobility was motivated by economic reasons, a sense of insecurity and increased vulnerability. Members of this minority group have faced various forms of discrimination and violence. From 1990 to 1995, 17 cases of mob violence directed against Roma communities led to the killing of ten Roma and the destruction of 295 of their homes. The hesitation of the authorities to prosecute the perpetrators or to take measures in order to prevent similar occurrences, led some Roma to leave the country and apply for asylum. Many of them went to Germany.[158]

An important number of citizens tried to reproduce migration practices from the Communist period and made ample use of asylum applications. At that time, it ap-

---

[156] Dana Diminescu, "La désinsitutionalisation de l'hospitalité et l'intégration par le bas. Le cas des migrants roumains," *Ville-École-Integration Enjeux* 131 (December 2002): 169–171. See also Vincent Maisongrande, "Les circulations migratoires roumaines en Europe: Réseaux sociaux et inscription dena l'espace" (M. A. diss., University of Poitiers, 2008), 3.
[157] Swanie Potot, "Circulation et réseaux de migrants roumains: une contribution à l'étude des nouvelles mobilités en Europe" (PhD diss., University of Nice-Sophie Antipolis, 2003), 92.
[158] Council of Europe, *Human Rights of Roma and Travellers in Europe* (Strasbourg: Council of Europe Publishing, 2012).

peared to be the best way of gaining legal status and residency abroad. In the early 1990s, Romanians represented the second largest group applying for asylum in Europe, outnumbered only by the citizens from the former Yugoslavia. Between 1990 and 1994, Romanian citizens submitted approximately 350,000 applications to Western countries, three quarters of them to Germany.[159] This phenomenon came as a surprise to Western countries that did not see why citizens from former Communist countries still wanted to emigrate, even after the fall of the regimes. These numbers rapidly amplified fears of mass immigration and triggered an upsurge in negative sentiment towards the influx of East-Central European immigrants. Immigration began to be perceived as a high-risk phenomenon and destination states rapidly changed their migration laws. The EU also started drawing up a common migration policy aimed at stopping "false" asylum applications.[160]

8.6 Archives and Literature

Archival fonds integral to the study of Romanian migration during the Cold War can be divided in two categories based on geographical criteria: archival funds kept in Romania and those that can be consulted abroad.

The three main archival funds in Romania where one can consult documents on Romanian migration are the National Council for the Study of *Securitate* Archives, the archives of the Romanian Ministry of Foreign Affairs and the archives at the Institute for the Study of Communist Crimes and Exile Memory. Documents can also be found at the National Romanian Archives in Bucharest. Selections of documents from these archives have been published over the past few years.

The National Council for the Study of the Securitate Archives (CNSAS) is the authority that administrates the archives of the former Communist secret services in Romania. Here one can find the personal files of those placed under surveillance by the *Securitate*, including reports, letters, conversation transcriptions, and pictures.

The Institute for the Investigation of Communist Crimes in Romania (IICCMER) is a government-sponsored organization founded in 2005. It investigates the crimes and abuses conducted while Romania was under Communist rule, prior to December 1989. Formerly named the Institute for the Investigation of Communist Crimes in Romania (IICCR), in 2009 it merged with the National Institute and Memory of Romanian Exile (INMER) and became IICCMER. It holds forty archival funds dealing with Romanian exile: the archives of several exile associations (e.g. ACARDA), per-

---

[159] Istvan Horvath and Remus Gabriel Anghel, "Migration and Its Consequences for Romania," *Südosteuropa. Seitschrift für Politik und Gesellschaft* 57 (2009): 388. See also United Nations High Commissioner for Refugees (UNHCR), *Asylum Applications in Industrialized Countries: 1980–1999* (Geneva: UNHCR, 2001).
[160] Monica Șerban, *Dinamica migrației internaționale: un exercitiu asupra migrației românești în Spania* (Iasi: Lumen, 2011), 118–119.

sonal archives of several migrants (e.g. Sanda Stolojan), several journals and newspapers published in exile (e.g. *BIRE*), and RFE reports. These documents are now reinventoried and digitalized. These actions are part of a bigger project, namely, the online archive of Romanian exile.[161]

The Romanian Ministry of Foreign Affairs mainly holds reports and information produced by the Romanian embassies abroad and the Romanian Ministry. These documents deal with Romanian migration in a more general way. It allows researchers to understand how Romanian officials perceived this situation from the perspective of international relations.

Information on Romanian migrants can be found in the archives of all the countries where they settled (e.g. Ministry of the Interior and Ministry of Foreign Affairs). The most important fonds are at the Open Society Archives (OSA) and the Hoover Archives.

The Open Society Archives at the Central European University (CEU) is a complex archival and research institute. Both "textual" and "moving image" archival documents dealing with Romania during the Cold War can be found: records of Radio Free Europe/Radio Liberty, Romanian Unit (1945–1995). Materials in the subfunds include press clippings, news agency releases, Radio Free Europe/Radio Liberty research papers and background analyzes, information items, transcripts of radio broadcasts, émigré publications, and letters. The website of the Open Society Archives notes that

> The records of the Romanian Unit give a broad picture of Romanian political life, economics, culture and arts, religions, media, social and military issues. Two series of this subfunds are of outstanding interest: the Records Relating to Romanian Opposition and Protest Movement offer an encompassing and detailed overview on the history of the Romanian anti-Communist opposition, dissent and dissenters; the RFE Confidential Reports on Romania consists of confidential reports from (often) anonymized, but usually reliable sources on various Romanian issues. The impressive quantity of documents on Romania's foreign and inter-party relations, as well as those on Communist propaganda included in the series Subject Files are also of great interest.[162]

The Hoover Archives cover Romanian history from the Balkan War (1912–1913) through the Ceaușescu era, until 1989. The complete list of the 1999 documents can be accessed online.[163] The documents concern either individuals that played an important role in Romanian history, or various organizations and associations and their activities (e.g. Constantin Vișoianu, National Romanian Council).

---

[161] Archiva online a exilului românesc, http://www.arhivaexilului.ro/ro/arhiva-online-a-exilului-romanesc/ (accessed 09 June 2017).
[162] "HU OSA 300–60 Romania Unit," http://catalog.osaarchivum.org/catalog/jDen7R9Q (accessed 19 July 2017).
[163] "Romania. List of Archival Holdings at the Hoover Institution Archives," http://www.hoover.org/sites/default/files/library/docs/romania_collections_english.pdf (accessed 2 February 2018).

Very useful documents can also be found in various centers, including the Bibliothèque de Documentation Internationale Contemporaine – BDIC (archives of the League for the Defense of Human Rights from Romania). Other relevant sources are the personal archives of émigrés, numerous memoirs, journals, biographies, autobiographies, and oral testimonies.

Research on Romanian migration during the Cold War has mainly focused on exile and ethnic migration. Due to the regime's negative perception of migration during the Communist period, the authorities did not encourage the development of this field of research. One of the earliest studies on contemporary Romanian migration, more specifically internal migration flows was written by Dumitru Sandu.[164] The situation has changed with the fall of the Communist regime and there is now a quite substantial body of research on the subject. A survey of migration literature shows a fragmented research field. A valuable starting point is Mihai Pelin and Florin Manolescu's works[165], which present the most famous members, organizations, and publications of Romanian migrants during the Cold War.

Cultural/Literary exile has received great attention from researchers, who focus mostly on initiatives in France and the United States (e.g. magazines, conferences, preeminent writers and journalists, radio shows). Studies on cultural/literary exile have been written mostly by linguists and literature experts, but also by historians and sociologists. Eva Behring's *Romanian authors in exile, 1945–1989* gives a general overview of the migration of authors during the Communist period (e.g. preeminent figures, publications, activities).[166] Monica Lovinescu and Virgil Ierunca are two of the most studied figures of Romanian migration during this period. Researchers focused on both their cultural and political activities, with a special emphasis on their work for RFE. Other authors, such as Mircea Eliade, Emil Cioran, Dumitru Țepeneag, or Norman Manea, have also received substantial attention. Current research has focused mainly on their literary work and very little attention is being given to their personal experiences abroad, their lives as immigrants, the difficulties they encountered when arriving in a new country.

The ethnic aspect of Romanian migration is another well-studied phenomenon, with researchers focusing on German and Jewish mobility.

Surprisingly, few studies deal with political exile and anti-Communist activities. Researchers have analyzed the aims and processes of creation of political groups (e.g. Romanian National Committee, National Peasant Party), associations and organizations (e.g. Free Romanians' Associations from RFG, Association of the Former Political Prisoners in Romania, League for the Defense of Human Rights in Romania) as well as their anti-Communist activities with the aim of delegitimizing the Romanian Communist regime and its leaders, especially Nicolae Ceausescu. Researchers

---

164 Dumitru Sandu, *Fluxurile de migrație în România* (Bucharest: Editura Albatros, 1984).
165 Pelin, *Opisul emigrației politice*; Manolescu, *Enciclopedia exilului literar românesc 1945–1989*.
166 Behring, *Scriitori români din exil*.

focus on well-known figures in the fight against Communism, such as Paul Goma, Ion Rațiu, Virgil-Viorel Tilea or Sanda Stolojan, whilst giving very little attention to the experiences of ordinary Romanian migrants involved in these associations or on the impact of these activities.

The experiences of migrants abroad, their perspectives and representations are topics which deserve more attention. Despite the existence of numerous diaries and memoirs that record the experiences of migrants and their perception and memories of emigration during the Cold War, these sources have not yet been used by researchers to their fullest potential. Moreover, exiles – especially those involved in anti-Communist actions – have published studies analyzing their mobilizations, thus blurring the line between actors/exiles and researchers.

Of paramount importance are oral interviews with Romanians who have migrated during the Cold War, the more and less famous, in order to create an archival database which researchers could use in the future.

The networks of Romanian migrants and their relations with other immigration groups is also an understudied aspect of East-Central European migrations during the Cold War. Exploring exile from a gender perspective is also urgent. Most studies focus on male figures; women and children are being given very little attention. A further research gap is the topic of the journeys undertook by migrants from their home country to their destination countries, including the means of transportation and difficulties encountered *en route*. In order to have a complete image of migration during this period, it is imperative these overlooked segments of the population be the focus of future research.

9 Ukraine
Anna Fiń

This chapter of the book is dedicated to the topic of Ukrainian emigration between 1945 and 1990.[1] Its main objective is to present general characteristics of Ukrainian emigration in the Cold War period. This chapter answers the following questions: What were the conditions and how did the process of Ukrainian migration look like? What was the scale of Ukrainian migration during the Cold War and what countries did the migrants choose as their destination? What was the socio-economic status of emigrants? What was the nature of the political (anti-Communist) activity of Ukrainian diaspora? The idea is to provide an overview of the Ukrainian emigration during the Cold War period, present its mechanisms and motives, as well as to offer the first synthesis of political emigration from Ukraine.

It is especially important mainly because Ukrainian emigration is a much-neglected topic of study. Until recently, this theme has rarely surfaced in scientific debate and the reference material is relatively poor, especially when compared with the literature on other European emigration groups: Poles, Czechs, Hungarians, or Germans. This is probably related to political and ideological factors that limited the scope of research on migration in Ukraine (especially in the Communist period) and the fact that this subject has been studied mainly in America. Only after the fall of Communism in Central and East Europe in 1989 and Ukrainian independence in 1991 did the Ukrainian migration processes begin to appear in scientific discourse and research.[2] Despite the significant increase in the interest of researchers in the processes of Ukrainian emigration, the gap in literature has not yet been filled. The review of contemporary bibliography also indicates that the existing positions on Ukrainian emigration are usually quite general and that some of them, as indicated by the Polish historian, Andrzej A. Zięba, still require fundamental review.[3] What is more, there are many discrepancies in the interpretation of the migration process itself – both in Ukrainian and English-language literature. These refer to the interpretation of the motives for emigration and the character of the migration processes.[4] There are also numerous discrepancies in the estimated size of Ukrainian emigration.

---

[1] This chapter would not have been possible without the help of Alla Karanukh from the Institute of Philosophy and Sociology at the Pedagogical University in Cracow, who translated parts of the study from Ukrainian, created final charts and with whom I have discussed each part of the analysis.

[2] The majority of these analyzes relate to the most recent emigration, referred to as the 4th wave of Ukrainian emigration that took place in 1991. It seems that the biggest contribution to research on the 4th wave of Ukrainian emigration was made by an American researcher, Oleh Wolowyna, as well as a Canadian researcher, Vic Satzewich.

[3] Andrzej A. Zięba, "Ukraińcy w Stanach Zjednoczonych. Rewizja przeszłości," *Przegląd Polonijny* 2 (1994): 117.

[4] The difference in the interpretation of motives of Ukrainian emigration concerns mostly the first two emigration waves. Ukrainian literature, along with economic, emphasizes the significance of political

The current state of research is not the only difficulty facing a prospective researcher. We can also point to the accessibility of archives on Ukrainian emigration. They are poorly organized and many of them remain in unorganized collections. It is therefore difficult to find certain source material. The other difficulty in examining the migration process is related to estimating the size of Ukrainian emigration. An exact number is impossible to provide due to several reasons:

a) The use of different criteria to define the immigrants' country of origin in different countries. In the case of Ukrainian migrants, one should remember that they were a group that both emigrated from the country of origin and were classified as a minority.[5] Official statistical data did not account for Ukrainian nationality, but published only size of emigration from individual countries;

b) A lack of reliable and precise statistical data on the scale of the first and second wave of Ukrainian emigration. Statistical data of host countries did not include nationality of migrants, but only their place of origin. This means that due to the complex geopolitical situation of Ukraine and incorporation of its parts into different individual states (Austria-Hungary, Russia, Poland, Czechoslovakia), Ukrainian migrants were registered as Austrians, Hungarians, Russians, or Poles. What is more, early migrants identified themselves not by their national origin but regional origin; many also had so called labile identity, which allowed them to identify themselves as belonging to other ethnic group, e.g. Polish. The process of their ethnic self-identification usually took place only in the destination country;[6]

c) It is also due to the fact that Ukraine later became part of the Soviet Union and thus the Ukrainian emigration was was treated as a part of Soviet emigration by the registers of the host countries. American censuses did not distinguish the influx of people from Ukraine, but only from the Soviet Union as a whole until 1989;

---

factors, which are much less emphasized in English literature. In terms of interpreting the characteristics of migration, the Ukrainian literature does not approach the issue of chain migration. The fact that Ukrainians emigrated with other members of ethnic groups and created multi-ethnic migration flows is somewhat neglected. Only one publication in Ukrainian refers to this issue, namely, the study by Julian Baczynskyj, who claimed that Ukrainians departed to the US in the footsteps of their Polish and Jewish neighbors, see: Julian Baczynskyj, *Ukraijnska immihracija w Spoluczenych Sztatach Ameryky* (Lviv, 1914, Kyjiw, 1994), 56. More information on the topic is available in t English and Polish. See: Emily Greene Balch, *Our Slavic Fellow Citizens*, (New York: Arno Press, 1969), 120–145; Dorota Praszałowicz, Andrzej A., Zięba, and Krzysztof Makowski, *Mechanizmy zamorskich migracji łańcuchowych w XIX wieku: Polacy, Niemcy, Żydzi, Rusini. Zarys problemu* (Kraków: Księgarnia Akademicka, 2004), 126,129–146; Andrzej Pilch, "Migracja zarobkowa z Galicji w XIX i XX wieku (do 1918 roku)," *Przegląd Polonijny* 1(1975): 5–15; Dmytro Bodnarczuk, *Ethno-national Consciousness of the Ukrainian Immigrants in the United States* (Clifton: Computoprint Corporation, 2000): 13–15; Vic Satzewich, *The Ukrainian Diaspora* (New York: Routledge, 2002), 35.

5 Satzewich, *The Ukrainian Diaspora*, 22.
6 Myron Kuropas, "The Centenary of the Ukrainian Emigration to the United States," in *The Ukrainian Experience in the United States: A Symposium*, ed. Paul R. Magocci (Cambridge Mass.: Harvard Ukrainian Research Institute, 1979), 41.

d) It is related to a diverse ethnic structure of Ukrainian population, which caused migration streams after World War II to be multi-ethnic.[7] It was also not included in the official statistics;[8]

To sum up, it needs to be noted that difficulties in the assessment of the size of each stream of Ukrainian emigration are caused by historical, geopolitical, and identity reasons but also stem from the census procedures employed in each host country. Thus, one needs to remember that all statistical data is based on estimates and does not fully reflect the actual size of Ukrainian emigration and diaspora.

This article is based on various source material. First, there are references to available English and Ukrainian secondary sources.[9] Furthermore, statistical data was used, both official Ukrainian data and immigration statistics of chosen host countries. The chapter is enriched by the conclusions of research project "Poles and Ukrainian in Pluralistic American Society" conducted by Anna Fiń between 2007 and 2009.[10] Although the research project deals with the relations between different immigrant groups, it provides substantial empirical material, which has been used for this study. The other sources used here include: press articles, documents and archival sources, memoirs, and autobiographies. Some references will also be made to interview statements by members of the Ukrainian diaspora, which will allow insight into the process of political emigration through the eyes of Ukrainian migrants, instead of focusing only on the national state aspect.

---

[7] This question will be studied in detail in the following part of this chapter.

[8] The ethnic structure and the composition of the Ukrainian emigration streams could be described only after 1991. The analysis of Ukrainian emigration to the United States after 1991 was carried out by Oleh Wolowyna, see: Oleh Wolowyna, "Recent Migration from Ukraine to the United States: Demographic and Socioeconomic Characteristic," *The Ukrainian Quarterly* 3 (2005): 253–269.

[9] There exist less Ukrainian studies (monographs, s statistical analyzes) related to the Ukrainian emigration before 1991. Among the most important papers in Ukrainian on migration issues are the works by Wołodymyr Maruniak, Ludmiła Strelczuk and Włodzimierz Jewtuch. See: Wołodymyr Maruniak, *Ukrainska emigracja w Nimeczczyni i Awstrii po Drugiej switowij wijni. Tom I. Roky 1945–1951* (Munich: Akademiczne Wydawnyctwo dr Petra Beleja, 1985); Ludmiła Strilczuk, *Ukrainski polityczni bizenci ta peremiseni osoby pisla Drugoi Switowoi wijny. Czerniwci,* 1999, http://disser.com.ua/contents/29338.html (accessed 6 May 2018); Jewhen Jewtuch et al., *Ukrainska diaspora. Sociologiczni ta istoryczni studii* (Kyjiw, 2003) http://enpuir.npu.edu.ua/handle/123456789/357 (accessed 6 May 2018).

[10] The study was financially supported by a grant from the Kosciuszko Foundation and the Shevchenko Scientific Society. The field study was conducted in New York City among Polish and Ukrainian immigrants. The collected empirical material originates from the following institutions: The Polish Institute of Arts and Science, Shevchenko Scientific Society, New York Public Library, The Immigration History Research Center of University of Minnesota, Library of Columbia University, The Pilsudski Institute of America, The Polish Veterans Army Association in New York City, The Ukrainian American Coordinating Council St. George Ukrainian Catholic Church in New York, Hoover Institution Archive at Stanford University. The results of the studies have been included in the doctoral dissertation and serve as a basis for several scientific articles.

9.1 Conditions and course of Ukrainian migration

The American researcher, Ann Lencyk Pawliczko, states, "The history of Ukrainian emigration is closely tied to both political and economic events in the country itself."[11] Generally, using the findings of other researchers, one can divide the process of Ukrainian emigration into four different periods called emigration waves. Each one of them was complex in terms of composition, origin, and the nature of emigration.

The first wave of Ukrainian emigration took place between 1870 and 1914. As Ukraine at that time was divided between various states s and did not exist as an autonomous state, Ukrainians were mainly leaving Austria-Hungary and only a small number of them left the Russian Empire.[12] Emigration was mainly motivated by economic reasons. This migration pattern was also a chain-reaction, which means that Ukrainians followed their neighbors: Poles, Jews, and Germans (especially to America). The socio-economic status of early Ukrainian emigrants was relatively low; among them were peasants, characterized by a high percentage of illiteracy.[13] Emigrants were mainly unqualified workers or farmers. The migration movement included mainly intercontinental migration to North and the South America (see table 9.1). There was also small internal migration, mainly to Czechoslovakia, Poland, Hungary, and Yugoslavia. It is difficult to estimate the size of this emigration stream. Every academic study presents different data.[14] Moreover, Ukrainian sources state that in this

---

11 Ann Lencyk Pawliczko, "Ukrainian Immigration: A Study in Ethnic Survival," in *The Immigration Experience in the United States: Policy Implications*, ed. Mary C. Powers and John J. Maciso (New York: Center for Migration Studies, 1994), 88.
12 the case of emigration of Ukrainians to the United States, nearly half of the emigrants came from Galicia, 30 percent from Rus, and the rest from Bukovina, Volhynia and the Eastern Ukraine, a significant part of the Ukrainian emigration to the USA was from the territory of the former Poland, constituting nearly 35 percent of its overall size. See: Andrzej A. Zięba, "Ukraińcy i karpaccy Rusini," in *Polska diaspora*, ed. Adam Walaszek (Kraków: Wydawnictwo Literackie, 2001), 450; Andrzej Pilch, "Emigracja z ziem polskich do Stanów Zjednoczonych Ameryki od lat pięćdziesiątych XIX w. do r. 1918," in *Polonia amerykańska. Przeszłość teraźniejszość współczesność*, ed. Hieronim Kubiak, Eugeniusz Kusielewicz and Tadeusz Gromada (Wrocław: Ossolineum, 1988), 42. See also: Baczynskyj, *Ukrajinska immihracija w Spoluczenych Sztatach Ameryky*, 56; Balch, *Our Slavic Fellow Citizens*, 120–145; Bodnarczuk, *Ethno-national Consciousness*, 13–15; Satzewich, *The Ukrainian Diaspora*, 35; Praszałowicz, Zięba and Makowski, *Mechanizmy zamorskich migracji łańcuchowych w XIX wieku*.
13 In the case of emigrants leaving for the United States, illiteracy was as high as 49 percent, see: Myron Kuropas, *The Ukrainian Americans: Roots and Aspirations 1884–1954* (Toronto: University Toronto Press, 1991), 23.
14 According to the Institute of Diaspora Studies in Kiev, these numbers were as follows: 256,000 people emigrated to the USA (among them 235,000 people from the territory of Austro-Hungary and 5,400 people from the Russian Empire), 135,000 went to Canada, 47,000 to Brazil, and 15,000 to Argentina, http://mihrantua.narod.ru/xvila1a.htm (accessed 2 March 2018).

period 1,619,000 Ukrainians departed to Siberia and East Asia as a result of mass migratory movements and the policy of populating virgin areas.[15]

The second wave of Ukrainian emigration took place during the interwar period. Its nature was mainly economic although some Ukrainian sources also point to political reasons (e.g. purge of "public enemies," division of Ukraine between Poland, Czechoslovakia and Romania, poor national relations inside Poland).[16] The estimated number of this emigration is 200,000 (see table 9.1).[17] The vast majority of the emigrants, similar to the previous wave, left for North and South America. Approximately 40,000 people migrated to France; one of the earliest destinations in Western Europe of Ukrainian emigrants. Ukrainian sources state that many of those who left for France later left for the USA and Canada. Generally, migration during the interwar period was characterized by significantly smaller number of emigrants. It was the continuation of previous processes (the first wave of emigration), especially in terms of the socio-economic status of emigrants.

Table 9.1: Main countries of destination and number of Ukrainian immigrants during the first and second wave of migration

1st Wave of Migration (1870–1914)		2nd Wave of Migration (1919–1939)	
United States	350,000	Canada	70,000
Canada	100,000	Argentina	50,000
Brazil	45,000	France	40,000
Argentina	10,000	United States	15,000
		Brazil	10,000
		Paraguay, Uruguay, Venezuela	10,000
		Belgium	1,000
		Great Britain	500
Total (approx.)	510,000	Total (approx.)	196,500

Source: Ann Lencyk Pawliczko, "Ukrainian Immigration: A study in Ethnic Survival," in *The Immigration Experience in the United States: Policy Implications*, ed. Mary C. Powers and John J. Maciso (New York: Center for Migration Studies, 1994), 90; Ann Lencyk Pawliczko ed., *Ukraine and Ukrainians throughout the World: A Demographic and Sociological Guide to the Homeland and Its Diaspora* (Toronto: University of Toronto Press), 116–117.

---

[15] According to Ludmila Strilczuk, migration was aided by the construction of the Trans-Siberian Railway between 1895–1905, see Strilczuk, *Ukrainski polityczni bizenci*, http://disser.com.ua/contents/29338.html (accessed 6 May 2018).

[16] Serhy Yekelchyk, *Ukraina. Narodziny nowoczesnego narodu* (Kraków: Wydawnictwo Uniwersytetu Jagiellońskiego, 2009), 153–171; *Zarubiżni Ukrajinci. Dwidnyk* (Kiev: Wydanystwo Ukrajina, 1991), 37.

[17] Forced emigration resulted from the policies of the Soviet Union. People were deported to Siberia, Central Asia, and the Soviet Pacific coast. The calculations made by Jewhen Jewtuch suggest that in the years 1926 to 1939, as a result of massive displacement of populations, 2,850,000 residents have left the URSR, see: Jewtuch et al., *Ukraińska diaspora*, 30.

9.2 The aftermath of World War II

World War II changed the nature of Ukrainian emigration and marked the beginning of the so-called third wave of Ukrainian emigration. It included, more or less, voluntary departures but also forced migration: deportation, exile, and repatriation. Ukrainian researchers estimate that in the beginning of World War II, about 312,000 families or 1,200,000 people from western Ukraine were deported to Siberia and the Soviet territories in Central Asia. Approximately 20 percent of those were of Ukrainian ethnicity.[18] Deportations continued also after the end of the war, encompassing 203,662 people between 1944 and 1950.[19] In 1944, under the agreement between the Polish Committee of National Liberation and the Soviet Union, the resettlement process of Ukrainians from Poland to the Soviet Union and Poles from the Soviet Union to Poland began.[20] It is estimated that 810,415 Poles left Ukraine and 482,880 Ukrainians arrived to Ukrainian Soviet Socialist Republic.[21] The changes of ethnic structures after World War II entailed not only a decrease in several of the national and ethnic minorities (e.g. Poles, Jews and Armenians), but also an increase of the number of Russians. Piotr Eberhardt states that the influx of Russians into the Soviet Union was so big that in 1970 they constituted 19% of the Ukrainian population, in 1979 – 21% and in 1989 – 22%.[22] The changes in the demographic structure between 1989 and 1989 are illustrated in table 9.2. and are based on Ukrainian statistical data.

Table 9.2: Ukrainian ethnic structure with changes between 1939 and 1989

Nationality	1939	%	1959	%	1970	%	1979	%	1989	%
Ukrainians	23667.5	76.48	32158.5	76.81	35283.9	74.87	36489.0	73.55	37419.1	72.73
Russians	4175.3	13.49	7090.8	16.94	9126.3	19.37	10471.6	21.11	11355.6	22.07
Belarusians	158.2	0.51	290.9	0.69	385.8	0.82	406.1	0.82	440.0	0.86
Crimean Tatars	—	--	0.193	0.00	3.554	0.008	6.636	0.01	46.807	0.09
Moldovans	260.4	0.84	241.7	0.58	265.9	0.56	293.6	0.59	324.5	0.63
Bulgarians	113.5	0.37	219.4	0.52	234.4	0.50	238.2	0.48	233.8	0.45
Hungarians	—	--	149.2	0.36	157.7	0.33	164.4	0.33	163.1	0.32
Romanians	0.825	0.003	100.9	0.24	112.1	0.24	121.8	0.25	134.8	0.26
Poles	357.7	1.16	363.3	0.87	295.1	0.63	258.3	0.52	219.2	0.43

---

18 Serhy Yekelchyk, *Ukraina*, 190.
19 Yekelchyk.
20 Repatriation campaigns were related to pre-war Poland loosing its eastern borderlands – *Kresy*. As a result of the decisions taken in Yalta, the borders of the Republic of Poland were shifted about 250 km to the west and the eastern areas, which used to be an integral part of Poland, were annexed to the USSR. The Podkarpacie and Chełm regions as well as a part of Lesser Poland perceived by the Ukrainians as "Ukrainian ethnographic territory" remained within Poland.
21 Serhy Yekelchyk, *Ukraina*, 212.
22 Piotr Eberhardt, *Przemiany narodowościowe na Ukrainie XX wieku* (Warsaw: Biblioteka Obozu, 1994), 121.

Table 9.2: Ukrainian ethnic structure with changes between 1939 and 1989 *(Continued)*

Nationality	1939	%	1959	%	1970	%	1979	%	1989	%
Jews	1532.8	4.95	840.3	2.01	776.1	1.65	632.9	1.28	486.6	0.95
Greeks	107.0	0.35	104.4	0.25	106.9	0.23	104.1	0.21	98.594	0.19
Armenians	21.688	0.07	28.024	0.07	33.439	0.07	38.646	0.08	54.200	0.11
Tatars	55.456	0.18	61.334	0.15	72.658	0.15	83.906	0.17	86.875	0.17
Roms	10.443	0.03	22.515	0.05	30.091	0.06	34.411	0.07	47.917	0.09
Azerbaijanis	4.626	0.015	6.680	0.02	10.769	0.02	17.235	0.03	36.961	0.07
Georgians	10.063	0.03	11.574	0.03	14.650	0.03	16.301	0.03	23.540	0.05
Germans	392.5	1.27	23.243	0.06	29.871	0.06	34.139	0.07	37.849	0.07
Gagauzes	–	–-	23.530	0.06	26.464	0.06	29.398	0.06	31.967	0.06
Total	30946.2	100.0	41869.0	100.0	47126.5	100.0	49609.3	100.0	51452.0	100.0

Source: *Nacionalnyj skład Ukrainy w 1926–2001 rokach*, http://ukrmap.org.ua/Statistika_nasel_ukr.htm (accessed 2 March 2015).

Although the demographic changes in Ukraine show a decrease in the percentage of specific national and ethnic groups in the overall population, they still show that "ethnic minorities represent a visible segment of the Ukrainian population (5.4%)."[23] This ethnic and cultural diversity of the Ukraine influenced the nature of migration streams. It this case, therefore, one cannot speak of emigration of one national/ethnic group, but about multi-ethnic migratory flows, composed of representatives of many different ethnic and national groups. Writing about migration from Soviet Ukraine, Oleg V. Shamshur clearly states that "migration out of the Soviet Union has had, since 1960s, almost exclusively an ethnic character. Jews, ethnic Germans, Greeks and Armenians make up the great bulk of Soviet emigration."[24] Nowadays, it is difficult to estimate the percentage of national minorities in the Ukrainian emigration in the Cold War era. There is no doubt, however, that other national groups left along with the Ukrainians.

Apart from demographic factors, political and economic factors also influenced emigration from Ukraine. Assimilation policy emphasizing the historical unity of Ukraine and Russia, and marginalizing Ukrainian culture was adopted. There was an attempt to create *Soviet man identity* with the help of propaganda, which in contemporary Ukrainian literature is defined as "full of Stalinist content."[25] In terms of the economy, it was both a period of development of the industry (mainly heavy industry) and an intense urbanization. It is estimated that in 1979, 53% of the population began living in urban areas.[26] These processes influenced the change of socio-labor and class structure of Ukrainian society. The dynamics of these changes are illustrated in table 9.3.

---

[23] Oleg V. Shamshur, "Ukraine in the context of new European Migrants," *International Migration Review* 2 (1992): 260.
[24] Shamshur, 259–260.
[25] Serhy Yekelchyk, *Ukraina*, 217.
[26] Bohdan Krawczenko, *Socialni zminy i nacionalna swidomist' w Ukraini*, 232–235.

Table 9.3: Class structure of Ukrainian society, 1939–1970

Class structure	1939		1959		1970	
	Total	%	Total	%	Total	%
Workers	10,362,000	32.6	17,123,000	40.9	23,430,000	49.8
Clerks	5,467,000	17.2	7,253,000	17.3	9,281,000	19.3
Farmers	15,956,000	50.2	17,472,000	41.7	14,230,000	30.3

Source: Bohdan Krawczenko, *Socialni zminy i nacionalna swidomist' w Ukraini w XX stolitti* (Kiev: Osnowy, 1999), 262–263.

The data clearly shows the decrease in the percentage of farmers and the increase in the number of workers in the social structure. The centrally planned economy and ineffectiveness of adopted solutions, especially the inefficiency of heavy industry caused stagnation and led to the collapse of the Ukrainian economy. It became noticeable in the 1980s and determined the social and economic situation of the state for the following decades. The results of the described phenomena of migratory processes (both during the Cold War and in the following decades) proved very serious. First, the described factors influenced the structure of emigration motivations and the increased the diversity of the migratory flows. Apart from peasants, other social classes started to migrate, including workers and the intellectual élite. Second, the described factors increased the intensity of migratory movements (constant migration and circular migration). Finally, yet importantly, the changes in social awareness (formation of *homo sovieticus*) as well as a division of Ukrainians into Ukrainian-speaking and Russian-speaking, influenced the relationships and social divisions of the Ukrainian diaspora. These changes in social awareness started to be visible in the 1980s and they lasted throughout the following decades.[27]

9.3 Major migration streams during the Cold War. The third wave of Ukrainian emigration

The third wave of Ukrainian emigration took place between 1945 and 1989. This wave can be further divided into four different periods of migratory movements:
a) the period of forced migrations within the Soviet Union: 1939–1956
b) "DP" Period: 1945–1955
c) migration in the period of "thaw": 1955–1989
d) The period of voluntary migration within the Soviet Union during the Cold War.

---

[27] Ihor V. Zielyk, "Ethnicity and Irredentism in Diaspora. Profile of an Ukrainian-American Community" (PhD diss., Columbia University, 1997).

Estimated data on the direction of this emigration and its size is included in the table 9.4.

Table 9.4: Main countries of destination and the number of Ukrainian immigrants during the third wave of migration

Years	Migration size	Main Directions
1939–1945	2,300,000	USSR: repatriations and deportations
1944–1952	200,000	Siberia: deportations
1945–1953	400,000	Russian the Far East. Kazakhstan. the Volga Region. North Caucasus. deportations and voluntary migrations
1954–1956	80,000	Siberia and Kazakhstan
1945–1955	250,000	North and South America. Australia and Oceania. Western Europe
1955–1989	Lack of accurate data	Indirect emigration to North America and Western Europe; emigration within USSR

Sources: Vic Satzewich, *The Ukrainian Diaspora* (New York: Routledge, 2002), 86–102; Ann Lencyk Pawliczko, ed., *Ukraine and Ukrainians throughout the World: A Demographic and Sociological Guide to the Homeland and Its Diaspora* (Toronto: University of Toronto Press, 1994); Serhy Yekelchyk, *Ukraina. Narodziny nowoczesnego narodu* (Kraków: Wydawnictwo Uniwersytetu Jagiellońskiego), 190–212.

The analysis of the data included in the table above leads to the conclusion that the period of Ukrainian migration after the war was diversified both in terms of size and nature of the diaspora. The starting period of emigration processes was characterized by forced migration and displacements, which were carried out under international agreements. The forced migration route led mainly to Siberia and deep into Russia to the border with Western Asia and the Middle East.

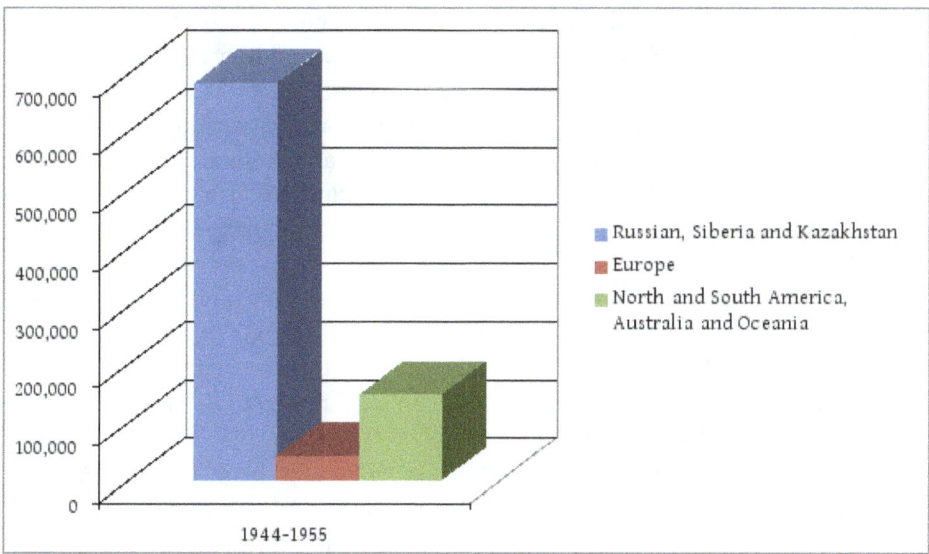

Chart 9.1: Countries of destination and the number of Ukrainian immigrants during the third wave of migration, 1944–1955
(* Europe: Western and Eastern Europe, without the Soviet Union)

The forced migration of Ukrainians ended with Stalin's death in 1953. His death enabled the so-called "thaw" or partial liberalization of political and cultural life. It did not, however, end the mobility movements into the Soviet Union. In fact, the whole Cold War era was characterized by internal migration, which took place within the various Soviet Republics. The most common destinations were Kazakhstan and areas along the Volga and Northern Caucasus. It is difficult to estimate the size of the movements. Their scope and intensity, however, were so vast that they formed Ukrainian communities in the various Russian Republics, the biggest clusters in Kazakhstan, the Republic of Moldova, and Russia.[28] During the "thaw" period, internal migrations stopped. The stagnation of external migratory movements was caused by political reasons connected to the laws limiting the departures from the Soviet Union. Small groups of Ukrainians who left to North America and Australia emigrated from other European countries: Poland, Czechoslovakia, Germany, or Great Britain. For instance, it is estimated that between 1960 and 1990, as many as 38,000 Ukrainians came to the United States, mostly via Poland, Germany and Canada.[29]

---

[28] In 1959, for example, the following numbers of Ukrainians were recorded in these republics: 762,131 (Kazakhstan); 420,820 (Moldova); 133,061 (Belarus); 3,359,083 (Russia). In 1970, the numbers were as follows: 930,158 (Kazakhstan); 506,560 (Moldova); 190,839 (Belarus); and 3,345,885 (Russia). This data was collected by the Institute of Demography, National Research Institute, http://demoscope.ru/weekly/ssp/census.php?cy=2 (accessed 6 May 2018).
[29] Oleh Wolowyna, "Immigration and Language of Ukrainians in the United States," *The Ukrainian Weekly*, 12 October 2003, http//www.ukweekly.com/old/archive/2003/410319.shtml?200m_hight=ukrainian

Similarly, between 1956 and 1986, approximately 17,800 people came to Canada, mainly from the United States, Great Britain, and Poland.[30] Roman Petryshyn, a researcher of Ukrainian immigration in Canada, confirms these numbers. He notes: "there has been no significant immigration of Ukrainians to Canada since that period. Although a few hundred do arrive annually from various Ukrainian settlement in the world."[31] In the context of social studies, the situation in which the sending country is different than the country of origin is called indirect/intermediate emigration.[32]

In the case of intermediate Ukrainian emigration in the period of "thaw," the reasons for departure were very complex. There were not only political but also economic factors and family ties that played a role in opting for emigration. Based on my research of the Ukrainian diaspora in the USA and the research results of various researchers, I established that: "the main reason for this migration was family reunification, less often it was refugee migration."[33] My interviews with Ukrainian emigrants who left during the "thaw" period may serve as a proof of this argument. One of the respondents recalled the following: " I emigrated from Germany to the USA in 1957. I came to New York and worked in an engineering company. (…) There were no perspectives in Germany at that time, so I had to leave." A similar experience was recalled by another interlocutor:

> In 1979. How did it look like? You are young and you want to leave. In Poland, at that time there wasn't … Let's say … I don't know … I … For me it was to leave from Poland. I had no ties there. I have an uncle here in America. I left because of him and I came to him (…) I don't know, because of uncle or someone else. But I got the passport and I came here to America, actually only for holidays. So I started to work but actually, I have never wanted to go back.

These statements show what reasons led to a decision to migrate and what were the real circumstances of Ukrainian indirect emigration during the "thaw" period. In the perspective of these subjective and biographical experiences, the reasons included personal factors, lack of perspective in the country of residence, family ties, and social networks. The significance of political factors seems to have been less significant.

+immigration+waves (accessed 6 May 2018). The issue is apparent in the case of Ukrainian diaspora in Australia, which is exclusively post-war. Population census from 1986 notes nearly 30,000 Ukrainians, 30% born in Ukraine, 10% in the camps in Germany and Austria, 4% t in Poland See: Pawliczko, *Ukraine and Ukrainians throughout the World,* 472.
30 Wsevolod W. Isajiw and Andrij, Makuch, "Ukrainians in Canada," in *Ukraine and Ukrainians throughout the World,* 328.
31 Roman W. Petrysyn, "The Ukrainian Canadians in Social Transition," in *Ukrainian Canadians, Multiculturalism and Separatism: An Assessment,* ed. Mandy R. Lupul (Edmonton: The Canadian Institute of Ukrainian Studies, 1978), 76.
32 Krystyna Iglicka, *Kontrasty migracyjne Polski. Wymiar transatlantycki* (Warsaw: Wydawnictwo Scholar, 2008), 15.
33 Anna Fiń, "Ukraińska imigracja w Stanach Zjednoczonych. Charakterystyka ogólna," *Studia Migracyjne-Przegląd Polonijny* 4 (2013): 41.

Although external emigration of Ukrainians was indirect between 1955 and 1989, it is worth to mention the departures of people connected with Ukrainian opposition. During the 1950s and 1960s, an opposition group named *szestydesiatnyky* was active in Ukraine. It consisted of young artists, the Ukrainian intellectual elite, whose activity was focused on anti-Communist acts and fighting for democratic freedoms.[34] In the beginning, its activity was limited to informal meetings. With time, however, the group created more formal structures, e.g. the Young Artists Club in Kiev[35] and cooperated with Ukrainian emigration intelligence.[36] Ukrainian opposition was not a unified movement. Although the *szestydesiatnyky* represented center opinions, the second important opposition movement in Ukraine was nationalist and its ideology referred to the Organization of Ukrainian Nationalists (OUN).[37] It propagated Ukraine integrity in the territories considered ethnic. Ukrainian sources state that the significant part of the people devoted to the movement came from Kiev (38% p) and Lvov (25%), while the rest came from East Ukraine.[38] Arrests of the Ukrainian oppositionists began in 1965. Attempts to stop the opposition continued until 1985.[39] In this period, many people who had engaged in opposition activities left the country. One needs to assume that it was enabled by the ties to various opposition groups in exile. Due to the lack of sources, we do not know the exact number of people who left the country in this manner. Taking into account the strict limits of spatial movement of people, we can infer that this number was small. Unfortunately, the lack of sources and documents on the subject makes it impossible to draw any conclusions.

The DP period between 1945 and 1955 was especially significant for the Ukrainian Cold War migration. After the end of World War II, over quarter of a million Ukrainians were in the Displaced Person Camps located in the Western Germany, Austria, and Italy. Detailed statistical data on the number of Ukrainians in DP camps can be found in table 9.5.

---

34 Among the most outstanding representatives of the *"szestydesiatnyky"* movement there are (or were?): Iwan Dracz, Lina Kostenko, Dmytro Pawłyczko, Wołodymir Drozd, Iwan Dziuba, Siergiej Parażanow, Iwan and Nadija Switłyczni, Wasyl Lisowyj see: Yekelchyk, *Ukraine*, 235.
35 The group's activities in the initial period were limited to the organization of conferences and the so-called *samwydat*, i.e. publishing and distributing illegal political publications, usually literary works. The book by Iwan Dziuba *Internacjonalizm czy rusyfikacja*, published in 1965, has gained a lot of publicity both in Ukraine and beyond. Since its official publication the fight with the movement really started and its members were arrested. Just a few people managed to emigrate, mostly to Germany. More on the subject: Yekelchyk, *Ukraina*, 240–241; Jarosław Hrycak, *Historia Ukrainy 1772– 1999. Narodziny nowoczesnego narodu* (Lublin: Instytut Europy Środkowo-Wschodniej, 2000), 284.
36 Jerzy Giedroyc, *Emigracja ukraińska. Listy 1950–1982*, ed. Bogumiła Berdychowska (Warsaw: Wydawnictwo Czytelnik, 2004), 42.
37 More information on the OUN can be found in Maruniak, *Ukrainska emigracja w Nimeczczyni i Awstrii*, 243–245.
38 Bohdan Krawczenko, *Socialni zminy i nacionalna swidomist' w Ukraini XX stolittia* (Kiev: Osnowy, 1997), 317–318.
39 Włodzimierz Pawluczuk, *Ukraina. Polityka i mistyka* (Kraków: Zakład Wydawniczy Nomos, 1998), 55.

Table 9.5: The number of Ukrainians in DP camps in Germany and Austria in the three occupation zones, 1946–1950

	1946	1947	1948	1949	1950
Germany (total)	177,630	140,555	119,742	85,608	55,183
American zone	104,024	85,646	78,504	56,611	39,359
British zone	54,580	44,987	35,108	24,923	12,983
French zone	19,026	9,922	6,130	4,074	2,841
Austria (total)	21,043	19,625	17,700	10,680	4,000
Total	**198,673**	**160,180**	**137,442**	**96,288**	**59,183**

Source: Wołodymyr Maruniak, *Ukrainska emigracja w Nimeczczyni i Awstrii po Drugiej switowij wijni*, vol. 1: *Roky 1945–1951* (Munich: Akademiczne Wydawnyctwo dr Petra Beleja, 1985), 86.

It is estimated that in 1946 about 180,000 people lived in the Germany, 30,000 in Austria, and 12,000 in Italy.[40] In Germany, Ukrainians were the second largest immigrant group after Poles. Half of them were in the American occupation zone, 30% in the British zone and 10% in the French zone. The number of Ukrainians in each occupation zone decreased every year due to the emigration of refugees to different countries. With the help of organizations such as the United Nations Relief and Rehabilitation Administration (UNRRA), the International Refuge Organization (IRO), the Church World Service, as well as the National Catholic Welfare Conference, Ukrainians emigrated mainly to North America, South America, and Western Europe. It is estimated that over 200,000 Ukrainians emigrated in this period. Data on the destinations of Ukrainian DPs and the size of migratory flows is shown in table 9.6 and 9.7 (the first table is more general and the second one detailed and compares the situation of Ukrainians with the situation of Poles and citizens of the Soviet Union).

Table 9.6: The number of Ukrainian refugees from Germany and Austria, 1947–1957

Country of Destination	Number of Ukrainians (in thousands)
USA	80
Canada	30
Australia. New Zeeland	20
Great Britain	20
Belgium	10
France	10

---

[40] Wolodymyr Maruniak, "Ukrainians in the Federal Republic of Germany," 254.

Table 9.6: The number of Ukrainian refugees from Germany and Austria, 1947–1957 *(Continued)*

Country of Destination	Number of Ukrainians (in thousands)
Brazil	7
Argentina	6
Venezuela	2
Other countries	2
Total	**187**

Source: Ann Lencyk Pawliczko, "Ukrainian Immigration: A Study in Ethnic Survivals," in *The Immigration Experience in the United States: Policy Implications*, ed. Mary G. Powers and John J. Macisco (New York: Center for Migration Studies 1994), 92.

Table 9.7: Emigration of Ukrainians and other nationalities from DP camps, 1947–1951

Host country	Total*	Ukrainians	Soviet Union Citizens	Poles
Argentina	32,712	2,283	2,071	6,536
Australia	182,159	19,607	4,944	60,308
Belgium	22,477	5,650	1,826	10,378
Bolivia	2,485	–	9	510
Brazil	28,848	4,609	1,427	7,770
Canada	123,479	14,877	8,158	46,961
Chile	5,108	319	320	516
France	38,445	3,342	735	11,882
Fr. Morocco	1,446	57	67	166
Israel	132,109	35	1,689	54,904
Netherlands	4,355	118	63	2,969
New Zeeland	4,837	179	275	847
Norway	1,105	58	41	232
Paraguay	5,887	146	2,665	1433
Peru	2,340	86	33	103
Sweden	4,330	46	12	563
Great Britain	86,346	15,001	459	35,780
USA	329,301	45,044	14,506	110,566
Uruguay	1,461	5	58	241
Venezuela	17,277	1,887	786	2,814
Other countries	13,094	328	1,181	1,929
Total	**1,039,601**	**113,677**	**41,325**	**357,435**

Source: Wołodymyr Maruniak, *Ukrainska emigracja w Nimeczczyni i Awstrii po Drugiej switowij wijni*. vol. 1: *Roky 1945–1951* (Munich: Akademiczne Wydawnyctwo dr Petra Beleja 1985), 87
*The total category includes the following nationalities: Poles, Ukrainians, Yugoslavians, Latvians, Hungarians, Lithuanians, Czechs and Slovaks, Estonians, Romanians, Soviet Union citizens and others.

It was a mass migration and the analysis of its course leads to two basic conclusions. First, emigrants used traditional migratory routes to the North America and South America. The biggest group of (80,000) Ukrainians emigrated to the United States between 1937 and 1957. At that time, migration to the Unites States was facilitated by American laws, especially the Displaced Persons Act of 1948, Refuge Relief Act of 1953, and the support of ethnical organizations such as the United Ukrainian-American Relief Committee (1944) or the Committee for the Aid of Refugee Ukrainian Scholars (1945).[41] A smaller group left for Canada (c. a. 30,000 people) and South America, mainly Brazil, Argentina and Venezuela (about 15,000 in total). Second, the DP period established new migration directions, both overseas and continental. After World War II, Australia became a new center of the Ukrainian diaspora. Nearly 20,000 Ukrainians emigrated there. The size of migration to Western Europe was entirely different. It is estimated that about 20,000 Ukrainians left for Great Britain, and groups of nearly 10,000 people went to France and Belgium.[42] Just a small number of Ukrainians stayed in the countries where the camps were located. For instance, only 20,000 people remained in Germany.

DP camps did not only send Ukrainians away. They were primarily a place of everyday life, where refugees tried to recreate social, cultural, and political life. In sociological terms, the process of creating/recreating institutions and organizations that aim to fulfill society's needs is called institutional completeness.[43] The development and maintenance of institutional completeness is a basic condition of survival of any ethnic community: institutional completeness supports group borders, consolidates, and mobilizes ethnic identity. Such was the case with Ukrainians. Vic Stazewicz states, "Ukrainians in the camps created a vibrant political, cultural and intellectual life."[44] Information on the organization of immigrant life in specific occupation zones is provided in table 9.8.

Table 9.8: Organization of Ukrainian life in DP camps in three occupation zones

	American zone	British zone	French zone
Camps	59	46	20
Ukrainians	60,759	31,083	5,785
Kindergardens	39	24	1
National schools	58	29	3
Junior High Schools (Gymnasiums)	26	7	-
Vocational Schools	31	7	-

---

41 Ihor Zielyk, "Ethnicity and Irredentism in Diaspora...," 102–103.
42 Vic Satzewich reports that in the UK members of the so-called Galicia Divison, who took advantage of the European Volunteer Worker Program belonged to the majority, see: Vic Satzewich, *The Ukrainian Diaspora*, 102.
43 Raymond Breton, "Institutional Completeness of Ethnic Communities and the Personal Relations of Immigrants," *The American Journal of Sociology* 2 (1964): 193–205.
44 Vic Satzewich, *The Ukrainian Diaspora*, 97.

Table 9.8: Organization of Ukrainian life in DP camps in three occupation zones *(Continued)*

	American zone	British zone	French zone
Libraries	35	26	-
Choir	41	19	-
Orchestra	13	8	-
Theatre Group	33	18	-
Puppet Theatres	2	-	-
Ballets	3	2	-
Professional Theatres	3	1	-
Exhibitions	1400	459	-
Concerts	957	544	-
Other events	335	303	-
Lectures/talks	1761	578	-
Folk Art Exhibitions	41	30	-
Specialist courses	288	129	-
Cooperatives	24	14	-
Shops	41	9.	-
Workshops	307	147	-
Local social organizations	225	80	-
Parishes	85	52	11
Church/Russian Orthodox Church Fraternities	49	36	5

Source: Wołodymyr Maruniak, *Ukrainska emigracja w Nimeczczyni i Awstrii po Drugiej switowij wijni.* Vol. 1: *Roky 1945–1951* (Munich: Akademiczne Wydawnyctwo dr Petra Beleja, 1985), 112.

9.4 Political activities in exile

The collected data suggests that the most vibrant immigrant life was led in Germany, in the American occupation zone. This fact should not come as a surprise as this particular zone encompassed the biggest number of camps and Ukrainians. Socio-cultural activity played a significant role in these communities. It is estimated that the camps held 160 cultural institutions and 70 ethnic organizations and institutions. There were artistic, student, trade, veteran, women, youth, and religious organizations. Created were also so-called umbrella organizations and general organizations, including the Ukrainian National Council and the Coordinating Ukrainian Committee, whose goal was not only the unification of politically and ideologically divided Ukrainian society but also political activity. An important part of their activities was directed at developing and upholding ties to country of origin. The forms of these contacts and cooperation varied. However, they were often ideological and their main goal was to defend Ukrainian national interests. Simultaneously, they strengthened national identity. Ihor Zielyk states "it was a heavily politicized identity. Formed and held together by adherence to nationalist symbols and rejection of status quo in Ukraine."[45]

---

[45] Ihor Zielyk, "Ethnicity and Irredentism in Diaspora," 106.

Undoubtedly, maintaining and creating Ukrainian identity and national consciousness enabled the recreation of religious structures of the Ukrainian population. The literature on the subject lists 148 parishes and 90 *Bratstva* (secular unions of Orthodox citizens). Most of the Ukrainian DPs declared themselves members of the Ukrainian Catholic Church (65%), while 35% were members of the Eastern Orthodox Church and 5% were members of other religious organizations.[46]

The camps were also a place of vivid artistic activity. Literary and artistic life revolved around institutions such as the Ukrainian Artistic Movements, the Ukrainian Associations of Artists, Associations of Ukrainian Musicians, and Theatrical Studio. Moreover, Weeks of Ukrainian Culture organized in Regensburg and Munich in 1948 can be considered as one of the most important artistic events.[47] It is also worth noting the large-scale publication activities. It is estimated that 327 periodicals, 1,200 books, including 250 literary works: poetry, drama, and prose, and pamphlets were published.[48]

Main Ukrainian educational and scientific institutions such as The Shevchenko Scientific Society (NTSH) and Ukrainian Free Academy of Science (UVAN) also started to operate in the DP camps. The scale of their development is shown in table 9.9, which includes their founding date and place of operation. Data shows that the main Ukrainian academic center was Munich. Smaller academic centers existed in Augsburg, Hirschberg, and Frankfurt. The schooling activity included broad academic education. For instance, students of the Ukrainian Free Academy of Science could study history, art, biology, mathematics, physics, economics, oriental literature studies, history of literature, botany, medicine, geography, zoology and socio-economic studies.[49] The development of UVAN's educational and scientific activity is best described by Lubomyr Wynar, who analyzed the Ukrainian migration schooling system during the DP period. He writes: "during the years 1946 through 1950, UVAN sponsored over fifty conferences and meetings in various DP camps at which Academy members presented over 500 papers. This impressive number of scientific communications indicates the dynamic nature and vitality of this major learned society."[50] Academic literature emphasizes that the schooling system was so well developed that Germany became the only European country with a private Ukrainian education-

---

[46] Wolodymyr Maruniak, "Ukrainians in the Federal Republic of Germany," 257.
[47] Maruniak, 260–261.
[48] Vic Satzewich, *The Ukrainian Diaspora*, 98. Wolodymyr Maruniak claims that in 1947 in Germany alone there were as many as 72 kindergartens with 139 teachers and 2,551 children; 87 elementary schools with 401 teachers and 5,300 pupils; 35 secondary schools with 461 teachers and 2,779 students; 8 other secondary schools with 58 teachers and 408 students; 39 trade schools with 217 teachers and 2,112 students and 5 institutions of high learning with 314 professors and 1,266 students. "Thus, in 1947, there was a Total of 246 educational institutions with 1590 teachers and 14, 416 students," see: Wolodymyr Maruniak, "Ukrainians in the Federal Republic of Germany," 258.
[49] Lubomyr Wynar, "Ukrainian Scholarship in exile: The DP Period, 1945–1952," *Ethnic Forum* 1 (1988): 59.
[50] Lubomyr Wynar, "Ukrainian Scholarship in exile," 61.

al system.⁵¹ The data speaks for itself. In total, there were 266 educational institutions created in DPs camps, 14,000 students attended classes, 1,600 teachers were employed, and there were 18 theatre groups.⁵²

Table 9.9: The chronological development of Ukrainian institutions of higher learning and research centers during the DP period

Institution of Higher Learning		
Founding Date	Educational Institution	Place
June 1945	Ukrainian Technical Institute	Regensburg; Munich
Oct. 1945	Ukrainian Higher School of Economics	Munich
Nov. 1945	Ukrainian Free University	Munich
Nov. 1945	Ukrainian Catholic Theological Seminary	Hirschberg
Nov. 1946	Theological-Pedagogic Academy Ukrainian Orthodox Church	Munich
Scholar Societies and Research Centers		
June 1945	Historical-Philological Society	Transfelden
Nov. 1945	Ukrainian Free Academy of Science	Augsburg
Nov. 1945	Ukrainian Scientific Society	Munich
June 1946	Ukrainian Black See Institute	Kastel
Aug. 1946	Institute of Ukrainian Martyrology	Munich
Aug. 1946	Ukrainian Genealogical Institute	Frankfurt
March 1947	Shevchenko Scientific Society	Munich

Source: Lubomyr Wynar, "Ukrainian Scholarship in exile: The Dp Period. 1945–1952," *Ethnic Forum* 1 (1988): 56–57.

At the end of the 1940s and the beginning of the 1950s, Ukrainian institutions and ethnic organizations in the camps became less active due to mass departures from the DP Camps. The indicator of the change underway was diminishing number of both organizations and their members. The number of Ukrainian ethnic organizations in Germany fell from seventy to just thirteen before 1962.⁵³ The disintegration of the institutions also affected the main ethnic organizations, including The Ukrainian National Council and other academic institutions. For example, UVAN's academic activity was decentralized and the organization split into three independent institutions: UVAN in Canada (established in 1949), UVAN in the United States (established in 1950), and UVAN in Europe with its headquarters in Munich.⁵⁴ Some organizations, like The Central Ukrainian Teachers Organization, with nearly 2,000 members between 1946 and 1951, ceased to exist completely.⁵⁵ The organized structure of

---

51 Wolodymyr Maruniak, "Ukrainians in the Federal Republic of Germany," 257.
52 Vic Satzewich, *The Ukrainian Diaspora*, 97–98.
53 Wolodymyr Maruniak, "Ukrainians in the Federal Republic of Germany," 264.
54 Lubomyr Wynar, "Ukrainian Scholarship in exile," 61.
55 Wolodymyr Maruniak, "Ukrainians in the Federal Republic of Germany," 258.

Ukrainian immigrant life in the Camps had disintegrated due to the massive departures. However, they did not disappear altogether. They were reconstructed in the new destination countries of the emigrants. It is also worth noting that "for Ukrainians from Soviet Union, the camps were their first contact with more nationally conscious western Ukrainians and their first systematic exposure to a specifically Ukrainian cultural, intellectual and social life."[56] Information about the life in DP camps, the circumstances that influenced departure and how individuals who participated in the migration experienced them can be found in the accounts of Ukrainian emigrants below. One of them recalled:

> "I left my home in 1944. I went to Austria and Vienna and I was there until the end of the war. After the war ended, I was in the DP camp in Salzburg. Meanwhile, I attended University to study Medicine … I was after two years of studying, so I wanted to try. I came to this country in 1948".

The following statement provides a more detailed account of emigration:

> "I come from Lvov and when I came here, I was really young. I was twelve when I came to this country. It was after the World War I; my father was a director at a printing house in Lvov. Before the Russians came, we had to leave the city, so we had to travel through Hungary, Slovakia, Austria and the camps in Germany (…) One day, someone came and told us not to stay there any longer because the Russians would come and they would take us to Russia. We slept in a forest that night. The entire family. We left everything and next day we went to Salzburg and my father found a big Ukrainian organization there. There were three Ukrainian camps and we were there. We had Ukrainian schools. At first I went to a German school, then a Hungarian one, but I did not learn Hungarian because it is very difficult. From Salzburg, we emigrated to America. It was 1948. We came to Connecticut, because my parents had some friends there and I have to say that everyone was very kind to us. The mayor of the town even gave us a big basket of fruit and flowers. I went to school there and after school I worked casually".

One of the respondents emphasized camp life:

> "We came in 1949, unemployment was quite big there. Truman ordered to let 350,000 refugees into the US and they were Jews, Poles, Ukrainians, Lithuanians. From the 350,000, 50,00 were Ukrainians. And everyone was there; it didn't matter who worked as who. Teachers could not work because they didn't know English. Only doctors could, in hospitals but only as assistants. They earned very little for that. Slowly, slowly, they then climbed up, but the first years were very difficult. And the language. I studied at a polytechnic, I knew chemistry so I got a job at a steel factory (…) I came here from Austria, Truman let us so we came for free, on warships from World War II. It took long, ten days. In Austria, we lived by ourselves, not in a camp. We went to the camp to do business. We smuggled cigarettes to Germany, we bought them in a Jewish camp. They were the biggest traders. A carton, ten packs cost $1.70. In Germany, it cost $2.70. It was a dollar difference for a pack. It was so much. If you had fifty cartons, you had fifty dollars. It was a lot of money. I needed about twenty dollars a month. There were Jews from the Ukraine in this camp. Not from Kiev, from the countryside. They were Jews from Ukraine."

---

56 Vic Satzewich, *The Ukrainian Diaspora*, 98.

These statements reflect the above-described issues the existence of education in the camps, the recreation of family life, social life, and the strategies of coping with the new reality (including informal and illegal ones). They also allow us to observe examples establishing relationships with other ethnic/immigrant groups: Jews, Poles, and Hungarians. In the perspective of subjective biographical experiences, the stay in the camp and the departure to another country are not interpreted negatively. In the reminiscences of Ukrainian emigrants, migration was facilitated by the liberal law of the host country (in this case the USA). What is more, these statements show the important role of social network in the process of emigration. Social networks appear to be the main factor facilitating the adaptation of emigrants to the new country.

The third wave of Ukrainian emigration differed from the earlier waves not only in nature but also composition. The representatives were mainly educated people with much higher professional qualifications than the previous emigrants. This difference was caused not only by educational development in the Central and Eastern Europe in the interwar period but also by the extensive educational activities in the refugee camps. Information on the socio-professional structure of the third wave of emigrants can be found in the statistics on Ukrainians leaving for the US. Myron Melnyk states that the occupational structure of emigrants from the camps in Germany in 1948 was as follows: 43% of Ukrainian migrants were farmers, 25.4% were skilled workers and 15.8% were unskilled and semi-skilled workers. The rest, so nearly 16% of emigrants, occupied high positions as specialist and managers.[57]

The demographic structure was also different. In contrast to the previous waves, it was not a highly masculinized emigration wave. Gender proportions were comparable, meaning that women migrated as often as men. They were mostly unmarried persons and about thirty years old.[58] The number of children who were either born in DP camps or found themselves in one as a result of the war was also significant. The core of the emigration consisted of persons from western Ukraine. Apart from differences in schooling and social and occupational standing, the emigrants after the war, in contrast to the previous wave, had a developed sense of national identity and national ties. They focused not only on participating in the social life of the host country but also on the relationship with their home country. The phenomenon is especially well visible in the case of Ukrainians migrating to the US. Some researchers believe that those migrants established a new type of Ukrainian-American loyalty to the new country, but remained emotionally tied to the old one. This relationship was expressed through the activities conducted in favor of the home country and a need to continue political and cultural life in a different country, which was visible in the recreation of old ethnic organizations and the formation of new ones. There were political institutions propagating various ideologies and policy options such as the Organization for the Defense of Four Freedoms of Ukraine (ODFFU),

---

57 Myron Melnyk, "Immigration of Ukrainians to the United States," *Ethnic Forum* 1–2 (1995): 122.
58 Ihor Zielyk, "Ethnicity and Irredentism in Diaspora," 103.

the Ukrainian American Youth Association (SUMA), and the Organization for the Rebirth of Ukraine (ODWU). An array of cultural, scientific and professional organizations was created, associating specialists from various professional categories e.g. doctors, engineers, historians etc. In the case of the Ukrainian diaspora in the US, the post-war migration founded the Ukrainian Historical Association (1965), the Ukrainian Medical Association (1950) and the Ukrainian American Bar Association (1977).[59] Different ways of adaptation to American host society, different worldview and political orientations as well as variances in the social and occupational composition influenced the long-lasting were the reasons for long-term process of adjustment of the "old" and the "new" (post-war) Ukrainian migration.[60]

Despite existing tensions between the representatives of the second and the third migration wave, it seems that the relations between post-war/political emigration and the newest "fourth" wave, which began in 1990s, are more complex. The divisions resulted from socio-economic differences and different social values of the diaspora and the newcomers.[61] The factor intensifying the tension within the Ukrainian diaspora is the complicated linguistic situation. Most of the recent emigrants (59%) use the Russian language in everyday communication and only two-fifths (41%) use Ukrainian at home. The influx of a significant number of Russian-speaking Ukrainians in 2000s resulted in a higher percentage of Ukrainians who speak Russian than those who speak Ukrainian.[62] It seems to be an additional factor influencing relations within the Ukrainian diaspora.

It is worth to note, however, that the influx of representatives of third wave of emigration also contributed to the change of status of Ukrainians in the stratification system of host communities, which were traditional clusters of Ukrainian diaspora. It is visible especially on the example of American and Canadian societies where the Ukrainians have occupied the lowest positions until the 1950s. The position of the group improved in the 1960s and 1970s. Oleh Wolwoyna pointed out that among

---

59 More on the subject: Anna Fiń, "Ukraińska imigracja w Stanach Zjednoczonych," 40–41, 48–50. Ihor Zielyk writes that the representatives of this migration wave "brought with them not only fresh talents but heart-stirring accounts of the incessant Ukrainian struggle for liberation and independence." See: Ihor Zielyk, "Ethnicity and Irredentism in Diaspora," 131.
60 Vic Satzevich, *The Ukrainian Diaspora*, 102–106; Ihor Zielyk, "Ethnicity and Irredentism in Diaspora," 226–231.
61 The analysis carried out so far suggest that the most recent immigrants brought up in the era of real socialism have shown little interest in the activities of ethnic institutions and organizations. In the opinion of the representatives of political emigration, they are mainly focused on "fast gathering mean"; for this reason, they are often referred to as a "homo sovieticus," "gold miners," "money-oriented people." It is emphasized that there is a different mentality and social awareness as well as different cultural behaviors, which usually manifests itself in the way of dressing (flashy appearance), behavior or manner of speaking, see more: Halyna Lemekh, "Immigrant Encounters in the Ukrainian Diaspora in New York," (PhD Diss., New School University, 2007), 47–63, 135–220; Vic Satzewich, *The Ukrainian* Diaspora, 195–197.
62 Oleh Wolowyna, "Immigration and Language..."

the members of the Ukrainian community in the United States there was an increase in employment in the category of a white-collar workers as well as a significant increase of the level of education.[63] The process depended in the following decades to the point that statistics from the 1980s and 1990s do not show any structural differences between the Ukrainian diaspora and the American society.[64] Academic literature emphasizes that the speed and nature of social mobility of the group was in reality caused by three factors: the influx of political emigrants, intergenerational social upgrade and overall socio-economic changes of the host society.

The analysis of the anti-Communist activities undertaken in exile is the another important issue with the description of Ukrainian emigration in the Cold War period. The issue, in particular the types of activities of the Ukrainian diaspora, needs closer examination.

9.4.1 Anti-Communist diaspora activity

Based on available sources, it can be said that anti-Communist activity of Ukrainian diaspora was very intense but Ukrainians never created a unified battlefront. It was related to internal political divisions and ideological tensions among the leftist group, the national group, and the moderate/center group.[65] Each of the fractions gathered different ethnic organizations and exhibited dissimilar attitudes toward the Ukrainian case.[66] Moreover, the conflicts and ideological dissimilarities existed within the fractions themselves.

---

63 Daria Markus and Oleh Wolowyna, "Ukrainian in the United States of America," in *Ukraine and Ukrainian throughout the World*, ed. Pawliczko, 69–372; OlehWolowyna, "Socioeconomic Characteristic," in *Ethnicity and National Identity: Demographic and Socioeconomic Characteristics of Persons with Ukrainian Mother Tongue in the US*, ed. Oleh Wolowyna (Cambridge: Harvard University Press, 1986): 98–117.
64 Anna Fiń, "Ukraińska imigracja," 45–47. Information on socio-occupational transformations in the Ukrainian diaspora can be found in Jaroslav Petryshyn, "The Ukrainian Canadians," 78–87; Oleh. W. Gerus and James E. Rea, *The Ukrainians in Canada* (Ottawa: Canadian Historical Association, 1985); Norbert J. Hartmann and Wsevolod Isajiw, "Ethnicity and Occupation: An Assessment of the Occupational Structure of Ukrainian Canadians in the 1960s," *Canadian Ethnic Studies* 12 (1980): 55–73.
65 Myron Kuropas writes about the reasons of ideological divisions within the Ukrainian diaspora and describes the phenomenon in relation to the Ukrainian immigration in the United States. See: Myron Kuropas, *The Ukrainian Americans*, 162–303. See also: Satzevich, *Ukrainian Diaspora*, 109–120.
66 Taking as an example the Ukrainian diaspora in the US, the following organizations representing various ideological camps could be enlisted: a) the leftist wing brought together, among others: the Ukrainian Workingsman's Ass. (UWA), Organization for the Rebirth of Ukraine (ODWU), The Union of Ukrainian Socialists, The Union of Ukrainian National Democrats (SUND); b) the right-wing groups were included, for example, Organizations for the Defense of Four Freedoms of Ukraine (ODFFU), The Ukrainian American Youth Association (SUMA), The Brotherhood of Former Soldiers of the last Ukrainian Division, The Brotherhood of Former Soldiers of the UPA, The Ukrainian Hetman Organization (UHO), and The Association of the Friends of the Ukrainian Liberation Struggle. These groups stood in opposition to democratic and leftist factions, and were against the two dangerous,

The leftist group, for example, was a divided into a pro-Communist (pro-Soviet) and a pro-socialist fraction; the right-wing group consisted of ultra-nationalist groups (the so-called Banderite groups), which derived their ideology from OUN UPA and a bit more moderate representatives of Ukrainian revolutionary and independence groups and the Ukrainian hetman movement. Generally speaking, among different migration groups (also Polish), there was a belief that the Ukrainian diaspora "is not a unified unit, even in the independence bloc there is an array of ideological shades which are a source of tensions and political struggle."[67] This fact was emphasized in the Polish newspaper of the diaspora, *Nowy Dziennik*, by the historian Konstantyn Zelenko, who wrote that, "as a result of different divisions and splits we have several versions of Ukrainian history and polemics within nationalist camp alone."[68] The ideological tensions within the diaspora in the discussed period are reflected in a statement of Ukrainian immigrant, who described the activities of New York and Ukrainian Communist fraction:

> "They were all Bolsheviks, this group on the fourth street, they were funded, because they had nothing here (...) I also want to say that in 1953 these Communists from the fourth street, they did, (...) Then Ukrainian anti-Communists wanted to disperse them and do not allow them to do this. I can speak accurately about this, as I participated in this. They, and I was at in the street. (...). Some group went inside. There was a coffin there and they organized a meeting. A fight broke out. They called the police, the police dispersed everyone. (...) They forbade them and us. Everyone went home. There were mainly older people, there were no young people, they belonged to the Communist party in the 1920s, after the revolution".

This statement also provides information about the social composition of each political group. Historical findings and current analyzes suggest that the nationalistic fraction composed mainly of newcomers, and as such, chiefly DPs and other political emigrants; the percentage of the so-called "old migration" was small. Members of moderate groups were mostly born in the US or have had American citizenship for a long time', among them were a large part of representatives of science and cultural world. On the other hand, socialist groups accommodated the participants of the second migration wave. It is worth mentioning that the ideologically divided Ukrainian diaspora was not even united by the World Congress of Free Ukrainians, which was

---

in their opinion,"imperialisms": the Polish imperialism and the Russian imperialism; c) to the centrist/ democratic groupings belonged: The Ukrainian National Association (UNA), The Ukrainian American Relief Committee (UUARC), The Ukrainian Youth League of America, and The Ukrainian American War Veterans. These organizations were amalgamated into The Ukrainian Congress Committee of America (UCCA), i.e. the primary organization established in 1940. The members of this wing advocated mainly for conducting lobbying and propaganda campaigns, cutting themselves off from the revolutionary movement.

67 Polish Consulate General in New York, "Raport sytuacyjny ukraiński za okres styczeń-luty 1944 r," Collection no. 10: 35, The Jozef Pilsudski Institute of America Archive. Archives are normally cited first in the footnotes

68 Konstatntyn Zelenko, "Emigracja Ukraińska," *Nowy Dziennik*, 6 January 1987, 6.

founded in 1967 (presently the Ukrainian World Congress). It was an international organization representing Ukrainian migration matters and aiming to consolidate different communities of the diaspora. K. Zelenko believes that in the analyzed period, the Congress was "vexed with different internal conflicts and rivalries of political groups fighting for influence and primacy and did not achieve its goal."[69]

Although the Ukrainian diaspora lacked ideological unity in the Cold War period, it started an ethnic mobilization, which relied on numerous activities aiming to "struggle" for Ukrainian independence. Based on the sources available, one can conclude that the immigrants in the United States and Canada were the most active, followed by those in Germany and Great Britain. The diaspora in South America had its representatives in The Ukrainian Pan-American Conference established in 1947,[70] but was not particularly active in this area. As the US constituted a very good base of strong and well-organized emigration, the anti-Communist activities of Ukrainian migrants will be described based on this example.[71] It will refer to Europe only in rare cases.

The analysis of available sources lets us extract four basic contexts of anti-Communist activity of the Ukrainian diaspora: a) context of political activity; b) context of activity in the symbolic and socio-cultural dimension; c) "identity" context; d) context of relations with different ethnic/immigrant groups. Although the contexts of anti-Communist activity of the Ukrainian diaspora have been distinguished for the sake of clarity of an analysis, in reality, they remained intertwined.

The first aspect refers to the political activity of Ukrainian organizations, lobbyist activities both on a federal and a local level, and a membership in captive nations organizations. Political activity of each ethnic organization was expressed primarily through Ukrainian emigrants' attitude to post-Yalta decisions. Disapproval towards the situation in Soviet Ukraine were declared openly, deeming Russian policy as aggressive and imperialist. Such attitudes were expressed by the Ukrainian Congress Committee of America (UCCA). It was established in 1940 and was represented by such men as, for instance, Lev Dobriansky. Based on archival documents, one can conclude that the main goal of the organization in the Cold War period was to sup-

---

69 Konstantyn Zelenko, "Emigracja Ukraińska," 6.
70 The Congress gathered representatives from both North and South America. It comprised the following primary organizations: The Ukrainian Congress Committee of America, The Committee of the Canadians of Ukrainian Origins, The Association of Friends of the Ukrainian Culture in Brazil, and The Ukrainian National Committee of Argentine, Paraguay and Uruguay.
71 For the actions taken by the Ukrainian diaspora in Canada see Roman March, "Political Mobility of Ukrainians in Canada," in *Changing Realities: Social Trends Among Ukrainian Canadians,* ed. Roman Petryshyn, (Edmonton: Canadian Institute of Ukrainian Studies Press, 1980), 213–224; Elizabeth D. Wangenheim, "The Ukrainians: A Case Study of the 'Third Force'," in *Nationalism in Canada,* ed. Peter Russell, (Toronto: McGraw-Hill Co., 1966), 72–91; Paul Yuzyk, "The Political Achievements of Ukrainians in Canada, 1891–1981," in *New Soil – Old Roots: The Ukrainian Experience in Canada,* ed. Jaroslav Rozumnyj (Winnipeg: Ukrainian Academy of Arts and Sciences in Canada, 1983), 303–316.

port the "struggle of the Ukrainian people against Moscow."[72] Such support was given in various ways: by sending memorandums and cablegrams to the American government, organizing conferences, lectures and spreading propaganda with the aim of raising awareness of the Ukrainian matter. As a centrist organization, the UCCA attempted to cooperate with other organizations representing other oppressed nations, in the question of anti-Communist activity. They expressed the view that the activities of the coalition were more effective. One example that proves this point was the UCCA's participation in a "Freedom Rally" in May 1949. It was an event organized by Common Cause Inc. Apart from the Ukrainians, the event was attended by Poles, Albanians, Czechoslovakians, Hungarians, and Bulgarians. An indicator of the attitudes towards the political situation in Eastern and Central Europe was the speech by the president of the UCCA, Lev Dobriansky, who said: "We fight against Soviet Communism – that is our negative action. We fight also for the eternal principles of free men – that, let us never forget, is our positive action."[73]

Attempts to consolidate of migration communities through organized congresses were important indicators of ethnic political mobilization. One of the first attempts was made in November 1947 in New York, where the already mentioned Ukrainian Pan-American Conference (PAUC) was established. The founding of the Pan-American Conference was an answer to the political situation in postwar Ukraine and an expression of disapproval toward such state of matters. The proof of the attitudes was the came in the form of adopted resolution, which stated the following: "The present Ukraine Republic, which is part of Soviet Russia, is not a free country. The Russians are trying to exterminate the Ukrainian nations (…) The present Bolshevik imperialism is the greatest danger to humanity and to the very existence of the West."[74]Simultaneously, the prevailing opinion was that the activities aiming to "liberate" Ukraine needed to be conducted while remaining loyal to American society.[75] Apart from propaganda and lobbying activities, PAUC also dealt with obtaining financial support. Information available to the public lets us conclude that the organization was mostly active in the US. In Canada, its activities were minimized by ideological divisions.

Another important attempt to consolidate Ukrainian diaspora was the creation of the World Congress of Free Ukrainians (WCFU) in November 1967. During the first con-

---

[72] Immigration History Research Center Archive, Collection, Walter Dushnyck, box 7, folder: Ukrainian Political Situation Today: Part Three: Ukrainians in Western Hemisphere, 123. Other important members of the UCCA included Dmytro Halychyn, Stephan Jarema, Michael Piznak, Dr. Luke Myshuha, Prof. Nicholas Chubaty, Wasyl Mudry, Julian Revay, Prof. Roman Smal-Stocky, Prof. Augustin Shtefan, and prof. Michael Vetukhiv.
[73] *The Ukrainian Bulletin*, 15 May 1949, 2.
[74] Polish Embassy in the USA, "Political Currents Among Ukrainian American," The Polish Institute of Arts and Science Archive, Collection no. 12, folder no. 13, 11.
[75] Polish Embassy in the USA, "Political Currents Among Ukrainian American," The Polish Institute of Arts and Science Archive, Collection no. 12, folder no. 13, 12.

gress, held in New York, *The first manifesto to the Ukrainian people in Ukraine and beyond its borders, in the U.S.S.R., and in the lands of the Russian Communist bloc* was adopted. The manifesto was a collection of rules for the migrant Ukrainians and a collection of goals. Among its goals were: nurturing social and cultural ties with Ukrainian migrants, cultivating national identity, and maintaining and developing religious traditions, history, culture and language.[76] Resolutions adopted by the congress supported the fight for a free and independent Ukraine. The statement issued at the time said: "with all our power and means, and within the laws of the countries of our domicile, to aid the Ukrainian people in their struggle for freedom and toward the re-establishment of an independent, united, democratic Ukrainian State."[77]

During the Cold War, many similar manifestos, resolutions, and cablegrams were made. On the level of politics, visible forms of protest were avoided and the activities were limited to propaganda and lobbying, which aimed to gain the support of the public opinion and the government for the Ukrainian interest. This activity was important as most Ukrainian political activists thought that Western countries and especially the American government ignored Ukraine's problems.[78] The establishment of the Captive Nation Week in 1959 by the US Congress is regarded as one of the greatest successes of the Ukrainian lobby.[79] As already mentioned, political activity of Ukrainian organizations was expressed through the cooperation with other captive nations. The Ukrainian diaspora joined various coalition organizations, which focused on anti-Soviet activities. The number of these organizations was quite high and the most important were: Conference of Americans of Central and Eastern European Descent (CACEED), The National Captive Nations Committee (NCNC), Federation of Americans of Central and East European Descent (FACEED), Central European Federation (CEF), Anti-Bolshevik Bloc of Nations (ABN), Americans from East Central Eu-

---

[76] "First Manifesto to the Ukrainian People in Ukraine and Beyond its Borders, in the U.S.S.R. and in the Lands of the Russian Communist Bloc," Immigration History Research Center Archive, Collection: Walter Dushnyck, box: 8

[77] "World Congress of Free Ukrainian: Resolutions, November 16–19, 1967, New York, USA," Immigration History Research Center Archive, Collection: Walter Dushnyck, box: 8, 2.

[78] Such proposals were formulated at the Fifth Session of the Ukrainian National Council, which took place in Europe and was attended by representatives of the Ukrainian diaspora from all over the Western world. The meetings were also attended by the representatives of the two Ukrainian churches. During the session it was claimed: "at the present moment the Ukrainian matter is not in the first place when it comes to international affairs. The Western world in their games against Moscow Bolshevism has no well-defined policy." See: "Przegląd Prasy Ukraińskiej, Grudzień 1961," The Hoover Institute Archive, Stanisław Mikołajczyk Collection, box 116: 1.

[79] The Captive Nations Week was initiated by the National Captive Nations Committee organization, the initiator and the long-term president of which was a Ukrainian activist Lev Dobriansky. Besides Polish and Ukrainian ethnic groups, the following ethnic groups also participated in the Captive Nations Week: Hungarian, Romanian, Belarusian, Estonian, Armenian, Lithuanian, and Yugoslavian. During the celebrations, usually a series of protests were organized. The event has aroused very ambivalent public opinion and has often been described in the American press as a conflict-generating factor in relations between the US and the USSR.

rope Coordination Committee and American Conference for the Liberation of the Non-Russian Nations of the USSR.[80] All these organizations associated several ethnic groups from East and Central Europe, which came territories under Soviet influence. For instance, the CACEED, created in 1956 in New York, associated the main organizations of the following ethnic communities in the US: Bulgarians, Hungarians, Lithuanians, Czechoslovakians, Estonians, Latvians, Poles, Ukrainians and Romanians. The main goal of this organization was to strengthen these countries position vis-à-vis the Soviet Union and was thus meant to help liberate them from the Soviets. The CACEED expressed its goal in the following statement: "merit support and encouragement in their struggle for freedom and national independence."[81] The ABN in their *Monthly Bulletin of ABN* postulated in three languages: English, German and French, this statement: "Freedom for Nations! Freedom of Individuals."[82]

The ethnic mobilization of migrants also took place in the different Soviet states. A good example is the activity of the so-called Helsinki Group operated in Armenia, Georgia, Lithuania, and Ukraine. It was established in 1976 as a result of Helsinki Accords, adopted during the Conference on Security and Co-operation in Europe in 1975 by the Soviet Union. The Helsinki Group was founded as a formal public institution that monitored the observance of human rights. In reality, the group associated many opposition activists. The activities of the group focused on publishing information about cases of human rights violations and sending the reports abroad. They cooperated very closely with the immigrant communities in Canada and the US. In the 1980s, because of repression, arrests, and compulsory emigration, the group stopped operating.[83]

The second aspect of anti-Communist activities of Ukrainian emigrants is of a symbolic and socio-cultural dimension. This aspect boiled down to the actions that were supposed to sensitize public opinion to the Ukrainian issue. Manifesta-

---

80 Interestingly, the Ukrainians did not have their representation in the leading coalition organization, which was the Assembly of Captive European Nation (ACEN). Available archival materials and statements by members of the Ukrainian and Polish diaspora (member of the ACEN) suggest that this situation was connected to the diplomatic activities of the US State Department, which did not recognize Ukraine diplomatically throughout the Cold War and treated it similarly to Belarus, Armenia or Georgia, namely, as a traditional part of the Soviet Union and not a captive nation. See: "Przegląd Prasy Ukraińskiej, Grudzień 1961," The Hoover Institute Archive, Stanisław Mikołajczyk Collection, box 116: 1. Some aspects of the activities of these organizations is also describe by Anna Mazurkiewicz see. Anna Mazurkiewicz, "Narody ujarzmione" – lobby polityczne czy projekt propagandowy?," *Studia Historica Gedanensia* 5 (2014): 354–392; Anna Mazurkiewicz, *Uchodźcy polityczni z Europy Środkowo-Wschodniej w amerykańskiej polityce zimnowojennej 1948–1954* (Warsaw: Instytut Pamięci Narodowej; Gdańsk: Uniwersytet Gdański, 2016).
81 "Przegląd Prasy Ukraińskiej, Grudzień 1961," The Hoover Institute Archive, Stanisław Mikołajczyk Collection, box 116: 1.
82 Immigration History Research Center Archive, Collection: Walter Dushnyck, box: 10.
83 See more: Jaroslav Hrycak, *Historia Ukrainy*, 300; Yekelchyk, *Ukraina*, 240–241. It is worth to mention, that the discussion of the detailed activities of the organization would be so vast that the phenomenon deserves its own study, thus it is only pointed out here

tions, demonstrations, publishing (books, articles, pamphlets), image building are examples of activities that aimed at showing the negative image of Soviet Russia and the organization of happenings. Many of these actions were symbolic and they tended to emphasize the differences between the Ukrainians and the Russians. They thereby built symbolic boundaries between Ukraine and the Soviet Union in the social consciousness of the Ukrainians and of the wider society. The use of the adjective "free" in the names of ethnic organizations and certain events was one way of serving this aim. Two such examples are the founding of the World Congress of Free Ukrainians and the Ukrainian Free University as an opposition to the Soviet Ukrainian Academy in Kiev. A number of social engineering activities were meant to create a negative stereotype of the Soviet Union. For this purpose, inter alia, in the ethnic press and even in official correspondence, the Soviet Union and its policies were referred to as "The evil dynamics of Communism"; "Bolshevik barbarian"; "Soviet tyranny," "The evil empire."[84]

The anti-Communist activity was also carried out through publishing activities. Books, brochures, and pamphlets were published. The UCCA was the main publisher and the scope of the publications focused on such issues such as Ukrainian history and culture and criticism of the Soviet Union. Examples of publications included *Experience with Russia* (1956) by Vasyl Hryshko; *The Soviet Union – A New Despotic Empire* (1958) by Dmytro Solovey or *Ukrainian Insurgent Army in Fight for Freedom* (1954), which has been distributed to various libraries throughout the United States.[85] At the same time, demonstrations were held practically in all major Ukrainian diaspora communities. On the one hand, they were held under the banner of fighting the Communist regime. On the other hand, however, they were held when other events took place, e.g. sporting events and national celebrations, such as the commemoration of the victims of the Great Famine in Ukraine. There are many examples of such actions.

In 1951 on the streets of New York, in Manhattan Center, there was an anti-Soviet demonstration in support for the Congressman Kersten's resolution, which called for support for the nations "enslaved" by Moscow. A number of similar events took place between 1952 and 1955.[86] In 1980, during the Winter Olympics in Lake Placid, a series of protests were held against the participation of USSR representatives in sports competitions. At that time, there appeared the signboards with the inscriptions: "Let Ukrainians Compete"; "Fixing the Gold-Medal for Murder in Ukraine"; "Move the Games

---

84 *The Ukrainian Bulletin*, 15 August, 1950, 2.; *The Ukrainian Bulletin*, 15 June, 1948, 3; "Address of the Secretary General of the World Congress of Free Ukrainian to the Annual Meeting of the Polish Rada Narodowa Canada Branch on 1 December 1980 in Toronto," Ukrainian Fraternal Association, Immigration History Research Center Archive, Log 594, box 2, folder 1.
85 Alexander Sokolyshn, "Ukrainian American Organizations in New York City, 1955," in *The Ukrainians in America 1608–1975*, ed. Vladimir Wertsman, (New York City: Oceana Publications, 1976), 74–79.
86 Alexander Sokolyshn, "Ukrainian American Organizations in New York City," 74–79.

from Moscow." Members of the so-called Ukrainians Liberation Front were involved in the distribution of thousands of brochures and pamphlets among the participants of the Olympic Games.[87] Representatives of other Communist bloc nations, mainly Poles and the Czechoslovaks, usually supported such actions. In 1984, the ABN organized the *Free Olympiad*, first in Toronto and then in Los Angeles, at which immigrant athletes representing Ukraine, Lithuania, Latvia and Estonia competed.[88]

This aspect of anti-Communist activities also covered concrete steps in the field of education, including the creation of ethnic studies programs, financial support for Ukrainians studying at American universities, donating book collections to libraries in the Ukraine and disseminating information about Ukrainian history and culture. Establishing relationships of diaspora with their homeland was another issue. Ihor Zielyk believes that there were two basic ways to keep in touch with Ukraine. The first one was through relationships with emissaries, who were most often representatives of the world of culture, science and art and who, according to Zielyk, were able to "provide valuable information and to convey a sense of concern with the fate of Ukrainian identity and culture."[89] The second way was through the dissemination of Ukrainian underground publications in the country of immigration by groups like The Prolog in New York and Smoloskyp Publishers in Baltimore.[90] Efforts were also made to organize and develop the liberation movement in Ukraine. For this purpose, financial and technical support was given mainly to The Rukh (Ukrainian National Movement).[91] Nationalist movement factions sought to maintain contacts and support the activities of the so-called *Grupa Objednannia* opposition movement, which had been operating since 1956.

The support for Ukraine took on less direct forms as well. For example, the Ukrainian diaspora in the United States organized fundraising campaigns in order to purchase a building for the Ukrainian embassy in Washington and for the consulates in Chicago and New York. Although it is not possible to present the entire spectrum of socio-cultural and symbolic activities in just few sentences, there is no doubt that they were not only significant for the in-exile fight against Communism. They also played an important role for the Ukrainian diaspora in terms of identity, integration and establishing ties.

Another aspect of ethnic mobilization of the Ukrainians in exile during the Cold War is "identity context." "Identity context" was connected with sustaining and stimulating the national identity of the Ukrainians in the diaspora. In fact, the context boiled down to two basic actions. Numerous attempts to build and strengthen group loyalty have been undertaken. In the case of the Ukrainian diaspora, it was about the "survival of the ethnic community abroad, with distinct cul-

---

[87] Vic Satzewich, *The Ukrainian Diaspora*, 161.
[88] Satzewich, 161.
[89] "Chronicle of Current Events," *The Ukrainian Quarterly* 1 (1980): 104–105.
[90] Vic Satzewich, *The Ukrainian Diaspora*, 161
[91] Ihor Zielyk, "Ethnicity and Irredentism in Diaspora," 83.

ture and self-awareness. and two, striving for political independence of the homeland."[92] It is probable that the best example of this type of action was the first WCFU congress, during which the above mentioned *First manifesto to the Ukrainian people in Ukraine and beyond its borders* and a special *Resolution*, which contained a separate provision: *Ideal of a Ukrainian in the Diaspora*, were adopted. The notation was as follows: "VII. The World Congress of Free Ukrainians defines the ideal of the Ukrainian in the diaspora as follows: 'A Ukrainian in the diaspora is a full-fledged citizen of his country, bound to the Ukrainian people by the bonds of the Ukrainian language and culture, and his personality characterized by Christian-ethical values and by his creative action for Ukraine."[93]

On the basis of this provision it can be deduced that group loyalty and collective identity were built primarily with reference to elements of the historical continuity (language, culture and Christian values, in other words, ancestral tradition) and with regard to contemporary reality, which meant an obligation to take action to protect the homeland. Research conducted by Ihor Zielyk suggests that these elements actually contributed to self-identification of the emigrants. Most of the examined representatives of the Ukrainian political emigration have defined national consciousness as the "awareness of what Ukraine was, and hopefully will be: free"; "awareness of problems-struggle for independence, freedom"; "Knowing what [the Ukrainian] people stand for"; "I know who is my enemy."[94] There were multiple ways of strengthening ethnic identity in exile. The organization of lectures, picnics, the so-called "culture week," and articles in the press aimed at building relationships and group loyalty. The second type of activities related to the "identity context" was the so-called "identity politics." Kenneth J. Gergen defined identity politics as a desire to obtain political recognition and legitimacy of ethnic identity by social groups, which to some extent have been experiencing marginalization.

This activity is based on two identification schemes: self-recognition and being recognized by others.[95] In the case of the Ukrainian diaspora, the efforts to recognize the Ukrainian people in official censuses and statistics were an example of this type of action. As already mentioned at the beginning of this chapter, the US census did not treat the immigrants from Ukraine as members of a separate nation but simply as Soviet citizens. Organizations such as the UCCA and the Ukrainian National Association made efforts to change this situation. An indicator of the undertaken activities has been, inter alia, the correspondence of the above ethnic organizations with the Bureau of the Census Department of Commerce. Meanwhile, members of the Ukrainian diaspora in the USA were urged to determine their Ukrainian origin in the American population censuses. One such large action took place in 1960 when, for the first

---

[92] Zielyk, 34.
[93] "World Congress of Free Ukrainian: Resolutions...," 3.
[94] Ihor Zielyk, "Ethnicity and Irredentism in Diaspora," 150.
[95] After: Katarzyna Warmińska, "Polityka a tożsamość. Kaszebsko Jednota," *Studia Migracyjne-Przegląd Polonijny* 1 (2013): 191–192.

time in the US census, Ukraine was recognized as a separate country and Ukrainian as a separate language. Thereafter, the UCCA published *Recognition of Ukrainians in the US Census*, which contained summary information about Ukrainian roots, ethnographic territory, as well as instructions for completing the questionnaire. The instructions began with the following words: "Our duty in the forthcoming US Population Census – we must acknowledge our Ukrainian origin."[96]

9.4.2 Interethnic cooperation

The last context of ethnic mobilization of the Ukrainians during the Cold War concerns intergroup relations. It mostly applies to relationships with other immigrant groups that were willing to fight against the Communist system. These relations were established mainly with representatives of the oppressed nations. Nonetheless, apart from cooperation within these mass (great) organizations, a series of smaller initiatives were also undertaken. Ukrainians had contacts mostly with the Slovaks, the Czechs, and the Poles. However, literature provides no detailed analysis of the relations among the European immigrant groups, especially after 1945. Therefore, when analyzing this issue will be use an example of the Polish-Ukrainian relations in the USA[97].

In general, the relationship between the Polish and the Ukrainian diaspora was shaped by various forms of intergroup references that were determined by the the heritage of the European neighborhood on the borderland and complex attitudes towards the country of origin.[98] These were multi-layered and diverse interactions, which mean that they included conflicts and tensions as well as various forms of cooperation. Between 1945 and 1989, intergroup cooperation was intensified by the existence of the Soviet Union as a common enemy. This cooperation was often instrumental and the participation in joint activities was dictated by their mutual goal to reinforce their position with regard to the Soviet Union. This cooperation was implemented at the political and cultural-scientific level. Cooperation at the political level manifested itself through belonging to the already mentioned coalitions and participation in events organized by several oppressed nations. In addition to the already mentioned *Freedom Rally* and the regular participation of both groups in the *Captive Nations Week*, another example of such cooperation was the conference organized in 1952 in Milwaukee as part of the so-called *Freedom Week*, where both Polish and Uk-

---

[96] "Recognition of Ukrainians in the U.S Census," Immigration History Research Center Archive, Collection: Walter Dushnyck, box 10; and "Ukrainian National Ass. Records," Immigration History Research Center Archive, Collection: Ukrainian National Association, box 3, folder: Census 1990.
[97] I refer to specific results of the research project mentioned in the introduction of the chapter
[98] Anna Fiń, "In the space of 'displaced borderland'. A few reflections on the relationships between Polish and Ukrainian immigrants in the United States," *Studia Migracyjne-Przegląd Polonijny* 1 (2014): 143–160.

rainian group leaders, Stanisław Mikołajczyk, Lev Dobriansky and Walter Dushnyck, met and debated.[99] There were also local initiatives, for example, the so-called Round Table Club in New York in the 1960s, and of The Czech-Polish-Ukrainian Society in Chicago in the 1960s and 1970s.[100] Unequivocal support from the American Polonia for Ukrainian state-building efforts was another evidence of cooperation. According to Polish activists, Ukraine's independence was crucial for Poland regaining its independence and for stability and security in Central and Eastern Europe. Expression of this support was evident at various, more or less formal meetings, in statements of ethnic organizations and in the Polish-American press.[101] Members of the Ukrainian community in the United States also expressed strong support for the Polish "Solidarity" movement.

Below are presented selected quotes of the members of Ukrainian community in the United States that illustrate the attitudes:

> "Wałęsa and this Polish *Solidarność* organization had a very positive impact on the Ukrainians, as it was a turn against Communism,"
> "What happened in Poland in the 1980s had a huge effect on what happened with the Soviet Union, many people think so (...) while the emigration community really supported Solidarność activity."

Similar ideas and opinions were expressed in special resolutions, declarations, and ethnic press as well as during the special meetings of the representatives of both ethnic groups:

> "We are not Russia's neighbors. Ukraine, Belarus and Lithuania are our Eastern neighbors." (From *The Program of the Coalition for Polish Independence*, The North American Study Center for Polish Affairs, 1977)[102];

---

99 "UCCA Delegates Participate in AntiCommunist Conference in Milwaukee," *The Ukrainian Bulletin*, 1 January 1952, 3
100 The Round Table Club in New York founded by representatives of the Ukrainian diaspora, aimed to organize discussions and seek a political agreement with various ethnic groups, mainly with the Jews, the Czechoslovak and the Poles. The statements collected during the research suggest that to the most engaged persons in the Club belonged such Ukrainian activists as Eugeniusz Stachiw, Mykola Haliv, and Ivan Rudnycki. The interviews are available in the co-author's, Anna Fiń's, archive. The analysis of archival documents showed that The Czech-Polish-Ukrainian Society in Chicago ceased operations due to the Polish-Ukrainian tensions caused by the issue of the eastern borders. The information has been gathered on a basis of the analysis of Wacław Jędrzejewicz's correspondence with Stanisław Paprocki, see: Document: "Archiwum Wacława Jędrzejewicza: Korespondencja Wacława Jędrzejewicza ze Stanisławem Paprockim rok 1971," The Jozef Pilsudski Institute of America Archive Archives, fond number 053, item 8.
101 This issue was stressed in the articles of Polonia activists, such as Stefan Korboński, Andrew Ehrenkreutz, or Zbigniew Brzeziński.
102 After "For a Double Understanding between Ukraine and its Neighbors," *The Ukrainian Quarterly* 3 (1977): 237.

"Strong, non-Communist Poland needs strong non-Communist Ukraine" (Polish Journalist Claude Hrabyk during the Meeting of the Association for Free Ukraine; New York, 1956)[103];

"Please accept our deep sympathy and support for gallant struggle of the Polish people led by Solidarity against alien, Moscow-directed Communist rule in Poland. The struggle by Solidarity leaders for genuine democracy has become a source of inspiration among the captive nations in the soviet Russian empire, especially in Ukraine (...) We hasten to assure you that Ukrainians in the United States fully understand the tragedy of the Polish people and stand with them on the same battle lines against the common enemy – Communist and totalitarian Moscow". (From the telegram from Lev E. Dobriansky, President of The UCCA to Alojzy Mazewski, President of Polish American Congress.)[104]

Cooperation in the field of culture and science manifested itself mostly through joint participation in various festivals (usually organized as part of the Slavic Culture Week and Slavic Evening), poetry evenings, lectures, and conferences. Such activities aimed at popularizing ethnic culture and were a deliberate way of changing the negative semantic context of mutual stereotypes. At the beginning of the 1950s, the idea arose to establish the Polish-Ukrainian Society in New York and a permanent Committee of Experts.[105] In June 1981, a Polish-Ukrainian conference was held in the Ukrainian National Association headquarters in Jersey City; in October 1982 at the Ukrainian Institute in New York; and in March 1984 at the headquarters of the Polish Institute of Science in New York.[106] Various lectures were also held at the Jozef Pilsudski Institute in New York, at the Kosciuszko Foundation House and the Consulate General of Poland in New York. Such cooperation took place not only in America but also in Europe.

The Polish-Ukrainian Society was founded in London in 1967. The Ukrainian Free University in Munich has offered a Polish-Ukrainian seminar organized by prof. Zinpowij Sokoluk and Ivan Besarab since 1975. The Polish-Ukrainian Society began its work in Germany in the 1980s and it has published the newsletter *Łącznik Polsko-Ukraiński*.[107] The Ukrainian intelligence in exile had particularly strong ties to the Parisian *Kultura* magazine published by Jerzy Giedroyc. Many representatives of the Ukrainian diaspora were involved in collaboration, including, Bohdan Osadczuk, Iwan Kedryn-Rudnycki, Iwan Lysiak-Rudnycki, and Borys Łewicki. Moreover, Parisian *Kultura* tried to maintain contact with the aforementioned *szestydesiatnicy* opposition

---

103 "Polish Writer Proposes Polish-Ukrainian Understanding," *The Ukrainian Bulletin*, 1 May 1956, 4.
104 Telegram from Lev E. Dobriansky, President of The UCCA to A. Mazewski, President of Polish American Congress, *The Ukrainian Quarterly* 4 (1981): 4, 436.
105 Correspondence between Ivan L. Rudnycki and Jerzy Giedroyc see: Jerzy Giedroyc, *Emigracja ukraińska*, 533–631.
106 Information on organized conferences and lectures has been obtained from the analysis of the ethnic press such ass: *The Ukrainian Weekley, Nowy Dziennik, The Ukrainian Quarterly* and from multimedia documentation: sound recordings from the archives of the Schevchenko Scientific Society and the Polish Institute of Science. See: Schevchenko Scientific Society Archive, K-383, K-384, K-075 and Conference on Polish-Ukrainian Relations, Oral History Recordings, 19 PIASA Archive, 013, 159–162.
107 Andrzej A. Zięba, "Ukraińcy u Karpaccy Rusini," in Polska diaspora, ed. Walaszek, 458–459.

movement. Ukrainian emigrants cooperated with Parisian *Kultura* on issues such as borders, the history of Polish-Ukrainian relations, the social transformation of the Soviet Ukraine, the presentation of Ukrainian culture and efforts at the "internationalization" of the Ukrainian matter.[108] The analysis of correspondence between Polish and Ukrainian representatives of émigré communities indicates that the collaboration of the Ukrainians and the Russians in exile was rather reluctant and careful.[109] All the activities intensified contacts between diasporic Poles and the Ukrainians and they enabled contacts with other ethnic groups, their culture and language.

Each of the anti-Communist activities by the Ukrainian diaspora could benefit from a separate study. Unfortunately, such studies are rare. The function of these activities for the diaspora is also worth mentioning. Social scientists argue that political activity in exile not only helped to strengthen intra-group ties, but it was also a tool to adapt to the host society. This observation applies not only to the Ukrainians, but also to representatives of other groups whose migration process during the Cold War developed similarly, including the Poles, the Lithuanians, and the Czechs. The activities of post-war emigrants were described in a similar way by Elliot Robert Barkan, who argued that, "for many such peoples a vital part of their adjustment was their rapid involvement in public affairs tied to homeland issues."[110]

9.5 Migration since 1989/1991

The Yalta provisions created a new socio-political situation in Europe. They also contributed to a number of changes in European migration processes. Although one can point to some similarities, many of the processes were typical for a particular sending country. It was related to its migration culture, economic, political, and social conditions. The consequences of this emigration processes were also of various kind. The Ukrainian emigration process during the Cold War period led to new directions for Ukrainian emigrants and to the formation of two Ukrainian diasporas: the east and the west (see: Table 9.10). Other researchers share this view and argue that "The Ukrainians living abroad as made up of two diasporas – an eastern diaspora, which lives in various countries in Eastern Europe and the former Soviet Union, and a "Western" diaspora, which lives in North and South America, Western Europe and Australia."[111] The differences between them are fundamental. Firstly, they differ when it comes to the degree of their organization, self-reliance, institutional completeness, and the identification with their homeland. Although the western diaspora was able to create certain solutions (institutions, actions) in their best interest, the

---

108 Bogumila Berdychowska, "Giedroyc i Ukraińcy," in *Emigracja ukraińska,* Jerzy Giedroyc, 5–55
109 Jerzy Giedroyc, *Emigracja ukraińska,* 97 and 145.
110 Elliot Robert Barkan, *And still they come: Immigrants and American Society 1920 to the 1990* (Wheeling, Illinois: Harlan Davidson Inc., 1996), 103.
111 Vic Satzewich, *The Ukrainian diaspora,* 9.

eastern diaspora still lacks such organizations and ability. It seems that the main reason for this situation is the fact that the eastern diaspora began creating institutional completeness only in the 1980s. Following the traditional concept of diasporas by Robin Cohen, because of post-war emigration, the Ukrainian diaspora has become not only the "diaspora of work" but also "diaspora of the victims." Their huge commitment to the homeland made it also a "diaspora of warriors."[112]

This analysis also points to characteristic features and general regularities of post-war emigration of the Ukrainians. At first, there were two great streams of this emigration as some people chose to go to various republics of the Soviet Union, while others migrated within Europe or overseas, which should be defined as indirect migration. Undoubtedly, these were multicultural streams, although it is difficult to estimate their ethnic composition. It is generally believed that the postwar wave of Ukrainian immigration was driven primarily by political reasons. In reality, however, other factors were responsible for the nature and scale of this phenomenon, including economic and social conditions such as family ties. Adam Walaszek is correct when arguing that the third wave of emigration from Eastern Europe "was a move towards achievement of their financial ambitions as well as escape from the narrow-minded and repressive countries of residence."[113] Hence, "it is impossible today to maintain the old, sharp distinctions between voluntary and forced migrations. Even in case of traditional movements formerly referred to as forced (...) in the light of literature the voluntary and autonomous decisions taken by migrants remain obvious, which bears a striking resemblance to other economic migrations."[114]

In sum, we can identify four different periods of migration movements of Ukrainians during the Cold War period: a) the period of forced migrations within the USSR, 1939–1956; b) DP Period, 1945–1955; c) Migration in the period of "thaw," 1955–1989; and d) the period of voluntary migration within the USSR during the Cold War. Migratory movements of Ukrainians during the Cold War include voluntary departures but also forced migration in the form of deportation, exile, and repatriation. The most popular destinations were various republics of the Soviet Union. In terms of overseas migration, USA and Canada were the most popular destinations. After 1955, overseas migration should be defined primarily as indirect/ intermediate migration.

The collapse of Communism in Central and Eastern Europe started a fourth stage of Ukrainian emigration. Recognition of citizens' right to freely leave their place of residence resulted in a significant increase in both continental and overseas emigration. New migration routes led to South European countries; mainly to Italy and Spain. Since the 1990s the composition of migration flows has changed and the reasons for migration have become more complex.

---

112 The typology of diasporas is described in Adam, Walaszek, "Diaspory," in *Etniczność – o przemianach społeczeństw narodowych*, ed. Maria Szmeja, (Kraków: Nomos, Kraków, 2008).
113 Adam Walaszek, "Diaspory," 263.
114 Walaszek, "Diaspory," 262.

Table 9.10: The estimated number of Ukrainian diaspora in 1989

Republics of the former Soviet Union	
Armenia	8,341
Azerbaijan	32,345
Belarus	291,008–1,000,0
Estonia	48,271
Georgia	52,443
Kazakhstan	896,240–4,000,0
Kyrgyzstan	108,027–300,0
Latvia	92,101
Lithuania	44,789
Moldova	600,366–800,000
Russia	4,362,872–8,600,000
Tajikistan	435,578
Turkmenistan	1,375
Uzbekistan	153,197
Eastern Europe	
Bulgaria	1,000
Czech and Slovak Republics	150,000–200,000
Hungary	11,000
Poland	250,000–500,000
Romania	150,000–300,000
Western Europe	
Austria	4,200
Belgium	2,332
Denmark	‹ 100
Finland	50–100
France	25,000–30,000
Germany	20,032
Italy and the Vatican	250
Luxembourg	100
Netherlands	80–100
Norway	50–100
Spain	140–150
Sweden	2,000
Switzerland	100
United Kingdom and Ireland	20,000–35,000
Republics of former Yugoslavia	45,000
North America	
Canada	963,310–1,000,000
United States	730,056–1,300,000
Central America	25–50

South America	
Argentina	220,000
Brazil	350,000
Paraguay	5,000–8,000
Uruguay	4,000–5,000
Venezuela	800–1,300
Other South American Countries	100–200
Australia and Oceania	
Australia	30,000
New Zealand	200–300
Africa, Asia, and the Middle East	
Former Soviet Far East	2,000,000

Source: Ann Lencyk Pawliczko, ed., *Ukraine and Ukrainians throughout the World: A Demographic and Sociological Guide to the Homeland and Its Diaspora* (Toronto: University of Toronto Press, 1994).

Ukrainian emigration as a subject of research still requires many detailed studies. This applies both to the history of Ukrainian emigration and sociological studies of migration processes, their determinants as well as to the formation and transformations of the Ukrainian diaspora.

9.6 Archives and Literature

Diaspora archives and individual émigré collections constitute the major source of information on the cultural heritage and historical development of ethnic groups.[115] Essential archival resources on migration issues of the Ukrainian diaspora can be found in the USA, Canada and Europe. The following archives can be found in the United States: The Shevchenko Scientific Society in America, New York City; Ukrainian Academy of Arts and Sciences in the United States, New York City; Ukrainian Heritage Studies Center, Manor College, Pennsylvania; Ukrainian Museum and Library of Stamford, Connecticut; Ukrainian-American Archives and Museum, Detroit; The Ukrainian Museum in New York City; The Ukrainian National Museum in Chicago; Ukrainian Museum-Archive in Cleveland; Immigration History Research Center, University of Minnesota; Harvard Ukrainian Research Institute.

The Shevchenko Scientific Society in America is a further significant institution whose archival holdings include material on the life and work of Ukrainians in dif-

---

[115] Lubomyr Wynar and Lois Buttler, *Guide to Ethnic Museums, Libraries and Archives in the United States* (Kent, Ohio: School of Library Science Kent State University, 1978), 9.

ferent parts of Europe and America since the 1840s. The Ukrainian Academy of Arts and Sciences in the United States is an association of scholars dedicated to the promotion and advancement of Ukrainian studies and culture in the United States and has an archive, which contains museum-archival holdings (over 500,000 items) of Ucrainica. The Ukrainian collection at the Harvard University Library (Harvard Ukrainian Research Institute) includes personal documents, correspondence, telegrams, minutes, financial and administrative records, manuscripts, publications, press clippings, and photographs. The collections are a particularly important historical resource for the study of Ukraine during the revolutionary years 1917 to 1921, and Ukrainian refugee and émigré life in Europe and the United States after the Second World War. Other archival holdings are available at the Immigration History Research Center at the University of Minnesota. The archive contains material on Ukrainians in the United States, documents about the organizational/institutional activity of the ethnic group, history as well as culture.

There are also many Ukrainian museums, which house libraries and archives. The main objective of the museums is to collect and preserve documents related to the history of the Ukrainian community in the United States, Ukrainian history and folk artifacts which depict Ukrainian culture. These museum collections contain material documenting the life, history, and cultural legacy of the Ukrainian people. They also hold documents on the history of the Ukrainian immigrant group. The most important museums are: Ukrainian Museum and Library of Stamford, Connecticut; Ukrainian-American Archives and Museum, Detroit; The Ukrainian Museum in New York City, The Ukrainian Museum-Archive in Cleveland and The Ukrainian National Museum in Chicago. In Canada, The Canadian Institute of Ukrainians Studies at the University of Alberta has collected material on Ukrainian heritage and history in Canada. The Ukrainian Canadian Research Center and Documentation Centre (UCRDC) in Toronto is a non-profit organization, which collects, catalogues, and preserves material documenting the history, culture, and contributions of Ukrainians throughout the world. The Center holds oral histories in audio and video formats, many digitized as well as textual and photographic records.

Essential archival resources on the Ukrainian issue can be found in different archives and libraries in Europe, mainly in the Ukraine, Poland, and Germany. Worth consulting are also the following research institutions: The Institute for Ukrainian Diaspora Studies in the National University of Ostroh Academy and The International Institute of Education, Culture and Contact with Diaspora, Lviv Polytechnic. In Poland, material related to Ukrainian emigration and history can be found in The National Archive in Przemyśl. In Germany, The Ukrainian Free University in Munich is a scholarly center specializing in the study of Ukraine in the USSR and of Ukrainians in the diaspora. The collections of The Ukrainian Free University serve as a resource for research of Ukrainian history, literature, culture, law, and politics. Additional information on Ukrainian (and also other ethnic groups) archives may be found in Lubomyr Wynar's and Lois Buttler's *Guide to Ethnic Museums, Libraries and Archives in the United States*.[116]

Academic debate on Ukrainian emigration (including the time of the Cold War) and the reference material (monographs, studies, statistical analyzes) is relatively poor, especially when compared to literature on other European emigration groups: Poles, Czechs, Hungarians, and Germans. Among the most important scholarly articles on migration issues, written in Ukrainian, are those by Julian Baczynskyj, Wołodymyr Maruniak, Ludmiła Strelczuk, and Jewhen Jewtuch.[117]

English-language literature on Ukrainian migration is much richer and heavily concentrated in the United States and Canada. Among the most outstanding contributions in English are those by Ann Lencyk Pawliczko, Vic Satzewich, Myron Kuropas, Paul S. Magosci, Wasyl Halich, Wsevolod Isajiw, Lubomyr Wynar, Dmytro Bodnarczuk, Mandy R. Lupul, Jaroslav Rozumnyj, Roman Petryshyn, Vladimir Wertsman as well as Oleh Wolowyna.[118]

There are also Polish studies of selected aspects of the Ukrainian emigration. Especially worth mentioning are Andrzej A. Zięba's study on Ukrainian immigrants and their relations with other ethnic group in *Ukraińcy i karpaccy Rusini* in *Polska dia-*

---

116 Wynar and Buttler, *Guide to Ethnic Museums*.
117 Baczynskyj, *Ukraijnska immihracija w Spoluczenych Sztatach Ameryky*; Wołodymyr Maruniak, *Ukrainska emigracja w Nimeczczyni i Awstrii po Drugiej switowij wijni. Tom I. Roky 1945–1951* (Munich: Akademiczne Wydawnyctwo dr Petra Beleja, 1985); Strilczuk, *Ukrainski polityczni bizenci ta peremiseni osoby pisla Drugoi Switowoi wijny. Czerniwci* (Chernivtsi 1999), http://disser.com.ua/contents/29338.html (accessed 20 February 2015); Jewhen Jewtuch et. al., "Ukrainska diaspora. Sociologiczni ta istoryczni studii" *Naukovi pratsi Fakul'tetu sotsial'no-ekonomichnoyi osvity ta upravlinnya* (2003): http://enpuir.npu.edu.ua/handle/123456789/357 (accessed 20 February 2015).
118 Ann Lencyk Pawliczko, ed., *Ukraine and Ukrainians throughout the World: A Demographic and Sociological Guide to the Homeland and its Dispora* (Toronto: University of Toronto Press, 1994); Ann Lencyk Pawliczko "Ukrainian Immigration: A study in Ethnic Survival," in *The immigration experience in the United States*; Myron Kuropas, *The Ukrainian Americans*; Myron Kuropas, "The Centenary of the Ukrainian Emigration to the United States," in *The Ukrainian Experience in the United States: A Symposium*, ed. Paul R. Magocci (Cambridge Mass: Harvard Ukrainian Research Institute, 1979); Paul S. Magosci, ed., *The Ukrainian Experience in the United States: A Symposium* (Cambridge Mass: Harvard Ukrainian Research Institute, 1979); Wasyl Halich, *Ukrainian in the US* (New York: Arno Press, 1970); Wsevolod Isajiw and Andrij Makuch, "Ukrainians in Canada," in *Ukraine and Ukrainians throughout the World*, 327–357; Lubomyr Wynar, "Ukrainian Scholarship in exile: The DP Period, 1945–1952," *Ethnic Forum* 1 (1988); Lubomyr Wynar, "Ethnic Press. The Ukrainian Press in the United States: Past and Present Development," *Ethnic Forum* 1–2 (1985); Dmytro Bodnarczuk, *Ethno-national Consciousness*; Mandy R. Lupul, ed., *Ukrainian Canadians, Mulicultarlism and Speratism: An Assessmen* (Edmonton: The Canadian Institute of Ukrainian Studies, 1978); Rozumnyj, ed., *New Soil*; Petryshyn, ed., *Changing Realities*; Vladimir Wertsman ed., *The Ukrainians in America 1608–1975. A Chronology & Fact Book* (New York: Oceana Publications, 1976); Oleh Wolowyna, ed., *Ethnicity and National Identity: Demographic and Socioeconomic Characteristics of Persons with Ukrainian Mother Tongue in the US* (Cambridge: Harvard University Press, 1986).

spora[119] as well as the studies by Anna Fiń on the relationship between the Polish and Ukrainian immigrants in the United States and her work on ethnic mobilization of Ukrainian immigrants.

Most recently, academic research has been complemented by the information collected by The Ukrainian Diaspora Studies Initiative in the form of an electronic newsletter entitled *Ukrainians Abroad: News and Views*.[120] The Diaspora Initiative is headed by historian Serge Cipko, who is the author of numerous studies on Ukrainian settlements abroad.

---

[119] Andrzej A.Zięba, "Ukraińcy i karpaccy Rusini," in *Polska diaspora*, ed. Walaszek; Andrzej A. Zięba, *Ukraińcy w Kanadzie wobec Polaków i Polski (1918–1939)* (Kraków: Księgarnia Akademicka, 1998); Anna Fiń, "Odtworzone sąsiedztwo. Polscy i ukraińscy imigranci w nowojorskiej East Village," *Studia Migracyjne-Przegląd Polonijny* 1 (2013); Fiń, "In the space of "displaced borderland"; Anna Fiń, "Ethnic Mobilization of Immigrants. Case Studies of Ukrainian Political Emigration in the United States," in *The United States Immigration Policy and Immigrants*; ed. Dorota Praszałowicz and Agnieszka Małek (Frankfurt am Main: Peter Lang, 2016).
[120] Kule Centre for Ukrainian Canadian Studies, http://www.artsrn.ualberta.ca/cius-sites/ukrcan/Diaspora/UDSI-News_Views.htm (accessed 6 May 2018).

10 USSR

Alexey Antoshin

10.1 Russian migrations in historical perspective

The history of political emigration from Russia began in the sixteenth century. The first Russian political émigré was Prince Andrey Kurbsky, who left Muscovy for Lithuania. In the next century, the official Grigory Kotoshihin also chose to emigrate from Russia. In exile, these individuals attempted to become politically active: they published essays criticizing the Russian autocracy and exposed corruption among officials. However, in this period, they were singular cases: there was no process of mass emigration from Russia. This can be explained by the fact that the vast territories of Eurasia had been opened up to Russians, which made it unnecessary to emigrate abroad. In the eighteenth and early nineteenth centuries, about 15 million Russians moved from the central regions of the country to its borders and empty spaces. In terms of living abroad, one should note that this was not an unusual experience for Russian noblemen in the nineteenth and early twentieth centuries. Many cultural actors and people from the intelligentsia (for example, the famous writers A. I. Turgenev, N.V. Gogol, F. M. Dostoevsky, and others) lived in Europe for considerable lengths of time, creating their most remarkable works whilst doing so. However, they did not understand their time abroad as 'emigration'. Many well-off Russians travelled annually to Europe for relaxation and medical reasons, amongst others. It was a common phenomenon for Russian students to live abroad while they studied at the universities of Germany, France, Belgium, and other countries.

The real process of mass emigration started in the second half of the nineteenth century. There were three main groups of émigrés from the Russian Empire:
- *labor émigrés*. This was the most numerous group. This emigration movement developed especially quickly at the end of nineteenth and the beginning of the twentieth centuries. Above all, emigrants left from the Russian Empire to North America,[1] South America,[2] and Australia.[3] Between 1861 and 1915, the total number of émigrés from the Russian Empire to the New World amounted to 4 million. The majority were not ethnic Russians: they were Jews, Polish, Ukrainians, Byelo-

---

[1] Simon Kuznets, "Immigration of Russian Jews to the US: Background and Structure," *Perspectives in American History* 9 (1975): 35–124; Nancy Eubank, *The Russians in America* (Minneapolis: Learner Publications, 1973); Paul Magocsi, *The Russian Americans* (New York: Chelsea House Publishers, 1989); Gerald Govorchin, *From Russia to America with Love: A Study of the Russian Immigrants in the United States* (Pittsburgh: Dorrance, 1993).
[2] Alexandr Sizonenko, *Russkie v Latinskoy Amerike* [Russians in Latin America] (Moscow: Avanglion, 2005).
[3] Glynn Barratt, *The Russians and Australia* (Vancouver: University of British Columbia Press, 1988); Elena Govor, *Australia in the Russian Mirror* (Melbourne: Melbourne University Press, 1997).

russians, and Lithuanians, all of whom formed their own diasporas in the New World. They belonged to the peasantry, artisans, and other less prestigious social estates of the empire. Some of them emigrated for reasons other than economic ones, especially the Jews, who constituted a separate group in Russian society and were strongly affected by governmental limitations.[4]

These émigrés were the part of Second Great Wave of American immigration.[5] In America, they formed the Russian Independent Mutual Aid Society (RIMAS), the American Russian Mutual Aid Society (ARMAS), and similar organizations. The main task of these structures was to provide social security and help members to survive during economic crises. The majority of ordinary "Russians" in America were workers in various factories in Detroit, Chicago, New York, and other cities. They had to toil in difficult conditions: "some jobs were hot, dirty and arduous; others were dangerous."[6] In part thanks to the influence of the left-wing intelligentsia, organizations like RIMAS and ARMAS frequently attempted to expand their activities into other spheres. They began to occupy themselves with cultural and educational work, carrying out various tasks in these areas. These processes were reflected in the establishment of the Society in the Name of N.G. Chernyshevsky in New York in 1930. In the 1930s and 1940s, the organizations created by labor émigrés in the United States were rapidly politicized. The difficult working conditions and the lives of labor émigrés, marked by the instability of their material position, led to them becoming propaganda targets of pro-Soviet groups in the USA. With the participation of the American left (in particular the Congress of Industrial Workers, which existed in Detroit in the 1940s),[7] the organizations created by 'Russian' labor émigrés were subjected to strong propaganda pressure from Soviet embassies and associated structures.[8]

– *Religious émigrés*. Old Believers, Molokans, and others communities pressured by the Russian Orthodox Church and governmental policy decided to immigrate to America and Canada, trying to save their identities in the New World.[9] During the Cold War (and especially in the second half of the 1940s), these migrants also

---

[4] Zvi Gitelman, *A Century of Ambivalence: The Jews of Russia and the Soviet Union, 1881 to the Present* (Bloomington: Indiana University Press, 2001).
[5] June Granatir Alexander, *Daily Life in Immigrant America, 1870–1920* (Chicago: Ivan R. Dee, 2007).
[6] Alexander, 111.
[7] Susan Stedman and Murray Stedman Jr., *Discontent at the Polls: A Study of Farmer and Labor Parties, 1827–1948* (New York: Columbia University Press, 1950); Mari Buhle, Paul Buhle, and Dan Georgakas, *Encyclopedia of the American Left* (Oxford: Oxford University Press, 1998).
[8] See the newspaper *Russky Golos*, published in New York from 1917. This publication was orientated towards labor migrants and their descendants and showed the common ground between their interests and the positions advocated by the Soviet Union.
[9] Marina Moseikina, *U istokov formirovania Russkogo mira (XIX – nachalo XX vv.)* [At the Origins of the Formation of the Russian World (the Nineteenth and Early Twentieth Centuries)] (Moscow: Aletiia, 2014), 141.

experienced intensive propaganda from Soviet diplomatic representatives and their press organs.[10]

– *Political émigrés.* One of the first Russian political émigrés was Alexander Herzen, who left the Russian Empire in 1847. In London, he founded the first Russian exile journal, *Kolokol* (The Bell). Between the 1860s and 1910s, many Russian revolutionaries (including the so-called *narodniks*, social democrats, and anarchists) left the Russian Empire for America and Europe. Among them were the future founders of Soviet Russia, Vladimir Lenin and Lev Trotsky.

The 1917 Revolution was a turning point in twentieth-century Russian history. The 'First Wave' of post-revolutionary Russian emigration began after the collapse of the monarchy in February 1917, when some former higher officials and aristocrats fled abroad. However, they did not do so in significant numbers. A much larger wave followed the defeat of the White Armies in the Russian Civil War (1917–1922), when the officers and soldiers of these forces had to leave Russia. In the beginning of the 1920s, many cultural activists and scientists left Soviet Russia although many of them were far from being principled opponents of the Bolshevik regime: very often, their departures were connected with the lack of opportunities for cultural and scientific work in Russia. Because of these movements, there arose a phenomenon dubbed 'Russia Abroad' in the Russian émigré literature; it flowered during the 1920s and 1930s. The most reliable data on the numbers and centers of the Russian diaspora in the inter-war period is given in the review composed by the Royal Institute of International Relations in London in 1937 (published by Sir John Simpson in 1939).[11]

Table 10.1: Numbers and centers of the Russian diaspora in the inter-war period

Country	1 January 1922	1 January 1930	1936–37
Austria	3,000–4,000	2,958	2,500
Belgium	3,823	7,000	8,000
Bulgaria	30,000–32,000	21,830	15,700
Cyprus	600–700	40	11
Czechoslovakia	5,000–6,000	15,184	9,000
Gdańsk	1,000	600	747
Denmark	800	300	600
Egypt	1,000–1,500	500	350
Estonia	14,000–16,000	11,200	5,283
Finland	19,000–20,000	10,000	7,932

---

10 See the newspaper *Vestnik*, published in Toronto from 1941. Many of the articles in this paper called on Old Believers living in Canada to support the foreign policy of the USSR during the Cold War.

11 Sir John Hope Simpson, *The Refugee Problem. Report of a Survey* (London: Oxford University Press, 1939), table 63.

Table 10.1: Numbers and centers of the Russian diaspora in the inter-war period *(Continued)*

Country	1 January 1922	1 January 1930	1936–37
France	67,000–75,000	150,000–200,000	100,000–120,000
Germany	230,000–250,000	90,000	45,000
Great Britain	8,000–10,000	4,000	2,000
Greece	3,000–3,200	2,000	2,205
Hungary	3,000–4,000	5,045	4,000
Italy	8,000–10,000	2,500	1,300
Latvia	16,000–17,000	15,646	12,800
Lithuania	4,000	5,000–8,000	5,000
Poland	150,000–200,000	80,000–90,000	80,000–100,000
Romania	35,000–40,000	12,000–15,000	11,000
Sweden and Norway	1,000–1,500	1,000	2,500
Switzerland	2,000–3,000	2,266	1,000
Turkey	30,000–35,000	1,400	1,211
Yugoslavia	33,500	29,500	27,000–28,000
The total number of non-naturalized Russian refugees in Europe and the Middle East	688,000–772,000	470,000–536,000	345,000–386,000

China was also a large center of post-revolutionary Soviet emigration. In 1922, there were 145,000 Russian migrants in the Far East. In 1930, this number had declined to 127,000, reaching around 94,000 by 1937.[12] In the 1920s and 1930s, the United States, Canada, Australia, and Latin America attracted few Russian refugees, since the majority of the participants in this wave hoped that the Bolshevik regime would fall in the near future and thus did not stray far from Russia.

In terms of ideology and politics, the Russian migrants of the post-revolutionary wave were divided into a few basic groups. Among the former officers of the White Army, the most popular were conservative political groups with a traditionalist orientation: a considerable number of them were monarchists and gathered around members of the Romanov dynasty. Others belonged to the so-called "undecided," who argued that the future form of government should be chosen by the Russian people in a referendum following the collapse of the Communist regime.[13]

Many representatives of the émigré intelligentsia held liberal democratic views and advocated forming a democratic republic in post-Communist Russia where civil and political liberties would be guaranteed. The most famous politician of

---

[12] Sir John Hope Simpson, table 64.
[13] Richard Pipes, *Struve – Liberal on the Right, 1905–1944* (Cambridge; Mass.: Harvard University Press, 1980).

this group was the historian Pavel Miliukov, the Provisional Government's minister of foreign affairs who now lived in Paris.[14]

Émigré groups propounding the idea of democratic socialism were very few in number. Alexander Kerensky, the former head of the Provisional Government, wielded little popularity in émigré circles, since they argued that his policies had allowed the Bolsheviks to rise to power.[15] However, the émigré social-democratic ('Menshevik') journal *Sotsialistichesky vestnik* (The Socialist Herald), published initially in Berlin and then in Paris and New York, distinguished itself by its deep analysis of the socio-economic and political evolution of the Stalinist USSR. During the Cold War, the intellectual heritage of the Menshevik historians Boris Nikolaevsky and David Dallin had a serious impact on American Sovietology.[16]

However, the younger generation of Russians who grew up in Europe had their own political attitudes. They were disappointed by the old politicians who "had lost" Russia in 1917. These young Russians were interested in the ideas of Fascism, which were quite popular in Europe in the 1930s.[17] They opposed liberal democracy, thinking that only a strong authority figure (even a dictatorship) could save Russia. The main such organization was "Young Russia," formed in Munich in 1923. Especially popular in 1930s, it tried to connect ideas of the Russian monarchy and the Soviet model of power: its main slogan was "The Tsar and Soviets!"[18]

Another group of young Russian émigrés chose a different path, forming The National Labor Union of the New Generation (Natsionalno-Trudovoy Sojuz Novogo Pokolenija, NTS) in 1930. This was one of the main structures of so-called émigré "activism," and it strove for active struggle against Soviet power. Its members tried to prepare for a "national revolution" in Russia, but their attempts to form an anti-Communist underground in the USSR in the 1930s were unsuccessful. The borders of the USSR were well guarded, so the majority of NTS activists who tried to enter the Soviet Union were killed or imprisoned.[19]

---

14 Robert H. Johnston, *New Mecca, New Babylon – Paris and the Russian Exiles, 1920–1945* (Kingston/Montreal: McGill-Quenn's University Press, 1988).
15 Richard Abraham, *Alexander Kerensky: The First Love of the Revolution* (New York: Columbia University Press, 1987).
16 Andre Liebich, *From the Other Shore: Russian Social-Democracy after 1921* (Cambridge, Mass.: Harvard University Press, 1997).
17 John J. Stephan, *The Russian Fascists – Tragedy and Farce in Exile, 1933–1945* (New York: Harper and Row, 1978).
18 Michail Nazarov, *Missija Russkoi emigratsii* [The Mission of the Russian Emigration] (Stavropol: Kavkazsky krai, 1992), 223–225.
19 Boris Pushkarev ed., *NTS: Mysl i Delo* [The NTS: Thoughts and Deeds] (Moscow: Posev, 2000).

10.2 The aftermath of World War II

Russian émigrés had a very difficult choice during World War II. Already in 1939/1940, some supporters of liberal and socialist ideas had left Europe for America, where they published newspapers supporting the anti-Nazi coalition. Some prominent Russian migrants were active participants in the Resistance movement in France. Among the heroes of the resistance were the sons of Russian émigrés Boris Vilde and Anatoly Levitsky. They were killed by the Gestapo in 1942. Some leaders of the Russian diaspora in France (the writer Ivan Bunin, General Anton Denikin, and the liberal politician Pavel Miliukov) refused to cooperate with Nazi Germany.

However, many Russian émigrés in Europe had a different stance and attempted to use World War II to overthrow Bolshevism. Some former "White" officers fought for the Nazi army, which also contained large military units made up of Russian Cossacks. In Yugoslavia, former "White" officers organized a Russian corps to help Nazi Germany battle the Communist partisans headed by Tito. The most famous such military unit was the Russian Liberation Army (RLA), led by the former Soviet general Andrey Vlasov. Consisting of imprisoned officers and soldiers from the Red Army who agreed to collaborate with Nazi Germany, the total number of RLA fighters amounted to about 124,000.[20] The RLA had close connections with the NTS, which tried to influence the ideological attitudes of the soldiers. The NTS also sought to use World War II for its own purposes, hoping to create groups in the Soviet Union. Its activists worked with the Nazi authorities in the occupied territories. After the retreat of the German Army, the NTS tried to save the underground structures it had created in the USSR.[21]

World War II deeply transformed the Russian diaspora. In 1940, after the arrival of the Red Army in the Baltic states, many Russian anti-Communists in Latvia, Lithuania, and Estonia were imprisoned, a policy which was followed from 1944 to 1945. The arrival of the Red Army in Eastern and Central Europe in 1944 and 1945 also ended important centers of the diaspora, bringing to a close the histories of Russian Sophia, Russian Belgrade, Russian Prague, and Russian Warsaw. The fate of Russian Harbin after the Red Army's descent into China was the same.

One of the main processes at work in the diaspora during World War II was the rise of Russian patriotism, an atmosphere that fostered pro-Soviet sentiments among émigrés in America and Europe. The political centers of pro-Soviet émigrés in the US were the newspaper Russky Golos and several clubs in New York City. These émigrés

---

[20] Catherine Andreyev, *Vlasov and the Russian Liberation Movement – Soviet Reality and Emigre Theories* (Cambridge: Cambridge University Press, 1987); Kirill Aleksandrov, *Ofitsersky Korpus Armii Generala-Leitenanta Vlasova* [Officer Corps of the Army of Lieutenant General Vlasov] (Moscow: Posev, 2009).
[21] Lev Rahr and Valerian Obolensky, *Rannie gody. Ocherk Istorii Natsionalno-Trudovogo Sojuza (1924–1948)* [The Early Years: An Overview of the History of the National-Labor Union (1924–1948)] (Moscow: Posev, 2006), 153–154.

were led by left-wing Russian intellectuals, who had left the Soviet Union but continued to support socialist ideas. These included famous men such as David Burliuk, a close friend of Vladimir Mayakovsky and a typical left-wing Russian intellectual who believed that the October Revolution of 1917 was the beginning of a deeper revolution affecting all spheres of life, most notably art. Unfortunately for thinkers like Burliuk, the development of Soviet society in the 1920s and 1930s resulted in the transition to strict control and the gradual limitation of creative freedom under the Stalinist regime. In response, Burliuk, like many others, fled the Soviet Union. In the United States, he continued to be a propagandist of Communist ideas, writing in his personal letters that the Soviet Union was "the state of the Great Stalin," where Soviet power nurtured the people.[22] Among the leaders of pro-Soviet structures in America were also some former Russian social democrats, whose ideological evolution during World War II led them to fully support Stalin's policies. For them, the social justice present in the Soviet Union was more important than the lack of freedom. The victory over Nazi Germany also demonstrated the effectiveness of the Soviet regime.[23]

However, the base for pro-Soviet structures in America was the great number of émigrés from the Russian Empire (see above). As former peasants and artisans, these émigrés detested the conservative social order of the former Russian monarchy. Without knowing much about the details of Soviet politics, they actively supported the Soviet Union, due largely in part to the impact of propaganda. Their leaders had to interact with main political authorities in America. They supported the left wing of the Democratic Party and formed the Russian Democratic Club in New York City. Such Russian émigrés strongly supported the ideas of the Roosevelt administration and tried to reinforce cooperation between America and the Soviet Union.[24] These émigré groups were closely connected with the Soviet embassy in the USA and their leaders were regularly invited to meetings there.

The supporters of the USSR were not simply "agents" of the Soviet state. These people really believed that the Soviet Union was an alternative, better path for the development of human civilization and that the Soviet people had built a society based on social justice. Recognizing the problems in American society, they idealized the radical new direction of the Soviet Union. Yet, some pro-Soviet émigrés gradually acknowledged that the Soviet Union was only using them in its grander political scheme.

Some Russian émigrés in Europe believed that World War II had led to a deep change in the Soviet regime. As a result, voluntary repatriation began after the end of the conflict. This process was connected with the formation of Unions of Rus-

---

22 "D. Burliuk to V. Kamensky. 1947," Rossiisky Gosydarstvenny Archiv Literatury i Iskusstva [Russian State Archive of Literature and the Arts], David Burliuk collection, folder 184, 32–33.
23 "Letters by A. Djubua 1944–1947," International Institute of Social History (IISH), A. Djubua collection, folder 3.
24 *Russky Golos*. New York, 3 July 1945, 1.

sian Patriots in different European states, such as France, Bulgaria, and Yugoslavia.[25] Initially, these organizations appeared spontaneously, but later the Soviet authorities sought to control them. Consequently, these new bodies were turned into Unions of Soviet Patriots. Their members wanted to return to the Motherland, having become tired of life abroad. Often, they had no success in European countries, having failed to achieve a high social status. The economic situation in Europe after World War II was grim, since prices were sky-high. Russian émigrés also felt a strong sense of nostalgia. They idealized the situation in the Soviet Union, arguing that it was a country built on the ideals of social justice. In 1945, 11,000 Russians in France proclaimed their desire to return home, while in Yugoslavia 6,000 Russians wanted to become Soviet citizens.[26]

10.3 Major migration streams from the USSR during the Cold War

10.3.1 Repatriation and the 'Second Wave' of Soviet emigration

The year 1946 was a very important point in the history of the Russian diaspora. In this year, the Soviet authorities promulgated a law, which gave Russian émigrés the opportunity to become Soviet citizens; it was an opportunity that many Russians in Europe were not slow to grasp. Consequently, pro-Soviet structures in Europe underwent another change and renamed themselves as Unions of Soviet Citizens.[27] These organizations were closely connected with the Soviet diplomatic apparatus, which strictly controlled this part of the Russian diaspora. There is no doubt that the Soviet authorities tried to use these structures during the Cold War, but this meant that it was more profitable for the USSR to have the new Soviet citizens remain in Europe. Although these individuals had Soviet citizenship, Moscow never offered them a real opportunity to return home. The Cold War changed the situation. In 1947, for example, the French government deported Soviet patriots to Eastern Germany.

The fates of deported individuals in the Soviet Union were very often tragic, with many becoming victims of Stalinist terror. Almost all the leaders of the Union of Soviet Citizens in France were repressed by the Soviet authorities and imprisoned in the gulags. They were freed only after Stalin's death in 1953. Some of their subsequent histories are especially interesting. For example, the hero of the Resistance, Igor Kri-

---

[25] *Dve moje domovine. Uspomene Jelizavete Zherardovne Giljoten* [My Two Motherlands. Memoirs by Elizabeth Gilioten] (Gorni Milanovats, 1991); Tsvetana K'oseva, *Bolgariya i Russkaja emigratsiya, 1920–1950-e gg.* [Bulgaria and Russian Emigration. 1920–1950s.] (Moscow: Russkii put, 2008).
[26] Natalia Pushkareva, "Vozniknovenie i formirovanie rossiiskoi diaspory za rubejom," *Otechestvennaja Istoria* 1 (1996): 61.
[27] Aleksej Timofejev, *Savez Sovjetskikh patriota – antifashistichka organizatsija russikh emigranata u Srbiji 1941–1945* [The Union of Soviet Patriots – The Anti-Fascist Organization of Russian Emigrants in Serbia 1941–1945], (Belgrade: Tokovi istorije, 2012), 257–277.

voshein, was deported from France to the Soviet Union in 1947, but was arrested in 1949. He was released from the gulag following Stalin's death and finally returned to France in the 1970s. His close friend, Alexander Ugrimov, the former leader of the Dourdane group of the Resistance, was also arrested in the Soviet Union and sent to a prison camp. In the 1970s, he was very close to Alexandr Solzhenitsyn and helped him work on the famous *Gulag Archipelago*.

Some active Soviet patriots received the opportunity to return only many years later. For example, General Iakhontov (former vice-minister of defense for the Provisional Government) received permission to repatriate only in 1975, despite the fact that Andrey Gromyko, the Soviet ambassador to the United States, tried to help Iakhontov receive permission for this in the 1940s.[28]

World War II led to the 'Second Wave' of Soviet emigration, which was made up of several different streams:

- Former Soviet officers and soldiers captured by the Nazis and then imprisoned in concentration camps. We have different data relating to the number of these people. According to official Soviet statistics, they numbered more than 4 million, while German statistics put the figure at 5.7 million.[29] However, it is necessary to take into consideration that many of them died in the camps. The majority who survived wanted to return to Russia, but sometimes their sentiments changed when they learned about Soviet authorities' negative attitude towards people who had been captured by Nazi Germany. One can point to the act adopted by the Soviet authorities on 16 August 1941, which ordered the repression of the family members of Soviet prisoners of war.
- Former *Ostarbeiter*, those who had been deported from occupied Soviet territories to the Third Reich, especially in 1942 and 1943. There were more than 4 million Soviet *Ostarbeiter*.[30] In Germany, they worked in factories owned by the Krupp and Flick companies or on numerous private farms. After World War II, many of those who returned to the Soviet Union also became victims of Stalinist repression, so some *Ostarbeiter* tried to stay in Europe.
- Former collaborators, especially the soldiers and officers of the Vlasov Army.[31] Unsurprisingly, those who had collaborated with Nazi Germany did not want to return to the Soviet Union.

The Second Wave could potentially have been even more sizeable. However, Moscow tried to have Soviet citizens returned to the USSR on the legal basis provided by the

---

28 Nikolay Kulikov, *Ja tvoy, Rossija* [I am Yours, Russia] (Moscow: Sov. Rossija, 1990), 21.
29 "Sudba voennoplennyh i deportirovannyh grajdan SSSR. Materialy comissii po reabilitatsii jertv politicheskih repressii," *Novaja i Noveishaja Istorija* 2 (1996): 92; Pavel Polian, *Jertvy dvuh diktatur* [The Victims of Two Dictators] (Moscow: ROSSPEN, 2002), 127.
30 Polian, *Jertvy dvuh diktatur*, 133.
31 Mark Edele, *Stalin's Defectors: How Red Army Soldiers Became Hitler's Collaborators, 1941–1945* (Oxford: Oxford University Press, 2017).

Yalta conference (February 1945). Here, the USA and Great Britain had agreed to help the Soviet Union with repatriation, although the question was the subject of debate among American and British political elites as early as 1944/1945. Winston Churchill, for example, was not sure whether it was necessary to assist Stalin with repatriation of Soviet citizens, although Anthony Eden was a more active supporter of cooperation with the USSR.[32]

One of the main conferences devoted to this question took place in Halle (Germany) in May 1945. The USA and Great Britain agreed to transfer all Soviet citizens to the USSR: this included residents of Latvia, Lithuania, and Estonia, which had been incorporated into the Soviet Union in 1940. Only two groups of people were free from repatriation: Soviet women who had married foreign citizens (there were about 8,000 such women in the different states where Soviet troops were located) and those from Bessarabia and Bukovina who had immigrated to Romania (4,000). However, this policy led to many scandals and victims. The most famous forced repatriation took place in Lienz (Austria), following which General D. Eisenhower, the commander of the American army in Europe, in September 1945 decided to stop the process of repatriation. By 1946/1947, forced repatriation had decreased in scope and the Soviet-French agreement on repatriation was terminated in 1947.[33]

By March 1946, 4,199,488 Soviet citizens had been repatriated, of whom 1,545,303 were prisoners of war.[34] Only 1,846,802 Soviet citizens were repatriated from territories occupied by Soviet troops (the Soviet zones of occupation in Germany and Austria, Romania, Poland, etc.). The majority (2,352,686) were repatriated from places under the control of American and British troops.

Table 10.2: Number of Soviet citizens repatriated with the assistance of Western Allies by March 1946

State (territory)	Number of repatriates
Western zones of occupation in Germany and Austria	2,031,925
France	121,005
Norway	84,775
Italy	53,240
The United Kingdom	26,329
Belgium	12,344
Switzerland	9,868

---

32 Nicholas Betell, *Posledhyaa Taina* [The Last Secret] (London: Stenvalli Press, 1974), 12.
33 Nikolay Ross, "Sovetskie lagerya vo Frantsii," *Russkaja Mysl* 4170 (1997): 16.
34 Viktor Zemskov, "K voprosu o repatriatsii sovetskih grajdan. 1944 – 1951," *Istoria SSSR* 4 (1990): 26–41. In the present case, by 'Soviet citizens' we also mean residents in the territories annexed by the USSR in 1939–1940.

Table 10.2: Number of Soviet citizens repatriated with the assistance of Western Allies by March 1946 *(Continued)*

State (territory)	Number of repatriates
Denmark	7,614
USA	3,950
Greece	1,402
The Netherlands	234

These people were repatriated with the assistance of American and British officials. After March 1946, the number of repatriations began to decline. Only 104,893 Soviet citizens were returned to the USSR between March 1946 and March 1952, bringing the total to 4,500,000.[35] Nonetheless, in speeches by, for example, Andrey Gromyko (UNO General Assembly, December 1946) and Andrey Vyshinsky (Moscow session of the Ministry of Foreign Affairs, March 1947) the Soviets repeatedly blamed Western states for creating obstacles in the way of repatriation.[36] The Cold War led to the end of cooperation between the USSR and its former allies in matters of repatriation.

The sources show that the personal positions of Western officers played a very important role in this process of repatriation of Soviet citizens. Some of them knew about the real situation in the Soviet Union, where many repatriates became the victims of repression. Therefore, they saved some people from Soviet officials and gave them opportunities to stay in Europe.[37] The Soviet authorities tried to use all the instruments at their disposal to facilitate repatriation, including organized propaganda campaigns. Some former émigrés who returned to the USSR took an active part in this campaign, including the famous Russian singer Alexander Vertinsky. However, while he was not a victim of Stalin's repressions, he had very limited outlets for his creative activity. His songs were not part of the Soviet musical mainstream, since Soviet radio stations did not broadcast his performances.[38] Nonetheless, Russian émigrés and former prisoners of Nazi camps were ignorant of this, believing that the Soviet authorities really did give newcomers every chance to lead a happy life.

The repatriation of Russians from China continued into the 1950s. For this part of the Russian diaspora, one of the main events was the establishment of Communist China in 1949. As the situation in China changed, Russian émigrés began to feel

---

[35] Viktor Zemskov, "K voprosu o repatriatsii sovetskih grajdan. 1944 – 1951," *Istoria SSSR* 4 (1990): 26–41.
[36] *Vneshnjaa politika Sovetskogo Sojuza. 1946. Dokumenty i materialy* [Foreign Policy of the Soviet Union. 1946. Documents and Materials] (Moscow, 1952), 535; *Vneshnjaa politika Sovetskogo Sojuza. 1947. Dokumenty i materialy* [Foreign Policy of the Soviet Union. 1947. Documents and Materials] (Moscow, 1952), 408.
[37] Eugene Romanov, *V borbe za Rossiju* [In the Struggle for Russia] (Moscow: Golos, 1999), 95–97.
[38] Alexander Vertinsky, *Dorogoy dlinnoju* [The Long Road] (Moscow: Pravda, 1991), 410–412.

that living conditions had become worse, making them receptive to the invitations of Soviet propaganda. As a result, Russians began to emigrate from China, either returning to Russia or travelling further to the USA, Australia, and New Zealand.[39]

By 1952, more than 4.5 million Soviet citizens and 430,000 "White" Russian émigrés had returned to the Soviet Union. The Soviet security services monitored them attentively, and some were imprisoned in the gulags very shortly upon arriving in the USSR. Many former émigrés were disappointed by the actual situation in the Soviet Union. In Europe, they had maintained the belief that the Soviet Union was a free and socially just country and had been ignorant of the Soviet security services, the gulags, and the prevalent poor living conditions. They soon saw that social justice in the Soviet Union was far from absolute; the fact that the bureaucracy had many privileges made many former émigrés indignant. The most difficult problem was with children who had grown up in Europe. They arrived in the USSR with their relatives and were not ready for Soviet life. Young Russians who had grown up in France were much more freedom loving than Soviet children, which led to many problems.[40]

Despite the policy of repatriation, some former Soviet citizens did not return to the USSR. One of the main issues at stake was the legal status of these people in Europe after World War II. They were situated in camps for Displaced Persons (DP), which were organized by the UN Relief and Rehabilitation Administration (UNRRA), later the International Refugees Organization (IRO).[41] The need for DP camps was connected with the situation in Germany at the end of the war. There were crowds of former prisoners, but food was scarce and many towns had neither electricity nor functioning water supply systems. Crime levels were also high.[42] Given these poor living conditions, former prisoners very often went voluntarily to the new DP camps, but, as their memoirs show, the psychological atmosphere of the DP camps was very hard to bear.[43] Frequently, these camps were established in the same buildings that had

---

39 Ekaterina Sofronova, *Gde ty, moja Rodina?* [Where are You, My Motherland?] (Moscow: Intellekt, 1999), 124–125.
40 Aleksandr Ugrimov, *Iz Moskvy v Moskvu cherez Parizh i Vorkutu* [From Moscow to Moscow via Paris and Vorkuta] (Moscow: RA, 2000); Nina Krivosheina, *Chetyre treti nashei zhizni* [Four Thirds of Our Life] (Moscow: Russkii Put', 2017); Nikita Krivoshein, "Surdokamera," *Zvezda* 3 (2011): 182.
41 Mark Wyman, *DP: Europe's Displaced Persons, 1945–1951* (Ithaca, NY: Cornell University Press, 1998); Michael Marrus, *The Unwanted: European Refugees From the 1st World War Through the Cold War* (Philadelphia: Temple University Press, 2002); Ted Gottfried, *Displaced Persons: The Liberation and Abuse of Holocaust Survivors*. (Brookfield, CT: Twenty-First Century Books, 2001); Gerard Daniel Cohen, *In War's Wake: Europe's Displaced Persons in the Postwar Order* (New York: Oxford University Press, 2011); Sheila Fitzpatrick, *Mischka's War: A European Odyssey of the 1940s* (Melbourne: Melbourne University Publishing, 2017).
42 Olga Chehova, *Moi chasy idut inache* [My Watch Runs in a Different Way] (Moscow: Vagrius, 1998), 223; Konstantin Boldyrev, "Menchegof – lager peremeschennyh lits (Zapadnaja Germanija)," *Voprosy Istorii* 7 (1998): 113.
43 Laura J. Hilton, *Prisoners of Peace: Rebuilding Community, Identity and Nationality in Displaced Persons Camps in Germany, 1945–1952* (PhD diss., Ohio State University, 2001); Anna Marta Holian,

once housed the Nazi prisons that the DPs had already survived over the last few years. Insecure about their futures, some were ready to move to the Soviet Union because it was a means of escaping this terrible life.[44]

International organizations helped DPs leave these camps. The most attractive way for the majority was immigration to the USA. This was not a coincidence as after World War II, the economic situation in America was better than in European countries and America had the highly positive image of a "country of unlimited opportunities." Russian DPs often idealized America, but this of course led some of them to be disappointed upon arrival. It was also rather difficult to immigrate to America, since American immigration policy was based on a national quota system. However, after the war, America adopted legislation, which gave new opportunities for DPs to travel to the USA. This led to the immigration of more than 30,000 Soviet DPs to the United States by the beginning of the 1950s.[45]

For different reasons, many Russians could not use these opportunities and had to agree to emigrate to Latin America instead. At this time, Brazil, Argentina, and Venezuela were trying to attract labor migrants and did not impose age limitations. For some Russians, this was the only way to leave Europe and its economic troubles behind, but they had no knowledge about the economic situation in these countries. Many experienced disillusionment when they arrived. They were confronted with hard living conditions, a terrible climate, and a lack of social infrastructure (e.g. Venezuela).[46] However, newcomers did receive support from Russians who had arrived in these countries earlier. Old Russian émigrés helped their new comrades find employment and rent rooms. For example, in Paraguay the old Russian general Nicholay Ern, the head of the "White" officers in that country, helped the new arrivals.[47]

Some Russians decided to emigrate to Australia and New Zealand, which were also trying to attract labor migrants[48]. Among these people were both refugees from Communist China and DPs.

However, all these countries were interested in young people, making it very difficult for older Russians to find a "new Motherland." As many of them were intellec-

---

Between National Socialism and Soviet Communism: Displaced Persons in Postwar Germany (Ann Arbor: University of Michigan Press, 2011).
44 "Letter by Z. Makarenko to D. Burliuk. 1947," in Rossiiskaya gosudarstvennaja biblioteka. Otdel rukopisey [Russian State Library. Manuscript Division]. David Burliuk collection.13\29.P. 1; "Letter by V. Stankevic to M. Aldanov," IISH, V. Stankevic collection, folder 1.
45 Dan Danilov and Howard Deutsch, *Immigrating to the USA* (Vancouver: Self-Counsel Press, 1994), xviii.
46 "Letter to Ph. Legostaev. 1951," Gosudarstvenny Archiv Rossiiskoi Federatsii [State Archive of the Russian Federation], Nikolay Troitsky collection, 4/24. P. 6.
47 "Vtoraya emigratsija," *Suvorovets* (Buenos-Aires), December 17, 1948, 2.
48 Boris Christa, "Great Bear and Southern Cross: The Russian Presence in Australia," in *Russia and the Fifth Continent: Aspects of Russian-Australian Relations*, ed. John McNair and Thomas Poole (Brisbane: University of Queensland Press, 1992), 100; James Jupp, *Immigration* (Sydney: University Press, 1991), 109.

tuals, they were not ready for hard physical labor, which became a problem when the only jobs available to them were those in agriculture and industry.

The size of the Second Wave of Soviet emigration is very debatable. Official Soviet data shows that this wave consisted of 451,000 former Soviet citizens, but it is necessary to add some new groups to this number (former Soviet Germans who gained citizenship in Western Germany, people from Bessarabia who emigrated to Romania, etc.).[49] The Russian historian Viktor Zemskov has written that the total number of people who emigrated in the Second Wave was about 620,000. It is necessary to stress that about 75% of these émigrés were people who had lived in the Baltic States or Poland before World War II.[50]

The ethnic composition of the Second Wave was as follows: 32% Ukrainians, 24% Latvians, 14% Lithuanians, 13% Estonians, and 7% Russians. By 1952, these new Soviet émigrés were living in many different states (table 10.2)[51]

Table 10.3: Distribution of Soviet émigrés around the world

State (territory)	Number of immigrants
Western Germany and Austria	103,716
The United Kingdom	100,036
Australia	50,307
Canada	38,681
The USA	35,251
Sweden	27,570
France	19,675
Belgium	14,729
Argentina	7,085
Finland	6,961
Brazil	3,710
Venezuela	2,804
The Netherlands	2,723
Norway	2,619
Denmark	1,540
Turkey	1,174
Paraguay	860
Palestine	692
New Zealand	631
Switzerland	489
Italy	437
Morocco	355

---

49 Alexey Sheviakov, "Tainy poslevoennoy repatriatsii," *Sociologicheskie issledovania* 8 (1993): 8. In the category of 'citizens of the USSR', Soviet bureaucratic structures also included the residents in territories added to the Soviet Union in 1939–1940.
50 Viktor Zemskov, "Repatriatsia i Vtoraja volna emigratsii," *Rodina* 6–7 (1991): 111.
51 Zemskov, "Repatriatsia i Vtoraja volna emigratsii," 111.

However, it is necessary to take into consideration that all these data is approximate. They are impossible to verify because many DPs changed their nationalities, surnames, and places of birth in order to avoid deportation to the Soviet Union.

Some others streams were also part of the Second Wave. At the end of the 1940s and the beginning of the 1950s, some Soviet citizens decided to stay in the West. The representatives of this stream were known as *perebezhchiki*. This term (used by the Russian émigré press in Europe and the US) included different types of people. Among them were some prominent *nevozvrashchentsy* (non-returners), such as the Soviet officer Grigory Klimov (author of the book *The Song of the Winner*), Viktor Kravchenko, who published a book entitled *I Chose Freedom* about Stalinist terror, and several others. The *perebezhchiki* were also deserters who fled the Soviet corps in Germany across the frontlines of the Cold War. Many of these individuals ended up in DP camps. Their relationships with former Vlasovites were extremely complicated. In order to distinguish these two groups, the press began to call those who were abroad as a result of the Second World War (former prisoners of war, *Ostarbeiter* and Vlasovites) 'new émigrés', while the *perebezhchiki* were dubbed the 'newest' émigrés from the USSR. American attitudes to this problem evolved over time. In the beginning, Americans were very cautious and did not believe that these persons were honest. Gradually, however, the CIA began to use such events in its propaganda.[52]

At the end of the 1940s and the beginning of the 1950s, the Soviet Union began pursuing the policy of repatriating Polish citizens who had been imprisoned during World War II. Some Soviet citizens tried to take advantage of this policy by marrying Polish citizens in an effort to emigrate from the USSR. By April 1946, 4,220 Polish citizens in Sverdlovsk region alone wanted to return home, along with 317 Soviet spouses.[53] The Soviet secret service paid great attention to this issue, especially since its agents had received information that some of these spouses had anti-Soviet beliefs while others were victims of Stalinist terror. As a result, some people did not receive permission to leave the USSR.

The death of Stalin in March 1953 and the beginning of reforms in the Soviet Union lessened, to a certain extent, the number of people who desired to leave the country. Some Soviet intellectuals believed that Khrushchev's policies would produce real change in the Soviet regime. Therefore, to their minds, it was not necessary to emigrate from USSR, since they wanted to remain in their homeland. However, this position was shared only by part of Soviet society. Other intellectuals maintained a different opinion, arguing that the reforms were just an attempt by the Soviet bureaucratic system to save itself from an inevitable collapse. They held that there was

---

[52] Simo Mikkonen, "Exploiting the Exiles: Soviet Emigres in US Cold War Strategy," *Journal of Cold War Studies* 14 (2012): 98–127; Grigory Klimov, *Pesn pobeditelya* [The Song of a Winner] (Krasnodar: Peresvet, 2002), 679–683.

[53] Alexey Antoshin, *Na frontah Vtoroi Mirovoi i Holodnoi voin: Russkie emigranty v 1939 – nachale 1950 h godov* [On the Fronts of the Second World War and the Cold War: Russian Émigrés from 1939 to the 1950s] (Moscow: Aleteia, 2014), 50.

no basis for a deep transformation of the Soviet regime. Thus, such individuals decided to emigrate from USSR at the end of the 1950s and the beginning of the 1960s. Among them were the historian and journalist Michail Heller and the internationally renowned musician Vladimir Ashkenazi.

10.3.2 Emigration of Soviet Jews in the 1960s–1980s.

The 'Third Wave' of Soviet emigration came about at the end of the 1960s. One of the most notable manifestations of this wave was the departure of Jews from the USSR.[54] Emigration from the Soviet Union to Israel began in 1955, but was rather insignificant. Only 12,000 Soviet Jews arrived to Israel in 1955. They had close relatives in Israel and were quickly absorbed by Israeli society. This movement was connected with Soviet foreign policy. Professor Theodor Fridgut from the Hebrew University in Jerusalem has argued that this process stopped after the Suez Crisis but then resumed after the normalization of relations between the USSR and Israel.[55]

A key moment in Jewish emigration from the USSR was the Six Days War in 1967. Jewish emigration was one of the main factors in this standoff and it became very important in the epoch of Détente in the 1970s. The year 1967 saw the rise of ethnic identity among Soviet Jews. Many wanted to immigrate to Israel to help their "historical Motherland" in the struggle against Islamic aggression. Documents provided by Soviet dissidents show that about 80,000 Jews wanted to leave the USSR in between 1968 and 1969.[56] The Russian-Jewish historian Valeriy Engel has commented that secret Ivrit courses were organized in many Soviet cities at the end of the 1960s, making this period a moment of recovery of ethnic identity among Soviet Jews.[57]

---

54 Victor Zaslavsky and Robert Brym, *Soviet Jewish Emigration and Soviet Nationality Policy* (New York: The Macmillan Press, 1983); Laurie Salitan, *Politics and Nationality in Contemporary Soviet-Jewish Emigration, 1968–1989* (London: St. Martin's Press, 1992); Nora Levin, *The Jews in the Soviet Union since 1917: Paradox of Survival* (New York/London: New York University Press, 1988); Alfred Low, *Soviet Jewry and Soviet Policy* (New York: Columbia University Press, 1990); Leonard Schroeter, *The Last Exodus* (New York: Universe Book, 1974); Edward Drachman, *Challenging the Kremlin: The Soviet Jewish Movement for Freedom, 1967–1990* (New York: Paragon House, 1992); Piet Buwalda, *They Did Not Dwell Alone: Jewish Emigration from the Soviet Union, 1967–1990* (Washington, D.C.: Woodrow Wilson Center Press; Baltimore; Johns Hopkins University Press, 1997); Murray Friedman and Albert Chernin ed., *A Second Exodus: The American Movement to Free Soviet Jews* (Hanover, NH: Brandies University Press, 1999); Martin Gilbert, "Soviet Jews: Their Situation in Recent Years," in *Vision Confronts Reality: Historical Perspectives on the Contemporary Jewish Agenda*, ed. by Ruth Kozodoy (Madison, New Jersey: Fairleigh Dickinson University Press, 1989).
55 Theodor Fridgut, "Vlijanie immigrantov iz SSSR/SNG na izrailskuju identichnost," in *"Russkoe" litso Israela: cherty sotcialnogo portreta* (Jerusalem/Moscow: Gesharim – Mosty kultury, 2007), 68.
56 International Memorial, Archive. Radio Liberty collection. Samizdat archives. 422/1.
57 Valeriy Engel, "Sotcialno-psihologicheskie aspecty evreiskoy emigratsii is SSSR/SNG poslednei trety XX – nachala XXI vekov (na primere Israela, SsHA i Germanii)" in *Istoria Rossiiskogo zarubejia. Emigratsia is SSSR – Rosssii. 1941 – 2001* (Moscow: Institut rossiiskoi istorii RAN, 2007), 174.

However, Soviet authorities understood that this process played an important role in the global confrontation between the West and the East. The United States tried to use Jewish emigration for propaganda aims, which led the Soviet government to reject Jewish applications to leave the USSR. Thus began the great campaign for the right to emigrate. One aspect of this was a petition campaign. Jews wrote open letters to different Soviet officials and international structure, including Leonid Brezhnev, UNO, the prime minister of Israel and the "World Jewish community."[58] They began to organize various activities to attract attention to their problems.

The West supported these campaigns. Jews became "exchange figures" in the game played by the USSR and the West. The development of Détente led to an increase in Jewish emigration. According to Soviet official data, there were: 2,700 émigrés in 1969; 992 in 1970; 13,700 in 1971; 29,800 in 1972; and 33,500 in 1973.[59]

However, Soviet bureaucratic organs placed many obstacles in the way of the departure process. In August 1972, the Presidium of the Supreme Soviet adopted the decree "On the reimbursement of state spending on education by citizens of the USSR who leave for permanent residence abroad". The Russian émigré press immediately shone a spotlight on this document. As the New York newspaper *Rossiya* noted, the intent of this edict was to increase the cost of exit visas for those Jews immigrating to Israel: "The cheapest price is 3,600 rubles ($4,200) for graduates of vocational schools. For those graduating from universities, [the cost is] 12,500 rubles (15,000 dollars), [and] for a person with a doctoral degree – 31,200 rubles (37,440 dollars)." The newspaper cited the case of a certain Mark Gorfinkel from Minsk, "studying for a doctorate in medicine," and his wife Svetlana, a biochemist: they were instructed to pay 21,600 rubles (25,920 dollars). Such costs meant, "that if petitioners do not have well-to-do relatives abroad, they can't actually leave, because it is unlikely that Soviet citizens have such savings."[60]

Colin Shindler has argued that the goal of this act was to extract money from the West, since Soviet Jews had to ask international Jewish organizations to send them cash for the visas.[61] Jewish communities claimed that they gave Soviet Jews a real opportunity to emigrate from the USSR. The highest point of this activity was the famous Jackson-Vanik amendment in 1974, which imposed trade restrictions on the Soviet Union. This document forbade granting countries which violated or seriously limited the human rights of their citizens, including their right to emigrate, most favored nation status in trade, state credit, and credit guarantees.

---

58 International Memorial, Archive, Radio Liberty collection, Samizdat archives, 267/1; 268/1; 282/1.
59 Boris Morozov, "Evreiskaya emigratsia iz SSSR kak factor mejdunarodnyh otnosheniy," in *"Russkoe" litso Israela: cherty sotcialnogo portreta* (Jerusalem/Moscow: Gesharim – Mosty kultury, 2007), 479.
60 "Evreiskaya emigratsia," *Rossiya*, September 22, 1972, 1
61 Colin Shindler, *Exit Visa: Détente, Human Rights and the Jewish Emigration Movement in the USSR* (London: Bachman and Turner, 1978), 3.

Several researchers (e.g. Nora Levin, Edward Drachman, and Josifs Steimanis) have focused on events like the Jackson-Vanik amendment, suggesting that external pressure forced the Soviet authorities to make concessions to Jewish emigration from the USSR.[62] However, while not ignoring the importance of external factors, the British historian Laurie Salitan and the American scholar Piet Buwalda propose that we should recall the contemporaneous political atmosphere in the Soviet Union. To their minds, the moral atmosphere of the Brezhnev era strengthened the desire of Soviet Jews to leave the country.[63]

Some specialists have argued that anti-Semitism was the main reason for Jewish emigration.[64] The Canadian authors Victor Zaslavsky and Robert Brym have demonstrated the close connection between Jewish emigration and Soviet nationality policy (the struggle against cosmopolitanism led by Stalin, discrimination in the educational system, etc.).[65] The historian Yaacov Roi has also written about the connection between the fate of Soviet Jewry and political processes in the USSR. He has pointed out that while the Soviet regime shifted through different policies between the 1940s and the 1960s, anti-Semitism was constant.[66] Benjamin Pinkus has underlined that 'popular' (everyday) anti-Semitism in the USSR played no less a role than 'official' anti-Semitism.[67]

Between the end of the 1960s and the mid-1970s, roughly 70,000 Jews left the Soviet Union. Valeriy Engel underscores that these people had very strong Jewish identities: "They wanted to immigrate only to Israel."[68] He thus argues that it is impossible to call this process "emigration," since for these Soviet Jews it was repatriation. These Jews did not want to go to USA or other countries, and they successfully assimilated into Israeli society.

The Israeli historian Boris Morozov has proposed that there was a relationship between the number of Soviet Jews who received permission to leave the USSR in the second half of the 1970s and the development of dialogue between the Soviet Union and the United States on various questions. The number of Jews who received permission to emigrate from the Soviet Union decreased in 1974 (20,600) and 1975 (13,200) thanks to the Soviet reaction against the Jackson-Vanik amendment. Howev-

---

62 Nora Levin, *The Jews in the Soviet Union since 1917: Paradox of Survival*, vol. 2 (New York/London: New York University Press, 1988), 708; Edward Drachman, *Challenging the Kremlin: The Soviet Jewish Movement for Freedom, 1967–1990* (New York: Paragon House, 1992), 35; Josifs Steimanis, *History of Latvian Jews* (New York: Columbia University Press, 2002), 155.
63 Salitan, *Politics and Nationality*, 105; Buwalda, *They Did Not Dwell Alone*.
64 Ben Zion Goldberg ed., *The Jewish Problem in the Soviet Union. Analysis and Solution* (New York: Crown Publishers, 1961), 231.
65 Zaslavsky and Brym, *Soviet Jewish Emigration*, 18.
66 Yaacov Roi, *The Struggle for Soviet-Jewish Emigration, 1948–1967* (Cambridge: Cambridge University Press, 1991), 341.
67 Benjamin Pinkus, *The Jews of the Soviet Union: The History of a National Minority* (Cambridge: Cambridge University Press, 1989), 231.
68 Engel, "Sotcialno-psihologicheskie aspect," 174.

er, with the Soviet-American conversation about nuclear security at the end of 1970s, the number once again rose: 28,800 Soviet citizens received permission to emigrate from the USSR in 1978, while 51,300 did so in 1979.[69]

Nonetheless, this conversation came at the tail end of the Détente era and the conflict in Afghanistan in 1979 marked its conclusion. As a result, the number of Soviet émigrés decreased: in 1980, there were 21,400, in 1981 only 9,400. The beginning of the Reagan era in the White House saw a new twist in Soviet-American relations. Reagan's rhetoric revived the atmosphere of the Cold War. The Soviet response was logical: Jews did not receive exit visas. Between 1982 and 1986, only 7,000 obtained permission to leave the USSR. In October 1984, for example, only twenty-nine Soviet Jews arrived in Vienna on their way to Israel. In comparison, 5,000 had emigrated in a single month in 1979.[70] With the new chill in the Cold War, the Soviet authorities began to arrest Jewish activists.

The motivation of Soviet Jewish émigrés is an issue to which significant attention should be devoted. The end of the 1960s and the beginning of the 1970s were dominated by Jewish activists in the USSR, since they were the single most important factor in the struggle for the right to emigrate. They emphasized the existence of governmental anti-Semitism and anti-Semitic sentiments among ordinary people, as can be seen in leaflets circulated in 1968 by Soviet Zionists.[71] They proclaimed that life in Israel was their dream, while others announced that Jews could live only in a Jewish country as other cultural milieus were not suitable for Jewish mentality.

However, this is too simple an explanation, since Jewish emigration in the 1970s was a highly complex phenomenon. Many Soviet Jews received official permission to immigrate to Israel but instead moved to America. Sometimes, even leading Jews did this. For example, the Soviet journalist Viktor Perelman dreamed of living in Israel at the end of the 1960s, writing that he wanted to be free: this, he argued, was impossible in the Soviet Union. He also highlighted that the Soviet authorities discriminated against Jews.[72] After a long struggle, Perelman received permission to emigrate in 1973, but very quickly chose to go to America. Later, he wrote that his image of Israel had been mistaken.[73]

The psychological attitudes of Jewish émigrés from the Soviet Union changed. Jewish activists opened the door to the West for ordinary Soviet Jews. For these people, economic reasons and good living conditions in the West were more important motivating factors than Zionism. Many did not want to live in Israel, instead often choosing immigration to America. The Russian historian Gennadiy Kostyrchenko

---

69 Morozov, "Evreiskaya emigratsia iz SSSR, 480.
70 Morozov, 481.
71 International Memorial, Archive. Radio Liberty collection. Samizdat archives. 334/1.
72 Viktor Perelman, *Pokinutaja Rossija. Jurnalist v zakrytom obschestve* [Forsaken Russia. A Journalist in a Closed Society] (New York/Jerusalem/Paris: Izdat. Vremya i My, 1989), 310.
73 Viktor Perelman, *Teatr absurda* [The Theater of the Absurd] (New York: Izdat. Vremya i My, 1984), 61.

has written that the key moment occurred in 1973, when the Austrian chancellor Bruno Kraysky closed the transit camp for Soviet Jews in Shenau castle.[74] This was connected to an attack by Arab terrorists in Vienna in October 1973. Thereafter, Soviet Jews received the opportunity to choose between immigrating to Israel or other countries. This irritated international Jewish organizations and Israel, who saw Soviet Jews as potential fighters against Islamic invasion in the Near East.

The leaders of the Soviet Jewish émigrés tried to understand the reasons for this situation. Debates on this problem were published by the journal *Vremja i my* (Us and the Times), which had been founded by former Soviet Jews in Tel-Aviv. Some authors (e.g. Asya Levina and Boris Orlov) stressed that only a small number of Soviet Jews had a strong ethnic identity.[75] In the opinion of these authors, the majority of Soviet Jews felt the effects of anti-Semitism in the USSR and wanted to leave. Soviet society labelled them "Jews" because they had Jewish roots and surnames. Only in Israel was it understood that this was inaccurate. These citizens had no Jewish identity, did not observe Jewish traditions, and very often did not go to synagogues. What they really wanted was to live in a free and cosmopolitan environment, which they found in the USA. Soviet policy influenced the image of the Third Wave. The only legal way to leave the USSR was by departing to one's 'historical motherland,' the country to which the potential émigré belonged ethnically. Israel was one of the few countries of this kind. Jewish activists at the end of the 1960s and beginning of the 1970s used this situation to draw the world's attention to Soviet emigration. As a result, this path came to be accepted as the main for those who desired to emigrate from the USSR. Soviet policy compelled potential émigrés to ask for visas to Israel, thus giving the impression that the wave was made up entirely of Jews. However, the reality was much more complex.

Some groups of Soviet dissidents (e.g. Moscow Helsinki group) paid special attention to the problem of emigration. In 1979, the dissident group "The Right to Emigrate" was organized in the USSR. Nonetheless, some leaders of the Soviet opposition were not supporters of such ideas. Alexandr Solzhenitsyn did not agree that emigration was a principal tenet of the anti-Communist movement, holding that it was more important to fight against the regime in the USSR than to emigrate.[76]

A sociological survey of new Soviet émigrés in America in the 1980s, conducted by the journalist Mark Popovsky, notes that 60% of respondents stated that they were opponents of the Soviet system, while 30% held that they had experienced anti-Semitism in the USSR. The majority were Jews, but about 50% had never been in a synagogue. A further 38% only visited a synagogue once or twice a

---

[74] Gennadiy Kostyrchenko, "Politika sovetskogo rukovodstva v otnoshenii evreiskoy emigratsii posle XX siezda CPSS (1956–1991)," in *Evreiskaja emigratsia is Rossii. 1881–2005* (Moscow: ROSSPEN, 2008), 202–219.
[75] Asya Levina, "Ljudi ostajutsja ludmi," *Vremja i My* 14 (1977): 115.
[76] Alexander Soljenitzin, *Publizistika* [Journalism] (Jaroslavl: Verhne-Voljskoe knijnoe izdatelstvo, 1996), 155.

year. This research provides a rather accurate picture of Jewish emigration from the Soviet Union.

10.3.3 Emigration of Soviet Germans

Soviet Germans also made up a considerable component of the Third Wave. This had deep historical roots. Germans had been invited to Russia in the eighteenth century by Catherine the Great to colonize underdeveloped and uncharted land on the Black Sea and on the banks of the Volga River and introduce more advanced German agriculture methods to rural Russia. By the 1920s, many of them lived in the German Republic in the Volga region. However, World War II led to the end of this Republic. In 1941, many Soviet Germans were deported to the Urals and Siberia and were forced to work in the Labor Army for the remainder of the conflict. Alfred Low has postulated that Germans had better lives than other ethnic groups in the USSR. They had their own national newspapers, schools, and cultural centers,[77] however, the cultural requirements of Germans in the USSR were far from fully met. In the 1950s, some began to ask for permission to emigrate from the USSR. Initially, this was not a particularly active movement, since they were promised that the German Republic in the Volga region would be reconstituted. However, in the 1960s it was evident that these promises had not been kept. The prominent Soviet dissident Ludmila Alexeeva has written that the movement for German emigration from the USSR became more active at the end of the 1960s, with most wanting to leave for Western Germany.[78]

From 1974, Western Germany began to help Soviet Germans emigrate from the USSR. At this point, the Social Democrats dominated West German governments. They sought cooperation with the Soviet Union in various spheres, including emigration. Before 1974, 40,000 Soviet Germans had asked permission to emigrate and had formed non-governmental committees in different regions. On 11 February 1974, Soviet Germans organized a demonstration in Moscow near the building that housed the Communist Party's Central Committee. Other demonstrations of this kind were also held when Soviet Germans who had been refused permission to emigrate rejected Soviet citizenship. The first action of this kind was organized by 300 Soviet Germans in Central Asia in 1976.

The number of Soviet Germans who left the USSR rose over several years. In 1971 as many as 1,145 Soviet Germans left the USSR, a year later that number rose to 3,423, in 1973 to 4,494 and in 1975 to 5,985. The climax of Soviet German emigration from the USSR came in 1976 when 9,704 German émigrés left the USSR.[79] This year was the high point of Détente.

---

77 Alfred Low, *Soviet Jewry and Soviet Policy* (New York: Columbia University Press, 1990), 167.
78 Ludmila Alexeeva, *Istorija inakomyslia v SSSR. Noveishii period* [A History of Dissent in the USSR: The Contemporary Period] (Vilnius/Moscow: Vest', 1992), 140.
79 Ludmila Alexeeva, 140.

The campaign against German emigration was renewed in 1977 when a new Soviet constitution was adopted. The secret services also took an active part in this campaign. Soviet authorities tried to destroy connections between Soviet Germans and their relatives in Western Germany by, for instance, limiting international phone calls. Soviet Germans who wanted to emigrate became the victims of propaganda campaigns, where they were smeared as "traitors" by the Soviet press.[80] As a result, the number of German émigrés from the USSR decreased. In 1977 as many as 9,274 Soviet Germans left the USSR, a year later that number lowered to 8,445, in 1979 to 7,226, in 1980 to 6,650, in 1981 to 3,273, in 1982 to 2,069, in 1983 to 1,447.[81]

The majority of Soviet Germans were denied emigration, as a consequence of which they organized demonstrations. At the beginning of the 1980s, the authorities began to arrest the organizers of these actions. For example, in 1984 German activists were arrested in Moscow.[82] The new political situation in Western Germany was an important contributing factor in the decline of migration, since this period saw the end of Social Democrat dominance and the rise of Helmut Kohl, who did not want to compromise with the Soviets, especially after the beginning of Soviet military operation in Afghanistan in 1979.

The Third Wave did not just consist of ethnic émigrés. Some leaders of the Soviet opposition, *dissidents*, also became émigrés. Very often, it was not a voluntary process. Alexandr Solzhenitsyn was deported from the Soviet Union in 1974. Another prominent dissident, Vladimir Bukovsky, was exchanged for the imprisoned leader of the Communist Party of Chile in 1976.

The "perestroika" begun by Gorbachev increased emigration from the Soviet Union. Official data demonstrates this: 1987 – 39,129 émigrés; 1988 – 108,189; 1989 – 234,994; 1990 – 453,600.[83]

Several changes led to this situation. Firstly, legislation was liberalized (supplements were adopted in August 1986) and Soviet citizens received real opportunity to emigrate. Secondly, political instability and economic troubles were also very important factors, leading many to seek emigration from the Soviet Union at the end of the 1980s and the beginning of the 1990s.

---

[80] The Urals was one of the regions where a considerable number of Germans lived in the 1950s and 1960s. Sverdlovsk region was one of the centers of the German emigration movement. Documents from the Center for the Documentation of the Social Organizations of Sverdlovsk Region (Tsentr dokumentatsii obshchestvennykh organizatsii Sverdlovskoi oblasti, TsDOOSO) show that the regional party leadership actively combated German emigration with various administrative measures and propaganda (see TsDOOSO, f. 4, op. 88, d. 164).
[81] "Emigratsija nemtzev iz SSSR," *Strana i Mir* 4 (1984): 28.
[82] "Emigratsija nemtzev iz SSSR," 28.
[83] Natalia Pushkareva, "Vozniknovenie i formirovanie rossiiskoi diaspory za rubejom," *Otechestvennaja Istoria* 1 (1996): 64.

10.3.4 The "Free World" and the Émigré

Many anti-Communist Russian émigrés believed that the Cold War was a better political situation than that which had existed between the First and Second World Wars. In the 1920s and 1930s, the context had been more complex due to the competition between different global powers. Russian Communism could justify itself through comparisons to Nazism. However, after World War II, things had drastically changed. Nazism had disappeared and Communist totalitarianism had become the only alternative and the sole enemy of the democratic world.

The rise of Russian anti-Communist activity in the USA was associated with the sharp aggravation of Soviet-American relations during the Korean War. It was not a coincidence that some Russian newspapers in the United States published articles entitled "If War Begins Tomorrow..." in 1950. Certainly, not all Russians in America hoped for a new global conflict. Some old intellectuals were afraid that a Third World War would be an absolute tragedy for humanity.[84] However, the position of the political elite of the Russian diaspora differed. Many authors within the Russian émigré press proposed defeating the Soviet Union in a new war, and were ready to support the West if this occurred. Some émigrés tried to declare that it was unpatriotic to not support the Motherland, but, as the liberal Prince Vladimir Obolensky wrote, "[w]e see that Stalin will not begin World War III in defense of Russian national interests. He will do it to expand the Communist regime. In this case, we must support the idea of the Soviet Union's defeat."[85]

However, among Russian liberals in America there was another point of view. The writer Mark Aldanov, for example, thought that Russian Americans had to adopt a position of "silence" should a new major conflict occur.[86] He presumed that such a war would lead to an anti-Russian sentiments in American society, a very dangerous situation for Russian Americans. Aldanov already felt that this was the case during the Korean War as some publishing houses refused to print his novels and argued that, "now American people do not want to read Russian authors."[87]

Even left-wing Russian political groups, such as Zagranichnaya Delegatia (RSDLP), supported the notion of a Soviet defeat in a future war, concluding that the Western states would fight for the "basic ideas of civilization." Of course, they tried to show that they were against any desire to initiate a world war and considered it vital that the true aspirations of Western democracy should be pursued if war did break out.[88] Most Russian anti-Communist groups declared that they would support

---

[84] "Letter by Lidia Dan to Nina Rubinstein. 1950," in IISH, Nina Rubinstein collection, folder 1.
[85] Vladimir Obolensky, "38 parallel," *Novoe russkoe slovo*, New York, 4 March 1951.
[86] "Letter by Mark Aldanov to Vasily Maklakov, 21 Nov.1949," in Hoover Institution Archives on War, Revolution and Peace (HIA), Vasily Maklakov papers. box 2, folder "M. Aldanov. 1949."
[87] "Letter by Mark Aldanov to Vasily Maklakov, 16.03.1951," in HIA, Vasily Maklakov papers, box 2, folder "M. Aldanov. 1951."
[88] "Zadachi i tactica RSDRP v emigratsii," in IISH, Boris Dvinov collection, folder 7.

Western democracy in a future war only if the West fought for the fall of Communism, and not the occupation of Russian territories. Immigrants who admired American action in Korea included Russian Orthodox priests. Archimandrite Konstantin later wrote that there had been "a growth in the civic courage and military bravery of Americans" in Korea.[89]

In these conditions, some of the American political elite decided to make use of Russian émigrés in their struggle against the Soviet Union. As the Russian historians Olga Zatsepina and Alexander Ruchkin note, the beginning of the Cold War made the Russian diaspora "interesting" to the American government.[90] During the Korean War, some Russian émigrés tried to obtain subsidies for their anti-Communist projects, taking advantage of the political situation. They even petitioned for financial support from American businesses for Russian anti-Communist military troops.[91]

The Korean War was the height of General McArthur's political career. In 1950, McArthur, who held an actively anti-Communist position during the Korean War, was a real hero for the conservative Russian diaspora in the USA. Former Russian generals from World War I and the Civil War wrote very emotional letters about the strategic wisdom and courage of McArthur, who had become, in their eyes, a real follower of famous "White" Russian heroes: the generals Kornilov, Vrangel. They believed that McArthur fought for the same traditional values as these men. This admiration went so far that K. Shevchenko and others created a political project in the Russian diaspora in the USA. They proposed that Congress form a "Government of Anti-Communist Dictatorship" that would consist of General McArthur, Senator Joseph McCarthy, Hoover, and others.[92] Conservative Russian émigrés thought that the American governmental machine had to be reorganized for victory in the Cold War. While expressing support for American democracy, they in fact wanted to recreate the traditional Russian political order, along with its autocracy. Entering into a ferocious battle with American liberal intellectuals, Russian conservatives rejected the freedom of political discussion in America, believing that this freedom allowed Communists and their supporters to instill dangerous ideas in the American public.[93]

For Russian anti-Communist groups in the United States, the "isolationist" ideas ingrained in the American establishment were very dangerous, because this meant losing the opportunity to see Communism crumble. Therefore, they earnestly cooperated with American organizations such as the Free Russia Foundation. Russian pol-

---

89 Arhimandrit Konstantin, "Bliz est, pri dvereh," *Pravoslavnaya Rus* 8 (1955), 10.
90 Olga Zatsepina and Alexander Ruchkin, *Russkiye v SShA* [Russians in the USA] (New York: Russian-American Cultural Center "Nasledie," 2011), 31.
91 "Letter by K. Shevchenko to B. Brasol. 17.06.1951," in Library of Congress. Manuscript Division (LoC MD). The papers of Boris Brasol, box 10, folder "Non English. 1951".
92 "Letter by K. Shevchenko to B. Brasol. 17 Jun. 1951".
93 "Letter by B. Brasol to E. Patterson. 09 Apr. 1951" in LoC MD, The papers of Boris Brasol, box 4, folder "Political correspondence. 1950–1952."

iticians like Ariadna Tyrkova-Williams, a participant in the liberal movement in prerevolutionary Russia, advocated that George Kennan head anti-Communist activities at the beginning of the 1950s.[94] However, these politicians were quickly disappointed when it became clear that the Ford Foundation, a leading sponsor, did not have much desire to fund anti-Communist activity.

Russian liberals and socialists took an active role in conversing with the American Committee for the Liberation from Bolshevism in the early 1950s. This group backed US policy towards the various peoples of the USSR during the Cold War. The Committee was a private organization incorporated under the laws of the state of Delaware. Its first president was Eugene Lyons and members included William Chamberlin, Charles Edison, William Elliott, Isaak Don Levin, and other American specialists on "Russian" problems.[95] Subsequently, its membership changed several times. In 1952, Admiral Alan Kirk became chairman, while Admiral L. Stevens was made president in 1953. Naturally, anti-Communism was at the core of their ideological worldview. Their main aim was to help various Soviet émigré groups all over the world in order to sustain the spirit of liberty among the peoples of the USSR. The founders of the American Committee believed that it was necessary to focus on opposition movements among these peoples in order to bring down the existing regime. For example, Charles Edison, the governor of the state of New Jersey and a soon-to-be member of the American Committee, stressed in a speech in May 1951: "The overthrow of the Soviet regime would be the best news for centuries. But only the peoples of Russia, the first and greatest victims of Communist tyranny, can do it."[96]

American governmental and non-governmental structures very often overestimated the real power of liberal groups in the Russian diaspora. Based on liberal and socialist immigrant groups, American experts on Russian problems organized the League of Struggle for the Freedom of Peoples.[97] One of its leaders was Alexander Kerensky, the former head of the Provisional Government during the Russian Revolution of 1917. However, he lacked popularity among Russian émigrés in USA because the majority strongly criticized his policies in 1917.

Perhaps, the most notable action of the American Committee was their attempt to form a Soviet 'government in exile' in the early 1950s. The Americans attempted to create a single body of representatives from the different peoples of the USSR and promised to give it a powerful modern anti-Communist propaganda tool, namely, a radio station. To achieve this, a large meeting was held in the West German city

---

[94] "Letter by Ariadna Tyrkova to Serge Melgunov. 19.05.1951," in Bakhmeteff Archive at Columbia University. Ariadna Tyrkova-Williams collection, box 2, folder "Melgunov S." See also John Lewis Gaddis, *George F. Kennan: An American Life* (New York: Penguin Press, 2011).
[95] "American Aid to Kremlin's Russian Enemies," in Georgetown University Libraries. Special Collections (GUL. SC), Robert F. Kelley papers, box 5, folder 1.
[96] "American Aid to Kremlin's Russian Enemies".
[97] "Letter by Mark Aldanov to Vasily Maklakov, 29 Oct. 1951," in HIA, Vasily Maklakov papers, box 2, folder "M. Aldanov. 1951."

of Wiesbaden in 1951.[98] However, it turned out to be hard for observers to find any ties connecting the Americans with the Soviet émigré associations. The only structure to represent peoples from Central Asia in this meeting was the Turkestan National Liberation Committee, *Turkeli*. This structure did not represent the political mood of émigrés of all the peoples of Central Asia (for example, there were no Tajiks and Uzbeks among the members of this structure).

In the early 1950s, it was already clear that the leaders of émigré political associations from Soviet Central Asia and the Caucasus were focusing on the struggle for the complete independence of their republics. Despite the fact that compromise between Russian and other émigré groups from the Soviet Union failed (the Russian organizations believed a post-Communist Russia must maintain the borders of the USSR), Radio Liberation (later Radio Liberty, RL) began broadcasting in March 1953. This was not by chance; it was in this year that the US Information Agency (USIA) was formed by President Eisenhower, with propaganda against the Soviet Union being one of its main aims.

RL, funded initially by the CIA, broadcast on nine transmitters located in central West Germany from studios in Munich.[99] Three of these nine transmitters broadcast fifteen-minute programs in the minority languages of the Soviet Union. About 40% of the scripts were prepared in New York, 30% in Munich, and 30% by external contributors.[100] The American management, therefore, determined a significant proportion of the program content. There was no music on this radio station.

Many Russian émigrés worked at RL as journalists and observers. Among them were Valerian Obolensky (program director at the New York department), Gleb Rahr, and Dmitry Pospelovsky. The majority of them were NTS members. Some of them had worked earlier at the European branch of "The Voice of America," which had closed in 1958.[101] RL attracted Russian émigrés by offering good salaries. There were a few other Russian-language radio stations during the Cold War. Some programs were broadcast from Rome, the Vatican, and Paris. Later, the Deutsche Welle also appeared. Russian émigrés worked at the Russian services of the BBC and Radio Madrid.[102]

From the outset, RL focused on the national contradictions that existed in the USSR. The basic principles of the radio stations were clearly expressed in 1954 in a memorandum by M. Williams, one of the managers. Williams particularly stressed

---

98 "Protocols of Wiesbaden Conference, 1951," in Gosudarstvenny Archiv Rossiiskoi Federatsii [State Archive of the Russian Federation], Nikolay Troitsky collection, 4/842.
99 On role of special services, see John N. L. Morrison, "Intelligence in the Cold War," *Cold War Histor* 14 (2014): 575–591.
100 Alan Snyder, *Warriors of Disinformation: American Propaganda, Soviet Lies and the Winning of the Cold War* (New York: Arcade Publishing, 1995), 34.
101 Ludmila Obolenskaya-Flam, "Vozdushnymi putyami," *Posev* 3 (2003): 11.
102 On Western propaganda activity see Patrick Major, "Listening behind the Curtain: BBC Broadcasting to East Germany and Its Cold War Echo," *Cold War History* 13 (2013): 255–275.

the following: "The sole purpose of Radio Liberation is the liberation of the peoples of the USSR from the Communist regime. All the peoples inhabiting the territory of the USSR have an unlimited right to determine their own destiny through the democratic expression of their will after the overthrow of the Communist regime."[103] Gradually, RL became the main political activity connected with the American Committee. By 1957, there were nine national desks at RL: Russian, Ukrainian, Byelorussian, Georgian, Armenian, Azerbaijani, North Caucasian, Turkestani, and Mataro-Bashkir.

However, strains in the relations between Russian politicians and the American Committee appeared very quickly. The American Committee continued to support close cooperation between émigrés from the different republics of the USSR, since this was one of the main aims of the Committee noted in the "Statement of mission, operating objectives and policy guides" (1954).[104] This document was written by L. Stevens, president of the Committee. He wrote that RL could help Americans receive new information about the situation in the Soviet Union, which would allow them to understand the prospects for a democratic transition in a post-Communist Russia.

However, some of the main questions were controversial even among the American management. In August 1955, Robert Kelley (vice-president of RL from 1953) sent a letter to R. Townsend, the vice-president of the American Committee, writing that it was necessary to remember that it was the Russians who were struggling against Communism: the US was only helping them. He also pointed out that the concept of America as a "Big Brother" was very dangerous.[105]

Later, Kelley continued to fight for a truly independent RL. He stressed that RL was important because it was impossible for opposition to exist in the USSR. In his opinion, RL had to be a truly independent radio station headed by émigrés from the Soviet Union.[106] In 1958, he wrote to the director of planning at RL that it was impossible for the station to be a "propaganda instrument" for American foreign policy as that would lead to a negative image of RL in the Soviet Union.[107] In February 1964, a briefing on these problems was held in Geneva, during which Kelley argued that RL was fundamentally different from the Voice of America, the BBC, and other Russian-language stations and programs. These stations served the interests of different governments and nations, whereas RL was a unique example of independent émigré activity.[108] This was an unrealistic picture. In 1956, Howland Sargeant, the president of

---

[103] "Radio Liberation – Staff Memorandum," in GUL.SC, Robert F. Kelley papers, box 5, folder 4.
[104] GUL.SC, Robert F. Kelley papers, box 5, folder 4.
[105] "Letter by R. Kelley to R. Townsend, 29 Aug. 1955," GUL.SC, Robert F. Kelley papers, box 5, folder 3.
[106] "Minutes of the Joint Meeting of the Management Policy and Program Advisory Committees, 15 Feb. 1956, New York," GUL.SC, Robert F. Kelley papers, box 5, folder 5.
[107] "Letter by R. Kelley to Director of Planning. 30.01.1958," GUL.SC, Robert F. Kelley papers, box 5, folder 3.
[108] "Briefing. Geneva, February 11, 1964," GUL.SC, Robert F. Kelley papers, box 5, folder 8.

RL, pointed out that it was impossible for the US to give émigrés real responsibility for RL policy and operations.[109]

In the 1960s, the American management of RL began paying more attention to the contradictions between different nations in the Soviet Union. In 1962, RL directors approved a special document entitled *Self-Determination for All Peoples*.[110] This document connected nationality conflicts in the USSR with the end of the global colonial system. The authors also wanted to show the close connection between self-determination for the peoples of the USSR and the transition to democracy. One of the questions raised in this era was whether RL should broadcast in Estonian, Lithuanian, and Latvian. Robert Kelley stressed that this region belonged to Radio Free Europe's sphere of activity. For him and the rest of the American management, the peoples of the Baltic republics were not nations of the Soviet Union; rather, they were similar to the East European "satellites."[111]

In the 1970s, special department of nationalities was organized at RL. It consisted of correspondents who were specialists on the various peoples of the Soviet Union. Broadcasting in the languages of the Baltic republics began in 1975. It was only in October 1984 that Baltic services were established by Radio Free Europe.[112]

Archival documents show that the American management of RL was very careful in the 1970s and 1980s. They tried to block the emotional scripts written by Russian émigrés, criticizing them for their "polemic style."[113] For example, RL experts pointed out that comparing the Soviet regime with Nazi Germany was "impossible."[114] This caution led to permanent conflicts between the American management of RL and Russian émigrés. The most active Russian anti-Communists did not agree with this political line. Alexandr Solzhenitsyn criticized it for being too limited, especially during Détente. According to him, the policy direction imposed a range of limitations on the active anti-Communist journalists at RL.[115]

Relations between the American managers of RL and the Third Wave of Soviet emigration were rather tense. The Americans did not agree with the content and style of the articles and speeches by the wave's prominent representatives. One of

---

109 "Minutes of the Joint Meeting of the Management Policy and Program Advisory Committees. February 15, 1956, New York," GUL.SC, Robert F. Kelley papers, box 5, folder 5.
110 "Radio Liberty Policy Position Statement. Self-determination for All Peoples. 22.03.1962," GUL.SC, Robert F. Kelley papers, box 5, folder 5.
111 "R. Kelley to Director, Audience Research Division. 12Jun. 1964," GUL.SC, Robert F. Kelley papers, box 5, folder 3.
112 "Radio Liberty. August 1, 1975," GUL.SC, The Jon Lodeesen papers, box 1, folder 66; "Letter by J. Pennar to K. Short. 09.01.1985," GUL.SC, The Jon Lodeesen papers, box 2, folder 33.
113 "Script by Garanin. 15–16 December 1967, Commentary on Soviet Affairs," GUL.SC, The Jon Lodeesen papers, box 1, folder 11, Evaluator 1.
114 "Response to W. Scott Letter of February 7, 1968 on Current Events Analysis, Mr. Neymirok," GUL.SC, The Jon Lodeesen papers, box 1,.folder 11.
115 "Letter by Alexandr Solzhenitsyn to F. Ronalds. 30 Oct. 1975," GUL.SC, The Jon Lodeesen papers, box 1, folder 71.

managers of RL, Lenn Savemark, called speeches by Alexander Galich, Vladimir Maksimov, Andrey Sinyavsky, and others "emotional," "naïve," and "silly," stating that it was impossible for RL to support them.[116]

When characterizing the propaganda spread by RL in the Soviet Union, we should pay attention to one further point. The services, which operated in Soviet Central Asia and the Caucasus enjoyed relative freedom, since the American management of these stations did not control them as tightly as they did the Russian service. Despite the lengthy struggle against 'Russian nationalism', this was not the case with the Central Asian and Caucasian stations. The reason for this was simple: the lack of specialists fluent in local languages. Even the American managers recognized this. In 1985, John Lodeesen, the director of US operations at RL, wrote that RL always checked texts before programs were aired. The exceptions to this rule were the "Caucasian and Tajik programs," because "among the members of the American management nobody understood the languages."[117] This situation was typical not only for Tajik programs, but also for news programs in the other languages of Central Asia.

RL tried to reach out to Soviet citizens. In the 1950s, it tried to spread anti-Communist propaganda appealing to the religious sentiments of the Soviet population. In particular, the author of one RL internal document wrote: "Tatar and Turkestan Soviet Muslim immigrants in the United States had some success in dispensing propaganda among pilgrims who were sent to Mecca by the Soviet government".[118] In 1960, at a special meeting of the Radio Liberty staff, the national services were instructed to prepare special programs "addressed to the Red Army units in the satellite countries."[119]

RL paid great attention to the study of relation of Soviet listeners to its programs. The management of the station knew the real situation and did not gloss over the fact that some Soviet people had negative attitudes towards RL's programs. In 1965, for example, R. Kelly wrote that over the past two or three years, the proportion of Soviet people who believed that RL was a 'free voice' had fallen from 44% to 37%. Indeed, the number of those who defined RL as 'the American station' greatly increased (from 4% to 18%).[120]

Former Worldnet director Alan Snyder has studied the jamming of American radio stations, a customary practice in the Soviet Union during those years.[121] As he writes, jamming was conducted in two ways: 'groundwave' (local) jamming, employed in large urban areas, and 'skywave' jamming, which covered broader, rural

---

[116] "Letter by L. Savemark to F. Ronalds. 06.12.1975," GUL.SC, The Jon Lodeesen papers,.box 1, folder 70.
[117] "Letter by J. Lodeesen to J. Buckley," GUL.SC, The Jon Lodeesen papers, box 2, folder 34.
[118] "Negotiations for an Effective Partnership," GUL.SC. Robert F. Kelley papers, box 5, folder 2.
[119] "Minutes Political Affairs – Émigré Relations Meeting with Mr. Kelley. 06 Jan. 1960," GUL.SC, Robert F. Kelley papers, box 5, folder 4.
[120] "R. Kelley to H. Sargeant," GUL.SC, Robert F. Kelley papers, box 5, folder 3.
[121] Snyder, *Warriors of Disinformation*, 26.

areas and was less effective. 'Skywave' transmitters were usually located thousands of miles apart, with jamming signals bouncing between the Earth and the ionosphere. Jamming was certainly a serious obstacle to anti-Communist propaganda in the Soviet Union.

Some structures affiliated with RL were centers of Soviet studies, including the Munich Institute for Soviet Studies founded in 1950. It received financial support from the American Committee and other organizations. However, this financial dependency led to it being dependent on American ideological approaches. The Munich Institute had the same problem as RL: conflicts of nationality among its staff. Separatist sentiments were popular among officers from the different republics of the Soviet Union. Some Russian specialists who wanted post-Communist Russia to maintain the borders of the USSR left the Munich Institute.[122] In the 1950s and 1960s, American liberal politicians and scholars (particularly from Harvard University) criticized the institute's activities. Employees of the Munich Institute studied psychological warfare, but some American liberals thought that it would be more useful to study the problems of cooperation between USSR and USA. As a result, the Munich Institute was closed during Détente in 1972.[123] This situation was rather typical of the Cold War. There were many disagreements between Russian émigrés and the US. Documents located at the RL/RFE Research Institute collection at the Open Society Archives (Budapest) show that Soviet émigrés very often criticized the "Free World" for compromises with the Soviet Union.[124] Russian émigrés wanted to be real partners of America in anti-Communist activity, but in reality, they were the subordinates of different US structures.

During the Cold War, Russian émigrés tried to receive financial support from different parts of the "Free World" by forging connections with European, Asian, and Latin American political elites. Between the 1950s and the 1980s, the NTS was connected with different organizations from seven countries. For example, Taiwan and South Korea gave the NTS radio stations, Western Germany helped them publish a journal, and American trade unions assisted the NTS with the development of propaganda activity among Soviet sailors at US seaports.[125]

The NTS tried to create a positive image of the Russian diaspora in *Europe*. In 1956, the leaders of the NTS were invited to an official meeting organized by the Council of Europe.[126] Russian politicians also tried to make connections with European colleagues. Some Russian émigrés understood that it was very important to make such links with Eastern European émigrés. For example, Russian-Polish unity was organized in Paris in the 1950s. It consisted of émigrés from Russia, Po-

---

[122] Dmitry Konstantinov, "Munhensky Institut. Is istorii vtoroy rossiskoy politiheskoy emigratsii," *Tribuna russkoy mysli* 4 (2002): 136.
[123] Dmitry Konstantinov, 142.
[124] Open Society Archives (HU OSA), 300/80/7, box 57, f.: Vladimir Bukovsky. 1978–1983.
[125] Boris Pushkarev ed., *NTS: Mysl i Delo*, 67.
[126] "Mejdunarodnaja dejatelnost NTS," *Posev* 1 (1957): 2.

land, and other countries (like Yugoslavia). Pan-Slavism was rather influential among old Russian émigrés.

The NTS tried to establish an image of itself as the representative of Russia abroad. Therefore, it organized summits with anti-Communist politicians in different countries. For example, in 1957 the leaders of the NTS made a long trip to Asia. During their travels, they met with Chan Quai-shek (Taiwan), the former prime minister of Japan Ioshida, and some politicians in Turkey, the Philippines, and Iran. Ngo Din Diem, the president of South Vietnam, met them as official guests. In the 1950s, the NTS had close connections with the Anti-Communist League of Asian Peoples. Russian émigrés participated in its conferences in Taiwan and tried to coordinate their activities with different anti-Communist structures in Asia. Some leaders of the NTS took an active part in regional anti-Communist activity. For example, at the end of 1950s and the beginning of the 1960s, Roman Redlih was an advisor to the South Vietnamese government on secret operations in North Vietnam. Some Russian politicians also tried to take an active part in anti-Communist activity in Latin America. Boris Holmston (Smyslovsky), the leader of the Russian anti-Communist émigrés in Argentina, advised the government on the struggle against terrorism.[127]

10.4 Political activities in exile

During the Cold War, the majority of politically active Russian émigrés supported the Western bloc and its political center, the United States of America. *Novoe Russkoe Slovo*, the most prominent Russian-language newspaper in the USA at this time, was based in New York City and voiced the opinions of the liberal-democratic diaspora. The majority of liberal Russian journalists in the United States worked for this newspaper, embellishing ideas of democracy, liberty, and human rights. It was a difficult task given the conservative political views of many average Russian émigrés. However, for American intellectuals, *Novoe Russkoe Slovo* appeared too conservative because of the implacable anti-Communist perspective of Russian liberal democrats and their refusal to acknowledge any agreements with the Soviets. Even when opportunities to compromise between the "Free World" and the Soviet bloc arose and some form of peace seemed attainable, Russian liberal democrats responded negatively. They always stressed that only the fall of Communism could bring true peace. The critics of Russian liberals often accused them of only propagating to the strongly grounded positions of the American establishment. However, this was not completely true. Russian liberals had their internal reasons for anti-Communist sentiments, which were always more aggressive than those of the American government. In fact, Russian liberals always thought that America was too "liberal" in its policy towards the Soviet Union.

---

[127] Vladimir Goldin, *Rokovoy vybor* [A Fateful Choice] (Archangelsk; Murmansk: Solti, 2005), 544.

The most widely read Russian liberal journal at the time was Novy Journal, which was founded by the prominent Russian writer Mark Aldanov and the Russian historian Michael Karpovich. They were merciless anti-Communists but their position on American foreign policy was controversial. They thought that the West could be more active in its anti-Communist policy, especially in Central and Eastern Europe, even going as far as saying that the Western bloc had relinquished this region to the Soviet Union. Russian émigrés wrote that such American policy in Central and Eastern Europe only showed Stalin the weakness of the Western bloc and led to new aggressive steps by the Soviet Union.[128] Many anti-Communist émigrés held the belief that the United States and its Western allies had the ability to stop the construction of the "socialist system" in Central and Eastern Europe, but did not want to.

Russian socialists in America also held strong anti-Communist beliefs, some of them successfully integrating into the American socialist movement. David Shub was on the editorial board of the American journal *Jewish Daily Forward*. He was also one of "sponsors" of the Cooperative Society Foundation in America, one of the most prominent left structures in the United States. Among the leaders of the American Socialist Party and different left-wing organizations were many members of the American Jewish community, some of whom belonged to different generations of Russian immigrants. Among Russian-born politicians, there were also leaders of the American labor movement. The main organizations of old Russian social democrats (Mensheviks) in America were the New York group of the Russian Social Democratic Labor Party (RSDLP) and the Zagranichnaya delegatiya (ZD) of the Russian social democrats. The leaders of the ZD were social democrats, including Boris Nikolaevsky and Rafail Abramovich. Russian socialists were connected with the American Federation of Labor and affiliated structures, and stood politically on the right wing of the socialist movement.[129] They actively supported all the anti-Communist actions of the Truman administration and stressed that Soviet foreign policy was dishonest. However, they were opponents of those anti-Communists who collaborated with the National Socialists during World War II. Excluding Boris Nikolaevsky, Russian socialists strongly criticized the attempts by General Andrey Vlasov to use Nazi Germany to overthrow the Stalinist dictatorship.[130] They thought that it was impossible to fight against Soviet totalitarianism under the leadership of the other version of totalitarianism.

Liberal democratic values and socialist ideas were popular only among some groups of intellectuals. Stalinist policies strengthened not only tough anti-Soviet attitudes but also traditionalist moods even among those immigrants who had previously been supporters of liberal reforms. The majority of old émigrés shared conser-

---

128 "Letter by Boris Nikolaevsky to Rafael Abramovich. 29 Aug. 1946," HIA. Boris Nikolaevsky collection, series 248, box 471, folder 2.
129 "Letter by Victor Chernov and Others to E. Eshurin. 12 May 1948," in Bakhmeteff Archive at Columbia University, Vladimir M. Zenzinov collection, box 6, folder "Correspondence. C-F."
130 IISH, Boris Dvinov collection, folder 7.

vative ideals. One of their leaders, Boris Brasol, was the chairman of the Pushkin Society in America. The main political organization of conservative Russian émigrés in the USA was the Association of Russian National Organizations in the United States, founded in 1948. Prince Serge Beloselsky-Belozersky was the chairman of this organization. They tried to show Americans the difference between the Russian people (who suffered under the Communist regime) and Soviet power. Conservative Russian émigrés stressed that Hitler had misunderstood this difference, contributing to his failure on the Eastern Front in World War II. His war against the Soviet Union had become a war against the Russian people, and even those Russians who did not like the Communist regime began to fight against Nazi aggression.

Throughout the Cold War, conservative émigrés in the USA came to realize that America and her allies were the enemies of the Russian monarchist's enemy – Communism. Only America could provide them with the money and support they needed. They were willing to declare that they were loyal American citizens, even patriots. As it became obvious that Communism was an enemy of the traditional American state and its values, most conservative Russians in America declared themselves supporters of American democracy. The most interesting example of this situation involved Nikolay Rybakoff, an editor of the right-wing Russian-language newspaper Rossiya, published in New York. He had been a colonel in the White Army during the Russian Civil War and was a supporter of the monarchy and traditional Russian values. However, he published articles about the problems that American democracy faced in an attempt to create an image himself as a real defender of the American Republic.[131]

The majority of conservative Russians in America preferred the Republican Party over the Democratic Party. Boris Brasol and Nikolay Rybakoff were connected with the National Committee of the Republican Party and its secretary Gui Gabrielson. In 1951, they sent fifty copies of their English-language newspaper Russia to Gabrielson in the hope that he would distribute them among "key-persons in the Republican Party and other important persons in the government." We do not know whether this action bore fruit, but Gui Gabrielson wrote to Boris Brasol that this conversation with the Russian diaspora was "very well-timed" (the Korean War was ongoing).[132]

Conservative Russian émigrés actively supported politicians (like Senator W. Jenner of Indiana) who strictly criticized the policies of the Roosevelt administration, but thought that even Truman's policies were not as active as they could be. Boris Brasol stressed in one letter: "Korea is but a bloody link in a long chain of disastrous events the source of which must be traced to Teheran, Yalta and Potsdam…Today the American people are paying with their lives for the treasonable undercover 'agree-

---

[131] Nikolay Rybakoff, "Glory to the Victors," *Russia*, November 1, 1945, 1.
[132] "Letter by G. Gabrielson to B. Brasol. 19.03.1951," in LoC MD, The papers of Boris Brasol, box 4, folder "Political Correspondence. 1950–1952."

ments', which I cannot term otherwise than a surrender of our national sovereignty to a gang of international criminals entrenched in the Kremlin."[133]

Conservative values were also rather popular among Russian émigrés in Europe. There were many small groups organized by veterans of the White Army in Western Germany, France, and some other countries. The main figure for Russian monarchists was Grand Prince Vladimir Kirillovich Romanov (his father was the cousin of Nicholas II). However, some monarchists did not recognize him as head of the Russian imperial house. They criticized his father, who had supported the Russian Revolution of March 1917.[134] However, other conservative émigrés thought that it was impossible to restore the political and social system of the Russian Empire. They understood that it was more fruitful to attempt to revive "the soul of the Russian monarchy."[135] As a result, they proclaimed that monarchy was not their goal. They wrote in their journals and newspapers that the form of government was not so important: post-Communist Russia could be a republic or a monarchy, but it was necessary to create it based on traditional Russian values.

One of the most active political organizations of Russian émigrés during the Cold War was the NTS.[136] The center of the NTS was situated in Western Germany, but it also had groups in the USA, Latin America, Australia, and Morocco. At the end of the 1940s and in the 1950s, the NTS was full of internal conflicts. NTS members living in different countries and continents had different psychological approaches. Germany was the main front of the Cold War and therefore NTS members there existed in an atmosphere of daily struggle. However, in Australia or Latin America, NTS activists lived as ordinary people and sometimes only published anti-Soviet leaflets. Some NTS members in Western Germany thought that their comrades had moved to Australia only to save themselves from the dangers of the Cold War.[137]

There was another important reason for the conflicts in the NTS after World War II. The leadership of the NTS gradually changed. The émigrés of the Second Wave, who had left the Soviet Union during World War II, became NTS leaders. They had grown up in the USSR and some of them were former Communist Party members. The old émigrés, many of whom were former White officers, thought that the new émigrés had a Soviet mentality. This situation led to a struggle within the NTS leadership and local groups. As a result, many old NTS members who had joined the organization before World War II left. During the Cold War, the NTS received financial support from the CIA. Its newspaper, *Posev*, became the most famous anti-Communist journal among Soviet intellectuals.

---

[133] "Letter by B. Brasol to F. Coudert. 05.09.1950," in LoC MD, The papers of Boris Brasol, box 4, folder "Political Correspondence. 1950–1952."
[134] "Vladimir Romanov," *Voskresenie* (Esslingen) 63 (1964): 21.
[135] "Rossija i Monarhija, *Pereklichka* (New York) 45 (1955): 3.
[136] For the NTS, See Benjamin Tromly, "The Making of a Myth: The National Labor Alliance, Russian Emigres, and Cold War Intelligence Activities," *Journal of Cold War Studies* 18 (2016): 80–111.
[137] "Nash Sojuz," Za Rossiju (Frankfurt am Main) 2 (1950): 3.

Some political groups in Western Germany were formed by veterans of the RLA. The main group was the Union of Struggle for the Liberation of the Peoples of Russian (Sojuz Borby za osvobojdenie narodov Rossii, SBONR). Gradually, however, its activities decreased. The majority of RLA veterans understood that almost all the anti-Communist actions of émigrés had no real results.[138]

In particular, the NTS and the SBONR tried to establish connections with underground groups in the Soviet Union. The NTS sought to maintain links with members who stayed in the USSR after World War II, but most of them had been arrested by the Soviet security services. The NTS attempted to prove in its leaflets that there was a "revolutionary situation" in the USSR in the 1940s and 1950s.[139] However, this was very far from the case. The Soviet people believed that the political system had been proven legitimate by its victory in World War II. Equally, the Soviet security services were very active. It was thus impossible to create strong underground groups in the USSR.

Initially, Russian émigrés had very little information about the real situation in the USSR. In the 1950s and 1960s, they realized the considerable gulf between their approaches and those of the underground opposition. Very often, Soviet nonconformists idealized émigrés (particularly the NTS). It seemed to them that *Posev* was published by a powerful anti-Communist organization, which led to disappointment when they learned the truth. Some leaders of the Soviet underground (particularly Jury Galanskov) were NTS members,[140] but many dissidents were not supporters of NTS ideas.[141] They did not want to cooperate with an organization connected with World War II collaborators, nor did they support the NTS's revolutionary methods, since they thought that reforms were the best way forward for Russia. Some dissidents (like Andrey Amalrik) criticized the national-patriotic ideology of the NTS.[142]

The NTS used different methods to influence the political mood of the Soviet people. From 1951 to 1957, it deployed aerostats to circulate leaflets. However, the Americans stopped this practice.[143] The NTS tried to infiltrate Soviet territory, but this was a very arduous task. The most famous incident occurred when a group of saboteurs, all of whom were young émigrés, was arrested and killed by the Soviet se-

---

138 Gosudarstvenny Archiv Rossiiskoi Federatsii [State Archive of the Russian Federation], Nikolay Troitsky Collection, 4/23. P. 1.
139 Gosudarstvenny Archiv Rossiiskoi Federatsii, Boris Pryanishnikov Collection, 1/33. P. 44.
140 Boris Pushkarev ed., *NTS: Mysl i Delo*, 57.
141 On dissidents, see Rudolf Tokes ed., *Dissent in the USSR: Politics, Ideology and People* (Baltimore/London: Johns Hopkins University Press, 1975); Walter Parchomenko, *Soviet Images of Dissidents and Nonconformists* (New York/ London: Praeger, 1986); Lisa C. Paul, *Swimming in the Daylight: An American Student, A Soviet-Jewish Dissident, and the Gift of Hope* (New York: Skyhorse Publishing, 2011).
142 Andrey Amalrik, *Zapiski dissidenta* [Notes of a Dissident] (Moscow: Slovo, 1991), 54.
143 Boris Pushkarev ed., *NTS: Mysl i Delo*, 37.

curity services in 1953.¹⁴⁴ This event led to a serious conflict between the NTS and émigré youth organizations. Consequently, the NTS put a stop to such actions.

The NTS tried to circulate *Posev* among Soviet tourists and sailors, but this rarely led to real results. More effective were the attempts to circulate Russian nonconformist literature (novels and poetry by Boris Pasternak, Bulat Okudjava, Andrey Sinyavsky, etc.) and religious texts (the Bible and Koran). These actions changed the moral atmosphere in the Soviet Union. The NTS also had its own radio station, Free Russia, but its broadcast signal was not as powerful as those of Radio Liberty or the BBC. Free Russia and BBC programs led to the formation of anti-Communist views among young people in Leningrad in the 1950s. They created a "Young Russia" group connected with the NTS, whose leader was Jury Levin. They circulated leaflets in Leningrad, particularly during the Hungarian uprising in 1956. However, this group did not last long as its young anti-Communists were arrested in December 1956.¹⁴⁵

The formation of this group was closely connected with the so-called molecular theory devised by Vladimir Poremsky, which was very popular among NTS leaders in the 1950s and 1960s. Poremsky thought that the most important goal was to distribute information about the NTS through radio programs and leaflets. Thereafter, each anti-Communist in the USSR could join an NTS organization. For Poremsky, this was the most effective approach in the context of the totalitarian Soviet regime, but it was very difficult to ascertain how many "revolutionary monads" were really created in this manner.¹⁴⁶

Working at RL, Free Russia, BBC, and several other radio stations, Soviet émigrés played a significant role in the fall of Communism. They changed the moral atmosphere in the Soviet Union and influenced the ideological attitudes of some Soviet intellectuals. Émigrés saved the ideological heritage of pre-revolutionary Russia and the political cultures of Russian liberalism, conservatism, and social democracy. Many of them also maintained the traditions of Russian culture. However, their participation in the overthrow of Communism was not the decisive factor. The main instigator was the internal crisis of the Soviet system. The reforms by Gorbachev destabilized this regime and made its substantial flaws apparent. The year 1991 was a great surprise even to the leaders of anti-Communist emigration. Furthermore, many were disappointed by the political processes in post-Communist Russia. They had hoped that the fall of Communism would lead to the formation of a real democracy in Russia. However, the result was a crisis in all spheres of society and the break-up of a united country. Émigré leaders have not found a place in the new post-Communist Russia. The position of Alexander Zinoviev, a prominent philosopher and émigré of the Third Wave, is highly symbolic. In 1996, he supported

---

144 Boris Pushkarev ed., *NTS: Mysl i Delo*, 38.
145 Viktor Dolinin, "KGB protiv NTS," *Posev* 5 (1999): 47.
146 Vladimir Poremsky, *Strategija antibolshevitskoy emigratsii* [The Strategy of the Anti-Bolshevik Emigration] (Moscow: Posev, 1998), 106.

the Communist leader Gennady Zuganov against Boris Eltzin during the presidential elections. Some NTS leaders also strongly criticized governmental policy in the 1990s.

10.5 Migration since 1991

Emigration continued after the collapse of the USSR. It was connected primarily with economic motives (the crisis of the Russian economy in the 1990s) and social and political instability. The majority of post-Soviet émigrés moved to Germany, the USA, and Israel. Gradually, Germany began to dominate as a recipient country for Russian émigrés. By the end of the 1990s, about 50 % of them moved there. This was connected with the increasing of activity of Palestinian terrorists in Israel and the difficulties some Russians faced when trying to adapt to Israeli society (the majority of the newcomers had no Jewish identity, only Jewish roots). Nonetheless, it was also very difficult for Russians to find their own place in German society. Therefore, they began emigrating from Germany to other countries (e. g. Canada).

It is very difficult to estimate the number of post-Soviet Russia émigrés in the USA. US officials have reported that many Russians immigrated to America illegally as former guests, scholars, students, etc. In the 1990s and 2000s, America continued to be attractive for Russian émigrés, but the restrictive nature of American immigration legislation placed many obstacles on this path. In the twenty-first century, the social and psychological character of Russian émigrés has begun to change. They are no longer men and women who want to escape from poverty and political volatility: the new Russian émigrés are young, well-educated people who know foreign languages better than their Soviet predecessors. Typically, they use "step-by-step" emigration (emigration after a long residence in a new country as scholars, students, etc.). Russian emigration is an ongoing process.

10.6 Archives and Literature

The main Russian archive dedicated to the history of Russian émigrés – The Alexandr Solzhenitsyn House of Russia Abroad (Dom Russkogo Zarubejia imeni Aleksandra Soljenitzina) in Moscow – was founded by Alexandr Solzhenitsyn after he returned to Russia in 1994. It has more than 60 archival collections produced by many Russian émigrés. There are numerous documents by Russian military organizations abroad, prominent Russian politicians, writers, painters, etc. There is also material on the history of the Second Wave of Soviet emigration and the activities of Radio Liberty.[147]

---

[147] Dom Russkogo Zarubejia imeni Aleksandra Soljenitzina, www.bfrz.ru (in Russian) (accessed 20 July 2018).

The State Archive of the Russian Federation (Gosudarstvenny Archiv Rossiiskoi Federatsii (State Archive of the Russian Federation) in Moscow has many collections from the famous "Prague Archive," an archive created by Russian émigrés in the 1920s and 1930s which was moved to the USSR after World War II. In the 1990s, it obtained the personal collections of some prominent leaders from the Second Wave of Soviet emigration (N. Troitsky, B. Pryanishnikov, D. Konstantinov, K. Shteppa).[148]

The International Memorial in Moscow is the main scholarly center dedicated to the history of Stalinist terror and dissident movement. It holds the collections of Andrey Amalrik, a prominent member of the Third Wave of Soviet emigration.[149] Research and Information Center Memorial in St Petersburg has a collection of anti-Soviet leaflets (particularly those published by the NTS).[150]

The Russian State Archive of Literature and the Arts (Rossiisky Gosudarstvenny Archiv Literatury i Iskusstva) in Moscow has many personal documents from prominent figures of Russian culture abroad, including writers Ivan Bunin, Boris Zaitsev, and Alexey Remizov, the painters Jury Annenkov and Sergey Makovsky.[151] The Russian State Library, Manuscript Division (Rossiiskaya gosudarstvennaja biblioteka. Otdel rukopisey) in Moscow contains collections by Russian writers and poets abroad (e.g. Ivan Shmelev and George Ivanov).[152]

The most famous and largest Russian archive in America is the Hoover Institution Archives on War, Revolution and Peace (HIA) – Stanford University, Palo-Alto, California. There are more than 12,500,000 documents in Slavic languages deposited in this archive. Herbert Hoover founded the archive in 1919. Russian and Soviet materials are among the most significant of the Hoover Institution's archival holdings, making up approximately 1,000 personal collections. The Hoover collection on the 1917 revolutions, the Provisional Government, and the Russian Civil War is probably the best in the West. Among the personal collections are the archives of Vasily Maklakov, Alexander Kerensky, well-known generals of the White Army, and many others.

The Russian politician Boris Nikolaevsky created one of the most valuable collections. He was a prominent Menshevik during the Russian Revolution. His collection contains rich documentation about the party and pre-revolutionary Russia, including letters and papers from many Russian politicians. He had close connections with

---

[148] Gosudarstvenny Archiv Rossiiskoi Federatsii, www.statearchive.ru (in Russian) (accessed 20 July 2018).
[149] International Memorial, www.memo.ru (in English) (accessed 20 July 2018).
[150] Research and Information Center "Memorial," www. memorial-nic.org (in Russian) (accessed 20 July 2018).
[151] Rossiisky Gosudarstvenny Archiv Literatury i Iskusstva, www.rgali.ru (in English) (accessed 20 July 2018).
[152] Rossiiskaya gosudarstvennaja biblioteka. Otdel rukopisey (in English) www.rsl.ru (accessed 20 July 2018).

many people who belonged to the Second Wave of Soviet emigration. The HIA has some interesting archives from prominent representatives of the Third Wave of Soviet emigration and Soviet dissidents/nonconformists (e.g. Alexander Nekrich, Alexander Ginzburg and Andrey Siniavsky).[153]

The Bakhmeteff Archive at Columbia University in New York was founded by the Russian diplomat Boris Bakhmeteff in 1951 as the Archive of Russian and Eastern European History and Culture. Among the many personal collections in this archive are those of Michail Karpovich, the editor of Novy Journal, the well-known Russian liberal politicians Sofia Panina, Ariadna Tyrkova, and Vladimir Zeeler, and the White Army general Alexey von Lampe. BAR also has a large collection of Boris Sapir, the last Russian Menshevik who died in 1989.[154]

The Archive of the Museum of Russian Culture (AMRC) in San Francisco, California was founded by the Russian Center in San Francisco in 1948. This is the main Russian émigré archive in the USA. It has many of the personal collections of Russian émigrés (mainly those who lived in California). There is also a collection of documents created by Russian DPs after World War II. The archive of the Russian Center in San Francisco is deposited at the AMRC.[155]

The Library of Congress. Manuscript Division (LoC.MD) in Washington, DC holds many Russian collections at the LoC.MD. Among them are the collections of the Pushkin Society in America and its leader Boris Brasol. The LoC.MD also holds the large collection of George Gamow, a world-renowned Russian-American scientist, and a small collection formerly belonging to the famous writer Vladimir Nabokov.[156]

The Georgetown University Library. Special collections (GUL.SC) in Washington, DC has the personal papers of people who significantly influenced the formation of the information policy of Radio Liberation/Radio Liberty, such as Robert Kelly, who spearheaded Radio Liberation in the 1950s, and John Lodeesen, who occupied a key position at the station from the late 1960s until the early 1980s. GUL.SC also has the collection of Victor Baydalakoff, the leader of the NTS in the 1930s and 1940s.[157]

The Leeds Russian Archive at the University of Leeds (LRA) in the United Kingdom is the largest Russian archive in Europe. It was founded in 1982. There are more than 650 collections of manuscripts, photographs, and other archival materials. There are also over 10,000 books, journals, newspapers, and other printed matter supplementary to the archival collections. Among the main collections on the Cold War epoch are the archives of the Russian diplomat Sablin (head of Russian

---

[153] Hoover Institution Archives on War, Revolution and Peace, www.hoover.org (accessed 3 May 2018).
[154] Bakhmeteff Archive of Russian and East European Culture, http://library.columbia.edu/locations/rbml/units/bakhmeteff.html (accessed 3 May 2018).
[155] Archive of the Museum of Russian Culture, www.mrcsf.org (accessed 3 May 2018).
[156] Library of Congress. Manuscript Division, www.loc.gov (accessed 3 May 2018).
[157] Georgetown University Library. Special collections, www.library.georgetown.edu (accessed 3 May 2018).

House in London until 1949) and the prominent writer of the Second Wave A. I. Pliushkov.[158]

The Forschungsstelle Osteuropa an der Universität Bremen. Historisches Archiv (FSO UB. HA) in Bremen, Germany is the main archive on Russian émigré political activity during the Cold War in Europe. It has many documents from the NTS, especially in the Gleb Rahr collection and the Possev Verlag archive. One can also find a collection of documents related to Kromiadi, who was one of the close collaborators of General Andrey Vlasov and a prominent politician of the Second Wave.[159]

The International Institute of Social History (IISH) in Amsterdam, Netherlands is the main archive on the history of left-wing political movements. It holds collections from Russian Mensheviks (Rafail Abramovich, Fedor Dan, Lidia Dan, Boris Dvinov, and others) and anarchists (Grigory Maksimov, Ida Lazarewitch, and Boris Yelensky).[160]

The Bibliotheque de Documentation Internationale Contemporaine, Departements Archives (BDIC) in Nanterre, France also specializes in the history of left-wing political culture. It has the collections of the prominent Russian socialist and historian Nikolay Valentinov (Volsky) and the anarchist Nikolay Lazarewitch.[161]

The Open Society Archives (HU OSA) in Budapest, Hungary. This archive has a collection entitled the "Soviet Red Archives," which was created by the Radio Free Europe/Radio Liberty Research Institute. It has different material on the activities of the leaders of the Third Wave of Soviet emigration (e. g. Vladimir Bukovsky and Petr Grigorenko).[162]

The majority of studies on the Russian diaspora are devoted to the period between the 1920s and the 1930s, the high point in the First Wave of post-revolutionary emigration. This was already being studied in the Soviet period[163] although such works were strongly influenced by the ideology of the Communist regime. This subject became especially attractive for scholars in the 1990s. Trying to find the roots of the new Russian state, historians have written some interesting works[164]. Among them are studies by Russian émigrés[165] (see Mark Raeff, *Russia Abroad*. New York/Oxford: Oxford University Press, 1990). The study of this wave of Russian emigration has

---

[158] Leeds Russian Archive at University of Leeds, www.library.leeds.ac.uk (accessed 3 May 2018).
[159] Forschungsstelle Osteuropa an der Universitat Bremen. Historisches Archiv, www.forschungsstelle.uni-bremen.de. (accessed 3 May 2018).
[160] International Institute of Social History, www.socialhistory.org. (accessed 20 July 2018).
[161] Bibliotheque de Documentation Internationale Contemporaine. Departements Archives, www.lacontemporaine.fr. (in French). (accessed 20 July 2018).
[162] Open Society Archives, www.osaarchivum.org. (accessed 20 July 2018).
[163] See Leonid Shkarenkov, *Agonija beloy emigratsii (*Moscow: Mysl', 1986).
[164] See Michail Nazarov, *Missija Russkoi emigratsii* (Stavropol: Kavkazsky krai, 1992).
[165] See Mark Raeff, *Russia Abroad* (New York/Oxford: Oxford University Press, 1990).

continued in the twenty-first century. Contemporary Russian historians actively use numerous materials deposited in Russian and foreign archives[166].

However, the Cold War period in the history of the Russian diaspora is understudied. Only a few Russian and foreign scholars have paid special attention to this epoch. The Second Wave of Soviet emigration was introduced to the Russian academic community by Viktor Zemskov[167]. It is also necessary to highlight the well-known Russian specialist on historical demography, Pavel Polian, who has published a well-researched volume on the formation of the Second Wave of Soviet emigration and repatriation into the USSR[168].

Several studies are devoted to the political activities of Russian exiles during the Cold War. Among Russian historians, we may note the works of Petr Bazanov. His monograph is devoted to the publishing activities of different political groups of the anti-Communist diaspora[169]. The Siberian historian Daniil Alekseev has studied the history of the NTS and its political activity[170].

European and American historians have also examined some aspects of this problem. It is necessary to highlight the studies by Andre Liebich[171], one of the main specialists in the history of Russian social democracy. One of the most popular subjects is the history of Jewish emigration from the Soviet Union. Many historians have scrutinized this issue, including Edward Drachmann, Laurie Salitan, Piet Buwalda[172] etc. However, many aspects of this subject await new researchers. Future scholars will need to work with documents from the archives of the Soviet and American security services. These will give scholars new data about the actual effectiveness of the activities of the Russian anti-Communist organizations. It is also very important to take into consideration the atmosphere in the recipient society for Russian émigrés. Almost no studies have been devoted to the conditions for Russian émigré political activity in West Germany, the USA, or France. Nonetheless, each country had its own characteristics during the Cold War. What can we say about the influence of

---

166 See Andrey Popov, *Rossiiskoye Pravoslavnoe Zarubejie: Istoriya i Istochniki* (Moscow: Istitute of Politicheskogo i Voennogo Analiza, 2005); Nikolay Bolhovitinov, *Russkie Uchenye-Emigranty (G. V. Vernadsky, M.M. Karpovich, M.T. Florinsky) i Stanovlenie Rusistiki v SShA* (Moscow: ROSSPEN, 2005); Amir Khisamutdinov, *Russkiy San-Francisco* (Moscow: Veche, 2010) etc.
167 Viktor Zemskov, "K voprosu o repatriatsii sovetskih grajdan," *Istoria SSSR*, 4 (1990): 26–41; Viktor Zemskov, "Repatriatsia sovetskih grajdan i ih dalneishaja sudba," *Socis*, 5 (1995): 109–112 etc.
168 See Pavel Polian, *Jertvy dvuh diktatur*. Moscow: ROSSPEN, 2002.
169 See Petr Bazanov, *Izdatelskaya Dejatelnost Politicheskih Organizatii Russkoi Emigratii (1917–1988)* (St Petersburg: St Petersburg gosudarstvenny universitet kultury i iskussv, 2008).
170 Daniil Alekseev, *NTS rossiiskih solidaristov v borbe protiv totalitarnogo rejima*. Abstract of candidate dissertation (Vladivostok, 1998).
171 See Andre Liebich, "Mensheviks Wage the Cold War" *Journal of Contemporary History* 30 (1995): 247–264; Andre Liebich, *From the Other Shore: Russian Social-Democracy after 1921* (Cambridge, Mass.: Harvard University Press, 1997).
172 Edward Drachmann, *Challenging the Kremlin. The Soviet Jewish Movement for Freedom. 1967–1990*. (New York: Paragon House, 1992); Salitan, *Politics and Nationality*; Buwalda, *They Did Not Dwell Alone*.

Russian political exiles in recipient societies and their cooperation with political elites? This is also a question for future scholars.

The majority of researchers usually write about key figures and organizations in the Russian diaspora. Unfortunately, we have practically no works devoted to "ordinary" people, even though they formed the largest part of the diaspora. It is necessary to write more about these "ordinary" émigrés and their political attitudes. This will require the examination of personal documents (letters, diaries, etc.) written by the émigrés and constitutes one of the primary tasks for future historians.

11 Yugoslavia

Brigitte Le Normand

11.1 Migrations in historical perspective

As Ulf Brunnbauer points out, emigration is a "longue durée phenomenon" in the Yugoslav region.[1] One might say the same of labor migration within the region. According to peasants interviewed by ethnographer Joel Halpern, for example, the pečalba tradition in Macedonia, in which rural dwellers would travel to neighboring Serbia for two to three years, had been going on "since Turkish times."[2] Both emigration – which involved long-term displacement, but was not always permanent – and labor migration were strategies for dealing with limited economic possibilities within the region. Statistics on emigration were first collected in the late nineteenth century, revealing the strong attraction of the North American "land of opportunity" in the prewar period. Total recorded migration to North America amounted to 165,960 out of a total 202,547 emigrants from Croatia and Slavonia between 1899 and 1913.[3] Although the newly founded Kingdom of Serbs, Croats, and Slovenes adopted a far more restrictive emigration regime, limiting the numbers of its citizens that could emigrate through quotas as well as bureaucratic inefficiencies, emigration did continue after the Great War, peaking in 1930 at nearly 39,000. Overseas emigration began to decline dramatically the following year, whereas emigration within Europe continued to play a significant role.[4]

11.2 The aftermath of World War II

Migration to and from Yugoslavia during the Cold War can best be understood by taking into account a number of critical factors. The first is the end of the Second World War and its aftermath, which continued have a lasting impact on migration well into the 1950s. The second, which dovetails with the first, is the geopolitical context of the Cold War, and Yugoslavia's evolving place within it. The third, also related to the sec-

---

[1] Ulf Brunnbauer, "Labor Emigration from the Yugoslav Region from the late 19th Century until the End of Socialism: Continuities and Changes," in *Transnational Societies, Transterritorial Politics: Migrations in the (Post-) Yugoslav Region 19th–21th Century*, vol. 141, ed. Ulf Brunnbauer (Munich: Oldenbourg, 2009), 17.
[2] Joel Halpern, "The Pečalba Tradition in Macedonia, A Case Study." (1975). *Anthropology Department Faculty Publication Series*. 58, 1.
[3] Ulf Brunnbauer, "Labor Emigration," 19.
[4] Aleksandar R. Miletić, "(Extra-)Institutional Practices, Restrictions, and Corruption. Emigration Policy in the Kingdom of Serbs, Croats, and Slovenes (1918–1928)," in *Transnational Societies, Transterritorial Politics: Migrations in the (Post-) Yugoslav Region 19th–21th century*, vol. 141, ed. Ulf Brunnbauer (Munich: Oldenbourg, 2009), 95–119.

ond, is the changing nature of Yugoslav state socialism, and its changing understanding of and attitude toward migration. The fourth is Yugoslavia's economic situation, which itself reflected the country's longstanding status as a predominantly agrarian state and its place within the European and global circulation of labor, as well as the consequences of the Yugoslav socialist model of economic development.

Cold War migration included a variety of migration types that cannot be easily distinguished from one another, but instead, overlap in important ways. Wartime refugees, political migrants, and economic migrants seem at first sight to be different categories, and yet the reality was more complicated. People fled Yugoslavia at the end of the war for multiple reasons that could not be separated so easily. Their material situation might have been difficult due to wartime destruction, dispossession due to identity, political views, general precarity at the end of the war, or all of the above. Labor migrants during the 1960s were sometimes hostile to Yugoslavia, or became so during their migration experience, associating with hostile political organizations.

This latter example suggests that we should be particularly skeptical of official categories, created by states and international organizations, that often oversimplify and even distort people's motivations. For example, refugees might have claimed this status because it was the easiest way to leave the country, but it seems that many were also motivated by the desire for a better life. It is difficult, in turn, to discern to what extent this desire was shaped by wariness of the new Communist authorities, the challenges of reconstruction, and a perceived awareness of greater opportunity in faraway lands. Furthermore, the motivations of many Yugoslav migrants were not starkly different from those of Dutch rural dwellers who, having similarly experienced occupation, an arduous reconstruction, and increasing government intervention, sought a new life in Canada.[5]

Reflecting the complexity of this migration story – or, more accurately, migration stories – this chapter is organized into two chronological sections, which correspond with two distinguishably different contexts. The first part deals with the period from the end of the Second World War until 1954. This period was characterized by the turmoil of the last struggles of the war, ethnic cleansing and retribution, mass confiscations and the establishment of new property relations, physical destruction and reconstruction, extreme material deprivation, border changes and disputes, and the political consolidation of a new Stalinist state. Globally, during this period, the Partisan state was first part of the Soviet Bloc, and then was expelled from it, forcing the Titoist regime to reassert control and legitimacy. From the perspective of migration, this period was characterized by mass emigration, both clandestine and at the behest of the Yugoslav state which sought to rid itself of populations considered polit-

---

[5] Frans J. Schryer, *The Netherlandic Presence in Ontario: Pillars, Class and Dutch Ethnicity* (Waterloo ON: Wilfrid Laurier University Press, 2006), 45–46, 48–53.

ically or ethnically problematic. All other types of movement across borders by Yugoslav citizens – whether labor migration, tourism, or other – was strictly limited and regulated.

The second part of this chapter, dealing with the period between 1954 and the dissolution of Yugoslavia, corresponds with a very different set of circumstances: economic stabilization and growth, political liberalization and decentralization, and relative political and economic stability. Having accepted its expulsion from the Soviet Bloc, Yugoslav innovated a brand of socialism characterized by self-management, openness, and non-alignment – a reorientation that was reflected in migration policy by the liberalization of borders, participation in global labor markets, and efforts to neutralize hostile diaspora organizations.

11.3 Major migration streams during the Cold War

11.3.1 1945–1954: Deciding who was in and who was out

At the end of the Second World War, Yugoslavia was in the hands of the Partisans, whose leadership was closely aligned with the Soviet Union. It adopted a Stalinist mode of government under the strict guidance of the Yugoslav Communist Party. In line with this orientation, Yugoslavia adopted a very restrictive passport regime. Passports and exit visas could only be obtained under exceptional circumstances, and largely at the request of state political organizations.[6]

Nevertheless, the decade after the Second World War was characterized by large-scale migration, primarily out of Yugoslavia, but also into the state. This out-migration is best understood in the context of the displacement caused by the Second World War in combination with the new socialist regime's consolidation over power. The fact that these migrations only ended in the mid-1950s testifies to the long shadow of the Second World War.

The end of the Second World War witnessed the flight and expulsion of civilians and fighters hostile to the Communists. These expulsions were not unique to Yugoslavia, but characteristic of the end of the war in Central and Eastern Europe. While these expellees and refugees often ended up in the same displaced persons camps and may have told very similar stories of persecution, dispossession, and other kinds of victimization, the reasons for their departure were different, if sometimes overlapping.

First, we must consider the political rivals and wartime enemies of the partisans fleeing their advance. This included large numbers of Croats, Serbs, and Slovenes, many of which were Ustaša fighters or members of the Domobranci (Slovene home

---

[6] Vladimir Ivanović, *Geburtstag pišeš normalno: jugoslovenski gastarbajteri u SR Nemačkoj i Austriji, 1965–1973* (Belgrade: Institut za savremenu istoriju, 2012), 50–51.

guard) or Četnik organizations. They were aggressively hunted down first by Partisan fighters seeking to exact retribution and then by the emerging Titoist regime in pursuit of a twofold objective: the neutralization of the threat they posed and the establishment of control over the People's Committees, and thus, a monopoly over violence. While the Titoist regime clearly sought to drive out the ethnic minorities discussed in the paragraphs below, in the case of its enemies, the goal was "disarming and, in many cases, physically liquidating these domestic rivals."[7] The most infamous instance of this is the Bleiburg repatriations. The Independent State of Croatia fascist puppet state organized a retreat of its soldiers and civilian supporters to Southern Austria. The fleeing columns were further inflated by Četniks and Slovenian home guard soldiers fleeing the Communists. While no precise records exist, the most credible estimate is that approximately 75,000 army personnel and 45,000 civilians crossed into Austria. Having reached Bleiburg, they attempted to surrender to the British, who returned them to the custody of the partisans, with deadly consequences, as an estimated 26,500 soldiers and 6,800 civilians were killed in the ensuing march back through Slovenia.[8]

Significant numbers were able to escape Yugoslavia and seek refuge in neighboring states or emigrate overseas. West Germany took in some 12,000 individuals who refused to be repatriated to Yugoslavia. This state would prove a welcoming place for anti-Communists until the 1960s, due in part to the support of German expellees from Communist states and of conservative political parties (CDU and CSU). A further 20,000 to 40,000 were able to journey to Latin America and Spain via escape routes organized by the Catholic Church. Those who were able to leave included a number of high-level Ustaša officials, such as Ante Pavelić, Maks Luburić, and Andrija Artuković, and others that would come to play a role in militant Croatian nationalist organizations, such as Branimir Jelić. Indeed, Pavelić, Luburić and Jelić would all go on to found the major organizations struggling for Croatian independence outside of Yugoslavia's borders. Thus, the Second World War set the stage for the development of anti-Yugoslav organizations during the Cold War.[9]

The second category of mass migrants during and after the war included minority ethnic populations: Italian, Hungarian, and German speakers. All three populations had been associated with the occupying regimes, in the sense that these regimes claimed them as members of their own nation-state, involved them in the

---

[7] Pamela Ballinger, "At the Borders of Force: Violence, Refugees, and the Reconfiguration of the Yugoslav and Italian States," *Past & Present* 210, no. 1 (2011): 164.
[8] Martina Grahek Ravančić, "Controversies about the Croatian Victims at Bleiburg and in 'Death Marches'," *Review of Croatian History* 2, no. 1 (2006): 46.
[9] Mate Nikola Tokić, Landscapes of Conflict: Unity and Disunity in Post-Second World War Croatian Emigre Separatism," *European Review of History—Revue européenne d'histoire* 16, no. 5 (2009): 740–742; Tokić, "The End of "Historical-Ideological Bedazzlement," *Social Science History* 36, no. 3 (2012): 427; Alexander Clarkson, *Fragmented Fatherland: Immigration and Cold War Conflict in the Federal Republic of Germany, 1945–1980*, (New York: Berghahn Books, 2013), 54–86.

occupation and gave them privileges. At the end of the war, members of those minorities were subjected to ill treatment ranging from harassment to systemic terror. It should be noted that the Yugoslav case was part of a much wider trend across Central and Eastern Europe, resulting in the displacement of millions, including 12 to 14 million ethnic Germans. At the conclusion of this period, hundreds of thousands of members of these ethnic minorities had fled or been expelled from Yugoslavia.

The expulsion of ethnic minorities, which took place across Central and Eastern Europe, was facilitated by a number of factors. One of them was the "directly punitive ethos" in Yugoslavia that may be difficult to understand for those who did not live through the atrocities of the Second World War.[10] In addition, the removal of ethnic minorities can be seen as one more step in the decades-long project of establishing nation-states in Europe. As Matthew Frank has pointed out, "a central component of post-war programs of national reconstruction and national revival, as well as a major source of their popular appeal, was the demand for the liquidation of the minority problem."[11] Pamela Ballinger makes a compelling argument in the Italian case against the concept of "ethnic cleansing" because it implied that these populations were targeted for elimination due to their origins. In her view, this assumption is not borne out by the evidence and obscures the actual dynamics of the early post-war period in Yugoslavia. Instead, the expulsion of a large part of the Italian-speaking community is best understood in the context of the Titoist regime's efforts to establish effective sovereignty over the territory that it claimed and controlled. In this case, Yugoslavia occupied and then obtained, through peace negotiation at the end of the war, territories that had been under Italian sovereignty since the end of the First World War. The reconfiguration of Yugoslavia's borders, which took place in several phases between 1945 and 1954, resulted in a large-scale exodus of Italians from the Istrian peninsula, Slovenian littoral, Dalmatia and the city of Rijeka. The widespread violence against Italians and perceived fascist collaborators that accompanied the partisan advance in 1945 generated a substantial exodus of Italians. Some 220,000 Italian-speakers left Istria, the Julian March, and the city of Rijeka in several distinct waves, both during the war and in the wake of several post-war international border settlements. The disputed territory was divided into two zones in 1945, the first of which was administered by the Anglo-American Allied Military Government, whereas the second one was governed by the Yugoslav military authorities. The Paris Peace Treaty of 1947 awarded southern Istria definitively to Yugoslavia and resulted in a modification of the zone boundaries. Per the conditions of the peace treaty, persons able to demonstrate that Italian was their primary language could opt for Italian citizenship. The memorandum of understanding of 1954 stabilized the Italian-Yugo-

---

10 Peter Gattrell, "Trajectories of Population Displacement in the Aftermaths of Two World Wars," in *The Disentanglement of Populations: Migration, Expulsion and Displacement in Post-War Europe, 1944–9*, ed. Jessica Reinisch and Elizabeth White (Basingstoke: Palgrave Macmillan, 2011), 7.
11 Matthew Frank, "Reconstructing the Nation-State: Population Transfer in Central and Eastern Europe, 1944–1948" in *The Disentanglement of Populations*, 28.

slav border, awarding the rest of Istria to Yugoslavia, and sparked a further exodus to Italy.[12]

Nonetheless, as Pamela Ballinger has argued, the concept ethnic cleansing does not sit easily with the facts on the ground. Indeed, many Italian-speakers who wished to "opt" for Italy and thus leave Yugoslavia were denied that possibility by the Yugoslav state. Ballinger sees the process of deciding which Italians should leave and which should stay in the context of the Communists' quest to establish a monopoly on violence, consolidate power, and validate its claims over formerly Italian territory. Consequently, they sought to establish which Italian-speakers, due to their political leanings and life experience, were loyal to the Italian state, and which were – or at the very least, could be – loyal to a socialist Yugoslav state. Framed in this manner, the emigration of Italian socialists into Yugoslavia – including two thousand Communists from Monfalcone – makes sense. The case of the Italian exodus not only illustrates Yugoslavia's desire to rid itself of potentially disloyal subjects, but it also highlights its desire to keep all the others within its borders.[13]

A better case for ethnic cleansing can be made for ethnic Germans, and potentially, for ethnic Hungarians. Unlike the case of Italian speakers, the territory inhabited by Hungarians and Germans had already been under Yugoslav sovereignty before the Second World War. It came under German and Hungarian occupation during the Second World War. The Hungarian population, which numbered some 466,000 in 1931, was concentrated in the former Hungarian "South Country" lost by Hungary and gained by Yugoslavia in the treaty of Trianon, including Banat and Bačka in Vojvodina, as well as Srem in Serbia and Baranja and Međumurje in Croatia, and Prekmurje in Slovenia.[14] By the end of the war, this population included both inhabitants of long standing and colonists and civil servants that came after Hungary occupied the territory in 1941. The German minority referred to as *Donauschwaben* or *Volksdeutscher*, totaling 496,000 inhabitants in 1931, was settled in Vojvodina, Slavonia and Slovenia, almost entirely prior to the Second World War. Out-migration began before the war's end, with large numbers of Hungarians and Germans fleeing in October and November 1944 with the retreating military forces.[15] This exodus would turn into forced expulsions after the war. While the partisan leadership clearly sanctioned this violence and endorsed it as its official policy, it also reflected popular pressures, as Yugoslavs perceived the Germans and the Hungarians as collaborators and supporters of the occupying regime. Expelling the Germans and Hungarians also fit in the Communists' broader project of confiscating property from collaborators in order to nationalize it (industry) or redistribute it (land), as part of its

---

12 Ballinger, "At the Borders of Force," 167–168.
13 Ballinger, "At the Borders of Force," 162–170.
14 Andrew Ludanyi, "Titoist Integration of Yugoslavia: The Partisan Myth & the Hungarians of the Vojvodina, 1945–1975," *Polity* 12 (1979): 233; Enikő A Sajti, *Hungarians in the Voivodina, 1918–1947* (Boulder: East European Monographs, 2003), xi.
15 Sajti, *Hungarians in the Voivodina*, 434.

program of popular revolution. This is particularly true of the Germans who, while only a quarter of the population of Vojvodina, reportedly accounted for 50% of the pre-World War II economy.[16]

The expulsion of Germans and Hungarians differed in some important ways. This is evident in the outcome, as virtually no ethnic Germans remained in Yugoslavia by 1960, while a substantial ethnic Hungarian minority did remain. Although it is debatable whether the Titoist regime pursued a consistent line on this issue, or whether its decisions are better seen as being *ad hoc*, in response to the evolving situation on the ground, there is credible evidence that it openly pursued a policy of ethnic cleansing of Germans, as demonstrated by Vladimir Geiger's research.[17]

In the German case, the international context created ideal conditions for ethnic cleansing. The use of ethnic cleansing was essentially endorsed by Yugoslavia's allies: the British and, in particular, the Soviets, who were eager to claim Polish territory East of the Oder-Neisse line and empty it of its Polish population. While the British were more ambivalent about the expulsion of the Germans, they ultimately endorsed this policy for a number of reasons. First, they regarded ethnic homogeneity as a precondition for stability and perceived the punishment of the Germans both as inevitable and as fruitful. The British had consequently tacitly approved of the expulsion of the Sudeten Germans as early as 1941. In spite of a growing awareness of the humanitarian catastrophe that loomed, in the months before and after the end of the war, they were eager not to alienate their Soviet allies.

Interestingly, Yugoslavia's idiosyncratic position in the postwar order, as a nominally "self-liberated state," meant that it was excluded from "Operation Swallow," the operation to facilitate the expulsions of ethnic Germans from the so-called "Potsdam States" – Czechoslovakia, Poland, and Hungary. Already overwhelmed by the seemingly unstaunchable flow of brutalized, sick and starving ethnic Germans flooding into a devastated Germany, the Big Three were eager to prevent any further swelling in their numbers. Consequently, they ignored Yugoslavia's request for the occupation zones to accept its own ethnic Germans. Anecdotal evidence suggests that this unwillingness to accommodate Yugoslavia's request increased the scale of the human rights catastrophe, as Yugoslavia resorted to trying to covertly smuggle its ethnic Germans across its borders, or intern them in concentration and work camps.[18]

---

[16] Ulrich Merten, *Forgotten Voices: The Expulsion of the Germans from Eastern Europe After World War II* (New Brunswick: Transaction Publishers, 2013), 210.

[17] Vladimir Geiger, "Josip Broz Tito i sudbina jugoslavenskih Nijemaca," *Časopis za suvremenu povijest* 3 (2008): 801–818.

[18] Marina Cattaruzza, "'Last Stop Expulsion" – The Minority Question and Forced Migration in East-Central Europe: 1918–49,' *Nations and Nationalism* 16, no. 1 (2010): 119; Ray M. Douglas, *Orderly and Humane: The Expulsion of the Germans after the Second World War* (New Haven/London: Yale University Press, 2012), 110–111, 122–123.

While rigorous numbers are hard to come by, Ulrich Merten provides the following figures for the German minority: "of the approximately 524,000 Germans living in prewar Yugoslavia, approximately 370,000 escaped to Austria and Germany in the last days of the War or were subsequently expelled by the Yugoslav government."[19] By 1948, only 55,000 Germans remained in Yugoslavia.[20] In 1948, Yugoslavia once again changed its policy toward its remaining ethnic Germans, releasing them from camps and putting them to work in Yugoslavia's campaign of rapid industrialization. Laborers were initially forced to sign three-year work contracts, and at the end of this period, they regained their civil rights and were offered Yugoslav citizenship. The final exodus of ethnic Germans would take place between 1950 and 1960 at the behest of the Federal Republic of Germany and with the assistance of the German and Yugoslav Red Cross, first through a repatriation program, and then a more generalized emigration program. According to official numbers, 53,000 ethnic Germans had left by 1960, although the numbers may have been even higher.[21]

Enikő A. Sajti has argued that the case of Yugoslav Hungarians is one of thwarted ethnic cleansing, but her case is not entirely persuasive. She supports her claim that there was an intention of ethnic cleansing by pointing to influential political figures who had previously argued for the wholesale elimination of the Hungarian minority, seeing them as a threat to Yugoslavia's control over the territory they inhabited. In her view, socialist Yugoslavia's relationship with the Hungarian People's Republic made it difficult to carry out this project. Hungary protested the abuse of its minority and was unwilling to take in large numbers of refugees that would put a further strain on its meager resources.

Ultimately, per the armistice and peace treaty with Hungary, Yugoslavia was allowed to deport Hungarians who had arrived following Hungary's occupation. In fact, however, a significant number of indigenous Hungarians were also forced out. By 1946, there were an estimated 84,800 Hungarians from Yugoslavia in Hungary. An earlier count had revealed that, of the 45,545 deportees and refugees, 13,521 were settlers, 9263 were public officials, most of which had come after 1941, and the remaining 15,626 – a full third – originated in the region.[22] While Hungary and Yugoslavia engaged in lengthy negotiations over a population transfer of 40,000 Hungarians and Slavs on the "wrong" side of the national border, they were unable to come to an agreement. Ultimately, according to the 1948 census, 496,492 persons claiming Hungarian ethnicity remained in Yugoslavia, primarily in Vojvodina.[23]

The case for thwarted ethnic cleansing is weakened by the fact that, pending further research, we have no strong evidence that the Titoist regime wished to expel all

---

19 Merten, *Forgotten Voices*, 208–209.
20 Ludanyi, "Titoist Integration of Yugoslavia," 233.
21 Merten, *Forgotten Voices*, 239.
22 Sajti, *Hungarians in the Voivodina*, 440.
23 Ludanyi, "Titoist Integration of Yugoslavia," 233.

its ethnic minorities. Whereas the regime issued calls for punishment and removal of Germans as a people, it did not do the same for the ethnic Hungarians. Rather, it distinguished between "good" and "bad" Hungarians – those who had supported the National Liberation Struggle and those who had collaborated with the occupier.[24] Unlike the Germans, the Hungarians were offered a place in the Yugoslav Partisan myth, with a focus on the exploits of the wartime Petőfi brigade. The very creation of this brigade, however insignificant in numbers, testifies to the Partisan's regime's willingness to make room for ethnic Hungarians in postwar Yugoslavia – this too is surely reflected in the much lower numbers of Hungarian expellees and the long-term persistence of the Hungarian community.

The significant flow of ethnic minorities and the more modest exodus of political enemies out of Yugoslavia can be seen as two manifestations of the larger tsunami of refugees after the Second World War, which also included significant numbers belonging to the recognized Yugoslav nationalities who left of their own accord. Aside from Italians, a number of Croats and Slovenes also left former Italian lands and sought asylum in Italy. Their motivations for leaving were diverse; they ranged from wartime devastation of their communities, the difficult realities of postwar reconstruction, an aversion to Communist ideology or to the practices of the Titoist regime, to a desire to reunite with family members across the border and aspirations for a better life in the land of emigration. These different populations coexisted in numerous refugee camps.[25]

In spite of the heterogeneity of this population, the discursive framework of the emerging Cold War on displaced persons tended to group them in the larger category of political refugees. As Francesca Rolandi shows, both due to its own territorial conflicts with Yugoslavia and pressure from its Cold War Allies, Italy had a policy of recognizing claims of political asylum. In turn, refugees claimed political refugee status, regardless of whether or not they had a political background, because such claims were likely to be successful. While they pointed to a general lack of freedoms in Yugoslavia, few gave specific instances of persecution. Rolandi concludes that many asylum seekers were likely also motivated by aspirations for a more prosperous life. Nonetheless, individuals and groups hostile to Yugoslavia and actively organizing against it were present in the displaced persons camps. Remarkably, in some cases, they even held informal authority over other displaced persons.[26]

The refugee camps that emerged after the Second World War continued to exist well into the 1960s. Aside from the lingering population of the so-called "hard core"

---

24 Geiger, *"Josip Broz Tito,"* 807.
25 Francesca Rolandi, "Escaping Yugoslavia: Italian and Austrian Refugee Policy toward Yugoslav Asylum Seekers after World War II," in *The 'Alpen-Adria' Region 1945–1955: International and Transnational Perspectives on a Conflicted European Region*, ed. Wolfgang Mueller, Karlo Ruzicic-Kessler and Philipp Greilinger (Vienna: New Academic Press, 2018).
26 Francesca Rolandi, "Heading Towards the West. Yugoslav Asylum Seekers in Italy (1955–1968)," *Acta Histriae* 23, no. 3 (2015): 562, 565.

cases, Yugoslav and otherwise, who refused to be repatriated and who were not accepted by any host country, Yugoslavs continued to seek asylum well into the Cold War era. Requests for asylum by Yugoslavs eventually slowed to a trickle in the second half of the 1960s, following the liberalization of the border regime, with only 994 applications in 1969, and 194 in 1974. However, the number of refugees from Eastern Bloc states transiting through Yugoslavia on their way to claiming asylum in Western Europe continued to increase, from 151 in 1969 to 3,275 in 1969.[27]

Aside from the significant flow out of Yugoslavia of groups who either wanted to leave or were considered undesirable by the Yugoslav authorities, there was a much smaller flow of repatriates and newcomers into the state. There were of course unwilling repatriates, including those returned to Yugoslavia by the British at Bleiburg, in Austria, and others political asylum seekers. However, the Department for Emigration in the Yugoslav Ministry of Labor also eagerly courted Yugoslav emigrants and their descendants living abroad. Brunnbauer argues that the main objective of attracting these emigrants was to create powerful propaganda contrasting the life of struggle and exploitation these repatriates had faced in capitalist states with the benefits of socialism, including social welfare, emancipation, and progress. In reality, returnees faced serious difficulties (re)integrating into society and the labor market, and many were deeply disappointed. Aware of the shortcomings of the program, and increasingly aware that it had unwittingly eliminated a potentially powerful pro-Yugoslav lobby abroad, Yugoslav authorities suspended the program in the early 1950s. It also disbanded the Department for Emigration in 1951, replacing it with a body that had consultative rather than executive function, signaling a decline in interest in emigrants.[28]

It is noteworthy that the repatriation program courted return-migrants not based on their citizenship or territorial belonging, but rather, of their ethnicity. Thus, members of the official Yugoslav nationalities were welcome to return, regardless of whether or not they held Yugoslav citizenship, or had ever even lived on Yugoslav territory. Conversely, Germans (because of their ethnicity) and Muslims (possibly because of their lower socio-economic status) were not welcome, and Magyars would be considered on a case-by-case basis, according to whether their return would be of benefit to Yugoslavia.[29] In addition to the returnees, there are some cases of non-Yugoslavs who immigrated to Yugoslavia immediately after the war – most notably, in 1946–1947, 2000 leftist shipyard workers moved to Rijeka from Monfalcone, near Trieste.[30]

---

[27] Rolandi, "Heading Towards the West," 555–556, 561.
[28] Ulf Brunnbauer, *Globalizing Southeastern Europe: Emigrants, America, and the State since the Late Nineteenth Century* (Landham, MD: Lexington Books, 2016), 263–270
[29] Brunnbauer, *Globalizing...*, 264–265, 268.
[30] Marco Abram, "Integrating Rijeka into Socialist Yugoslavia: The Politics of National Identity and the New City's Image (1947–1955)," *Nationalities Papers* 46, no. 1 (2018): 72.

One last case that defies neat categorization deserves mention here, namely, the 1953 migration agreement between Yugoslavia and Turkey permitting members of the Turkish minority to leave Macedonia. On the one hand, this episode can be considered as belonging to this earlier era of Cold War migration, in that it defined migrants according to ethnicity, and may have reflected a desire to get rid of an undesirable minority and boost the Macedonian nation-building project; thus, it has some parallels with the German, Hungarian, and Italian minority cases. On the other hand, it took place a decade after the war had ended, in a significantly altered context – both domestically and internationally – between two friendly states. Interestingly, a number of non-Turkish Muslims took advantage of the policy, impersonating Turkish nationality in order to emigrate to Turkey. By 1956, more than 86,000 people had relinquished their Yugoslav citizenship through this program, with a further 50,000 leaving the following year.[31]

The anomalous Macedonian Turkish case aside, the aforementioned examples highlight the untidiness of the end of the Second World War. Settlings of account, border changes, and the new regime's consolidation of its power all entailed large-scale population movement. While the Yugoslav authorities were eager to bring this flux to a close, by expelling its perceived enemies, repatriating its citizens, and establishing the loyalty of the ethnic minorities that remained, the context of the Cold War, particularly in the handling of refugee cases, and the lingering Istrian question, continued to foster a steady stream of illegal migration.

11.3.2 1954–1990: Opening the borders

The Tito-Stalin split initially provoked a hardening and retrenchment of the Titoist regime. A generalized sense that Yugoslavia was surrounded by enemies, both from without and within, was not a favorable context for a relaxation of its border regime. However, by 1953, Yugoslavia had developed a new identity as the beacon for a new, more humane form of socialism. It built closer relations to the United States and eased tensions with the Soviet Union. In addition to this, the Istrian question was essentially settled by the Treaty of London in 1954. All this set the stage for a new approach to cross-border migration.

First and foremost was a quest to depoliticize the Yugoslav emigrant population. Yugoslavia's strict border policy meant that a large number of Yugoslavs who had left during or after the war were in violation of Yugoslav law, and consequently, at odds with the state. Federal authorities were cognizant that their citizens who were crossing the border illegally in search of a better life were swelling the ranks of hostile emigrant organizations. The government attempted to improve relations with emigrants by passing an amnesty law in 1962, which indemnified Yugoslavs that had

---

31 Brunnbauer, *Globalizing Southeastern Europe*, 291–294.

crossed the border illegally, as well as by rescinding the "Law on the removal of citizenship from officers and non-commissioned officers of the former Yugoslav army, which will not return to the homeland, as well as members of military formations which served the occupier and fled abroad, as well as persons who fled after the liberation."[32] Yugoslav authorities were convinced that, aside from hard-core anti-Yugoslav emigrants who were exempt from amnesty, the majority of these emigrants would welcome the opportunity to resume a normal relationship with Yugoslavia, transitioning from political to economic migrants. This would in turn promote a greater flow of foreign currency back to Yugoslavia. A 1963 memo of the Socialist Alliance of Workers (Socijalistički savez radnog naroda Jugoslavije), the primary organization for mass mobilization, credited these two laws for changing the attitudes of the emigrant community.[33] Approximately 50,000 migrants were able to obtain a passport through amnesty. While some officials believed the amnesty had succeeded in undercutting hostile emigrant organizations, others were less satisfied – and indeed, hostile emigrant organizations would not only survive but also grow in the coming decade.[34]

Yugoslavia had a particularly strong interest in trying to improve its relations with its citizens living abroad, because growing numbers of Yugoslavs were crossing the border to seek employment in Western Europe. As noted in the introduction to this chapter, there was nothing novel about labor migration in Yugoslavia. Inhabitants of the South Slavic lands had long migrated for work, either seasonally or for longer durations. During the Ottoman Empire, for example, Macedonians from the Lake Ohrid region would work in Serbia, Bulgaria, and Romania for two or three years at a time.[35] The region of Gorizia in the Habsburg Empire provides another pre-Yugoslav example of labor migration, with its largely Slovene population migrating seasonally to other parts of the Empire, as well as to Germany and Switzerland, to work as peddlers, lumberjacks, and construction workers.[36] Hundreds of

---

[32] In the original, this law was called "Zakon o prestanku važenja Zakona o oduzimanju državljanstva oficirima i podoficirima bivše jugoslavenske vojske, koji ne će da se vrate u domovinu, te pripadnicima vojnih formacija, koji su služili okupatora i odbjegli u inozemstvo, kao i licima odbjeglim poslije oslobodjenja."

[33] "IO GO SSRNH. Svim Kotarskim i općinskim odborima SSRN Hrvatske. 1 Nov. 1963." Arhiv Jugoslavije, 142–492.

[34] For a positive evaluation, see Iva Kraljević, "Matica iseljenika Hrvatske 1964–1968," *Časopis za suvremenu povijest* 41, no. 1 (2009): 75; For a more skeptical view, see "*XI Sjednica savjeta za pitanja iseljenika, održana 14.IX 1966. g. u 9 časova*," Hrvatski Državni Arhiv, 562 Savezna Komisija za pitanja iseljenika, 1965 od br. 201–311.

[35] Joel Halpern, "The Pečalba Tradition in Macedonia, A Case Study", 1–3; See also Petko Hristov, "The Balkan Gurbet: Traditional Patterns and New Trends," in *Migration in the Southern Balkans*, ed. Hans Vermeulen, Martin Baldwin-Edwards, Riki van Boeschoten (New York: Springer International Publishing, 2015), 31–46.

[36] Aleksej Kalc, "Migration Movements in Goriška in the Time of Aleksandrinke," in *From Slovenia to Egypt: Aleksandrinke's Trans-Mediterranean Domestic Workers' Migration and National Imagination*, Mirjam Hladnik ed. (Göttingen: V&R unipress, 2015), 49–72.

thousands had left the Habsburg Empire and, after the First World War, the Kingdom of Yugoslavia, to seek their fortunes across the oceans.

Although socialist Yugoslavia adopted a much more restrictive passport regime than its predecessors; one which did not permit its citizens to leave the country to work abroad, Yugoslavs kept crossing the border illegally for that very purpose. Indeed, Francesca Rolandi has shown that the Yugoslav-Italian border was oddly porous, and punishments for illegal border crossing became milder over time.[37] Motivations for border-crossing varied and included a desire to avoid military service, aspirations to higher income, and for some, simply employment. As Susan Woodward has shown, Yugoslavia dealt with significant unemployment even before the 1965 economic reforms created large-scale unemployment.[38] Starting in 1957, requests by Yugoslavs judged to be poor and unemployed, and who wished to look abroad for work, were approved. The figures testify to a growing interest in this possibility. In Bosnia-Herzegovina, 179 passports were issued in 1957 and almost the exact same number the second year, with an unexplained dip in 1959 to 90 passports. Then, in 1960, 366 passports were approved, followed by 1776 in 1961 and 5003 in 1962.[39] Numbers of Yugoslav workers in Europe increased from 3,000 in 1954 to 28,000 in 1961.[40]

Although no formal changes in Yugoslavia's border regime are recorded, 1962 seems to have been the watershed year in that a general relaxation of the border and of the process of obtaining passports can be observed at this time. The opening of the borders was linked directly to political liberalization in Yugoslavia following Aleksandar Ranković's fall. According to William Zimmerman, this shift was explicitly tied to a desire to facilitate labor migration, which policy-makers justified on the grounds that Yugoslav citizens had "the right to seek and find better working and living conditions".[41] They would also later claim that participating in the global exchange of labor was an essential step in Yugoslavia's economic development. In addition to popular pressure to work abroad, the liberalization of the border regime was driven by Yugoslavia's wish to participate in the global tourism boom, as Igor Tchoukarine has demonstrated.[42]

---

37 Rolandi, "Heading Towards the West," 568–569.
38 Susan Woodward, *Socialist Unemployment: The Political Economy of Yugoslavia 1945–1990* (Princeton: Princeton University Press, 1995), 180–190, 191–208.
39 Boško Jović, sekretar Matice. Informacija o odlasku naših građana na rad u inostranstvo sent to savet za pitanje iseljenika 11. Juni 1963. AJ, 562 Savezna Komisija za pitanja iseljenika, Kutija "1963 – pov. Arhiva i str. Pov. R-2"
40 William Zimmerman, *Open Borders, Nonalignment, and the Political Evolution of Yugoslavia* (Princeton: Princeton University Press, 1987), 75. Nikola Baković, "Tending the "oasis of socialism." Transnational political mobilization of Yugoslav economic emigrants in the FR Germany in the late 1960s and 1970s." Nationalities Papers 42, no. 4 (2014): 674–690.
41 Zimmerman, *Open Borders*, 76–77.
42 Igor Tchoukarine, "Yugoslavia's Open-Door Policy and Global Tourism in the 1950s and 1960s." *East European Politics & Societies and Cultures* 29, no.1 (2015): 168–188.

Brunnbauer makes a compelling case that Yugoslavia's adoption of an open-border policy was based on a multi-year process of learning and debate that began in 1960. Policy-makers gained their knowledge about the behavior of migrants and the potential threats and opportunities that came with open borders, by observing and interacting with emigrants. In particular, Brunnbauer stresses the role of Matica iseljenika organizations, which were Republican-level cultural associations whose purpose was to maintain ties with emigrants. Policy-makers were also impressed by the important sums of foreign currency coming from migrant transfers and repatriated savings, which at the time even dwarfed profits from tourism. Policy-makers debated the benefits and risks of opening the border over the course of 1962–1963. Recognizing that illegal cross-border flows were significant and that the cost of enforcing the border or ignoring its violations was too high, they opted to provide legal channels that they could hopefully steer and supervise.[43]

Just as Tito's regime had opted to expel thousands of ethnic minorities from its borders as a means of bolstering its legitimacy, so it now opted to open its borders as a means of attending to both its domestic legitimacy – by providing a solution for unemployment – and its international prestige – by showcasing Yugoslavia's natural and cultural wealth and representing itself as a "different" kind of socialist state. These motivations overpowered the Communists' deep reservations about labor migration, based both on misgivings toward the strategy of addressing economic underdevelopment by sending workers abroad to labor in the capitalist economy, and concerns that workers would be subject to anti-Yugoslav propaganda. Concerns about the negative influence of foreigners on Yugoslav tourists were similarly ignored.[44]

Beyond simply opening up the border, federal authorities sought to regulate the flow of workers across its border. Starting in 1964, workers could seek employment through official channels, as Republican employment bureaus were empowered to strike agreements with foreign employers. The Yugoslav state also signed several bilateral labor agreements, with France in 1965, with Austria and Sweden in 1966, and finally, with the Federal Republic of Germany (FRG) in 1968. Thus, the designation "worker temporarily employed abroad" was born.

Showcasing the opening of the border, while only 1850 requests for an exit visa were received in the Republic of Croatia in 1961 – of which 1138 were approved and 712 turned down – 14,933 were received the following year (11,320 were approved). A further 25,121 were received in just the first half of 1963, but a significant proportion of these were turned down (9,584), most likely pointing to the authorities' concerns that labor migration had spun out of control.[45] The opening of the border is also reflected in the increasing numbers of Yugoslav workers living abroad in Europe, including those who received permission to work abroad, those who exited on a tourist

---

43 Brunnbauer, *Globalizing Southeastern Europe,* 270–290.
44 Tchoukarine, "Yugoslavia's Open-Door Policy," 177.
45 Zapisnik sa sastanka Komisije za društveno-ekonomski razvoj Glavnog odbora SSRN Hrvatske, održanog 13. travnja 1964. godine. HR HDA 1220 CK SKJ, D-666.

visa, and those who left illegally. Ivo Baučić estimated that the population of Yugoslavs working in the FRG increased from 23,608 in 1962 to 44,428 in 1963 and to 53,057 in 1964. The figures for Yugoslavs living abroad in all European states was 42,000, 80,000 and 105,000, respectively.[46]

The restructuring of the Yugoslav economy that began in 1962 and culminated in 1965, aimed at improving its efficiency and global competitiveness, further fueled labor migration by further increasing unemployment. The official unemployment rate increased from approximately 6% in 1959 to nearly 9% a decade later, and the real figures were most likely significantly higher.[47] Thus, the number of Yugoslavs working in Germany increased from 64,060 in 1965 to 96,675 the following year. They would peak in 1973, with 535,000 Yugoslavs employed in the FRG, and 860,000 in all European states. Large numbers of Yugoslavs also left for overseas – in particular, Canada, the United States, and Australia. According to the 1971 census, 33,000 Yugoslavs were living in the United States, 60,000 in Australia, 41,000 in Canada, and another 9,500 in other non-European states.[48]

Migrant workers came from a variety of geographical, socio-economic, and educational backgrounds, but the typical migrant of the 1960s was likely to be young male from rural Croatia with a basic education. While women were less well represented, they still accounted for 32 percent of migrant workers. According to the 1971 census, the vast majority of migrant workers – 412,000 out of 597,000 Yugoslavs in Europe – ended up in the FRG, with Austria in distant second place. More than 60 percent of Yugoslav migrants were between the ages of twenty and thirty-five. Seventy-eight percent had no more than the eight years of elementary school. Migrant workers were predominantly from underdeveloped regions of Yugoslavia, in particular, Croatia, Bosnia-Herzegovina, and Macedonia. Fifty-seven percent of migrants had worked in agriculture, forestry or fishing prior to leaving the country. Five of the ten communes with the highest number of migrants per capita were located in the region of Dalmatian Zagora and Western Herzegovina, with the town of Imotski topping the list at 18.6 percent of inhabitants.[49]

While a non-negligible number of migrants were skilled workers and professionals who sought to participate in the societies they inhabited – in spite of efforts by Yugoslav policy makers to prevent such citizens from leaving – the majority of migrant workers were unskilled or semi-skilled workers whose primary aim was to save up and return home. These migrants tended to live in modest circumstances, quite commonly in dormitories with other migrant workers, and many did not learn the local language beyond what was necessary to get by. All in all, they

---

46 Ivo Baučić, *Stanje vanjskih migracija iz Jugoslavije krajem sedamdesetih godina* (Zagreb: Centar za istraživanje migracija, 1979), 6.
47 Woodward, *Socialist Unemployment*, 180–90, 191–208.
48 Ivo Baučić, *Radnici u inozemstvu prema popisu stanovnistva Jugoslavije 1971* (Zagreb: Studies of the Institute of Geography University of Zagreb, 1973), 38.
49 Baučić, *Radnici u inozemstvu*, 26, 44, 46, 52, 69, 97.

lived a life of privation in order to use their earnings to improve their living conditions and advance their social status and that of their families in Yugoslavia. A study carried out by Ivo Baučić and Vera Pavlaković in 1975 amongst migrants from Medjumurje indicated that 27 percent of migrants had chosen to work abroad in order to purchase, build, or add to a home. A further 20 percent were enticed by the attraction of higher earnings and savings, and 13 percent sought an improvement in their living standards. The 33 percent that cited unemployment as their primary reason for leaving were obviously also attracted by a desire to improve their standard of living.[50]

Migrants returned regularly to Yugoslavia on visits, particularly during holidays. During these visits, they spent time with friends and relatives – particularly important for the migrants who had left their spouses and children behind. They either distributed goods that they had bought abroad, or else purchased them locally. In Medjumurje in 1971 and 1972, 61 percent of migrants spent at least part of their earnings on acquiring a building site, building or adding to and furnishing a house. A further 9 percent admitted to spending their savings exclusively on furnishings and appliances. Eleven percent spent at least part of their remittances on purchasing a car.[51] labor migration had a major impact on communities, many of which were otherwise isolated and economically stagnant. However, such conspicuous consumption did not lead to local economic development, leading Carl-Ulrich Schierup to identify it as an example of "modernization without development."[52]

While labor migration was clearly an opportunity for Yugoslavia to decrease unemployment and to access foreign currency through remittances, Yugoslav authorities also quickly recognized the unique challenge posed by its migrant workers in Europe. Whereas it considered those who had moved overseas as diaspora – having an emotional connection to Yugoslavia, but unlikely to return – Yugoslavs working in Europe were citizens, expected to return after a few years. Moreover, they had grown so numerous as to be referred to as a virtual "Seventh Republic." Authorities also rightly feared that they would be manipulated by groups hostile to Yugoslavia, not the least of which were émigré organizations. While Yugoslavia had opened borders, the League of Communists and the government intended to maintain close ties with – and a close eye on – migrant workers. Beyond operating the usual consular services and enforcing the bilateral agreements related to working conditions and so-

---

[50] Ivo Baučić and Vera Pavlaković, *Basic Aspects of External Migration from Medjimurje* (Zagreb: Centre for migration studies, 1975), 29. See also Brigitte Le Normand, "The Gastarbajteri as a Transnational Yugoslav Working Class," in *Social Inequalities and Discontent in Yugoslav Socialism*, ed. Rory Archer and Igor Duda (London: Routledge, 2016), 38–57.
[51] Baučić and Pavlaković, *Basic aspects*, 30.
[52] Carl-Ulrik Schierup, *Migration, Socialism, and the International Division of Labor: The Yugoslavian Experience*. (Aldershot: Avebury, 1990); 219; Carl-Ulrik Schierup, *Houses, Tractors, Golden Ducats: Prestige Game and Migration: A Study of Migrants to Denmark from a Yugoslav Village* (Århus: Århus Universitet, 1973).

cial security, the various levels of government, ranging from the federal down through to the local, administered a variety of programs aimed at including migrants in Yugoslav political, cultural, social and economic life. These activities ranged from broadcasting specialized radio shows, publishing newspapers, organizing tours of folkloric groups, and sending social workers, to conducting sociological studies on migrants, holding meetings with migrants about their regular visits home, and seeking to channel remittances into investments in industrial activities. The League of Communists also sought a presence amongst workers abroad.[53]

Important changes in the character of labor migration came into effect starting at the end of the 1960s. First, the profile of the migrant worker changed. The proportion of Croats amongst migrant workers began to decline, while migrants from rural Serbia, Kosovo, Macedonia, and Montenegro were more strongly represented than ever before. According to the 1971 census, the Republic of Croatia had 224,722 workers living abroad, whereas in 1981, it had only 135,244. Meanwhile, during the same period, the number of workers from Serbia had increased from 114,581 to 139,157. In both instances, the number of dependents increased, in the case of Croatia from 30,134 to 53,673, and in the case of Serbia, from 18,808 to 45,961.[54] Second, due to economic recession, the FRG decided to restrict its use of migrant workers by limiting the number of work visas that it issued. The oil crisis of 1973 and the ensuing economic crisis led to a further restriction of labor opportunities for Yugoslavs. Far from triggering the return of migrant workers, these challenges provoked an entrenchment of current migrant workers who, afraid that they would lose their employment if they returned home, now sought to bring their families to live with them. As a result, more and more women and children now lived abroad, and the ties binding workers to their home villages and towns became weaker. Writing in 1990, before the outbreak of hostilities in Yugoslavia, Schierup noted that "[m]igrants' commitment to return has become increasingly vague during the 1970s and 1980s."[55]

The Yugoslav state took note of this evolution and developed policies to respond to them. On the one hand, it became increasingly preoccupied with the perceived "alienation" of its workers, and sought to further strengthen the migrants' attachment to their homeland through cultural programing and educational programs for Yugoslav children. On the other hand, it seemed incapable of responding to the sincere aspiration on the part of many migrants to return home, by providing opportunities for employment. Belying one of the arguments for labor migration, Yugoslavia had not been successful in tapping into the remittances of its migrant workers

---

[53] Nikola Baković, "Song of Brotherhood, Dance of Unity: Cultural-Entertainment Activities for Yugoslav Economic Emigrants in the West in the 1960s and 1970s," *Journal of Contemporary History* 50, no. 2 (2015): 354–375; Nikola Baković, "Tending the 'oasis of socialism'. Transnational political mobilization of Yugoslav economic emigrants in the FR Germany in the late 1960s and 1970s." *Nationalities Papers* 42, no. 4 (2014): 674–690; Zimmerman, *Open Borders*, 74–132.
[54] Schierup, *Migration, Socialism*, 111.
[55] Schierup, *Migration, Socialism*, 110–120.

and transforming them into opportunities for development.[56] In spite of the efforts of Yugoslav banks to attract their savings, migrants had tended to invest their savings abroad, and migrant spending had been largely for non-productive purposes. While efforts were made to create opportunities for migrants to invest in new factories – and thus new jobs – only a few such projects came to fruition, such as the Pionirka textile factory in the region of Imotska Krajina.[57] Yugoslavia also participated in programs managed by the OECD aimed at facilitating the repatriation of surplus migrant workers from Western Europe.[58]

The inability of the Yugoslav state to translate migrant earnings into development, the overrepresentation of ethnic Croats amongst the labor migrants in the 1960s, and the worrying realization that skilled workers, rather than unskilled workers, were the ones leaving to work abroad, would contribute to the politicization of the labor migration. During the period of nationalist unrest cresting in 1971, known as the Croatian Spring, Yugoslavia's facilitation of labor migration was held up as an example of the exploitation of the Croatian people by the supposedly Serb-dominated federation, artificially holding back Croatia's economic development, rather than building it.[59] Opinions such as these continued to be popular long after the Croatian Spring was repressed, even if the proportion of Croats among migrant workers continued to decline in the 1980s.

11.4 Political activities in exile

The wave of migration that immediately followed the Second World War fostered the proliferation of political exile organizations across Europe, in Australia and the Americas. Much to the chagrin of the Yugoslav authorities, the majority of émigré organizations appear to have been both hostile to Yugoslavia and highly active. Of the 191 emigrant organizations inventoried in 1963, 135 were listed as "very hostile" and of 136 newspapers, 126 were deemed "overwhelmingly hostile."[60]

In Europe, the arrival of migrant workers first disturbed, then ultimately rejuvenated the ailing Croatian nationalist organizations that had crystallized in the immediate post-war period. Groups had until that point focused their efforts on lobbying foreign governments and disseminating anti-Yugoslav propaganda to persuade host societies to reject the Titoist state and support their struggle for independence. These

---

56 Sara Bernard, "Developing the Yugoslav Gastarbeiter Reintegration Policy. Political and Economic Aspects (1969–1974)," Working paper 5 (Graz: Centre for Southeast European Studies, 2012).
57 Jenny Winterhagen, "Die Pioniere von Imotski. Die Verwendung von remittances am Beispiel des ehemaligen Jugoslawien," *Südosteuropa Jahrbuch* 38 (2011): 61–92.
58 Schierup, *Migration, Socialism*, 129–130.
59 See, for example, Zvonimir Komarica, "Povijesna pouka o hrvatskim selenjima," in *Imotska Krajina*, 1 February, 14, February 15, and 1 March 1971.
60 Brunnbauer, *Globalizing Southeastern Europe*, 287–288.

strategies proved futile. Croatian nationalists living in the FRG had become increasingly hopeless as the German leadership shifted its foreign policy towards supporting Tito and towards an *Ostpolitik* of rapprochement with the Soviet Bloc more generally. Extremist nationalist groups were also prone to infighting and fracturing. Although the influx of migrant workers in the 1960s first provoked suspicion and even antagonism toward the new arrivals as holders of the hated "Red Passport," as Mate Tokić notes, attitudes quickly changed as different factions recognized the potential to dominate other groups and pick up new momentum by recruiting new and younger members.[61] Although Serbian anti-Titoist organizations also existed, they were even more divided over their aims than the Croatians. Moreover, given the preponderance of Croats among the first wave of labor migrants, it was really the Croatian nationalist organizations that were able to take advantage of the influx.

From the outset, migrant workers were the target of both harassment and seduction by anti-Yugoslav émigré organizations. As in the days of displaced persons camps, migrant workers were vulnerable to pressures from nationalist organizations. In unfamiliar surroundings and without an effective support network, and possibly already hostile to some or all aspects of the Yugoslav state, they were easy prey for emigrants who provided a listening ear, advice, assistance, and a compelling and empowering narrative. Extreme nationalist groups were aggressive in their outreach to migrant workers, operating in ways reminiscent of organized crime: those susceptible to supporting the groups were pressured either to join or to make a financial contribution, and those identified as alien or hostile would be harassed and even physically attacked.[62] In some ways, the recruiting of labor migrants into extremist organizations seems to prefigure modern day radicalization, but more research would have to be done to establish if the comparison stands to scrutiny.

As Tokić has noted, migrant workers were "well-suited" (though "not pre-destined") to political radicalization – young, uneducated, and disproportionately from impoverished regions that were strongholds of anti-Titoist activity.[63] Indeed, a number of labor migrants did become actively involved in anti-Yugoslav activities, ranging from the peaceful (answering surveys in the separatist newspaper *Nova Hrvatska*) to the violent (participating in terrorist attacks.) Alexander Clarkson, for example, has highlighted that the majority of the foot-soldiers in the *Kreuzbruderschaft* (Crusaders, or Križari), that carried out the 1962 terrorist attack on the Yugoslav trade mission in Bonn-Mehlem, were in fact radicalized migrant workers.[64]

It is difficult to establish how representative this type of active opposition to the Yugoslav regime was among migrant workers, in part because it is difficult to find reliable sources on this topic. A survey of migrant workers on the possibility of returning to Yugoslavia, conducted by the Institute for the Study of Migration and Eth-

---

61 Tokić, "Landscapes of Conflict," 743.
62 Tokić, "Landscapes of Conflict," 745.
63 Tokić, "The End of "Historical-Ideological Bedazzlement," 421–45.
64 Clarkson, *Fragmented Fatherland*, 68.

nicity of the Republic of Croatia in 1970–1971, provides a very diverse snapshot of migrants. The survey was taken at the height of the Croatian Spring, when the Croatian Communist Party mobilized the population in favor of increasing Croatia's cultural and political autonomy. While many of the responses were neutral or positively disposed toward Yugoslavia, a significant number of responses were highly critical and even hostile. Some of the critical responses interpreted Yugoslavia's reliance on labor migration as a policy failure, noting the ideological paradox of being sent abroad to build capitalism. Respondents criticized, in particular, poor management of the economy, nepotism, and corruption. Significantly, migrants emphasized the differences between how things worked in Yugoslavia and in their host states. In other words, their politicization was rooted in their personal experience of migration.[65]

Hostile responses went beyond criticism. They openly identified with a political alternative to the Yugoslav federation, framing the respondent's predicament in explicitly nationalist terms, which pitted Croats and Croatia against other ethnic groups and the federal government in a zero-sum game. Some of these respondents sent in formulaic statements instead of completing the survey, indicating that they were receiving guidance in how to respond, potentially by hostile émigré groups. More frequently, responses lifted language and arguments directly out of the reformist Communist movement. The most common grievances, which surface in numerous letters, were that the Croatian language and culture were not respected and that Croatia was being exploited by the federation ("Belgrade" in shorthand). In terms of economic exploitation, migrants complained bitterly that the foreign currency they worked so hard to earn somehow ended up being spent in Belgrade instead of being used to finance development in the economically depressed parts of Croatia from where the migrants came.[66] Another frequent complaint was that Croats were barred from leadership positions in the army, police, and even the workplace, such that they were in effect "ruled" by other ethnic groups.[67]

The case of these critical and hostile survey responses highlights the fact that migrant workers were being mobilized against Yugoslavia not only by exile groups hostile to Yugoslavia in their host states, but also by actors within the Yugoslav state – such as the reformist Croatian Communists and Matica Hrvatska. Even so, it would be hasty to assume that overt hostility, as expressed in an anonymous survey, reflected active political engagement. After all, labor migrants who were flagged as hostile to Yugoslavia risked losing their passport, and most intended to return to Yugoslavia once they had reached their savings target. It is perhaps useful to think of the politicization of migrant workers as being on a spectrum, ranging from active involvement in Yugoslav organizations, on the one end, to active involvement in anti-Yugo-

---

[65] Le Normand, "The Gastarbajteri," 2016.
[66] *Response from 28 year old male dated 28.10.1970,* HR HDA, Fond 1611, Registrator 18.
[67] See, for example, Response no. 369, 381; HR HDA, Fond 1611, Registrator 18; Response from Linz dated 29.10.70, HR HDA, Fond 1611, Registrator 15.

slav organizations on the other, with the majority of migrant workers clustered somewhere in the middle. Thus, until further research can be done on this topic, it is safe to assume that the number of migrants participating in extremist organizations was limited.

This reinvigoration of extremist nationalist Croatian organizations by new arrivals coincided with a shift in strategies used to achieve independence, not only in Europe but also overseas, in Australia, Canada, and later, the United States. Militant Croatian nationalists had become disillusioned with the tactics of the past, which they perceived as innefectual. In addition, in the German case, the fiercely anti-Communist atmosphere of the CDU/CSU coalition was replaced by a more conciliatory approach toward Yugoslavia and the Eastern Bloc that would eventually culminate in Willy Brandt's *Ostpolitik*. This in turn led to the marginalization of extremist Croatian groups that had previously enjoyed at least the tacit support of conservative politicians. These groups now resorted to terrorist attacks on Yugoslav institutions and commercial offices, in the belief that, only by dealing a spectacular blow to Yugoslavia, could they gain credibility and support for the establishment of an independent homeland. Security forces were caught off guard in both Germany and Australia, at least in part due to anti-Communist sympathies with Croatian nationalists that had led them to underestimate the threat they posed. The emergence of Croatian terrorism highlights the impact of the domestic politics of host societies as well as their changing foreign policy during the Cold War, and the transnational connectedness of militant Croatian nationalist groups.[68]

11.5 Migration since 1989

Migration across Yugoslavia's borders during the Cold War was shaped both by the dictates of the Yugoslav state and by broader global forces, including the Cold War and the global labor market, as well as historical legacies. Indeed, state policy itself was not entirely determined by ideology, but was very much influenced by pragmatic considerations, including how to establish its legitimacy and secure monopoly over violence, and what modernization strategy to pursue. Insofar as ideology did shape policy, that ideology itself evolved over time, from one that rejected relations with the capitalist West to one that eagerly sought engagement; and from one that strictly limited personal freedoms in the name of revolution to one that celebrated freedom of movement as a hallmark of self-managed socialism. The limits of the power of the state also come through, whether in the porousness of the border, or its inability to police hostile émigré communities, or prevent its migrant workers from switching

---

[68] Tokić, "Landscapes of Conflict"; Tokić, "The End of "Historical-Ideological Bedazzlement," 421–445; Mate Nikola Tokić, "Party Politics, National Security, and Émigré Political Violence in Australia, 1949–1973," in *Control of Violence*, ed. Wilhelm Heitmeyer et al. (New York: Springer, 2011), 395–414.

allegiances. Ultimately, rather than persist in its policy of enforcing a border that was only sealed on paper, the Yugoslav state opted to manage migration, allowing Yugoslavs to pursue the income strategy that they had inherited from previous generations. While opening its borders may have increased its prestige globally, ultimately, neither strategy enabled it to deal with its considerable domestic political and economic challenges. In contrast to socialist Yugoslavia's deliberate and intentional border and migration policies, migration following Yugoslavia's break-up has been characterized by confusion, created and exploited by various competing state and non-state actors.

The final denouement of the 1990s would produce yet another series of war-induced mass migrations, the product of three related but distinct conflicts. In Bosnia Herzegovina, between 1992 and 1995, conflicting parties engaged in ethnic cleansing as a strategy to gain control of territory, including terrorizing and coercing inhabitants of other ethnicities to leave their communities. In Croatia, there were two major waves of displacement: at the beginning of the war in 1991–1992, and in August 1995 as a result of Operation Storm when the Croatian army, in collaboration with the Croatian police and the Army of Bosnia Herzegovina, successfully defeated the separatist Republic of the Serbian Krajina, and effectively expelled the majority of Croatian Serbs. Finally, the intensification of conflict in Kosovo in 1998 under the leadership of Slobodan Milošević, president of what remained of Yugoslavia, provoked a new wave of refugees.

While reliable figures are hard to come by, a product of the chaos of war, the United Nations High Commissioner for Refugees estimates that 1.3 million people were displaced by the war in Bosnia-Herzegovina.[69] Figures given for Croatia vary from 220,000 to 384,000, the majority of which were ethnic Serbs who fled Croatia.[70] The conflict in Kosovo displaced approximately 1.1 million ethnic Albanians and Serbs.[71] These figures include those who were internally displaced, those who sought refuge in neighboring Yugoslavia or post-Yugoslav Republics, as well as in Albania in the case of ethnic Albanians, and those who sought asylum in states around the world. Once these conflicts ended, international actors put pressure on states to put in place measures to facilitate return migration for those who wished to return, although, ironically, the Dayton Accord actually accelerated ethnic cleansing in its immediate aftermath.[72] Return migration has had mixed results due to a combination

---

[69] Florence Kondylis, "Conflict Displacement and Labor Market Outcomes in Post-War Bosnia and Herzegovina," *Journal of Development Economics* 2, no. 93 (2010): 235.
[70] Brad K. Blitz, "Refugee Returns in Croatia: Contradictions and Reform," *Politics* 23, no. 3 (2003): 182; Joanna Harvey, "Return Dynamics in Bosnia and Croatia: A Comparative Analysis," *International Migration* 44, no. 3 (2006): 89–114.
[71] A.R. Kushner, "Kosovo and the Refugee Crisis, 1999: The Search for Patterns Amidst the Prejudice," *Patterns of Prejudice* 33, no. 3 (1999): 74.
[72] Gerard Toal and Carl Dahlman, *Bosnia Remade: Ethnic Cleansing and its Reversal* (New York: Oxford University Press, 2011), 161–166.

of factors, including obstacles that are understandable in the context of wartime trauma and destruction, but also obstructionist laws and harassment by authorities of return migrants. It is estimated that only 105,467 former inhabitants had returned to Croatia by 2002.[73] In the same year, of the initial 1.3 million displaced from Bosnia, according to the United States Committee for Refugees and Immigrants, "more than 528,000 Bosnians remained uprooted [...] including 368,000 internally displaced persons and more than 160,000 refugees and asylum seekers abroad."[74]

As with migration after the Second World War, a hard line cannot be drawn between migration due to war and economic migration. Some of those who have opted not to return have based their decision on a desire to take advantage of a new life situation that offered better economic prospects. Indeed, following in the aspirational footsteps of the migrant workers of the 1960s, numerous inhabitants of the post-Yugoslav space have emigrated, primarily to escape the economic stagnation that followed war and returned in the wake of the global economic crisis beginning in 2008. While there are problems with the figures presented in Serbia's census, as a general indication, roughly 415,000 Serbian citizens lived abroad in 2002, decreasing to 313,000 in 2011.[75]

Interestingly, the post-Yugoslav territory has become a space of transit migration, a phenomenon highlighted by the dramatic and ongoing refugee crisis that resulted in Syrian and other refugees journeying on foot on the so-called Western Balkan route through Macedonia to Serbia, only to become stranded there in dire circumstances.[76] While this trajectory may seem to be the outcome of a specific crisis, by 2000 migrants and asylum-seekers were already choosing Bosnia Herzegovina in increasing numbers as a country of transit on their way to Western European destinations, due to its liberal visa policy.[77] On a darker note, the post-Yugoslav space has also become involved in human trafficking networks. As Friman and Reich have pointed out, while the region has been depicted as a transit hub in the hands of Balkan organized crime, the presence of international troops during the war actually helped foster the growth of trafficking in Bosnia Herzegovina by providing a demand for prostitution. As of 2007, Croatia and Macedonia were primarily points of transit and destination, whereas Kosovo and Serbia were primarily points of transit and de-

---

73 Blitz, "Refugee Returns," 181–191.
74 United States Committee for Refugees and Immigrants, *US Committee for Refugees World Refugee Survey 2003 – Bosnia and Herzegovina*, 1 June 2003, available at: http://www.refworld.org/docid/3eddc4962.html (accessed 12 April 2017).
75 Jelena Predojević-Despić and Goran Penev, "Emigration Zones in Serbia: 2011 Census Results," *Zbornik Matice Srpske za društvene nauke* 148 (2014): 386.
76 Zsuzsa Gille, "Introduction: From Comparison to Relationality," *Slavic Review* 76, no. 2 (2017): 285–290.
77 United States Committee for Refugees and Immigrants, *US Committee for Refugees World Refugee Survey 2001 – Bosnia and Herzegovina*, 20 June 2001, available at: http://www.refworld.org/docid/3b31e15f0.html (accessed 12 April 2017).

parture.[78] To fully understand the role of the region as a point of transit within Europe for migrants seeking to enter the European Union (EU), it would be necessary to examine EU border and immigration policy, as well as the EU's relationship to the states on its borders, which is beyond the scope of this essay.

11.6 Archives and Literature

The following bibliographical survey will limit itself to works on Cold-war migration written in English, Bosnian, Croatian, and Serbian, partly reflecting the author's linguistic competences. It should be noted that there is rich scholarship on labor migration in the German language, which focuses particularly on the migrants' experiences in their host societies – unsurprising, given how prominent Germany was as a country of destination. An equally abundant literature on the expulsion of ethnic minorities after the Second World War also exists, in the languages spoken by those minorities.

The first studies on migration from Yugoslavia during the Cold War were written by contemporaries, primarily geographers, sociologists, and ethnographers. These studies constitute a formidable wealth of knowledge, both quantitative and qualitative, on a variety of topics, including the motivations for migration, the impact of migration on families and localities, and the migrants' everyday life and trajectories. The Zagreb-based Institute for the Study of Migration and Ethnicity (Institut za migracije i narodnosti) was particularly productive, overseeing the journal *Migracijske Teme* (later renamed *Migracijske i etničke teme*) and regularly publishing studies as part of its *Rasprave o Migracijama* series. Geographer Ivo Baučić, who was one of its most important directors, published several comprehensive and sophisticated studies on the impact of labor migration on Yugoslavia.[79] Silva Mežnarić published a rather comprehensive overview and bibliography of Yugoslav publications on this topic in the inaugural issue of *Migracijske Teme*.[80]

The first scholars in the Anglo-sphere to interest themselves in labor migration were ethnographers Joel Halpern and Carl-Ulrich Schierup. Halpern was interested in relating present-day migration to traditional migration patterns, as well as in looking at how migration was traditionally understood in the village.[81] In his first study,

---

[78] H. Richard Friman and Simon Reich, *Human Trafficking, Human Security, and the Balkans* (Pittsburgh: University of Pittsburgh Press, 2007), 2.
[79] See, for example, Baučić, *Stanje vanjskih migracija*; Baučić and Pavlakoviić, *Basic Aspects*; Baučić, *Radnici u inozemstvu*. Full biblio unless already cited elsewhere
[80] Silva Mežnarić, "Jugoslavenska sociologija (vanjskih) migracija – pokušaj sistematizacije," *Migracijske teme* 1 (1985): 77–96.
[81] Joel Halpern, "Yugoslav Migration Process and Employment in Western Europe: a Historical Perspective," in *Migrants in Europe: The Role of Family, Labor, and Politics*, ed. Hans Christian Buechler

Schierup was interested in how peasants used migration to advance their status within the village.⁸² Their later studies broadened the scope and framing of the inquiry, explicitly recognizing and embracing the transnational nature of migration and situating Yugoslav labor migration within the global, political, and economic system. Schierup examined the role of Yugoslav labor migration in the international division of labor, arguing that Yugoslavia's position within that system would have undermined any potential of such migration to fuel economic development within Yugoslavia.⁸³ While Schierup emphasized the powerlessnes of the Yugoslav state, political scientist William Zimmerman, in contrast, focused on its agency. He examined the role that open borders played in elite strategies for maintaining independence and reinforcing autonomy.⁸⁴ These two works highlight how labor migration might seem disadvantageous to authorities from one perspective, and advantageous from another.

With the end of the Cold War and Yugoslavia's final demise, post-war migration became the purview of historians. A number of English-language scholarly monographs and articles have been written on the expulsion and willing departure of the German, Hungarian and Italian ethnic minorities from Yugoslav territory.⁸⁵ While monographs by Merten, Sajti and Ballinger have largely approached the topic from the perspective of the victimized minorities and their ethnic homelands, Dota, Geiger, Janjetović, Ludanji, and Ballinger (in an article) have also tried to incorporate the Yugoslav perspective. In general, more research is needed to understand the specific factors shaping Yugoslav policy-making at this time, and to examine the interactions between local conditions and policy.

More recently, there has been renewed scholarly interest in postwar migration, focusing not only on the trauma of the war and its immediate aftermath, but also

---

and Judith-Maria Buechler (New York: Greenwood Press, 1987); Halpern, "The Pečalba Tradition in Macedonia."

82 Schierup, *Houses, Tractors.*
83 Schierup. *Migration, Socialism.*
84 Zimmerman, *Open Borders.*
85 On the German case, see Merten, *Forgotten Voices;* Geiger, "Josip Broz Tito"; Zoran Janjetović, *Between Hitler and Tito: The Disappearance of the Vojvodina Germans* (Belgrade: s.n., 2000); Zoran Janjetović, "The disappearance of the Germans from Yugoslavia: Expulsion or emigration?" *Revue des études sud-est européennes* 40, no. 1–4 (2002): 215–231. On the Hungarian case, see Sajti, *Hungarians in the Voivodina, 1918–1947*; Ludany, "Titoist Integration." On the Italian case, see Ballinger, "At the Borders of Force"; Pamela Ballinger, *History in Exile: Memory and Identity at the Borders of the Balkans* (Princeton: Princeton University Press, 2003); Cattaruzza, "'Last Stop Expulsion"; Franko Dota, *Zaraćeno poraće. Konfliktni i konkurentski narativi o stradanju i iseljavanju Talijana Istre* (Zagreb: Srednja Europa, 2010); Marica Karakaš Obradov, "Emigracija talijanskog stanovništva s hrvatskog područja tijekom Drugog svjetskog rata i poraća," *Radovi Zavoda za povijesne znanosti HAZU u Zadru* 55 (2013): 204–225; Marino Manin, "O ljudskim gubicima Istre u Drugom svjetskom ratu i poraću," in *Identitet Istre – ishodišta i perspective*, ed. Marino Manin et al. (Zagreb: Institut društvenih znanosti Ivo Pilar, 2006); Maruša Zgradnik, "Optiranje za italijansko državljanstvo s priključenega ozemlja," *Prispevki za novejšto zgodovino* 36, no. 1–2 (1996): 95–107.

on the long-term evolution of postwar emigration in the context of the Cold War. Methodologically, this literature adopts an explicitly transnational analytical framework. A number of works have documented the activities of Croatian émigrés hostile to Yugoslavia.[86] Tokić work is particularly interesting in that it explores the evolution of the strategies of émigré organizations as a response to East-West relations during the Cold War and domestic policies of host states. Francesca Rolandi's ground-breaking work has examined the role of Italian and Austrian asylum policy in dictating the fate of those fleeing across the Yugoslav border, once again situating policy in the context of the Cold War.[87] Tatjana Šarić has investigated the characteristics of illegal cross-border flows prior to the liberalization of Yugoslavia's borders.[88]

A number of new studies have also enriched our understanding of postwar voluntary migration. Ulf Brunnbauer's work has helped to contextualize this emigration within continuities and shifts across the long twentieth century. In focusing on the rural character of emigration, long-term trends and the role of state-building projects, his monograph *Globalizing Southeastern Europe* develops some of the earlier insights of Halpern, Schierup and Zimmerman. In applying the questions and methods of migration history, he has also brought to light the mechanisms of migration and the experiences of migrants, highlighting their agency and reminding us that they were not just an amorphous, passive mass that was simply acted upon.[89]

In the last decade, several articles and one book-length study, Vladimir Ivanović's *Geburtstag pišeš normalno*, have shed light on various aspects of labor migration. Nikola Baković and Sara Bernard have scrutinized Yugoslav state policy-making towards migrants, focusing on cultural outreach and return-migration policy. Karolina Novinšćsak and Ivanović have both examined the role of Germany's larger foreign policy objectives toward the Eastern Bloc in shaping Yugoslav-German negotiations for a bilateral migrant worker agreement. Ivanović and Brigitte Le Normand have focused on the experiences and self-understanding of migrant workers, while Le Normand has analyzed perceptions of migrant workers in Yugoslav film.[90] There is scope

---

[86] Clarkson, *Fragmented Fatherland*; Vladimir Ivanović, "Ekstremna emigracija u SR Nemačkoj i Jugoslavija," *Istorija 20. veka*. 1 (2009): 139–147; Bernd Robionek, *Croatian Political Refugees and the Western Allies: A Documented Survey from the Second World War to the Year 1948* (Berlin: Osteuropa-Zentrum Berlin, 2009); Tokić, 'The End of "Historical-Ideological Bedazzlement"'; Tokić, "Party Politics"; Tokić, "Landscapes of Conflict."
[87] Rolandi, "Heading towards the West"; Francesca Rolandi, "Escaping Yugoslavia."
[88] Tatjana Šarić, "Bijeg iz socijalističke Jugoslavije – ilegalna emigracija iz Hrvatske od 1945. do početka šezdesetih godina 20. stoljeća, " *Migracijske i etničke teme* 31:2 (2015): 195–220.
[89] Brunnbauer, *Transnational Societies*; Brunnbauer, *Globalizing Southeastern Europe*.
[90] Baković, "Song of Brotherhood"; Baković, "Tending the "oasis of socialism""; Bernard, "Developing the Yugoslav Gastarbeiter Reintegration Policy"; Ivana Dobrivojević, "U potrazi za blagostanjem. Odlazak jugoslovenskih državljana u zemlje zapadne Evrope 1960–1970," *Istorija 20. veka* 2 (2007): 89–100; Petar Dragišić, "Searching for El Dorado. Workers from Serbia Temporary Employed Abroad from the 1960s to the Dissolution of Yugoslavia," *Tokovi istorije* 3 (2014): 131–142; Vladimir Ivanović, "Zaključivanje sporazuma o angažovanju jugoslovenske radne snage sa SR Nemačkom," *Hereticus*.

for more research in this area, including work that would examine the politicization of migrant workers. More generally, as Brunnbauer has noted, "there is still no comprehensive analysis of the Yugoslav *Gastarbeiter* experience despite the ubiquity of this phenomenon."[91]

This essay concludes with some recommendations of where to start when researching Cold War migration from Yugoslavia. These suggestions should not be understood as exhaustive. Rather, they largely reflect the author's own research agenda and the work of other scholars who have relied extensively on archival material. Archives internal to Yugoslavia reflect the state's federal structure: relevant fonds can be found at both the federal level, in the Arhiv Jugoslavije (AJ), located in Belgrade, the Republican level, and even, occasionally, at the local level. Interesting material on migrants from Yugoslavia can also be found at the archives of the states where these migrants lived. Aside from archives, the Institute for the Study of Migration and Ethnicity in Zagreb has a rich library of rare published materials.

For those interested in migration as an outcome of the Second World War, the Arhiv Jugoslavije contains several fonds with relevant material, including fond 97. *Komisija za agrarnu reformu i kolonizaciju vlade FNRJ, 1946–1948* and fond 110. *Državna komisija za utvrđivanje zločina okupatora i njihovih pomagača u zemlji* on ethnic Germans. The Diplomatic Archive of the Yugoslav Ministry of Foreign Affairs, which is maintained by the Serbian Ministry of Foreign Affairs, also holds useful material. Eniko Sajti's work has demonstrated that the Hungarian National Archives contain copious material pertaining to ethnic Hungarians. With regard to Italian-speaking emigrants, scholars may want to consult the Arhiv Jugoslavije, Fond 314: *Komitet za kulturu i umetnost Vlade FNRJ*, as well as the fond 1086. *Ministarstvo za novooslobođene krajeve FNRJ 1948–1951*, which is found at the Hrvatski državni arhiv in Zagreb. Finer-grain detail, however, will be found at the local level. For example, the Hrvatski državni arhiv in Rijeka (HDAR) contains the individual records of persons who applied for the "option" of emigrating to Italy. The Italian Archivio Centrale dello Stato – in particular the fond of the *Ministero dell'Interno*, and the sousfonds of the *Gabinetto and Direzione Generale Affari Politici* also contains valuable material concerning individuals both claiming Italian citizenship and seeking political asylum. The *Ufficio Zone di Confine* fond at the Archivio della Presidenza del consiglio dei ministry also contains useful records on this topic.

Scholars working on labor migration and political exiles will find abundant material at the Arhiv Jugoslavije, especially in fonds 837: *Arhiv predsednika republike, 142. Socijalistički savez radnog naroda, and 562. Savezna komisija za pitanja iseljenika*. In the case of Croatian migration, the Hrvatski državni arhiv in Zagreb (HR HDA) has

---

Časopis za preispitivanje prošlosti 7, no. 4 (2009): 25–40; Ivanović, *Geburtstag pišeš normalno*; Le Normand, "The Gastarbajteri"; Karolina Novinšćak, 'The Recruiting and Sending of Yugoslav "Gastarbeiter" to Germany: Between Socialist Demands and Economic Needs,' in *Transnational Societies*, ed. Brunnbauer, 121–144.

91 Brunnbauer, *Globalizing Southeastern Europe*, 258.

numerous fonds with rich documentation, including HR HDA 1220 *Centralni komitet SKH*, HR HDA 1228 *Republička konferencija* SSRNH, HR HDA 1409 *Izvršno vijeće Sabora – Savjet o odnose s inoz*emstvom. It is anticipated that other Republics also contain significant material. While both archives are a great source of information on policy and data related to migration, the Republican level archive is the most useful in terms of material on the interactions between state and migrants. Archival collections outside Yugoslavia also contain materials related to political exiles, seen through the lens of the surveillance activities of host states. Mate Tokić, for example, has made fruitful use of the Politisches Archiv des Auswärtiges Amt in Germany, the National Archives of Australia (Canberra), and the Malcolm Fraser Archives at the University of Melbourne Archives.

Selected Bibliography

For desciption of primary sources and annotated bibliography please consult relevant sections following each chapter.

Abraham, Richard. *Alexander Kerensky: The First Love of the Revolution* (New York: Columbia University Press, 1987).
Achim, Viorel (ed.). *România și Transnistria: problema Holocaustului. Perspective istorice și comparative* (Bucharest: Curtea Veche, 2004).
Ackermann, Volker. *Der "echte" Flüchtlinge: Deutscher Vertriebene und Flüchtlinge aus der DDR, 1945–1961* (Osnabrück: Universitätsverlag Rasch, 1995).
Adamczyk, Arkadiusz. *Piłsudczycy w izolacji (1939–1954). Studium z dziejów struktur i myśli politycznej* (Warszawa: Instytut Józefa Piłsudskiego; Bełchatów: Związek Strzelecki 'Strzelec', 2008).
Ahonen, Pertti. *After the Expulsion: West Germany and Eastern Europe 1945–1990* (Oxford: Oxford University Press, 2003).
Akerlof, George, et. al. "East Germany in from the Cold: The Economic Aftermath of the Currency Union," *Brookings Papers on Economic Activity* 1 (1991): 1–105.
Albu, Mihaela. "Presa literară din exil – Mijloc și sursă de continuitate a culturii românești" (Luceafărul. Paris, 1948–1949), *Studii de Știința și Cultură* 5, no. 3 (2009): 72–77.
Albu, Mihaela. Anghelescu Dan, *Luceafarul – o reconstituire* (Bucharest: Ideea Europeană, 2009).
Aleksandrov, Kirill. *Ofitsersky Korpus Armii General-Leitenanta Vlasova* (Moscow: Posev, 2009).
Alekseev, Daniil. *NTS rossiiskih solidaristov v borbe protiv totalitarnogo rejima*. Abstract of candidate dissertation (Vladivostok, 1998).
Alexander, June Granatir. *Daily Life in Immigrant America, 1870–1920* (Chicago: Ivan R. Dee, 2007).
Alexeeva, Ludmila. *Istorija inakomyslia v SSS:. Noveishii period* (Vilnius / Moscow: Vest', 1992).
Altankov, Nikolay G. *The Bulgarian-Americans* (Palo Alto, California: Ragusan Press, 1979).
Amalrik, Andrey. *Zapiski dissidenta* (Moscow: Slovo, 1991).
Anders, Władysław. *Bez ostatniego rozdziału* (Newtown: Montgomeryshire Printing Co., 1949).
Andrew, Christopher, and Mitrokhin, Vasili. *The Sword and the Shield: The Mitrokhin Archive and the Secret History of the KGB* (New York: Basic Books, 1999).
Andreyev, Catherine. *Vlasov and the Russian Liberation Movement – Soviet Reality and Émigré Theories* (Cambridge: Cambridge University Press, 1987).
Anghel, Florin, and Bednarek, Jerzy (et al., eds.). *Polscy uchodźcy w Rumunii 1939–1947. Dokumenty z Narodowych Archiwów Rumunii / Refugiații polonezi în România 1939–1947. Documente din Arhivele Naționale ale României*, vol. 1, part 1 and 2 (Warszawa/Bucharest: Instytut Pamięci Narodowej/Arhivele Naționale ale României, 2013).
Anniste, Kristi, Kumer-Haukanõmm, Kaja, and Tammaru, Tiit (eds.). *Sõna jõul. Diasporaa roll Eesti iseseisvuse taastamisel*, (Tartu: Tartu ülikooli kirjastus, 2008).
Ant, Jüri. *August Rei: Eesti riigimees, poliitik, diplomat* (Tartu: Rahvusarhiiv, 2012).
Anusauskas, Arvydas, ed. *The Anti-Soviet Resistance in the Baltic States* (Vilnius: Genocide and Resistance Research Centre of Lithuania, 2002).
Antoshin, Alexey. *Na frontah Vtoroi Mirovoi i Holodnoi voin: Russkie emigranty v 1939 – nachale 1950 h godov* (Moscow: Aleteia, 2014).
Appelyard, Reginald. "International Migration Policies: 1950–2000," *International Migration* 39 (2001): 7–20.
Applebaum, Anne. *Iron Curtain: The Crushing of Eastern Europe 1944–1956* (New York/London: Doubleday, 2012).

Archer, Rory, Duda, Igor, ed. *Social Inequalities and Discontent in Yugoslav Socialism*, (London: Routledge, 2016).
Audebert, Cédric, and Ma Mung, Emmanuel, eds. *Les migrations internationals: enjeux contemporains et questions nouvelles*, (Bilbao: Université de Deusto, 2007).
Aun, Karl. *Political Refugees: A History of the Estonians in Canada* (Toronto: McClelland and Stewart, 1985).
Babiński, Grzegorz, and Chałupczak, Henryk, eds. *Diaspora polska w procesach globalizacji. Stan i perspektywy badań* (Kraków: Komitet Badania Polonii PAN, 2006).
Baczynskyj, Julian. *Ukraijnska immihracija w Spoluczenych Sztatach Ameryky* (Lviv, 1914, Kyjiw, 1994).
Bade, Klaus J. *Europa in Bewegung: Migration vom späten 18. Jahrhundert bis zur Gegenwart* (Munich: C.H. Beck).
Bade, Klaus J. et. at., eds. *The Encyclopedia of Migration and Minorities in Europe: From the 17th century to the present* (in German: *Enzyklopädie Migration in Europa. Vom 17. Jahrhundert bis zur Gegenwart.* (Munich: Schöningh, 2007), in English: Cambridge: Cambridge University Press, 2011).
Bade, Klaus J., and Oltmer, Jochen, ed. *Zuwanderung und Integration seit dem Zweiten Weltkrieg*, (Osnabrück: Universitätsverlag Rasch, 2002).
Bagieński, Witold. *Wywiad cywilny Polski Ludowej w latach 1945–1961*, vol. 2 (Warszawa: Instytut Pamięci Narodowej, 2017).
Bagieński, Witold et al., eds. *Stanisław Mikołajczyk w dokumentach aparatu bezpieczeństwa*, vol. 1–3, (Łódź/Warszawa: Instytut Pamięci Narodowej, 2010).
Baicoianu, Anca. "Exile and Identity Reconfiguration," *Journal of World Literature* 3 (2018): 10–22.
Baković, Nikola. "Song of Brotherhood, Dance of Unity: Cultural-Entertainment Activities for Yugoslav Economic Emigrants in the West in the 1960s and 1970s," *Journal of Contemporary History* 50, no. 2 (2015): 354–375.
Ballinger, Pamela. "At the Borders of Force: Violence, Refugees, and the Reconfiguration of the Yugoslav and Italian States," *Past & Present* 210, no. 1 (2011): 158–176.
Ballinger, Pamela. *History in Exile: Memory and Identity at the Borders of the Balkans* (Princeton: Princeton University Press, 2003).
Balys, Jonas. "The American Lithuanian Press," *Lituanus* 22 (1976): http://www.lituanus.org/1976/76_1_02.htm.
Banasiak, Stefan. *Działalność osadnicza Państwowego Urzędu Repatriacyjnego na Ziemiach Odzyskanych w latach 1945–1947* (Poznań: Instytut Zachodni, 1963).
Banionis, Juozas. *Lietuvos laisves byla vakaruose 1975–1990: Istorine apzvalga* (Vilnius: Genocide and Resistance Research Centre of Lithuania, 2002).
Bar-Zohar, Michael. *Beyond Hitler's Grasp: The Heroic Rescue of Bulgaria's Jews* (Holbrook, Massachusetts: Adams Media, 1998).
Barbu, Bogdan. *Vin Americanii! Prezența simbolică a Statelor Unite în România Războiului Rece* (Bucharest: Humanitas, 2006).
Barbu, Eugen. "'Mămica" Lovinescu față cu refugiații,' *Săptămâna* (December 1975).
Bárdi, Nándor, Fedinec, Csilla, and Szarka, László (eds.). *Minority Hungarian Communities in the 20th Century*, (Boulder: Social Science Monographs, Atlantic Research and Publications, 2011).
Barev, Tsenko. *S pero v izgnanie*, book 1–3 (Sofia: Robinzon, 1993).
Barratt, Glynn. *The Russians and Australia* (Vancouver: University of British Columbia Press, 1988).
Barkan, Elliot Robert. *And still they come: Immigrants and American Society 1920 to the 1990* (Wheeling, Illinois: Harlan Davidson Inc., 1996).
Baučić, Ivo. *Radnici u inozemstvu prema popisu stanovnistva Jugoslavije 1971* (Zagreb: Studies of the Institute of Geography University of Zagreb, 1973).

Baučić, Ivo. *Stanje vanjskih migracija iz Jugoslavije krajem sedamdesetih godina* (Zagreb: Centar za istraživanje migracija, 1979).
Baučić, Ivo. Pavlaković Vera, *Basic Aspects of External Migration from Medjimurje* (Zagreb: Centre for Migration Studies, 1975).
Bazanov, Petr. *Izdatelskaya Dejatelnost Politicheskih Organizatii Russkoi Emigratii (1917–1988)* (St Petersburg: St Petersburg gosudarstvenny universitet kultury i iskussv, 2008).
Behring, Eva. *Scriitori români din exil, 1945–1989* (Bucharest: Editura Fundaţiei Culturale Române, 2001).
Berdychowska, Bogumiła, ed., Jerzy Giedroyc. *Emigracja ukraińska. Listy 1950–1982* (Warszawa: Spółdzielnia Wydawnicza Czytelnik, 2004).
Bernard, Sara. "Developing the Yugoslav Gastarbeiter Reintegration Policy. Political and Economic Aspects (1969–1974)," Working paper 5 (Graz: Centre for Southeast European Studies, 2012).
Bertheleu, Hélène, ed. *Identifications ethniques. Rapport de pouvoir, Compromis, Territoire*, (Paris: Armand Colin, 1995).
Best, Heinrich. "Cadres into Managers: Structural Changes of East German Economic Elites before and after Unification," *Historical Social Research* 30, no. 2 (Spring 2005): 6–24.
Betell, Nicholas. *Posledhyaa Taina* (London: Stenvalli Press, 1974).
Białokura, Marek, and Jakóbczyk-Adamczyk, Patrycja, eds. *Polska a Hiszpania. Z dziejów koegzystencji dwóch narodów w XX wieku*, (Toruń: Duet, 2012).
Biberaj, Elez. *Shqipëria në tranzicion: rruga e vështirë drejt demokracisë: 1990–2010* (Tirana: AIIS, 2011).
Bischof, Günter, (ed. et al.). *The Prague Spring and the Warsaw Pact Invasion of Czechoslovakia in 1968* (Lanham: Lexington, 2010).
Biskupski, Mieczysław B. B. "Spy, Patriot, or Internationalist? The Early Career of Józef Retinger, the Polish Patriarch of the European Union," *Polish Review* 43, no. 1 (1998): 23–67.
Błażyński, Zbigniew, ed. *Władze RP na obczyźnie podczas II wojny światowej* (London: Polskie Towarzystwo Naukowe na Obczyźnie, 1994).
Bleiere, Daina et al., eds. *The Occupation Regimes in the Baltic States 1940–1991* (Riga: Institute of the History of Latvia, 2009).
Blitz, Brad K. "Refugee Returns in Croatia: Contradictions and Reform," *Politics* 23, no. 3 (2003): 181–191.
Bobelis, Kazys, and Aničas, Jonas. *VLIK: Vyriausiasis Lietuvos išlaisvinimo komitetas 1943–1992* (Vilnius: Vaga, 2011).
Bogdan, Magdalena. *Radio Madryt 1949–1955: powstanie, organizacja oraz funkcjonowanie polskiej sekcji Radio Nacional de España w pierwszym okresie działalności* (Łomianki/Warszawa: Wydawnictwo LTW/Uniwersytet Kardynała Stefana Wyszyńskiego, 2011).
Bogdani, Mirela, and Loughlin John. *Albania and the European Union: The Tumultuous Journey towards Integration and Accession* (London: Tauris, 2007).
Boia, Lucian. *La Roumanie. Un pays à la frontière de l'Europe* (Paris: Les Belles Lettres, 2003).
Boldea, Iulian. "Exilul literar românesc. Dileme și trauma identitare," *Comunicare interculturală și Literatură* 21 (2014): 59–69.
Boldyrev, Konstantin. "Menchegof – lager peremeschennyh lits (Zapadnaja Germanija)," *Voprosy Istorii* 7 (1998): 110–141.
Bolhovitinov, Nikolay. *Russkie Uchenye-Emigranty (G. V. Vernadsky, M. M. Karpovich, M. T. Florinsky) i Stanovlenie Rusistiki v SShA* (Moscow: ROSSPEN, 2005).
Bodnarczuk, Dmytro. *Ethno-national Consciousness of the Ukrainian Immigrants in the United States* (Clifton: Computoprint Corporation, 2000): 13–15.
Borbándi, Gyula. *A magyar emigráció életrajza: 1945–1985* (Bern: Európái Protestáns Magyar Szabadegyetem, 1985).

Borzym, Andrzej, and Sadowski, Jeremi. *Polscy ojcowie Europy* (Warszawa: Wydawnictwo Trio, 2007).
Botezatu, Elena. "Fragmente de 'destin'. Dramaturgi români din diaspora de limbă franceză," *Comunicare interculturală și literatură* 1 (2017): 94–106.
Bozhilov, Ivan et al. *Istoria na Bulgaria* (Sofia: Izdatelska kashta "Hristo Botev," 1994).
Bozhinova, Blagorodna. *Zhertveno pokolenie* (Sofia: Bulgarika, 1996).
Breton, Raymond. "Institutional Completeness of Ethnic Communities and the Personal Relations of Immigrants," *The American Journal of Sociology* 2 (1964): 193–205.
Brinson, Charmian, and Malet, Marian, eds. *Exile in and from Czechoslovakia during the 1930s and 1940s* (Amsterdam: Rodopi, 2009).
Brown, James F. *Radio Free Europe: An Insider's View* (Washington, DC: New Academia, 2013).
Brunnbauer, Ulf. *Globalizing Southeastern Europe: Emigrants, America, and the State since the Late Nineteenth Century* (Landham, MD: Lexington Books, 2016).
Brunnbauer, Ulf, ed. *Transnational Societies, Transterritorial Politics: Migrations in the (Post-)Yugoslav Region 19th–21th Century*, vol. 141, (Munich: Oldenbourg, 2009).
Buc, Bonaventure S. "The Role of Emigrants in Slovak Nationalism," *Slovakia* 9, no.4 (March 1959), 32–47.
Buczek, Roman. *Stanisław Mikołajczyk*, vol. 1–2 (Toronto: Century Publishing Company, 1996).
Buda, Dumitru-Mircea. "Două jurnale din exil în lecture contemporane," *Studia Universitatis Petru Maior* 10 (2011): 109–119.
Budeanca, Cosmin, and Olteanu Florentin, eds. *Forme de represiune în regimurile comuniste* (Iasi: Polirom, 2009).
Budnitzkiy, Oleg, ed. *Evreiskaja emigratsia is Rossii. 1881 – 2005* (Moscow: ROSSPEN, 2008).
Buechtemann, Christoph, and Schupp, Jürgen. "Repercussions of Unification: Patterns and Trends in the Socio-Economic Transformation of East Germany," *Industrial Relations Journal* 23, no. 2 (Spring 1992): 90–106.
Buechler, Hans Christian, and Buechler Judith-Maria, eds. *Migrants in Europe: The Role of Family, Labor, and Politics*, (New York: Greenwood Press, 1987).
Buhle, Mari, Buhle, Paul, and Georgakas, Dan. *Encyclopedia of the American Left* (Oxford: Oxford University Press, 1998).
Bułhak, Władysław, and Pleskot, Patryk. *Szpiedzy PRL-u* (Kraków: Znak Horyzont, 2014).
Burant, Stephen R., *East Germany: A Country Study* (Washington D.C.: Library of Congress, 1988).
Burch, Cecilia Notini. *A Cold War Pursuit: Soviet Refugees in Sweden, 1945–54* (Stockholm: Santérus Academic Press, 2014).
Burrell, Kathy, and Hörschelmann, Kathhrin, eds. *Mobilities in Socialist and Post-Socialist States: Societies on the Move*, (Hampshire/New York: Palgrave Macmillan, 2014).
Buwalda, Piet. *They Did Not Dwell Alone: Jewish Emigration from the Soviet Union, 1967–1990* (Washington, D.C.: Woodrow Wilson Center Press, 1997).
Caccamo, Francesco. *Jiří Pelikán a jeho cesta socialismem 20. Století* (Brno: Doplněk, 2008).
Calafeteanu, Ion. *Politică și exil. 1946–1950. Din istoria exilului românesc* (Bucharest: Editura enciclopedica, 2000).
Calda, Milos. "Demographic Slump vs. Immigration Policy. The Case of the Czech Republic," The Center for Comparative Immigration Studies, University of California, San Diego, Working Paper 127 (Nov. 2005), https://ccis.ucsd.edu/_files/wp127.pdf.
Campani, Giovama. "Albanian Refugees in Italy," *Refuge* 12, no. 4 (October 1992): 7–10.
Cătănuș, Dan. "Divergențele româno-sovietice din CAER și consecințele lor asupra politicii externe a României, 1962–1963," *Arhivele totalitarismului* 46–47 (2005), 68–80.
Cattaruzza, Marina. "'Last Stop Expulsion" – The Minority Question and Forced Migration in East-Central Europe: 1918–49,' *Nations and Nationalism* 16 no. 1 (2010): 108–126.
Çeku, Ethem. *Struktura politike e ilegales së Kosovës* (Tirana: Argeta-LMG, 2006).

Celovský, Boris. *Politici bez moci: první léta exilové Rady svobodného Československa* (Senov near Ostrava: Tilia, 2000).
Cenckiewicz, Sławomir. *Oczami bezpieki. Szkice i materiały z dziejów aparatu bezpieczeństwa PRL* (Łomianki: LTW, 2012).
Cenckiewicz, Sławomir, ed. *Polska emigracja polityczna. Informator (reprint of 1962 edition)*, (Warszawa: Adiutor and Instytut Pamięci Narodowej, 2004).
Chehova, Olga. *Moi chasy idut inache* (Moscow: Vagrius, 1998).
Chin, Rita C. K. *The Guestworker Question in postwar Germany* (Cambridge: Cambridge University Press, 2007).
Chioveanu, Mihai. *Faces of Facism* (Bucharest: University of Bucharest, 2005).
Cioroianu, Adrian. *Pe umerii lui Marx. O introducere în istoria comunismului românesc* (Bucharest Curtea Veche, 2007).
Clarkson, Alexander. *Fragmented Fatherland: Immigration and Cold War Conflict in the Federal Republic of Germany, 1945–1980*, (New York: Berghahn Books, 2013).
Cloyes, DioGuardi Shirley. "Jewish Survival in Albania & the Ethics of 'Besa,'" *Congress Monthly*, (January/February 2006): 7–10.
Cohen, Gerard Daniel. *In War's Wake: Europe's Displaced Persons in the Postwar Order* (New York: Oxford University Press, 2011).
Connor, Ian. *Refugees and Expellees in Post-War Germany* (Manchester: University of Manchester Press, 2007).
Constantin, Marie-Viorica. *Umorul politic românesc in perioda comunistă. Perspective lingvistice* (Bucharest: Editura Universitatii din Bucuresti, 2012).
Constantiniu, Florin. *O istorie sinceră a poporului român* (Bucharest: Editura Univers Enciclopedic, 1997).
Cordell, Karl. "The Role of the Evangelical Church in the GDR," *Government and Opposition* 25, no. 1 (Winter 2007): 48–59.
Corobca, Liliana, ed. *Paul Goma și exilul etern*, (Oradea: Ratio et Revelatio, 2016).
Crampton, Richard J. *The Balkans since the Second World War* (London/New York: Longman, 2002).
Cude, Michael. "Transatlantic Perspectives on the Slovak Question, 1914–1948" (PhD diss., University of Colorado-Boulder, 2013).
Culic, Irina. "One Hundred Years of Solitude: Romanian Immigrants in Canada," *Studia UBB Sociologia* 2 (2011): 27–49.
Cummings, Richard H. *Cold War Radio: The Dangerous History of American Broadcasting in Europe, 1950–1989* (Jefferson, NC: McFarland, 2009).
Czekalski, Tadeusz. "Between Longstanding Hostilities and Unwanted Alliances – the Crucial Aspects of Balkan Policy of Albanian State in Twentieth Century," Suleyman Demirel University. Journal of Social Sciences: Special issue on Balkans 2, (December 2012): 87–96.
Czekalski, Tadeusz. *The Shining Beacon of Socialism in Europe: The Albanian State and Society in the Period of Communist Dictatorship 1944–1992* (Kraków: Wydawnictwo Uniwersytetu Jagiellońskiego, 2013).
Czerniakiewicz, Jan, and Czerniakiewicz, Monika. *Przesiedlenia ludności w Europie 1915–1959* (Warszawa: Wydawnictwo Wyższej Szkoły Pedagogicznej TWP, 2005).
Damyanov, Simeon, and Berov, Lyuben. *Balgarite v Avstralia* (Sofia: Izdatelstvo na BAN, 1986).
Danilov, Dan, and Deutsch, Howard. *Immigrating to the USA* (Vancouver: Self-Counsel Press, 1994).
Danyte, Milda, ed. *Beginnings and Ends of Immigration: Life without Borders in the Contemporary World*, (Vilnius: Versus Aureus, 2005).
Dapkute, Daiva. "Between Organization and Informality: A few Pages from the History of Santara-Šviesa," *Lituanus* 52 (2006): http://www.lituanus.org/2006/06_3_01%20Dapkute.htm

Decressin, Jörg. "Internal Migration in West Germany and Implications for East-West Salary Convergence," *Review of World Economics* 130, no. 2 (1994): 231–257.

Denéchère, Yves. *Des enfants venus de loin. Histoire de l'adoption internationale en France* (Paris: Armand Colin, 2011).

Denéchère, Yves. "L'adoption des "enfants de Ceauşescu": un fait social au cœur des relations franco-roumaines," *Cahier d'Histoire Immédiate* 44 (2013): 171–184.

Denéchère, Yves, and Niget, David, eds. *Droits des enfants au XXe siècle. Pour une histoire transnationale*, (Rennes: Presses Universitaires de Rennes, 2014).

Denéchère, Yves, and Scutaru, Beatrice. "International adoption of Romanian children and Romania's admission to the European Union (1990–2007)," *Eastern Journal of European Studies* 1 (June 2010): 135–151.

Dervishi, Kastriot. *Sigurimi i Shtetit 1944–1991. Historia e policisë politike të regjimit komunist* (Tirana: Shtëpia Botuese 55, 2012).

Diminescu, Dana. "Deplasările oşenilor în străinătate, un nou model de migraţie," *Revista de Cercetări Sociale* 2 (1996): 16–32.

Diminescu, Dana. "La désinsitutionalisation de l'hospitalité et l'intégration par le bas. Le cas des migrants roumains," *Ville-École-Integration Enjeux* 131 (December 2002): 167–175.

Dobrivojević, Ivana. "U potrazi za blagostanjem. Odlazak jugoslovenskih državljana u zemlje zapadne Evrope 1960–1970," *Istorija 20. veka* 2 (2007): 89–100.

Dota, Franko. *Zaraćeno poraće. Konfliktni i konkurentski narativi o stradanju i iseljavanju Talijana Istre* (Zagreb: Srednja Europa, 2010).

Drachman, Edward. *Challenging the Kremlin: The Soviet Jewish Movement for Freedom, 1967–1990* (New York: Paragon House, 1992).

Draus, Jan. *Nauka polska na emigracji w latach 1945–1990* (Warszawa: Instytut Historii Nauki PAN/ASPRA-JR, 2015).

Dreyfus-Armand, Geneviève. *L'exil des républicains espagnols en France de la guerre civile à la mort de Franco* (Paris: Albin Michel, 1999).

Diefendorf, Jeffery. *In the Wake of the War: The Reconstruction of German Cities after World War II* (New York: Oxford University Press, 1993).

Diminescu, Dana, ed. *Visibles mais peu nombreux ... Les circulations migratoires roumaines* (Paris: Éditions de la Maison des sciences de l'homme, 2003).

Dineva, Detelina. "The 'Master of Several Trades' and the Historian: The Stories of Two Exiled Bulgarian Intellectuals during the Cold War Years," *Bulgarian Historical Review* 3/4 (2014): 220–230.

Dochev, Ivan. *Shest desetiletia borba protiv komunizma za svobodata na Bulgaria* (Plovdiv: Pigmalion, 1995).

Dolinin, Viktor. "KGB protiv NTS," *Posev* 5 (1999): 45–47.

Dongen, van Luc, Roulin, Stéphanie, and Scott-Smith, Giles, eds. *Transnational anti-Communism and the Cold War: agents, activities, and networks*, (Basingstoke: Palgrave Macmillan, 2014).

Dorril, Stephen. *MI6: Inside the Covert World of Her Majesty's Secret Intelligence Service* (New York: Touchstone, 2002).

Douglas, Ray M. *Orderly and Humane: The Expulsion of the Germans after the Second World War* (New Haven/London: Yale University Press, 2012).

Dowty, Alan. *Closed Borders: The Contemporary Assault on Freedom of Movement* (Binghamton: Vail-Ballou Press, 1987).

Doynov, Doyno. *Kresnensko-Razlozhkoto vastanie, 1878–1879* (Sofia: Balgarska akademia na naukite, 1979).

Doynov, Stefan. *Balgarite v Ukrayna i Moldova prez Vazrazhdaneto, 1751–1877* (Sofia: Marin Drinov, 2005).

Drachman, Edward. *Challenging the Kremlin: The Soviet Jewish Movement for Freedom, 1967–1990* (New York: Paragon House, 1992).
Dragišić, Petar. "Searching for El Dorado. Workers from Serbia Temporary Employed Abroad from the 1960s to the Dissolution of Yugoslavia," *Tokovi istorije* 3 (2014): 131–142.
Dragostinova, Theodora. *Between Two Motherlands: Nationality and Emigration among the Greeks of Bulgaria, 1900–1949* (Ithaca/London: Cornell University Press, 2011).
Drozdowski, Marian Marek (ed. et al.). *Archiwum polityczne Ignacego Jana Paderewskiego*, vol. 6, *1915–1941* (Warszawa: Wydawnictwo DiG, 2007).
Dufoix, Stéphane. "Sertorius ou Prospero?," *Socio-anthropologie* 9 (2001): https://journals.openedition.org/socio-anthropologie/8
Durandin, Caherine. *Europe: l'utopie et le chaos* (Paris: Armand Colin, 2005).
Eberhardt, Piotr. *Migracje polityczne na ziemiach polskich: 1939–1950* (Poznań: Instytut Zachodni, 2010).
Eberhardt, Piotr. *Przemiany narodowościowe na Ukrainie XX wieku* (Warszawa: Biblioteka Obozu, 1994).
Edele, Mark. *Stalin's Defectors: How Red Army Soldiers Became Hitler's Collaborators, 1941–1945* (Oxford: Oxford University Press, 2017).
Eidintas, Alfonsas. *Lithuanian Emigration to the United States 1868–1950* (Vilnius: Mokslo ir enciklopediju leidybos institutas, 2003).
Elliot, Mark. "The United States and Forced Repatriation of Soviet Citizens," *Political Science Quarterly* 88 no. 2 (Spring 1973).
Elsie, Robert. *Historical Dictionary of Albania* (Plymouth: Scarecrow Press, 2010).
Elsie, Robert. *Historical Dictionary of Kosovo* (Plymouth: Scarecrow Press, 2011).
Emmer, Pieter C., Lucassen, Leo, and Oltmer, Jochen, ed. *Enzyklopädie Migration in Europa: vom 17. Jahrhundert bis zur Gegenwart*, (Munich: Schöningh, 2007).
Erdmans, Mary P. *Opposite Poles: Immigrants and Ethnics in Polish Chicago, 1976–1990* (University Park, PA: Penn. State University Press, 1990).
Eubank, Nancy. *The Russians in America* (Minneapolis: Learner Publications, 1973).
Fassmann, Heinz, and Munz Rainer. "European East-West Migration, 1945–1992," *International Migration Review* 28, no. 3 (Autumn 1994): 520–538.
Feherváry, István. *The Long Road to Revolution: The Hungarian Gulag 1945–1956* (Santa Fe.: Pro Libertate Publishing, 1989).
Ficeac, Bogdan. *Cenzura comunistă și formarea "omului nou"* (Bucharest: Nemira, 1999).
Fiń, Anna. "In the space of 'displaced borderland'. A few reflections on the relationships between Polish and Ukrainian immigrants in the United States," *Studia Migracyjne-Przegląd Polonijny* 1 (2014): 143–160.
Fiń, Anna. "Odtworzone sąsiedztwo. Polscy i ukraińscy imigranci w nowojorskiej East Village," *Studia Migracyjne – Przegląd Polonijny* 1 (2013): 150–128.
Fiń, Anna. "Ukraińska imigracja w Stanach Zjednoczonych. Charakterystyka ogólna," *Studia Migracyjne-Przegląd Polonijny* 4 (2013): 35–56.
Fischer, Bernd Jürgen. *Albania at War 1939–1945* (London: Purdue University Press, 1999).
Fitzpatrick, Sheila. *Mischka's War: A European Odyssey of the 1940s* (Melbourne: Melbourne University Publishing, 2017).
Fotache, Oana. "Troubled Heritage. Monica Lovinescu and the Aestretical Tradition in Romanian Literary Historiography," *Studia UBB Philologia* 2 (2012): 53–61.
Frank, Matthew. *Making Minorities History: Population Transfer in Twentieth-Century Europe* (Oxford: Oxford University Press, 2017).
Freidman, Murray, and Chernin, Albert, ed. *A Second Exodus: The American Movement to Free Soviet Jews* (Hanover, NH: Brandies University Press, 1999).

Friman, Richard H., and Reich, Simon, *Human Trafficking, Human Security, and the Balkans* (Pittsburgh: University of Pittsburgh Press, 2007).
Friszke, Andrzej. *Życie polityczne emigracji* (Warszawa: Biblioteka Więzi 1999).
Gaddis, John Lewis. *George F. Kennan: An American Life* (New York: Penguin Press, 2011).
Gadjev, Ivan. *Istoria na balgarskata emigratsia v Severna Amerika*, vol. 2: *Bulgaria, mashteha nasha, 1944–1989* (Sofia: Institut po istoria na balgarskata emigratsia "Ilia Todorov Gadjev," 2006).
Gadomski, Feliks. *Zgromadzenie Europejskich Narodów Ujarzmionych: krótki zarys* (New York: Nowy Dziennik Bicentennial Publishing Corporation, 1995).
Galița, Andrei Catalin. "Instituții ale exilului românesc din Franța și Marea Britanie. O abordare comparativă" (M.A. diss., University of Bucharest, 2014).
Garliński, Józef. *Politycy i żołnierze* (London: Odnowa, 1968).
Gawenda, Jerzy A. *Legalizm Polski w świetle Prawa Publicznego* (London: White Eagle Press, 1959).
Gawlikowski, Lechosław. *Pracownicy Radia Wolna Europa. Biografie zwykłe i niezwykłe* (Warszawa: Instytut Studiów Politycznych Polskiej Akademii Nauk; Naczelna Dyrekcja Archiwów Państwowych, 2015).
Gawryszewski, Andrzej. *Ludność Polski w XX wieku* (Warszawa: Instytut Geografii i Przestrzennego Zagospodarowania, 2005).
Geiger, Vladimir. "Josip Broz Tito i sudbina jugoslavenskih Nijemaca," *Časopis za suvremenu povijest 3* (2008): 801–818.
Gerus, Oleh.W., and Rea, James.E. *The Ukrainians in Canada* (Ottawa: Canadian Historical Association, 1985).
Gilad, Margolit. "The Foreign Policy of the German Sudeten Council and Hans-Christoph Seebohm, 1956–1964," *Central European History* 43 (2010): 464–583.
Gilbert, Emily. *Changing Identities: Latvians, Lithuanians and Estonians in Great Britain* (Devon UK: Create Space, 2013).
Gilioten, Elizabeth. *Dve moje domovine. Uspomene Jelizavete Zherardovne Giljoten* (Gorni Milanovats, 1991).
Gille, Zsuzsa. "Introduction: From Comparison to Relationality," *Slavic Review* 76, no. 2 (2017): 285–290.
Gitelman, Zvi. *A Century of Ambivalence: The Jews of Russia and the Soviet Union, 1881 to the Present* (Bloomington: Indiana University Press, 2001).
Giurescu, Dinu. "Cu patru decenii în urmă 'Declarația' din aprilie 1964," *Dosarele istoriei* 4 (2004): 17.
Glodeanu, Gheorghe, ed. *Incursiuni în literatura diasporei și a disidenței* (Bucharest: Libra, 1999).
Gloviczki, Peter J. "Ceaușescu's Children: The Process of Democratization and the Plight of Romania's Orphans," *Critique: A Worldwide Journal of Politics* (2004): 117–123.
Gmitruk, Janusz et al., eds. *Stanisław Mikołajczyk w dokumentach aparatu bezpieczeństwa*, vol. 1–3, (Warszawa/Łódź: Instytut Pamięci Narodowej, 2010).
Goddeeris, Idesbald. *Polonia w Belgii w pierwszych latach po II wojnie światowej* (Warszawa: Wydawnictwo Naukowe Semper, 2005).
Goeken-Haidl, Ulrike. *Der Weg zurück: Die Repatriierung Sowjetischer Zwangsarbeiter während und nach dem zweiten Weltkrieg* (Essen: Klartext Verlag, 2006).
Goldberg, Ben Zion, ed. *The Jewish Problem in the Soviet Union. Analysis and Solution* (New York: Crown Publishers, 1961).
Goldin, Vladimir. *Rokovoy vybor* (Archangelsk; Murmansk: Solti, 2005).
Goldman, Minton F. *Revolution and Change in Central and Eastern Europe: Political, Economic and Social Challenges* (New York: M.E. Sharpe, 1997).
Goněc, Vladimír. *Za sjednocenou Evropu: z myšlenek a programů Huberta Ripky* (Brno: Vyd. Masarykova univerzita v Brně, 2004).

Gottfried, Ted. *Displaced Persons: The Liberation and Abuse of Holocaust Survivors*. (Brookfield, CT: Twenty-First Century Books, 2001).

Górecki, Dariusz. *Polskie naczelne władze państwowe na uchodźstwie w latach 1939–1990* (Warszawa: Wydawnictwo Sejmowe, 2002).

Götürk, Deniz, Gramling, David, and Kaes, Anton. *Germany in Transit: Nation and Migration, 1955–2005* (Berkeley: University of California Press, 2007).

Govor, Elena. *Australia in the Russian Mirror* (Melbourne: Melbourne University Press, 1997).

Govorchin, Gerald. *From Russia to America with Love: A Study of the Russian Immigrants in the United States* (Pittsburgh: Dorrance, 1993).

Grebenarov, Aleksandar, and Nikolova, Nadya (compilers). *Balgarskoto upravlenie vav Vardarska Makedonia, 1941–1944* (Sofia: Darzhavna agentsia arhivi, 2012).

Greene, Balch Emily. *Our Slavic Fellow Citizens*, (New York: Arno Press, 1969).

Gremion, Pierre. *Intelligence de l'antiCommunisme: le Congrès pour la liberté de la culture à Paris (1950–1975)* (Paris: Fayard, 1995).

Gribnicea, Mihai. *Basarabia în primii ani de ocupaţie sovietică 1944–1950* (Cluj-Napoca: Dacia, 1995).

Gridan, Irina. "Le 'nouveau cours' des relations roumano-soviétiques (années 1950): un assouplissement consenti ou octroyé depuis Moscou?," *Relations internationales* 2 (2015): 111–124.

Gridan, Irina. "Du Communisme national au national-Communisme. Réactions à la soviétisation dans la Roumanie des années 1960," *Vingtième siècle. Revue d'histoire* 109 (January–March 2011): 113–127.

Gross, Feliks. "Political Emigration from Iron Curtain Countries," *The Annals of the American Academy of Political and Social Science* 271 (September 1950): 175–184.

Gruev, Stefan. *Moyata odiseya* (Sofia: Obsidian, 2002).

Grundmann. Siegfried, *Bevölkerungsentwicklung in Ostdeutschland: Demographische Strukturen und räumliche Wandlungsprozesse seit 1945* (Opladen: Leske und Büdrich, 1998).

Grzybowski, Jerzy. *Pogoń między Orłem Białym, Swastyką i Czerwoną Gwiazdą. Białoruski ruch niepodległościowy w latach 1939–1956* (Warszawa: Bel Studio, 2011).

Haas, Õie, and Siska, Voldemar, eds. *Eestlased Austraalias I* (Adelaide: Austraalia Eesti Seltside Liit, 1988).

Habielski, Rafał. *Życie społeczne i kulturalne emigracji* (Warszawa: Biblioteka Więzi 1999).

Halich, Wasyl. *Ukrainian in the US* (New York: Arno Press, 1970).

Hallik, Terje et al., ed. *Eestlaste põgenemine läände teise maailmasõja ajal* (Tartu: Filiae Patriae, 2009).

Halpern, Joel. "The Pečalba Tradition in Macedonia, A Case Study." (Jan. 1975), *Anthropology Department Faculty Publication Series* 58, https://scholarworks.umass.edu/cgi/viewcontent.cgi?article=1057&context=anthro_faculty_pubs.

Hartman, Gary. *The Immigrant as Diplomat: Ethnicity, Nationalism, and the Shaping of Foreign Policy in the Lithuanian-American Community, 1870–1922* (Chicago: Lithuanian Research and Studies Center, 2002).

Hartmann, Norbert J., and Isajiw, Wsevolod. "Ethnicity and Occupation: An Assessment of the Occupational Structure of Ukrainian Canadians in the 1960s," *Canadian Ethnic Studies* 12 (1980): 55–73.

Harvey, Joanna. "Return Dynamics in Bosnia and Croatia: A Comparative Analysis," *International Migration* 44, no. 3 (2006): 89–114.

Haxhia, Ljarjaa Nertila. "An Analysis of the Consequences of the Ideological and Cultural Revolution," *Sociology Study* 1, no. 6 (2011): 315–322.

Heidemeyer, Helge. *Flucht und Zuwanderung aus der SBZ/DDR: Die Flüchtlingspolitik der Bundesrepublik Deutschland bis zum Bau der Berliner Mauer* (Düsseldorf: Droste Verlag, 1993).
Heikkilä, Pauli. *Estonians for Europe: National Activism for European Integration, 1922 – 1991* (Brussels: Peter Lang, 2014).
Heitmeyer, Wilhelm, Haupt, Heinz-Gerhard, Malthaner, Stefan, and Kirschner, Andrea, eds. *Control of Violence* (New York: Springer, 2011).
Herbert, Ulrich. *Hitler's Foreign Workers: Enforced Foreign Labour in Germany under the Third Reich* (Cambridge: Cambridge University Press, 2007).
Herbert, Ulrich. *Geschichte der Ausländerpolitik in Deutschland: Saisonarbeiter, Zwangsarbeiter, Gastarbeiter, Flüchtlinge* (München: C.H. Beck, 2001).
Heruday-Kiełczewska, Magdalena. *"Solidarność" nad Sekwaną: działalność Komitetu Koordynacyjnego NSZZ "Solidarność" w Paryżu 1981 – 1989* (Gdańsk: Europejskie Centrum Solidarności, 2016).
Hiden, John, Made, Vahur, and Smith, David J., eds. *The Baltic Question during the Cold War* (Abingdon: Routledge, 2008).
Hilton, Laura J. *Prisoners of Peace: Rebuilding Community, Identity and Nationality in Displaced Persons Camps in Germany, 1945 – 1952* (PhD diss., Ohio State University, 2001).
Hladnik, Mirjam, ed. *From Slovenia to Egypt: Aleksandrinke's Trans-Mediterranean Domestic Workers' Migration and National Imagination* (Göttingen: V&R unipress, 2015).
Hochstadt, Steve. *Mobility and Modernity: Migration in Germany 1820 – 1989* (Ann Arbor: University of Michigan Press, 1999).
Hoerder, Dirk. *Cultures in Contact: World Migrations in the Second Millennium* (Durham: Duke University Press, 2002).
Holian, Anna Marta. *Between National Socialism and Soviet Communism: Displaced Persons in Postwar Germany* (Ann Arbor: University of Michigan Press, 2011).
Horvath, Istvan. "Migrația din România și Republica Moldova de la mijlocul secolului XIX pâna în present, cu accent pe migrația minorităților," *Working Papers in Romanian Minority Studies*, Cluj Napoca: Institutul Pentru Studierea Problemelor Minoritatilor Nationale 40 (2011): 1 – 14.
Horvath, Istvan, and Anghel Remus Gabriel. "Migration and Its Consequences for Romania," *Südosteuropa. Seitschrift für Politik und Gesellschaft* 57 (2009): 386 – 403.
Hough, William J.H. "The Annexation of the Baltic States and its Effect on the Development of Law Prohibiting Forcible Seizure of Territory," *New York Law School Journal of International and Comparative Law* 6, no. 2 (1985): 301 – 533.
Hovi, Kalervo, ed. *Relations between the Nordic Countries and the Baltic Nations in the XX Century* (Turku: University of Turku, 1998).
Hristov, Hristo. *Darzhavna sigurnost sreshtu balgarskata emigratsia* (Sofia: Izdatelska kashta "Ivan Vazov," 2000).
Hristov, Hristo. *Dvoyniyat zhivot na agent "Pikadili"* (Sofia: Ikonomedia, 2008).
Hristov, Hristo. *Ubiyte "Skitnik": Balgarskata i britanskata politika po sluchaya "Georgi Markov"* (Sofia: Siela, 2005).
Hron, Madeleine. "The Czech Émigré Experience of Return after 1989," *The Slavonic and East European Review* 85, no. 1 (Jan. 2007): 47 – 78.
Hrycak, Jarosław. *Historia Ukrainy 1772 – 1999. Narodziny nowoczesnego narodu* (Lublin: Instytut Europy Środkowo-Wschodniej, 2000).
Hułas, Magdalena. *Goście czy intruzi. Rząd polski na uchodźstwie wrzesień 1939 – lipiec 1943* (Warszawa: Instytut Historii PAN, 1996).
Hysi, Shyqyri. *Histori e trojeve dhe e diasporës shqiptare* (Tirana: Shtëpia Botuese e Librit Universitar, 2007).

Ilmjärv, Magnus. *Silent Submission: Formation of Foreign Policy of Estonia, Latvia and Lithuania: Period from mid-1920s to Annexation in 1940* (Stockholm: Stockholm University, 2004).
Iglicka, Krystyna. *Kontrasty migracyjne Polski. Wymiar transatlantycki* (Warszawa: Wydawnictwo Scholar, 2008).
Iglicka, Krystyna. "Mechanisms of Migration from Poland before and during the Transition Period," *Journal of Ethnic and Migration Studies* 26, no. 1 (2000): 61–73.
Iglicka, Krystyna, ed. *Migracje powrotne Polaków. Powroty sukcesu czy rozczarowania?* (Warszawa: Instytut Spraw Publicznych, 2002).
Iglicka, Krystyna. *Poland's Post-War Dynamic of Migration* (Aldershot: Ashgate, 2001).
Ioanid, Radu. "The Sacralised Politics of the Romanian Iron Guard," *Totalitarian Movements & Political Religions* 4 (2004): 419–453.
Ioniță, Sorin Gabriel. *Publicațiile românești din exil despre problematica respectării drepturilor omului în România, 1975–1989* (Bucharest: Institutul Național pentru Memoria Exilului Românesc, 2009).
Irie, Akira, and Saunier, Pierre-Yves, eds. *The Palgrave Dictionary of Transnational History*, (Hampshire: Palgrave Macmillan, 2009).
Ivan, Ruxandra. *La politique étrangère roumaine (1990–2006)* (Brussels: Éditions de l'Université de Bruxelles, 2009).
Ivan, Ruxandra, ed. *Transformarea socialistă. Politici ale regimului Communist ântre ideologie și administratie* (Bucharest: Polirom, 2009).
Ivanov, Martin, Todorova, Tsvetana, and Vachkov, Daniel. *Istoria na vanshnia darzhaven dalg na Bulgaria, 1878–1990* (Sofia: Balgarska Narodna Banka, 2009).
Ivanova, Ivanka, ed. *Tendentsii v transgranichnata migratsia na rabotna sila i svobodnoto dvizhenie na hora – efekti za Bulgaria: Doklad* (Sofia: Institut "Otvoreno obshtestvo," 2010).
Ivanović, Vladimir. *Geburtstag pišeš normalno: jugoslovenski gastarbajteri u SR Nemačkoj i Austriji, 1965–1973* (Belgrade: Institut za savremenu istoriju, 2012).
Ivanović, Vladimir. "Ekstremna emigracija u SR Nemačkoj i Jugoslavija," *Istorija 20. veka.* 1 (2009): 139–147.
Ivanović, Vladimir. "Zaključivanje sporazuma o angažovanju jugoslovenske radne snage sa SR Nemačkom," *Hereticus. Časopis za preispitivanje prošlosti* 7, no. 4 (2009): 25–40.
Jaakson, Ernst. *Eestile* (Tallinn: SE&JS, 1995).
Jackson, James Harvey. *Migration and Urbanization in the Ruhr Valley, 1812–1914* (Boston: Brill, 1997).
Jaczyńska, Agnieszka, Łukasiewicz, Sławomir, and Pleskot, Patryk, eds. *Wasza solidarność – nasza wolność. Reakcje emigracji polskiej i świata na wprowadzenie stanu wojennego*, (Lublin/Gdańsk: Instytut Pamięci Narodowej/Europejskie Centrum Solidarności, 2017).
Janauskas, Giedrius. *Kongresine akcija: JAV ir Kanados lietuviu politinis lobizmas XX amziaus 6–9 desimtceciais* (Vilnius: Versus Aureus, 2009).
Janjetović, Zoran. *Between Hitler and Tito: The Disappearance of the Vojvodina Germans* (Belgrade: s. n., 2000).
Janjetović, Zoran. "The disappearance of the Germans from Yugoslavia: Expulsion or emigration?" *Revue des études sud-est européennes* 40, no. 1–4 (2002): 215–231.
Jarausch, Konrad, ed. *After Unity: Reconfiguring German Identities* (Providence: Berghahn Books, 1997).
Jarausch, Konrad, and Gransow, Volker, ed. *United Germany: Documents and Debates, 1944–1993*, (Providence: Berghahn Books, 1994).
Jaroszyńska-Kirchmann, Anna. *The Exile Mission. The Polish Political Diaspora and Polish Americans, 1939–1956* (Athens: Ohio University Press, 2004).
Jasek, Peter, ed. *Anti-Communist Resistance in Central and Eastern Europe*, (Bratislava: Ustav Pamati Naroda, 2011).

Jeffery, Keith. *MI6: The History of the Secret Intelligence Service 1909–1949* (London: Crowd, 2010).
Jeřábek, Vojtěch. *Československi uprchlici ve studene valce: dějiny American Fund for Czechoslovak Refugees* (Brno: Stilus, 2005).
Jewtuch, Jewhen et. al. 'Ukrainska diaspora. Sociologiczni ta istoryczni studii," *Naukovi pratsi Fakul'tetu sotsial'no-ekonomichnoyi osvity ta upravlinnya* (2003): http://enpuir.npu.edu.ua/handle/123456789/357 (accessed 20 February 2015).
Jinga, Luciana M., and Soare, Florin S., eds. *Politica pronatalistă a regimului Ceaușescu*, 2nd vol., *Instituții și practici* (Iasi: Polirom, 2001), 248–249.
Johnson, A. Ross. *Radio Free Europe and Radio Liberty: The CIA Years and Beyond* (Washington DC: Wilson Center Press, 2010).
Johnson, A. Ross. Parta Russell Eugene, eds. *Cold War Broadcasting: Impact on the Soviet Union and Eastern Europe: A Collection of Studies and Documents*, (Budapest/New York: Central European University Press, 2010).
Johnston, Robert H. *New Mecca, New Babylon – Paris and the Russian Exiles, 1920–1945* (Kingston/Montreal: McGill-Quenn's University Press, 1988).
Jonušauskas, Laurynas. *Likimo vedami: Lietuvos diplomatinės tarnybos egzilyje veikla 1940–1991* (Vilnius: Genocide and Resistance Research Centre of Lithuania, 2003).
Junek, Marek (ed. et al.). *Svobodně!: Radio Svobodná Evropa 1951–2011*, (Prague: Radioservis, 2011).
Jupp, James. *Immigration* (Sydney: University Press, 1991).
Jürjo, Indrek. *Pagulus ja Nõukogude Eesti: Vaateid KGB, EKP ja VEKSA arhiividokumentide põhjal* (Tartu: Tammerraamat, 2014).
Kaba, Hamit. *"Vatra" gjatë luftës së dytë botërore dhe luftës së ftohtë* in Roli i Mërgatës në Shtetformim (Prishtina: Ministria e Diasporës, 2012).
Kádár, Lynn Katalin, ed. *The Inauguration of Organized Political Warfare: Cold War Organizations sponsored by the National Committee for a Free Europe / Free Europe Committee* (St. Helena: Helena History Press, 2013).
Kalbarczyk, Sławomir, ed. *Zbrodnia katyńska: w kręgu prawdy i kłamstwa*, (Warszawa: Instytut Pamięci Narodowej, 2010).
Kalm, Arne. *Balti musketärid USA Kongressis* (Tallinn: Aade, 2015).
Kamiński, Łukasz, and Waligóra, Grzegorz, eds. *NSZZ "Solidarność" 1980–1989*, vol. 2: *Ruch społeczny* (Warszawa: Instytut Pamięci Narodowej, 2010).
Kaplan, Marion A. *From Dignity to Despair: Jewish Life in Nazi Germany* (Oxford: Oxford University Press, 2005).
Karabulkov, Toncho. *Za da ne ichezne nashiyat svyat s nas: Spomeni na edin politicheski emigrant* (Paris/Sofia: Svetat utre, 1999).
Kardela, Piotr. *Stowarzyszenie Polskich Kombatantów w Stanach Zjednoczonych w latach 1953–1990* (Olsztyn/Białystok: Instytut Pamięci Narodowej, 2015).
Karoly, Bela, and Richardson, Nancy Anna. *Feel no Fear: The Power, Passion and Politics of a Life in Gymnastics* (New York: Hyperion, 1994).
Kasekamp, Andres. *A History of the Baltic States* (Basingstoke: Palgrave Macmillan, 2010).
Kello, Petrit. *Emigrant në Australi* (London: Balli i Kombit, 2010).
Kenigshtein, Moshe, ed. *"Russkoe" litso Israela: cherty sotcialnogo portreta* (Jerusalem/Moscow: Gesharim – Mosty kultury, 2007).
Kersten, Krystyna. *Repatriacja ludności polskiej po II wojnie światowej (studium historyczne)* (Wrocław: Ossolineum, 1974).
Kesting, Robert W. "American Support of Polish Refugees and Their Santa Rosa Camp," *Polish American Studies* 48, no. 1 (Spring 1991): 79–90.
Khisamutdinov, Amir. *Russkiy San-Francisco* (Moscow: Veche, 2010).

Kilian, Stanisław. *Myśl społeczno-polityczna Tadeusza Bieleckiego* (Kraków: Wydawn. Naukowe Akademii Pedagogicznej, 2000).

Kilgman, Gail. *Politica duplicității. Controlul reproducerii în Romania lui Ceaușescu* (Bucharest: Humanitas, 2000).

Kilgman, Gail, and Verdery, Katherine. *Peasants Under Siege: The Collectivization of Romanian Agriculture, 1949–1962* (Princeton: Princeton University Press, 2011).

Kind-Kovács, Friederike, and Labov, Jessie, eds. *Samizdat, Tamizdat, and Beyond: Transnational Media During and After Socialism* (New York: Berghahn, 2013).

King, Russell, and Mai, Nicola. *Out Of Albania: From Crisis Migration to Social Inclusion in Italy* (London: Berghahn Books, 2008).

King, Russell. "Across the Sea and Over the Mountains: Documenting Albanian Migration," *Scottish Geographical Journal* 119, no. 3 (2003): 283–309.

King, Russell. "Albania as a laboratory for the study of migration and development," *Journal of Southern Europe and the Balkans* 7, no. 1 (August 2005): 133–155.

Kirkpatrick, Evron M. "A Chronology of Events: The Collapse of the German Democratic Republic and steps toward German Unity: May 1989 – January 1991," *World Affairs* 152 (1990): 195–197.

Kirschbaum, Joseph M. "Dr. Paučo's Writings and the History of American Slovaks," *Furdek* 13 (1974): 75–80.

Kirschbaum, Joseph M., ed. *Slovakia in the 19th & 20th Centuries*, Proceedings of the Conference on Slovakia held during the General Meeting of the Slovak World Congress on June 17–18, 1971 in Toronto, Ontario, Canada (Toronto: Slovak World Congress, 1973).

Kirschbaum, Stanislav J., ed. *Slovak Politics: Essays on Slovak History in Honor of Joseph M. Kirschbaum*, (Cleveland: Slovak Institute, 1983).

Kłaczkow, Jarosław. *Na emigracji. Losy polskiego wychodźstwa ewangelickiego w XX wieku* (Toruń: Wydawnictwo Adam Marszałek, 2013).

Klimov, Grigory. *Pesn pobeditelya* (Krasnodar: Peresvet, 2002).

Kłonczyński, Arnold. *My w Szwecji nie porastamy mchem…: emigranci z Polski w Szwecji w latach 1945–1980* (Gdańsk: Wydawnictwo Uniwersytetu Gdańskiego, 2012).

Knight, Robert, ed. *Ethnicity, Nationalism and the European Cold War* (London/New York: Continuum, 2012).

Kolarska-Bobińska, Lena, ed. *Emigrować i wracać. Migracje zarobkowe Polaków a polityka państwa* (Warszawa: Instytut Spraw Publicznych, 2007).

Kolinsky, Eva, Nickel Hildegard Maria, eds. *Reinventing Gender: Women in Eastern Germany since Unification* (Portland: Frank Cass, 2003).

Kondracki, Tadeusz. *Historia Stowarzyszenia Polskich Kombatantów w Wielkiej Brytanii 1946–1996* (London: Zarząd Główny SPK w Wielkiej Brytanii, 1996).

Kondylis, Florence. "Conflict Displacement and Labor Market Outcomes in Post-War Bosnia and Herzegovina," *Journal of Development Economics* 2, no. 93 (2010): 235–248.

Konstantinov, Dmitry. "Munhensky Institut. Is istorii vtoroy rossiskoy politiheskoy emigratsii," *Tribuna russkoy mysli* 4 (2002): 133–144.

Kool, Ferdinand. *DP Kroonika: Eesti pagulased Saksamaal 1944–1951* (Lakewood: Eesti Arhiiv Ühendriikides, 1999).

Kosatík, Pavel. *Ferdinand Peroutka: pozdější život, 1938–1978* (Prague: Paseka, 2000).

K'oseva, Tsvetana. *Bolgariya i Russkaja emigratsiya, 1920–1950-e gg.* (Moscow: Russkii put, 2008).

Kostov, Chris. *Contested Ethnic Identity: The Case of Macedonian Immigrants in Toronto, 1900–1996* (Bern: Peter Lang AG, 2010).

Kovrig, Bennett. *Of Walls and Bridges: The United States and Eastern Europe* (New York: New York University Press, 1991).

Kozodoy, Ruth, ed. *Vision Confronts Reality: Historical Perspectives on the Contemporary Jewish Agenda* (Madison, New Jersey: Fairleigh Dickinson University Press, 1989).

Krajsa, Joseph C., (ed. et al.). *Slovaks in America: A Bicentennial Study*, (Middletown, PA: Slovak League of America, 1978).

Kraljević, Iva. "Matica iseljenika Hrvatske 1964–1968." *Časopis za suvremenu povijest* 41, no. 1 (2009): 71–92.

Krasteva, Anna, ed. *Imigratsiyata v Bulgaria*, (Sofia: Mezhdunaroden tsentar za izsledvane na maltsinstvata i kulturnite vzaimodeystvia, 2005).

Krawczenko, Bohdan. *Socialni zminy i nacionalna swidomist' w Ukraini XX stolittia* (Kiev: Osnowy, 1997).

Krebs, Gilbert, and Schneilin, Gérard, eds. *Exil et Résistance au National-socialisme 1933–1945*, (Paris: Université de la Sorbonne Nouvelle, Publications de l'Institut d'allemand, 1998).

Krebs, Ronald R. *Dueling visions: US strategy toward Eastern Europe under Eisenhower* (College Station, TX: Texas A & M University Press, 2001).

Křen, Jan. *Česi-Němci-odsun* (Prague: Academia, 1990).

Krivosheina, Nina. *Chetyre treti nashei zhizni* (Moscow: Russkii Put', 2017).

Krivoshein, Nikita. "Surdokamera," *Zvezda* 3 (2011):178–187.

Kröhnert, Steffen, and Klingholz, Reiner. *Not am Mann: Von Helden der Arbeit zur neuen Unterschicht?* (Berlin: Berlin Institut für Bevölkerung und Entwicklung, 2007).

Kubiak, Hieronim, Kusielewicz, Eugeniusz, and Gromada, Tadeusz, ed. *Polonia amerykańska. Przeszłość teraźniejszość współczesność* (Wrocław: Ossolineum, 1988).

Kula, Marcin. 'Emigracja z realnego socjalizmu: ekonomiczna i polityczna zarazem,' *Sprawy Narodowościowe. Seria Nowa* 4, no. 2 (1995): 141–146.

Kulikov, Nikolay. *Ja tvoy, Rossija* (Moscow: Sov. Rossija, 1990).

Kulischer, Eugene. "Displaced Persons in the Modern World," *Annals of the American Academy of Political and Social Science* 262 (1949): 166–177.

Kuropas, Myron. *The Ukrainian Americans: Roots and Aspirations 1884–1954* (Toronto: University Toronto Press, 1991).

Kushner, A. R. "Kosovo and the Refugee Crisis, 1999: The Search for Patterns Amidst the Prejudice," *Patterns of Prejudice* 33, no. 3 (1999): 73–86.

Kuznets, Simon. "Immigration of Russian Jews to the US: Background and Structure," *Perspectives in American History* 9 (1975): 35–124.

Lääne, Tiit. *Välis-Eesti spordielu 1940–1991 Austraalias ja Uus-Meremaal, Saksamaal, Rootsis, Kanadas, USAs ja teistes riikides* (Tallinn: Maaleht, 2000).

Lane, Thomas. *Victims of Stalin and Hitler: The Exodus of Poles and Balts to Britain* (Basingstoke: Palgrave Macmillan, 2004).

Łabędzki, Jan, and Strużyński, Marian. *Z doświadczeń pracownika operacyjnego SB. Sprawa kryptonim "Cezary"* (Warszawa: Departament Szkolenia i Doskonalenia Zawodowego MSW, 1972).

Łaptos, Józef. *Europa marzycieli: wizje i projekty integracyjne środkowoeuropejskiej emigracji politycznej 1940–1956* (Kraków: Wydawnictwo Naukowe Uniwersytetu Pedagogicznego, 2013).

Lemekh, Halyna. "Immigrant Encounters in the Ukrainian Diaspora in New York," (PhD Diss., New School University, 2007).

Levin, Nora. *The Jews in the Soviet Union since 1917: Paradox of Survival* (New York/London: New York University Press, 1988).

Liebich, Andre. *From the Other Shore: Russian Social-Democracy after 1921* (Cambridge, Mass.: Harvard University Press, 1997).

Liebich, Andre. "Mensheviks Wage the Cold War" *Journal of Contemporary History* 30 (1995): 247–264.

Likaj, Matilda. "*Migration as a Challenge for Albanian Post-Communist Society*," *Journal of Educational and Social Research* 4, no. 2 (2014): 143–149.

Litván, György, ed. *The Hungarian Revolution of 1956: Reform, Revolt and Repression 1953–1963* (London: Longman, 1996).

Lipski, Aleksander. Walkowska Wiesława, eds. *Emigracja jako problem lokalny i globalny*, (Mysłowice: GWSP, 2010).

Liszewicz, Leonidas et al., eds. *Materiały do dziejów polskiego uchodźstwa niepodległościowego*, vol. 1–8 (London: Polskie Towarzystwo Naukowe na Obczyźnie, 1994–1996).

Lencznarowicz, Jan. 'Rola Towarzystwa "Polonia" w polityce PRL wobec Polonii w krajach zachodnich,' *Przegląd Polonijny* no. 1 (1996): 43–60.

Levin, Nora. *The Jews in the Soviet Union since 1917: Paradox of Survival*, vol. 2 (New York/London: New York University Press, 1988).

Lhomel, Édith. "Monica Lovinescu, la force d'une voix," *Le Courrier des pays de l'Est* 1067 (2008): 109–112.

Low, Alfred. *Soviet Jewry and Soviet Policy* (New York: Columbia University Press, 1990).

Łuczak, Czesław. *Polacy w okupowanych Niemczech 1945–1949* (Poznań: Pracownia Serwisu Oprogramowania, 1993).

Łuczak, Czesław. *Polityka ludnościowa i ekonomiczna hitlerowskich Niemiec w okupowanej Polsce* (Poznań: Wydawnictwo Poznańskie, 1979).

Lukeš, Igor. "Czechoslovak Political Exile in the Cold War: The Early Years," *The Polish Review* 47, no. 3 (2002): 332–343.

Lukeš, Igor. *Czechoslovakia Between Stalin and Hitler: The Diplomacy of Edvard Beneš in the 1930s* (New York: Oxford University Press, 1996).

Lukeš, Igor. "Československý politický exil za studené války: první roky," *Střední Evropa* 119 (February 2004): 1–13.

Lukeš, Igor. *On the Edge of the Cold War: American Diplomats and Spies in Postwar Prague* (Oxford: Oxford University Press, 2012).

Lulushi, Albert. *Operation Valuable Fiend: The CIA's First Paramilitary Strike Against the Iron Curtain* (New York: Arcade Publishing, 2014).

Ludanyi, Andrew. "Titoist Integration of Yugoslavia: The Partisan Myth & the Hungarians of the Vojvodina, 1945–1975," *Polity* 12 (1979): 225–252.

Łukasiewicz, Sławomir. *Partia w warunkach emigracji. Dylematy Polskiego Ruchu Wolnościowego "Niepodległość i Demokracja"* (Lublin/Warszawa: IPN, Instytut Studiów Politycznych PAN, 2014).

Łukasiewicz, Sławomir. "Polska emigracja polityczna w XX wieku i pamięć historyczna," *Przegląd Zachodni* no. 1 (2007): 63–76.

Łukasiewicz, Sławomir. *Third Europe: Polish Federalist Thought in the United States – 1940s–1970s* (Budapest: Helena History Press, 2016).

Łukasiewicz, Sławomir, ed. *Polska Emigracja polityczna 1939–1990. Stan badań*, (Lublin: IPN, 2015).

Łukasiewicz, Sławomir, ed. *Tajny oręż czy ofiary zimnej wojny? Emigracje polityczne z Europy Środkowej i Wschodniej*, ed. Sławomir Łukasiewicz (Lublin/Warszawa: IPN, 2010).

Łukasiewicz, Sławomir, ed. *Towards a United Europe: An Anthology of Twentieth Century Polish Thought on Europe*, transl. Robert Looby (Warszawa: Ministry of Foreign Affairs of the Republic of Poland, 2011).

Lupul, Mandy R., ed. *Ukrainian Canadians, Multiculturalism and Separatism: An Assessment*, (Edmonton: The Canadian Institute of Ukrainian Studies, 1978).

Luža, Radomír. *The Transfer of the Sudeten Germans: A Study of Czech-German Relations, 1933–1962* (New York: New York University Press, 1964).

Macartney, Carlile Aylmer. *Refugees: The Work of the League* (London: League of Nations Union, 1931).
Machcewicz, Paweł. *Emigracja w polityce międzynarodowej* (Warszawa: Biblioteka Więzi 1999).
Machcewicz, Paweł. *Monachijska menażeria. Walka z Radiem Wolna Europa 1950–1989* (Warszawa: IPN; Instytut Studiów Politycznych PAN, 2007).
Machcewicz, Paweł, and Habielski, Rafał, eds. *Rozgłośnia Polska RWE 1952–1975*, (Wrocław: Zakład Narodowy im. Ossolińskich, 2018).
Macrea-Toma, Ioana. *Radio Free Europe in Paris: The Paradoxes of an Ethereal Opposition* (M.A. diss., Central European University, 2008).
Maegi, Bernard John. *Dangerous People, Delayed Pilgrims: Baltic Displaced Persons and the Making of Cold War America, 1945–1952* (PhD diss., University of Minnesota, 2008).
Magocsi, Paul R. *Historical Altas of East Central Europe* (Seattle/London: University of Washington Press, 1993).
Magocsi, Paul R. *Historical Atlas of Central Europe* (Seattle: University of Washington Press, 2002).
Magocsi, Paul R. "Magyars and Carpatho-Rusyns: On the Seventieth Anniversary of the Founding of Czechoslovakia," *Harvard Ukrainian Studies* 14, no. 3 (December 1990): 442–457.
Magocsi, Paul R. *Of the Making of Nationalities There is No End* (New York: Columbia University Press, 1999).
Magocsi, Paul R. *The Russian Americans* (New York: Chelsea House Publishers, 1989).
Magocsi, Paul R., ed. *Encyclopedia of Canada's Peoples* (Toronto: University of Toronto Press, 1999).
Magocci, Paul R., ed. *The Ukrainian Experience in the United States: A Symposium*, (Cambridge Mass.: Harvard Ukrainian Research Institute, 1979).
Mai, Nicola. "Looking for a More Modern Life...': The Role of Italian Television in then Albanian Migration to Italy," *Westminster Paper in Communication and Culture* 1, (2004): 3–22.
Maisongrande, Vincent. "Les circulations migratoires roumaines en Europe: Réseaux sociaux et inscription dena l'espace" (M.A. diss., University of Poitiers, 2008).
Major, Patrick. "Listening behind the Curtain: BBC Broadcasting to East Germany and Its Cold War Echo," *Cold War History* 13 (2013): 255–275.
Malkavaara, Mikko. *Kahtia jakautuneet Baltian luterilaiset kirkot ja Luterilainen maailmanliitto 1944–1963* (Helsinki: Suomen kirkkohistoriallinen seura, 2002).
Mälksoo, Lauri. *Illegal Annexation and State Continuity: The Case of the Incorporation of the Baltic States by the USSR: A Study of the Tension between Normativity and Power in International Law* (Leiden: Martinus Nijhoff Publishers, 2003).
Mamatey, Victor S. *The United States and East Central Europe, 1914–1918: A Study in Wilsonian Diplomacy and Propaganda* (Princeton: Princeton University Press, 1957).
Mamatey, Victor S., and Luža, Radomir, eds. *History of the Czechoslovak Republic, 1918–1948* (Princeton: Princeton University Press, 1973).
Manea, Gabriel Stelian. "O lovitură de imagine pentru Nicolae Ceaușescu. Vizita președintelui Richard Nixon la București, 2–3 august 1969," *Studii și materiale de istorie contemporană* 1 (2012): 170–183.
Manin, Marino et al., eds. *Identitet Istre – ishodišta i perspective*, (Zagreb: Institut društvenih znanosti Ivo Pilar, 2006).
Manolescu, Florin. *Enciclopedia exilului literar românesc 1945–1989. Scriitori, reviste, instituții, organizații* (Bucharest: Compania, 2003).
Marco, Abram. "Integrating Rijeka into Socialist Yugoslavia: The Politics of National Identity and the New City's Image (1947–1955)," *Nationalities Papers* 46, no. 1 (2018): 69–85.
Marès, Antoine, and Milza, Pierre, ed. *Le Paris des étrangers depuis 1945* (Paris: Publications de la Sorbonne, 1994).

Maresch, Eugenia. *Katyn 1940: The Documentary Evidence of the West's Betrayal* (Stroud: Spellmount, 2010).
Markov, Atanas. *Balgari v Tavria i tavriytsi v Bulgaria* (Dobrich: Matador 74, 2012).
Marks, Shula, Weindling, Paul, and Wintour, Laura, eds. *In Defense of Learning: The Plight, Persecution, and Placement of Academic Refugees, 1933–1980s*, Proceedings of the British Academy, vol. 169 (Oxford: Oxford University Press, 2011).
Marmullaku, Ramadan. *Albania and the Albanians* (London: Hurst, 1975).
Marrus, Michael. *The Unwanted: European Refugees from the 1st World War Through the Cold War* (Philadelphia: Temple University Press, 2002).
Maruniak, Wołodymyr. *Ukrainska emigracja w Nimeczczyni i Awstrii po Drugiej switowij wijni. Tom I. Roky 1945–1951* (Munich: Akademiczne Wydawnyctwo dr Petra Beleja, 1985).
Mâța, Dan Constantin. "Relațiile franco-române în perioada 1964–1968. Dialog în anii destinderii" (PhD diss., Universitaty "Al. I. Cuza," 2011).
Mazurkiewicz, Anna. *Uchodźcy polityczni z Europy Środkowo-Wschodniej w amerykańskiej polityce zimnowojennej 1948–1954* (Warszawa: Instytut Pamięci Narodowej; Gdańsk: Uniwersytet Gdański, 2016).
Mazurkiewicz, Anna. "Narody ujarzmione" – lobby polityczne czy projekt propagandowy?," *Studia Historica Gedanensia* 5 (2014): 354–392.
Mazurkiewicz, Anna. "Political Emigration from East Central Europe during the Cold War," *Polish American Studies* 72, no. 2 (Autumn 2015): 65–82.
Mazurkiewicz, Anna, ed. *East Central Europe in Exile: Transatlantic Identities*, vols. 1–2 (Newcastle: Cambridge Scholars Publishing, 2013).
Mazurkiewicz, Anna, ed. *From Exsilium to Exile: Coercion in Migration*, Studia Historica Gedanensia, vol. 5, (Gdańsk: Wydawnictwo Uniwersytetu Gdańskiego, 2014).
Merten, Ulrich. *Forgotten Voices: The Expulsion of the Germans from Eastern Europe After World War II* (New Brunswick: Transaction Publishers, 2013).
Mertelsmann, Olaf. Piirimäe Kaarel, eds. *The Baltic Sea Region and the Cold War* (Frankfurt: Peter Lang, 2012).
Maruniak, Wołodymyr. *Ukrainska emigracja w Nimeczczyni i Awstrii po Drugiej switowij wijni. Tom I. Roky 1945–1951* (Munich: Akademiczne Wydawnyctwo dr Petra Beleja, 1985).
Meyer, Henry C. *Drang nach Osten: Fortunes of a Slogan-Concept in German-Slavic Relations, 1849–1990* (Bern: Peter Lang, 1996).
McNair, John, Poole Thomas. *Russia and the Fifth Continent: Aspects of Russian-Australian Relations* (Brisbane: University of Queensland Press, 1992).
Medved, Felicita, ed. *Proliferation of Migration Transition: Selected New EU Member States* (Brussels: European Liberal Forum/Novum Institute, 2014).
Mežnarić, Silva. "Jugoslavenska sociologija (vanjskih) migracija – pokušaj sistematizacije," *Migracijske teme* 1 (1985): 77–96.
Michálek, Slavomír. *Diplomat Štefan Osuský: 1889–1973* (Bratislava: Veda, 1999).
Michálek, Slavomír. *Ján Papánek: politik, diplomat, humanista, 1896–1991* (Bratislava: Veda, 1996).
Michálek, Slavomír. *Nádeje a vytriezvenia: československo-americké hospodárske vzťahy v rokoch 1945–1951* (Bratislava: Veda, 1995).
Michálek, Slavomir. "Rada slobodného Československa, 1949–1960," *Historický Časopis*, 4 (1999): 327–344.
Michálek, Slavomír (et al. eds.). *Juraj Slávik Neresnický: od politiky cez diplomaciu po exil 1890–1969* (Bratislava: Prodama, 2006).
Michalon, Bénédicte, and Nedelcu, Mihaela. "Histoire, constantes et transformations récentes des dynamiques migratoires en Roumanie," *Revue d'Études Comparatives Est-Ouest* 4 (2010): 5–27.

Michev, Dobrin. *Makedonskiyat vapros i balgaro-yugoslavskite otnoshenia, 9 septemvri 1944–1949* (Sofia: Universitetsko izdatelstvo "Sv. Kliment Ohridski," 1994).
Mikkonen, Simo. "Exploiting the Exiles: Soviet Émigrés in US Cold War Strategy," *Journal of Cold War Studies* 14 (2012): 98–127.
Mikkonen, Simo, and Koivunen, Pia, eds. *Beyond the Divide. Entangled Histories of Cold War Europe* (New York, Oxford: Berghahn Books, 2015).
Mintchev, Vesselin. "External Migration and External Migration Policies in Bulgaria," *South-East Europe Review for Labor and Social Affairs* 2, no. 3 (1999): 123–150.
Mitseva, Evgenia. *Armentsite v Bulgaria – kultura i identichnost* (Sofia: IMIR, 2001).
Molenda, Jarosław. *Ucieczki z PRL* (Warszawa: Bellona, 2015).
Morrison, John N. L. "Intelligence in the Cold War," *Cold War Histor* 14 (2014): 575–591.
Moseikina, Marina. *U istokov formirovania Russkogo mira (XIX – nachalo XX vv.)* (Moscow: Aletiia, 2014).
Mueller, Carol. "Escape from the GDR, 1961–1989: Hybrid Exit Repertoires in a Disintegrating Leninist Regime," *The American Journal of Sociology* 105 no. 3 (1999): 697–735.
Mueller, Wolfgang, Ruzicic-Kessler, Karlo, and Greilinger, Philipp, eds. *The 'Alpen-Adria' Region 1945–1955: International and Transnational Perspectives on a Conflicted European Region* (Vienna: New Academic Press, 2018).
Murgescu, Bogdan. *România şi Europa. Acumularea decalajelor economice (1500–2010)* (Iasi: Polirom, 2010).
Nagórski, Jr. Zygmunt. "Liberation Movements in Exile," *Journal of Central European Affairs* 10, no. 2 (July 1950): 128–144.
Nazarov, Michail. *Missija Russkoi emigratsii* (Stavropol: Kavkazsky krai, 1992).
Neblich, Esther. "Das Umsiedlerproblem der Jahre 1945–1955 in der SBZ/DDR am Beispiel des Oberen Vogtlandes," in *Agenda DDR-Forschung*, ed. Heiner Timmermann (Berlin: LIT Verlag, 2005).
Nekola, Martin. *Petr Zenkl: politik a člověk* (Prague: Mladá Fronta, 2014).
Nelson, Michael. *War of the Black Heavens: The Battles of Western Broadcasting in the Cold War* (Syracuse, NY: Syracuse University Press, 1997).
Neubauer, John, and Török, Borbála Zsuzsanna, eds. *The Exile and Return of Writers from East-Central Europe: A Compendium* (Berlin: De Gruyter, 2009).
Nešpor, Zdeněk. "The Disappointed and Disgruntled: A Study of the Return in the 1990s of Czech Emigrants from the Communist Era," *Czech Sociological Review* 38, no. 6 (2002); 789–808.
Nisiobęcka, Aneta. *Reemigration of Poles from France and Their Adaptation in People's Poland in 1945–1950* (PhD diss., University of Warsaw, 2015).
Nové, Béla. *Patria Nostra – doctoral dissertation* (Budapest: Balassi Kiadó Kft., 2016), dis szertacio.uni-eger.hu/17/13Nóve_Béla_tézisek_angol.pdf
Nowicka, Ewa, Firouzbakhch Hanna, eds. *Homecoming. An Anthology of Return Migrations* (Kraków: Nomos, 2008).
Nurek, Mieczysław. *Gorycz zwycięstwa. Los Polskich Sił Zbrojnych na Zachodzie po II wojnie światowej. 1945–1949* (Gdańsk: Wydawnictwo Univwersytetu Gdańskiego, 2009).
Obolenskaya-Flam, Ludmila. "Vozdushnymi putyami," *Posev* 3 (2003): 9–12.
Obradov. "Emigracija talijanskog stanovništva s hrvatskog područja tijekom Drugog svjetskog rata i poraća," *Radovi Zavoda* Marica Karakaš *za povijesne znanosti HAZU u Zadru* 55 (2013): 204–225.
Oddo, Gilbert. *Slovakia and Its People* (New York: Robert Speller & Sons, 1960).
O'Donnell, James S. *A Coming of Age: Albania under Enver Hoxha* (New York: Columbia University Press, 1999).
Ogoyski, Petko. *Zapiski za balgarskite stradania 1944–1989*, vol. 3 (Sofia: Izdatelstvo "Vulkan-4," 2000).

Ogoyski, Petko. *Zapiski za balgarskite stradania 1944–1989*, vol. 2 (Sofia: IK Fenomen, 2008).
O'Grady, Joseph P., ed. *The Immigrants' Influence on Wilson's Peace Policies*, (Lexington: University of Kentucky, 1967).
Okólski, Marek, ed. *European immigrations: trends, structures and policy implications* (Amsterdam: Amsterdam University Press, 2012).
Oltmer, Jochen, ed. *Handbuch Staat und Migration in Deutschland seit dem 17. Jahrhundert*, (Oldenbourg: De Gruyter, 2015).
Oltmer, Jochen. *Migration und Politik in der Weimarer Republik* (Göttingen: Vandenhoek & Ruprecht, 2005).
Olszewski, Edward. *Emigracja polska w Danii 1893–1983* (Warszawa-Lublin: ISP PAN, 1993).
Orłowski, Hubert Sakson Andrzej. *Utracona ojczyzna: przymusowe wysiedlenia, deportacje i przesiedlenia jako wspólne doświadczenie* (Poznań: Instytut Zachodni, 1996).
Paczkowski, Andrzej. *Trzy twarze Józefa Światły. Przyczynek do historii komunizmu w Polsce* (Warszawa: Prószyński i S-ka, 2009).
Pajo, Erind. *International Migration, Social Demotion, and Imagined Advancement: An Ethnography of Socioglobal Mobility* (New York: Springer, 2008).
Papathimiu, Sonila. "The demographic and economic development of Albania during and after the decline of Communist regime (1945–2010)," *Treballs de la Societat Catalana de Geografia* 73 (Juny 2012): 101–118.
Panayotov, Panayot. *Moyat zhiteyski pat: Misli za Bulgaria* (Sofia: Gutenberg, 2002).
Paprikoff, George I. *Works of Bulgarian Emigrants: An Annotated Bibliography* (Chicago: Stanka K. Paprikoff, 1985).
Paraschiv, Vasile. *Lupta mea pentru sindicatele libere din România* (Iasi: Polirom, 2005).
Parchomenko, Walter. *Soviet Images of Dissidents and Nonconformists* (New York/London: Praeger, 1986).
Paučo, Joseph. "Twenty Years of the Slovak Institute in Cleveland" *Slovakia* 23, no. 46 (1973): 16–21.
Paul, Lisa C. *Swimming in the Daylight: An American Student, A Soviet-Jewish Dissident, and the Gift of Hope* (New York: Skyhorse Publishing, 2011).
Păunescu, Adrian. "Aici e țara," *România Liberă* (December 1975).
Pawliczko, Ann, Lencyk, ed. *Ukraine and Ukrainians throughout the World: A Demographic and Sociological Guide to the Homeland and its Dispora* (Toronto: University of Toronto Press, 1994).
Pawluczuk, Włodzimierz. *Ukraina. Polityka i mistyka* (Kraków: Zakład Wydawniczy Nomos, 1998).
Payne, Jason. "Projekti Bunkerizimit: The Strange Case of the Albanian Bunker," *Log*, 31, (Spring/Summer 2014): 161–168.
Pawlikowicz, Leszek. *Tajny front zimnej wojny. Uciekinierzy z polskich służb specjalnych* (Warszawa: Rytm, 2004).
Pawlikowicz, Leszek, and Zapart, Robert, ed. *Służby wywiadowcze jako narzędzia realizacji polityki państwa w XX wieku. Wybrane zagadnienia* (Rzeszów: Wydawnictwo Uniwersytetu Rzeszowskiego, 2014).
Pearson, Owen. *Albania in the Twentieth Century, A History*, vol. 3: *Albania as Dictatorship and Democracy, 1945–98* (New York: Tauris, 2007).
Pehe, Jiří. "Czechoslovakia. Émigrés in the Postcommunist Era: New Data, New Policies," *Report on Eastern Europe* (26 April 1991): 11–15.
Pelin, Mihai. *Opisul emigrației politice: destine în 1222 de fișe alcătuite pe baza dosarelor din arhivele Securității* (Bucharest: Compania, 2002).
Pennar, Jaan, ed. *Estonians in America 1627–1975: A Chronology and Fact Book* (New York: Oceana, 1975).

Péteri, György. "Nylon Curtain – Transnational and Transsystemic Tendencies in the Cultural Life of State-Socialist Russia and East-Central Europe," *Slavonica* 2 (November 2004): 113–122.
Perelman, Viktor. *Pokinutaja Rossija. Jurnalist v zakrytom obschestve* (New York/Jerusalem/Paris: Izdat. Vremya i My, 1989).
Perelman, Viktor. *Teatr absurda* (New York: Izdat. Vremya i My, 1984).
Peykovska, Penka, and Kiselkova, Nina. "Ruskata imigratsia v Bulgaria spored prebroyavaniyata na naselenieto prez 1920 i 1926 godina," *Statistika* 3–4 (2013).
Petkova, Lidia. "The Ethnic Turks in Bulgaria: Social Integration and Impact on Bulgarian-Turkish Relations, 1947–2000," *The Global Review of Ethnopolitics* 4 (2002): 42–59.
Petryshyn, Roman, ed. *Changing Realities: Social Trends Among Ukrainian Canadians* (Edmonton: Canadian Institute of Ukrainian Studies Press, 1980).
Pfaff, Steven. "The Politics of Peace in the GDR: The Independent Peace Movement, the Church, and the Origins of the East German Opposition," *Peace and Change* 26, no. 3 (Summer 2002): 280–300.
Pichler, Robert, ed. *Legacy and Change: Albanian Transformation from Multidisciplinary Perspectives* (Zurich: LIT Verlag, 2014).
Piesakowski, Tomasz, ed. *Akcja niepodległościowa na terenie międzynarodowym 1945–1990* (London: Polskie Towarzystwo Naukowe na Obczyźnie, 1999).
Pilch, Andrzej. "Migracja zarobkowa z Galicji w XIX i XX wieku (do 1918 roku)," *Przegląd Polonijny* 1 (1975): 5–15.
Pinkus, Benjamin. *The Jews of the Soviet Union: The History of a National Minority* (Cambridge: Cambridge University Press, 1989).
Piotrowski, Jacek, ed. *Dzienniki czynności Prezydenta RP Władysława Raczkiewicza 1939–1947*, vol. 1–2 (Wrocław: Wydawnictwo Uniwersytetu Wrocławskiego, 2004).
Piotrowski, Jacek. *Piłsudczycy bez lidera* (Toruń: Adam Marszałek, 2003).
Pipa, Arshi. *Albanian Stalinism: Ideo-Political Aspects* (New York: Columbia University Press, 1990).
Pipes, Richard. *Struve – Liberal on the Right, 1905–1944* (Cambridge; Mass.: Harvard University Press, 1980).
Pistrick, Eckehard. "Singing back the kurbetlli – Responses to migration in Albanian folk culture as a culturally innovative practice," *Anthropological Notebooks* 16 (2010): 29–37.
Pisuliński, Jan. *Akcja specjalna "Wisła"* (Rzeszów: Libra, 2017).
Plakans, Andrejs. *A Concise History of the Baltic States* (Cambridge: Cambridge University Press, 2011).
Pletzing, Christian. Pletzing Marianne, eds. *Displaced Persons: Flüchtlinge aus den baltischen Staaten in Deutschland* (Munich: Martin Meidenbauer, 2007).
Pleskot, Patryk. *Solidarność na Antypodach. Inicjatywy solidarnościowe polskiej diaspory w Australii* (Warszawa: Instytut Pamięci Narodowej, 2014).
Pleskot, Patryk, ed. *Za naszą i waszą Solidarność. Inicjatyw solidarnościowe z udziałem Polonii podejmowane na świecie (1980–1989)*, ed., vols. 1–2 (Warszawa: Instytut Pamięci Narodowej, 2018).
Podgórski, Bogdan. *Józef Retinger: prywatny polityk* (Kraków: Universitas, 2013).
Poliakov, Juriy, and Tarle, Galina, eds. *Istoria Rossiiskogo zarubejia. Emigratsia is SSSR – Rosssii. 1941 – 2001* (Moscow: Institut rossiiskoi istorii RAN, 2007).
Polakovič, Štefan, and Vnuk, František. *Zahraničné' akcie na záchranu o obnovenie slovenskej samostatnosti (1943–1948)* (Lakewood-Hamilton: Slovak Research Institute of America, 1988).
Polian, Pavel. *Jertvy dvuh diktatur* (Moscow: ROSSPEN, 2002).
Polian, Pavel. *Against Their Will: The History and Geography of Forced Migrations in the USSR* (Budapest: Central European University Press, 2004).
Polišenská, Milada. *Diplomatické vztahy Československa a USA 1918–1968* (Prague: Libri, 2012).

Polišenská, Milada. *Zapomenutý 'nepřítel' Josef Josten: Free Czechoslovakia Information na pozadí československo-britských diplomatických styků 1948–1985* (Prague: Libri, 2009).
Pomian, Grażyna, ed. *Wizja Polski na łamach Kultury 1947–1976*, vols. 1–2 (Lublin: UMCS, 1999).
Popa, Ioana. "Dépasser l'exil. Degrés de médiation et stratégies de transfert littéraire chez les exilés de l'Europe de l'Est en France," *Genèses* 38 (2000): 5–32.
Popescu, Dumitru, and Vulcanescu, Mihu. *Un om în Agora* (Bucharest: Editura Eminescu, 1972).
Popescu, Titu. *Convorbiri despre exil și literatură* (Bucharest: Jurnalul literar, 2001).
Popov, Andrey. *Rossiiskoye Pravoslavnoe Zarubejie: Istoriya i Istochniki* (Moscow: Istitute of Politicheskogo i Voennogo Analiza, 2005).
Poremsky, Vladimir. *Strategija antibolshevitskoy emigratsii* (Moscow: Posev, 1998).
Potot, Swanie. "Circulation et réseaux de migrants roumains: une contribution à l'étude des nouvelles mobilités en Europe" (PhD diss., University of Nice-Sophie Antipolis, 2003).
Povolný, Mojmír. *Zápas o lidská práva: Rada Svobodného Čeakoslovenska a helsinský process, 1975–1989* (Brno: Stilus Press, 2007).
Powers, Mary C., and Maciso, John J., eds. *The Immigration Experience in the United States: Policy Implications* (New York: Center for Migration Studies, 1994).
Predojević-Despić, Jelena, and Penev, Goran. "Emigration Zones in Serbia: 2011 Census Results," *Zbornik Matice Srpske za drustvene nauke* 148 (2014): 383–397.
Praszałowicz, Dorota, and Zięba, Andrzej A. Makowski Krzysztof, *Mechanizmy zamorskich migracji łańcuchowych w XIX wieku: Polacy, Niemcy, Żydzi, Rusini. Zarys problemu* (Kraków: Księgarnia Akademicka, 2004).
Praszałowicz, Dorota, and Małek, Agnieszka, eds. *The United States Immigration Policy and Immigrants' Responses: Past and Present* (Frankfurt am Main: Peter Lang, 2016).
Prokš, Petr. *Československo a Západ, 1945–1948: vztahy Československa se Spojenými státy, Velkou Británií a Francií v letech 1945–1948* (Prague: ISV, 2001).
Proudfoot, Malcolm J. *European Refugees –1939–1952: A Study in Forced Population Movement* (Evanston: Northwestern University Press, 1956).
Promitzer, Christian, Klaus-Jurgen, Hermanik, and Eduard, Staudinger, eds. *(Hidden) Minorities: Language and Ethnic Identity between Central Europe and the Balkans* (Berlin: Lit, 2009).
Pszenicki, Krzysztof. *Tu mówi London: Historia Sekcji Polskiej BBC* (Warszawa: Rosner & Wspólnicy, 2009).
Puddington, Arch. *Broadcasting Freedom: The Cold War Triumph of Radio Free Europe and Radio Liberty* (Lexington: University Press of Kentucky, 2000).
Puskás, Julianna. *Ties that Bind, Ties that Divide: 100 Years of Hungarian Experience in the United States* (New York: Holmes & Meier, 2000).
Pushkarev, Boris, ed. *NTS: Mysl i Delo* (Moscow: Posev, 2000).
Pushkareva, Natalia. "Vozniknovenie i formirovanie rossiiskoi diaspory za rubejom," *Otechestvennaja Istoria* 1 (1996): 53–69.
Raag, Raimo. *Eestlane väljaspool Eestit: Ajalooline ülevaade* (Tartu: Tartu ülikooli kirjastus, 1999).
Raag, Raimo, and Runblom, Harald, eds. *Estländare i Sverige: Historia, språk, kultur* (Uppsala: Centre for Multiethnic Research, 1988).
Raeff, Mark. *Russia Abroad* (New York/Oxford: Oxford University Press, 1990).
Rad, Ilie, ed. *Jurnalism românesc in exil și diaspora* (Bucharest: Tritonic, 2012).
Radut-Draghi, Luciana. "'Luceafarul' et 'Kultura', deux premises de modèles de pratiques diasporiques parisiennes," *Revista comunicare* 27 (2012): 163–180.
Rahr, Lev, and Obolensky, Valerian. *Rannie gody. Ocherk Istorii Natsionalno-Trudovogo Sojuza (1924–1948)* (Moscow: Posev, 2006).
Raikin, Spas. *Politicheski problemi pred balgarskata obshtestvenost v chuzhbina*, vol. 2 (Sofia: Izdatelstvo "Damyan Yakov," 1993).
Raikin, Spas. *Politichesko pateshestvie sreshtu vetrovete na XX vek*, vol. 7 (Sofia: Pensoft, 2004).

Raikin, Spas. *Politichesko pateshestvie sreshtu vetrovete na XX v.* vol. 1: *Sinya i chervena Bulgaria* (Sofia-Moskva: Pensoft, 2000).
Raška, Francis D. *Fighting Communism from Afar: The Council of Free Czechoslovakia* (Boulder: East European Monographs, 2008).
Raška, Francis D. *Long Road to Victory: A History or Czechoslovak Exile Organizations after 1968* (Boulder: East European Monographs, 2012).
Ravančić, Martina Grahek. "Controversies about the Croatian Victims at Bleiburg and in" Death Marches," *Review of Croatian History* 2, no. 1 (2006): 27–46.
Rechcígl, Jr. Miloslav. *Czechoslovak American Archivalia* (Olomouc-Ostrava: Repronis, 2004).
Reichling, Gerhard. *Die Deutschen Vertriebenen in Zählen: Umsiedler, Verschleppte, Vertriebene, Aussiedler, 1940–1985* (Bonn: Kulturstiftung der Deutschen Vertriebenen, 1995).
Reinisch, Jessica, and White Elizabeth, eds. *The Disentanglement of Populations: Migration, Expulsion and Displacement in Post-War Europe, 1944–9* (Basingstoke: Palgrave Macmillan, 2011).
Reisch, Alfred A. *Hot Books in the Cold War: The CIA-Funded Secret Western Book Distribution Program Behind the Iron Curtain* (Budapest/New York: Central European University Press, 2013).
Robionek, Bernd. *Croatian Political Refugees and the Western Allies: A Documented Survey from the Second World War to the Year 1948* (Berlin: Osteuropa-Zentrum Berlin, 2009).
Rock, David, and Wolff, Stefan, eds. *Coming Home to Germany? The Integration of Ethnic Germans from Central and Eastern Europe in the Federal Republic* (Oxford: Berghahn, 2002).
Roesler, Jörg. "Privatization in Eastern Germany, Experience with the Treuhand," *Europe-Asia Studies* 46 no. 3 (Summer 1994): 505–517.
Roi, Yaacov. *The Struggle for Soviet-Jewish Emigration, 1948–1967* (Cambridge: Cambridge University Press, 1991).
Rolandi, Francesca. "Heading Towards the West. Yugoslav Asylum Seekers in Italy (1955–1968)," *Acta Histriae* 23, no. 3 (2015): 555–574.
Roman, Wanda K., ed. Sabbat Kazimierz, *Polska na drodze do wolności i niepodległości. Pisma polityczne* (Toruń: Wydawnictwo Adam Marszałek, 2009).
Romanov, Eugene. *V borbe za Rossiju* (Moscow: Golos, 1999).
Roper, Steven D. *Romania: The Unfinished Revolution* (Amsterdam: Harwood Academic Publishers, 2000).
Ross, Corey. "Before the Wall: East German Communist Authority and the Mass Exodus to the West," *The Historical Journal* 45, no. 2 (Spring 2002): 462–469.
Ross, Nikolay. "Sovetskie lagerya vo Frantsii," *Russkaja Mysl* 4170 (1997): 15–16.
Rotariu, Traian. Voineagu, Virgil, eds. *Inerție și schimbare. Dimensiuni sociale ale tranziției în România* (Iasi: Polirom, 2012).
Rothschild, Joseph. *East Central Europe between the Two World Wars* (Seattle/London: University of WashingtonPress, 1998).
Rotman, Liviu. *Evreii din România în perioada comunistă. 1944–1965* (Iasi-Bucharest: Polirom, 2004).
Rozumnyj, Jaroslav, ed. *New Soil – Old Roots: The Ukrainian Experience in Canada* (Winnipeg: Ukrainian Academy of Arts and Sciences in Canada, 1983).
Russell, Peter, ed. *Nationalism in Canada* (Toronto: McGraw-Hill Co., 1966).
Rusu, Valeriu. *Migrația forței de muncă în Europa* (Bucharest: Arvin Press, 2003).
Sajti, Enikő A. *Hungarians in the Voivodina, 1918–1947* (Boulder: East European Monographs, 2003).
Salitan, Laurie. *Politics and Nationality in Contemporary Soviet-Jewish Emigration, 1968–1989* (London: St. Martin's Press, 1992).

Salomon, Kim. *Refugees in the Cold War: Toward a New International Refugee Regime in the Early Postwar Era* (Lund: Lund University Press, 1991).
Sălcudeanu, Nicoleta. "The Cultural Cold War in Romania," *Studia Universitatis Petru Maior* 12 (2012): 30–35.
Salitan, Laurie. *Politics and Nationality in Contemporary Soviet – Jewish Emigration. 1968–1989* (London: St. Martin's Press, 1992).
Sandu, Dumitru. *Fluxurile de migrație în România* (Bucharest: Editura Albatros, 1984).
Sandu, Dumitru, ed. *Locuirea temporară in străinătate. Migrația economică a românilor 1990–2006* (Bucharest: Fundația pentru o Societate Deschisă, 2006).
ŠarićTatjana. "Bijeg iz socijalističke Jugoslavije – ilegalna emigracija iz Hrvatske od 1945. do početka šezdesetih godina 20. stoljeća," *Migracijske i etničke teme* 31:2 (2015): 195–220.
Satzewich, Vic. *The Ukrainian Diaspora* (New York: Routledge, 2002).
Sazdov, Dimitar, and Penchev, Pencho. "Angorskiyat dogovor i spogodbata Mollov-Kafandaris," *Sbornik Trakia*, vol. 1 (Haskovo: Trakiyski nauchen institut, 2001).
Schierup, Carl-Ulrik. *Migration, Socialism, and the International Division of Labor: The Yugoslavian Experience* (Aldershot: Avebury, 1990).
Schierup, Carl-Ulrik. *Houses, Tractors, Golden Ducats: Prestige Game and Migration: A Study of Migrants to Denmark from a Yugoslav Village* (Århus: Århus Universitet, 1973).
Scholz, Hannelore. "East-West Women's Culture in Transition: Are East German Women the Losers of Unification?" *Journal of Women's History* 5, no.3 (Summer 1994): 109–116.
Schroeder, Gregory F. "Ties of Urban Heimat: West German Cities and Their Wartime Evacuees in the 1950s," *German Studies Review* 27 no.2 (May 2004): 307–324.
Schroeter, Leonard. *The Last Exodus* (New York: Universe Book, 1974).
Schryer, Frans J. *The Netherlandic Presence in Ontario: Pillars, Class and Dutch Ethnicity* (Waterloo ON: Wilfrid Laurier University Press, 2006).
Scutaru, Beatrice. "Ambassadeurs en pays étranger: la place des lecteurs dans la dipomatie culturelle franco-roumaine (années 1960–1970)," *Valahian Journal of Historical Studies* 20 (2013): 169–185.
Scutaru, Beatrice. "Images d'enfants roumains et médias occidentaux. La construction d'une cause (1989–1990)," *Relations internationales* 161 (2015): 99–112.
Scutaru, Beatrice. "La Roumanie à Paris: exil politique et lutte anti-Communiste," *Histoire@Politique. Politique, culture, société* 23 (2014): https://www.histoire-politique.fr/index.php?numero=23&rub=autres-articles&item=83
Scutaru, Beatrice. "Les relations entre les sociétés française et roumaine des années 1960 à 1995: un atout pour l'ancrage de la Roumanie à l'Europe?" (PhD diss., University of Angers, 2013).
Scurtu, Ioan. *Istoria contemporană a României (1918–2001)* (București: Editura Fundatiei Eomania de Maine, 2002) 106–112.
Șerban, Monica. *Dinamica migrației internaționale: un exercitiu asupra migrației românești în Spania* (Iasi: Lumen, 2011).
Șerban, Nicoleta. "Românii din exilul American și poziția lor față de proiectul de sistematizare rurală," *Studii și Materiale de Istorie Contemporană* 15 (2016): 80–92.
Șerban-Oprescu, Teodora, and Șerban-Oprescu, George. "Overview of Romanian Emigration to America during Communism and PostCommunism: Cultural Dimensions of Quality of Life," *International Journal of Humanities and Social Science* 23 (December 2012): 45–53.
Shamshur, Oleg V. "Ukraine in the context of new European Migrants," *International Migration Review* 26 no. 2 (1992): 258–268.
Sienkiewicz, Jan Wiktor. *Artyści Andersa: continuità e novità* (Warszawa/Toruń: Polski Instytut Studiów nad Sztuką Świata/Tako, 2016).
Simuț, Ion. "Cronologia exilului literar postbelic," *România literară*, 23 (June 2008): http://www.romlit.ro/index.pl/cronologia_exilului_literar_postbelic.

Simuț, Ion. "Comentarii critice: Cronologia exilului literar postbelic (II)," *România literară* 24 (2008): http://www.romlit.ro/index.pl/cronologia_exilului_literar_postbelic_ii?caut=cronologia %20exilului
Sinani, Shaban. *Hebrenjtë në Shqipëri: prania dhe shpëtimi: studim monografik* (Tirana: Naimi, 2009).
Siwik, Anna. *Polska Partia Socjalistyczna na emigracji w latach 1945–1956* (Kraków: Księgarnia Akademicka, 1998).
Siwik, Anna. *Polskie uchodźstwo polityczne. Socjaliści na emigracji w latach 1956–1990* (Kraków: Abrys, 2002).
Siwik, Anna. "Sprawa Bergu. Współpraca emigracyjnej Rady Politycznej z zachodnim wywiadem," *Studia Historyczne* 2 (2001): 267–288.
Sizonenko, Alexandr. *Russkie v Latinskoy Amerike* (Moscow: Avanglion, 2005).
Sharp, Tony. *Stalin's American Spy: Noel Field, Allen Dulles and the East European Show Trials* (London: Hurst, 2014).
Sheviakov, Alexey. "Tainy poslevoennoy repatriatsii," *Sociologicheskie issledovania* 8 (1993): 3–11.
Shindler, Colin. *Exit Visa: Détente, Human Rights and the Jewish Emigration Movement in the USSR* (London: Bachman and Turner, 1978).
Shkarenkov, Leonid. *Agonija beloy emigratsii* (Moscow: Mysl', 1986).
Skirius, Juozas. "Prezidento Antano Smetonos atvykimas į JAV 1941 metais ir išeivijos pozicija," *Lietuvos Istorijos Metraštis* 22 (2010): 77–91.
Škvorecký, Josef. "Bohemia of the Soul," *Daedalus* 119, no. 1 (Winter 1990): 111–139.
Slany, Krystyna. *Między przymusem a wyborem. Kontynentalne i zamorskie emigracje z krajów Europy Środkowo-Wschodniej (1939–1989)* (Kraków: Wydawnictwo Uniwerystetu Jagiellońskiego, 1995).
Smith, William Thomas. *Encyclopedia of the Central Intelligence Agency* (New York: Factson File, 2003).
Snyder, Alan. *Warriors of Disinformation: American Propaganda, Soviet Lies and the Winning of the Cold War* (New York: Arcade Publishing, 1995).
Snyder, Timothy. *Black Earth: The Holocaust as History and Warning* (London: Vintage, 2016).
Sofronova, Ekaterina. *Gde ty, moja Rodina?* (Moscow: Intellekt, 1999).
Solonari, Vladimir. *Purificarea națiunii: dislocări forțate de populație și epurări etnice în România lui Ion Antonescu, 1940–1944* (Iasi: Polirom, 2015).
Solzhenitsyn, Alexandr. *Publizistika* (Jaroslavl, Verhne-Voljskoe knijnoe izdatelstvo, 1996).
Sonila, Papathimiu. "The demographic and economic development of Albania during and after the decline of Communist regime (1945–2010)," *Treballs de la Societat Catalana de Geografia* 73 (2012): 101–118.
Spałek, Robert, ed. *Polska Partia Socjalistyczna. Dlaczego się nie udało? Szkice – polemiki – wspomnienia* (Warszawa: Instytut Pamięci Narodowej, 2010).
Spetko, Jozef. *Líšky kontra ježe: slovenská politická emigrácia 1948–1989* (Bratislava: Kalligram, 2002).
Spurný, Matěj. "Czech and German Memories of Forced Migration," *Hungarian Historical Review* 1, no. 3–4 (2012): 353–367.
Staikova, Evelina. "Emigration and Immigration: Bulgarian Dilemmas," *SEER Journal for Labor and Social Affairs in Eastern Europe* 16 (2013): 403–415.
Statelova, Elena, and Tankova, Vaska. *Prokudenite* (Plovdiv: Zhanet-45 Publishing House, 2002).
Stanek, Piotr. "Figurant "Tybr". Nieudany werbunek niedoszłego ministra" *Pamięć i Sprawiedliwość* no. 1 (2010): 117–138.
Stanek, Piotr. *Stefan Korboński (1901–1989): działalność polityczna i społeczna* (Warszawa: IPN, 2014).

Stańczyk, Henryk, and Zwoliński Stefan. *Wojsko Berlinga i Żymierskiego* (Warszawa: Rytm, 2015).
Statelova, Elena et al. *Drugata Bulgaria: Dokumenti za organizatsiite na balgarskata politicheska emigratsia 1944–1989* (Sofia: Anubis, 2000).
Stedman, Susan, and Stedman Jr. Murray. *Discontent at the Polls: A Study of Farmer and Labor Parties, 1827–1948* (New York: Columbia University Press, 1950).
Ştefănescu, Călin-Bogdan, and Pop, Mihai. *10 ani de umor negru românesc: jurnal de bancuri politice* (Bucharest: Metropol-Paideia, 1991).
Ştefănescu, Călin-Bogdan. *Umorul român in faza terminală a socialismului* (Bucharest: Paideia, 2014).
Steimanis, Josifs. *History of Latvian Jews* (New York: Columbia University Press, 2002).
Steiner, Johann, and Magheti, Doina. *Mormintele tac: relatări de la cea mai sângeroasă graniţa a Europei* (Iasi: Polirom, 2009).
Stephan, John J. *The Russian Fascists – Tragedy and Farce in Exile, 1933–1945* (New York: Harper and Row, 1978).
Stobiecki, Rafał. *Klio na wygnaniu: z dziejów polskiej historiografii na uchodźstwie w Wielkiej Brytanii po 1945 r.* (Poznań: Wydawnictwo Poznańskie, 2005).
Stobiecki, Rafał. *Klio za wielką wodą: polscy historycy w Stanach Zjednoczonych po 1945 roku* (Warszawa: Instytut Pamięci Narodowej, 2017).
Stobiecki, Rafał. Nowinowski Sławomir (eds.), *Władysław Pobóg-Malinowski and Wacław Jędrzejewicz, Listy 1945–1962* (Warszawa: Instytut Pamięci Narodowej, 2016).
Stöcker, Lars Fredrik. "Nylon Stockings and Samizdat: The 'White Ship' between Helsinki and Tallinn in the Light of Its Unintended Economic and Political Consequences," *Zeitschrift für Ostmitteleuropaforschung* 3 (2014): 374–398.
Stola, Dariusz. "Forced Migrations in Central European History," *International Migration Review* 26, no. 2 (1992): 324–341.
Stola, Dariusz. *Kraj bez wyjścia. Migracje z Polski 1949–1989* (Warszawa: Instytut Pamięci Narodowej, 2010).
Stolarik, Marian Mark. "The Slovak League of America and the Canadian League in the Struggle for the Self-determination of the Nation, 1907–1992," *Slovakia* 39, 72 and 73 (2007): 7–35.
Stolarik, Marian Mark. *Where is my Home? Slovak Immigration to North America (1870–2010)* (Bern: Peter Lang, 2012).
Stolojan, Sanda. *Au balcon de l'exil roumain à Paris avec Cioran, Eugène Ionesco, Mircea Eliade, Vintilă Horia* (Paris: l'Harmattan, 1999).
Stonor, Saunders Frances. *The Cultural Cold War: CIA and the World of Arts and Letters* (New York/London: The New Press, 2001).
Stravinskienė, Vitalija. *Pasaulio lietuvių bendruomenė 1949–2003* (Vilnius: Artlora, 2004).
Suchcitz, Andrzej, Maik, Ludwik, and Rojek, Wojciech, eds. *Wybór dokumentów do dziejów polskiego uchodźstwa niepodległościowego 1939–1990* (London: Polskie Towarzystwo Naukowe na Obczyźnie, 1997).
Suppan, Arnold. "Austrians, Czechs, and Sudeten Germans as a Community of Conflict in the Twentieth Century," Working Paper 06–1, *CAS Working Papers in Austrian Studies*, Center for Austrian Studies, University of Minnesota (October 2006): https://conservancy.umn.edu/handle/11299/90505.
Supruniuk, Mirosław A. *Przyjaciele wolności. Kongres Wolności Kultury i Polacy* (Warszawa: DiG, 2008).
Szczurowski, Maciej. "Sprawa obywatelstwa polskiego generałów i oficerów, którzy wstąpili do Polskiego Korpusu Przysposobienia i Rozmieszczenia w świetle dokumentów Urzędu Rady Ministrów w Warszawie," *Teki Historyczne* 23 (2004).
Szkuta, Aleksander, ed. *Kierownictwo obozu niepodległościowego na obczyźnie 1945–1990* (London: Polskie Towarzystwo Naukowe na Obczyźnie, 1996).

Szmeja, Maria, ed. *Etniczność – o przemianach społeczeństw narodowych* (Kraków: Nomos, Kraków, 2008).
Taagepera, Rein. "Baltic Quest for a Hungarian Path, 1965," *Journal of Baltic Studies* 44 (2013): 19–47.
Tamman, Tiina. *The Last Ambassador: August Torma, Soldier, Diplomat, Spy* (Amsterdam: Rodopi, 2011).
Tammaru, Tiit, Kumer-Haukanõmm, Kaja, and Anniste, Kristi. "The Formation and Development of the Estonian Diaspora," *Journal of Ethnic and Migration Studies* 18 (2010): 1157–1174.
Tănase, Virgil. *Portrait d'un homme à la faux dans un paysage marin* (Paris: Flammarion, 1976).
Târău, Virgil, ed. *Învățând istoria prin experiențele trecutului: Cetățenii obișnuiți supravegheați de Securitate în anii 70–80* (Bucharest: CNSAS, 2009).
Tarifa, Fatos. "Albania's road from Communism: political and social change, 1990–1993," *Development and Change* 26, vol. 1 (1995): 133–162.
Tarka, Krzysztof. *Emigracyjna dyplomacja* (Warszawa: Rytm, 2003).
Tarka, Krzyszof. *Mackiewicz i inni. Wywiad PRL wobec emigrantów* (Łomianki: LTW, 2007).
Tarka, Krzysztof. *Emigranci na celowniku. Władze Polski Ludowej wobec wychodźstwa* (Łomianki: LTW, 2012).
Tarka, Krzysztof. *Jest tylko jedna Polska. Emigranci w służbie PRL* (Łomianki: LTW, 2014).
Tase, Peter. "Italy and Albania: The political and economic alliance and the Italian invasion of 1939," Academicus International Scientific Journal 6 (2012), http://www.academicus.edu.al/nr6/Academicus-MMXII-6-062-070.pdf
Tchoukarine, Igor. "Yugoslavia's Open-Door Policy and Global Tourism in the 1950s and 1960s." *East European Politics & Societies and Cultures* 29, no.1 (2015): 168–188.
Terlecki, Ryszard, ed. *Aparat bezpieczeństwa wobec emigracji politycznej i Polonii* (Warszawa: Instytut Pamięci Narodowej 2005).
Terlecki, Tymon, ed. *Literatura polska na obczyźnie 1940–1960* (London: B. Świderski, 1964–1965).
Tézé-Delafon, Blandine, and Tănase, Virgil. *Ma Roumanie: Entretiens avec Blandine Tézé-Delafon* (Paris: Ramsay, 1990).
Ther, Philipp. "The Integration of Expellees in Germany and Poland after World War II: A Historical Reassessment," *Slavic Review* 55 no. 4 (1996): 779–805.
Timofejev, Aleksej. *Savez Sovjetskikh patriota – antifashistichka organizatsija russikh emigranata u Srbiji 1941–1945* (Belgrade: Tokovi istorije, 2012).
Tiu, Ilarion. "Migrația ilegală a românilor în anul 1989. Aspecte socio-demografice," *Sfera politicii* 166 (2011): 116–122.
Toal, Gerard, and Dahlman, Carl. *Bosnia Remade: Ethnic Cleansing and its Reversal* (New York: Oxford University Press, 2011).
Tokes, Rudolf, ed. *Dissent in the USSR: Politics, Ideology and People* (Baltimore/London: Johns Hopkins University Press, 1975).
Tokić, Mate Nikola. "Landscapes of Conflict: Unity and Disunity in Post-Second World War Croatian Émigré Separatism," *European Review of History: Revue europeenne d'histoire* 16, no. 5 (2009): 739–53.
Tokić. "The End of 'Historical-Ideological Bedazzlement'," *Social Science History* 36, no. 3 (2012): 442–445.
Tomek, Prokop. *Československé bezpečnostní složky proti Rádiu Svobodná Evropa "Objekt ALFA"* (Prague: Úřad dokumentace a vyšetřování zločinů komunismu, 2006).
Tomek, Prokop. *Nejlepší Propaganda je Pravda: Pavel Pecháček v Československém Rozhlase, v Hlasu Ameriky a ve Svobodné Evropě* (Prague: Nakladatelství Lidové noviny, 2014).
Tóth, Heléna. *An Exiled Generation: German and Hungarian Refugees of Revolution, 1848–1871* (Cambridge: Cambridge University Press, 2014).

Trahair, Richard, C. *Encyclopedia of Cold War Espionage, Spies, and Secret Operations* (New York: Enigma Books, 2012).
Trahair, Richard C. S., and Robert, Miller. *Encyclopedia of Cold War Espionage, Spies and Secret Operations* (New York: Enigma Books, 2013).
Traykov, Veselin. *Istoria na balgarskata emigratsia v Severna Amerika* (Sofia: Universitetsko izdatelstvo "Sv. Kliment Ohridski," 1993).
Tromly, Benjamin. "The Making of a Myth: The National Labor Alliance, Russian Émigrés, and Cold War Intelligence Activities," *Journal of Cold War Studies* 18 (2016): 80–111.
Troncota, Tiberiu. *România comunistă. Propagandă și cenzură* (Bucharest; Tritonic, 2006).
Trubinsky, Jozef C. *Slovenský exil za suverenitu a štátnosť slovenského národa* (Martin: Matica slovenská, 2003).
Tucholski, Jędrzej. *Cichociemni. Historia legendarnych spadochroniarzy* (Wrocław: Wydawnictwo Dolnośląskie, 2010).
Turek, Wojciech. *Arka Przymierza. Wojciech Wasiutyński 1910–1994. Biografia polityczna* (Kraków: Arkana, 2008).
Turkowski, Romuald. *Parlamentaryzm polski na uchodźstwie 1945–1972 w okresie rozbicia emigracji politycznej w Londonie* (Warszawa: Wydawnictwo Sejmowe, 2001).
Turkowski, Romuald. *Parlamentaryzm polski na uchodźstwie 1972–1991 po zjednoczeniu emigracji politycznej w Londynie* (Warszawa: Wydawnictwo Sejmowe, 2002).
Turkowski, Romulad, ed. *Polski ruch ludowy na emigracji. Dokumenty i materiały*, part 1: *1944–1954*, part 2: *1954–1968*, part 3: *1968–1991* (Kielce-Pińczów: Wyższa Szkoła Umiejętności Zawodowych, 2005–2007).
Tzavella, Hristofor, ed. *Dnevnik na kosturskiya voyvoda Lazar Kiselinchev* (Sofia: Makedonia Pres, 2003).
Tzvetkov, Plamen S. *A History of the Balkans: A Regional Overview from a Bulgarian Perspective*, vol. 2 (New York: Edwin Mellen Press, 1993).
Ugrimov, Aleksandr. *Iz Moskvy v Moskvu cherez Parizh i Vorkutu* (Moscow: RA, 2000).
Ungváry, Krisztián. *The Siege of Budapest: 100 Days in World War II* (New Haven: Yale University Press, 2002).
Urzyńska, Dorota. *Polski ruch socjalistyczny na obczyźnie w latach 1939–1945* (Poznań: Instytut Historii UAM, 2000).
Vachkov, Daniel. "Makedonskite bezhantsi i tyahnoto nastanyavane v Bulgaria – finansovo-ikonomicheski aspekti na problema (1878 – 30-te godini na XX v.)," *Makedonski pregled* 1 (2016): 7–17.
Vadura, Katherine. "Exile, Return and Restitution in the Czech Republic," *Portal* (January 2005): https://epress.lib.uts.edu.au/journals/index.php/portal/article/view/73.
Valmas, Anne. *Eestlaste kirjastustegevus välismaal 1944–2000 I* (Tallinn: Tallinna pedagoogikaülikooli kirjastus, 2003).
Várdy, Steven Béla, and Várdy, Agnes Huszár. *Stalin's Gulag: The Hungarian Experience* (Naples: Universita degli Studi di Napoli L'Orientale, 2007).
Varinský, Vladimír. *Jozef Vicen a Biela légia* (Banská Bystrica: Univerzita Mateja Bela, 2003).
Vasileva, Boyka. *Balgarskata politicheska emigratsia sled Vtorata svetovna voyna* (Sofia: Universitetsko izdatelstvo "Sv. Kliment Ohridski," 1999).
Vasileva, Boyka. "Balgarskata politicheska emigratsia sled 9 septemvri 1944 g." *Izvestia na Balgarskoto istorichesko druzhestvo* 39 (1987), 257–288.
Vedder, Richard K., Gallaway, Lowell E., and Chapin, Gene L. "The Determinants of Internal Migration in West Germany," *Weltwirtschaftliches Archiv* 106, no. 2 (1967): 309–317.
Veigners, Ilgvars. *Latvieši Rietumzemē – un vēl dažās zemēs* (Riga: Drukātava, 2009).
Vermeulen, Hans, Baldwin-Edwards, Martin, and van Boeschoten, Riki. *Migration in the Southern Balkans* (New York: Springer International Publishing, 2015).

Vernant, Jacques. *The Refugee in the Post-War World* (Edinburgh: T. & A. Constable, 1953).
Vertinsky, Alexander. *Dorogoy dlinnoju* (Moscow: Pravda, 1991).
Várdy, Steven Béla. *The Hungarian Americans* (Boston: Twayne Publishing, 1985).
Vidra, Zsuzsanna, ed. *Roma Migration to and from Canada: The Czech, Hungarian and Slovak Case* (Budapest: Central European University Press, 2013).
Vladimirov, Iulia. *Monica Lovinescu în documentele Securității. 1949–1989* (Bucharest: Humanitas, 2012).
Vullnetari, Julie. *Albania on the Move: Links Between Internal and International Migration* (Amsterdam: Amsterdam University Press, 2012).
Vullnetari, Julie. "Albanian migration and development: state of the art review," IMISCO Working Paper (September 2007): 1–94.
Vultur, Smaranda. "Pentru un dicționar al lumii comuniste," *Colloquium politicum* 2 (July–December 2010): 104.
Vychytil-Baudoux, Florence. "Le Comité éléctoral des Polonais naturalisés (1953–1976). Une expérience *polonienne* en France," *Relations internationales* no. 141 (2010): 65–81.
Wagner, Gerd, ed. "An der Schwelle zur Sozialen Marktwirtschaft: Ergebnisse aus der Basiserhebung des Sozio-ökonomischen Panels in der DDR im Juni 1990." Beiträge Aus Der Arbeitsmarkt- und Berufs Forschung 143 (1991): https://www.iab.de/179/section.aspx/Publikation/i910516d14
Walaszek, Adam, ed. *Polska diaspora* (Kraków: Wydawnictwo Literackie, 2001).
Waldinger, Robert. *The Cross-Border Connection: Immigrants, Emigrants, and Their Homelands* (Cambridge and London: Harvard University Press, 2015).
Wallace, Claire, and Palyanitsya, Andrii. "East-West Migration and the Czech Republic," *Journal of Public Policy*, 15, no. 1 (Jan–Apr 1995): 89–109.
Wallace, Claire and Stola, Dariusz, ed. *Patterns of Migration in Central Europe* (New York: Palgrave, 2001).
Warmińska, Katarzyna. "Polityka a tożsamość. Kaszebsko Jednota," *Studia Migracyjne-Przegląd Polonijny* 1 (2013): 189–206.
Wejs-Milewska, Violetta. *Radio Wolna Europa na emigracyjnych szlakach pisarzy: Gustaw Herling-Grudziński, Tadeusz Nowakowski, Roman Palester, Czesław Straszewicz, Tymon Terlecki* (Kraków: Wydawnictwo Arcana, 2007).
Wejs-Milewska, Violetta, Rogalewska Ewa, eds. *Powrześniowa emigracja niepodległościowa na mapie kultury nie tylko polskiej: Paryż, London, Monachium, Nowy Jork* (Białystok: Trans Humana, 2009); vol. 2: Białystok: Instytut Pamięci Narodowej/Uniwersytet w Białymstoku, 2016).
Wertsman, Vladimir, ed. *The Ukrainians in America 1608–1975* (New York City: Oceana Publications, 1976).
Winterhagen, Jenny. "Die Pioniere von Imotski. Die Verwendung von remittances am Beispiel des ehemaligen Jugoslawien," *Südosteuropa Jahrbuch* 38 (2011): 61–92.
Wittlichová, Lucie, ed. *Vzkazy domů/Messages Home: Stories of Czechs who went abroad (Emigration and Exile 1848–1989)*, (Prague: Labyrint, 2012).
Wnuk, Rafał. 'Dwie prowokacje – Piąta Komenda Zrzeszenia "WiN" i Berg,' *Zeszyty Historyczne* no. 141 (2002): 71–112.
Wojdon, Joanna. *White and Red Umbrella: The Polish American Congress in the Cold War Era, 1944–1988* (Saint Helena, CA: Helena History Press, 2015).
Wölben, Jan Philipp. "Die Entstehung des "Häftlingsfreikaufs" aus der DDR, 1962 – 1964," *Deutschland Archiv* 41 (June 2008): 856–867.
Wolowyna, Oleh. "Recent Migration from Ukraine to the United States: Demographic and Socioeconomic Characteristic," *The Ukrainian Quarterly* 3 (2005): 253–269.

Wolowyna, Oleh, ed. *Ethnicity and National Identity: Demographic and Socioeconomic Characteristics of Persons with Ukrainian Mother Tongue in the US* (Cambridge: Harvard University Press, 1986).

Woodward, Susan. *Socialist Unemployment: The Political Economy of Yugoslavia 1945–1990* (Princeton: Princeton University Press, 1995).

Wróbel, Janusz. *Na rozdrożu historii. Repatriacje obywateli polskich z Zachodu w latach 1945–1949* (Łódź: Instytut Pamięci Narodowej, 2009).

Wróbel, Elżbieta, and Wróbel, Janusz. *Rozproszeni po świecie: Obozy i osiedla uchodźców polskich ze Związku Sowieckiego, 1942–1950* (Chicago: Panorama, 1992).

Wyman, Mark. *DP: Europe's Displaced Persons, 1945–1951* (Ithaca, NY: Cornell University Press, 1998).

Wynar, Lubomyr, and Buttler Lois. *Guide to Ethnic Museums, Libraries and Archives in the United States* (Kent, Ohio: School of Library Science Kent State University, 1978).

Wynar, Lubomyr. "Ukrainian Scholarship in exile: The DP Period, 1945–1952," *Ethnic Forum* 8, no. 1 (1988): 40–72.

Wynar, Lubomyr. "Ethnic Press. The Ukrainian Press in the United States: Past and Present Development," *Ethnic Forum* 1–2 (1985).

Yekelchyk, Serhy. *Ukraina. Narodziny nowoczesnego narodu* (Kraków: Wydawnictwo Uniwersytetu Jagiellońskiego, 2009).

Yonchev, Dimitar. *Bulgaria i Belomorieto (oktomvri 1940 – 9 septemvri 1944 g.): Voennopoliticheski aspekti* (Sofia: Dirum, 1993).

Zabłocki, Janusz. *Chrześcijańska demokracja w kraju i na emigracji 1947–1970* (Lublin, Ośrodek studiów polonijnych i społecznych PZKS w Lublinie, 1999).

Zaķe, Ieva. "'The Secret Nazi Network' and Post-World War II Latvian Émigrés in the United States," *Journal of Baltic Studies* 41 (2010): 91–117.

Zaķe, Ieva. *American Latvians: Politics of a Refugee Community* (Piscataway, NJ: Transaction, 2010).

Zaķe, Ieva, ed. *Anti-Communist Minorities in the US. Political Activism of Ethnic Refugees*, (New York: Palgrave Macmillan, 2009).

Zaķe, Ieva. *Nineteenth-Century Nationalism and Twentieth-Century Anti-Democratic Ideals: The Case of Latvia, 1840s to 1980s* (Lewinston: Edwin Mellen Press, 2008).

Zalkans, Lilita. *Back to the Motherland: Repatriation and Latvian Émigrés 1955–1958* (Stockholm: Stockholm University, 2014).

Zaslavsky, Victor, and Brym, Robert. *Soviet Jewish Emigration and Soviet Nationality Policy* (New York: St. Martin's Press, 1983).

Zatsepina, Olga, and Ruchkin Alexander. *Russkiye v SShA* (New York: Russian-American Cultural Center "Nasledie," 2011).

Zawodny, Janusz. *Death in the forest: the story of the Katyn Forest Massacre* (University of Notre Dame Press, 1962).

Zeman, Zbyněk. *The Masaryks: The Making of Czechoslovakia* (New York: Harper and Row, 1976).

Zemskov, Viktor. "K voprosu o repatriatsii sovetskih grajdan. 1944–1951," *Istoria SSSR* 4 (1990): 26–41.

Zemskov, Viktor. "Repatriatsia sovetskih grajdan i ih dalneishaja sudba," *Socis* 5 (1995): 109–112.

Zemskov, Viktor. "Repatriatsia i Vtoraja volna emigratsii," *Rodina* 6–7 (1991): 111.

Zgradnik, Maruša. "Optiranje za italijansko državljanstvo s priključenega ozemlja," *Prispevki za novejšto zgodovino* 36, no. 1–2 (1996): 95–107.

Zhelyazkova, Antonia, ed. *Albania and the Albanian identities* (Sofia: International Center for Minority Studies and Intercultural Relations, 2000).

Zielyk, Ihor V. "Ethnicity and Irredentism in Diaspora. Profile of an Ukrainian-American Community" (PhD diss., Columbia University, 1997).

Zięba, Andrzej A. *Ukraińcy w Kanadzie wobec Polaków i Polski (1918–1939)* (Kraków: Księgarnia Akademicka, 1998).

Zięba, Andrzej A. "Ukraińcy w Stanach Zjednoczonych. Rewizja przeszłości," *Przegląd Polonijny* 2 (1994): 117–131.

Ziętara, Paweł. *Emigracja wobec Października. Postawy polskich środowisk emigracyjnych wobec liberalizacji w PRL w latach 1955–1957* (Warszawa: LTW, 2001).

Ziętara, Paweł. "Konrad Sieniewicz w dokumentach bezpieki' *Pamięć i Sprawiedliwość* no. 1 (2010): 89–110.

Zimmerman, William. *Open Borders, Nonalignment, and the Political Evolution of Yugoslavia* (Princeton: Princeton University Press, 1987).

Żaryn, Jan. *"Taniec na linie, nad przepaścią": Organizacja Polska na wychodźstwie i jej łączność z krajem w latach 1945–1955* (Warszawa: IPN, 2011).

Żurawski, Radosław Paweł, ed. *Rządy bez ziemi. Struktury władzy na uchodźstwie* (Warszawa: Wydawnictwo DiG, 2014).

Authors' Biographical Notes

Alexey Antoshin
Ph.D., historian at the Ural Federal University (Russia, Ekaterinburg). Research areas: history of the Russian diaspora, Russian political history in the twentieth century, Russia and Africa. Internships at Kennan Institute (Washington, DC, USA), Center of East European Studies (Bremen University, Germany), Belgrade University (Serbia), International Institute of Social History (Amsterdam, Netherlands), Bibliotheque de Documentation Internationale Contemporaine (Nanterre, France), Tehran University (Iran). Main publications (in Russian): *Rossiiskie emigranty v uslovijah holodnoy voyny* [*Russian émigrés in conditions of Cold War*] (Ekaterinburg; Ural University Publishing, 2008); Ot Russkogo Monmartra k Braiton Bich: Evolutsija Russkogo mira v 1950–1980-e gg. [*From Russian Montmartre to Brighton Beach: Evolution of the Russian diaspora in 1950s – 1980s*] (Moscow: AIRO-XXI, 2014).

Michael R. Cude
Ph.D., historian, Schreiner University in Kerrville (USA, Texas). Research areas: Slovak immigration and its impact on Slovak national identity and transatlantic politics and diplomacy in the twentieth century, immigration. Publications: "Wilsonian National Self-determination and the Slovak Question during the Founding of Czechoslovakia, 1918–1921," *Diplomatic History* 40, no. 1 (2016): 155–180; "The Imagined Exiles: Slovak-Americans and the Slovak Question during the First Czechoslovak Republic," in "From Exsilium to Exile: Coercion in Migration," *Studia Historica Gedanensia* 5, ed. Anna Mazurkiewicz (Gdańsk: University of Gdańsk History Institute, 2014), 287–305.

Detelina Dineva
Ph.D., historian, Institute for Historical Studies, Bulgarian Academy of Sciences (Sofia, Bulgaria). Research areas: post-World War II political history of East-Central Europe; history of the idea of Europe; lobbies and lobbying in the European Union and in Washington, D.C. Recent publications: "Bulgaria," in *Lobbying in Europe: Public Affairs and the Lobbying Industry in 28 EU Countries*, ed. Alberto Bitonti and Phil Harris (London: Palgrave Macmillan, 2017), 69–78; "The Disillusionment with the Cost of Transition," *Bulgarian Historical Review*, 3–4 (2015): 41–47; "The Initial Stages of Bulgaria's Transition to Democracy and US Policy," in *Rethinking the Past – Looking to the Future*, ed. Anissava Miltenova, Cynthia Vakareliyska and Christine Holden (Sofia: Boyan Penev Publishing Center, 2015), 53–70; "The 'Master of Several Trades' and the Historian: The Stories of Two Exiled Bulgarian Intellectuals during the Cold War Years," *Bulgarian Historical Review*, 3–4 (2014): 220–230.

Agata Beata Domachowska

Ph.D., political scientist and philologist; assistant professor at the Faculty of Languages Nicolaus Copernicus University (Toruń, Poland). Recipient of numerous scholarships and grants including a grant from the Kosciuszko Foundation in New York, the 2015 ASEEES Davis Travel Grant from the Polish Ministry of Education, the Theodor Koerner Grant from the Ministry of Education and Culture in Croatia. Research areas: migration from South East Europe, ethnicity, national/ethnic identity, politics of memory, and the history, politics and culture of post-Yugoslav states. Selected publications: *Od reminiscencji do realizacji wielkiej idei? Działalność polityczna Albańczyków na Bałkanach na przełomie XX i XXI wieku* (Toruń: Wydawnictwo Naukowe Uniwersytetu Mikołaja Kopernika, 2017); *Powojenne rozliczenie zbrodni ustaszy popełnionych w czasie II wojny światowej*, in "Wina i kara: społeczeństwa wobec rozliczeń zbrodni popełnionych przez reżimy totalitarne w latach 1939–1956: studia i materiały," ed. Patryk Pleskot (Warszawa: IPN, 2015); "An Introduction to the Analysis of Serbian-Albanian Relations (2001–2016)," in *Republika Serbii: aspekty polityki wewnętrznej i międzynarodowej*, ed. Anna Jagiełło-Szostak (Wrocław: ATUT, 2016); "Albania and Albanian Émigrés in the United States before World War II," in *East Central Europe in Exile, vol.1: Transatlantic Migrations*, ed. Anna Mazurkiewicz (Newcastle upon Tyne: Cambridge Scholars Publishing, 2013).

Anna Fiń

Ph.D., sociologist, Pedagogical University in Kraków (Poland). Research areas: sociology of migration, methods of social research, sociology of culture, contemporary migrations of Poles to the United States (with special emphasis on Polonia in New York City), Ukrainian immigration in the United States and on contemporary migration of Europeans to the United States. Recent Publications: "Ethnic Mobilization of Immigrants: Case Studies of Ukrainian Political Emigration in the United States," in *The United States Immigration Policy and Immigrants; Dorota Praszałowicz*, ed. Agnieszka Małek (Frankfurt am Main: Peter Lang, 2016), 107–125; "*The Newest Polish New Yorkers: Social and Demographic Profile*" Migration Studies-Polish Diaspora Review/Studia Migracyjne – Przegląd Polonijny 4 (2015): 193–214; With Łucja Kapralska, editor of: *Sieć pamięci. Cyfrowe postaci pamięci zbiorowej* (Kraków, Nomos, 2015).

Pauli Heikkilä

Ph.D., historian, Research Fellow at the University of Helsinki (Finland). Research areas: Estonian political diaspora during the Cold War, Estonian discussions on the European unification. Publications: *Estonians for Europe: National Activism for European Integration, 1922–1991* (Bruxelles-New York: P.I.E. Peter Lang, 2014) and *Tasavalta vai tasapaino? Suomalaiset keskustelut Euroopan yhdentymissuunnitelmista 1923–1944* [Republic or Equilibrium? Finnish Discussions on the Plans for European Unification, 1923–1944] (Helsinki: SKS, 2017). Heikkilä is currently writing a book on the Estonian participation in the Assembly of Captive European Nations.

Bethany Hicks
Ph.D., historian, Ouachita Baptist University in Arkadelphia (USA, Arkansas). Research areas: German Cold War and post-Cold War migration, gender dynamics of the East-West migration before and after the German revolution of 1989. Between 2008 and 2009 Fulbright IIE scholar in residence at the Institute for Migration and Intercultural Studies (University of Osnabrück). Her current research interests include state ransoming schemes involving political prisoners and CIA involvement in family reunification negotiations in divided Germany.

Brigitte Le Normand
Ph.D., historian, University of British Columbia Okanagan (Canada). Research areas: urban history, history of state-socialism, and the related topics of identity, ethnicity, and nationalism. Recent publications: "The Gastarbajters as a Transnational Yugoslav Working Class," in *Bringing Class Back In. The Dynamics of Social Change in (Post) Yugoslavia*, ed. Paul Stubbs, Igor Duda, and Rory Archer (Aldershot: Ashgate, 2016); "The Contested Place of the Detached Home in Yugoslavia's Socialist Cities," in *The Cultural Life of Capitalism in Yugoslavia: (Post) Socialism and its Other*, ed. Dijana Jelača, Maša Kolanović and Danijela Lugarić (London: Palgrave Macmillan, 2017); *Designing Tito's Capital: Urban Planners, Modernism and Socialism* (Pittsburgh: University of Pittsburgh Press, 2014.) She is currently leading a collaborative project examining the impact of the relocation of the Italo-Yugoslav border after the Second World War on the city of Rijeka.

Katalin Kádár Lynn
Ph.D., historian, based in Budapest and California (Hungary and USA). She is the founder and Editor in Chief of Helena History Press, LLC a publishing house specializing in scholarship about and from Central and East Europe in English. She is also an external member of the Hungarian Academy of Sciences. Research areas: World War II and the Cold War with an emphasis on Central and East European émigré political activities and organizations. Editor and contributor to *The Inauguration of Organized Political Warfare: Cold War Organizations sponsored by the National Committee for a Free Europe/Free Europe Committee* (St. Helena, CA: Helena History Press, 2013). She is the biographer of the Hungarian political figure Tibor Eckhardt titled *Tibor Eckhardt: His American Years 1941–1972* published in English and Hungarian (Boulder, CO: East European Monographs, L'Harmattan Press). She edited and published Eckhardt's memoir, *Tibor Eckhardt: In His Own Words* (Boulder, CO: East European Monographs, 2005).

Sławomir Łukasiewicz
Hab. Ph.D., historian, political scientist and Europeanist, university professor, chair of the Department of Political Science and director of the Institute of European Studies at John Paul II Catholic University of Lublin (Poland). Staff historian at the Institute of National Remembrance (Lublin branch). Research areas: European integra-

tion with a special emphasis on Polish post-1939 émigré, East Central European political parties and groups in exile in comparative perspective, history of historiography and Soviet studies as well as history of Polish Communist civilian intelligence. Recent publications: *Third Europe: Polish Federalist Thought in the United States 1940–1970s* (Budapest: Helena History Press, 2016); *Partia w warunkach emigracji. Dylematy Polskiego Ruchu Wolnościowego "Niepodległość i Demokracja" 1945–1994* (Lublin/Warszawa: Instytut Pamięci Narodowej Oddział w Lublinie, Instytut Studiów Politycznych PAN, 2014). Co-editor (with Piotr H. Kosicki) of *Christian Democracy across the Iron Curtain – Europe Redefined* (Cham, Switzerland: Palgrave-Macmillan 2018).

Anna Mazurkiewicz
Ph. D., historian the University of Gdańsk (Poland). Research areas: Cold War, public diplomacy, US-Polish relations; Polish diaspora in the USA; political activity of refugees from East Central Europe in the United States after World War II. Author of books on American diplomatic and press responses to elections in Poland in 1947 and 1989 and on political exiles from East Central Europe in American Cold War Politics,1948 to 1954 (published in Polish). For overview see: "Join, or Die"—The Road to Cooperation among East European Exiled Political Leaders in the United States, 1949–1954," *Polish American Studies* 69, no. 2 (2012): 5–43; "American Attitudes on Two Attempts to Establish Democracy in Poland, 1947 and 1989," *Polish American Studies* 62, no. 1 (2005): 67–96. Editor of a two-volume publication: *East Central Europe in Exile*, vol. 1: *Transatlantic Migrations* and vol. 2: *Transatlantic Identities* (Newcastle upon Tyne: Cambridge Scholars Publishing, 2013); *Od exsilli do exile. Migracje przymusowe w perspektywie historycznej*, "Studia Historica Gedanensia," vol. 5 (Gdańsk: University of Gdańsk Press, 2014).

Ellen L. Paul
Ph. D., historian at Fort Lewis College (USA, Colorado). Research areas: Modern East Central Europe. Publications: "Safety & Nutrition in the Socialist Outdoors: Improving Conditions for Communist-era Youth Hops Brigades in Czechoslovakia in the 1960s," *Kosmas: Czechoslovak and Central European Journal* 23, no. 2 (Spring 2010): 72–78; "Perception vs. Reality: Slovak Views of the Hungarian Minority in Slovakia," *Nationalities Papers* 31, no. 4 (December 2003): 484–493.

Beatrice Scutaru
Ph. D., historian, Assistant Professor in European History at Dublin City University (Ireland). She was a Marie Curie Intra-European Fellow at the University of Padua (Italy) between 2015 and 2017. Research interests: migration and childhood/youth, identities and belonging, migrant life narratives. She has conducted research on (1) Romanian migration to Western Europe since 1945, (2) child mobility and protection and (3) East-West relations and exchanges. She has published extensively on the French and Romanian contexts analysing such issues as political exile, migrants' ex-

periences and activism and children at risk. Publications: "Romanian Roma on the move: international belonging *versus* European problem" (*Journal of European Integration History*, 2016); "" Se trouver une place " en exil. Dumitru Tepeneag et la création de nouveaux savoirs sur la Roumanie Communiste," in *Exils d'Europe Médiane en France dans la Seconde moitié du XX^{e}siècle*, ed. Antoine Marès (Paris: Institut d'Études Slaves, 2017), 109–122; "International adoption of Romanian children and Romania's admission to the European Union (1990–2007)," *Eastern Journal of European Studies* 1 (2010): 135–151.

Index

Abraham, Richard 330
Abram, Marco 377
Abramovich, Rafail 357, 365
Academy of the Socialist Republic of Romania 259
Achim, Viorel 246
Ackermann, Volker 146, 166 f.
Adamczyk, Arkadiusz 219 f.
Adamkus, Valdas 64
adaptation (of migrants) 6, 165, 214, 305 f.
Adenauer, Konrad 117 f., 124, 161
Aegean Macedonia 69, 78
Aegean Thrace 73–75
Africa 19, 196, 203, 213, 218, 322, 426
Agency for Bulgarians Abroad 97
Agrarian League (Lidhja Agrare) 29
agreement 44, 109 157, 205, 269, 317, 356
– bilateral, on migration 9 f., 10, 19, 37, 70, 73, 81–83, 205, 207, 213, 237, 254, 258 f., 259, 264, 291, 335, 375, 378, 381, 383, 393
– Craiova 71
– International agreements 3, 75, 140 f., 204 f., 294
– Mollov-Kafandaris 71–72
– Mukje 13
– Munich 118
– Prespa 89
– Sikorski-Mayski 196, 200, 219
Agushi, Ali 15
Ahonen, Pertti 117, 119, 134 f.
airplane hijacking 210
Akerlof, George 163
Aktion Link 206
Alaska House 105
Albania 2 f., 8–44, 81, 228, 389, 427
– Republic of Albania 9, 44
– Nikaj-Mërtur (region) 39
Albanian Agrarian Party (Lidhja Kombëtare e Fshatarëve) 28
Albanian-American National Organization (Organizatën Kombëtare Shqiptaro Amerikane) 33
Albanian government in exile (Qeveria e Përbashkët Anti-komuniste në Emigracion, QPAE) 26 f., 32, 34
Albanian Independent Democratic Group 32
Albanian Legation 9
Albanian Ministry of Internal Affairs 20

Albanian Ministry of People's Defense 20
Albanians 9–16, 18, 20–28, 30, 33–38, 40–43, 310, 389
Albu, Mihaela 278
Aldanov, Mark 338, 348, 350, 357
Alekseev, Daniil 366
Alexander, June Granatir 327
Alexeeva, Ludmila 346
Ali, Muḥammad 10
Ali bey Këlcyra (Ali bey Klissura) 15, 26, 33
Alia, Ramiz 39
Aliyah 205
Alizoti, Fejzi 16
All-Bulgarian Union for National Salvation (Obshtobalgarski sayuz za natsionalno spasenie) 88
Alldeutscher Verband 136
Allied Control Commission 75, 173, 175
Allied Military Government 372
Altankov, Nikolay 99
Altona 15
Altötting 185
Amalrik, Andrey 360, 363
American-Bulgarian League (Amerikano-balgarska liga) 88
American Committee for the Liberation from Bolshevism 350, 352, 355
American Conference for the Liberation of the Non-Russian Nations of the USSR 312
American Friends of the Anti-Bolshevik Bloc of Nations 94
American Fund for Czechoslovak Refugees (AFCR) 106, 134
American Hungarian Federation 187
American Hungarian Federation Executive Committee 188
American Hungarian Foundation Library and Archive 192
American Hungarian Library and Historical Society 192
American Jewish Joint Distribution Committee 181
American Latvian Association (Amerikas latviešu apvienība) 55, 61, 65
American Lithuanian Cultural Archives (Amerikos Lietuvių Kultūros Archyvas) 65
American Russian Mutual Aid Society (ARMAS) 327

American Slav Committee 88
American Socialist Party 357
Americans for Congressional Action to Free the Baltic States 62
Americans from East Central Europe Coordination Committee 312
amnesty 47, 180, 378–379
Amnesty International 261, 275
Amsterdam 23, 44, 52, 101, 241, 255, 365, 426
ancestry 76, 143, 182, 206f., 217
Anders, Władysław 196, 200, 221, 231
Andoni, Vasil 13, 29f.
Andrew, Christopher 232, 317, 373
Andreyev, Catherine 331
Aneks 225
Angelov, Georgi 96
Anghel, Florin 213
Anghel, Remus Gabriel 254, 282
Anghelescu, Dan 278
Anglo-Czechoslovak Refugee Welfare Organization 106
Aničas, Jonas 54, 66
Annenkov, Jury 363
Anniste, Kristi 45, 55, 66
Anti-Bolshevik Bloc of Nations (ABN) 90, 311f., 314
Anti-Communist League of Asian Peoples 356
Anti-Fascist Congress for National Liberation 14
Anti-Fascist National Committee for National Liberation 14
anti-Semitism 169, 173, 205f., 343f.
Anti Yalta League 271
Antoshin, Alexey 326, 340, 426
Anusauskas, Arvydas 46, 58
Apennine Peninsula 216
Appelyard, Reginald 260
Applebaum, Anne 3, 170, 181f.
Apulia 15, 40, 42
Çarçani, Daut 16
Archer, Rory 383, 428
Arciszewski, Tomasz 219–221
Argentina 52, 174, 184, 202, 213, 217, 244, 277, 289f., 299f., 322, 338f., 356
Armenia 71, 82, 311f., 321, 352
Armenian Red Cross 71
Armenian Relief Society 71
Arrow Cross (Hungarian fascist party) 171, 185
Artuković, Andrija 371

Ash, Mitchell 150
Ashkenazi, Vladimir 341
assault 72, 147
Assembly of Captive European Nations 5, 35, 37, 55, 90, 110, 121, 188, 192, 228, 312, 427
assimilation policy 292
assistance 10, 19, 40, 46, 229, 386
– foreign, to refugees 4, 6–8, 48f., 139, 154, 202, 240, 281, 335f., 375
Association for Technical Internships in France (ASTEF) 259
Association for the Advancement of Baltic Studies 61
Association for the Protection of Sudeten German Interests (AG) 77, 118
Association of Albanian Political Ex-prisoners (Asociacioni i ish të Burgosurve Politikë të Shqipërisë) 22
Association of Bulgarian Refugees 85
Association of Estonians in the UK (Inglismaa Eestlaste Ühing) 56
Association of Friends of the Ukrainian Culture 309
Association of Polish War Refugees (Zjednoczenie Polskiego Uchodźstwa Wojennego) 222
Association of Russian National Organizations 358
Association of the Former Political Prisoners in Romania 272, 284
Association of the Friends of the Ukrainian Liberation Struggle 307
Associations of Ukrainian Musicians and Theatrical Studio 302
asylum 40, 53, 80, 111, 153, 173, 210, 248, 256, 259, 265, 272, 281f., 376f., 389f., 393
– applications for asylum 256
– asylum seekers 153, 155, 158, 259f., 376, 390
– political asylum 21, 40f., 215, 259f., 376f., 394
Athanas, Andoni 32
Audebert, Cédric 245
Augsburg 302f.
Aun, Karl 51, 66
Aussiedler 141, 281
Australia 10, 15, 29, 34, 50f., 58, 61, 85, 89f., 98, 139, 174, 177, 184f., 192, 202, 209f.,

213 f., 218, 238, 264, 277, 294–296, 298–300, 319, 322, 326, 329, 337–339, 359, 382, 385, 388
Austrālijas Latvietis 58
Austria 2, 15 f., 27, 31, 34, 48, 73, 75, 84, 86, 101, 105–107, 119, 122, 125 f., 129, 133, 141, 153–155, 171 f., 174, 176, 179 f., 185, 189, 199, 202, 210, 213, 215, 253, 257, 264, 296–298, 304, 321, 328, 335, 339, 345, 371, 375–377, 381 f., 393
Austria-Hungary 68, 287, 289
Aversa 86

Babiński, Grzegorz 241
Bačka 373
Bačkis, Stasys Antanas 53
Bácska region 170
Bączkowski, Włodzimierz 229
Baczynskyj, Julian 287, 289, 324
Bade, Klaus J. 137, 139, 142, 149, 166
Baev, Jordan 91–93, 95
Bagieński, Witold 218, 232
Bahro, Rudolf 160
Baicoianu, Anca 268
Bajraktari, Mark (Kashnjet) 39
Bajraktari, Muharrem 12, 15, 29–31
Bajraktari, Ndue (Kushneni) 39
Bakhmeteff, Boris 364
Baković, Nikola 380, 384, 393
Bălcescu, Ncolae 245
Balch, Emily Greene 287
Baldwin-Edwards, Martin 379
Balgarsko ognishte 88
Balkan Mountains 68
Balla, Halil 15
Balla, Shaban 17
Balli Kombëtar Agrarian (Partia Agrare Demokratike e Ballit Kombëta) 33
Balli Kombëtar Organization (Balli i Vjetër Kombëtar) 11, 33 f., 107
Ballinger, Pamela 371–373, 392
Baltic American Freedom League 62, 64
Baltic Appeal to the United Nations (BATUN); United Baltic Appeal Inc. 61, 64, 66
Baltic Audiovisual Archival Council 64
Baltic Council in Australia 62
Baltic Council of European Movement 56
Baltic Federation 65
Baltic Freedom Day 62
Baltic Germans 48

Baltic Heritage Network 64
Baltic Peace and Freedom Cruise 63
Baltic tribunal (Copenhagen) 63
Baltic University (Hamburg) 57
Baltic Welfare, Education and Employment Organization 48
Baltic Women's Council 61, 64
Baltimore 314, 341, 360
Balys, Jonas 58
Banasiak, Stefan 202
Banat 244, 253, 373
Bańczyk, Stanisław 228
Banionis, Juozas 60, 62 f.
Bar-Zohar, Michael 74
Baranja 373
Barbu, Bogdan 253
Barbu, Eugen 251
Bárdi, Nándor 182
Barev, Tsenko 91 f., 95, 99
Barkan, Elliot Robert 319
Barratt, Glynn 326
Bartkowiak, Danuta 216
Basel 113
Bashkimi i Kombit (Unity of the Nation) 27
Bashkimi Shqiptar 36
Baučić, Ivo 382 f., 391
Bavaria 142, 148, 154, 182
Baydalakoff, Victor 364
Bazanov, Petr 366
Becher, Walter 118
Bednarek, Jerzy 213
Begolli, Rifat 16
Behring, Eva 252 f., 284
Behuncik, Edward J. 134
Belarus 2, 77, 295, 312, 317, 321
Belgium 35, 51, 56, 137, 139, 168, 177, 184, 199, 202 f., 213, 215, 237, 267, 277, 290, 298–300, 321, 326, 328, 335, 339
Belgrade 12, 19, 30 f., 37, 128, 331, 333, 370, 387, 392, 394, 426
Belluš, Samuel 124
Beloselsky-Belozersky, Serge 358
Beneš, Edvard 101, 108, 113, 117, 124
Berdychowska, Bogumiła 229, 297, 319
Berindei, Mihnea 273
Berlin 152, 155
Bernard, Noël 275 f.
Bernard, Sara 385, 393
Berov, Lyuben 98
Bessarabia 69, 71, 140, 245 f., 335, 339

Bessarabian Bulgarians 68
Best, Heinrich 164
Betell, Nicholas 335
Białokura, Marek 216
Biberaj, Elez 12
Biçaku, Ibrahim 16
Biega, Bolesław 228
Bielański, Stefan 216
Biermann, Wolf 152, 160
Bilisht 41
Bilyarski, Tsocho 85
Biryuzov, Sergey 75
Bischof, Günter 127
Bischof, Anna 8
Bishqeni, Tahsim 16
Biskupski, Mieczysław B. B. 231
Bitoński, Adam 233
Black Sea 2f., 68, 245, 346
Blaive, Muriel 123
Błażyński, Zbigniew 200
Bleiburg 371, 377
Bleiere, Daina 58
Blejwas, Stanisław A. 217
Blitz, Brad K. 389f.
Bloku Kombëtar i Pavarur (National Independent Block/Independent Group (Partia Grupi Independent/Bloku Kombëtar Indipendent) 26, 30f., 34
Bobelis, Kazys 54, 66
Bocheński, Józef Innocenty Maria 230
Bogdan, Magdalena 225
Bogdani, Aleksandra 21
Bogdani, Mirela 17f., 22
Bogonaş, Mihai 261
Boia, Lucian 245
Bolhovitinov, Nikolay 366
Bolivia 174, 184, 299
bombing 10, 74, 127, 140
Boniver, Margherita 42
Bonn-Mehlem 386
Borbándi, Gyula 171, 177, 179f., 185, 192
border 3, 6, 8, 12, 20f., 41, 47, 62, 69, 71, 73, 75, 79–82, 84, 87, 100, 104, 111f., 125f., 129, 145–148, 151, 153–158, 170–173, 176, 180, 193, 195, 198, 201, 203f., 210, 212, 229, 245–248, 252, 257, 260–263, 267, 277, 291, 294, 300, 311, 315, 317, 319, 326, 330, 351, 355, 370–376, 378–381, 383f., 388f., 391–393, 428
– border changes 5, 48, 204, 215, 369, 378

– border crossing 20, 155f., 172
 – illegal border crossing 204, 263, 380
– border militia/troops 4, 9f., 47, 75, 79f., 100, 129, 171–173, 177, 196f., 223, 228, 246, 255, 335, 349, 390
– border offenders 80
– border regime 377f., 380
– border zone 79
– displaced borderland 316, 325
– open-border policy 381
Boris III, King of Bulgaria 74, 76
Borshi, Shyqyri 16
Borzym, Andrzej 231
Bosilegrad 70
Bosnia-Herzegovina 2, 380, 382, 389
Bosnians 390
Bosnief-Paraschivescu, Dan 273
Bozhilov, Ivan 74
Bozhinova, Blagorodna 85
Braho, Lediona 40
Brandt, Willy 388
Brasol, Boris 349, 358f., 364
Brătianu, Maria 273, 275
Brazil 52, 85, 174, 184, 202, 213, 217, 289f., 299f., 309, 322, 338f.
Bregman, Aleksander 229f.
Bregu, Bahri 15
Breitzner, Richard 118
Bremen 155f., 158f., 365, 426
Bremen-Vegesack 156, 158
Brezhnev, Leonid 342f.
Brindisi 15, 42
Brinson, Charmian 101
British Broadcasting Corporation (BBC) 122, 130, 190, 225, 272, 275, 351f., 361
British Isles 192, 197, 213f., 224
British-Romanian Association (ACARDA) 272, 282
British Special Operation Executive (SOE) 196
Brīvā Latvijā 58
Brotherhood of Former Soldiers of the last Ukrainian Division 307
Brotherhood of Former Soldiers of the UPA 307
Brown, James F. 124, 131
Brunnbauer, Ulf 368, 377f., 381, 385, 393f.
Brym, Robert 341, 343
Brzeziński, Zbigniew 227, 317
Buc, Bonaventure S. 116

Bucharest   213, 243f., 246, 248–253, 255f., 259, 262, 266, 270–272, 274–278, 280, 282, 284
Budapest   95, 131, 153, 155, 172–175, 181, 183, 192, 226f., 235, 355, 365, 428f.
Buechler, Judith-Maria   391f.
Buechtemann, Christoph   163
Buhle, Mari   327
Buhle, Paul   327
Bukovina   170, 244, 246, 289, 335
Bukovsky, Vladimir   347, 355, 365
Bulcha, Mekuria   194
Buletini, Bajzit   26
Bulgaria   2f., 35, 68–100, 186, 190, 228, 245, 257, 279, 321, 328, 333, 379, 426
– General Directorate for Settlement of Refugees   70
Bulgarian Agrarian National Union   83, 88, 90
Bulgarian Anti-Bolshevik Union (Balgarski protivobolshevishki sayuz)   88
Bulgarian Communist Party   72, 82, 97
– Politburo of the Bulgarian Communist Party   83
– Politburo of the Central Committee of the Bulgarian Communist Party   72
Bulgarian Free Centre   98
Bulgarian Immigrant Society   98
Bulgarian Jurists in Exile   98
Bulgarian League for Rights of Exiled Persons (Balgarska liga za pravata na choveka v izgnanie)   88
Bulgarian Liberation Movement (Balgarsko osvoboditelno dvizhenie)   88, 92
Bulgarian Liberation Organization   95
Bulgarian National Committee for a Free and Independent Bulgaria (BNC)   88, 90–93
Bulgarian National Front (BNF)   88, 90–93, 95
Bulgarian National Revival   68
Bulgarian Orthodox Church   74
Bulgarian Provisional Representation   88
Bulgarian state authorities 79, 82f., 85, 97f., 283
– Directorate of Migration   97
Bulgarian State Security Service (State Security Committee)   80, 95–97, 99f., 190, 192
Bulgarian Turks   72, 82, 87
Bulgarians   68–77, 79, 81, 83–87, 91, 93, 95, 97f., 245, 291, 310, 312
Bułhak, Władysław   234
Bund der Evangelischen Kirchen (BEK)   152

Bundesministerium für Vertriebenen, Flüchtlinge und Kriegsgeschädigte   133
Bunin, Ivan   331, 363
Burant, Stephen R.   141
Burch, Cecilia Notini   49
Burliuk, David   332, 338
Burrell, Kathy   257f.
Buttler, Lois   322, 324
Buwalda, Piet   341, 343, 366
Byelorussia, Soviet Republic of   202, 352

Caccamo, Francesco   112, 129
Cadrilater   245
Calafeteanu, Ion   253, 262, 264f., 268f.
Calda, Milos   105
California   36, 62, 73, 87, 105, 133, 148, 191, 238, 363f., 428
Cami, Dik   16
Campani, Giovama   43f.
Câmpeanu, Radu   271
Canada   50–52, 56, 58, 62, 64–66, 73, 78, 89f., 98, 106f., 114, 116, 119, 138f., 169, 174, 177, 181, 183f., 189, 192, 202, 209f., 213f., 217, 238, 244, 261, 264, 267, 277, 289f., 295f., 298–300, 303, 307, 309f., 312f., 320–324, 327–329, 339, 362, 369, 382, 388, 428
Canadian Institute of Ukrainians Studies at the University of Alberta   323
Canberra   395
Canës Bazi I, see Kupi, Abaz
captive nations   4, 6, 122, 309, 311, 318
Captive Nations Week   311, 316
Capua   86
Cara, Et'hem   16
Caritas   150
Carter, Jimmy   131
Carpathian Mountains   244
– Carpathian Germans   117
– Carpatho-Rusyns   119f., 134, 377
– Sub-Carpathia   119, 170
– Sub-Carpathian Rusyns/Ruthenians   119, 134
Cătănuș, Ana-Maria   250, 257, 272
Cătănuș, Dan   254
Catherine the Great   346
Catholic Church   224, 302, 371
Cattaruzza, Marina   374, 392
Catthorpe Manor   65
Ceaușescu, Nicolae   250f., 256f., 261, 265–267, 270, 274, 283

Cedar Rapids 134
Čelovský, Boris 110, 115, 119, 121, 123–125, 134
Cenckiewicz, Sławomir 208, 233 f., 241
Center for Albanian Studies (CAS) 43
Center for the Study of Czechoslovak Exiles (Centrum pro Československá exilová studia) 133
Central Asia, Soviet territories in 46, 77, 81, 290 f., 346, 351, 354
Central European Federation (CEF) 108, 311
Central Intelligence Agency (CIA) 26–32, 38 f., 91–93, 122 f., 125, 127, 226, 230, 340, 351, 359, 428
Central Office for German Resettlers (Zentralverwaltung für deutsche Umsiedler) 143
Central Ukrainian Teachers Organization 303
Černý, Karel 125
Cesianu, Constantin 248, 273
Chałupczak, Henryk 241
Chamberlin, William 350
Chameria (Çamëria, gr. Τσαμουριά). 9, 36
Chapin, Gene L. 148
Charter 77 112, 128–132, 272
Chehova, Olga 337
Chemnitz 166
Chernin, Albert 341
Chernyshevsky, N.G. 327
Chetniks 14
Chicago 33, 45, 61, 65, 87, 99, 212 f., 314, 317, 322 f., 327
children 10, 59, 62, 69, 75, 80 f., 145, 156, 162, 199, 206, 261, 265–268, 285, 302, 305, 337, 383 f., 430
– international adoption 265–268, 430
Chile 184, 217, 299
Chin, Rita C. K. 149
Chodyłowa, Elżbieta Later 216 f.
Choroszewski, Walery E. 220
Christa, Boris 338
Christian Democratic Party 118
Christian Democratic Union of Central Europe (CDUCE) 186, 227
Christian Democratic Union of Germany (Christlich Demokratische Union Deutschlands, CDU) 144, 159, 220, 229, 371, 388
Christian Social Union in Bavaria (Christlich-Soziale Union in Bayern, CSU) 371
Chubaty, Nicholas 310
Chunchukov, Georgi 76

Church World Service 298
Churchill, Winston 121, 196, 335
Cico, Hysni 15
Ciglerova, Jana 112, 129
Ciano, Galeazzo 9
Cioran, Emil 247, 284
Cioroianu, Adrian 280
Cipko, Serge 325
Circassians 74
Citaku, Ramadan 11
citizenship 75 f., 79, 85, 110, 116, 119, 126, 132 f., 149, 152, 193, 202, 206, 215, 224, 231, 236, 281, 308, 333, 339, 346, 372, 375, 377–379, 394
Civici, Adrian 24
Clarkson, Alexander 371, 386, 393
Cleveland 45, 53, 87, 107, 115 f., 134, 185, 322 f.
Cluj 244 f., 273
Codreanu, Corneliu Zelea 253
Cohen, Gerard Daniel 337
Cohen, Robin 194, 320
Çokon, Profi 17
Cologne 140, 166
Colombia 217
Comăneci, Nadia 261
Commission for the Development of Cultural Ties with Estonians Abroad (Välismaaga Sõpruse ja Kultuurisidemete Arendamise Eesti Ühing) 59
Commission on Security and Cooperation in Europe (CSCE) 63, 124, 128 f., 131
Committee for a Return to the Motherland 58
Committee for the Aid of Refugee Ukrainian Scholars 300
Committee for the Defense of the Unjustly Prosecuted (CDUP) 127 f.
Committee for the Salvation of Albania 13 f.
Committee of Free Czechoslovakia 110, 114
Committee of Naturalized Poles in France (Komitet Polaków Naturalizowanych we Francji) 224
Committee of the Canadians of Ukrainian Origins 309
Communism 3, 7, 9, 11, 15, 17–19, 21–23, 25, 40, 87, 90, 94, 96, 102, 104 f., 110 f., 116, 120–123, 129–132, 134 f., 230, 238, 240,

252f., 255f., 272, 280, 285f., 310, 313f., 317, 320, 338, 348f., 352, 356, 358, 361
- anti-Communism 55, 60, 83, 115, 188f., 229f., 350
- Communists 3f., 6, 9, 11–30, 32–35, 37f., 40–42, 44, 46, 50, 52, 55, 72, 76–78, 80, 82–84, 87, 89–94, 96, 98, 101–105, 107–109, 111, 114, 117, 119–122, 124–126, 129–133, 135, 147, 155, 178, 189–191, 196, 201, 203f., 206, 208f., 212, 217, 219, 221, 224, 228–235, 237, 243, 248, 250, 252, 254f., 257, 260, 265–267, 269f., 272–278, 280–286, 297, 307–310, 312–314, 316, 318f., 329–332, 336, 338, 345f., 348–357, 359–362, 366, 369–371, 373, 376, 381, 383f., 387f., 429f.
- Communist bloc 1, 18, 122, 128, 130, 209, 311, 314
- communist regime 7, 9, 16, 18, 20–23, 25, 29, 32f., 36–39, 43f., 87, 105, 123, 197, 203–205, 210, 229, 231f., 243, 247–249, 251, 253, 257, 259, 265, 267, 270, 272–274, 277, 284, 313, 329, 348, 352, 358, 365
Communist Party of Albania (Partia Komuniste e Shqipërisë, PKSH) 11, 17, 39
Communist Party of Chile 347
concentration camp 16, 72, 74, 85, 108, 139, 174, 177, 199, 334
Conference of Americans of Central and Eastern European Descent (CACEED) 311f.
Conference on Security and Cooperation in Europe (CSCE) 37, 63
Congress for Cultural Freedom 226
Connecticut 65, 304, 322f.
Connelly, Kate 112, 129
Connor, Ian 143f., 167
Constantiniu, Florin 244
convention 70, 188
Cooperative Society Foundation 357
Coordinating Ukrainian Committee 301
Copenhagen 63, 211
coping strategies 269
Cordell, Karl 152
Corfu 37, 40f.
Cornea, Doina 275
Corobca, Liliana 272, 277
Coudenys, Wim 8
Council for Education and Socialist Culture 251

Council for Mutual Economic Assistance (CMEA) 19
Council of Europe 7, 63, 227, 281, 355
Council of Free Czechoslovakia (CFC) 102, 106, 108–111, 114, 116–125, 128f., 131, 134
Council of Lithuanian Americans (Amerikos Lietuviu Taryba) 50
Council of the Three (Rada Trzech) 221
counter-intelligence 232
coup d'état 77, 85, 97
Crampton, Richard J. 14, 82
Crisana 170
Croatia 2, 27, 34, 279, 368, 371, 373, 381f., 384–391, 393f., 427
- Independent State of Croatia 371
Croatian Communist Party 387
Croatian Spring 385, 387
Croats 69, 368, 370, 376, 384–387
Cuba 138, 149, 210, 226
Cude, Michael 101, 107, 114, 116, 124, 426
Čulen, Konštantín 113, 115, 134
Culic, Irina 244
Čulík, Jan 131
Cultural, Literary and Artistic Publications 251
cultural/expression/resistance/opposition 3, 7, 12, 19, 35, 43, 57, 59, 63–65, 77, 93, 105, 108, 112, 115, 129f., 132, 134, 142, 162, 172, 178, 184f., 188, 191, 194, 204, 208f., 223–226, 233, 237f., 240, 242f., 246, 251f., 258, 269, 276–279, 284, 292, 295, 300f., 304–306, 308f., 311f., 314, 316, 322f., 326–328, 344, 346, 349, 381, 384, 387, 393, 428
Cummings, Richard H. 123, 125, 127
Czapski, Józef 216, 224
Czech and Slovak Solidarity Council 116
Czech-Polish-Ukrainian Society 317
Czech Refugee Trust Fund 106
Czech Republic 2, 105, 132f.
Czechoslovak Academy of Sciences 104
Czechoslovak Advisory Committee 111
Czechoslovak American Fund 126
Czechoslovak National Committee 108, 120
Czechoslovak National Council of America (CNCA) 106, 111, 121, 128, 134
Czechoslovak Newsletter 112
Czechoslovak Relief Committee for Political Refugees 106

Czechoslovak Society of Arts and Sciences (Společnosti pro vědy a umění, SVU) 111–113
Czechoslovak State Security (Státní bezpečnost, StB) 104, 125–127
Czechoslovakia 3, 8, 35, 73, 81, 101–114, 116–123, 125–135, 155, 170, 228, 256 f., 279, 287, 289 f., 295, 328, 374, 426, 429
– First Czechoslovak Republic 101, 426
– Third Czechoslovak Republic 101, 107
Czechs 82, 101 f., 104–106, 108 f., 113 f., 118 f., 123, 125 f., 133, 286, 299, 316, 319, 324
Czekalski, Tadeusz 11, 14
Czerniakiewicz, Jan and Monika 202

Dahlman, Carl 389
Dako, Christo Anastas 32
Dallin, David 330
Dalmatia 372, 382
Damyanov, Simeon 98
Dan, Fedor 365
Dan, Lidia 348, 365
Dandenong 15
Danilov, Dan 338
Danube 68, 263
Danville 134
Danyte, Milda 62
Dapkute, Daiva 60
Daudze, Argita 58
Dayton 87, 389
de Gaulle, Charles 256, 270, 273
Decressin, Jörg 148
defection 94, 147, 232, 261
defectors 52, 63, 173, 208, 232, 334
Deksnis, Eduards Bruno 8
Delvina, Hiqmet 16, 26
Dema, Hysai 31
Demneri, Said 15
Democracy 34, 90, 330, 366, 426, 429
Democratic Concentration and the Coalition of the Democratic Parties 220
Democratic Party (Stronnictwo Demokratyczne, SD) 42, 133, 219, 332, 358
Democratic Union (Bashkimi Demokratik) 17, 34
demographic structure 291, 305
Dempsey, Sean 172
Denéchère, Yves 265–268
Denikin, Anton 331

Denmark 48, 63, 104, 213, 216, 321, 328, 336, 339, 383
departure 171, 176, 181, 190, 194, 209, 211, 248, 250, 254 f., 257, 260, 267, 291, 295–297, 303–305, 320, 328, 341 f., 370, 391 f.
– clandestine departures 92, 197, 204, 261, 369
deportations 5 f., 46, 182, 198, 291, 294
deportees 76, 200, 375
Der Spiegel 144 f., 147, 150, 155, 158
Dervishi, Ferid 21, 31
d'Estaing, Valéry Giscard 275
Detroit 33, 87, 322 f., 327
Deutsch, Howard 338
Deutsche Welle 122, 351
Deutsches Ostdienst 261 f.
Deva, Djafer 31
Deva, Xhafer 14 f., 26 f., 30
development 18, 20, 24 f., 40, 42–45, 49, 52, 63 f., 66, 70, 88 f., 94, 97, 110, 115, 137, 143 f., 150 f., 164, 227 f., 231, 255 f., 267, 273 f., 284, 292, 300, 302 f., 305, 322, 324, 332, 342 f., 355, 369, 371, 380, 383, 385, 387, 389, 392
Dhimitraj, Vasil 30
Diaspora 45, 66, 202, 240 f., 287, 289 f., 293 f., 300–307, 314 f., 322 f., 325, 427
– diaspora of fighters 194
– diaspora of victims 194
– diaspora of warriors 320
– diaspora of work 320
– diaspora organizations 370
Dibra, Qenan 17
Die Zeit 154–157, 159, 164
Diefendorf, Jeffery 140
Dilo, Jani 30
Diminescu, Dana 244, 264, 279–281
Dimitrov, Georgi 72, 77 f., 82, 90–93
Dine, Fiqri 12
Dineva, Detelina 68, 94, 426
discrimination 211, 281, 343
Dishnica, Ymer 13
displacement 161 f., 164, 218, 290, 294, 368, 370, 372, 389
Displaced Person (DP) 15, 47–50, 57, 61, 64, 66, 139 f., 174, 176 f., 180, 192, 215, 293, 297–300, 302–305, 320, 324, 337 f., 340
– Displaced Person's Act 106
dissent 112, 114, 123, 129, 152, 172, 189, 234 f., 276, 283, 346, 360

Djadjuli, Asaf   31
Dobriansky, Lev   309–311, 317 f.
Dobruja (Dobrudzha)   70, 76 f., 244–246
   Northern   68, 71
   Southern   69–71, 75
Dochev, Ivan   90, 92 f., 95, 99
Dodbiba, Sokrat   16
Dolinin, Viktor   361
Domachowska, Agata   9, 427
Dongen, Luc van   230
Dorril, Stephen   38, 230
Dósa, Attila   189
Dosti, Hasan   13, 28–30, 33 f.
Dostoevsky, Fyodor M.   326
Dota, Franko   392
Douba, Honza (Měkota, Jan)   130 f.
Douglass, Ray M.   117
Dowty, Alan   147
Doynov, Doyno   68 f.
Drachman, Edward   341, 343, 366
Dracz, Iwan   297
Dragostinova, Theodora   81
Draus, Jan   242
Drenikoff, Kyril   98
Dresden   140, 166
Drozd, Wołodymir   297
Drozdowski, Marian Marek   195
Dubček, Alexander   129 f.
Duda, Igor   383, 428
Dufoix, Stéphane   247
Dumitreasa, Caliciu   275
Dumitriu, Ion   270
Dumitriu, Victor   259
Durandin, Catherine   243, 279
Ďurčanský, Ferdinand   107, 113, 115 f., 134
Ďurica, Milan   113
Durres   42
Dushnyck, Walter   310–312, 316 f.
Dvinov, Boris   348, 357, 365
Dziennik Polski i Dziennik Żołnierza   225
Dziewanowski, Marian Kamil   230
Dzimtenes Balss (Voice of Motherland)   59
Dziuba, Iwan   297

East and Central Europe   1–5, 17, 24, 35, 42, 55, 61, 95, 100, 104 f., 117 f., 121, 131 f., 135, 137, 143, 151, 154, 164, 167 f., 170, 176, 181, 183, 186, 188, 190, 235, 248, 270, 273, 275, 281, 295, 305, 312, 317, 319–321, 357, 370, 372, 374
East Frisian Islands   143
Eastern Macedonia   75
Eastern Orthodox Church   302
Eastern Rumelia   68
Eberhardt, Piotr   198–203, 205 f., 241, 291
Eberle, Brigitte   158
Eckhardt, Tibor   186, 188, 428
Ecuador   217
Edele, Mark   334
Eder, Wiesława   215
Edison, Charles   350
Eesti Hääl   57
Egypt   10, 15, 26 f., 31, 34, 36, 328, 379
Ehrenkreutz, Andrew   317
Eidintas, Alfonsas   45, 47, 49 f., 52, 57, 64, 66
Einstein, Albert   16
Eisenhower, Dwight   92, 121 f., 335, 351
Eisler, Gerhard   145
Elezi, Cen   12
Eliade, Mircea   247, 252, 278, 284
Elliot, Mark   140
Elliott, William   350
Elsie, Robert   10, 12–15, 27–29, 32, 34, 37 f.
Eltzin, Boris   362
Emigration   24, 45, 47, 49 f., 52, 57, 64, 66, 70, 81 f., 87, 99 f., 105 f., 146, 170, 193 f., 205, 237, 240, 252, 287, 289, 299, 324, 330, 333, 341–343, 346, 361 f., 368, 390
– criminalization of emigration   146
– economic emigration   97, 105
– emigration limitation   252
– emigration restriction   138, 146, 169, 181, 217, 248, 266, 362, 368, 370, 380
– indirect/intermediate emigration   294, 296, 320
– motives for emigration; also known as „emigration motivations" or „reasons of emigration"   144, 286, 293
– political emigration   1, 7, 72, 83, 95 f., 98 f., 224, 227, 236, 240, 248, 262, 286, 288, 306, 315, 325 f., 427
– size of emigration; also known as „migration size"   287, 294
– tax on emigrants   159, 251 f.
émigré   3–7, 25, 32, 35, 39, 58 f., 64, 80, 84, 88, 90–96, 98–100, 104, 116, 127, 130, 132 f., 171, 176 f., 185–192, 194, 197, 203, 205, 208, 213, 219–242, 247, 284, 319,

322 f., 326–333, 336–340, 342, 344–353, 355–367, 383, 385–388, 393, 426, 428 f.
– émigré religious   327
employment bureaus   381
Emsland   143
Engel, Valeriy   341, 343
England   36, 86, 106, 196, 271, 277
Entente   69
Țepeneag, Dumitru   269, 278 f., 284
Șerban, Monica   282
Șerban, Nicoleta   271
Șerban-Oprescu, George   252
Erdmans, Mary P.   212
Erfurt   166
Ermenji, Abas   16, 26, 29 f., 33
Ern, Nicholay   338
escape   5, 20–22, 53, 76, 80, 101, 104 f., 197 f., 208, 248, 320, 362, 371, 390
escapee   5 f., 20, 80, 105, 123, 126, 133, 208
Estonia   35, 45–48, 50–60, 64–67, 186, 228, 311, 314, 321, 328, 331, 335, 353, 427
Estonian American National Council   55, 61
Estonian Central Council in Canada (Eesti Kesknõukogu Kanadas)   56
Estonian Committee (Eesti Komitee)   65
Estonian Consulate General in New York   53, 65
Estonian Federation in Canada (Eesti Liit Kanadas)   56
Estonian House   64
Estonian Literary Museum (Eesti Kirjandusmuuseum)   65
Estonian National Committee   54
Estonian National Congress (Rootsi Eestlaste Esindus, later Rootsi Eestlaste Liit)   56
Estonian National Council (Eesti Rahvusnõukogu)   56, 63, 65 f.
Estonian National Fund, Eesti Rahvusfond, the Estonian Information Centre   57
Estonian World Council   56, 61, 63
Estonians   45–51, 54–57, 59–61, 63–66, 299, 312, 339, 427
'Ethnic Albania'   12, 14, 36 f.
ethnic cleansing   117, 369, 372–375, 389
ethnic community   300, 314
ethnic groups, minorities   6, 9, 51, 55, 70 f., 73, 83, 100 f., 103, 114, 116 f., 119, 134 f., 166, 181 f., 189 f., 204 f., 228, 243, 245 f.,
251, 281, 287, 291 f., 311 f., 317, 319, 322 f., 346, 371 f., 376, 378, 381, 387, 391 f.
– interethnic relations   316
ethnic migration   249, 263, 281, 284, 287
ethnic mobilization   309, 312, 314, 316, 325, 427
ethnic organizations   188, 301, 303, 305, 307, 313, 315, 317
ethnic self-identification; also known as „ethnic identity"; or „national identity"   73, 77 f., 287, 300 f., 305, 307, 311, 314 f., 324, 341, 345, 377, 426 f.
ethnic structure   71, 288, 291
ethnicity   61, 77, 82, 207, 244 f., 257, 291, 293, 300 f., 305–307, 314 f., 324, 369, 375, 377 f., 427 f.
Eubank, Nancy   326
Eurasia   326
European Day of Remembrance for Victims of Stalinism and Nazism   62
European Movement   56, 230
European Parliament   63, 131
European Union (EU)   17, 22, 40, 62, 79, 96, 119, 183, 231, 236 f., 265, 268, 279 f., 282, 391, 426, 430
evacuation   5, 118, 140, 171, 196 f., 201
evacuees   140–142
Evangelical Lutheran Church (EvKD)   150, 152
exchange: scholarship/grant/internship/training   37 f., 42, 57, 92, 103, 152, 163, 183, 191, 232, 257–260, 269, 276, 288, 302 f., 324, 391, 426–428
Executive Committee (Komiteti i Ekzekutiv)   28, 33
Executive of National Unity (Egzekutywa Zjednoczenia Narodowego, EZN)   221
exile   3–7, 15, 26, 30–34, 36, 38–40, 53–55, 57–61, 63–67, 80, 84, 88–90, 101–115, 117–135, 160, 171, 174 f., 184–186, 188 f., 191, 193, 195–198, 202 f., 213 f., 216, 218–222, 224, 226–235, 238–242, 247 f., 251–253, 255, 261 f., 264, 266, 268–272, 274 f., 277 f., 282–285, 291, 297, 301–303, 307, 314 f., 318–320, 324, 326, 328, 330, 340, 350, 356, 366 f., 385, 387, 392, 394 f., 426 f., 429
– government-in-exile 37, 53 f., 65 f., 88
– Polish   196, 201, 208, 213, 219, 221 f., 225 f., 233, 236, 241
exo-polity   247

expellee   117 f., 139, 141–144, 167, 370, 376
– Ethnic German expellees   141–143, 167, 201, 371
Expellees' and Disenfranchised People's Bloc (Block der Heimatsvertriebenen und Entrechteten)   118
expulsion   4–6, 117–119, 135, 137, 152, 193, 198 f., 201, 206, 370, 372–374, 391 f.

Familial Association of Hungarian Gendarmerie (Magyar Csendőrok Családi Közössége, MCsCSK)   185
Far East   198, 294, 322, 329
Farébersviller   157
Farouk I, King of Egypt   10
Fassmann, Heinz   193, 201
Fatherland Front   76, 79, 83, 85, 89 f.
Federal Republic of Germany (FRG)   38, 142–145, 147–149, 152–154, 156, 159 f., 164 f., 167, 207, 214, 257, 271, 281, 298, 302 f., 371, 375, 381 f., 384, 386
Federation of Americans of Central and East European Descent (FACEED)   311
Federation of Democratic Movements   221
Federation of Poles in Great Britain (Zjednoczenie Polskie w Wielkiej Brytanii)   223
Federative Estonian World Council (Ülemaailmne Eesti Kesknõukogu)   54
Fedinec, Csilla   182
Fehérváry, István   189 f.
Feierabend, Ladislav   105
Ficeac, Bogdan   256
Ființa Românească (The Romanian Being).   277
Filiates   41
Fiń, Anna   286, 288, 296, 306 f., 316, 325, 427
Finland   2, 45, 49, 168, 217, 277, 321, 328, 339, 427
Fiorina   41
Firouzbakhch, Hanna   214
Fischer, Bernd Jürgen   13
Fitzpatrick, Sheila   337
Florkowska-Frančić, Halina   215
Footscray   15
Ford Foundation   350
Fort Wayne   87, 89
Fotache, Oana   277
France   267
Frank, Matthew   35, 38, 117, 162, 372
Frankfurt (Main)   105, 271, 302 f.
Frankfurt (Oder)   166

Frankfurter Allgemeine Zeitung   146
Frashëri, Abdyl bey   11
Frashëri, Mehdi   12, 31
Frashëri, Mithat (Mid'hat bey Frashëri)   11 f., 15, 27 f., 30, 33
Frashëri, Nami   11
Frashëri, Sami   11
Fraternal Organization of Hungarian Veterans (Magyar Harcosok Bajtársi Közössége, MHBK)   184 f., 189
Free Albania Committees
– Anti-Communist National Democratic Committee for a Free Albania (Shqypnja e lire)   29
– Free Albania National Committee   35
– „Free Albania" National Committee Archive (Arkivi i Komitetit „Shqipnia e Lirë")   27, 43
– „Free Albania" National Committee (Komiteti Kombëtar „Shqipëria e Lirë", NCFA)   27–35, 38
Free Albania (Shqipëria e lirë)   28–30, 32
Free Bulgarian Center   88
Free Central European News Agency   111
Free Europe Committee (FEC)/National Committee for a Free Europe (NCFE)   4 f., 27, 55, 90–93, 110, 121 f., 124 f., 176, 186, 188, 220, 225, 227 f., 233, 235, 238, 271, 428
– Mid-European Studies Center   55
Free Romanians' Associations from RFG   271, 284
Free Russia   361
Free Russia Foundation   349
Free Trade Union of the American Federation of Labor (AFL)   186
Free Trade Union of the Working People in Romania   272
Free World   3 f., 7, 123, 348, 355 f.
freedom   4, 6, 17 f., 40, 55 f., 63, 90, 116, 119, 122 f., 129, 147, 152, 177 f., 187, 191, 203, 209, 238, 247 f., 250, 271, 273, 275, 277, 280, 297, 310–313, 315 f., 332, 337, 340 f., 343, 349, 354, 366, 376, 388
– free movement   23, 280
– freedom of association   273
Freedom and Independence organization (Wolność i Niezawisłość, WiN)   232
Frenzen, Niels   42
Fridgut, Theodor   341
Friedman, Murray   341
Friman, H. Richard   391
Friszke, Andrzej   193, 218, 231, 240

Fröbelstraße Gymnasium 156
frontier 10, 20f., 79f., 83, 229, 260, 263 see also borders
Fundo, Llazar 12

Gabensky, Dora 98
Gabrielson, Gui 358
Gaddis, John Lewis 350
Gadjev, Ilia 89
Gadjev, Ivan 80, 85, 88–90, 93, 98f.
Gadomski, Feliks 228
Gafencu, Gregoire 188
Galanskov, Jury 360
Galița, Andrei Catalin 272
Galich, Alexander 354
Galicia 289, 300
Gallaway, Lowell E. 148
Gamow, George 364
Garliński, Józef 196
Gary 61, 87
Gattrell, Peter 372
Gawenda, Jerzy August 221f.
Gawlikowski, Lechosław 225
Gawlina, Józef 224
Gawryszewski, Andrzej 198, 200–203, 206, 212, 241
Gdańsk 5f., 91, 101, 196, 198, 208, 216, 236, 241, 312, 328, 426, 429
Gebhardt, Stanisław 229
Gedeshi, Ilir 24
Gega (Petrich region) 85
Gega, Antanas 36
Geiger, Vladimir 374, 376, 392
Geislingen 64
Gémes, Andreas 172, 180
General Committee (Komiteti i Pergjitshem) 28f.
Geneva 70, 256, 282, 352
Georgakas, Dan 327
Georgi Mihov Dimitrov/ Gemeto 88
Georgia 312, 321, 352
Georgiev, Kimon 76
Gergen, Kenneth J. 315
German Democratic Republic (GDR) 3, 5f., 142–165, 182, 248
Germans 5, 12, 14, 21, 27, 30, 47f., 108, 117–119, 137, 140f., 143f., 146–152, 154–162, 171, 174, 182f., 198–201, 205–207, 212, 246, 253, 263, 281, 286, 289, 292, 324, 346f., 372–377, 392, 394

Germany 2, 5, 9, 34, 39, 43, 47–54, 57f., 61, 75, 85f., 89, 106, 117–119, 122, 125, 127, 133, 136–141, 143, 145, 148–150, 153f., 160, 162–169, 171, 173f., 177, 179, 182–185, 199, 202, 206f., 209–211, 213, 215, 220, 229, 237f., 245f., 253, 259f., 262, 264f., 270–272, 277, 281f., 295–298, 300–305, 309, 318, 321, 323, 326, 329, 333–335, 337–340, 346f., 351, 355, 359f., 362, 365f., 371, 374f., 379f., 382, 384, 388, 391, 394f., 426, 428
Germenji, Themistokli 35
Germenji, Vasil 35
Gerus, Oleh.W. 307
Gerutis, Albertas 54
Gestapo 331
Gheorghiu-Dej, Gheorghe 255
Ghica, Ion 245
Giedroyc, Jerzy 216, 225, 229, 236, 239, 297, 318f.
Gilbert, Emily 47
Gilbert, Martin 341
Gille, Zsuzsa 390
Ginzburg, Alexander 364
Gitelman, Zvi 327
Giurescu, Dinu 256
Gjakova 12, 34
Gjana, Sulejman 36f.
Gjinishi, Mustafa 13
Gjomarkaj, Kole Bibe Mirakaj dhe Ndue 26
Gjoni, Nduc Marko 34
Gjonin, Gjon Marka (Markagjoni, Gjon) 26
Glanville, Jo 112, 129
Global Union of Poles Abroad (Światpol) 195
Glodeanu, Gheorghe 252
Gloviczki, Peter J. 266
Glüsing, Jens 155
Gochev, Yanko 68, 76
Goddeeris, Idesbald 215
Goeken-Haidl, Ulrike 140, 166
Gogo, Caqo 29, 31
Gogol, Nikolai V. 326
Goldberg, Ben Zion 343
Goldin, Vladimir 356
Golemi, Ismail 16
Goleniewski, Michał 232
Golescu, A.G. 245
Goma, Paul 250, 272, 275–277, 279, 285
Gombrowicz, Witold 224
Gomułka, Władysław 235

Goněc, Vladimír 108, 134
Gorbachev, Mikhail 155, 347, 361
Gorfinkel, Mark 342
Gorfinkel, Svetlana 342
Gorizia 379
Gorna Oryahovitsa 69
Gotse Delchev 98
Gottfried, Ted 337
Götürk, Deniz 148
Government of Anti-Communist Dictatorship 349
Govor, Elena 326
Gramling, David 148
Grancharov, Stoycho 74
Gransow, Volker 153
Graz 31, 86, 385
Great Britain 9f., 15, 32, 34, 43, 47, 177, 196f., 213f., 216, 223, 238, 290, 295f., 298–300, 309, 329, 335, see also British Isles
Grebenarov, Aleksandar 69, 75, 81
Greece 2, 10, 15f., 20f., 29–31, 34, 38f., 41, 43, 69–71, 75, 79–81, 84, 89, 92, 94, 148, 259, 267, 329, 336
Greilinger, Philipp 376
Gremion, Pierre 226
Grenoble 260
Gribnicea, Mihai 245
Gridan, Irina 254–256
Grigorenko, Petr 365
Grocholski, Stanisław 230
Gromada, Tadeusz 289
Gromyko, Andrey 334, 336
Gross, Feliks 227
Gruenther, Alfred 92
Gruev, Stefan 99
Grundmann, Siegfried 156
Grupa Objednannia (Ukraine) 314
Grzybowski, Jerzy 205
guest workers, see migration/labor
Gulag 76, 140, 182, 190, 270, 334
Gurakuqi, Shuk 16

Habielski, Rafał 193, 203, 225, 239f., 242
Habsburg Empire 109, 379f.
Habšudová, Zuzana 133
Hála, František 126
Halecki, Oskar 230
Haliv, Mykola 317
Halle 155, 157f., 166, 335

Haller, Józef 195
Halpern, Joel 368, 379, 391–393
Halychyn, Dmytro 310
Hamburg 57, 154, 158
– Hamburg-Eidelstedt 154
– Hamburg Social Service 158
Hanke, Hugon 208, 233
Hareshiti, Javer 16
Hartman, Gary 61, 307
Harvard Ukrainian Research Institute 287, 322–324
Harvey, Joanna 389
Haskovo 69, 71
Hauner, Milan 113
Havel, Václav 112, 128–130, 132
Havlík, Iva 127
Hebrew University in Jerusalem 341
Heidemeyer, Helge 144, 167
Heidrich, Arnošt 110
Heikkilä, Pauli 45, 56, 427
Hein, Christoph 143, 153
Heller, Michail 341
Helsinki 37, 59f., 63, 112, 128, 131, 250, 274, 312, 345, 427
Helsinki (Final) Act 63, 112, 128f., 131, 250, 256, 270–273
– Helsinki Group 312
– Helsinki Watch 251, 274f.
Hemar, Marian 224
Henney, Árpád 185
Herbert, Ulrich 138, 149, 166
Herling-Grudziński, Gustaw 224f.
Hermanik, Klaus-Jurgen 73
Heroizma Shqiptare 36
Herzen, Alexander 328
Hicks, Bethany 136, 428
Hiden, John 54, 60
Hilton, Laura J. 337
Hirschberg 302f.
Historical Society of Pennsylvania / the Balch Institute 65, 134
Hladnik, Mirjam 379
Hlavatý, Václav 110, 112
Hletko, Peter 115
Hochstadt, Steve 136
Hodža, Fedor 113
Hodža, Milan 108
Hoerder, Dirk 138, 166
Holian, Anna Marta 337
Holmston, Boris (Smyslovsky) 356

Holodomor (Great Famine) 76
homo sovieticus 256, 293, 306
Honecker, Erich 155
Hoover, Herbert 363
Horia, Vintilă 247, 278
Hörschelmann, Kathhrin 257 f.
Horthy, Regent 184 f.
Horvath, Istvan 244, 246, 249 f., 254, 261, 279, 282
Horyzonty 225, 233
host countries; also known as „destination country" or „countries of destination" or „host society" 50, 138, 207, 213, 264, 278, 280 f., 285, 287 f., 290, 294 f., 298 f., 304–307, 319, 377, 385, 388, 391
Hough, William J. H. 63
Hovi, Kalervo 63
Hoxha, Enver 11 f., 14, 17, 20, 39
Hrabyk, Klaudiusz 233, 318
Hristov, Hristo 96, 99 f.
Hristov, Petko 379
Hron, Madeleine 104, 133, 135
Hruby, Karel 113
Hrušovský, František 113, 115
Hrycak, Jarosław 297, 312
Hryshko, Vasyl 313
Hułas, Magdalena 200
human rights 18, 35, 63, 117, 128 f., 132, 250–252, 267, 271–274, 279, 281, 312, 342, 356, 374
– human rights violations/abuses 128, 131, 271, 273–275, 312
human trafficking 390 f.
Hungarian Arrow Cross 183
Hungarian Authorities
– Central Statistical Office (HSCO) 182, 192
– Foreign Ministry 180
– Katonapolitikai Osztály 189
Hungarian Freedom Fighters Federation (HFFF) 187
Hungarian Freedom Fighters Movement (HFFM) 187
Hungarian Gendarmerie Benevolent Aassociation (Magyar Királyi Csendőr Bajtársi Közössége, MKCSBK) 185
Hungarian Movement for Freedom (Magyar Szabadságmozgalom) 185
Hungarian National Council (Magyar Nemzeti Bizottmány, HNC) 176, 186–189
Hungarian Royal Army 171

Hungarian State Security (Államvedelmi Osztály, ÁVO) 189
Hungarians 116 f., 120, 134, 168–172, 174, 176 f., 179 f., 184, 186, 188 f., 191 f., 244–246, 253, 281, 286 f., 291, 299, 305, 310, 312, 324, 373–376, 392, 394
Hungary 2 f., 35, 73, 81, 101, 120, 129, 153, 155, 168–184, 186–190, 192, 198, 213, 228, 245 f., 251, 257, 261, 263 f., 289, 304, 321, 329, 365, 373–375, 428
Hurban, Vladimir 134
Hysi, Shyqyri 33, 44

Iakhontov, Gen. 334
Iberian Peninsula 216
identity 78, 113, 116 f., 119, 161, 268, 277, 287 f., 301 f., 309, 314 f., 337, 345, 362, 369, 378, 392, 428
– identity politics 315
Iepan, Florin 266
Ierunca, Virgil 278, 284
Iglicka, Krystyna 204–206, 212, 237, 241, 296
Illinois 87, 319
Ilmjärv, Magnus 53
immigrant 42, 61, 68, 71–73, 76–78, 81, 84–87, 89, 91, 93, 98, 101, 134, 149, 157, 168 f., 177, 189, 192, 210, 212, 214–217, 244, 247, 255, 262, 264, 269, 274, 282, 284, 287 f., 290, 294 f., 298, 300 f., 304–306, 308 f., 312, 314–316, 319, 323–327, 339, 349 f., 354, 357, 390, 427
Immigration History Research Center 64, 134, 191, 239, 288, 310–313, 316, 322 f.
immigration laws 6, 101, 168, 217
Imotski 382, 385
imprisonment 16, 79, 180, 189, 261, 269
independence 11, 13 f., 18, 30, 35, 46, 50, 56, 61, 64, 66–68, 90, 113–117, 255 f., 271, 286, 306, 308 f., 312, 315, 317, 351, 371, 385, 388, 392
Independent Fighting Group (Grupi Luftëtar i Pavarur) 29
Independent Social Group (Niezależna Grupa Społeczna) 220
India 213, 267
Indiana 87, 89, 124, 327, 358
Indianapolis 87
Innsbruck 86, 189

Institute for the Investigation of Communist Crimes in Romania and the Memory of the Romanian Exile (IICCMER)   266, 282
– Institute for the Investigation of Communist Crimes in Romania (IICCR)   282
– National Institute and Memory of Romanian Exile (INMER)   282
Institute for the Studies of Communist Crimes and its Consequences in Albania (Instituti i Studimeve për Krimet dhe Pasojat e Komunizmit)   43
Institute for the Study of Communist Crimes and Exile Memory   282
Institute for the Study of Migration and Ethnicity (Institut za migracije i narodnosti)   387, 391, 394
Institute for Ukrainian Diaspora Studies   323
Institute of Diaspora Studies, Kiev   289
Institute of National Remembrance (IPN; Instytut Pamięci Narodowej)   1, 5, 91, 193 f., 200, 205, 208, 210 f., 213 f., 218–220, 222, 228, 230, 232–234, 236, 239–242, 312, 429
institutional completeness   300, 319 f.
Instytut Literacki [Literary Institute] (Maisons-Laffitte)   216, 225, 235, 238
integration   6 f., 17, 22, 32, 36, 56, 72, 97, 132, 141–143, 149, 165, 167, 223, 230 f., 281, 314, 373, 375, 392, 427, 429 f.
intelligence activities   6, 79, 359
Internal Macedonian Revolutionary Organization (IMRO)   77, 89
International Center of Free Trade Unionists in Exile   186
international cooperation   1, 67
International Federation for Human Rights   275
International Institute of Education, Culture and Contact with Diaspora   323
International Institute of Social History (IISH)   332, 338, 348, 357, 365, 426
International Memorial in Moscow   341 f., 344, 363
International Organization for Migration (IOM)   43
International Peasant Union   90, 186, 227
International Red Cross (IRC)   139
International Refugee Organization (IRO)   49, 83, 106 f., 174, 178 f., 184, 192, 298, 337
Ioanid, Radu   253
Ioannina   41
Ionesco, Marie-France   247, 273
Ioniță, Sorin Gabriel   271
Ioshida   356
Iowa   134
Iran   213, 356, 426
Iron Curtain   3, 7, 38, 57, 87, 91, 102, 160, 170, 173, 176, 181 f., 186, 188, 208, 218, 225–227, 247, 268, 274 f., 429
Iron Guard   253
Isajiw, Wsevolod W.   296, 307, 324
Israel   16, 82, 139, 174, 181, 184, 202, 205 f., 209, 214, 254, 264 f., 299, 341–345, 362
Istoc, Marin   261
Istrian peninsula   372
Italy   9 f., 12, 15 f., 21, 23, 27–31, 34, 41–43, 48, 84, 86, 89, 111, 148, 168, 173 f., 196, 200, 213, 215 f., 220, 238, 260, 262, 267 f., 277, 297 f., 320 f., 329, 335, 339, 373, 376, 394, 429
Ivan, Ruxandra   245, 255, 266
Ivanov, George   70 f., 363
Ivanova, Ivanka   96
Ivanović, Vladimir   370, 393 f.
Ivaylovgrad   69

Jaakson, Ernst   52 f.
Jackson, James Harvey   136
Jadrná-Pokorná, Rozina   130
Jakeš, Miloš   131
Jakimova, Marijana   73, 86
Jakóbczyk-Adamczyk, Patrycja   216
Jakova, Asim   31
Jakova, Tuk   11
jamming of radio stations   122 f., 125 f., 130, 275, 354 f.
Janauskas, Giedrius   60, 62 f.
Janjetović, Zoran   392
Jankola Library   134
Jankowski, Jerzy   224, 229 f.
Janouch, František   128
Janoušek, Karel   126
Japan   198, 257, 356
Jarausch, Konrad   150, 153
Jarema, Stephan   310
Jaroszyńska-Kirchmann, Anna   202
Jaruzelski, Wojciech   211
Jaunā Gaita   58
Jędrzejewicz, Wacław   239
Jenner, William E.   358
Jeřábek, Vojtěch   106, 135
Jerusalem   341 f., 344

Jewish Daily Forward 357
Jews 6, 45, 123, 244–45, 357
– See also: anti-Semitism
– Jewish refugees 138–139, 174, 181, 198, 216, 253, 304f.
– Migration 16, 71, 82, 137, 205f., 209, 212, 224, 251, 254, 256, 261, 264, 284, 287, 289, 326f., 341–345, 362, 366
– persecution of 74, 137, 173f., 181, 200, 246, 342f.
– rescue/saving of 16, 73f., 198
– wartime extermination 47, 73f., 191, 199f., 291f.
Jewtuch, Jewhen 288, 290, 324
Jewtuch, Włodzimierz 288
Jezdinský, Karel 105
Jinga, Luciana M. 266
Jiu Valley 272
Joanine 11
Johnson, A. Ross 95, 123, 125, 131, 235
Johnston, Robert H. 131, 330
Joint Baltic American National Committee 61, 66
Jonušauskas, Laurynas 52f., 66
Jordan, Zbigniew 91, 95, 230
Jorgoni, Elira 24
Josten, Josef 111f., 129, 134
Jović, Boško 380
Józef Piłsudski Institute of America 233, 238f., 308, 317
Judeţul Timiş 263
Juka, Musa 31
Junek, Marek 114, 123f., 131, 135
Jupp, James 338
Jüri Ant 56
Jürjo, Indrek 49, 58–60
Just, Vladimír 131
Jutro Polski 193, 197f., 200–203, 205f., 210–212, 215f., 218, 220–222, 225f., 229, 232, 234, 238–242, 296, 325

Kaba, Hamit 32f.
Kaczorowski, Ryszard 222, 236
Kádár, Janos 172
Kádár Lynn, Katalin 55, 90, 102, 135, 168, 176, 271, 428
Kadarja, Zef 16
Kaes, Anton 148
Kaiv, Johannes 53f.
Kakavi 41
Kalamäe, Raivo 62
Kalbarczyk, Sławomir 200
Kalc, Aleksej 379
Kalm, Arne 62
Kaloyanov, Vladimir 76
Kaplan, Marion A. 137
Karabulkov, Toncho 99
Karanukh, Alla 8, 286
Karel Kyncl 128
Karelia 46
Karoly, Bela 261
Karpovich, Michail 357, 364, 366
Karvelis, Petras 54
Kasekamp, Andres 46–48
Kastoria 41
Kastrati, Rexhep 29
Katek, Charles 105, 125
Katyń forest massacre 200f.
Kaunas 65
Kavan, Jan 111f., 128f., 132
Kazakhstan 200, 294f., 321
Kedryn-Rudnycki, Iwan 318
Këlcyra, Ali bey 15, 34
Kelley, Robert F. 350, 352–354, 364
Kello, Petrit 15
Kennan, George 350, 426
Kerensky, Alexander 188, 330, 350, 363
Kersten, Charles J. 61, 121, 313
Kesting, Robert W. 213
Khisamutdinov, Amir 366
Khrushchev, Nikita 19, 58, 78, 340
Kiev 289f., 293, 297, 304, 313
Kilgman, Gail 253, 266
Kilian, Stanisław 219
Kind-Kovács, Friederike 112
King, Russell 24f., 41, 43f.
Kingdom of Serbs, Croats, and Slovenes 69, 368
Kiraly, Béla 187
Kiripolský, Štefan 126
Kirk, Alan 350
Kirkpatrick, Evron M. 153
Kirschbaum, Jozef M. 107, 113, 116
Ķirsons, Māris 63
Kiryakov, Boyko 80, 84, 99
Kisbarnaki-Farkas, Ferenc 185
Kiselkova, Nina 71
Kłaczkow, Jarosław 224
Klagenfurt 86
Klaipėda 47f.

Klimov, Grigory   340
Klingholz, Reiner   161
Klisura, Ali   31
Kłonczyński, Arnold   216
Knight, Robert   82
Koblenz   133
Koci, Jake   31
Kodra e Priftit in Tirana   16
Kodumaa (Homeland)   59
Kogalniceanu, Mihail   245
Kohl, Helmut   149, 159, 161, 347
Kõiv, Enn   66
Koivunen, Pia   247, 259
Kojiš, Abbot Theodore   115
Koka, Sami   17
Kokalari, Musine   17
Kokojka, Mali   12
Kokoncheva, Maria   90
Kola, Bilal   39
Kołakowski, Leszek   230
Kolarska-Bobińska, Lena   237
Kolin, Ludwig   133
Kolinsky, Eva   162
Koliqi, Ernest   15, 26, 31
Komarica, Zvonimir   385
Kondylis, Florence   389
Konica, Faik   32, 36
Konstantin, Arhimandrit   53, 337, 349
Konstantinov, Dmitry   355, 363
Kool, Ferdinand   48, 66
Kopecký, Rudolf   134
Korboński, Stefan   228, 317
Korça, Xhevat   16
Korça Group   11
Korne, Mihai   273
Kosatík, Pavel   108, 134
Kosciuszko Foundation   288, 318, 427
K'oseva, Tsvetana   333
Kosovo   9f., 12–14, 16, 22, 25, 27, 34–36, 43, 384, 389f.
– Republic of Kosovo   9
Kosta, Fred   33
Koste, Çekrezi (also known as Kost/Kostandin/ Constantine Chekrezi)   32
Kostenko, Lina   297
Kostlán, Antonín   104f.
Kostov, Chris   77f.
Kostyrchenko, Gennadiy   344f.
Kota, Koço   16
Kote, Kostandin   16

Kotoshihin, Grigory   326
Kotta, Nuçi   29
Koura, Petr   106, 109, 127
Kovacs, Attila   189
Kovrig, Bennett   121, 127
Kozielsk   200
Kozłowski, Jerzy   199, 202, 215
Kozmaçi, Andon   16
Kozodoy, Ruth   341
Kraft, Waldemar   118
Krajina, Imotska   385
Krajina, Vladimir   105
Krajsa, Joseph C.   116
Kraków   11, 193f., 214, 218f., 225, 231, 234, 238, 241, 287, 289f., 294, 297, 320, 325, 427
Krasniqi, Rexhep   34f.
Krasteva, Anna   78f., 81, 83f., 96f., 100
Kravarev, Dimitar Petkov   92
Kravchenko, Viktor   340
Krawczenko, Bohdan   292f., 297
Kraysky, Bruno   345
Krebs, Ronald R.   121, 247
Kremlin   1, 4, 7, 341, 343, 350, 359, 366
Křen, Jan   119
Krenz, Egon   155
Kreuzbruderschaft (Crusaders, or Križari)   386
Krivoshein, Nikita   334, 337
Krivosheina, Nina   337
Kröhnert, Steffen   161
Krug, Manfred   152
Kruja, Mustafa   13, 26
Krumovgrad   69
Kryeziu brothers (Kryeziu, Said bey; Kryeziu, Gani bey and Kryeziu, Cano bey)   12, 28, 31
Kubiak, Hieronim   289
Kubičko, Radko   131
Kucharski, Władysław S.   215
Kula, Marcin   70, 203
Kułakowski, Jan   227, 236
Kulikov, Nikolay   334
Kulischer, Eugene   139f.
Kultura   220, 225, 229, 234f., 239, 278f., 318f.
Kumer-Haukanõmm, Kaja   45, 48–51, 55, 64, 66
Kun, Béla   170
Kupi, Abaz (also called Bazi i Canës)   12–16, 26

Kurbsky, Andrey 326
Kuropas, Myron 287, 289, 307, 324
Kushner, A.R. 389
Kusielewicz, Eugeniusz 289
Kuznets, Simon 326
Kvetko, Martin 111
Kyhn, Peter 63

Łabędzki, Jan 232
labor, forced 14, 17, 22, 24, 40, 42, 50, 68, 78, 96, 100, 121, 123, 125, 138–140, 142, 144, 148f., 162–164, 166, 168, 182f., 198f., 208f., 215, 220, 231, 237, 292, 326f., 331, 338f., 346, 357, 359, 368–370, 377, 380f., 383–389, 391f.
labor camp 21, 75f., 78, 200, 273
Labov, Jessie 112
Lafontaine, Oskar 159
Laiks 58
Lake Placid 313
Lakewood, New Jersey 48, 64, 114
Lalor 15
Lane, Thomas 46
Lange, Fritz 144
Larrabee, F. Stephen 19
Latin America 15, 19, 169, 173f., 184f., 192, 203, 217, 326, 329, 338, 355f., 359, 371
Latvia 35, 45–49, 52–55, 57–60, 63–67, 186, 228, 314, 321, 329, 331, 335, 343, 353
Latvian Association of Australia (Latviešu apvienība Austrālijā) 55
Latvian Association of Brazil (Latviešu apvienība Brazīlijā) 55
Latvian Documentation Centre 65
Latvian Liberation Committee of the European Centre (Latvijas atbrīvošanas komitejas Eiropas centrs) 55
Latvian National Association in Canada (Latviešu nacionālā apvienība Kanādā) 55
Latvian Social Democrat Workers' Party 57
Latvian Welfare Fund (Daugavas Vanagi; Hawks of the river Daugava) 56
Latvians 45–51, 55, 66, 299, 312, 339
Latvija Amerikā 58
Lauer Rice, Andrea 192
Lázár, George 190
Lazarewitch, Ida 365
Lazarewitch, Nikolay 365
Lăzăroiu, Sebastian 280

Le Normand, Brigitte 368, 383, 387, 393f., 428
League for Independent Poland (Liga Niepodległości Polski, LNP) 219f.
League for the Defense of Human Rights of Romania (LDHR) 272–274, 284
League of Communists of Yugoslavia 11
League of Nations 61, 70
– Commissioner for Refugees 70
League of Struggle for the Freedom of Peoples 350
Lefterov, Zhivko 80
Legaliteti (Legaliteti/Lëvizja e Legalitetit; eng. Legality Movement) 12, 14f., 25–29, 31f., 35f.
legionnaires 180, 253, 262
legislation, repressive 118, 146, 169, 257, 268, 273, 338, 347, 362
Lehrbach 157f.
Leicestershire 65
Leipzig 152, 166
Leka I Zogu 10f., 36f.
Leka, Hilmi 16
Lemekh, Halyna 306
Lemke, Christian 150
Lencznarowicz, Jan 208, 218
Lenin, Vladimir 328
Leningrad 47, 59, 361
Leoben 86
Leskoviku, Xhavit 16
Lettrich, Jozef 108, 113
Levin, Isaak Don 350
Levin, Jury 361
Levin, Nora 341, 343
Levina, Asya 345
Levitsky, Anatoly 331
Levy, Daniel 143
Łewicki, Borys 318
Ležák-Borin, Vladimir 106
Lhomel, Édith 276
L'Hommedieu, Jonathan 55f.
Liaison Committee for Cultural Relations with Compatriots Abroad (Kultūras sakaru biedrība) 59
Libera, Paweł 216
Liberal-Democratic Union of Central Eastern Europe 227
Liberty of the Nation (Liria e Kombit) 35
Liebich, Andre 330, 366
Lienz 335

Liepiņš, Robert 54
Lipski, Józef 198, 226
Liquidation Commission (Polish) 236
Lisowyj, Wasyl 297
Listy Group 111f., 128
Liszewicz, Leonidas 240
Lithuania 2, 35, 45–50, 52–61, 63–67, 186, 202, 228, 311f., 314, 317, 321, 326, 329, 331, 335, 353
Lithuanian American Council 61
Lithuanian Association in the UK (Didžiosios Britanijos Lietuvių Sąjunga) 56
Lithuanian Emigration Institute (Lietuvių išeivijos institutas) 65
Lithuanian Museum-Archives of Canada 65
Lithuanian Research and Studies Center (Lituanistikos tyrimo ir studijų centras) 61, 65
Lithuanian Soviet Socialist Republic 229
Lithuanian World Center 65
Lithuanian World Community (Pasaulio lietuvių bendruomenė, PLB) 54, 56f., 63, 65f.
Lithuanians 45–54, 57, 60, 62, 65, 200, 204, 299, 304, 312, 319, 327, 339
Litván, György 172
Ljarjaa, Nertila Haxhia 35
Łobodowski, Józef 216, 229
Lodeesen, John 353f., 364
Łódź 194, 198f., 218, 239
Logoreci, Anton 19
Londonas Avīze 58
Looby, Robert 230
Lorraine 157
Los Angeles 87, 314
Loughlin, John 17–19, 22
Lovejoy, Alice 112, 129
Lovinescu, Monica 251f., 254f., 276f., 284
Low, Alfred 341, 346
Lower Saxony 142f.
Loyer, Emmanuelle 248
Lozoraitis, Stasys 53f.
Lublin 1, 216, 218, 220, 229f., 232, 234, 236, 238, 241, 297, 428f.
Luburić, Maks 371
Łuczak, Czesław 194, 199
Ludanyi, Andrew 373, 375
Ludogorie 76
Ludwig, Bernard 230
Łukasiewicz, Juliusz 226

Łukasiewicz, Sławomir 1, 193f., 205, 210f., 214, 218, 220, 227, 230, 232, 234, 236, 240f., 428
Łukaszewski, Jerzy 227, 236
Lukeš, Igor 101–103, 106, 109f., 115, 119, 121–125, 127, 134f.
Lupul, Mandy R. 296, 324
Lushaku, Hilë 12
Luža, Radomír 111, 119
Lviv 229, 297, 304, 323
Lyon 260
Lyons, Eugene 350
Lysiak-Rudnycki, Iwan 318

Ma Mung, Emmanuel 245
Mâța, Dan Constantin 256
Macartney, Carlile Aylmer 69f.
Macedonia 2, 9f., 12, 15, 36, 43, 68f., 74, 77f., 81, 85, 89, 368, 378f., 382, 384, 390, 392
– Republic of North Macedonia 89
Macedonian Patriotic Organization / Macedonian Political Organization (MPO) 89
Macedonization of the Bulgarians 78
Machewicz, Paweł 193, 225, 233f., 240f.
Maçi, Halil 29
Maciso, John J. 289f.
Mackiewicz, Stanisław 208, 219, 233f., 241
Macrea-Toma, Ioana 275–277
Maczek, Stanisław 215
Madden, Ray J. 124
Made, Vahur 54, 60
Madrid 36, 52, 63, 86, 90, 124, 129, 226, 273f.
Magdeburg 166
Magheti, Doina 263
Magocsi, Paul Robert 2, 119f., 134, 244, 326
Magyars 119f., 134, 377
Mai, Nicola 23, 41, 44
Maik, Ludwik 197
Majer, Václav 108
Majko, Pandeli 40
Major, Patrick 351
Maklakov, Vasily 348, 350, 363
Makovsky, Sergey 363
Makowski, Krzysztof 287
Maksimov, Grigory 365
Maksimov, Vladimir 354
Malczewski, Zdzisław 217
Malet, Marian 101

Malkavaara, Mikko 60
Mälksoo, Lauri 52
Maloki, Kristo 31
Malosmani, Ismail 12
Mămăliga, Leonid 278
Mamatey, Victor S. 101
Manea, Gabriel Stelian 256
Manea, Norman 284
Maniku, Tut 17
Manin, Marino 392
Manolescu, Florin 277 f., 284
March, Roman 309
Marès, Antoine 253, 279, 430
Maresch, Eugenia 200
Margolit, Gilad 119
marielitos 210
Markagjoni, Gzon 30
Markagjoni, Ndue 26, 30
Marko, Vasil 32
Markov, Atanas 76
Markov, Georgi 99 f., 190
Marks, Shula 104
Marku, Gjin 11
Markus, Daria 307
Marmullaku, Ramadan 10
Marrus, Michael 337
Martaneshi, Baba Faja 12
martial law 209 f., 236
Maruniak, Wolodymyr 288, 297–299, 301–303, 324
Masaryk, Tomáš 101, 120
Māsēns, Vilis 55
massacre 71, 200
Matica
– Hrvatska 386 f.
– iseljenika organizations 381
– Slovenská 129, 133
Mattes, Monika 166 f.
Mayakovsky, Vladimir 332
Mayski, Ivan 196
Mazurkiewicz, Anna 1, 5, 91–93, 101 f., 117, 135, 208, 223, 225, 227 f., 233, 235, 241, 312, 426 f., 429
Mbroja, Tefik 16
McCargar, James 175
McCarthy, Joseph 349
Medek, Ivan 128, 130, 132
Međumurje 373, 383
Meie Elu 57
Melbourne 15, 326, 337

Melnyk, Myron 305
Merits, Helga 57
Merkuriusz Polski 225
Merlika, Reshit 16
Mertelsmann, Olaf 60
Merten, Ulrich 374 f., 392
Mexico 213, 217
Meyer, Henry Cord 136
Mežnarić, Silva 391
Michálek, Slavomír 108 f., 121, 134
Michalon, Bénédicte 244 f.
Michałowski, Roman 227
Michev, Dobrin 77 f.
Michigan 87, 136, 338
Middle East 196, 200, 203, 213, 218, 294, 322, 329
Mieroszewski, Juliusz 229, 239
migration 1, 3–9, 15 f., 20 f., 23–25, 39–47, 51 f., 64, 66, 68, 71, 73, 78–80, 82–84, 86, 96–98, 100 f., 104 f., 107, 132, 136–139, 142, 146, 148–151, 155, 159 f., 162–171, 173, 175, 179, 181, 183, 187, 190–195, 197–199, 201, 203–207, 209–216, 236–241, 243–248, 251–254, 256–258, 260 f., 264 f., 268–270, 278–290, 292–297, 299 f., 302, 304–306, 308–310, 319 f., 322, 324, 326, 333, 347, 362, 368–370, 372 f., 378 f., 383–385, 387–395, 426–429
– migrant integration, see integration
– migration, agreement, see agreement
– migration, external 68, 70 f., 74, 81–83, 96, 383
– migration, forced 118, 173, 198 f., 201, 245 f., 291, 293–295, 320, 374
– migration, intercontinental; also known as „overseas migration" 289, 320
– migration, internal 9, 23–25, 44, 97, 136, 142, 148, 161 f., 164, 204, 284, 289, 295
– migration, labor 79, 83, 138, 148–150, 168, 257, 368, 370, 379–385, 387, 391–394
– migration, legal/illegal 43, 137, 147, 208, 237, 250, 254, 257, 261 f., 281, 378
– migration, pattern 1, 6, 8 f., 136 f., 169, 204, 289, 391
– migration, permanent/temporary 211, 257–259
– migration, stream 1, 6, 8, 20, 52, 69, 78, 104 f., 142, 148, 156, 158, 165 f., 173, 197, 204,

206f., 209f., 213–215, 229, 234, 246, 252, 288f., 292f., 320, 333f., 340, 370, 378
- migration, voluntary   173, 293f., 320, 393
- migration flows   193, 320
- migration policy   78, 96f., 207, 210f., 282, 370, 393
- migration/transit   137, 148, 179, 210, 345, 377, 379, 390f.
- migratory movements   290, 293, 295, 320
- multi-ethnic migratory flows   292
Mihaylov, Ivan   89
Mikkonen, Simo   247, 259, 340
Mikołajczyk, Stanisław   204, 218–220, 228, 231, 239, 311f., 317
Milanovats, Gorni   333
Miletić, Aleksandar R.   368
Miliukov, Pavel   330f.
Milošević, Slobodan   389
Miłosz, Czesław   224, 234, 239
Milza, Pierre   253, 279
Minařík, Pavel   127
Ministry/Committee for State Security (MGB/KGB)   58f.
Minneapolis   64, 134, 191, 239, 326
minority (ethnic population)   10, 41, 48, 57, 70, 77f., 82, 103, 108, 113, 120, 133, 181f., 206f., 244, 246, 257, 281, 287, 343, 351, 371–375, 378, 429
Minsk   342
Mintchev, Vesselin   68, 70, 81
Mirakaj, Kol Bit   31
Mirakaj, Ndoc (Puka)   39
Mirdashi, Gustav   16
Mississauga   65
Mitev, Trendafil   89
Mitrokhin, Vasili   232
Mitrovica, Redjip   31
Mitrovica, Rexhep   14f., 27
Mitrovica, Xhelal   34
Mitseva, Evgenia   71, 81
Mitterrand, François   267
mobilization, political   117, 137f., 220, 224, 243, 270, 285, 310, 379f., 384
Moczar, Mieczysław   233
Modelski, Izydor   232
Moesia   68
Moldova   2, 68, 137, 170, 243f., 246, 295, 321
Molenda, Jarosław   204
Molotov-Ribbentrop Pact   46, 62, 198

monarchy   10f., 26f., 37, 90, 168, 328, 330, 332, 358f.
Monat, Paweł   232
Monfalcone   373, 377
Montenegro   9, 12, 384
Morawiecki, Kornel   210
Morawski, Kajetan   226
Morocco   184
Morozov, Boris   342–344
Morris, Helen M.   60f., 63
Morrison, John N.L.   351
Mościcki, Ignacy   195
Moseikina, Marina   327
Most Favored Nation (MFN)   172f., 251f.
Mudry, Wasyl   310
Mueller, Carol   248
Mueller, Wolfgang   376
Mugoša, Dušan   11
Muka, Koco   26, 31
Mulleti, Hysni   29
Mulletti, Qazim   31
Mungiu, Cristian   266
Munich Institute for Soviet Studies   355
Muntele, Ionuț   244, 252f., 264
Munz, Rainer   193, 201
Murgescu, Bogdan   247, 255
Murin, Charles   107
Muscovy   326
Museum of Memory in Shkodër (Muzeu i Kujtesës, Shkodër)   43
Museum of Memory (Muzeu i Memories)   21, 43
Museum of the Occupation of Latvia (Latvijas Okupācijas muzejs)   65
Muslims   15f., 72, 74, 244, 354, 377f.
Mussolini, Benito   10
Mustafa, Kruja   15
Myftiu, Sali   26
Myshuha, Dr. Luke   310

Nabokov, Vladimir   364
Naegele, Jolyon   130
Nagy, Ferenc   175, 186
Nagy, Imre   172
Najder, Zdzisław   230
Nanterre   99, 365, 426
Naraçi, Ndoc   16
nation   3, 5, 7, 16, 27, 30, 36f., 47, 62f., 65, 67, 74, 77f., 89, 93, 101, 114, 117, 129, 137, 139f., 148, 160, 168f., 173f., 178, 181, 187,

189, 191, 221f., 247, 271, 310–316, 342, 352f., 371f., 374, 378
National Captive Nations Committee (NCNC) 311
National Catholic Welfare Conference 298
National Committee of Hungarians from Czechoslovakia 120
National Committee of the Republican Party 358
National Committees for a free Estonia, Latvia and Lithuania 55
National Council for the Study of the Securitate Archives (CNSAS) 249, 282
National Front for Romanians' Union 271
National Legionary State (Romania) 272
National Liberal Party of Romania (Partidul Naţional Liberal) 253
National Liberation Front (of Albania) 13
National Liberation General Council (of Albania) 13
National Liberation Movement (Lëvizje Nacionalçlirimtare, NLM) 13f., 17
National Peasant Party of Romania (Partidul Naţional Ţărănesc) 253, 271
National Social Movement (Bulgaria) 88
National Socialist Party (Czechoslovakia) 105, 107–110, 114, 117,
National Socialist German Workers' Party (Nazi Party) 137, 229, 338, 357
nationalists 5, 11f., 12, 48, 58–61, 66, 82, 113–116, 118, 136, 189, 256, 297, 301, 308f., 314, 354, 371, 374, 385–388, 428
Nazarov, Michail 330, 365
Nazi Germany 3, 13, 46, 59, 92, 114, 137, 198, 253, 331f., 334, 353, 357
Neblich, Esther 143
Nedelcu, Mihaela 244f., 272
Nekola, Martin 102, 108
Nekrich, Alexander 364
Nelson, Michael 122f., 125, 127, 131, 275
Němec, Jaroslav 112f.
Nemtsanov, Serguei 260
Nepriklausoma Lietuva 58
Nešpor, Zdeněk 133
Netherlands 51, 137, 184, 202, 299, 321, 336, 339, 365, 426
Neubauer, John 112
New Brunswick 192, 374
New Jersey 64, 341, 350

New York City 87, 112, 192, 288, 313, 322f., 331f., 356, 427
New York Daily Mail 147
New York Times 147, 189, 261
New Zealand 51, 174, 184, 210, 213, 322, 337–339
newspaper/émigré publishing/media coverage of migration 27–29, 34f., 57–59, 98, 146, 153, 160, 179, 189, 225, 263, 270, 274f., 277, 283, 308, 327f., 331, 342, 346, 348, 356, 358f., 364, 384–386
Ngo Din Diem 356
Nicholas II of Russia 359
Nichols, David 172
Nicholson, Emma (baroness) 268
Nickel, Hildegard Maria 162
Nicolescu, Vasile 251
Niebieszczański, Adam 228
Niedersächsische 263
Nikolaevsky, Boris 330, 357, 363
Nikolaikirche 152
Nikolova, Nadya 75
Nikopol 69
Niš 69
Nisiobęcka, Aneta 214
Nixon, Richard 256, 270
Noli, Fan 32f., 36, 43
normalization 104, 111, 160, 190, 341
North Rhine-Westphalia 154, 203
Northern Caucasus 295
Nõu, Enn 66
Nova Zagora 69
Novinšćsak, Karolina 393
Novoe Russkoe Slovo 356
Novy Journal 357, 364
Nowak, Magdalena 8, 239
Nowicka, Ewa 214
Nowy Dziennik 228, 308, 318
NTS (National Labor Union of the New Generation/Natsionalno-Trudovoy Sojuz Novogo Pokolenija) 330f., 351, 355f., 359–366
Nurek, Mieczysław 196, 203, 241
nylon curtain 246

Oberlander, Theodor 118
Obolenskaya-Flam, Ludmila 351
Obolensky, Valerian 331, 351
Obolensky, Vladimir 348
Obradov, Marica Karakaš 392

occupation 5, 10–12, 22, 26 f., 35, 48, 52, 58, 64, 76, 117 f., 138–143, 170 f., 173, 175 f., 191, 197 f., 201, 253, 307, 335, 349, 369, 372 f., 375
occupation zone 86, 139–141, 183, 202, 298, 300 f., 374
Oddo, Gilbert 107
Oder-Neisse line 141, 203, 229, 374
Odložilík, Otakar 101
O'Donnell, James S. 20
Office of Policy Coordination (OPC) 38
O'Grady, Joseph P. 101
Ohio 53, 87, 134, 185, 202, 322, 337
Ohrid (lake) 379
oil crisis 148 f., 384
Okólski, Marek 212, 241
Okudjava, Bulat 361
Olomouc 133 f.
Olszewski, Edward 216
Olszewski, Stanisław 228
Olszewski, Witold 233
Oltmer, Jochen 137, 139, 141 f., 149, 166
Omari, Bahri 16
Opisul emigrației politice [The register of political emigration] 262, 273, 284
Opole 238
opposition 4, 7, 15, 17, 21, 25, 37, 42, 59, 63, 74, 83, 93, 110, 151 f., 159, 175, 179, 204, 210 f., 221, 231, 233 f., 275, 283, 297, 307, 312–314, 318, 345, 347, 350, 352, 360, 386
Orav, Mart 66
Organization for the Defense of Four Freedoms of Ukraine (ODFFU) 305, 307
Organization for the Rebirth of Ukraine (ODWU) 306 f.
Organization of Free Bulgarians (Organizatsia na svobodnite balgari) 88
Organization of Ukrainian Nationalists (OUN) 297, 308
origin, country of/place of 1, 4, 10 f., 56, 139, 149, 152, 178, 191, 205, 215, 217, 227, 229, 245, 254, 264, 268, 287, 289, 296, 301, 315 f., 327, 372
Orlov, Boris 345
Orłowski, Hubert 197
O'Rourke, John 74
Orzeł Biały 205, 225
Osadczuk, Bohdan 318
Osóbka-Morawski, Edward 231

Ostalgie 165
Ostaszków 200
Ostpolitik 127, 386, 388
Ostsiedlung 136
Osuský, Štefan 107 f., 110, 113 f., 116, 121, 133 f.
Ottawa 62, 129, 192, 307
Ottoman Empire 10 f., 68 f., 71–73, 76, 136, 379

Paderewski, Ignacy 195
Padova 113
Pahiatua 213
Paisiy, Otets 90
Paix et Liberté 230
Palach Press 111 f.
Palestine 174, 181, 202, 205, 213, 244, 339
Pali, Zef 28 f., 33
Palyanitsya, Andrii 132
Panayotov, Panayot 99
Panina, Sofia 364
Papánek, Ján 106–108, 113 f., 125, 134
Papathimiu, Sonila 25, 43 f.
Papée, Kazimierz 226
Paprikoff, George I. 93, 99
Paraguay 184, 202, 217, 290, 299, 309, 322, 338 f.
Paraschiv, Vasile 273, 275
Paraskevov, Vasil 82–84, 90 f., 190
Parażanow, Siergiej 297
Paris 9, 11, 27, 29, 36, 75, 85 f., 92, 96, 99, 107–109, 113, 120, 137, 186, 195, 210, 216, 224, 226, 229, 234 f., 238, 243–245, 247 f., 252 f., 255, 258–261, 264 f., 269 f., 272 f., 275–279, 330, 337, 344, 351, 355, 372 f., 430
Parisius, Bernhard 143
Parta, Russell Eugene 95
Partia Agrarare Shqiptare (Albanian Agrarian Party) 29
Partia Grupi i Kosovës (Grupi i Kosovarëve/Partia Irendentiste/The „Kosovo group" Party/The Kosovars' Group/the Irredentist Party) 26
Partisans 11, 14, 370
Party of Labor of Albania 14, 17, 39
passport 6, 40, 73, 104, 146, 204, 210 f., 214, 235, 248–250, 279, 296, 370, 379 f., 386 f.
– regime/application 249 f., 370, 380
Patek, Artur 200

Päts, Konstantin 53
Paučo, Jozef 113, 116
Paul, Ellen 101
Pavelić, Ante 371
Pavlaković, Vera 383, 391
Pawliczko, Ann Lencyk 289f., 294, 296, 299, 307, 322, 324
Pawlikowicz, Leszek 226, 232
Pawluczuk, Włodzimierz 297
Pawłyczko, Dmytro 297
Payne, Jason 23
Pearson, Owen 34
Peasant League (Lidhja Katundare) 29
pečalba 368, 379, 392
Pecháček, Pavel 130f.
Peci, Sotir 17, 32
Peck, Jeffrey 150
Pehe, Jiří 104f., 133
Pehr, Otto 228
Pejani, Bedri 14
Peka, Sejdi 34
Pelikán, Jiří 111f., 128f., 131
Pelin, Mihai 262, 284
penal law/penal code 79, 204, 261
Penev, Goran 390
Pennar, Jaan 50, 55f., 61, 66, 353
Pennsylvania 87, 134, 322
People's Party (Stronnictwo Ludowe, SL) 107, 126, 218f.
People's Republic of China 19
People's Republic of Poland 194, 206, 231, 239f.
People's Socialist Republic of Albania 17f.
Perelman, Viktor 344
Pergega, Zef 29
Permanent Conference of Slovak Democratic Exiles 114
Përmeti, Aqif 16
Peroutka, Ferdinand 108f., 121f., 124, 134
persecution, religious 71, 77, 104, 113, 129, 131, 144, 182, 204, 272f., 370, 376
Peru 174, 184, 217, 299
Pervisi, Prenk 31
Peshev, Dimitar 73
Péteri, György 246
Petkov, Nikola 83, 92
Petkova, Lidia 72
Petraru, Marius 8, 271
Petryshyn, Jaroslav 307
Petryshyn, Roman 296, 309, 324

Peykovska, Penka 71
Peza, Myslym 12
Pfaff, Steven 152
Pfeiffer, Zoltan 186
Philadelphia 33, 65, 87, 188, 337
Philby, Kim 39
Philippines 356
Piesakowski, Tomasz 215
Pigniczky, Réka 192
Piirimäe, Kaarel 60
Pilch, Andrzej 287, 289
Piłsudski, Józef 195, 219
Pilsudski Institute of America 223, 288
Pinkus, Benjamin 343
Piotrowski, Jacek 197, 219f.
Pipa, Arshi 11, 22
Pipes, Richard 329
Pirin Macedonia 77f.
Pirot 69, 74
Pisuliński, Jan 204
Piznak, Michael 310
Plakans, Andrejs 46–48, 64
Planche, Anne 273
Planche, François 273
Pleskot, Patryk 210f., 234, 236, 241, 427
Pletzing, Christian 48
Pletzing, Marianne 48
Pliushkov, A. I. 365
Plovdid 69
Pobóg-Malinowski, Władysław 239
Podgórski, Bogdan 231
Podkarpacie 291
Podkrivacký, Adam 134
Pogradec 16
Polakovič, Štefan 114, 116, 124
Poland 1–3, 35, 45, 47f., 73, 81, 119, 137, 140f., 154f., 174, 186, 193–199, 201–217, 219f., 222, 224–229, 231–240, 257, 287, 289–291, 295f., 317f., 321, 323, 329, 335, 339, 356, 374, 427–429
– Republic of Poland 198f., 230, 291
Poles 3, 46, 138, 157, 194–196, 198–205, 208–218, 222–224, 226f., 230f., 233, 236f., 239–241, 286–289, 291, 298f., 304f., 310, 312, 314, 316f., 319, 324, 427
Polian, Pavel 334, 366
Polish Armed Forces in the West 194–196, 200, 203, 214, 217, 223

Polish Army Veterans Association of America (Stowarzyszenie Weteranów Armii Polskiej w Ameryce, SWAP) 223
Polish Christian Labor Party (Stronnictwo Pracy, SP) 218
Polish Committee of National Liberation 291
Polish Communist Ministry of Public Security 232
Polish Consulate General (New York) 308
Polish Ex-Combatants Association/Polish Veterans Army Association (Stowarzyszenie Polskich Kombatantów, SPK) 222, 224, 288
Polish Federalists' Association (Związek Polskich Federalistów) 230
Polish First Corps 196
Polish Freedom Movement „Independence and Democracy" (Polski Ruch Wolnościowy „Niepodległość i Demokracja," PRW NiD) 220
Polish Home Army Ex-Servicemen Association (Związek byłych Żołnierzy Armii Krajowej) 222
Polish Institute of Arts and Sciences of America 223, 318, 238
Polish National Democratic Committee (Polski Narodowy Komitet Demokratyczny) 220, 227
Polish National Union (Polskie Zjednoczenie Narodowe) 221
Polish People's Republic 205, 207, 230 f., 234, 239
Polish Resettlement Corps 197, 223
Polish Second Corps 196 f.
Polish Socialist Party (Polska Partia Socjalistyczna, PPS) 218, 225
Polish Underground Movement Study Trust (Studium Polski Podziemnej) 238
Polish University Abroad in London (Polski Uniwersytet na Obczyźnie, PUNO) 223
Political Council (Rada Polityczna) 220, 223, 227, 232
political refugee 42, 51, 56 f., 60, 62, 66, 117, 126, 137, 170, 191, 217, 376, 393
Polonia (Poles and their descendants abroad) 203, 208, 210, 212, 215, 223, 232, 239, 289, 317, 427
„Polonia" Society for Liaison with Poles Abroad (Towarzystwo Łączności z Polonią Zagraniczną „Polonia") 208, 239

Pomerania 199, 201
Pomian, Grażyna 229
Pomian, Jan (Bławdziewicz) 230
Pop, Mihai 243
Popa, Ioana 255
Pope John Paul II 129, 132, 224
Popescu, Dumitru 250 f.
Popescu, Titu 270
Popiel, Karol 228
Popov, Andrey 366
Popović, Miladin 11
Popovsky, Mark 345
populating virgin areas 290
population exchange 5, 71, 202
population transfers 1, 6, 68, 117, 193, 198, 200, 206
Poremsky, Vladimir 361
Porta, Eugene 235
Posen, see Poznań
Posev 330 f., 351, 355, 359–361
Pospelovsky, Dmitry 351
Possev Verlag 365
Potocki, Józef 226
Potot, Swanie 269, 281
Potsdam Agreement 3, 5, 140 f., 166, 201 f., 204, 374
Poutrus, Patrice G. 166
Povolný, Mojmír 111 f., 129, 134
Powers, Mary C. 289 f.
Poznań 137, 194, 197–199, 202, 218, 242
Prague 103, 105 f., 108, 112, 114, 119, 121, 123 f., 127, 131, 135, 153, 331
Prague Spring 104, 110 f., 127–131, 133, 270
Praszałowicz, Dorota 287, 289, 325, 427
Prchala, Lev 108, 118, 120
Prečan, Vilém 133
Predojević-Despić, Jelena 390
Preka, Zef (Zadrima) 39
Prekmurje 373
Preparatory Commission for the International Refugee Organization (PCIRO) 174, 179
Preševo Valley 9, 12
Prešov 119
Preston 15
Prídavok, Peter 115
prisoners, political 21, 138–140, 150 f., 199, 215, 246, 248, 253, 256, 264, 273, 334–337, 340, 428
Prokop, Tomek 123
Prokš, Petr 103, 121

Promeny („Metamorphosis")   112
Promitzer, Christian   73
propaganda   4, 6, 18, 22 f., 26, 28, 35, 38, 101, 120–123, 126 f., 129, 131, 135, 145, 147, 178, 180, 189, 201, 208, 230, 234, 250, 283, 292, 308, 310 f., 327 f., 332, 336 f., 340, 342, 347, 350–352, 354 f., 377, 381, 385
Protectorate of Bohemia and Moravia   137
Proudfoot, Malcom Jarvis   169, 174–176, 178–184, 192
Provisional Council of National Unity (Tymczasowa Rada Jedności Narodowej, TRJN)   219, 221, 223, 227
Prussia   201
Pryanishnikov, B.   360, 363
Przemyśl   323
psychological warfare   4, 7, 225, 235, 355
Pszenicki, Krzysztof   225
public opinion   91, 94, 210 f., 272, 311 f.
publications/exile/émigré   134, 283
Puddington, Arch   119, 123–125, 127, 131, 275
Pułtusk   239
Pushkarev, Boris   330, 355, 360 f.
Pushkareva, Natalia   333, 347
Pushkin Society   358, 364
Puskás, Julianna   168–173, 175 f., 179, 192
Pusta, Kaarel Robert   65
Pustina, Bajram   16
Putnam   65

Qeribashi, Sami   17
Qerolli, Nexhmedin   26
Quai d'Orsay   226
Quai-shek, Chan   356
Queen Geraldine   10

Raag, Raimo   45, 49–52, 57, 60
Raczkiewicz, Władysław   195 f., 220
Raczyński, Edward   221, 226, 230
Rad, Ilie   278
Radi, Lazër   16, 233
radicalization   386
Radio   55, 59, 100, 103, 114, 123–125, 127, 130 f., 135, 225, 277
– Radio Canada International   122
– Radio France Internationale   122, 225
– Radio Free Europe (RFE)   28, 55 f., 95, 105, 109, 119, 121–127, 129–131, 133–135, 220, 233–235, 239, 272, 275 f., 283 f., 353, 355, 365
– Polish Section of Radio Free Europe   225, 230
– Radio Liberation (Radio Liberty, RL)   4, 56, 119, 123, 275, 283, 341 f., 344, 351–355, 361 f., 364 f.
– Radio Madrid   216, 225, 351
– Radio Prague   130
– Vatican Radio   56, 122, 131
Rădulescu, Ion Heliade   245
Radut-Draghi, Luciana   278 f.
Radzik, Tadeusz   214
Radziłowski, John   188 f.
Raeff, Mark   365
Rahr, Gleb   351, 365
Rahr, Lev   331
Raikin, Spas   85, 90, 93 f., 98 f.
Rațiu, Ion   271 f., 285
Rákosi, Mátyás   175
Rakovski, Georgi Sava   68
Rampe, Leonid   51
Ranković, Aleksandar   380
ransom   150 f., 160, 428
Raška, Francis Dostál   8, 102 f., 105 f., 109 f., 112, 115 f., 119–125, 127, 129, 131 f., 134
Ratnik   90
Rauziński, Robert   198
Ravančić, Martina Grahek   371
Raymond Breton   300
Rea, James E.   307
Readman, Kristina Spohr   54
Reagan, Ronald   36, 131
Rebas, Hain   57
reception centers   147, 153
Rechcígl, Miloslav   110, 113, 134
Reczyńska, Anna   217
Red/Soviet Army   113, 140 f., 182, 194, 200 f., 246, 255, 331, 334, 354
Redlih, Roman   356
refugee   5 f., 8, 15, 26, 30, 33 f., 40 f., 43, 46–52, 55, 57–59, 62, 66, 69–72, 75, 77 f., 81, 83–86, 102–107, 118, 121, 125, 135 f., 139, 141–147, 153–160, 163, 167, 169–174, 176–184, 187–192, 210, 213, 217, 228, 245, 255, 296, 298, 300, 304, 323, 328 f., 337 f., 369–371, 375–378, 389 f., 429
– refugee camps   84, 93, 105 f., 144, 178, 305, 376

– refugee reception 153
Regensburg 302f.
Řehák, Edmund 111
Rei, August 53, 56
Reich, Simon 391
Reich-Ranicki, Marceli 208
Reichling, Gerhard 141
Reichsgau Wartheland 199
Reisch, Alfred A. 226, 235
relocation 25, 106, 157, 196, 214, 245–247, 254, 264, 428
Remizov, Alexey 363
repatriates 145, 335f., 377
repatriation 48, 58f., 139f., 142, 166, 174, 176–180, 202, 205, 207, 217, 245, 291, 294, 320, 332f., 335–337, 343, 366, 375, 377, 385
– repatriation, forced 140, 335
– repatriation campaign 6f., 207f., 233, 291
Republikflucht 145–147
resettlement 6f., 57, 142f., 178, 184, 190, 198, 204, 206f., 291
resistance 10, 94, 190, 247, 277–8
– armed 12–15, 28–29, 35, 38–39, 47, 68–69, 92, 196, 199, 331–334
retribution 117, 126, 369, 371
Rettinger, Józef 230
return, rights 145, 154, 206
returnees 7, 48, 64, 237, 377
reunification/families 150f., 165, 207, 250, 273, 296, 428
Revay, Julian 310
revolt 69, 82, 172
Rexhepi, Baba 15
Rhodope Mountains 68
Ribbentrop-Molotov Pact, see Molotov-Ribbentrop Pact
Richardson, Nancy Anna 261
Riga 47, 49, 58, 65
Rijeka 372, 377, 428
Rink-Abel, Marju 55
Ripka, Hubert 105, 107, 109, 121, 124
Rock, David 143, 167
Roesler, Jörg 164
Rogalewska, Ewa 242
Roi, Yaacov 343
Rojek, Wojciech 197
Rolandi, Francesca 8, 376f., 380, 393
Roma (ethnic group) 47, 116, 183, 218, 225, 227, 246, 281, 296, 310, 356, 430

Roman, Stephen 116
Roman, Wanda K. 197
Roman, W. Petrysyn 296
Romania 2f., 35, 69, 71, 75, 81, 170, 173, 182, 186, 188f., 191, 195, 198, 213, 228, 243–285, 290, 311, 321, 329, 335, 339, 379, 429f.
– Communist Party (PCR) 250f., 256
– government 248–250, 267, 282f
– Greater Romania 244
– legations abroad 264, 269, 272
– The Old Kingdom 244
Romanian National Committee (in exile) 271, 284
Romanian National Liberal Party 248
Romanian Writers' Union 272, 276
Romanians 71f., 243–254, 256–259, 261–264, 268–282, 285, 291, 299, 312
Romanians' Association 271
Romanov, Eugene 336
Romanov, Vladimir Kirillovich 359
Roosevelt, Franklin D. 26, 332, 358
Roper, Steven D. 255
Rosetti, C. A. 245
Ross, Corey 146f.
Ross, Nikolay 335
Rossiya 342, 358
Rostock 166
Rothschild, Joseph 75
Rotman, Liviu 246
Roulin, Stéphanie 230
Royal Institute of International Relations (UK) 328
Rozumnyj, Jaroslav 309, 324
Rubin, Władysław 224
Ruchkin, Alexander 349
Rudnycki, Ivan L. 317f.
Ruhr 136, 138
Rukh 314
Runblom, Harald 57
Rupnik, Jacques 112, 129
Ruse 69
Russell, Peter 309
Russia 4, 45, 53, 68f., 71–73, 76, 101, 137, 145, 168, 170f., 188, 196, 200, 246, 255, 287, 289, 292–295, 304, 306, 308–311, 313, 318, 321, 326–334, 336–342, 344, 346, 348–367, 426
Russian Center in San Francisco 364

Russian conservative émigrés (also conservative Russians)   349, 358
Russian Democratic Club   332
Russian Independent Mutual Aid Society (RIMAS)   327
Russian liberals (also Russian liberal democrats)   348, 350, 356
Russian Liberation Army (RLA)   331, 360
Russian Orthodox Church   301, 327
Russian Social Democratic Labor Party (Zagranichnaya Delegatia, RSDLP)   348, 357
Russians   48, 71f., 74, 82, 200, 287, 291, 304, 310, 313, 319, 326f., 330, 333, 336–339, 348f., 352, 358, 362
Rusu, Valeriu   280
Rusyn   101, 116, 119f., 134
Ruzicic-Kessler, Karlo   376
Rybakoff, Nikolay   358
Rydz-Śmigły, Edward   195

Saarland   157–159
Sabbat, Kazimierz   197
Sablin   364
Saint George Albanian Orthodox Cathedral   43
Sajti, Enikő A.   373, 375, 392, 394
Sakharov, Andrei   128
Sakson, Andrzej   197
Sakson, Barbara   212
Sălcudeanu, Nicoleta   278
Salerno   86
Salitan, Laurie   341, 343, 366
Salomon, Kim   47
Salzburg   86, 304
Samaritan Alliance   154f.
Sandhurst   36
Sandu, Dumitru   280, 284
Santa Rosa   213
Santara-Šviesa organization   59
Sapir, Boris   364
Săptămana (The Week)   251
Sarandë   41
Šarić, Tatjana   393
Satzewich, Vic   286f., 289, 294, 300, 302–304, 306, 314, 319, 324
Saunders, Frances Stonor   226
Savemark, Lenn   354
Sawicki, Krzysztof   218
Saxony   144
Scandinavia   168, 198, 206, 213
Schabowski, Günter   155
Schierup, Carl-Ulrich   383–385, 391–393
Schleswig-Holstein   142, 154
Schmidt, Klaus-Peter   159
Scholz, Hannelore   162
Schönhuber, Franz   159
Schroeder, Gregory F.   141
Schroeter, Leonard   341
Schryer, Frans J.   369
Schultz, George   131
Schupp, Jürgen   163
Schütz, Hans   118
Schweiger, Franz von   14
Schwerin   166
Scott-Smith, Giles   230
Scurtu, Ioan   246
Scutaru, Beatrice   243, 248–250, 252, 259f., 265–268, 273–275, 277f., 429
Second League of Prizren (Lidhja e Dytë e Prizrenit)   14, 27, 30, 36
Securitate (Romania)   248f., 262, 272f., 282
security   4, 6, 20f., 39, 80, 91, 94–97, 99f., 105, 108, 126f., 177, 189, 208, 213, 227, 232–235, 239, 247, 312, 317, 327, 337, 344, 360f., 366, 384, 388, 391
– security forces/police   39, 41, 46, 85, 105, 122, 126, 131, 158, 175, 189, 231, 234, 248–250, 263, 308, 387–389
Seebohm, Hans-Christoph   118f.
Selge, Eduard   61
Selman, Peter   268
Selmani, Hysen   26
Selter, Karl   54
Semmering   129
Serbia   4, 12, 68f., 73, 85, 260, 279, 333, 368, 373, 379, 384, 386, 390f., 393f., 426f.
– Republic of Serbia   9
– Republic of Serbian Krajina   389
Serbs   14, 73, 370, 389
Sereqi, Zef   31
Shamshur, Oleg V.   292
Shanghai   213
Shar (organization)   77
Sharp, Tony   127
Shehut, Musa   14
Sheldija, Martin   39
Shenau   345
Shevchenko, K.   349
Shevchenko Scientific Society (NTSH)   288, 302f., 322
Sheviakov, Alexey   339

Shindler, Colin   342
Shkarenkov, Leonid   365
Shkodër Group   11
Shkodra   10
Shkumbin river   12
Shmelev, Ivan   363
Shqipëria   12, 28 f., 32
Shtefan, Augustin   310
Shteppa, K.   363
Shub, David   357
Siberia   46, 198, 200, 290 f., 294, 346, 366
Sidor, Karol   107, 113, 115, 134
Sigurimi (State Security, Albania)   21
Sikorski, Władysław   195, 219
Silesia   199, 201
– Upper Silesia   137
Simeon II, Zsar of Bulgaria   86, 90
Simpson, John H.   169, 328 f.
Simuţ, Ion   252, 265
Sinyavsky, Andrey   354, 361, 364
Siwik, Anna   218, 232
Sizonenko, Alexandr   326
Sjöberg, Örjan   25
Skendi, Stavro   30, 32
Skëndo, Lumo   12
Skirius, Juozas   53
Škvorecký, Josef   105, 133
Śladkowski, Wiesław   215
Slany, Krystyna   193, 241
Slávik, Juraj   106 – 108, 113, 133
Slavonia   368, 373
Sławoj-Składkowski, Felicjan   195
Slovak Action Committee (SAC)   115
Slovak Democrat Party   113
Slovak Institute in Cleveland   107, 115 f., 134
Slovak Leagues   107, 115
– Slovak League of America (SLA)   101, 106 f., 115 f., 124, 134
– Slovak League of Canada   101, 106, 115
Slovak Liberation Council   115
Slovak National Council Abroad (SNCA)   115
Slovak question   101, 107, 114, 117, 124, 426
Slovak White Legion   125
Slovak World Congress   116, 129, 131, 134
Slovakia   2, 101, 107, 113 – 116, 119 f., 125 f., 129, 133, 304, 429
Slovaks   82, 101 f., 104 – 106, 109, 113 – 116, 119, 123 – 125, 129 f., 134, 299, 316
Slovenes   69, 368, 370, 376
Slovenia   2, 137, 371 – 373, 379

Smal-Stocky, Roman   310
Smallholder Party (Hungarian)   175, 186
Smith, David J.   54, 60
Smith, William Thomas   38
Smolana, Krzysztof   217
Smoloskyp Publishers   314
Smolyan   69
smuggling   60, 127, 210, 212, 226, 260 f., 304, 374
Snyder, Alan   351, 354
Snyder, Timothy   199
Social Democrat Party of Romania (Partidul Social Democrat)   253
social networks   296, 305
Socialist Alliance of Workers (Socijalistički savez radnog naroda Jugoslavije)   379
Socialist Union of Central Eastern Europe (SUCEE)   227
Socialist Unity Party, Germany (SED)   142 f., 145 – 147, 150 – 152, 155
Society for Human Rights   271
Society of Bulgarian Gardeners   86
socio-economic status   286, 289 f., 377
Sofronova, Ekaterina   337
Sokoli, Nik   39
Sokolnicki, Juliusz   221
Sokolyshn, Alexander   313
soldiers   43, 49, 137 f., 140, 194, 196 – 201, 204, 213 – 218, 222 f., 241, 260, 328, 331, 334, 371, 386
Solidarity (Solidarność)   209 f., 214 – 218, 234, 236, 240 f., 317 f.
Solidarity diaspora   210 – 212
Solonari, Vladimir   246
Solovey, Dmytro   313
Solzhenitsyn, Alexandr   270, 334, 345, 347, 353, 362
South Africa   37, 51, 177, 210, 214, 218
South Korea   267, 355
Southern Macedonia   41
Soviet Germans   339, 346 f.
Soviet Union   2, 4, 19, 25, 32, 45 f., 49, 52, 55, 58 f., 64, 67, 72, 74 – 77, 81, 83, 91, 95, 119, 128, 131, 137, 139 – 141, 144, 153 – 155, 167, 170, 172, 175, 178, 181 – 183, 188, 196, 198, 200 – 202, 207, 229, 235, 245, 275, 277, 281, 287, 290 – 293, 295, 298 f., 304, 312 f., 316 f., 319 – 321, 327, 330 – 344, 346 – 349, 351 – 361, 366, 370, 378

Sowjetzonenflüchtling (SBZ-Flüchtlinge/SBZ-refugees) 144, 146
Spain 37, 52, 98, 148, 216, 226, 253, 262, 320f., 371
Spałek, Robert 218
Spekke, Arnolds 53
Špetko, Jozef 114, 116, 124, 134
Spira, Steffi 153
Sport 18, 42, 61, 156f., 211, 313
Šprinc, Mikuláš 113
Spurný, Matěj 118f., 135
Šrámek, Jan 126
Srem 373
St Albans 15
St. Andrew's Abbey 115
St. George Ukrainian Catholic Church 288
St. Louis (Missouri) 87
St. Nedelya Church 72
St. Petersburg 363, 366
Stachiw, Eugeniusz 317
Stafa, Qemal 11
Stamford 322f.
Stańczyk, Henryk 201
Stanek, Piotr 218, 228
Stara Zagora 69
Stark, Tamás 182
Starobielsk 200
Štastny, Marián 129
State Agency for Refugees (Bulgaria) 97
Statelova, Elena 79, 83–86, 88, 98–100
Statev, Hristo 90
Staudinger, Eduard 73
Stedman, Susan 327
Stedman Jr., Murray 327
Stefan, Metropolitan of Sofia and Kiril, Metropolitan of Plovdiv 13, 68, 74, 99, 152, 201f., 216, 228, 317
Steimanis, Josifs 343
Steiner, Johann 263
Stephan, John J. 310, 330
stereotype 313, 318
Stevens, Admiral L. 350, 352
Stewart, Neil 51, 112, 120f., 129
Stöcker, Lars Fredrik 59f.
Stockholm 49, 53, 59, 63, 65, 128
Stockholm Tidning Eestlastele / Eesti Päevaleht 57
Stokes, Lee 21
Stola, Dariusz 193f., 199, 201, 203f., 206–212, 214, 240f., 245

Stolarik, Marian Mark 101, 107, 114, 116, 124f., 129, 131f., 134
Stolojan, Sanda 247, 273, 283, 285
Stoyanov, Lachezar 80
Stoyanova, Virzhinia 76f.
Stozher 90
Strasbourg 260, 281
Stravinskienė, Vitalija 54, 56f., 66
Štrbáňová, Soňa 104f.
Strelczuk, Ludmiła 288, 324
Stronnictwo Narodowe (Polish National Party) 218f., 221
Strumica 85
Strużyński, Marian 232
Study of Migration and Ethnicity (Institut za migracije i narodnosti) 391
Suchcitz, Andrzej 197
Sudeten Germans 102–104, 108, 116–120, 124f., 133, 135, 374
Sugihara, Chiune 198
Sukiennicki, Wiktor 230
Sula, Abdul 31
Sulyok, Dezső 186
Suppan, Arnold 119, 133
Supreme Committee for the Liberation of Lithuania (Vyriausiasis Lietuvos išlaisvinimo komitetas, VLIK) 54, 58, 61, 63, 66
Supreme Headquarter Allied Expeditionary Force (SHAEF) 179, 192
Supruniuk, Mirosław A. 226
Svědectví („Testimony") 112, 120
Sverdlovsk 340, 347
Svilengrad 69
Svishtov 69
Svoboda 90, 189
Swedish Latvian Central Council 57
Swedish Latvian National Council 57
Światło, Józef 208, 225, 232
Świnoujście 211
Switłyczni, Iwan 297
Switłyczni, Nadija 297
Switzerland 9, 36, 43, 104, 107, 113, 136, 174, 177, 215, 267, 321, 329, 335, 339, 379, 429
Syrena 225
Syria 15, 27, 31, 390
Szalási, Ferenc 170
Szarka, László 182
Szaynok, Bożena 205f.
Szczurowski, Maciej 231

szestydesiatnyky 297
Szkuta, Aleksander 220

Taagepera, Rein 60, 64
Tafili, Gani 29
Taiwan 355 f.
Tallinn 47, 52–54, 57, 59, 61 f., 65
Tamman, Tiina 52
Tammaru, Tiit 45, 49, 55, 64, 66
Tănase, Virgil 269
Tankova, Vasilka 79, 83–86, 88, 98 f.
Tărău, Virgil 249
Tarifa, Fatos 18, 42, 44
Tarka, Krzysztof 208, 226, 233–235, 241
Tartu 45, 48 f., 55 f., 65
Tase, Peter 9
Tasi, Koço 16
Tautininkai 50
Tavrian Bulgarians 76
Tchoukarine, Igor 380 f.
Teataja 57
Ştefan, Adelina Oana 257 f.
Ştefănescu, Călin-Bogdan 243
Tegeler, Tillman 48–50, 57
Teheran 3, 5, 358
Telhai, Ekrem 29
terrorism 356, 388
Tėviškės Žiburiai 58
Tézé-Delafon, Blandine 269
Thanasi, Kristo 32
Thatcher, Margaret 132
thaw 58, 235, 246, 293, 295 f., 320
The Central European Federalist 227
The Prolog 314
'the silent unseens' (cichociemni) 196
Themelko, Kristo 11
Ther, Philipp 6, 9, 11 f., 14, 17 f., 22, 32 f., 43, 45, 52 f., 66, 73, 79, 83, 86, 108, 119, 133–135, 141, 153, 157, 162, 171 f., 176, 178, 180, 185, 187 f., 191, 194, 196–200, 205, 215 f., 219, 222, 224, 232, 234, 237, 239, 241, 261, 266, 274 f., 286, 288 f., 292, 296, 301, 304 f., 308, 313, 315, 317, 323 f., 326, 333 f., 337, 351, 355, 359, 362–364, 377, 393
Thessaloniki 41
Third Reich 138, 166, 198, 201–203, 334
Thomastown 15
Thrace 68 f.
Thuringia 144

Tigrid, Pavel 109, 112 f., 120, 122
Timmermann, Heiner 143
Timofejev, Aleksej 333
Tirana 10–12, 14, 16 f., 19, 21, 24 f., 30, 33, 35, 37 f., 40, 43 f.
Tirana Treaty (of the Tirana Pact) 10
Tiso, Jozef 107
Tito, Josip Broz 4, 11, 19, 38, 77 f., 85, 331, 374, 376, 378, 381, 386, 392, 428
Tiu, Ilarion 261, 263
Toal, Gerard 389
Toçi, Terenc 16
Todd, Jim 8
Tokes, Rudolf 360
Tokić, Mate Nikola 371, 386, 388, 393, 395
Tokyo 210
Tolbukhin, Fyodor 75
Tomek, Prokop 8, 103, 106, 109, 115, 119, 122–125, 127, 131, 135
Toptani, Ishan 15, 29, 31
Toronto 51, 56 f., 65, 77, 116, 218, 244, 289 f., 294, 309, 313 f., 322–324, 328
Toruń 197, 216, 219, 224, 238, 242, 427
Tóth, Heléna 116, 136
tourism/tourist 58–60, 80, 208 f., 212, 217, 257–259, 361, 370, 380 f.
Trahair, Richard C. 38 f.
Traiskirchen 210
Tran 70
transnational ties/aspects 1, 6–7, 228, 235, 247, 388, 393
Transylvania 170, 244–246
Trapp, Frithjof 247
travel 8, 16, 20, 58, 105 f., 152, 156, 176, 204, 209 f., 237, 243, 245, 249, 257–259, 262, 279, 304, 338, 356, 368, 427
– travel document 210, 248
– travel liberalization 237, 280
Travemünde 211
Traykov, Veselin 73, 78, 87
treaty 19, 68 f., 72, 75, 137 f., 159 f., 164, 168, 213, 245, 372 f., 375
Treaty of London 378
Treuhandanstalt/ Treuhand 161
Trieste 27, 86, 377
Troitsky, N. 338, 351, 360, 363
Tromara, Kol 16
Tromly, Benjamin 8, 359
Troncota, Tiberiu 256
Trotsky, Lev 328

Trubinsky, Jozef C. 116, 134
Truman, Harry S. 121, 304, 357 f.
Trybuna 225
Tsamandas 41
Tsankov, Aleksandar 88 f.
Tsaribrod 70
Tubin, Eduard 59
Tucholski, Jędrzej 196
Turek, Wojciech 219
Turgenev, Alexander I. 326
Turin 30
Turkestan National Liberation Committee/ Turkeli 351
Turkey 2, 9, 15, 30 f., 70, 72, 79 f., 82 – 84, 92, 148, 184, 244, 329, 339, 356, 378
Turkowski, Romulad 218, 239, 241
Tyrkova-Williams, Ariadna 350, 364
Tzavella, Hristofor 69
Tzvetkov, Plamen S. 74 – 76

Udine 86
Ugrimov, Alexander 334, 337
Ukraine 2, 46, 71, 119, 137, 186, 202, 246, 286 – 292, 294, 296 f., 301, 304 f., 307, 309 – 319, 322 – 324
– Eastern Ukraine 289
Ukrainian Academy of Arts and Sciences 309, 322 f.
Ukrainian American Bar Association 306
Ukrainian American Coordinating Council 288
Ukrainian American Relief Committee (UUARC) 308
Ukrainian American War Veterans 308
Ukrainian American Youth Association (SUMA) 306 f.
Ukrainian Artistic Movements 302
Ukrainian Associations of Artists 302
Ukrainian Canadian Research Center and Documentation Centre (UCRDC) 323
Ukrainian Congress Committee of America (UCCA) 308 – 310, 313, 315 – 318
Ukrainian Diaspora Studies Initiative 325
Ukrainian Free University 303, 313, 318, 323
Ukrainian Heritage Studies Center 322
Ukrainian Hetman Organization (UHO) 307
Ukrainian Historical Association 306
Ukrainian Medical Association 306
Ukrainian National Association (UNA) 308, 315 f., 318

Ukrainian National Committee of Argentina, Paraguay and Uruguay 309
Ukrainian National Council 301, 303, 311
Ukrainian Soviet Socialist Republic 229, 291
Ukrainian Workingsman's Ass. (UWA) 307
Ukrainian World Congress 309
Ukrainian Youth League of America, 308
Ulbricht, Walter 147
Ulici, Laurențiu 252
Ulmanis, Kārlis 53
Umsiedler 141, 143, 148, 155
unemployment 138, 148, 160 f., 163 – 165, 237, 304, 380 – 383
Ungváry, Krisztián 174
Union Européenne des Fédéralistes 230
Union of Free Bulgarians 88
Union of Polish Patriots 201
Union of Struggle for the Liberation of the Peoples of Russian (Sojuz Borby za osvobojdenie narodov Rossii, SBONR) 360
Union of the Bulgarian National Legions 90
Union of Ukrainian National Democrats (SUND) 307
Union of Ukrainian Socialists 307
United Lithuanian Relief Fund of America (Bendras Amerikos Lietuviu Fondas) 50
United Nations 7, 32, 48, 61, 106, 128, 132, 178, 180, 188, 196, 227 f.
– United Nations High Commissioner for Refugees (UNHCR) 180, 256, 282, 389
– United Nations Human Rights Committee 128
– United Nations Relief and Rehabilitation Administration (UNRRA) 48 f., 139 f., 179, 192, 202, 298, 337
United States of America 4, 15 f., 19, 22, 26 – 30, 32 – 37, 42, 45 f., 48 – 53, 55, 57 f., 61 f., 64 – 66, 71 f., 74, 78, 83, 87, 89 – 93, 98, 101 – 109, 114, 116, 121 – 127, 130 – 136, 138 – 141, 168 f., 172 – 177, 179, 181, 184 – 190, 192, 195, 202, 208 – 210, 213 f., 217, 220, 223, 227 f., 232 f., 237 f., 241, 244, 251 f., 258, 264 f., 267 f., 270 f., 277, 284, 287 – 290, 295 f., 298 – 300, 303 – 318, 320 – 327, 329, 331 f., 334 – 340, 342 f., 345, 348 – 350, 352 – 359, 362, 364, 366, 378, 382, 388, 390, 426 – 429
– US Escapee Program 106
– US government 3 – 5, 32, 74, 105 f., 110, 121 f., 124, 126, 186, 190, 228

– US Information Agency (USIA) 351
United Ukrainian-American Relief Committee 300
unity camp (obóz zjednoczenia) 221
uprising 69, 72, 123, 146, 199, 361
Urals 346f.
Uruguay 184, 217, 290, 299, 309, 322
Urzyńska, Dorota 218
Ustaša 370f.

Vaba Eesti Sõna 57
Vaba Eestlane 57
Vachkov, Daniel 70f.
Vadura, Katherine 133, 135
Valencia 6
Valentinov, Nikolay 365
Välis-Eesti 57, 61
Valiukas, Leonardas 62
Valmas, Anne 57f.
Valteri, Beqir 16
van Boeschoten, Riki 379
Vankova, Zvezda 96
Vardar Macedonia 69, 73, 75, 78, 85
Várdy, Agnes Huszár 182
Várdy, Steven Béla 174, 182
Varga, Béla 175, 186, 189
Varinský, Vladimír 125
Varna 69
Vasileva, Boyka 84, 86, 98f.
Vata, Gjergj 39
Vatican 26, 30, 129, 226, 321, 351
Vatra – Pan-Albanian Federation of America 32, 34, 36, 43
Vedder, Richard K. 148
Veigners, Ilgvars 49
Velvet Revolution 116, 129–131, 133
Venezuela 50, 174, 184, 202, 217, 290, 299f., 322, 338f.
Verdery, Katherine 253
Vërlaci, Ismail 26, 30, 34
Vërlaci, Shefqet Bey 34
Vermeulen, Hans 379
Vernant, Jacques 179
Vertinsky, Alexander 336
Vertragsarbeiter (foreign contract workers) 149f.
Vertriebene 141, 143–146, 167
Vesilind, Priit 66

victims 21, 46f., 49, 51, 56f., 64, 72, 76, 114, 126, 201, 253, 273f., 313, 320, 333–336, 340, 347, 350, 371
Victor Emmanuel III 10
Victoria 15, 36
Vida, István 8
Vidin 69
Vidra, Zsuzsanna 183
Vienna 6, 27, 86, 88, 125f., 129f., 132f., 170, 172, 183, 189, 191, 280, 304, 344f., 376
Vietnam 19, 81, 149, 356
– North Vietnam 356
– South Vietnam 356
Vietnamese 81, 356
Vīķe-Freiberga, Vaira 64
Vilare Ailange College 36
Vilde, Boris 331
Vilím, Blažej 107, 121
Vilímek, Tomáš 105, 112, 127, 129
Vilnius 45–48, 52, 54, 58, 60, 62, 65, 346
violence 93, 127, 130, 281, 371–373, 388
visa application 152
Vladimirov, Iulia 276
Vlasov, Andrey 331, 334, 357, 365
Vlora 16, 42
Vlora, Muredin 31
Vnuk, František 114, 116, 124
Voice of America, VOA 28, 55, 122, 124f., 128, 130f., 225, 272, 275, 351f.
Voice of Czechoslovakia 120
Voice of Free Czechoslovakia 122, 126, 129
Vojvodina 373–375, 392
Vokri, Mark Bib 39
Volga 294f., 346
Volhynia 289
von Lampe, Alexey 364
Vranje 69
Vremja i my (Us and the Times) 345
Vrioni, Ali 30
Vrioni, Qemal 16
Vuçiterni, Sulejman 17
Vullnetari, Julie 23–25, 40, 42, 44
Vultur, Smaranda 249, 251, 263
Vychytil-Baudoux, Florence 224
Vyshinsky, Andrey 336

Wagner, Gerd 162
Wajs-Milewska, Wioletta 242
wakacjusze 212

Walaszek, Adam 194, 199f., 202, 205, 214–218, 240, 289, 318, 320, 325
Waldinger, Robert 247
Wallace, Claire 132, 193
Wallachia 68, 243
Wandycz, Piotr 230
Wangenheim, Elizabeth D. 309
Wańkowicz, Melchior 224, 233
war 1–9, 13f., 16, 20f., 25f., 28f., 32f., 37–39, 44–52, 54–63, 65f., 70–72, 74f., 78, 80–84, 86f., 89–91, 94f., 97, 102f., 105, 107, 109, 111f., 115–120, 122–132, 134f., 137–144, 146, 148, 153f., 160, 163–165, 167–174, 176, 178f., 182f., 185f., 188f., 192–207, 209, 212–220, 222–224, 226, 228–232, 234–236, 238–243, 246f., 253, 259, 264, 268, 270f., 275, 278, 282–286, 291–297, 304–307, 309, 311f., 314, 316, 319f., 324, 327f., 330, 333–338, 340f., 344, 348–351, 355f., 358f., 363–366, 368–378, 385, 388–394, 426–429
– Balkan Wars 69, 71, 283
– Russian-Turkish Wars 68
– World War I 45, 61, 69f., 101, 111, 136–138, 166, 169f., 195, 223, 244, 304, 349, 372, 380
– World War II 1, 5f., 9–11, 14–17, 21, 25, 27–30, 32–35, 37, 42, 45–47, 49–52, 54, 63, 71, 73f., 77, 85–87, 89f., 99, 101f., 104f., 107f., 113, 115, 117f., 121, 133, 138, 140f., 147, 166, 169–171, 174, 177, 181–183, 185f., 188, 191, 193–195, 197f., 202, 205, 213, 215–217, 219f., 222–224, 238–241, 243, 245–247, 253, 271, 274, 288, 291, 297, 300, 304, 323, 331–334, 337–340, 346, 348, 357–360, 363f., 368–374, 376, 378, 385, 390f., 393f., 426–429
Warmińska, Katarzyna 315
Warsaw 5f., 53, 91, 153, 193–195, 198–202, 204–208, 210f., 213–216, 218–222, 225f., 228–242, 291, 296f., 312, 331
Warsaw Treaty Organization (Warsaw Pact) 19, 127, 251, 271
Washington 2, 20, 39, 53, 75, 91, 107f., 112f., 123f., 139, 141, 186, 210, 220, 226, 232, 239, 251, 264, 314, 341, 364, 426
Wawer, Zbigniew 200
Weindling, Paul 104
Wejs-Milewska, Violetta 225, 242
Wesoły, Szczepan 224

West German Agency for Refugee Matters (Westdeutscher Senat für Flüchtlingsfragen) 144
West Prussia 137
Western Herzegovina 382
Western Thrace 69f., 75
Wiadomości Literackie 225
Wiedemeier, Klaus 159
Wieniawa-Długoszowski, Bolesław 195
Williams, M. 351
Williamsburg 188
Wilno 229
Winterhagen, Jenny 385
Wintour, Laura 104
Wittlichová, Lucie 105f.
Wojtyła, Karol 224, see also: Pope John Paul II
Wölben, Jan Philipp 150
Wolf, Christa 152f.
Wolff, Frank 166
Wolff, Stefan 143, 167
Wolowyna, Oleh 286, 288, 295, 306f., 324
Woodward, Susan 380, 382
World Anti-Communist League (WACL) 91
World Association of Estonians (Ülemaailmne Eesti Ühing) 54
World Confederation of Labor 227
World Congress of Free Ukrainians (WCFU) 308, 310, 313, 315
World Federation of Free Latvians (Brīvās pasaules latviešu apvienības) 55, 61, 63
World Organization of Free Estonians (Vabade Eestlaste Keskorganisatsioon) 56
writer(s) exile/émigré 22, 112, 152, 224f., 250, 265, 269, 272, 276–278, 284, 318, 326, 331, 348, 357, 362–365
Wróbel, Janusz 194, 203–205, 213f.
Wrocław 196f., 202, 225, 238, 289, 427
Wszelaki, Jan 226
Würzburg 140
Wyman, Mark 47, 49–52, 57, 61, 64, 337
Wynar, Lubomyr 302f., 322, 324

Xoxe, Koci 11

Yalta 3–5, 140, 196, 201f., 204, 291, 309, 319, 335, 358
Yarraville 15
Yekelchyk, Serhy 290–292, 294, 297, 312
Yelensky, Boris 365
Young Artists Club 297

Youth Group (of Albania)   11
Yugoslav Communist Party   370
Yugoslav Federation   78
Yugoslav nationalities   376 f.
Yugoslav Red Cross   375
Yugoslavia   2–5, 8–11, 13 f., 16, 19–22, 32, 34 f., 75, 77, 80 f., 84–86, 89, 148, 170, 172 f., 186, 261, 263, 277, 282, 289, 311, 321, 329, 331, 333, 356, 368–389, 391–395, 428
– break-up   389
– Department for Emigration   377
– Kingdom of Yugoslavia   73, 380
– Ministry of Labor   377

Zabłocki, Janusz   218
Zagora, Dalmatian   382
Zagreb   382 f., 391 f., 394
Zaitsev, Boris   363
Zake, Ieva   189 f.
Zákó, András   184, 189
Zakšauskienė, Inga   8
Zaleski, August   219, 221, 231
Zalkans, Lilita   59
Zallari, Mihal   16
Zamfirescu, Dinu   249
Zamość   199, 201
Zapart, Robert   226
Zariņš, Kārlis   53 f.

Żaryn, Jan   219
Zaslavsky, Victor   341, 343
Zatsepina, Olga   349
Zavalani, Tajar   31 f.
Zawodny, Janusz   200
Zeeler, Vladimir   364
Zeineli, Asllan   29
Zelenko, Konstantyn   308 f.
Zeman, Zbyněk   101
Zemskov, Viktor   335 f., 339, 366
Zenkl, Petr   102, 105, 108–111, 114, 121, 126 f., 134
Zeqo, Njazi   15
Zeszyty Literackie   194, 225, 289
Zgradnik, Maruša   392
Zhelyazkova, Antonina   10
Zięba, Andrzej A.   205, 286 f., 289, 318, 324 f.
Zielyk, Ihor V.   293, 300 f., 305 f., 314 f.
Ziętara, Paweł   208, 218, 235, 241
Zimmerman, William   380, 384, 392 f.
Zog I (Ahmet Zogu), King of Albania   9–11, 15, 26, 28, 31 f., 36 f.
Zogists   31
Zprávy SVU   112
Zsitnyányi, Ildikó   189
Zuganov, Gennady   362
Zurawski, Radosław Paweł   53
Zwoliński, Stefan   201

www.ingramcontent.com/pod-product-compliance
Lightning Source LLC
Chambersburg PA
CBHW082057230426
43670CB00017B/2879